M

THE JEWISH WORLD IN THE MODERN AGE

THE JEWISH WORLD IN THE MODERN AGE

Jon Bloomberg

KTAV Publishing House
930 Newark Avenue
Jersey City, NJ 07360

Library of Congress Cataloging-in-Publication Data

Bloomberg, Jon.
 The Jewish world in the modern age / Jon Bloomberg.
    p. cm.
 Includes bibliographical references and index.
 ISBN 0-88125-844-X
 1. Jews--Europe--History--18th century. 2. Jews--Europe--History--19th century. 3.
Jews--Europe--History--20th century. 4. Judaism--History--Modern period, 1750- I.
Title.
DS135.E83B56 2004
909'.04924--dc22
                                        2004008845

                                    Published by
                              KTAV Publishing House, Inc.
                                   930 Newark Avenue
                                  Jersey City, NJ 07306
                                  Email: info@ktav.com
                                      www.ktav.com
                                    (201) 963-9524
                                  Fax (201) 963-0102

CONTENTS

Introduction

Today's readers have many interests. Computers and other advances in technology have provided enormous resources of knowledge that were not available in the past. Why should one explore the Jewish past when there are so many other possibilities, so many other avenues to pursue? The answer is simple: those who do not acquaint themselves with the Jewish past cannot pretend to understand the Jewish present. Anti-Semitism, for example, cannot be fully understood without an examination of its roots in history, its development over time, and the myths about Jews and Judaism that it has promoted. Zionism and the State of Israel cannot be understood without a study of their history, nor can the emergence of Reform Judaism, Conservative Judaism, and other denominational movements be appreciated without careful historical study.

Jewish identity is strengthened, moreover, as one becomes more fully acquainted with the many significant accomplishments and contributions of Jews throughout history. Those who come to know the Jewish past will take pride in it and identify with it, so that it becomes part of their own being. They will also become sensitive to the continuities in the history of the Jews, as well as to the changes. They will see, as well, how many of today's issues, problems, and challenges were confronted in the past.

My goals in this book are to offer a readable narrative, introduce some of the classical texts of Jewish literature in translation, present primary sources, stimulate readers to confront some of the questions raised by these texts, and motivate them to want to study the history of the Jews in greater depth.

Among the major developments of the modern period were the emancipation of the Jews in the countries of Western Europe. The Jews of the 18th century were exposed to the thought of the Enlightenment; this exposure led to the Haskalah, the Jewish Enlightenment. Reform and Conservative Judaism and modern Orthodoxy emerged in 19th-century Germany, and Hasidism was born in 18th-century Poland. The Zionist movement developed under the leadership of Theodor Herzl. Despite these trends, anti-Semitism remained a constant of Jewish history.

Each chapter of this book opens with an introductory essay that presents the subject at hand. For example, the essay that opens Chapter 1, "Politics and Community in Eastern Europe," speaks of the poverty of Polish and Russian Jews, the power of the church, the Czars and the Pale of Settlement, the pogroms, the Communist Revolution, and so on. It is followed by a selection of primary source readings and questions addressing these texts. At the end of the book is an index and an extensive bibliography.

Dr. Robert Shapiro of the Ramaz School read this book, critiqued it, and offered ideas for refinements and improvements. His suggestions, many of which I have incorporated in the text, have upgraded the book's content immeasurably. Dr. Shapiro's efforts are much appreciated.

My publisher, Mr. Bernard Scharfstein of KTAV Publishing House, continues to encourage my work. The publication of this book is but one expression of that caring.

Ilene McGrath and Robert Milch were the copy editors for this book. They invested enormous energy in this effort.

Like my earlier work, *The Jewish World in the Middle Ages,* this book is dedicated to my children, Adina, Mordechai, and Zehava. Above all, though, it is dedicated to my wife, Miriam, whose counsel I have always sought.

ACKNOWLEDGMENTS

We acknowledge the use of selections from

A. Altmann. *Moses Mendelssohn: A Biographical Study.* Philadelphia: Jewish Society, 1973.

S. Bayme. *Understanding Jewish History.* New York: KTAV Publishing House, 1997.

L. Berson. *Case Study of a Riot: the Philadelphia Story.* New York: American Jewish Committee, 1966.

I. Bickerton and M. N. Pearson. *The Arab-Israeli Conflict: A History.* Melbourne, Australia: Longman Cheshire, 1993.

A. Davis, Black Jewish Relations, © 1984, Greenwood Press. Reproduced with permission of Greenwood Publishing Group, Inc. Westport, CT.

Documents on the Holocaust (Yad Vashem). Ed. Y. Arad. Jerusalem: KTAV Publishing House, 1981.

E. Ginzberg, *Employing the Unemployed,* Edited by Eli Ginzberg. © 1980, Basic Books, Inc. Reprinted by permission of Basic Books, a member of Perseus Books, L.L.C.

Hadoar, Volume 40:8.

A Holocaust Reader. Ed. L. Davidowicz, © Behrman House, Inc. Reprinted with permission. www.behrmanhouse.com

Israel in the Middle East. Edited by Itamar Rabinovich and Jehuda Reinharz. © 1984, Oxford University Press, Inc. Used by permission of Oxford University Press, Inc.

The Jew in the Modern World: A Documentary History. Edited by P. Mendes-Flohr and J. Reinharz. New York: Oxford University Press, 1980, 1995.

Jewish Emancipation: A Selection of Documents. Ed. Raphael Mahler. New York: American Jewish Committee, 1941.

Norman Lamm. *The Religious Thought of Hasidism.* New York: KTAV Publishing House, 1999.

J.R. Marcus. *The American Jewish Woman.* New York: KTAV Publishing House, 1981.

Moses Mendelssohn. Translated by Allan Arkush, pp. 89-90, 128-128 from *Jerusalem, or on Religious Power and Judaism,* © 1983, by the Trustees of Brandeis University, Reprinted by permission. University Press of New England.

W. Gunther Plaut. *The Rise of Reform Judaism: a Sourcebook of Its Origins.* New York: World Union for Progressive Judaism, 1963.

The Zionist Idea, A. Hertzberg. © 1966 by the Jewish Publication Society. Reprinted with permission.

We are also grateful to WNET/Channel 13 in New York City for permitting us to use maps from the Heritage Series.

If we have inadvertently omitted any acknowledgement, we would be grateful if you would bring that fact to our attention.

1

POLITICS AND COMMUNITY IN EASTERN EUROPE

INTRODUCTION

This chapter will examine the situation of Jews in Eastern Europe from the middle of the 18th century to the present day.

In the 18th century, there were major Jewish communities in Western Europe (England, France, and Germany), Central Europe (Austria-Hungary), and Eastern Europe (Poland and Russia). There were approximately 500,000 Jews in Western Europe, about 150,00 in Central Europe, and roughly 5 million in Poland.

The Jewish communities of Western Europe and Central Europe faced challenges that were both similar to and different from those confronted by the Jewish communities in Eastern Europe.

Throughout Europe most Jews were poor. Their poverty resulted from the heavy taxation imposed upon them by their local rulers. Jews also lacked the freedom to work where and in whatever capacity they desired, the right to participate in government through the vote, and freedom of movement. Any privileges they had were just that, and not rights they enjoyed as citizens, although, as we will see in Chapter 2, French Jews became citizens after the French Revolution of 1789. Jews experienced social isolation from Christians. While the Jews of Europe had some control over their own affairs, they were almost always isolated from the Christian society in which they lived.

There were, however, major differences between the Jewish experience in Western and Central Europe and in Eastern Europe. The Jews of Poland constituted an autonomous community, governed by a national federation known as the Council of the Four Lands—the four major provinces of the Kingdom of Poland. This federation enabled Jews to protect their own interests to some extent, serving as a middleman between the Jews and the Sejm (parliament). The Council apportioned and collected taxes, and governed the inner life of the various Jewish communities (kahals) by regulating their economic, judicial, cultural, and administrative activities.

Most Polish Jews lived in cities, towns, and villages. A 1764 census showed that about 70 percent lived in towns and cities, with less than one-third in villages (shtetls). More than two-thirds lived in the country's eastern provinces; that is, in Ukraine and Lithuania/White Russia. Agricultural workers lived in houses in the villages, while the fields lay beyond the dwelling area. A neighboring town served as administrative and shopping center.

In Germany and Italy, by contrast, the Jews lived in ghettos. Overcrowded and lacking in hygiene, ghettos were located in the worst sections of town. Jews lived in them because they had to, not because they wanted to. Jews in Western Europe, moreover, were restricted in occupations. They were banned from agriculture and commerce, and most other fields, and as a result were forced into such occupations as moneylending and petty trade. Jews in Poland were able to engage in a wider range of activities, although they too were subject to many occupational restrictions. Among other things they were permitted to be tradesmen, lumberjacks, farmers, and the like. Some served as estate managers and stewards for the Poland nobility. They did not have to engage in moneylending.

The Polish monarchy was weak, which made it easier for the Jewish communities, but on the other hand the Roman Catholic Church in Poland was very powerful, and the anti-Semitic teachings it disseminated aroused intense hatred. Much the same was true in Russia, where the Greek Orthodox Church prevailed. In 1762, for instance, Empress Elizabeth Petrovna of Russia ordered that

All Jews, male and female, of whatever occupation and standing, shall be immediately deported, together with all their property, from Our whole Empire. They shall henceforth not be admitted to Our Empire unless they be willing to accept Christianity of the Greek persuasion.

In Western Europe and in the Habsburg Empire, by contrast, the emergence of absolute monarchies had led to a corresponding decline in the influence of the church. Moreover, the Protestant Reformation in the 16th century had created more tolerance for different religious beliefs and traditions.

As one weighs the similarities and the differences in the mid-18th century, the similarities seem to outweigh the differences. All of Europe's Jewish communities were socially isolated from the world of the Christians, each governed itself for the most part, each was impoverished and barely surviving. Perhaps the greatest difference is that there were no ghettos in Central or Eastern Europe.

LIFE UNDER THE CZARS

The latter part of the 18th century brought major changes to Eastern Europe. Both Prussia and Russia wanted Poland, as did the Austro-Hungarian Empire. They agreed to divide Poland among them. Prussia took the area called Great Poland. The Habsburg Empire took Galicia, and Russia took Lithuania and Ukraine. Thus most of Poland's territory, and with it most of its Jews, now became part of the Russian Empire. As a result, the policy of expelling Jews adopted by Elizabeth Petrovna was no longer applicable. Catherine II (Catherine the Great) was now the ruler of the world's largest Jewish community.

The Pale of Settlement

In 1794 Empress Catherine II created the Pale of Settlement, although its final contours were not set until 1812 by Alexander II (1777–1825). The Pale—the area in which Jews were permitted to reside—took in Russia's 25 westernmost provinces from the Baltic to the Black Sea. It included most of eastern Poland, Lithuania, White Russia (Byelorussia, now known as Belarus), Ukraine, the Crimea, and Bessarabia. Jews had no choice but to live within the Pale. They could not leave it without special permission from the government. An official census in 1897 showed that by

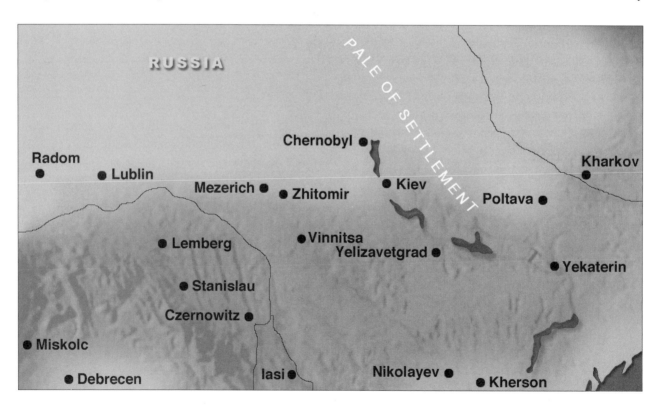

1825 Map of Eastern Europe, including the Pale of Settlement

then there were close to 5 million Jews living in this area of 386,100 square miles. They represented 11.6 percent of the total population of the Pale.

In 1802 Czar Alexander I ruled that Jews could not live or work in incorporated villages. Although the liquor trade was a traditional Jewish business in Europe, they were also forbidden to sell liquor to the local peasants. These regulations destroyed the livelihood of one-third of the Jews, since these unfortunates held village leases or ran villages inns; another third were in trade, and most of the rest were craftsmen. The Czar explained that he wanted the Jews to be involved in "productive labor"—farming and timber. There was little land available, however. The real aim was to bring the Jews to baptism or induce them to leave Russia. Neither choice was taken, and the Jew of the Pale became completely impoverished.

Nicholas I

The year 1825 brought the death of Alexander, who was succeeded by his younger brother, Nicholas I (1796–1855). Nicholas was a professional soldier who came to be known as the "Iron Czar." His agenda included nationalism, loyalty to Russian Orthodox teachings, and autocracy, or absolute government by the Czar. Nicholas saw the Jews as an alien people who must adapt themselves rapidly to the Russian Orthodox majority or suffer fearful consequences. The Jews were, in short, a threat to "Holy Mother Russia."

In 1827 Nicholas issued the Cantonist Decrees, which conscripted male Jews aged 12 to 25. Approximately 50,000 Jews were conscripted at this time. The 12-year-olds were to be trained and educated at the local canton (military depot), and at age 18 they were inducted into the Russian army for a term of 25 years. Based on published recruitment lists for the empire, about 70,000 Jews were conscripted between 1827 and 1854. Some 50,000 of the recruits were minors. Many of these young people died from malnutrition, beatings, disease, or loneliness. Some broke under the pressure and converted to the Russian Orthodox Church, but most remained Jewish under the difficult circumstances. Fewer than half of the cantonists ever returned home.

The quota of recruits was to be filled by the leadership of the Jewish communities. More fortunate families and better-connected families could buy their way out, so it was usually the children of the poor, the defenseless, and the downtrodden who were conscripted. In order to make their quotas, Jewish communities were forced to hire special agents, known as kidnappers (*khappers*), who roamed the streets looking for candidates, delivering them to the Russian army for a fee.

The Minister of Public Education under Nicholas was Count Sergei S. Uvarov. A man of great intellect, he was literate in French and German as well as in Russian. Uvarov had formulated the essential themes of the regime of Nicholas: Orthodoxy, Autocracy, and Nationalism. He became the intellectual leader of Russian nationalism.

Uvarov concluded that Jews must be introduced to a curriculum of secular studies. The Talmud, he thought, was the text that kept Jews a separate people, for it taught them superstitions and prejudices about non-Jews. If they could be separated from the Talmud, they could be more easily exposed and attracted to the teachings of Christianity. The purpose of this new approach could be hidden from the Jews by implementing it in Jewish schools, not Russian schools. Students would be taught the Russian language, secular sciences, Hebrew, and "religion according to the Holy Writ."

Sir Moses Montefiore speaking to Czar Nicholas I in 1846 in St. Petersburg.

The teachers would be Jews who could be relied upon to carry out the goals of the new crown schools. The principals of primary schools would be Christians. There would be three theological seminaries, in Vilna, Warsaw, and Zhitomir, whose purpose would be to train teachers and rabbis. The directors of the theological seminaries would be Jews.

It would be necessary, though, to find a capable Jewish educator to be placed in charge, one who was a "modern" enlightened Jew but would not look too closely into the government's ulterior motives. Uvarov's choice was Max Lilienthal. Lilienthal was a young German Jew, educated at the University of Munich. He was a rabbi, but also a doctor of philosophy. He had established, in the city of Riga in Lithuania, a modern secular school for the more prosperous Jews of the community, a school that had been remarkably successful.

When approached to be in charge, Lilienthal wondered why a literate people like Jews needed educational efforts more than the illiterate masses of Russian people. Uvarov's response was that secular education was indispensable if Jews sought emancipation. Lilienthal asked permission to consult with colleagues, which he was granted. Abraham Geiger, leader of Reform Judaism in Germany, Adolphe Crémieux, a distinguished French politician, and Sir Moses Montefiore, a wealthy English banker and stockbroker, agreed that secular education, no matter what the underlying motives, would be a great opportunity for the pious but unenlightened Jews of Russia. Lilienthal agreed to take on the challenge.

Lilienthal began with a public-relations campaign on behalf of the new schools. He decided to tour the communities in the Pale of Settlement in an effort to gain support. He visited Vilna, where Jews told him that the motives of the Russians were obvious, that they sought to bring Jews to Christianity. In Minsk, Jews refused to speak with him. In Berditchev and Odessa, where maskilim, or enlightened Jews, were more numerous, he was greeted like royalty. Support came as well from maskilim living outside Russia.

In 1844 Uvarov decided that the time had come to announce the establishment of the Jewish crown schools. Much ceremony was attached to the opening of these schools. They might have experienced more success were it not for a memorandum sent by Nicholas to Uvarov, reaffirming that the real goal was to make the Jews more like Christians and remove from them the prejudices against Christians emerging from the Talmud. Uvarov responded with his own memorandum, indicating that soon all the "Jewish" courses would be eliminated and displaced by instruction in the Orthodox faith. The Jews' skepticism had been justified all along.

Lilienthal himself had come to realize the government's intention, so in 1844 he left Russia for America. There he lived until 1882, occupying distinguished rabbinic positions in Cincinnati and New York.

By 1855 the Pale of Settlement was reduced to include only Lithuania, New Russia, Little Russia, and sections of Ukraine. New regulations were introduced. Traditional Jewish clothing was prohibited or taxed heavily. Jews could not employ non-Jews as domestics, nor could they marry before the age of 18. Jewish agricultural settlements were now prohibited. Jewish education was to be strictly supervised. The Jewish quota for the Russian army was tripled, and there were decrees against the study of Talmud. Jews were forbidden to practice many professions unless they first converted to Christianity. Jews were classified as "useful" (farmers, artisans, skilled workers, the "educated") or "useless" (teamsters, unskilled laborers, rabbis, teachers, unemployed, sick, orphans); the "useless" had a higher conscription quota for the army.

The Russian rabbinate suffered another compromise of its authority when the government required the Jews to have official rabbis. These rabbis were to be responsible for keeping track of births, deaths, marriages, and divorces, but official rabbis had to be literate in Russian and able to meet the government standards for clergymen. This meant that almost all traditional rabbis were excluded from official recognition. More important, they lost the basis of their salaries and whatever official powers they held. For the most part the official rabbis were ready to accept the authority of the unofficial but recognized rabbis, but many of the official rabbis were of low character and ignorant in Jewish law. Some were "enlightened"

Jews, whose loyalty to Jewish tradition and Torah observance was under question.

Alexander II

The Crimean War (1854–1856) pitted Russia against Turkey; England, France, and Sardinia came to Turkey's aid and helped defeat Russia. Supposedly this war related to protection of the holy places in Palestine; it brought disastrous military defeats to Russia. Many lives were lost, but, more important, Nicholas's major theme, military efficiency, was discredited. The year 1855 brought the death of Nicholas, however, and Russia looked for changes under the rule of his successor, Alexander II.

After his coronation, Alexander promised "education, equal justice, tolerance, and humaneness" to all Russians. He rescinded the decree of cantonism, the conscription of young Jews, and the Jewish community rejoiced. He abolished serfdom, granting Russia's 47 million serfs legal freedom. He introduced jury trials for the first time in Russia's history. In addition, he reduced military service from 25 years to a more tolerable six years. Crowds of Jews gathering in the public square of St. Petersburg hailed Alexander as "Czar-Liberator."

A decree of 1865 permitted large-scale Jewish merchants, Jewish university graduates, and skilled Jewish artisans to move out of the Pale of Settlement into the interior of Russia. Jewish peddlers and storekeepers, for whom congestion remained a problem, were denied permission to settle outside the Pale; some did anyway, sometimes disguising themselves as artisans. Needless to say, this was a very risky thing to do.

The Jews who were living outside the Pale of Settlement began to take full advantage of this privilege. New Jewish communities were established, populated by merchants, industrialists, financiers, academicians, artisans, and discharged veterans. Jews began to adopt the Russian language and Russian manner of dress and behavior, becoming the new "aristocrats" of Russian-Jewish life, encouraging their fellow Jews to become more Russian. They expressed their affection for the Russian language and for the culture of "Mother Russia."

Czar Alexander II (1818–1881)

Jews involved themselves in establishing the Russian railroad system, with three-fourths of the railroads supported by them alone. Among the prominent investors were the Poliakovs, the Nathansons, and the Gunzbergs. In addition, Baron Horace Gunzberg laid the foundations for one of the largest banking systems in Russia. Jews were engaged as well in the sugar industry.

Congress Poland, the core of ethnic Poland, was the center of Polish politics and culture, and an area of great economic importance. It became part of the Russian Empire as a result of the partitions of Poland in 1772, 1793, and 1795, just as Galicia went to the Austrian Empire, and Poznan, Silesia, and Pomerania to Prussia. In 1863 Congress Poland rebelled against Russia. This uprising was long, bloody, and a failure, and it led to greater anti-Semitism in Russia. It stimulated Russian patriotism and reinforced the xenophobia of the Russian people; those who suffered as a result were the non-Russian minorities, especially the Jews.

Alexander's first eight years cultivated justice and equal rights, but the Polish revolt led him to conclude that what Russia needed most was a firm hand and a clear policy of strict conservatism. All reforms were halted abruptly. The secret police became particularly harsh with the minority groups, suspecting them of disloyalty. Meanwhile greater attention was given to promoting Slavophilism, a philosophy that endorsed both religious Orthodoxy—that is, Russian Orthodoxy, not autocratic Roman Catholicism—and

What's in a name? Jewish names have great significance. They may express the values of the community. They may indicate the acculturation or the assimilation of one's family. They may demonstrate desire to change one's identity and become part of the surrounding society, or they may indicate one's profession.

Consider my own surname. Conventionally it is assumed to come from the German word for "flower," Blume. Actually it is a mangled version of the Spanish Paloma, "dove." It is spelled "Bloomberg," not "Blumberg," but the genesis of the name is the same. It was fashionable at one time to add a suffix to Bloom or Blum, so Jews added -stein, or -feld, or -thal. Although there are dozens of communities in Germany named Blumberg, the name is really just an extension of Blum.

Consider some other Jewish surnames:

Eckstein: Eckstein means "cornerstone" and is a reference to Psalm 118:22: "The stone that the builders rejected has become a cornerstone." This has been viewed traditionally as a reference to the tragic fate of Israel and expressed the hope that in the future its fortunes would rise.

Hefter: This name indicates a worker with gold braid and lacing. Jews in the 17th and 18th centuries were very involved in this trade.

Kaganoff: Kahn, a form of kohen, becomes Kagan among Russian Jews. The suffix -off indicates descent, so Kaganoff means "descended from a kohen."

Krauss: This name describes a curly-headed person.

Schick: Schich, Shick, or Shik is the acronym for Shem Yisrael Kodesh, "the name of Israel is holy."

Weinreb: Weinreb means "vine" in German, and Weinraub is the Yiddish form. Weinstock is a vine garland that decorated a wine shop. When Joseph II issued a law compelling Austrian Jews to assume family names, they were forbidden to take Hebrew names. Jews eluded the restriction by preserving a Hebrew name symbolically. In Jeremiah 6:9 Israel is compared to a vine. Jeremiah's comparison is reflected in the Jews' choice of surnames.

Zackheim: The name Zackheim is an acronym for zera kodesh hem, "they are the children of holy seed," indicating Jews who are the descendants of martyrs.

Do you know the history of your surname?

Great Russian nationalism, while rejecting Western ideals and liberalism.

Russian leaders began to ask themselves about the Jews: Were Jews useful or harmful to the state? To what extent had the Jews made themselves part of the Russian people? The conclusions reached were that although the new Jewish intelligentsia and industrial aristocracy desired to become more Russified, the masses did not. They were not at all part of the state, despite the favors that had been offered them, such as the reduction of the term of military service.

This thinking led Alexander to restore his decree against the traditional form of Jewish dress. All Jewish government schools were closed; even the official rabbinical seminaries established to prepare rabbis who would "modernize" Judaism were closed. Alexander rejected the advice of some of his ministers to abolish the Pale of Settlement.

In their periodicals the advocates of Jewish Enlightenment, the maskilim, encouraged Jews to become familiar with Russian language and culture and to abandon traditional Jewish studies, dress, and lifestyle. They expected that such changes and assimilation to the surrounding culture would be rewarded with full and equal rights under Russian law and acceptance into Russian society. However, 1871 brought with it a major pogrom in Odessa, the prime center of Jewish Enlightenment, or Haskalah. This did much to undercut the message of the maskilim.

The May Laws

On March 13, 1881, Alexander II was killed by a bomb thrown into his carriage. He was succeeded by his son, Alexander III (1845–1894). Alexander was an autocrat. He rejected the advances of the Western world in favor

1881 Map of part of Russia

of Slavophilism, and he was an uncompromising nationalist. In his youth, Alexander had been tutored by Constantin Pobedonostsev, a reactionary and fanatic, who served from 1880 to 1905 as Chief Procurator of the Orthodox Church. He was taught hatred for democratic reform, firm belief in the principle of the divinity of autocratic government, unswerving loyalty to the narrowest interpretation of Russian Orthodox Christianity, and a mystical trust in the *narodnost* (belief in the Russian people) system. In April 1891 he announced, "We can have no other policy except one that is purely Russian and national." For Alexander the ideal nation had only one nationality, one language, one religion, and one form of administration.

Alexander's policies were placed in the hands of Pobedonostsev, who quickly became the most powerful man in Russia. He began by drafting the "Police Constitution," which gave arbitrary powers of arrest to the governors of the various provinces. The judicial and educational systems were redesigned so that they would favor the aristocracy. Every medium of public opinion was made subject to censorship. Germans, Poles, Ukranians, Estonians, Latvians, Finns, and Armenians all saw their school systems restructured and their religious institutions restaffed with Russians. These non-Russian minorities were forbidden to use their native languages in school, the courtroom, state banks, railway offices, or any other state enterprise.

The Jews felt the effects of the new policies as well. Jews were identified as the central group at fault—they were the group responsible for the ills of Russia. It was, after all, the Jews who had crucified Jesus and spilled his holy blood. The Jews, it was said, were involved in the assassination of Alexander II; it was suggested that there was a "secret Jewish conspiracy" against Mother Russia.

The spring and summer of 1881 brought pogroms—"spontaneous" outbreaks—throughout southern Russia and Ukraine. Hundreds of Jewish homes were looted in Kiev, in Balta, even in Warsaw, and nearly 100 Jews were killed or maimed; the police watched but did not intervene. Jews were plagued by expulsions, deportations, arrests, and beatings. The lower class was affected, but so were the middle class and the Jewish intelligentsia.

In August 1881 Alexander appointed a new Minister of the Interior, Nikolai Ignatiev. Ignatiev was a Slavophile and, more important, he hated Jews. In October 1881 he appointed a "Central Committee for the Revision of the Jewish Question"; this Central Committee determined the fate of Jews until the end of the Russian Empire in March 1917, placing them under a dizzying and paralyzing collection of legal disabilities. The beginning was the May Laws.

The Central Committee submitted its report in the spring of 1882. Its recommendations were enacted by the Czar on May 3, 1882, and came to be known as the "May Laws." Jews were told that no Jew would be permitted to settle in any rural area in Russia, not even within the Pale of Settlement. Jews already living in the villages of the Pale—two-fifths of the Pale's inhabitants—could be evicted, so long as they were determined to be "vicious" inhabitants. Jews looking for work and thus circulating among the villages were classified as "new settlers" and expelled. A Jew could not take in his widowed mother when she lived in a different village, nor could he inherit a father's business in another village, nor could he go to a hospital in another village without facing expulsion. Thousands of small towns were reclassified as villages; thus they became off limits to Jews. Jews began to leave the newly restricted countryside for the already congested cities.

The May Laws also restricted the access of Jews to the Russian school system. The quotas for Jews in the secondary schools and universities were reduced dramatically, so that many thousands of young Jews had to leave Russia to study in Central and Western Europe. Doctors, lawyers, or artisans, who were considered to be pursuing a "respectable" occupation and thus were permitted to live outside the Pale, were nevertheless discouraged from doing so.

The most stunning outcome of the May Laws was the eviction in 1891 of the 20,000 Jews living in Moscow. On the first day of Passover the Jews were told to pack up. They were manacled and taken to the railroad station. The famous synagogue of Moscow was boarded up and could not be used. Similar mass expulsions took place in Kharkov and St. Petersburg.

The Bund: A Mass Jewish Socialist Movement

Life in the Pale of Settlement presented a number of features that made it ready for the emergence of a Jewish socialist movement. One feature was the secularism supported by the Haskalah, or Jewish Enlightenment, without which any political activism would have been inconceivable. A second feature was the *hevras,* which were forerunners to trade unions. A third was the yearning for social justice, an ideal which persisted even in the absence of religious observance.

Most importantly, however, the structure of the Jewish economy in the Pale was altered dramatically by the Russian economic boom of the late 19th century. Textile plants, tanneries, and tobacco factories appeared in the Pale. Perhaps 40 percent of the Jews in the Pale worked in these factories. Working conditions in the textile plants were terrible. Looms were tended 17 and 18 hours a day, men and women worked under exceptionally dangerous conditions, and the wages were the lowest in Russia.

In the early 1890s, a group of rabbinical students, who felt that their studies were not addressing the burning social issues of the day, began to preach Marxism to the impoverished people of the Pale of Settlement. They encountered great difficulty in communicating their message, for Marxism was assimilationist in character and Russian in form and content. The majority of Jewish workers wanted to remain Jewish in their personal and cultural lives and were opposed to any kind of bloody class revolution. They were most interested in higher wages and shorter hours and less interested in abstract theorizing.

Successful strikes in 1895 and 1896, initiated and sustained by the workers, changed everything. The

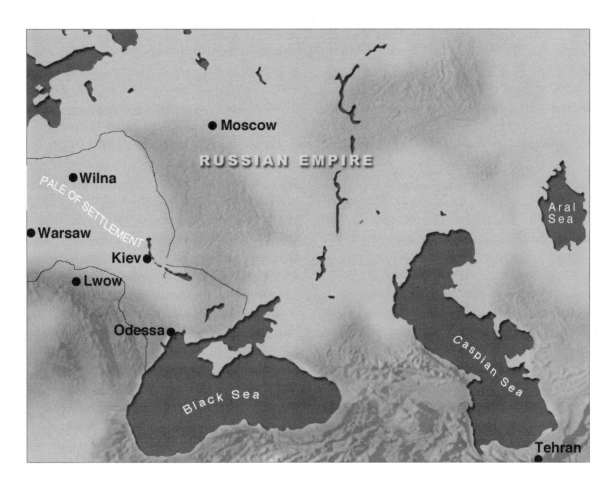

1885 Map of Russian Empire

founders decided to shift their focus to strike agitation. They also decided reluctantly that the language of Jewish socialism would have to be Yiddish. An independent Yiddish-speaking labor group would have to be established.

In the winter of 1897, the same year in which Theodor Herzl conducted the First Zionist Congress, to be discussed in Chapter 7, 15 Jewish socialists met in the back room of a Vilna blacksmith's house to establish the Jewish socialist organization, the Bund. The Bund entered the Russian Social Democratic Labor Party as an autonomous body with its first president, Arkady Kremer, elected as a member of the party's central committee.

Although Kremer said at the founding meeting that

it will have the special task of defending the specific interests of the Jewish workers, carry on the struggle for the civic rights of the Jewish workers and above all carry on the struggle against discriminatory anti-Jewish laws,

he paid minimal attention to this commitment. His focus was on organizing strikes in the Jewish industrial areas of the Pale. His success in these efforts bore fruit, as tens of thousands of young Jewish men and women joined the Bund.

In its early years, however, the Bund was simply imitating the formulas and programs of the Russian Social Democratic Party. It needed to define itself as a Jewish socialist party. A distinguished Jewish historian, Dr. Simon Dubnow, attempted to accomplish this. The Jews are, to be sure, a separate nation, he said, but Jewish national autonomy can be achieved outside of Palestine, perhaps even within the Russian Empire. The fourth convention of the Bund endorsed this view, which called for Jewish autonomism in Russia.

A Russian police raid on a revolutionary organization. From a French illustrated weekly, 1881.

The Bund needed a leader, however, who could make the case for Jewish autonomism. A 24-year-old young man, Vladimir Medem, took the reins of Bund leadership from Kremer. Medem came from a completely assimilated family and had been baptized as a child, but, as he read about Marxism and socialism, he was simultaneously drawn back to the Jewish people. It was Medem who became the Bund's most eloquent spokesman for Jewish autonomism.

At the second congress of the Russian Social Democrats, Medem demanded autonomy for the Bund within the party. When this was refused, he declared independence for the Bund and left the convention hall. In 1905 Medem and his colleagues endorsed cultural autonomy for Russian Jewry, demanding that the state recognize Yiddish as a legal language of Russia and provide funds for the establishment of a Yiddish school system.

During 1904 and 1905, the Bund organized massive strikes in the industrial cities of Lodz and Bialystok, distributing leaflets in the hundreds of thousands and organizing street demonstrations that attracted tens of thousands. On May Day in 1905, the Bund participated in a nationwide walkout. During 1905, there were countless strikes in factories, on railroads, in sweatshops, and in textile mills.

Bundist strength peaked in 1905. From 1905 until the First World War, however, it went into a rapid decline. In any case, Jewish socialism was an expression of national consciousness. Secularism, dignity, national revival, and greater economic security were the major themes of the period in which the Bund was founded.

Nicholas II

Alexander III died in November 1894 and was succeeded by his son, Nicholas II (1868–1918). Whereas Alexander was stern and inflexible, Nicholas was inept, shallow, timid, and shy. He was influenced by the opinions of Pobedonostsev and the views of his wife, Alexandra, granddaughter of England's Queen Victoria, but, more important, by the counsel of Grigori Rasputin.

Nicholas was more of an anti-Semite than his father. His ministers realized this and tried to win his favor by issuing new anti-Semitic decrees. This became the way to get ahead, to achieve prominence and power in the court of the Czar. Pogroms occurred throughout Russia, organized and supported by the government. There were more expulsions, more diminishing of basic human rights, more enforcement of school admission quotas, more restrictions on Jewish learning and observance. When these conditions were accompanied by poverty and a high infant mortality rate, Jewish life became even more intolerable than it had been.

The year 1891 brought a famine to Russia. Drought and terrible weather combined with poor transportation, governmental corruption, and inefficiency led to a severe food shortage. More than 400,000 peasants died in the famine.

But who was to blame? The Jews! Nicholas became determined to blame the Jews for the famine and for Russian poverty. He appointed von Plehve, a Baltic German, as Minister of the Interior. Plehve concluded that it had now become necessary to engage in systematic murder and pillage, to move toward violence. The Russian people needed to be encouraged to carry out "spontaneous" uprisings against Jewish "exploitation."

Kishinev, the capital city of Bessarabia, the westernmost province of Russia at the beginning of the 20th century, provided the first test of Russia's readiness for violence. Russians and Jews had always lived there in friendship. Some peasants living outside Kishinev discovered the mutilated body of a little boy.

The boy's uncle confessed to the crime, but the local anti-Semitic newspaper accused the Jews of having used the boy's body for ritual murder. In April 1903, government representatives met with the editor of the newspaper and provincial officials and urged them to circulate handbills encouraging the town's residents to inflict what they called a "bloody punishment" on the Jews. On Sunday, April 6, 1903, a mob of Russian teenagers—perhaps having been given a signal—went on a rampage, looting Jewish stores and homes. Forty-five Jews were murdered, more than 600 were severely injured, and 1,300 homes were destroyed. Rapes, beatings, torture, and other atrocities took place; the police watched but did not interfere.

The year 1904 brought the Russo-Japanese War. Russia was experiencing severe internal problems, as workers' strikes took place and the threat of revolution lurked. Nicholas, acting on the advice of Plehve, now his chief minister, attempted to distract his people with a patriotic war. With Russia's defeat, however, Nicholas lost the people's tolerance for autocratic monarchy. Sailors mutinied, the army's loyalty became suspect, and revolutionary violence began again.

Plehve was assassinated by terrorists in July 1904 when a bomb was thrown under his carriage while he was on his way to report to Nicholas. Nicholas, extremely frightened by this act and by the threat of other strikes and assassinations, made some concessions; thus, for example, censorship was relaxed and state workmen's insurance was established. The strikes and assassinations continued, however.

On January 22, 1905, came "Bloody Sunday." Czarist guards fired into a working people's parade, killing and wounding some 1,500 men and women. The revolutionaries responded by assassinating the Grand Duke Sergei Aleksandrovich, the Czar's brother. In October 1905 the Marxist Social Democrats called a massive nationwide strike, which paralyzed Russia's entire economy.

On October 30 Nicholas capitulated, issuing a manifesto which promised the Russian people a constitution, basic civil rights, and a Duma, a parliament, to be chosen by election. This parliament would have the power of veto, the last say regarding any proposed laws. Reactions to this manifesto varied, however.

The revolutionaries saw it as indecisive and insincere; the moderates, or Constitutional Democrats ("Cadets"), were grateful but cautious; the monarchists and conservatives were aghast at the concessions made by the Czar.

Nicholas allowed the first Duma to meet. The Jews had participated in the election campaign, with 12 Jewish deputies becoming members of the Duma. The spokesman for this group was a lawyer from St. Petersburg, Maxim M. Vinaver, a highly regarded member of the Constitutional Democrats. The Jews wanted the enactment of a law on civil equality for every inhabitant of the Russian Empire.

Such a law was proposed in the Duma, with 151 members supporting it. Unfortunately this law was never enacted, for by April 1906 an Imperial Decree had restored power to the Czar. There were later Dumas, but these bodies lacked real power. For example, the second Duma convened in 1907; it had many members of the extreme right, a very strong representation from the left, and a very weak center. Without any common ideological ground, this Duma was essentially useless. The fourth Duma similarly became nothing more than a rubber stamp.

Among the anti-Semites of Russia, the most notorious was Peter Stolypin. Stolypin was governor of the provinces of Saratov and Grodno and was notable for his ability to suppress peasant uprisings. In 1906 he was appointed Minister of the Interior, as his administrative skills, personal courage, and militant Russian nationalism caught the Czar's attention. From this juncture on he was Russia's prime minister without holding that title.

Stolypin was determined to crush the incipient revolution. This meant oppression and terror, and it meant extremes of Russification. It also meant drowning the revolution in Jewish blood. Ready for Stolypin's use was the Union of the Russian People and its activist arm, the "Black Hundreds." This organization, established in St. Petersburg in October 1904, drew upon Russia's lower middle class and minor government officials, people who believed they were being excluded from the benefits of growing capitalism in Russia. The Union also had the blessing of the Czar. It was the first really modern instrument of Russian anti-Semitism, as it aimed at the emerging liberal middle class of Russia, which it called the "Jewish middle class." A list of proposed assassination victims was drawn up, most of them bourgeois liberals, including several Jewish members of the Duma. Hundreds of assassinations were carried out by the Black Hundreds.

With Stolypin's accession to power, the Black Hundreds continued their work. They carried out pogroms in the Jewish districts of Kiev, Odessa, Bialystok, and Minsk. At the same time, members of the Union published and distributed handbills in town squares, warning Russians that the Jews were their oppressors. The Jews, said the handbills, shared opinions similar to those of the German factory-owners, the Japanese, the Poles, and the English. The Black Hundreds, with the tacit support of the Czar, moved through the Pale, burning, raping, and killing. Demonstrating their patriotism, they carried with them portraits of the Czar, national flags, and church banners.

In addition to pogroms, Stolypin intensified legal assaults on the Jews. The May Laws had made the lives of Jews more miserable, but Stolypin wanted them to be applied with the utmost brutality. The expulsion of Jews from cities outside the Pale had to be immediate; the movement of Jews from villages to towns of the Pale could not be postponed. Jews were told they could not be educated by the Russian school system. Jewish religious and cultural institutions were denied police protection, and many were forced to close. Jews were labeled "werewolves," "bloodsuckers," and "traitors" by the government newspapers.

In 1911 the "blood libel" accusation was revived. A Christian child was murdered in Kiev, most likely by a criminal named Vera Cheberiak, because he had threatened to expose a band of thieves of which she was the leader. The Kiev cell of the Union of the Russian People saw an opportunity to organize a major demonstration and accuse the Jews of ritual murder. Two professors of medicine, who later admitted that they had been bribed, testified that the child's blood had been drained while he was still alive. Mendel Beilis, a Jewish manager of a brick factory, was arrested and accused of carrying out this crime and providing the Jews with the blood needed for ritual purposes.

The district attorney in Kiev used every means of cross-examination and torture to "persuade" Beilis to confess, but could not make him do so. Beilis was eventually brought to trial at the end of 1913. No real evidence was available. Moreover, it was discovered by a liberal journalist that Vera Cheberiak had cooperated with the government in planting the dead boy's clothing in Beilis's home. In addition, she had killed her own son, lest he disclose the facts regarding the boy's murder. Beilis was found not guilty, but this verdict did not mean that the ritual murder charge had been discredited.

RUSSIAN REVOLUTION

The invasion of Russia by the powerful German army during World War I brought the Czar's forces to their knees. The Russian war effort was crippled by corruption and mismanagement. Soldiers, insufficiently clothed, were found frozen in the trenches; workers, weakened by hunger and fatigue, were collapsing at their workbenches. Russia was plagued by bread riots and mutinies of the troops.

As the Russians retreated before the Germans, Grand Duke Sergei, the army's commander-in-chief, announced that the Jews living in the Pale of Settlement could not be trusted to remain in territory invaded by the Germans. In March 1915, therefore, the Russian army began to expel Jews from the Polish provinces and from Kovno in Lithuania. Had the Germans not entered Russia so quickly, every one of

Mendel Beilis on trial.

the 2 million Jews living in the Pale might have been expelled. As it was, 600,000 were forced to move into the interior of Russia. About 100,000 Jews died from starvation and exposure during this expulsion.

In March 1917 Nicholas II, Czar of all the Russias, was forced to abdicate. The Jews of Russia rejoiced. No longer would they be subject to the Romanovs. Instead the "February Revolution" installed a Provisional Government led by Alexander Kerensky.

Kerensky had complete support of the Jews. He advocated democracy, although it was to be led by the bourgeois. He promised national autonomy to non-Russian people and began to make changes in policy for the Jews of Ukraine. In April 1917, all 650 anti-Jewish laws in Russia were abolished. Would Kerensky have given the Jews the degree of national and cultural autonomy they sought? Who is to say, for November brought the Bolshevik faction of the Russian Social Democratic Party to power in his place.

The Bolsheviks wished to establish a totalitarian Communist regime. Many Jews were prominent among the Bolsheviks: Jacob Sverdlov was the first president of the Central Executive Committee; Grigori Zinoviev became the president of the Third International; Maxim Litvinov became Commissar for Foreign Affairs; Karl Radek was Press Commissar; D. Riazanov was chairman of the Marx-Engels Institute and the leading Marxist historian; Jakob Yoffe, Lev Kamenev, and Lazar Kaganovich became major figures in the Soviet regime. All of these, however, were not only non-Jewish Jews but anti-Jewish Jews.

Of all the Jewish Bolsheviks, the most prominent was Leon Trotsky (1879–1940). Trotsky was the son of a Ukrainian Jewish farmer. While still a teenager, he became acquainted with Marxist ideology and concluded that he ought to become a member of the Russian Social Democratic Party; he also decided at some point to dedicate his life to establishing a proletarian dictatorship in Russia. By virtue of his powerful intellect and his enormous energy, Trotsky had access to the inner councils of the party before he was 20. After the Bolshevik Revolution, the party appointed him Commissar of Foreign Affairs, then Commissar of Defense. The Red Army was organized by Trotsky, a Jew. He was its commander-in-chief. He planned its campaigns and personally led it against the counterrevolutionary forces. With the death of Lenin in 1924, Trotsky was exiled. He was later assassinated in 1940 near Mexico City at the command of Joseph Stalin (1879–1953).

The Jewish Communists were known as the Yevsektsiya. Semyon M. Dimanshtein led this group but also directed the Commissariat for Jewish National Affairs. Dimanshtein had studied in the Telshe yeshiva but had been forced to leave after leading a student demonstration. He later studied in the Slobodka yeshiva, where he was attracted to the Musar movement. Then he studied in the Lubavitcher yeshiva, since he was attracted to Hasidism. He received rabbinical ordination from the renowned Rabbi Chaim Ozer Grodzensky of Vilna. The establishment of the great yeshivot, the creation of the Musar movement, and the history of Hasidism will all be examined in later chapters.

The Jews of the Yevsektsiya were ruthless and fanatical in their treatment of Judaism and Jewish society. Observant Jews were persecuted, religious schools and synagogues were closed, leading rabbinic scholars and laypersons were exiled or executed and religious artifacts were confiscated. By 1919 all local religious *kehillot* (communities), the agencies of Jewish self-government for centuries, had been abolished, and their assets and functions were taken over by the Yevsektsiya. Zionism was seen as the enemy, so all organized Zionist activity was forced underground. The Hebrew language was banned, although Yiddish was not; presumably Yiddish was viewed as a secular, proletarian, progressive language—unlike Hebrew, which was a holy, religious tongue that had no place in Russia, the new utopia.

Lenin (1870–1924) led the Bolshevik faction within the Russian Social Democratic Workers Party. His motto was "Bread, Peace, and Land." In accordance with this slogan, the Bolsheviks began with peace when, on March 3, 1918, Russia and Germany signed the Treaty of Brest-Litovsk. Large areas of land were then confiscated and transformed into collective settlements. Factories were organized around workers, soldiers, and Communist bureaucrats. But the speed with which this happened led to major economic troubles in 1920. Lenin was forced to create a New Economic

Lev Davidovich Bronstein, known as Trotsky, arrives in Mexico, 1936.

Policy. This was helpful but not before the famines of 1921–1922 had taken the lives of hundreds of thousands of Russians, who starved to death; thus the "bread" of Lenin's motto was still lacking.

After Lenin died in 1924, his "leadership" continued as Russia was introduced to the Five Year Plan. This plan was aimed at developing a truly Communist economy instead of the capitalist economy in place. The idea was to bring Russia to industrialization within five years.

The Five Year Plan was quite successful. Post–World War I Russia had about 2.5 million Jews. Other Jews, who had previously been citizens of the Czarist Empire, were now in the successor states. Most Russian Jews lived in Ukraine and White Russia, areas that were previously in the Pale of Settlement; the Soviet government had abolished the Pale as one of its first acts.

Without being restricted to the Pale, many thousands of Jews, perhaps as many as 750,000, moved into the interior of Russia. This migration brought some relief from the economic stresses of the Pale, as some 400,000 Jews were employed by the Soviet government while another 750,000 worked in factories and other forms of industrial labor. However, some 1 million Jews who were petty tradesmen and artisans found no such relief. They were no better off than in czarist times.

The Soviets realized that the difficulties experienced by the Jews were simply the consequence of what the czars had done. It was decided to offer the Jews the opportunity to settle on land in Ukraine and the Crimea. The Jews were promised full government assistance. When this idea was communicated to Western philanthropic agencies, they welcomed it and offered their financial support. Some Jews seized the opportunity to own land, perhaps 175,000, but many more did not.

The Five Year Plan did more. As Russia became industrialized, hundreds of thousands of Jews took great advantage of the new vocational possibilities. Jewish tailors went down into the mines, shoemakers went to the timber regions of Russia, peddlers went to the oil fields. Industrial cities were built under the supervision of Jewish engineers, with Jewish workers in the thousands working in the plants. By 1932, the end of the Five Year Plan, 750,000 Jews were involved in the enormous process of industrialization.

JOSEPH STALIN

Joseph Stalin (1879–1953) succeeded Lenin as ruler of the Soviet Union and leader of the world Communist movement. Stalin was born in Gori in Georgia, the son of a shoemaker. His father was an alcoholic who was stabbed to death in a drunken brawl when Stalin was 11. His mother enrolled him in a local religious school, hoping he would choose to be a Russian Orthodox priest.

In his early years Stalin was supportive of the Jews as a nationality whose distinct culture and language would have to be considered if effective revolutionary work were to be performed among them. Thus he encouraged Yiddish culture and lent support to Jewish administrative institutions and agricultural settlements.

In 1926 Soviet officials were becoming greatly concerned by an increasing Chinese presence in the province of Birobidzhan, located in eastern Russia north of Manchuria. In order to protect Russia in case of a war in the Far East, it was decided to establish a Jewish Autonomous Region in eastern Russia. Although the harsh climate of Birobidzhan made it unlikely that Jews would seize the opportunity to settle there, the hope was that the idea of "national autonomy" would draw them.

From left to right: Stalin, Lenin, and Kalinin in February 1918.

As things turned out, most of the Jews who settled in Birobidzhan between 1927 and 1939 could not tolerate the climate. Some chose to stay, working on collective farm settlements. There were 70 of these by World War II. Most chose to leave, however, and in 1939 there were only 20,000 Jews in Birobidzhan, less than 1 percent of the Jewish population of Russia. The Birobidzhan project had failed.

At the beginning of his rule Stalin discouraged anti-Semitism, but the late 1930s brought a resurgence of anti-Semitism. For example, Stalin permitted the revival of anti-Semitic stereotypes and prejudices; those who were accused of anti-Semitism now received only light sentences. Stalin purged Jews from leadership positions in the Communist Party. Only Lazar Kaganovich, Stalin's trusted henchman, remained in a position of power. His family relationship with Stalin and his undoubted personal loyalty protected him from Stalin's purges of Jews.

Jewish culture suffered under Stalin as well. Jewish culture was seen as a nationalist deviation. Religious education was banned. Zionism was outlawed and Hebrew books were suppressed. Circumcision or synagogue attendance would lead to banishment from the Communist Party and loss of employment. Jews chose to forgo circumcision and they remained uneducated Jewishly. As we will see in Chapter 5, Lubavitcher Hasidim resisted these efforts and sought to rebuild Jewish life. Their efforts were frustrated, however, when their leader, R. Joseph Isaac Schneersohn (1880–1950), was forced to leave Russia.

On August 23, 1939, the Nazis and Soviets signed a Non-Aggression Pact. On September 1, 1939, World War II began, as Germany invaded Poland. Just two weeks later, Russia invaded Poland. Germany and the Soviet Union agreed to divide Poland, bringing another 2 million Jews under Russian rule.

Hitler invaded Russia in June 1941 with Operation Barbarossa. The impact on Russian Jews was tragic. Nazi *Einsatzgruppen* (special-duty groups) accompanied the German army. They rounded up the Jews of every community, forced them to dig large pits outside the town, and then shot them into the pits. Approximately 1.5 million died in the *Einsatzgruppen* massacres. Unfortunately the Soviet government did very little to stand in the way of these mass murders. The best-known massacre took place at Babi Yar in Ukraine.

Particularly distressing for Jews was the participation of the Ukrainians, who collaborated with the Nazis, one form of response to the fact that the Soviets had denied them independence. The Ukrainian partisan movement killed Jews, Soviet prisoners of war, and Poles.

The "black years" of Soviet Jewry began in 1948. Purges against Jews in public life were renewed. Jews could not serve in the foreign service or on the general staff of the Communist Party. Stalin began to see Jews as "cosmopolitan nationalists" whose interests lay in America and in the new state of Israel. When Jews welcomed Golda Meir as the first Israeli ambassador to Moscow, Stalin saw this as a symbol of continued Jewish internationalism and cosmopolitanism, as a deficiency in their Soviet patriotism.

The black years peaked with the "Doctors' Plot" of 1953, when Stalin claimed that a group of prominent Soviet Jewish physicians were plotting to poison Soviet leaders. Although Stalin died before the full impact of these accusations could be felt, this "plot" served as the basis for more purges and deportations.

NIKITA KHRUSHCHEV

Nikita Khrushchev succeeded Stalin. Khrushchev opposed the Doctors' Plot from the beginning. Upon Stalin's death, he revoked it and charged Stalin with anti-Semitism. But Khrushchev had his own methods of anti-Semitism. Jews could not hold high positions within the Soviet leadership. All but a few synagogues were closed. Jews could not produce matzot for Passover. Jews were blamed for the Hungarian Revolution of 1956. Jews were charged with economic crimes, such as black marketeering within the Soviet Union, and thus were singled out for undermining socialism. Fifty percent of the 250 individuals executed for economic crimes were Jews!

LEONID BREZHNEV AND THE REFUSENIKS

The stunning June 1967 Israel-Arab war, the Six-Day War, changed everything, making Jewish emigration the prime focus of Soviet Jews. The Russians had provided the Arabs with military equipment, but no less than $2 billion in Russian arms had been destroyed or captured by Israel. This humiliating defeat led the Soviets to engage in a massive propaganda effort that labeled Zionism a "world threat." Jews were depicted as sinister power brokers funded in secret by the unlimited wealth of world Jewry.

This propaganda campaign strengthened the Jews' desire to emigrate. Some had become convinced that the Soviet system was flawed and preferred to live in the Jewish homeland. Others saw that economic opportunities were unavailable in the Soviet Union, for an unofficial quota system for Jews in many professions stood in the way. A small minority sought to recover their religious roots.

The Soviets sought an opportunity to crush the campaign for emigration. In the spring of 1970, just such an opportunity presented itself. In December 1969 three Soviet-Jewish activists, Mark Dymshits, Edward Kuznetsov, and Sylva Zalmanson, decided to hijack a Soviet airliner, thereby calling attention to the emigration campaign. They intended to seize the airplane before takeoff and force the crew to fly to Stockholm, from where the three of them would proceed to Israel. The problem was that the KGB, the Soviet intelligence service, arrested them before takeoff, at the same time arresting 232 Jews in other cities.

One of the great heroic figures in the history of Soviet Jewry is Natan (Anatoly) Scharansky. Born in 1948 in Ukraine, he graduated from the Physical Technical Institute in Moscow with a degree in computer sciences.

Scharansky was one of Soviet Jewry's refuseniks. When he applied to emigrate in 1973, his visa was denied for "security" reasons. Refusing to accept this denial, he continued to engage in underground Zionist activities until the Soviets arrested him for treason and espionage in 1977. Although the United States denied that Scharansky was working for the CIA, he was found guilty and sentenced to 13 years' imprisonment. Scharansky's wife, Avital, waged an ongoing international campaign for his release, with the support of organizations around the world. These efforts resulted in his release by the Soviets in Berlin, Germany, on February 11, 1986. Scharansky was transported to Frankfurt, Germany, *where he boarded a plane that would bring him to Israel that same night.*

Scharansky has devoted himself to the cause of Soviet Jewry. When the Soviet Union collapsed in 1989 and mass immigration of Soviet Jews resulted, he urged that immigration and absorption of immigrants be high on Israel's agenda. It is for this reason that he established the Yisrael b'Aliya party.

From June 1996 to June 1999 Scharansky served as Minister of Industry and Trade in Israel, and from July 1999 until July 2000 he served as Minister of the Interior. Until the election of January 28, 2003, he was the Deputy Prime Minister and the Minister of Housing and Construction. After the election, Prime Minister Sharon persuaded him to resign his seat in the Knesset and join the government as a minister without portfolio, responsible for Jerusalem and Diaspora Affairs

Leonid Brezhnev presenting a decoration to his predecessor, Nikita S. Khrushchev.

The Soviets should have prosecuted the offenders for aerial hijacking, which was a crime everywhere, even in Israel and the United States. They chose instead to challenge the entire emigration movement, equating it with "treason and betrayal of the fatherland" and "anti-Soviet activity." The prosecution demanded the death penalty for the defendants, although there had been no actual hijacking! This was a major public relations gaffe, for protests came from all parts of the world. The governments of 24 nations intervened on behalf of the defendants. The Pope, Protestant religious leaders, Nobel Prize laureates, and others protested. Six days after the trial, the Supreme Court of the Russian Federal Republic commuted the death sentences to life imprisonment.

The lesson learned from the trial of the "hijackers" was the power of making the world aware of the situation of Soviet Jews. Petitions and letter-writing campaigns were organized. Posters appeared in American synagogues appealing to Jews to "Save Soviet Jewry" and to "Let My People Go." Rallies, lectures, "remembrance days," television interviews, and editorials all combined to make the world aware of the situation of Soviet Jewry.

During 1971 and 1972 tens of thousands of Jews applied for exit visas. The Jews of Moscow, of whom there were about 340,000, were especially important.

They lived in Russia's capital city and were in contact with members of the foreign diplomatic corps and with foreign journalists and tourists, many of whom were Jews. When denied visas, the Moscow Jews would engage in public demonstrations in the streets, sit-down strikes in government offices, hunger strikes in jail. The assumption was that the Russians would prefer not to look bad in the eyes of the world.

Supporters of Soviet Jews in the West called them "refuseniks." The Soviets denied them visas, dismissed them from employment, and imposed on them crippling exit taxes, but all this did not undermine the emigration campaign. In fact, from January 1968 to mid-1973 no fewer than 62,000 Jews left the Soviet Union, most leaving the Soviet republics of Georgia and Azerbaijan.

Why were so many Jews being permitted to leave? The General Secretary of the Soviet Communist Party and President of the USSR from 1964 to his death in 1982 was Leonid Brezhnev. He wanted to gain access to American technology and to be accorded the status of most-favored-nation, provided to America's closest partners in trade. To qualify as a most-favored-nation meant that goods produced in the Soviet Union could be imported into the United States without high tariffs. It also meant that increased commercial credits would be offered by the United States. Clearly it was in the interest of the Soviet Union to enjoy such privileges.

Senator Henry Jackson, a powerful Democrat and supporter of the National Conference on Soviet Jewry, sponsored a resolution that would deny most-favored-nation status to any Communist nation "unless that country permits its citizens to emigrate to the country of their choice." The thinking in this resolution, known as the Jackson-Vanik amendment, was to link most-favored-nation status to emigration policy.

After two years of negotiation, an agreement was reached, in October 1975, between the United States and Russia. The Soviets agreed to permit the departure of not less than 60,000 applicants per year. The Soviets did not, however, take advantage of the most-favored-nation rights. Moreover, so bitter were they about the Jackson-Vanik amendment that between 1975 and 1983, the total number of Jews permitted to leave Russia was only 150,000.

MIKHAIL GORBACHEV AND THE COLLAPSE OF THE SOVIET UNION

Things improved for the Jews under President Mikhail Gorbachev, who governed the Soviet Union from June 1985 to December 1991. Gorbachev was most interested in improving the image of the Soviet Union abroad and restructuring the Soviet economy. He wanted to cultivate better relations with Israel, and he permitted the expression of Jewish culture within the Soviet Union. Gorbachev also permitted Jewish emigration from the Soviet Union. By the early 1990s, hundreds of thousands of Jews were emigrating from Russia to Israel; as will be told in Chapter 6, Israel would face the daunting task of absorbing and acculturating them.

In August 1991, Gorbachev was suddenly ousted from power by Soviet military leaders and hard-line Communists. This challenge lasted for only two days, though, with Gorbachev returning to power. By this time, Communism was no longer an ideological and political force. Gorbachev resigned as head of the Communist party on August 23 and the Supreme Soviet banned Communists from all political activity in the Soviet Union.

In December 1991, the Soviet Union dissolved and Mikhail Gorbachev resigned from the presidency. At this time, 11 former republics of the Soviet Union constituted themselves as the Commonwealth of Independent States.

BORIS YELTSIN

The successor to Gorbachev as leader of Russia was Boris Yeltsin. President Yeltsin governed from December 1991 until his resignation in December 1999. Yeltsin was born in 1931 in the village of Butka, located in western Siberia. Trained as an engineer at the Ural Polytechnic Institute, he spent his early working years in local housing construction. At age 30 he became a member of the Communist Party.

As Jews evaluated Yeltsin, they were concerned with his views on three central issues: anti-Semitism, Russian nationalism, and populism. The major threat to the Jews was Pamyat, an ultra-nationalist group known for its virulent anti-Semitism. Yeltsin had a number of opportunities to disavow this group but did not take advantage of them. Called upon to condemn anti-Semitism, he did not do so. Does this mean that Yeltsin was an anti-Semite? Not necessarily. Perhaps he was trying not to offend Pamyat, while not sharing its views at all.

Pamyat supported Russian nationalism, as do most Russians. The theme of "Mother Russia" continues to be a popular one in Russian literature, film, and music. If Yeltsin had been too friendly with Jews, people might have questioned his nationalism. As far as populism is concerned, to label Yeltsin a populist is to oversimplify a man talented enough to make it through both the difficult Brezhnev years and the dynamic Gorbachev years. Yeltsin also led the popular resistance to an attempted coup against Gorbachev.

VLADIMIR PUTIN

The successor to Yeltsin was Vladimir Putin, elected President of Russia in 2000 and still holding office. Putin was a colonel in the KGB and thus was expected to return Russia to hard-core Communism. Surprisingly, he has provided Russia with stability and predictability. In addition, he has aligned Russia with the West, leading to economic benefit and increased personal popularity.

Putin, who has become a close ally and personal confidante of President George W. Bush, has encouraged Bush to overturn the 1974 Jackson-Vanik amendment, discussed earlier in this chapter. This was a Cold War law imposing trade restrictions on nations that limited emigration and persecuted those who sought to leave.

Vladimir Putin

Putin has made a number of goodwill gestures toward Russia's Jews. Thus he attended the opening of Russia's first Jewish community center. Present for this occasion were Anatoly Scharansky, the Chief Rabbi of Israel, Mordechai Eliyahu, and the ambassadors of Israel and the United States. Putin later appeared with Hasidic rabbis at an outdoor lighting of Hanukah candles. Finally, he hosted Moshe Katsav, the President of Israel, at the Kremlin. For this event, the Kremlin created a kosher kitchen, requiring the presence of a group of rabbis, all-new cooking utensils, and a blowtorch.

These are positive signs, given Russia's history of anti-Semitism. Putin has not yet condemned expressions of racial hatred, however, nor has he moved to enforce the laws against such expressions.

SUMMARY

This chapter has examined the history of the Jews in Eastern Europe from the middle of the 18th century to the present day. Jews were forced to live in the Pale of Settlement, which had been created by Czarina Catherine II. Among the difficulties confronted by Soviet Jews were the May Laws, the pogroms, and oppression by the notorious anti-Semite Peter Stolypin.

Although Jews welcomed the fall of the czars, the Russian Revolution had a profound impact on their lives. The years of Stalin were difficult for Russian Jews, as were the years under Khrushchev. Jews fared somewhat better under Brezhnev, as the desire of many Jews to leave Russia became more apparent and as Brezhnev looked for access to American science and technology. Gorbachev's treatment of Jews was even more open, as all Russian citizens were free to emigrate by virtue of a law passed in the Soviet parliament. Hundreds of thousands of Jews left for Israel and other destinations, as the Soviet Union collapsed in December 1991 and the Commonwealth of Independent States took its place.

Boris Yeltsin succeeded Gorbachev. Yeltsin was something of an unknown, leading Jews to be concerned that he might be an anti-Semite. His repeated reluctance to publicly disavow Pamyat, an ultra-nationalist, anti-Semitic group, supported their concern. Yeltsin resigned abruptly in December 1999, however, leading to a new election. Vladimir Putin, formerly a colonel in the KGB, won this election. Putin was expected to return to hardcore Communism, but surprised Russians by aligning himself with the West and becoming a close ally of President Bush. A number of goodwill gestures were made toward the Jews, awaking hope that their lives would be improved under his rule.

Documents

ALEXANDER I: STATUTES CONCERNING THE ORGANIZATION OF THE JEWS (DECEMBER 9, 1804)

This document contains the first Russian legislation dealing with the Jews. In 1802 Alexander, who ruled from 1801 to 1825, appointed a Committee for the Amelioration of the Jews. He accepted its recommendations and proposals, incorporating them as legislation.

Numerous complaints have been submitted to us regarding the abuse and exploitation of native farmers and laborers in those provinces in which the Jews are permitted to reside. . . . The following regulations are in accord both with our concern with the true happiness of the Jews and with the needs of the principal inhabitants of those provinces. . . .

I. Education and Language

1. Jewish children may study in all the public schools, secondary schools and universities in Russia, on equal terms with other children.

2. Jewish pupils will neither be required to renounce their religion nor will they be compelled to study subjects which are contrary to their religion. . . .

6. If the Jews refuse, despite all these encouragements, to send their children to public schools, special schools must be built at their expense. For this purpose a special tax will be levied. The study of either Polish, Russian, or German must be included in the curriculum. . . .

8. All the Jews residing in the Russian Empire, although free to use their native language in all their religious and domestic affairs, are obliged, as of January 1807, to use the Russian, Polish, or German language in all public documents, contracts, and bills of sale. Otherwise these documents will not be registered. . . .

In accordance with these regulations, Jews who are elected as members of the municipal councils in the former Polish province shall, for the sake of order and uniformity, dress in the Russian or Polish fashion; whereas Jews elected to the municipal councils in those Russian provinces in which they are permitted to reside permanently shall dress in the German fashion. As of the year 1808, a Jew who cannot read and write either Russian, German, or Polish may not be elected to the municipal councils. . . .

10. As of the year 1812, a person who is not literate in one of the previously mentioned languages may not be appointed to a communal position or to the rabbinate.

II. The Status, Occupations, and Rights of the Jews

11. All the Jews are divided into four classes: (a) farmers, (b) manufacturers and craftsmen, (c) merchants, and (d) city dwellers. . . .

13. Jews who are farmers, as well as those who are manufacturers, craftsmen, merchants, and city dwellers, are allowed to purchase and own property in the unpopulated areas of the provinces of Lithuania, Belorussia, Little Russia, Kiev, Minsk, Volhynia, Podolia, Astrakhan, Caucasus, Ekaterinoslav, Kherson, and Tsabaria. They may sell the land, lease it, bequeath it, or bestow it as a gift. . . .

18. No Jew will be compelled to engage in agriculture in the aforementioned provinces, but those who do shall be exempt from payment of taxes for a period of ten years. This exemption, however, does not extend to debts related to the purchase of land. They will receive loans which will be repayable after a few years, on terms under which similar loans are given to settlers from abroad. . . .

20. Jews are permitted to establish factories of all kinds, in those provinces in which they are permitted to settle, with the same freedom and on the same basis as that granted to all subjects of Russia. . . .

23. In the aforementioned provinces, Jewish craftsmen may engage in any craft not prohibited by law. Managers of workshops or organizations of craftsmen may not interfere in their rights. They [i.e., Jews] are permitted to register as members of a craftsmen's association if it is not in conflict with local regulations. . . .

29. When all the Jews shall evince diligence and industry in agriculture, commerce, and manufacturing, the government will take steps to equalize their taxes to those of other Russian citizens.

III. The Duties of the Jews According to Their Aforementioned Class

30. If he is not registered in one of these classes, a Jew will not be tolerated anywhere in Russia. Jews who will not present a written document in standard legal form certifying their membership in a class will be regarded as vagrants and will be treated according to the full severity of the law. . . .

34. As of January 1, 1807, in Astrakhan, the Caucasus, Little Russia, and New Russia, and the other provinces mentioned, no Jew is permitted to hold rented property in any village or settlement. They may not own taverns, pubs, or inns, either in their own name or in that of a monitor. . . .

IV. The Legal Status of Jews

44. . . . No persons may coerce [the Jews], or disturb them in matters of their religious practice, and in civilian life generally, either in word or in deed. Their complaints, whatever they may be, will be heard before the courts and will be satisfied according to the strict letter of the law as it applies to all the citizens of Russia. . . .

NICHOLAS I: STATUTES REGARDING THE MILITARY SERVICE OF JEWS (AUGUST 26, 1827)

Nicholas I (1821–1855) thought that the problem of the Jews could best be resolved through coerced assimilation. This law was in effect until 1859. During the years it was in force, between 40,000 and 50,000 Jewish minors served in cantonist units.

I. General Rules Applying to the Jewish People

1. Upon being called to military service, Jews shall fulfill their obligation in a manner identical to that of other citizens who are members of that class which is required to serve in the armed forces. . . .

II. Manner of Fulfilling Military Draft Obligations

6. If, at the time of the call to service, it is generally permitted to substitute a sum of money for a recruit, this privilege shall be extended to Jews under the following conditions: (a) The Jewish community owes no back taxes to the government; (b) The community is not in debt to other communities or individuals. . . .

8. Jews presented by the community for the purpose of military service must be no younger than twelve and no older than twenty-five years of age. . . .

13. the Jews of each province must fill their quota of recruits independently of the Gentile population thereof. . . .

24. The responsibility for fulfilling the military obligations falls upon the Jewish communities themselves. They shall follow the dictates of the appropriate provincial authority. . . .

Exemptions:

58. In addition to merchants, rabbis also are exempt from military service. They must show proper documents proving their title. . . .

62. Jewish youths who are enrolled in general schools for a minimum of three years and who perform adequately

and those apprenticed to Gentile artisans are exempt from military service for the duration of their studies. . . .

64. Jews who have settled and who work upon land designated for agricultural purposes are exempt. . . .

X. The Assignment of Jews to Various Branches of the Military

74. Jewish minors—those under eighteen—shall be sent to preparatory institutions for military training [i.e., cantonist units].

75. Jews from the age of eighteen and upwards shall be assigned to active military duty according to their physical condition, as ordered by the military command.

XI. Jews Evading the Draft

87. Whoever discloses the names of those who hide a Jew escaping the draft shall receive a reward in the sum of one hundred rubles from the treasury. . . .

90. For the purpose of release from the draft, only time spent in active duty after the age of eighteen shall be taken into account.

91. Jews in active military duty are permitted to observe their religious customs during their spare time. This is in accordance with the law of the land concerning accepted religions. Commanding officers shall protect the Jews from disturbances or abuses which may be caused by their religious affiliation.

ALEXANDER III: THE MAY LAWS (MAY 3, 1882)

In response to the assassination of Alexander II in 1881, pogroms broke out against Jews. A commission established to investigate concluded that "Jewish exploitation" was the principal cause. As a result, the May Laws imposed further restrictions on the Jews.

The Council of Ministers, having heard the presentation made by the Minister of Internal Affairs regarding the execution of the Temporary Regulations regarding the Jews, has concluded as follows:

1. As a temporary measure, and until a general reexamination of the laws pertaining to the Jews takes place by set order, it is henceforth forbidden for Jews to settle outside the cities and townships. Existing Jewish settlements which are engaged in agricultural work are exempted [from this ban].

2. The registration of property and mortgages in the name of Jews is to be halted temporarily; the approval of the leasing by Jews of real estate beyond the precincts of the cities and townships is also to be halted temporarily. Jews are also prohibited from administering such properties.

3. It is forbidden for Jews to engage in commerce on Sundays and Christian holidays. . . .

4. The regulations contained in paragraphs one through three apply to those provinces in which the Jews permanently reside.

ON THE LATEST WAVE OF EMIGRATION (1891)

The year 1891 brought a sudden increase in Jews seeking to leave Russia, the numbers more than doubling. Their desire to leave resulted from concern about additional discriminatory laws, the expulsion of Jews from Moscow and other Russian cities, and severe economic depression in the Pale of Settlement.

With respect to the exodus of Jews from Russia—which has recently gained in momentum—the following letter appeared in the journal *Novoe Vremya:*

Since the spring of this year almost all the Jews living in the southern provinces of Russia have been seized by the urge to leave for abroad. The success of some few Jews who went to America; the false tales spread among the Jews by shipowners' agents about the success and happiness awaiting those who go; and the rumors circulated in anti-Jewish periodicals about the laws soon to be promulgated against them—all these have strengthened the desire of the Jews to leave Russia and go to Palestine or America, with no heed to the danger of this step and no fear of the evil into which they may fall. . . .

Those Jews who wish to go to America make every effort to find the money for the journey, and in anticipation of the success and happiness to come they sell all of their movable possessions. When they are unable to take their families with them, as is frequently the case, they go without them, leaving their wives and children to be a burden on the Jewish community. In most cases the fate of these abandoned wretches is miserable and bitter, for the charity of the Jewish community rarely suffices to meet their needs. And from the husbands and fathers in America come letters full of moans and wails about their bitter lot in the new country, for they soon realize there is no chance of success, it is difficult to find work, and their pay is sufficient only to buy themselves a few crusts of bread. How then could they save even a penny to send home to their families? Those who leave yearn with all their hearts to return to their homeland but are unable to find the money for the journey. Many of the refugees who went to America last year are in this miserable state. . . .

[An appeal from a Jewish immigration relief committee in Memel.] May it please you, dear Sir, to publish this letter to all the residents of this city cautioning them against leaving their homes for England or America without sufficient funds to cover the entire cost of the journey and assuming that help will be forthcoming from the committee in this city or in Hamburg. We feel compelled to issue a solemn warning that anyone doing so is bringing a grave disaster upon himself. We are unable to offer any monetary help whatsoever, and the police may seize him and expel him across the border back to his point of origin. . . . His blood is upon his own head, for we must abide by our warning. . . .

N. TCHAYKOVSKY: THE MASSACRE OF JEWS AT KISHINEV (JUNE 1, 1903)

As this document indicates, the town of Kishinev, capital of Bessarabia at the time, experienced a pogrom during Easter, on April 6 and 7, 1903. Approximately 50,000 Jews lived in Kishinev, about 45 percent of the population. Jews were accused of killing a Christian child in order to use his blood for their religious observances. More than 100 Jews died in the attack, and hundreds were injured.

. . . Shortly before Easter, when the Bishop of the Greek Church in the Kishinev province was asked to contradict the absurd rumor that the Jews murdered a young man for their ritual [at Passover], . . . this high priest publicly stated that he himself believed the story of Jews using Christian blood for ritualistic purposes.

The semi-official paper . . . openly preached the extermination of Jews for months . . . All applicants for permission to publish a more impartial paper having been repeatedly refused. . . .

And still, when the actual massacres began, the Governor—it is said now—failed for two days to obtain orders from the Ministry and the Czar at St. Petersburg to use military force against the housebreakers and murderers. Moreover, he refused in the course of those two days any communication with the suffering Jewish population, never left his private quarters, closed all the telephones in the town to the public, and prohibited [the sending of] any private telegrams from Kishinev to St. Petersburg.

The police of the town not only refused to render any efficient protection and assistance to the . . . attacked and murdered Jewish population, but deliberately prevented by force any assistance being rendered to them by those private persons who were willing to do so. The police actually pointed out Jewish houses to the rioters. Whenever Jews themselves attempted to gather to show armed resistance, the police and military instantly attacked, disarmed, and dispersed them.

The results of this terrible circumstance are awful: 118 Jews, men, women, and children, have already been buried; over 200 cases of serious injuries are still in the hospitals; and over 1,000 cases of lighter injuries [have been] attended [to] in infirmaries; 800 Jewish houses destroyed and demolished; 600 shops and stores broken into and looted; over 4,000 Jewish families have been rendered homeless and destitute. . . .

It has been learned that there were about 12,000 troops in Kishinev at the time, against 200 to 300 active rioters and housebreakers. And as soon as the Government chose to proclaim martial law, after two days of delay, all disorders instantly stopped. . . .

H. N. BIALIK: THE CITY OF SLAUGHTER (1903)

Bialik (1873–1934) was a great poet who lived in the Pale of Settlement and wrote his verse in modern Hebrew. He was sent to Kishinev by the Historical Commission in Odessa to interview survivors of the pogrom and record the atrocities.

Arise and go now to the city of slaughter;
Into its courtyard wind thy way;
There with thine own hand touch, and with the eyes of
 thine head,
Behold on tree, on stone, on fence, on mural clay;
The spattered blood and dried brains of the dead.
Proceed thence to the ruins, the split walls reach,
Where wider grows the hollow, and greater grows the
 breach;
Pass over the shattered hearth, attain the broken wall
Whose burnt and barren brick, whose charred stones
 reveal
The open mouths of such wounds, that no mending
Shall ever mend, nor healing ever heal.
There will thy feet in feathers sink, and stumble
On wreckage doubly wrecked, scroll heaped on manuscript,
Fragments against fragmented—
Pause not upon this havoc; go thy way. . . .

Descend then, to the cellars of the town,
There where the virginal daughters of thy folk were fouled,
Where seven heathens flung a woman down,
The daughter in the presence of her mother,
The mother in the presence of her daughter,
Before slaughter, during slaughter, and after slaughter!
Touch with thy hand the cushion stained, touch
The pillow incarnadined;
This is the place the wild ones of the wood, the beasts of
 the field
With bloody axes in their paws compelled thy daughters
 yield;
Beasted and swined!
Note also, do not fail to note,
In that dark corner, and behind that cask

Crouched husbands, bridegrooms, brothers, peering from
  the cracks,
Watching the sacred bodies struggling underneath
The bestial breath,
Stifled in filth, and swallowing their blood!
The lecherous rabble portioning for booty
Their kindred and their flesh!
Crushed in their shame, they saw it all;
They did not stir nor move;
They did not pluck their eyes out; they
Beat not their brains against the wall!

Perhaps, perhaps, each watcher had it in his heart to pray:
A miracle, O Lord,—and spare my skin this day!
Those who survived this foulness, who from their blood
  awoke,
Beheld their life polluted, the light of their world gone out—
How did their menfolk bear it, how did they bear this yoke?
They crawled forth from their holes, they fled to the
  house of the Lord,
They offered thanks to Him, the sweet benedictory word.
The *kohanim* [descendants of priestly families] sallied
  forth, to the Rabbi's house they flitted:
Tell me, O Rabbi, tell, is my own wife permitted?[1]
The matter ends; and nothing more.
And all is as it was before. . . .

Come, now, and I will bring thee to their lairs
The privies, jakes and pigpens where the heirs
Of Hasmoneans lay, with trembling knees,
Concealed and cowering,—the sons of the Maccabees!
The seed of saints, the scions of the lions!
Who, crammed by scores in all the sanctuaries of their
  shame,
So sanctified My name!
It was the flight of mice they fled,
The scurrying of roaches was their flight;
They died like dogs, and they were dead!

L. TROTSKY: A SOCIAL DEMOCRAT ONLY—FROM THE AUTOBIOGRAPHY PUBLISHED IN 1930 UNDER THE TITLE MY LIFE

Leon Trotsky (1879–1940), a Jew, born Lev
Davidovich Bronstein, was a Russian revolutionary,
Soviet, and Communist leader in early 20th-century
Russia. In this document, he presents his views.

In the spheres of religion and nationality, there was no
opposition between the country and the town; on the con-

---

[1]The *kohanim* are subject to strict laws of purity.

trary, they complemented one another in various respects.
In my father's family there was no strict observance of religion. At first, appearances were kept up through sheer in-
ertia: on holy days my parents journeyed to the synagogue
in the colony; Mother abstained from sewing on Saturdays,
at least within the sight of others. But all this ceremonial
observance of religion lessened as years went on—as the
children grew up and the prosperity of the family increased. Father did not believe in God from his youth, and
in later years spoke openly about it in front of Mother and
the children. Mother preferred to avoid the subject, but
when occasion required would raise her eyes in prayer.

In my mother's family, the Schpentzers, religion was
not observed at all, not counting the old aunt, who did not
matter. My father, however, wanted me to know the Bible
in the original, this being one of the marks of his parental
vanity, and therefore I took private lessons in the Bible
from a very learned old man in Odessa. My studies lasted
only a few months and did little to confirm me in the ancestral faith. . . .

Did the Schpentzer family have any political views?
Those of Moissey Filippovich, my mother's nephew,
were moderately liberal in a humanitarian way. They
were lightly touched by vague socialist sympathies,
tinged with Populist and Tolstoyan ideas. Political subjects were never openly discussed, especially in my presence; probably that was because they were afraid that I
might say something censurable at school and get myself
in trouble. And when casual reference to what was going
on or had taken place within the revolutionary movement
was made in the grown-ups' conversation, such as, for
example, "This was in the year of the assassination of
Czar Alexander II," it had the ring of a past as far removed as if they had said, "This was in the year
Columbus discovered America." The people who surrounded me were outside of politics.

During my school years I held no political views, nor for
that matter had I any desire to acquire them. At the same
time my subconscious strivings were tinged by a spirit of
opposition. I had an intense hatred of the existing order, of
injustice, of tyranny. Whence did it come? It came from the
conditions existing during the reign of Alexander III; the
highhandedness of the police; the exploitation practiced by
landlords; the grafting by officials; the nationalistic restrictions; the cases of injustice at school and in the street;
the close contact with children, servants, and laborers in
the country; the conversations in the workshop; the hu-
mane spirit in the Schpentzer family; the reading of
Nekrasov's poems and of all kinds of other books, and, in
general, the entire social atmosphere of the time. . . .

After the seizure of power, I tried to stay out of the government and offered to undertake the direction of the
press. It is quite possible that the nervous reaction after

the victory had something to do with that; the months that had preceded it had been too closely tied up with the preparatory work for the revolution. Every fiber of my entire being was strained to its limit. Lunacharsky [Anatoly Lunacharsky, Commissar for Education and Culture] wrote somewhere in the papers that Trotsky walked about like an electric battery and that each contact with him brought forth a discharge. The twenty-fifth of October brought the letdown. I felt like a surgeon who has finished a difficult and dangerous operation—I must wash my hands, take off my apron, and rest.

Lenin was in a different position. He had just arrived from his refuge, after spending three and a half months cut off from real, practical direction. One thing coincided with the other, and this only added to my desire to retire behind the scenes for a while. Lenin would not hear of it, however. He insisted that I take over the commissariat of the interior, saying that the most important task at the moment was to fight off counterrevolution. I objected and brought up, among other arguments, the question of a nationality. Was it worthwhile to put into our enemies' hands such an additional weapon as my Jewish origin?

Lenin almost lost his temper. "We are having a great international revolution. Of what importance are such trifles?"

A good-humored bickering began. "No doubt the revolution is great," I answered, "but there are still a good many fools left."

"But surely we don't keep step with the fools?"

"Probably we don't, but sometimes one has to make some allowance for stupidity. Why create additional complications at the outset?"

I have already had occasion to observe that the national question, so important in the life of Russia, had practically no personal significance for me. Even in my early youth, the national bias and national prejudices had only bewildered my sense of reason, in some cases stirring in me nothing but disdain and even a moral nausea. My Marxist education deepened this feeling and changed my attitude to that of an active internationalism. My life in so many countries, my acquaintance with so many different languages, political systems, and cultures only helped me to absorb that internationalism into my very flesh and blood. If, in 1917 and later, I occasionally pointed to my Jewish origin as an argument against some appointment, it was simply because of political considerations.

Sverdlov [Yakov Sverdlov, a Lithuanian Jew, who was a Russian revolutionary and Communist leader, one of the outstanding figures of the Bolshevik Revolution] and other members of the Central Committee were won over to my side. Lenin was in the minority. He shrugged his shoulders, sighed, shook his head reproachfully, and consoled himself with the thought that we should all have to fight the counterrevolution anyway, no matter what departments of the government we were in. But my going over to the press was also firmly opposed by Sverdlov; Bukharin [Nikolai Bukharin, a brilliant Russian who aided Lenin in building the Communist Party], he said, was the man for that. "Lev Davidovich should be set up against the rest of Europe. Let him take charge of foreign affairs."

"What foreign affairs will we have now?" retorted Lenin. But reluctantly he finally agreed, and I, likewise with reluctance, consented. And thus, at the instigation of Sverdlov, I came to head the Soviet diplomacy for a quarter of a year.

When I was declining the commissariat of home affairs on the second day after the revolution, I brought up, among other things, the question of race. It would seem that in war business this consideration should have involved even greater complications than in civil administration. But Lenin proved to be right. In the years of the revolutionary *ascendancy,* this question never had the slightest importance. Of course, the Whites tried to develop anti-Semitic motifs in their propaganda in the Red Army, but they failed signally. There are many testimonials to this, even in the White press. In *Archives of the Russian Revolution,* published in Berlin, a White Guard writer relates the following striking episode: "A Cossack who came to see us was hurt by someone's taunt that he not only served under, but fought under the command of a Jew—Trotsky—and retorted with warm conviction: 'Nothing of the sort. Trotsky is not a Jew. Trotsky is a fighter. He's ours . . . Russian! . . . It is Lenin who is a Communist, a Jew, but Trotsky is ours . . . a fighter . . . Russian . . . our own!' "

The same motif will be found in *The Red Cavalry,* by Babel [Isaac Babel, a Jew, regarded as one of the best Russian writers of the 20th century], the most talented of our younger writers. The question of my Jewish origin acquired importance only after I had become a subject for political baiting. Anti-Semitism raised its head with that of anti-Trotskyism. They both derived from the same source—the petit bourgeois reaction against October [i.e., the Bolshevik Revolution].

YEVSEKTSIYA: THE LIQUIDATION OF BOURGEOIS JEWISH INSTITUTIONS (OCTOBER 1918)

As the Communists assumed power in November 1917, they attempted to bring the various nationalities and ethnic groups into the revolution and into the ideological structure of the new Russia. To accomplish this purpose, special "national" sections were established; the Jewish section was called Yevsektsiya. The first conference, held in Moscow in October 1918, made several resolutions, included in this document.

Our Cultural Tasks: Education has always been a powerful means in the hands of the ruling classes. The bourgeoisie claims that schooling and education are beyond class interests and politics. At the same time, however, it makes sure that the broad masses will obtain neither knowledge nor enlightenment.

The Jewish community has hitherto been dominated by the members of the propertied class who want to keep the masses in the dark by superimposing a Hebrew culture upon them. While the upper classes have been sending their own children to public schools, they have provided only dark primary schools and synagogues for the offspring of the proletariat, in which nothing but nonsense is taught.

Only the proletariat, defending the interests of their class, and thus defending the interests of all mankind, will be able to open the treasures of human culture to the broad masses.

Only the proletariat is strong enough to forge the golden chain of human culture, freeing it from the bloody hands of the decadent bourgeoisie.

From now on, the Jewish proletariat will assume the reins of power in the Jewish community.

Only the Jewish worker and the Jewish laboring masses will create a free Jewish culture for themselves and arm themselves with the strong weaponry of knowledge.

Our Relations with the [Jewish] Community and Other Bourgeois Societies: The First Conference of Jewish Communities and Communist Yevsektsiya declares that the various institutions which have so far ruled the traditional communal organization, the so-called kehile . . . have no further function in our life.

In the struggle against the organized Jewish community, no compromise can be made with the bourgeoisie. All its institutions are harmful to the interests of the Jewish masses, who are seduced by sweet lullabies of alleged democracy.

Following the proletarian victory in the October Revolution, the Jewish workers have assumed power and have established the dictatorship of the proletariat in the Jewish community. They now call upon the Jewish masses to unite around the Jewish commissariat in order to strengthen its rule.

The first all-Russian conference of Jewish Communists authorizes the members of the Central Commissariat for Jewish Affairs to take steps toward a systematic liquidation of the institutions of the Jewish bourgeoisie. . . .

The Liquidation of the Zionist Party—A Memorandum [Submitted July 4, 1919]: The General Council of the Jewish Communist Union in Ukraine, in full agreement with the resolution adopted by the conference of Jewish Communist sections of the Russian Communist party in Moscow, has decided to suspend immediately all activities of the Zionist party and its affiliated institutions and organizations.

This decision has been taken for the following reasons: Proclaiming the dictatorship of the proletariat, the Soviet has suspended the activities of all bourgeois parties and organizations and discontinued the publication of all their printed periodicals. The free existence of these organs and institutions would merely have interfered with the creative activity of the proletarian power, for they surely would have been used to support the counterrevolution which aims at the reestablishment of the old order. Only a misunderstanding deriving from the incomplete organization of the Soviets can explain, but not justify, the exception that is being made of the Zionists. They are still allowed to publish their official organ, *Khronik fun yidishen lebn* [Chronicle of Jewish life], and to employ their entire party organization. [But we must not forget that] by its political and social structure, the Zionist party is a Jewish version of the General Russian Cadet party. By forging together the representatives of big and small capital with the Jewish petty bourgeoisie and cementing their union with a nationalistic ideology, this party—in close cooperation with clerical groups—constitutes a natural political center for all Jews who support the counterrevolution and wish to regain their freedom of exploitation and speculation. The pogroms that recently took place in Ukraine and in Poland have stirred nationalistic tendencies among reactionary Jews and are now being exploited by the Zionist party to strengthen its position. It is natural that in its most recent circular, the central committee of the Zionists in Ukraine has reported a major increase of its organization, in spite of numerous cases in which local authorities have tried to interfere with this development.

The Zionists often protest their loyalty and pretend to be interested only in their work concerning Palestine. But in reality, their Palestinian agitation is nothing but a nationalistic response to the political events of the day. At the present time when the authorities and the Communist party are trying with all their might to mobilize the laboring masses for the struggle against local and Polish gangs, when they are committing themselves to liberating thousands of Jewish workers from the ideological influence of the petty bourgeoisie and to enlisting them in the revolutionary Red Army—at this time the Zionist agitation, even where it is performed by the Zionist left, is harmful because it hinders the mobilization of the workers just as it had previously interfered with the attempts to make the Jewish masses a part of the revolutionary movement.

It must further be noted that the Palestinian ideal of the Zionists is in its very content a bourgeois one. Moreover, the current international situation has firmly established the Zionist party in the camp of the international imperialistic counterrevolution.

The Zionist party has linked its fate with the powers of the Entente [the British-French alliance in World War I] who, upon dividing the Turkish Empire, have made certain promises to the Zionists which force them to support their coalition. The Peace of Versailles, forging chains for the enslavement of the proletariat and for entire peoples, is welcomed by the Zionists. This is a logical consequence of their bourgeois nature. Furthermore, the Zionists are directly interested in a victory of the Entente in Eastern Europe. Only a victory of these powers will get them a little closer to the practical realization of their hopes. Under these circumstances, the continued activity of the Zionist party would be harmful to the interests of the Soviet Union and her international policies. Any protestation on the part of the Zionists that they are not interested in the victory of the reactionary forces cannot be taken seriously if one remembers that the Jewish bourgeoisie, and the Zionists among them, were able to accept even Plehve's regime.

Simultaneously with its political activity, the Zionist party is also engaged in cultural and economic activities which interfere with the cultural and economic policies of the Soviet Union. The Zionists endeavor to defend the vested interests of the petty bourgeoisie, of the middle class, and even of the patricians. . . .

The Zionist party puts special emphasis on its cultural and educational institutions. . . . The Zionist cultural and educational programs, however, do not even pretend to share the liberalism adopted by the Cadet party. All they endeavor to achieve is the strengthening of the clerical spirit in the Jewish *shul*. Furthermore, they support the religious instruction in the [traditional Jewish] schools as the mainstay of their nationalistic education. Their energies are directed toward an artificial revival of the Hebrew language, thereby endangering the daily language of the Jewish laboring masses. The cultural and educational activities of the Zionist party persistently undermine—too often successfully—the budding culture of socialism which has been emerging from within the Jewish proletarian movement throughout the last few decades. In this respect, positive action has already been undertaken in Greater Russia where Hebrew schools are now forbidden. . . .

That is why we must urgently proceed to suspend all activities of the Zionist party, not only where its central and local committees are concerned, but also the economic, cultural, and professional organizations centered around the party. In doing so we shall only be taking the steps necessary for the propagation of communistic ideas among the Jewish working class and the younger generation of the Jewish petty bourgeoisie.

Reference Works

S. W. Baron, *The Russian Jew under Tsars and Soviets*

L. Dawidowicz, *The Golden Tradition*

Zvi Gitelman, *Jewish Nationality and Soviet Politics*

P. Mendes-Flohr and J. Reinharz, *The Jew in the Modern World: A Documentary History*

L. Rappoport, *Stalin's War Against the Jews*

H. M. Sachar, *The Course of Modern Jewish History*

M. Stanislawski, *Nicholas I and the Jews*

Chronology

1764	Polish Sejm abolishes the Council of the Four Lands.
1772	First partition of Poland. Poland loses one-third of its territory.
1793	Second partition of Poland.
1794	Czarina Catherine II's decree establishes Russian Pale of Settlement.
1795	Third partition of Poland. All of Poland divided among Prussia, Russia, and Austria.
1804	Czar Alexander I promulgates first Constitution of the Jews.
1827	Czar Nicholas I issues the Cantonist Decrees.
1844	Sergei Uvarov announces establishment of Jewish crown schools.
	R. Moses Lilienthal appointed to direct them.
1856	Czar Alexander II abolishes the Cantonist System.
1881	Czar Alexander II is assassinated.
1882	May Laws are enacted.
1884	First Conference of Hibbat Zion takes place at Kattowitz, Germany.
1897	First Russian census indicates 5.2 million Jews live in the Russian Empire; all but 300,000 live in the Pale of Settlement.
1901	No more than 3 percent of students at Russian universities are to be Jews. Jews are forbidden to attend the University of Moscow.
1902	Mizrachi party is founded at Vilna.
1903	Kishinev pogrom.

1903–1905	Government-inspired pogroms in 660 Russian communities in one week; 1,000 are dead, 7,000 to 8,000 are wounded. First Russian edition of *Protocols of the Elders of Zion* appears.
1912	Agudas Yisrael is founded in Kattowitz.
1914	World War I breaks out.
1915	Russian government abolishes Pale of Settlement.
1915	Russian Revolution. Bolsheviks take control of Russia, led by Lenin and Trotsky.
1918	Jewish Commissariat and Yevsektsiya (Jewish sections of the Communist Party) are established. November 11, 1918, World War I ends.
1921	Two thousand pogroms are carried out during Russian civil war.
1922	Stalin becomes General Secretary of the Communist Party; in December 1922, USSR is formed.
1924	Lenin dies. Stalin challenges Trotsky's leadership and prevails.
1926	Jewish Autonomous Region is established in Birobidzhan.
1933	Soviet Union is recognized by the United States; trade relations are opened.
1939	Molotov-Ribbentrop Pact.
1940	Trotsky is assassinated in Mexico City on orders from Stalin.
1945	Soviet Army liberates Auschwitz.
1948	Stalin begins anti-Jewish campaign. Soviet Union recognizes Israel.
1951	Mass deportation of Jews from border areas of Soviet Union to Siberia.
1953	Doctors' Plot—seven Jewish physicians are arrested and accused of murdering Soviet leaders and being Western espionage agents. The charges are determined to be false, and the accused are released. Stalin dies March 5.
1955	Nikita Khrushchev becomes leader of Soviet Union. He denounces Stalin and begins to ease repression.
1964	Khrushchev is ousted by Leonid Brezhnev.
1970	Soviet Union begins intensive anti-Israel campaign. The Soviets maintain that Russian Jews have no desire to emigrate to Israel. On Simchat Torah, more than 15,000 Jews gather in front of the Moscow synagogue; large numbers gather in other cities.
1975	Jackson-Vanik Amendment ties most-favored-nation status to emigration policies.
1978	Anatoly Scharansky is convicted of espionage and given a 13-year sentence.
1985	Gorbachev becomes the Soviet leader. He advocates more openness and frankness in Soviet society.
1986	Scharansky is released from prison and exchanged in Berlin.
1989	Over 70,000 Jews leave the Soviet Union in 1989.
1991	Soviet Union collapses and Gorbachev resigns. Boris Yeltsin elected President of Russia
2000	Yeltsin resigns as President. Vladimir Putin wins election to succeed him.

2

POLITICS AND COMMUNITY IN WESTERN AND CENTRAL EUROPE

INTRODUCTION

This chapter deals with the history of the Jews of Western Europe, Britain, France, and Germany, from the middle of the 18th century to the latter part of the 19th century. It deals as well with the Jewish communities of Central Europe, that is, the Jews living in the Habsburg Empire.

The experience of Jews in Western and Central Europe was significantly different from that in Eastern Europe. In France, and later in England, Germany, and the Habsburg Empire, Jews were emancipated. Eastern Europe's Jews, by contrast, were never emancipated. Western and Central European Jews saw the ghetto walls fall and began to enjoy full legal rights. They could now move freely, practice any profession, and reside wherever they chose. For some Jews this meant full assimilation to the surrounding culture and its val-

ues, but for most it simply meant acculturation, taking on the forms and customs of the surrounding culture.

FRANCE

About 40,000 Jews lived in France in 1750. A few thousand Sephardic Jews lived in Bordeaux and Bayonne in western France, and in Avignon in southern France. Eight hundred Sephardic Jews lived in Paris in the north of France. The largest number, however, about 30,000, were Ashkenazic Jews living in the German-speaking provinces of Alsace and Lorraine, located in the east of France.

On the Eve of the Revolution

The king of France in the late 18th century was Louis XVI. He claimed absolute power, and thus

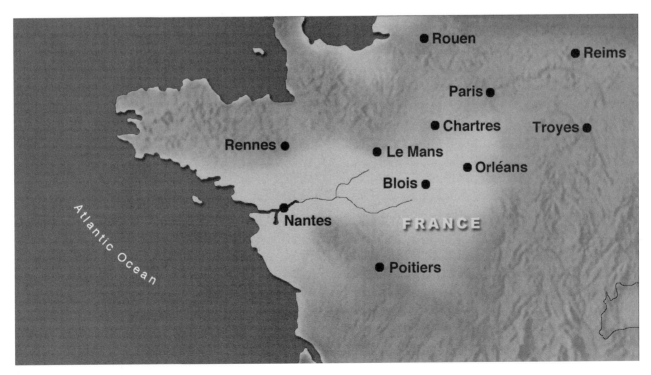

1791 Map of France.

First page of a petition by Metz Jews to Louis XV in 1745, requesting permission to engage freely in commerce and industry.

was empowered by his law to assess and collect taxes. When he tried to do so, however, he encountered resistance. Judicial bodies known as Parlements refused to acknowledge the royal decrees as law enforceable in the courts. This meant, in fact, that the Parlements, the members of which were royal officials, were taking a stand against absolute monarchy.

Louis's response in 1787 was to convene an Assembly of Notables, hoping that the representatives of the nobility and the higher clergy would agree to higher taxation of their property—but this strategy failed. Support began to come instead for the revival of an old medieval body, the Estates General, which had not met since 1614. At that time it was composed of representatives of the three "estates" of France: the clergy, the nobility, and the commoners (Third Estate). The members of each estate would meet and vote separately.

The Estates General convened at Versailles in May 1789. One major issue remained on the table, however. The king had agreed that the number of representatives of the Third Estate should equal the number of representatives of the other two orders combined. The Third Estate would have 600 representatives, while each of the other estates would have 300. Still unresolved was the question of whether the voting should be by head—which would favor the Third Estate and had some additional support from clergy and nobility—or by estate, in which case the status quo would be maintained.

The Third Estate went on the offensive, refusing to take their place as a separate chamber and urging members of the clergy and the nobility to join them in forming a National Assembly. The king was so disturbed by what he saw as insubordination that he had the meeting room of the Third Estate locked up and put under military guard. The Third Estate responded by convening on an indoor tennis court, taking an oath never to disband until France had a constitution; this oath was called the "Oath of the Tennis Court." With it, they were declaring that the king had no power to dismiss them and that they had every intention to put an end to royal absolutism.

King Louis was a weak king. Thus, on June 27 he gave in to the Third Estate's wishes, ordering all three estates to sit together and vote by head. This meant that the Estates General had been transformed into the National Assembly.

Jews on the Eve of the Revolution

Jews living in France experienced no physical persecution. They were permitted to worship as they pleased and to build synagogues for that worship. Only in 1787, though, was a law passed in Alsace permitting them to participate freely in commerce and the crafts. Most Jews still felt the misfortune of remaining second-class citizens.

In Paris, for example, Jews had no legally recognized status. The city's 800 Sephardic Jews lived there only through bribing the police. In Strasbourg, the capital of Alsace, Jews could not reside at all. Thousands of Jews in Alsace, only recently having been permitted to engage in commerce, continued to make their living through peddling, pawnbroking, and moneylending. As a result, these Jews were very poor. In some cities "Jew-taxes" remained, while in others Jewish testimony would not be admitted against Christians.

The French Revolution

In July 1789 suspicion was rampant that Louis, yielding to pressure from those who opposed any government reform, was prepared to dissolve the National Assembly. This suspicion was strengthened when the liberally minded Controller General of Finance, Jacques Necker, was dismissed. A committee of citizens seized the government of Paris and ordered its citizens to organize a National Guard to protect liberties and maintain order. On July 14 the Bastille, a royal fortress and prison in central Paris, was attacked. After a siege of several hours, the Bastille surrendered.

In later years the fall of the Bastille would be observed as a holiday in France; it was viewed as the beginning of the Revolution. It was also the point at which the people of Paris became involved in its politics. The revolutionary government of Paris, called the Commune, was often able to compel the king, and sometimes the National Assembly, to follow its dictates.

Over the next two years the National Assembly sought to draw up a constitution. They began, in August 1789, with a first statement of political principles, known as the Declaration of the Rights of Man and the Citizen. Here it was declared that all citizens were free and equal in rights and that the cardinal rights of man were liberty, property, security, and resistance to oppression. It was declared as well that the nation was the source of all political authority.

The National Assembly found itself dealing with two preliminary issues, however. The first was taxes. By the fall of 1789 the government found itself insolvent. In November the National Assembly decided to confront the problem by confiscating all land belonging to the Catholic Church and issuing paper currency, assignats, with which the confiscated land could be purchased.

The second major problem was how the National Assembly should relate to the king. Many of Louis's closest advisers were opposed to the activities of the National Assembly. Louis's queen, Marie Antoinette, was opposed to the revolutionaries. In addition to these challenges facing the National Assembly, the power of the people of Paris over this body continued to grow.

Meanwhile the National Assembly was working on the formulation of a constitution. The new constitution reorganized the government, limiting the king's power and increasing the power of the Legislative Assembly. The assembly was to have control of taxation, the right to impeach ministers or call them to account, and supreme appellate jurisdiction; it was given, then, essential sovereign powers. The king, however, was given veto power over laws of which he disapproved; this meant that he could postpone but not prevent passage of such laws. The king also was given the right to choose ministers for the executive branch as well as to appoint diplomats and army officers.

Local government was reorganized and decentralized as well. New administrative units, departments, were created. Administrative districts, judicial organization, and church dioceses were to coincide with the new departmental boundaries. The newly organized government would stand for Liberty, Equality and Fraternity—the slogan of the French Revolution.

King Louis expressed his readiness to accept a constitution, and elections were organized in conformity with it. On September 30, 1791, the National Assembly adjourned; on the next day the new Legislative Assembly began to sit.

To all appearances the Revolution was over. The king had accepted reordering of the French government. Nobles and clergymen were now ordinary citizens. Peasants had been freed from previous feudal obligations. The middle class had secured a dominant voice in the control of government. But the Revolution was not yet over.

The Declaration of the Rights of Man, 1789

Emancipation of French Jews

The new governmental system presented the Jews with an opportunity to achieve emancipation. The Jews needed to consider how to approach the issue. Should they appeal to members of the Legislative Assembly? Should they expect emancipation to come "automatically," without any appeal to the Assembly? What arguments should be made on their behalf? Who should speak for them?

In the summer of 1789 the corporate autonomy of Jews was abolished. Before this, they had run their own communities, providing their own educational, religious, administrative, social, and medical services. As long as they paid taxes, the local authorities had no objection to the Jews running their own communities. Now Jews, along with all other religious, social, economic, and political groups, lost their right to autonomy. The Jews anticipated that this significant change would be followed by full emancipation, for it seemed the next logical step. This would happen, but not so quickly as the French Jews thought.

In 1787 Count de Mirabeau, a distinguished rationalist, had published an essay entitled *On Moses Mendelssohn and Political Reform of the Jews,* in which he suggested that Mendelssohn was merely one outstanding example of the great intellectual talents of the Jews which were waiting to be tapped. Abbé Grégoire, in an essay entitled *On the Physical, Moral and Political Regeneration of the Jews,* wrote: "If the Jew has faults, it is Christian society which is responsible. . . . In their place would we not be worse?" Similar remarks were made repeatedly by Grégoire in sessions of the Assembly, of which he was a member.

A distinguished Jew of Strasbourg, Lippman Cerf-Berr, appealed to Mirabeau and Abbé Grégoire, two supporters of Jewish rights, expecting emancipation to follow, but it did not. There was instead intense opposition from the people of Alsace and Lorraine, where the Jews were hated for being moneylenders. In December 1789 the Assembly granted civil and political rights to non-Catholics—but not to Jews! In January 1790 emancipation was granted to the Sephardic Jews of southern France by the Legislative Assembly. These Jews had broken off from their coreligionists, understanding that they, who were not

moneylenders, would be in a better position. Argument was made that Jews would be better citizens were their disabilities removed. Reason demanded equal rights for all, moreover, as had been stated in the Declaration of the Rights of Man. It was argued as well that the French Revolution spoke of fraternity—why should anyone be excluded? The economic benefits that Jews might bring to France were noted, for after all, the international connections of Jews would be enormously beneficial in a capitalist economy.

But what about the Ashkenazic Jews, who lived in Alsace and Lorraine? Here enters Godard, a brilliant lawyer and delegate to the Legislative Assembly. Godard, a Christian, thought that if members of the Commune of Paris, the up-and-comers in French politics, could be convinced that emancipation of the Jews was desirable, they would do the job of convincing the Legislative Assembly. Moreover, Godard agreed to appear himself before the Commune of Paris. He spoke well, but it was not just oratory that worked in favor of the Jews. It was the realization on the part of delegates, first of all, that they could not be inconsistent in applying the ideals of the Revolution. Beyond this, most of the delegates were merchants and lawyers, who understood the positive economic role that Jews could play in France.

In September 1791 emancipation was granted to all French Jews. This was a great victory. As we will see shortly, the problem of usury never went away and needed eventually to be addressed by Napoleon.

Moses Mendelssohn

The Reign of Terror

According to the new constitution, France was to be a constitutional monarchy. In September 1792 the Jacobins seized power and declared a democratic republic. Led by Robespierre, a lawyer turned politician, the Jacobins declared Louis XVI a traitor and had him guillotined on January 21, 1793. The Jacobins ruled France from 1792 to June 1794. Their rule was strong-armed and iron-handed. The period between September 1793 and June 1794 was the "Reign of Terror," during which the Jacobins attempted to exterminate all opponents of the Revolution. In 1794, however, the Jacobins fell and Robespierre was guillotined.

At this time it was decided to abrogate the constitution of 1791 and draw up a new one. The National Convention, a successor to the Legislative Assembly, was assigned this task. By 1795 the new constitution was completed. It determined that executive power should be in the hands of five directors, representatives of the bourgeoisie. This group came to be known as the Directory.

As an institution, however, the Directory was weak, heavily dependent on the French army. The Directory ruled from 1794 to 1799, when a young general, Napoleon Bonaparte, carried out a coup d'état. He had support from the military and from the nation; he was viewed as a hero among corrupt politicians.

Assembly of Jewish Notables

In 1806 Napoleon issued a two-part decree. First, there would be a one-year moratorium on the repayment of debts to the Jews of Alsace and Lorraine. Second, Napoleon ordered the convening of an Assembly of Jewish Notables in Paris, to begin on July 29, 1806. The notables would be 112 Jews appointed by French officials.

Napoleon was attempting to achieve two goals with this decree. He saw a need to respond to the complaints of the people of Alsace and Lorraine about what they saw as usury on the Jews' part. At the same time he sought to solidify his relationship with Jews, to ensure their loyalty to him. He wanted the Jews to declare publicly, officially, and unequivocally that they were loyal Frenchmen above all. He wanted them to affirm that they were not a "state within a state," that they gave precedence to French law over Jewish law.

The Assembly of Jewish Notables was presented with twelve questions. Some of these addressed the question of precedence of law and whether Jews were French above all. Others asked whether Judaism preached immorality. Some questions were answered correctly, but in some cases, incorrect answers were offered.

The Jews were asked, for example, whether the Jewish religion permitted divorce, even when French law and Jewish law were in conflict. They answered that a Jewish divorce in such a case would be judged invalid. This is untrue according to the halacha. They were asked, in addition, whether personal loans at interest between Jew and non-Jew were permitted and they answered that such loans were acceptable according to the halacha. This answer is also incorrect.

The most distinguished rabbinic figure in 19th century France was Rabbi Joseph David Sinzheim (1745–1812), who was the first chief rabbi of France. During the Jacobins' Reign of Terror, from September 1793 to June 1794, he was forced to leave France for a time, but he returned to serve as rabbi of Strasbourg.

In 1806 he was appointed to the Assembly of Jewish Notables and impressed those who did not know him yet with his extensive learning and his astuteness. Sinzhheim was chosen to formulate answers to Napoleon's questions, succeeding in convincing Napoleon that Jews could accept the authority of the state and fulfill their obligations as citizens without giving up their principles of faith and their traditions. When Napoleon announced the convening of the ancient institution of the Sanhedrin, in order to accord canon law status to the answers of the Assembly, Sinzheim was appointed president of the Great Sanhedrin.

Rabbi Sinzheim wrote numerous volumes of Talmud commentary as well as many responsa. Only one volume of responsa, Yad David, was published during his lifetime; a halakhic encyclopedia, Minhat Ani, remained unpublished because of Sinzheim's burden of rabbinic responsibilities.

The Great Sanhedrin

Once the answers had been given, Napoleon announced that in February 1807 the venerated ancient institution of the Jewish people, the Great Sanhedrin, would be reconstituted. Napoleon's declared purpose was to accord to the answers of the Notables the status of canon law, to ensure that the Jews were committing themselves to the answers given. Napoleon had underlying motives, however; he had much to gain. He sought to arouse Jewish national pride, thereby stimulating Jewish leaders to work toward transforming the Jews of France into the most loyal and devoted Frenchmen—especially loyal to him. He wanted as well to secure the loyalty of Polish Jews. His intention was to move against Russia, and he would need food supplies for his troops; he wanted to make good use of the Polish Jews in this regard. Finally, he wanted to camouflage, and soften, his plan to reverse some of the gains of Jewish emancipation.

Napoleon's Decrees

March 1808 brought two decrees connected with reversing some gains of emancipation. The first was the Infamous Decree. Arbitrary restrictions were intro-

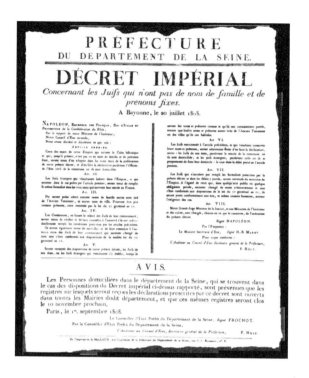

Napoleonic decree ordering the Jews of France to adopt definitive family and first names, July 20. 1808.

duced to Jewish moneylending; for example, Jews now had to request permission from their local government to engage in this practice. Jews were not to be allowed to change their residence unless they purchased rural

In 1806 Napoleon convened an assembly of Jewish notables and announced that Jews were now officially citizens of the French nation. The Emperor is shown raising the Jewish woman while the rabbis kneel at his feet.

property and promised to engage in agriculture rather than moneylending. Part of this decree told Jews that they could no longer send substitutes to serve in the army, as other Frenchmen could; the Jews needed to be impressed with the "sacred obligation" of military service.

The second decree was the Organic Regulation on the Mosaic Religion, by which the French established the Consistory System. The Jewish community was divided into districts, and the central office was in Paris. Local officials and rabbis were to be responsible for implementing Napoleon's policy regarding Jews. In particular they were to emphasize the importance of loyalty to France and obedience to French law. They were to reprimand Jews who had left moneylending but had now decided to return to it. They were to ensure that every Jew of age made himself available to the French army if called. In short, local officials and rabbis became a "police force" regarding the moral conduct of French Jews.

Fall of Napoleon

Napoleon was a man of great gifts. He was a brilliant general. He knew how to appoint effective officers and how to win the loyalty of soldiers. He drew on the French military tradition of the revolution, but he also innovated. Most important, he made greater use of field artillery, using lighter weapons even before the infantry was engaged in battle. This new approach provided Napoleon with great advantage until his opponents began to imitate his system.

Between 1806 and 1812 Napoleon redesigned Europe. The borders of France were expanded, extending from Holland and the North Sea coast of Germany in the north to the Illyrian Provinces, which border on the Adriatic Sea, in the east. Italy was completely under French control; part of it became a kingdom of Italy, with Napoleon as king, and another part became a kingdom of Naples, with Napoleon's relative in charge.

The changes in Germany were most dramatic though. The German states bordering France became the Confederation of the Rhine, while in north-central Germany a new kingdom of Westphalia was created. Territory that Napoleon had taken from Prussia and Austria became the Grand Duchy of Warsaw.

Only in 1812 did Napoleon finally experience defeat. The powerful British navy had triumphed over him at Trafalgar. Invasion of Britain was ill advised. Napoleon chose instead an economic blockade that would devastate the British economy. Czar Alexander I supported this approach at first, but his support eventually faded due to its damaging effect on the Russian economy. The blockade against British goods was lifted.

Napoleon's response to what he saw as betrayal by the Czar was to invade Russia in 1812. He marched to Moscow but was forced to retreat. Prussia was encouraged to attack Napoleon, as was Germany. A new coalition was formed, consisting of Russia, Prussia, Great Britain, and Austria. Many great battles were fought, and finally Napoleon was driven back inside France and forced to abdicate. Napoleon returned to power, however, and took to the battlefield again. In June 1815 he was defeated at the battle of Waterloo and forced to abdicate once more. He was sent by the British to a desolate island and died there in 1821.

Congress of Vienna

Waterloo had brought defeat to Napoleon. Now Europe had to put itself together again. The Congress of Vienna, held in 1815, was to serve this purpose. Representatives of the four great powers, Austria, Russia, Prussia, and Great Britain, met to seek ways to preserve peace. France too joined what would come to be called the Concert of Europe.

Charles Maurice Talleyrand (1754–1838), the main diplomatic representative of the restored Bourbon king, represented France at the Congress of Vienna. Talleyrand wanted to be sure that the territorial integrity of France would not be compromised, and he worked in that direction at Vienna. He felt as well that the internal life of France should be dealt with thoughtfully and that therefore the dynasty of the Bourbons should be restored, with Louis XVIII in charge. Louis XVIII recognized, however, that he could not rule absolutely as previous kings had, for the gains of the Revolution could not be reversed. Thus he agreed with Talleyrand that France should be a constitutional monarchy.

The Revolution stood for equality before the law, and this commitment could not be undercut. After 1815 the decrees of Napoleon regarding the Jews were revoked. The Infamous Decree, which had placed

1789 Map of Western Europe.

commercial restrictions on the Jews, was not renewed when it expired in 1818. The Consistory System remained, with rabbis and laymen continuing to supervise the religious lives of Jews. However, the humiliating examination of Jewish business behavior, of Jewish "patriotism," and of Jewish participation in military service was eliminated. In brief, Jewish emancipation was renewed in France.

GERMANY

German Jews numbered 300,000 in the middle of the 18th century. Most were poor, since they were excluded from farming and from commercial activity. They also were required to pay high taxes and were restricted in travel from one town to another. A few wealthy Jews did live in Frankfurt, Berlin, or Hamburg, but the vast majority of Jews in Germany struggled just to support themselves.

The Jew regarded by enlightened Germans as the model Jew was Moses Mendelssohn (1729–1786). He will be discussed at greater length in a later chapter. It was he and friends in France and Germany who called upon a distinguished German diplomat, historian, and economist, Christian Wilhelm Dohm, to write an essay in defense of the Jews of Alsace and Lorraine, where much anti-Semitic propaganda was being circulated. Dohm responded in 1781 with his "Considering the Amelioration of the Civil Status of the Jews." He considered the justifications that had been offered for discrimination and then made recommendations of a program that would make Jews "better members of civil societies." He urged that Jews be granted equal rights and be emancipated. Much benefit would come

The Alliance Israélite Française, the first modern international Jewish organization was founded in 1860. Its central office was in Paris.

The establishment of the Alliance relates directly to events in the 19th century. The first of these was the Damascus Affair, a notorious blood libel in 1840, which brought together Christian anti-Semitism and popular Muslim anti-Jewish feelings. On February 5, 1840, in the city of Damascus in Syria, Friar Thomas and his Muslim servant disappeared. The local monks circulated a rumor that Jews had murdered both in order to use their blood for Passover rituals. Two Jews were arrested and tortured, both dying from the torture. Prominent Jews from England and France, including Sir Moses Montefiore and Adolphe Crémieux, made efforts to get the others released, and this did happen, as Muhammed Ali, ruler of Egypt and Syria, signed a liberation order in August 1840.

The second precipitating event was the Mortara Affair, in which a 6-year-old Jewish child was forcibly abducted by Catholic conversionists. On June 24, 1858, Edgardo Mortara was seized by the papal police and taken to Rome. The boy had been secretly baptized by a Christian domestic servant, and the church maintained that the baptism of a child in danger of death was valid, even if carried out against the will of the parents. Pope Pius IX rejected all petitions to overturn the baptism. Mortara remained with the church and was educated by it. In due course he became a priest and a professor of theology. He also became an ardent conversionist.

These two events made it clear that an organization needed to be created for Jewish self-help. Thus the Alliance was established. It would work everywhere for the emancipation and moral progress of the Jews, and it would seek to provide effective assistance to Jews suffering from anti-Semitism. In addition, it would encourage publications calculated to achieve these goals.

The Alliance conducted its activities in the diplomatic, social, and educational spheres. It became the place to which persecuted Jewish communities turned for help and the organization that provided assistance to Jews suffering from anti-Semitism. It began to concentrate its efforts as well on Jewish education, especially in the Balkans and the Middle Eastern countries.

Among the leaders of the Alliance was Adolphe Crémieux, who served as president from 1863 to 1880. Crémieux was a distinguished French lawyer and statesman, who served for a time in the Chamber of Deputies. He was extremely helpful to the Alliance in its efforts to aid oppressed Jewish minorities.

to those societies that accepted Jews, he wrote. There remained, however, a long way to go before that would happen.

Habsburg Empire

In the middle of the 18th century, about 150,000 Jews lived in Austria-Hungary, also known as the Habsburg Empire. On the occasion of the first partition of Poland in 1772, however, Austria took over Galicia, increasing the Jewish population under the empire's control to 400,000.

The Habsburg Empire was a bastion of the Catholic faith, and the Catholic clergy had enormous influence over the governing authorities. Evidence of this influence is the expulsion of the Jews of Prague by Queen Maria Theresa of Austria in 1744–1745. The Jews of Prague were rumored to have been disloyal during the French and Prussian conquest. These rumors were proven false, but a scapegoat had been found to blame for Austria's military failures. The expulsion was reversed only after the intervention of diplomatic representatives under the influence of court Jews and Jewish bankers.

The Habsburgs ruled Vienna and Lower Austria, Hungary, Bohemia, and Moravia. Quite apart from the attempted expulsion from Prague, their policy toward Jews was a restrictive one regarding numbers of Jews, places of residence, and freedom of movement. Maria Theresa, whose hostility toward the Jews was deeply entrenched, was very upset by the enormous

Medal commemorating Joseph II's Edict of Tolerance, Vienna, 1782.

increase in the empire's Jewish population. She tried on more than one occasion to reduce the Jewish population of Galicia by expelling the "beggars."

The end of the 18th century produced a new concept of political leadership, "enlightened absolutism." This concept saw the welfare of the state as supreme and regarded the ruler as the first servant of the state. At the same time, however, the public good and the interest of the subjects were viewed as one and the same. The "enlightened" rulers sought to bring the Jews closer to the state and integrate them within it. They believed that this could be accomplished by the reformation of Jews through education, redirecting them to new and useful occupations, and granting them their "human rights," meaning the abolition of the discrimination against them in matters of personal status.

This new concept of leadership led Emperor Joseph II to promulgate an Edict of Tolerance for the Jews of Vienna in early 1782. Jews living in other parts of the empire, in Bohemia, Moravia, Silesia, and Hungary, were included in separate edicts. These edicts canceled movement and residence restrictions, made concessions regarding Jewish occupations, and gave Jews the right to send their children to public schools and to establish their own schools. At the same time, though, Jews became obligated to serve in the military, were prohibited from using Hebrew and Yiddish for commercial or public purposes, and had their internal Jewish autonomy restricted by revoking the communities' legal and economic power.

Joseph died in 1790 and was succeeded by his brother Leopold II, who ruled until his own death in 1792. Francis I (1792–1835) succeeded Leopold. The Edict of Tolerance remained in place, but Francis ordered that measures be taken against "Jewish superstition" and "vain rabbinical argumentation."

Despite what appeared to be a reversal of policy, Jews became active in the expansion and modernization of industry, transportation, commerce, and banking in the Habsburg Empire. They developed its textile industry and built its first railroad. Some, like the famous Rothschild family, became leading bankers and served on the board of the newly established National Bank. Many Jews had a university education and became prominent in journalism and literature. Less wealthy classes of Jews prospered as well, opening workshops, or selling and peddling products of the developing industries.

Metternich

The great moving spirit after the Congress of Vienna was Prince Metternich (1773–1859), chief minister of the Austrian Empire. Metternich held control over Austria, of course, but also Germany and Italy; the period between 1815 and 1848 is often referred to as the era of Metternich. In an effort to forestall any revolutionary outbursts, Metternich encouraged conservative politics and discouraged liberalism. He wanted, above all, to maintain the status quo in Europe.

How were German Jews affected by these political attitudes? The simple answer is that Germany wanted to erase all the changes that Napoleon had brought to French Jews, the emancipation of French Jews representing a likely target. Much lobbying was done by the Jewish bankers of Berlin, Frankfurt, and Vienna, as they promoted the cause of Jewish emancipation. The living rooms and salons of the Rothschilds, the von Herzs, the Itzigs, and the von Arnsteins hosted Metternich, Humboldt, Hardenberg, and the princes and dukes of smaller German states. Lavish banquets and gifts of fine jewelry were provided the honored guests.

Humboldt and Hardenberg responded with an effort to include Jewish emancipation in the new constitution of the German Federation. Numerous drafts of such a measure were prepared, revised, but then discarded. Finally the Prussian delegates suggested a formulation that would be acceptable to all, ensuring Jews "all rights heretofore accorded them in the several states." Just before acceptance, however, a delegate changed the meaning of the clause by substituting the word "by" for "in." This meant that Jews would receive the civil "rights heretofore accorded them by the several states." Other than Prussia, no German states had accorded Jews rights voluntarily. They had done so only because Napoleon and his military forces had forced them to do this.

Thinking they had been granted emancipation but then realizing they had not, Jews were crushed. They were encouraged, however, by the simple fact that, for the first time, Jews had been the subject of discussion at an international conference. Distinguished figures, some of the greatest statesmen of Europe present at the Congress of Vienna, had supported the cause of Jewish emancipation. Many were convinced that emancipation was on the horizon.

1848 Revolutions

Despite Metternich's efforts to discourage liberalism, it would not go away. The year 1848 brought revolutions all over Europe. The first was in France, where the people preferred a republic to a weak constitutional monarchy. Mobs in the streets expressed that preference.

Then came the revolution in Venice. In March 1848 a republic was proclaimed, which would stand for complete civil and political equality for all inhabitants, whatever their race or creed. Similar revolutions took place in Rome, Lombardy, Naples-Sicily, and the smaller states of Italy.

Germany too was affected by revolution. Rioting crowds of students and workers demanded constitutional reform. In Prussia and Saxony, basic civil rights were given recognition and supported by the authority of law. Other German states, such as Baden and Hanover, felt compelled to provide residents with liberal constitutions.

Austria was affected as well. Metternich's desires to the contrary, an uprising in Vienna forced him out. Bohemia too experienced revolution, as the Czechs rose up against the Austrian forces, demanding autonomy.

Revolution came to Hungary as well. The leader of this revolution, Louis Kossuth, came to a synagogue in Grosswardein to ask forgiveness for past persecutions and promise to work for the equality of all citizens. In response to Kossuth's pledge, some 20,000 Jews joined the Hungarian National Army. In addition, distinguished rabbinical figures conducted prayer meetings on behalf of the revolutionary cause. The Hungarian Diet, the parliament, reacted to the revolution by granting equal civil and political rights to all minorities.

Jews were extraordinarily active in the revolutions of 1848. In Germany many participated actively in the uprisings. Thus, for example, many Jews fell in the Berlin uprising. Jews became involved in the drafting of a new Prussian constitution, and a Jew, Gabriel

Riesser, served as the Prussian National Assembly's vice-president. In Brunswick, Saxony, and Hamburg, Jews sat as delegates in the assemblies. In Frankfurt, too, Jews participated, with no less than seven Jews sitting in the parliament of this city.

Jews anticipated the coming of emancipation, but, unfortunately they were disappointed. The armed forces of Prussia, Germany, Austria, and Italy fought back and restored their governments, governments that rejected liberalism in favor of conservatism.

Was the fight for emancipation over? It certainly seemed that way. The only consolation was that Jews had been turned into activists. They had participated in the uprisings and they had participated in politics. They had battled for the wider goal of constitutionalism. They had not just looked at what was good for the Jews and what was bad for the Jews. Perhaps emancipation would come in its own time.

Emancipation of the Jews

Indeed emancipation of the Jews did come, as liberalism, which seemed dead, came alive; the conservatives made very grudging concessions to the liberals, and among these concessions was emancipation of the Jews.

How did this come about? In 1866 the Habsburg Empire was defeated at the hands of Prussia. The Emperor, Franz Josef, was desperate to hold on to

Gabriel Riesser

The founders of the German Empire: William I, Crown Prince Frederick William, Prince Frederick-Charles, Bismarck and Moltke. German Postcard

Bohemia, Moravia, Slovakia, Hungary, and Galicia. In order to do so, he issued a constitution that divided his empire in two. The Hungarians were given complete autonomy in internal affairs. Residents of the other part of the Hapsburg Empire, which included Christians, Jews, and Muslims, were given all rights of citizenship, including equality before the law; there would be no limitations of residence or of occupation. Thus did half a million Jews become equal citizens.

Meanwhile the Prussian victors in the war saw the need to carry out their own reform. In 1850 King Frederick William issued his own constitution, and it extended Jews the right to vote, to own land, and to enter professions. In 1866 the famous Otto von Bismarck (1815–1898), the "Iron Chancellor," became the first minister. Bismarck brought about the unification of Germany. At first he went to war with Austria, and the German states of the north joined together in a North German Confederation. Later he went to war with France; this time the south German states joined the Confederation. Now Germany had become one and the provisions of its constitution were to be applied to all its citizens, Christians and Jews alike; equality before the law was to be the rule. Thus did the Jews of Prussia become emancipated in 1871.

ENGLAND

By 1720 approximately 3,000 Jews lived in England. Most of the Jewish population at this juncture were Ashkenazic Jews, immigrants from the German states, while a minority were Sephardic Jews, who

had come from Spain and Portugal. By the middle of the century, 7,000 Jews resided in England, with at least two-thirds of them Ashkenazim.

Jews were involved in a variety of occupations. Most Jewish immigrants to England came with few material resources or artisan skills, so they earned a living by buying and selling old clothes or peddling notions and inexpensive jewelry. Jews also dealt in oranges and lemons, sponges, lead pencils, glassware, and so on. Since many Jews traded in substandard watches, these came to be called "Jew watches."

Jewish communal life in England centered on the synagogue. The first synagogue was established in 1657 and located on Creechurch Lane in London. Samuel Pepys, who visited this synagogue on Simchat Torah and included this visit in his famous diary, commented on the "disorder, laughing, sporting, and no attention" in the service, "confusion . . . more like brutes than people knowing the true God." In 1701 Bevis Marks, the chief Sephardi synagogue, opened in place of the Creechurch Lane synagogue. The first Ashkenazi synagogue in London, called the Great Synagogue, opened in 1690, a second in 1706, and a third in 1761.

The institution most critical for the formation of the identity of British Jews was its chief religious authority, the Chief Rabbinate, established in 1764. A controversy over the appointment of a rabbi in Portsmouth led the rabbi of the Great Synagogue to be named the

"The Rothschild Family at Prayer," by Moritz Daniel Oppenheim.

Chief Rabbi of Great Britain, a position he had held unofficially before. As is the case with today's Chief Rabbi, Rabbi Jonathan Sacks, unwavering loyalty to Orthodox belief and practice is combined with adherence to the principles and etiquette of English society.

Did the Jews of England encounter anti-Semitism? Were they subject to violent pogroms as were the Jews in Russia's Pale of Settlement? Did they experience other forms of persecution? Were they subjected to discrimination? These are far from simple questions. On the one hand, despite its avowed liberalism, England was unprepared to accept cultural diversity; on the other hand, England was prepared to defend individual freedoms from racial conceptions of the nation.

Consider the case of the Jew Bill of 1753. Jews born in England were citizens of the state, unlike residents of other countries before the French Revolution. Like others who were not members of the Church of England, however, they could not serve in Parliament, vote in parliamentary elections, hold municipal office, be called to the bar, obtain a naval commission, or matriculate or take a degree at Oxford or Cambridge. These restrictions could be removed, though, were they to take a christological oath or take the sacrament in the Church of England.

Foreign-born Jews, by distinction, were not citizens of England. They could apply to become naturalized citizens, but this required that they receive a sacrament. Professing Jews would never do this. They were free to engage in business and trade, but the duties imposed were twice as high as those for British citizens. The Jew Bill, or Jewish Naturalization Bill, was an attempt to remove the obligation of taking the sacrament.

The initiators of the Jew Bill were Sephardi Jews. Many were foreign-born and thus could gain advantage from the passage of the bill. The bill passed and became law in May 1753. The opponents of the bill refused to give up, however, claiming that Britain would shortly be overrun by unscrupulous brokers and moneylenders seeking to acquire the estates of ruined landowners. Jews would control Parliament, they said, convert St. Paul's to a synagogue, and circumcise their tenants. The campaign was a successful one, for the bill was repealed in November 1753.

By 1851 the Jewish population of England reached 35,000. Approximately 25,000 lived in London, but Jews settled in other towns in the provinces. Birmingham, for example, had a Jewish population of 780, while Manchester had 1,100 Jews and Liverpool 1,500 Jews by 1850.

The synagogue continued to be the center of Jewish communal life in the 19th century. As Jews began to live in different parts of London, it became necessary to consider forming new congregations. In 1853 a Sephardi synagogue opened, while in 1855 the West End Branch Synagogue opened. A major influence in the Jewish community was the Chief Rabbi elected in 1845, Rabbi Nathan Marcus Adler.

Jews became involved in British politics in the 19th century. They could not take part in politics, however, without first achieving emancipation. The struggle for emancipation began in 1830. The first bill introduced in the House of Commons was defeated, but a second bill passed in 1832. The House of Lords, though, defeated it. The same pattern prevailed in 1834, 1836, 1841, 1848, 1849, 1851, 1853, 1856, and 1857, as the House of Commons passed the measure and the House of Lords rejected it.

Support for Jewish emancipation came from four political groups: the Whigs, liberals who were ideologically committed to religious freedom and civil rights; progressive Tories, conservatives who had broken with their party and supported religious liberty; evangelical Tories, who thought their support would encourage Jews to convert; and Radicals and Non-Conformists, who saw their support as a challenge to the Church of England. Opposition came mainly from the Tory High Churchmen, who were less than sympathetic to Jews and Judaism.

The strategy recommended by David Salomons was to have Jews run as candidates of the Whigs, the Liberal Party, for Parliament. In 1847, five Jews were selected as candidates. Only Lionel Rothschild won his election in 1847, although Salomons won in 1851. Salomans spoke and voted before being excluded, but the issue had been framed as a specific question: Could the Parliament exclude the legally elected representatives of British voters, especially when the house to which they were elected saw no impediment to their admission? The Conservative leadership, the Tories, saw that they could not hold to their position and the Jews of England were emancipated in 1858.

Did emancipation remove from the Jews of England the challenge of anti-Semitism? Benjamin Disraeli (1804–1881), a convert from Judaism who was a member of the Conservative Party and subsequently British Prime Minister, addressed the following words to fellow members of Parliament:

> You are influenced by the darkest superstitions of the darkest ages that have ever existed in this country. It is this feeling that has been kept out of this debate; indeed, that has been kept secret in yourselves—enlightened as you are—and that is unknowingly influencing you as it is influencing others abroad.

The Jews had achieved emancipation, but anti-Semitism remained.

SUMMARY

We have considered the history of French, German, and British Jews from the middle of the 18th century until their emancipation. Louis XVI ruled France until the French Revolution of 1789, which brought major changes to France. The government was reorganized, a constitution was written and the Jews were emancipated. Napoleon seized power in 1799, ruling France until his defeat at Waterloo in 1815. In order to solidify his relationship with the Jews, he convened the Assembly of Jewish Notables in 1806, later convening the Great Sanhedrin, to be certain that Jews saw the answers of the Notables as authoritative and binding.

Emancipation was on the minds of German Jews as well. After the defeat of Napoleon, the Congress of Vienna met to redraw the map of Europe. On this occasion, Jewish emancipation was considered but not put into effect. Europe was beset with revolutions in 1848, affecting Italy, Germany, Prussia, and Austria, among other places. Jews participated actively in these revolutions. Only in 1871 were all Jews in the German states finally granted emancipation.

The partitions of Poland in the late 18th century brought many more Jews into the Habsburg Empire. Joseph II's Edict of Tolerance seemed aimed at integrating all Jews into the empire, and this did take place gradually. Emancipation did not come, however, until Prussia defeated the military forces of the Habsburg Empire in 1866. Jews benefited from this defeat, as those living in Hungary were emancipated in 1867, and so too were those living in other parts of the empire.

The Jews of England also aspired to emancipation, but this was not achieved until 1858. Jewish communal life centered in the synagogue in both the 18th and 19th centuries. An important institution for British Jews was the Chief Rabbinate, established in 1764. The Chief Rabbinate helped set the agenda of the British Jewish community. Despite being emancipated, and despite being elected members of the House of Commons, anti-Semitism was never removed from the concerns of British Jews.

Documents

CHRISTIAN WILHELM VON DOHM: CONCERNING THE AMELIORATION OF THE CIVIL STATUS OF THE JEWS (1781)

Dohm (1751–1820), active in Enlightenment circles in Berlin and a scholar of law and history, wrote this essay in response to a request from his friend Moses Mendelssohn. The thinking was that Dohm's prominence in the Prussian government would put the issue on the table for discussion. He argued in favor of Jewish emancipation and Jewish citizenship.

What might be the reasons that induced the governments of almost all European states unanimously to deal so harshly with the Jewish nation? What has induced them (even the wisest) to make this one exception from the laws of an otherwise enlightened policy according to which all citizens should be incited by uniform justice, support of trade and the greatest possible freedom of action so as to contribute to the general welfare? Should a number of industrious and law-abiding citizens be less useful to the state because they stem from Asia and differ from others by beard, circumcision, and a special way—transmitted to them from their ancient forefathers—of worshipping the Supreme Being? This latter would certainly disqualify them from full rights of citizenship, and justify all restrictive measures, if it contained principles which would keep the Jews from fulfilling their duties to the state, and from keeping faith in their actions within the community and with single members of the community; and if hatred against those who do not belong to their faith would make them feel an obligation to deal crookedly with others and to disregard their rights.

It would have to be clearly proved that the religion of the Jews contains such antisocial principles, that their divine laws are contrary to the laws of justice and charity, if one were to justify before the eyes of reason that the rights of citizenship should be withheld entirely only from the Jew, and that he should be permitted only partially to enjoy the rights of man. According to what has become known about the Jewish religion so far, it does not contain such harmful principles. The most important book of the Jews, the Law of Moses, is looked upon by Christians with reverence and it is ascribed by them to divine revelation. This belief in its divine origin alone must banish every thought that this law could prescribe any vicious thing, or that its followers must be bad citizens. But even those who did not start from this assumption have found after investigation that the Mosaic law contains the most correct principle of moral law, justice and order. . . .

More than anything else a life of normal civil happiness in a well-ordered state, enjoying the long withheld freedom, would tend to do away with clannish religious opinions. The Jew is even more man than Jew, and how would it be possible for him not to love a state where he could freely acquire property and freely enjoy it, where his taxes would be not heavier than those of the other citizens, where he could reach positions of honor and enjoy general esteem? Why should he hate people who are no longer distinguished from him by offensive prerogatives, who share with him equal rights and duties? The novelty of this happiness, and unfortunately, the probability that this will not in the near future happen in all states, would make it even more precious to the Jew, and gratitude alone would make him the most patriotic citizen. He would look at his country with the eyes of a long misjudged, and finally after long banishment, reinstated son. These human emotions would talk louder in his heart than the sophistic sayings of his rabbis. . . .

If I am not entirely mistaken, there is one error in this reasoning, namely, that one states as cause what in reality is the effect, quoting the evil wrought by the past erroneous policy as an excuse for it. Let us concede that the Jews may be more morally corrupt than other nations; that they are guilty of a proportionately greater number of crimes than the Christians; that their character in general inclines more toward usury and fraud in commerce, that their religious prejudice is more antisocial and clannish; but I must add that this supposed greater moral corruption of the Jews is a necessary and natural consequence of the oppressed condition in which they have been living for so many centuries. A calm and impartial consideration will prove the correctness of this assertion. . . .

If this reasoning is correct, then we have found in the oppression and in the restricted occupation of the Jews the true source of their corruption. Then we have discovered also at the same time the means of healing this corruption and of making the Jews better men and useful citizens. With the elimination of the unjust and unpolitical treatment of the Jews will also disappear the consequences of it; and when we cease to limit them to one kind of occupation, then the detrimental influence of that occupation will no longer be so noticeable. With the modesty that a private citizen should always show when expressing his thoughts about public affairs, and with the certain conviction that general proposals should always be tailored, if they should be useful, to the special local conditions in every state, I dare now, after these remarks, to submit my ideas as to the manner in which the Jews could become happier and better members of civil societies.

To make them such it is FIRST necessary to give them equal rights with all other subjects. Since they are able to fulfill the duties they should be allowed to claim the equal impartial love and care of the state. No humiliating discrimination should be tolerated, no way of earning a living should be closed to them, none other than the regular taxes demanded from them. They would have to pay all the usual taxes in the states, but they would not have to pay protection money for the mere right to exist, no special fee for the permission to earn a living. It is obvious that in accordance with the principle of equal rights, also special privileges favoring the Jews—which exist in some states—would have to be abolished. These sometimes owed their existence to a feeling of pity which would be without basis under more just conditions. When no occupation will be closed to Jews, then they should, in all fairness, not have a monopoly on any occupation in preference to other citizens. When the government will decide to fix the rate of interest by law, the Jew will not be able to ask for any more than the legal rate of interest. If it will be prohibited to private citizens to lend money on pawns, or do so only under certain conditions, the Jews will have to observe these rules.

Since it is primarily the limitation of the Jews to commerce which has had a detrimental influence on their moral and political character, a perfect freedom in the choice of a livelihood would serve justice, as well as represent a humanitarian policy which would make of the Jews more useful and happier members of society.

It might even be useful, in order to achieve this great purpose, if the government would first try to dissuade the Jews from the occupation of commerce and endeavor to weaken its influence by encouraging them to prefer such kinds of earning a living as are the most apt to create a diametrically opposed spirit and character—I mean artisan occupations. . . .

The Jews should not be excluded from agriculture. Unless the purchase of landed property is restricted in a country to certain classes of the inhabitants, the Jews should not be excluded, and they should have equal rights to lease land. . . .

From several sides the proposal has been made that the Jews should be allotted separate districts for settlement and be kept isolated there from the rest of the subjects. In my opinion it would not be advisable to make the religious difference more noticeable and probably more permanent by this step. The Jews, left entirely to themselves, would be strengthened in their prejudices against Christians, and vice versa. Frequent intercourse and sharing the burdens and advantages of the state equally is the most certain way to dull the edge of the hostile prejudices on both sides. The *Judengasse* (*Juiveries* in France) [ghetto] and restricted districts of Jewish residence in many cities are remnants of the old harsh principles. In many places (for instance, Frankfurt on the Main, where the *Judengasse* is locked up every night) the evil consequence is that the Jews are forced to build their houses many stories high and live under very crowded conditions resulting in uncleanliness, diseases, and bad policing, and greater danger of fire. . . .

It should be a special endeavor of a wise government to care for the moral education and enlightenment of the Jews, in order to make at least the coming generations more receptive to a milder treatment and the enjoyment of all advantage of our society. The state should not look further into their religious education than would perhaps be necessary to prevent the teaching of antisocial opinions against men of other persuasions. But the government should take care that, besides the holy teachings of his fathers, the Jew is taught to develop his reason by the clear light of knowledge, the science of nature and its great creator, and that his heart is warmed by the principles of order, honesty, love for all men and the great society in which he lives; that the Jew, too, is led at an early age to the sciences required more or less for his future profession. This would have to be done either in the Jewish schools, or if teachers and funds are for the time being lacking, the Jews should be permitted to send their children to the Christian schools (except for the hours reserved for religious instruction). As some Jews perhaps would be kept from making use of this permission by prejudice, they should even be required to send their children to certain classes in accordance with their future vocations. That department of the government which is in charge of public education (an office which should always belong to the state, not to a religious party) should extend its supervision over the education of the Jews, except only for their religious instruction. Regarding all other subjects Jewish schools should be organized just like the best Christian schools, or the Department should order the Jewish children to be admitted to these latter and take care to make sure that Jewish parents need not be afraid that their children might be lured away from the religion of their father. No doubt it would be useful for the education of the moral and civil character of the Jew if the government

would arrange that in the synagogues, besides the religious instruction which is not to be interfered with, instruction be given sometimes in the pure and holy truths of reason, and especially on the relationship of all citizens to the state and their duties to it. An institution which would, in fact, be highly desirable also for the Christians!

With the moral improvement of the Jews there should go hand in hand efforts of the Christians to get rid of their prejudices and uncharitable opinions.

An important part of civil rights would be the right for Jews in all places of free worship, to build synagogues and employ teachers at their own expense.

The written law of Moses, which does not refer to Palestine, and the old judicial and ritual organization, as the oral law, are regarded by the Jews as permanently binding divine commandments. Besides, various commentaries to these laws and argumentations from them by famous Jewish scholars are held in the same respects as laws. Therefore, if they are to be granted full human rights, one has to permit them to live and be judged according to these laws. This will no more isolate them from the rest of the citizens of the state than a city or community living according to their own statutes; and the experience made with Jewish autonomy during the first centuries in the Roman Empire as also in some modern states has shown that no inconvenient or detrimental consequences are to be feared. Although this does not necessarily mean that the laws should be administered by Jewish judges, this would always be more agreeable to them and would avoid many difficulties arising from ignorance of the complicated Jewish jurisprudence in Christian judges, which requires the knowledge of the Hebrew language and Rabbinics. It would therefore be better to leave litigation between Jew and Jew in civil cases to their own judges in the first instance, but also to permit the Jews to start court proceedings at the court of the regular Christian judges. These courts as well as the higher instances to which Jews might appeal from the decision of the Jewish judge, would of course have to decide according to Jewish laws; for if they would decide according to the common law, great confusion would be unavoidable, and besides the litigants would have the unfair advantage that he could file his claim with the judge whose decision he would expect to be favorable to him.

JOSEPH II: EDICT OF TOLERANCE (JANUARY 2, 1782)

Joseph II (1741–1790) was king of Germany and Holy Roman Emperor. The policy expressed in this "Edict of Tolerance" is one of enlightened absolutism: religious tolerance, the encouragement of education, and unrestricted trade. Joseph issued a number of edicts, of which this is the first, all designed to end the social and economic isolation of the Jews and make them more useful to the state.

We, Joseph the Second by the Grace of God, elected Roman Emperor, at all times the Enlarger of the Empire, King of Germany, Hungary and Bohemia, etc., Archduke in Austria, Duke of Burgundy, and Lorraine, send our Grace to all and graciously make known the following:

From the ascension to Our reign We have directed Our most preeminent attention to the end that all Our subjects without distinction of nationality and religion, once they have been admitted and tolerated in Our States, shall participate in common public welfare, the increase of which is Our care, shall enjoy legal freedom and not find any obstacles in any honest ways of gaining their livelihood and increasing general industriousness.

Since, however, the laws and the so-called Jewish Regulations pertaining to the Jewish nation prevailing in Our hereditary countries in general and particularly in Vienna and Lower Austria [Vienna was Joseph's city of residence and Lower Austria was one of the provinces of the Habsburg monarchy] are not always compatible with these Our most gracious intentions, We hereby will amend them by the virtue of this present edict in so far as the difference in times and conditions necessitates it.

The favors granted to the Jewish nation [the Jewish people] by this present amendment, whereby the latest Jewish Regulation of May 5, 1764, is fully repealed consist of the following:

As it is our goal to make the Jewish nation useful and serviceable to the State, mainly through better education and enlightenment of its youth as well as by directing them to the sciences, the arts and the crafts, We hereby grant and order. . . .

1. It certainly is not at all Our supreme wish herewith to grant the Jews residing in Vienna an expansion [of rights] with respect to external tolerance. On the contrary, in the future it will remain that they do not constitute an actual community under a designated leader from their own nation, but as hitherto each family, considered separately, will serenely enjoy the protection of the laws of the land in accordance with the tolerance specifically given it by Our government of Lower Austria. Further, as hitherto they will not be allowed public religious worship or public synagogues; they will not be permitted to establish their own press for the printing of prayer books and other Hebrew books, but when necessary they are to turn to available printing presses in Bohemia; should they wish to import Jewish books from foreign lands, which in general is forbidden, they are accordingly obligated in each such instance to apply for permission and, like all other subjects, to submit imported books to the censor.

2. Likewise, We have no intention by virtue of these new ordinances to increase the number of the members of the Jewish religion in Vienna or in general elsewhere in Our states; nor do we wish to bring foreign [Jews] here without important cause and special merits recommending them.

Rather we expressly wish that the number of Jews, and the manner with which they are tolerated, currently in Lower Austria will remain unchanged; and in the places where Jews never resided they will not in the future be granted the right of residence. Only in accordance with specific circumstances and for good cause, We will find it tolerable to make one or two exceptions.

3. In consonance with these limitations to tolerance ["tolerance" is a technical term designating residence rights, freedom of movement to another town, freedom of profession, and so on], which remains valid, Jews from other lands of Our Inheritance will therefore also not be allowed in the future to come to Vienna in order to stay here permanently, unless they have received a permit from Our government of Lower Austria. And should foreign Jews wish to seek such permission, they would have to apply directly to Us.

4. In order to receive such permission, each and every applicant must indicate without deceit what trade he intends to engage in, or the means of livelihood he wishes to pursue; he must also indicate that he has the assets necessary to support his occupation and to securing the local tolerance. At the same time, he is to indicate to the governments of Lower Austria what he believes he can pay for the tolerance to be granted him. The government will then determine the actual sum of the protection money or the so-called tolerance, and in such a manner that after due consideration the government could increase or lower the sum should the circumstances of the tolerated [Jew] improve or worsen.

5. In exchange for payment of the protection money, one will be allowed together with his wife and his children who do not have a trade of their own and who do not independently conduct any commerce, but are still dependent on him, to live in Vienna, to enjoy Our protection and to conduct activities allowed to his nation, or to engage in the means of livelihood opened to him.

6. This protection, however, does not apply to the son of the tolerated head of a household who is married and has begun to maintain his own household, nor to a daughter who is married to a Jew who is not yet tolerated, or is married to a foreign Jew. The father is obliged forthwith to announce such marriages, and should the son-in-law choose to stay here, he must pay a special tolerance [fee] or, if he should receive permission to leave, pay an exit fee. A son-in-law who is yet tolerated but who contemplates living here must seek to attain permission—should he be a foreigner, from Us, and should he be a subject of one of the states of our Empire, from the government of Lower Austria. In such cases in which permission was granted the daughter to marry a foreigner, the bridegroom must pay an exit fee from the dowry that he will take with him.

7. As in the past, it is forbidden for Jews to live in rural regions of Lower Austria, except if they wish to establish a

factory or pursue a useful trade in some village, in one of the market towns, in a provincial city, or perhaps in a desolate area. In such an instance, they must request permission of the government, but after they receive it their rights and freedoms will be the same as their co-religionists in the capital city [Vienna].

The favors granted to the Jewish nation by this present amendment, whereby the latest Jewish Regulation of May 5, 1764, is fully repealed, consist of the following:

As it is Our goal to make the Jewish nation useful and serviceable to the State, mainly through better education and enlightenment of its youth as well as by directing them to the sciences, the arts and the crafts, We hereby grant and order:

8. Graciously, that the tolerated Jews may send their children to the Christian primary and secondary schools so that they have at least the opportunity to learn reading, writing, and arithmetic. And although they do not have in Our capital a real synagogue, We nonetheless allow them to establish for their children and at their own expense a school of their own, organized in the standard fashion with teachers of their own religion. Toward this end, they are to select three suitable young people to be instructed by the administration of local primary schools in the acceptable pedagogical practice. Their future primary school will be under the aforementioned administration like all local German primary schools, and with respect to the specific equipment, particularly as regards books of a moral content, the most fundamental will be legislated as soon as possible. In the meantime, it is Our wish to announce to them that in order to remove any worry regarding matters of religion and opinion, that we are inclined to leave it to them to compose these books, on the one condition that they must submit them to the superintendent of schools for inspection and approval.

9. With regard to schools of higher degrees which were never forbidden to Jewish co-religionists, We hereby merely renew and confirm this permission.

10. In order to facilitate their future means of support and to prepare the necessary ways of gaining a livelihood, We hereby most graciously permit them from now to learn all kinds of crafts or trades here as well as elsewhere from Christian masters, certainly also amongst themselves, and to this end to apprentice themselves to Christian masters to work as their journeymen, and the latter [the Christian craftsmen] may accept them without hesitation. This, however, should not be interpreted as if We wish to exercise any compulsion on Jews and Christians. We merely grant both sides full freedom to come to an understanding about this amongst themselves to their satisfaction.

11. We hereby further grant to the Jewish nation the general license to carry on all kinds of trade, without however the right of citizenship and mastership from which they re-

main excluded, to be carried on by them freely, only consequently as it is usual here and even then not before having obtained, same as Christians do, the consent of the Magistrate in the city, and the government of Lower Austria.

12. These authorities will grant or decline this consent in accordance with the circumstances. The final decision will be in the hands of the bureau of Our royal court in the same manner that matters of the freedoms requested by Christians are. Painting, sculpture and the practice of the other free arts are granted them as to Christians; and We further grant to the Jewish co-religionists the completely free choice of all non-civic branches of commerce and authorize them to apply for the right of wholesale trade under the same conditions and with the same liberties as are obtained by Our Christian subjects. . . .

13. Since the investment in factories and manufacture has always been permitted them, We only use this opportunity to renew this permission in order to encourage them openly to such undertakings that benefit the public.

14. Furthermore, in order to allow them to invest their capital and to secure it, they will be permitted to borrow against real estate, although they do not have the right to assess the latter themselves.

15. Considering the numerous openings in trades and manifold contacts with Christians resulting therefrom, the care for maintaining common confidence requires that the Hebrew and the so-called Jewish language and writing of Hebrew intermixed with German be abolished. . . . We therefore explicitly forbid their use in all public transactions in and out of the courts; in the future the vernacular of the land is to be used instead. In order to obviate all excuses or objections that such a hasty transition would be impossible, We will allow a period of two years, to be calculated from the day of the promulgation of this decree, in which it should be possible to carry out all the necessary changes and arrangements. We, accordingly, herewith announce that after this period all legal instruments written in Hebrew or written only in the Hebrew and Jewish letters will be invalid and null and void.

16. In order to facilitate the tolerated Jews in their trades also with regard to the question of servants, it shall be permitted to them from now on to employ as many Jewish as well as Christian servants as their business requires. . . . Nonetheless, they will be required, not as in the past every quarter of a year but once a year, to submit to the government a trustworthy testimony noting together with the children and other family members beholden to their care and fatherly charge also their servants, their names, ages and religion. Every head of a [Jewish] household is required not only to lodge in their homes their Jewish servants but also to ensure that they will not engage in any trade of their own, which is prohibited to Jews who are not tolerated.

Moreover, We expect that they [the heads of Jewish households] will not allow foreign Jews residence [in their homes] on the pretext that they are servants and through such a ruse violate Our commandment. Should such violations be discovered, they will be severely punished.

17. It is self-evident that these Jewish servants must be unmarried, and should they have a family, their wives, husbands, or adult children must also be in the service of the same household or in that of another [tolerated] Jew or have the right to engage in a trade, otherwise they will not have the right to reside here [in Vienna] without being tolerated or servants.

18. By the present Decree We hereby permit the existing restrictions with regard to definite Jewish houses to lapse and allow tolerated Jews to lease at their choice their own residences in the city as well as in the suburbs.

19. No less do We hereby completely abolish the head toll hitherto levied on foreign Jews and permit them to enter Our residence [Vienna] from time to time in order to carry on their business.

20. Since we have already announced that We do not wish to increase the number of Jewish families residing here, any foreign Jew who comes here must immediately upon his arrival register with the government of Lower Austria and indicate the business [that has brought him to Vienna] and the time required in order to complete it, to wait for the approval, or in any case an answer from the appropriate office. When this period of time is over, they must either leave [Vienna] or request from the government an extension. All those who hide or stay here without the required license or stay beyond the time allotted them will be sought out, arrested and evicted from here. We, therefore, impose upon Our government in Lower Austria the explicit task constantly to keep a watchful eye through the police that these foreign Jews will depart [at the appointed time]. To facilitate this surveillance, We also order those Christians and [tolerated] Jews at whose homes alien Jews may be lodging to report this to the authorities, which they are in any case required to do, immediately.

21. With respect to such arrivals it is self-evident that they cannot be treated equally with the local tolerated Jews in transactions and in the management of food shops. Accordingly, they do not have the license to deal in such goods for which only authorized merchants and tolerated Jews have been granted permission. Similarly, the general prohibition, applying to them as well as others, against peddling (that is, the selling of goods from house to house in the city and also in the country) still remains and with the [threat of] confiscation of these goods.

22. On the other hand, foreign Jews are permitted during the period of fairs to deal in all goods that one is generally allowed to import; at other times, however, they are only permitted to deal in those goods that foreign merchants are permitted to sell. Similarly, like all others, they are permitted to take orders from factories and licensed merchants and craftsmen for raw and uncooked materials, and equipment that they have imported here. They are, however, warned to take care not to buy or even help conceal stolen goods and moveable property, a [crime] for which they will be punished with all severity in accordance with the law.

23. In addition, the special double court and notary taxes incumbent upon Jews that hitherto existed are herewith cancelled and [We remove],

24. In general all hitherto customary distinctive marks and distinctions, such as the wearing of beards, the prohibition of leaving their homes before twelve o'clock on Sundays and holidays, the frequenting of public places and the like; on the contrary, it shall be permitted to wholesale merchants and their sons as well as to people of such rank to carry swords.

25. Since by these favors We almost place the Jewish nation on an equal level with adherents of other religious associations in respect to trade and employment of civil and domestic facilities, We hereby earnestly advise them to observe scrupulously all political, civil and judicial laws of the country to which they are bound as all other inhabitants, just as they remain subject with respect to all political and legal matters to the provincial and municipal authorities within their jurisdiction and pertinent activities.

Done in our city of Residence Vienna, the second day of January, 1782, in the eighteenth year of Our reign in the Roman Empire and in the second year of reign in Our hereditary lands.

ABBÉ GRÉGOIRE: AN ESSAY ON THE PHYSICAL, MORAL, AND POLITICAL REFORMATION OF THE JEWS (1789)

Abbé Grégoire (1750–1831) favored the granting of equal rights to Jews and spoke on their behalf in the French National Assembly, presenting a motion for Jewish emancipation. His arguments on behalf of the Jews are noteworthy, since they were offered by a professing Catholic and priest.

But the Jews, I shall be told, are incapable of being reformed, because they are absolutely worthless. I reply, that we see few of them commit murder, or other enormous crimes, that call forth public vengeance; but their abominable meanness produces base actions. Mr. Michaelis assures us that in Germany, of twenty-five criminals imprisoned or condemned, twenty-four are always Jews. This is the assertion of Mr. Michaelis—but, in the first place, an assertion is no proof. The truth of this, however, might have been easily ascertained by examining and producing the criminals. Secondly, supposing the circumstances to be as true as it is doubtful, this would prove nothing but against the German Jews; and lastly, it would still be necessary to establish as a certainty that this perversity proceeds immediately from their religion, or their natural disposition. That it is not inspired by the law is evident; shall we believe, then, that it is innate? Some peevish philosophers, indeed, have pretended that man is born wicked; but happily for the honor and comfort of humanity, this system has been banished to the class of absurd and mortifying hypotheses. So many laws made against the Jews always suppose in them a natural and indelible worthlessness; but these laws, which are the fruit of hatred or prejudice, have no other foundation but the motive which gives rise to them. This perversity is not so inherent in their character as to affect every individual. We see talents and virtues shine forth in them wherever they begin to be treated as men, especially in the territories of the Pope [the Papal States, although located in Italy, functioned independently], which have so long been their terrestrial paradise; in Holland, Prussia, and even among us. Hertz [Markus Hertz, German-Jewish physician, friend and disciple of Immanuel Kant] and Bloch [Markus (Mordechai) Eliezer Bloch, German-Jewish physician, famed zoologist, friend of Moses Mendelssohn] render the Jewish nation illustrious at present in Germany; and the Hague is honored by a Pinto [Isaac de Pinto, philosopher and economist of Portuguese-Jewish descent from France, lived most of his life in Holland]. We must, therefore, believe these people susceptible of morality, until we are shown that they have invincible obstacles in their physical organization, and in their religious and moral constitution.

Let us cherish morality, but let us not be so unreasonable as to require it of those whom we have compelled to become vicious. Let us reform their education, to reform their hearts; it has long been observed that they are men as well as we, and they are so before they are Jews.

Mr. Michaelis objects also that this nation, being in constant opposition to general manners, will never become patriotic. We allow that it will be difficult to incorporate them into universal society; but between difficulty and impossibility, there is the same difference as between impossibility and possibility. I have myself remarked, and even proved, that hitherto the Jews have been invariable in their manners and customs; but the greater part of their customs are not contrary to civil functions; and with regard to those which may appear to be incompatible with the duties of the citizen, they are preserved only by the uniformity of that conduct which all nations observe towards them. If we do not maintain, with Helvetius [Claude Adrien Helvetius, French philosopher, one of the Encyclopedists], that the character and disposition of man depend altogether on his education, we at least allow that in a great measure they are

the result of circumstances. Can the Jews ever become patriots? This is a question proposed by those who reproach them with not loving a country that drove them from its bosom; and with not cherishing people who exercised their fury against them—that is to say, who were their executioners. . . .

The Jews, everywhere dispersed, yet nowhere established, have only had the spirit of a body, which is entirely different from the spirit of a nation; for this reason, as has been observed, it is neither that of the English at London, nor that of the Dutch at the Hague, nor that of the French at Metz; they form always a state within a state, because they are never treated as children of the country. In republics even, where the people taking an active part in the legislation are subject only to themselves, the Jews are always passive, and counted as nothing; they possess no landed property, though commerce, which generally renders men citizens of the world, procures them portable riches, that afford them a small consolation of the opprobrium thrown upon them, and the load of oppressive laws under which they groan. You require that they should love their country—first give them one. . . .

Lavater [Johann Caspar Lavater, Swiss clergyman and theologian] the philosopher, who may be considered as a legislator in whatever relates to physiognomy, told me that according to his observations, the Jews in general had sallow complexions, hooked noses, hollow eyes, prominent chins, and the constrictory muscles of the mouth very apparent. . . .

It is added, that the Jews abound with bad humors; are very much subject to those disorders which indicate that the general mass of the blood is corrupted, as appears from their being formerly troubled with leprosy, and at present with the scurvy, which has so much affinity to it, and with the scrophula, bloody-flux, etc. If to the testimony of those who make the above assertion, we join the acknowledgement of Abrabanel [Judah Abrabanel, Jewish physician and poet, one of the foremost philosophers of the Italian Renaissance], we shall be tempted to believe, that the hemorrhoids are endemic among them; and as this malady has sometimes periodical returns, several writers have seriously concluded that the Jews are subject to menstrual evacuations. Cardoso [Isaac (Fernando) Cardoso, Marrano physician and scientist] quotes and refutes various authors, who have propagated these ridiculous notions.

It is contended also, that the Jews constantly exhale a bad smell. This, indeed, is not a new opinion; for we find frequent mention made of it in old authors; and this accusation, repeated in all ages, has perpetuated the same prejudice. Ramazzini [Bernardo Ramazzini, Italian physician], in his *Treatise on the Diseases of Tradesmen,* has inserted a chapter on those of the Jews. He has no doubt that the Jews exhaled a very fetid smell when they lived amidst the splendor of Jerusalem; and he assigns as the cause of this pretended stink, and of their paleness, which is more real, their occupations (such as that of selling old clothes) and their poverty. Others ascribe these effects to the frequent use of herbs, such as onions and garlic, the smell of which is penetrating; and some to their eating the flesh of he-goats; while others pretend that the flesh of geese, which they are remarkably fond of, renders them melancholy and livid, as this food abounds with viscous and gross juices.

I admit the influence of these particular causes upon the constitution, but the inductions thence drawn are not satisfactory. Who will believe, for example, that selling old clothes is sufficient to render the complexion dark? Are the inhabitants of the street Tirechape at Paris, or the Ray-fair at Strasbourg, less blooming than those of other streets in the neighborhood? Besides, the Jews are neither all poor, nor sellers of old clothes; and the custom of Metz, already mentioned, is not general. Mr. Venel, after remarking that epilepsy is common among the Jews, that the greater part of them soon appear old, and that they seldom attain to a great age, pretends that their ablutions [ritual baths] contribute much to enervate their constitutions. In answer to this it may be said that the continual use of the bath did not enervate the Romans; that the Turks, subjected in this respect to more legal ceremonies than the Jews, are not effeminated; and that besides, cold ablutions, such as those used by the latter, instead of relaxing the body, ought to strengthen the muscles and give them more elasticity.

THE ASSEMBLY OF JEWISH NOTABLES: ANSWERS TO NAPOLEON (1806)

This document presents the answers offered to Napoleon at the Assembly. A committee of Assembly members formulated the answers, which were subsequently ratified by the entire 112-member Assembly in August 1806.

Resolved, by the French deputies professing the religion of Moses, that the following Declaration shall precede the answers returned to the questions proposed by the Commissioners of His Imperial and Royal Majesty.

The assembly, impressed with a deep sense of gratitude, love, respect, and admiration for the sacred person of His Imperial and Royal Majesty, declares, in the name of all Frenchmen professing the religion of Moses, that they are fully determined to prove worthy of the favors His Majesty intends for them, by scrupulously conforming to his paternal intentions; that their religion makes it their duty to consider the law of the prince as the supreme law in civil and political matters; that consequently, should their religious code, or its various interpretations, contain civil or politi-cal commands at variance with those of the French code, those commands would, of course, cease to influence and govern them, since they must, above all, acknowledge and obey the laws of the prince.

That, in consequence of this principle, the Jews have, at all times, considered it their duty to obey the laws of the state, and that, since the revolution, they, like all Frenchmen, have acknowledged no others.

First Question: *Is it lawful for Jews to marry more than one wife?*

Answer: It is not lawful for Jews to marry more than one wife: in all European countries they conform to the general practice marrying only one.

Moses does not command expressly to take several, but he does not forbid it. He seems even to adopt that custom as generally prevailing, since he settles the rights of inheritance between children of different wives. Although this practice still prevails in the East, yet their ancient doctors have enjoined them to restrain from taking more than one wife, except when the man is enabled by his fortune to maintain several.

The case has been different in the West; the wish of adopting the customs of the inhabitants of this part of the world has induced the Jews to renounce polygamy. But as several individuals still indulged in that practice, a synod was convened at Worms in the eleventh century, composed of one hundred Rabbis, with Gershom at their head. This assembly pronounced an anathema against every Israelite who should, in future, take more than one wife.

Although this prohibition was not to last forever, the influence of European manners has universally prevailed.

Second Question: *Is divorce allowed by the Jewish religion? Is divorce valid when not pronounced by courts of justice by virtue of laws in contradiction with those of the French Code?*

Answer: Repudiation is allowed by the law of Moses; but it is not valid if not previously pronounced by the French code.

In the eyes of every Israelite, without exception, submission to the prince is the first of duties. It is a principle generally acknowledged among them, that in every thing relating to civil or political interests, the law of the state is the supreme law. Before they were admitted in France to share the right of all citizens, and when they lived under a particular legislation which set them at liberty to follow their religious customs, they had the ability to divorce their wives; but it was extremely rare to see it put into practice.

Since the revolution, they have acknowledged no other laws on this head but those of the empire. At the epoch when they were admitted to the rank of citizens, the Rabbis and the principal Jews appeared before the municipalities of their respective places of abode and took an oath to conform, in every thing to the laws, and to acknowledge no other rules in all civil matters. . . .

Third Question: *Can a Jewess marry a Christian, and a Jew a Christian woman? Or does the law allow the Jews to marry only among themselves?*

Answer: The law does not say that a Jewess cannot marry a Christian, nor a Jew a Christian woman; nor does it state that the Jews can only marry among themselves.

The only marriages expressly forbidden by the law are those with the seven Canaanite nations, with Ammon and Moab, and with the Egyptians. The prohibition is absolute concerning the seven Canaanite nations: with regard to Ammon and Moab, it is limited, according to many Talmudists, to the men of those nations, and does not extend to the women; it is even thought that these last would have embraced the Jewish religion. As to Egyptians, the prohibition is limited to the third generation. The prohibition in general applies only to nations in idolatry. The Talmud declares formally that modern nations are not to be considered as such, since they worship, like us, the God of heaven and earth. And, accordingly, there have been, at several periods, intermarriages between Jews and Christians in France, in Spain, and in Germany: these marriages were sometimes tolerated and sometimes forbidden by the laws of those sovereigns, who had received Jews into their dominions.

Unions of this kind are still found in France; but we cannot deny that the opinion of the Rabbis is against these marriages. According to their doctrine, although the religion of Moses has not forbidden the Jews from intermarrying with nations not of their religion, yet, as marriage, according to the Talmud, requires religious ceremonies called Kiddushin, with the benediction used in such cases, no marriage can be religiously valid unless these ceremonies have been performed. This could not be done towards persons who would not both of them consider these ceremonies as sacred; and in that case the married couple could separate without the religious divorce; they would then be considered as married civilly but not religiously.

Such is the opinion of the Rabbis, members of this assembly. In general, they would be no more inclined to bless the union of Jewess with a Christian, or of a Jew with a Christian woman, than Catholic priests themselves would be disposed to sanction unions of this kind. The Rabbis acknowledge, however, that a Jew who marries a Christian woman does not cease on that account to be considered as a Jew by his brethren, any more than if he had married a Jewess civilly and not religiously.

Fourth Question: *In the eyes of Jews, are Frenchmen considered as their brethren? Or are they considered as strangers?*

Answer: In the eyes of Jews, Frenchmen are their brethren and are not strangers.

The true spirit of the law of Moses is consonant with this mode of considering Frenchmen.

When the Israelites formed a settled and independent nation, their law made it a rule for them to consider strangers as their brethren.

With the most tender care for their welfare, their lawgiver commands to love them, "Love ye therefore the strangers," says he to the Israelites, "for ye were strangers in the land of Egypt." Respect and benevolence towards strangers are enforced by Moses, not as an exhortation to the practice of social morality only, but as an obligation imposed by God himself.

A religion whose fundamental maxims are such—a religion which makes a duty of loving the stranger—which enforces the practice of social virtues, must surely require that its followers should consider their fellow-citizens as brethren.

And how could they consider them otherwise when they inhabit the same land, when they are ruled and protected by the same government, and by the same laws? When they enjoy the same rights and have the same duties to fulfill? There exists, even between the Jew and Christian, a tie which abundantly compensates for religion—it is the tie of gratitude. This sentiment was at first excited in us by the mere grant of toleration. It has been increased, these eighteen years, by new favors from government, to such a degree of energy, that now our fate is irrevocably linked with the common fate of all Frenchmen. Yes, France is our country; all Frenchmen are our brethren, and this glorious title, by raising us in our own esteem, becomes a sure pledge that we shall never cease to be worthy of it.

Fifth Question: *In either case, what line of conduct does their law prescribe towards Frenchmen not of their religion?*

Answer: The line of conduct prescribed towards Frenchmen not of our religion is the same as that prescribed between Jews themselves; we admit of no difference but that of worshipping the Supreme Being, every one in his own way.

The answer to the preceding question has explained the line of conduct which the law of Moses and the Talmud prescribe towards Frenchmen not of our religion. At the present time, when the Jews no longer form a separate people, but enjoy the advantage of being incorporated with the great Nation (which privilege they consider as a kind of political redemption), it is impossible that a Jew should treat a Frenchman not of his religion in any other manner than he would treat one of his Israelite brethren.

Sixth Question: *Do Jews born in France, and treated by the laws as French citizens, consider France their country? Are they bound to defend it? Are they bound to obey the laws and to conform to the dispositions of the civil code?*

Answer: Men who have adopted a country, who have resided in it these many generations—who, even under the restraint of particular laws which abridged their civil rights, were so attached to it that they preferred being debarred from the advantages common to all other citizens, rather than leave it—cannot but consider themselves as equally sacred and honorable the bounden duty of defending their country.

Jeremiah (chapter 29) exhorts the Jews to consider Babylon as their country, although they were to remain in it only for seventy years. He exhorts them to till the ground, to build houses, to sow, and to plant. His recommendation was so much attended to, that Ezra (chapter 2) says that when Cyrus allowed them to return to Jerusalem to rebuild the Temple, 42,360 only, left Babylon; and that this number was mostly composed of poor people, the wealthy having remained in that city.

The love of the country is in the heart of Jews a sentiment so natural, so powerful, and so consonant to their religious opinions, that a French Jew considers himself in England as among strangers, although he may be among Jews; and the case is the same with English Jews in France.

To such a pitch is this sentiment carried among them, that during the last war, French Jews have been seen fighting desperately against other Jews, the subjects of countries then at war with France.

Many of them are covered with honorable wounds, and others have obtained, in the field of honor, the noble rewards of bravery.

Seventh Question: *Who names the Rabbis?*

Answer: Since the revolution, the majority of the chiefs of families names the Rabbi, wherever there is a sufficient number of Jews to maintain one, after previous inquiries as to the morality and learning of the candidate. This mode of election is not, however, uniform: it varies according to place, and, to this day, whatever concerns the elections of Rabbis is still in a state of uncertainty.

Eighth Question: *What police jurisdiction do Rabbis exercise among the Jews? What judicial power do they enjoy among them?*

Answer: The Rabbis exercise no manner of Police Jurisdiction among the Jews.

It is only in the Mishnah and in the Talmud that the word Rabbi is found for the first time applied to a doctor in the law; and he was commonly indebted for this qualification to his reputation, and to the opinion generally entertained of his learning.

When the Israelites were totally dispersed, they formed small communities in those places where they were allowed to settle in certain numbers.

Sometimes, in these circumstances, a Rabbi and two other doctors formed a kind of tribunal, named Beth Din, that is, House of Justice; the Rabbi fulfilled the functions of judge, and the other two those of his assessors.

The attributes, and even the existence of these tribunals, have, to this day, always depended on the will of governments under which the Jews have lived, and on the degree of tolerance they have enjoyed. Since the revolution those rabbinical tribunals are totally suppressed in France, and in Italy. The Jews, raised to the rank of citizens, have conformed in every thing to the laws of the state; and, accordingly, the functions of Rabbis, wherever any are established, are limited to preaching morality in the temples, blessing marriages, and pronouncing divorces. . . .

Ninth Question: *Are these forms of Election, and that police-jurisdiction, regulated by law, or are they only sanctioned by custom?*

Answer: The answer to the preceding questions makes it useless to say much on this, only it may be remarked, that, even supposing that Rabbis should have, to this day preserved some kind of police-judicial jurisdiction among us, which is not the case, neither such jurisdiction, nor the forms of the elections, could be said to be sanctioned by the law; they should be attributed solely to custom.

Tenth Question: *Are there professions which the law of the Jews forbids them from exercising?*

Answer: There are none: on the contrary, the Talmud (*vide* Kiddushin, chapter 1) expressly declares that "the father who does not teach a profession to his child rears him up to be a villain."

Eleventh Question: *Does the law forbid the Jews from taking usury from their brethren?*

Answer: Deuteronomy says, "thou shalt not lend upon interest to thy brother, interest of money, interest of victuals, interest of any thing that is lent upon interest."

The Hebrew word *neshekh* has been improperly translated by the word "usury": in the Hebrew language it means interest of any kind, and not usurious interest. It cannot then be taken in the meaning now given the word "usury".

Twelfth Question: *Does it forbid or does it allow to take usury from strangers?*

Answer: We have seen, in the answer to the foregoing question, that the prohibition of usury, considered as the smallest interest, was a maxim of charity and of benevolence, rather than a commercial regulation. In this point of view it is equally condemned by the law of Moses and by the Talmud: we are generally forbidden, always on the score of charity, to lend upon interest to our fellow-citizens of different persuasions, as well as our fellow-Jews.

The disposition of the law, which allows to take interest from the stranger, evidently refers only to nations in commercial intercourse with us; otherwise there would be an evident contradiction between this passage and twenty others of the sacred writings.

Thus the prohibition extended to the stranger who dealt in Israel; the Holy Writ places them under the safeguard of God; he is a sacred guest, and God orders us to treat him like the widow and like the orphan.

Can Moses be considered as the lawgiver of the universe because he was the lawgiver of the Jews? Were the laws he gave to the people, which God had entrusted to his care, likely to become the general laws of mankind? Thou shalt not lend upon interest to thy brother. What security had he that, in the intercourse which would be naturally established between the Jews and foreign nations, these last would renounce customs generally prevailing in trade, and lend to the Jews without requiring any interest? Was he then bound to sacrifice the interest of his people, and to impoverish the Jews to enrich foreign nations? Is it not absolutely absurd to reproach him with having put a restriction to the precept contained in Deuteronomy? What a lawgiver but would have considered such a restriction as a natural principle of reciprocity?

How far superior in simplicity, generosity, justice, and humanity is the law of Moses, on this matter, to those of the Greeks and of the Romans! Can we find, in the history of the ancient Israelites, those scandalous scenes of rebellion excited by the harshness of creditors towards their debtors, those frequent abolitions of debts to prevent the multitude, impoverished by the extortions of lenders, from being driven to despair?

The law of Moses and its interpreters have distinguished, with a praiseworthy humanity, the different uses of borrowed money. Is it to maintain a family? Interest is forbidden. Is it to undertake a commercial speculation, by which the principal is adventured? Interest is allowed, even between Jews. Lend to the poor, says Moses. Here the tribute of gratitude is the only kind of interest allowed; the satisfaction of obliging is the sole recompense of the conferred benefit. The case is different in regard to capital employed in extensive commerce: there, Moses allows the lender to come in for a share of the profits of the borrower; and as commerce was scarcely known among the Israelites, who were exclusively addicted to agricultural pursuits, and as it was carried on only with strangers, that is, with neighboring nations, it was allowed to share its profits with them. . . .

It is an incontrovertible point, according to the Talmud, that interest, even among Israelites, is lawful in commercial operations, where the lender, running some of the risk of the borrower, becomes a sharer in his profits. This is the opinion of all Jewish doctors.

It is evident that our opinions, teeming with absurdities, and contrary to all rules of social morality, although advanced by a Rabbi, can no more be imputed to the general doctrine of the Jews than similar notions if advanced by Catholic theologians, could be attributed to the evangelical doctrine. The same may be said of the general charge made against the Hebrews, that they are naturally inclined to usury: it cannot be denied that some of them are to be found, though not so many as is generally supposed, who follow that nefarious traffic condemned by their religion.

But if there are some not over-nice in this particular, is it just to accuse one hundred thousand individuals of this vice? Would it not be deemed an injustice to lay the same imputation on all Christians because some of them are guilty of usury?

THE "INFAMOUS DECREE" (MARCH 17, 1808)

The "Infamous Decree" placed restrictions on the economic activities of Jews, as well as on their rights of residence. It was very much contrary to the ideals of the French Revolution.

Decree on the Regulation of Commercial Transactions and Residence of Jews
(March 17, 1808)

Napoleon, Emperor of the French, etc., etc.; On the report of our Minister of the Interior; Our Council of State in agreement, We have decreed and do decree that which follows:

Title I

Article 1. From the date of the publication of this decree, the moratorium declared by our decree of May 30, 1806, on the payment of debts to Jews is cancelled.

2. The aforesaid debts, however, shall be subject to the following provisions.

3. Any transaction for a loan made by Jews: to minors without the consent of their guardians; to women without the consent of their husbands; to the lower ranks of military personnel without consent of their officers, or to the higher ranks, without the consent of superiors; shall be considered void so that the holder of the debt cannot take unfair advantage. And our courts may not authorize any suits for the recovery of such loans.

4. No bill of exchange, no promissory note, and no obligation nor promise signed by one of our non-commercial subjects in favor of a Jew shall be collectable unless the holder of the debt can prove that the complete value of the note has been rendered to the debtor without any fraud.

5. Any debt, the capital of which shall be increased as a matter of course or the capital of which shall become entirely hidden by the accumulation of interest in excess of five percent, shall be reduced by our courts. If the interest attached to the capital exceeds ten percent, the debt shall be declared usurious and, thus, cancelled.

6. For legitimate and non-usurious debts, our courts are authorized to grant extensions to the debtors in conformity with equity.

Title II

7. From the first day of the coming July and thenceforth, no Jew shall be permitted to devote himself to any business, negotiation, or any type of commerce without having received a specific license from the prefect of the department in which he resides. This license will only be granted on the receipt of precise information and of certification: a) from the municipal council stating that the said Jew does not devote himself to an illicit business; b) from the consistory of the district in which he lives attesting to his good conduct and his integrity.

8. This license shall be renewed annually.

9. The attorneys-general of our courts are specifically instructed to revoke these licenses on the decision of the court whenever it comes to their attention that a licensed Jew is engaging in usury or devoting himself to fraudulent business.

10. Any commercial action undertaken by an unlicensed Jew shall be null and of no value.

11. The preceding shall also apply to any mortgage taken on property by an unlicensed Jew, whenever it can be proven that the said mortgage was taken in payment of a debt resulting from a bill of exchange or from any commercial enterprise whatsoever.

12. All contracts or obligations endorsed for the profit of an unlicensed Jew, in matters foreign to regular commerce, may be annulled after an inquiry by our courts. The debtor shall be allowed to prove that there was usury or some fraudulent transaction, and, if the proof is valid, these debts shall be liable either to arbitrary reduction by the courts or to annulment if the usury exceeds ten percent.

13. The provisions of article 4, title 1, of this decree, concerning bills of exchange, promissory notes, etc., are applicable for the future as well as the past.

14. No Jew shall be allowed to lend money on collateral to servants or hired people nor to lend money on collateral to any other persons unless the document be drawn up by a notary who will certify in the document that the items were counted in his presence and in the presence of witnesses. Otherwise he shall forfeit all rights to the debtor's wages, and our courts will, in such a case, be able to order free restitution.

15. Jews may not be allowed, under the same penalties, to receive the tools, utensils, implements, or clothing of day workers or servants in lieu of payment of debts.

Title III

16. No Jew not actually now living in our departments (provinces) of Haut- and Bas-Rhin shall be hereafter admitted to take up residence there.

In the other departments of the Empire, no Jew not actually now living in them shall be admitted to take up residence except in a case where he acquires a rural property and devotes himself to agriculture, without entering into any commercial or business transactions. It shall be possible to make exceptions to the provisions of this article by means of a special dispensation from us.

17. The Jewish population in our departments shall never be allowed to supply replacements for conscription; consequently, every Jewish conscript shall be subject to personal service.

General Provisions

18. The provisions included in this decree shall remain in effect for ten years in the hope that, at the end of this period and as a result of these various measures made necessary because of the Jews, there will no longer be any difference between them and the other citizens of our Empire. But, nevertheless, if our hope is disappointed these provisions shall be extended until whatever time shall be judged convenient.

19. The Jews living in Bordeaux and in the departments of Gironde and Landes, not having caused any complaints and not ever having devoted themselves to illicit business, are not included under the provisions of this decree.

Signed, Napoleon
For the Emperor:
The Minister Secretary of State,
Signed, Hugues B. Maret

THE FRANKFURT PARLIAMENT: RELIGIOUS EQUALITY (DECEMBER 27, 1848)

1848 was a year of revolutions in Europe—revolutions in which liberal democratic principles were prominent themes, including full civil and political equality for Jews. A provisional government was established in Germany by the Frankfurt National Parliament, but it had only a short life. Nevertheless, the right of Jews to vote and to be elected to office remained. In addition, the cause of Jewish emancipation had strong support from the liberals.

The Imperial Regent [*Reichsverweser*] in execution of the resolution of the National Assembly of December 21, 1848, proclaims as law:

1. The Fundamental Rights of the German People. The following rights shall be granted to the German people. They shall serve as a norm for the constitutions of the individual German states and no constitution or legislation of an individual German state may abolish or restrict them. . . .

Article 5. . . . Paragraph 14. Every German has full freedom of faith and conscience. Nobody shall be forced to disclose his religious creed. . . .

Paragraph 16. The enjoyment of civil or political rights shall be neither conditioned nor limited by religious confession.

The same religious confession should not impair civil duties.

Paragraph 17. . . . No religious association shall benefit from any state prerogatives before others. No state church shall exist henceforth.

WILHELM I: EMANCIPATION IN BAVARIA (APRIL 22, 1871)

By 1864, two of the three South German states, Baden and Wuerttemberg, had given Jews full rights. This act extended these rights to the Jews in Bavaria as well. This meant that the process of emancipation in Germany was now complete.

We, Wilhelm, by the grace of God, German Emperor, King of Prussia, etc., Decree, in the name of the German Reich, following the approval of the Bundesrath and the Reichstag, as follows:

1. The laws of the North German Confederation cited in the following paragraphs shall be introduced

in the Kingdom of Bavaria as laws of the Reich, according to the detailed stipulations contained in these paragraphs.

2. From the day on which the present law goes into effect the following shall be in force: . . . (10) the law of July 3, 1869, concerning the equality of confessions with respect to civil and political rights.

Authentically under Our Most High Signature and with the Imperial Seal affixed.

Done in Berlin, April 22, 1871.

Reference Works

J. Berkovitz, *The Shaping of Jewish Identity in 19th Century France*

A. Hertzberg, *The French Enlightenment and the Jews*

J. Katz, *Out of the Ghetto: The Social Background of Jewish Emancipation, 1770–1870*

P. Mendes-Flohr and J. Reinharz, *The Jew in the Modern World: A Documentary History*

M. Meyer, *The Origins of the Modern Jew: Jewish Identity and European Culture in Germany, 1749–1824*

H. M. Sachar, *The Course of Modern Jewish History*

Chronology

1775	Pius VI issues Edict on the Jews.
1781	Joseph II, Holy Roman Emperor, issues Edict of Toleration.
1789	French Revolution begins. French National Assembly adopts the Declaration of the Rights of Man and the Citizen.
1790	French National Assembly adopts a constitution, establishing a limited monarchy. Sephardic Jews of France are emancipated.
1791	All French Jews are emancipated.
1792	French monarchy is abolished. King Louis XVI and Marie Antoinette are executed. Republic is established.
1799	Napoleon overthrows Directory.
1804	Napoleon is proclaimed Emperor of France.
1806	Assembly of Jewish Notables is convened.
1807	Great Sanhedrin is reconstituted.
1812	War between United States and England. United States defeats England on Lake Champlain, winning War of 1812.
1815	Napoleon is defeated by British and Russian armies at Waterloo. Congress of Vienna redraws map of Europe. German states form a Confederation of 39 kingdoms, duchies, principalities, and free cities. The Congress is dominated by Prussia and Austria.
1831	Judaism is granted equal legal status with other religions in France. King Louis-Philippe agrees to include salaries of rabbis in national budget.
1837	Victoria (1819–1901) becomes queen of Great Britain and Ireland.
1840	Damascus Blood Libel begins.
1848	Marx and Engels publish the *Communist Manifesto*.
1852	French approve new constitution and establishment of Second Empire. President Louis Napoleon proclaims himself Emperor Napoleon III.
1854	Crimean War—Turkey, Britain, and France against Russia. Russia is defeated. Zechariah Frankel is appointed first head of Jewish Theological Seminary in Breslau.
1858	Edgardo Mortara Affair takes place.
1862	Otto von Bismarck (1815–1898) becomes Chancellor of Prussia.
1869	North German Federation abolishes all remaining civil and political disabilities due to differences in religious affiliation.
1870	Franco-Prussian War. Prussia defeats France. Bloodless revolution in France deposes Napoleon III; Third French Republic is established.
1885	Bismarck supports expulsion from Germany of 30,000 Russian and Austrian citizens, 33 percent of whom are Jews.
1890	Bismarck is dismissed as Chancellor of Germany by Emperor William III.
1894	Dreyfus Affair.
1909	Herbert Samuel (1870–1963) becomes Britain's first Jewish cabinet minister.
1914	Archduke Franz Ferdinand is assassinated at Sarajevo; World War I results.
1919	League of Nations is created by agreement at Paris Peace Conference after World War I. Weimar Republic is established in Germany.

1936   Léon Blum is first Jew and first Socialist to become premier of France.

1939   Cardinal Pacelli (1876–1958) is elected Pope Pius XII.

1941   United States enters World War II.

1945   World War II ends in Europe on May 8.

1951   Konrad Adenauer wins approval from Bundestag to make reparation payments to Jews of Israel.
Agreement is signed between West Germany and Israel regarding reparation payments.

1954   Pierre-Mendes France (1907–1982) becomes third Jewish premier of France.

1958   New constitution for Fifth French Republic, to be headed by General Charles de Gaulle.

1969   De Gaulle resigns after defeat of national referendum.
Georges Pompidou is elected to take his place.
Willy Brandt is elected Chancellor of Germany

1978   John Paul II becomes Pope.

3

CULTURAL AND INTELLECTUAL HISTORY

INTRODUCTION

This chapter considers the cultural and intellectual history of Jews in Western and Eastern Europe.

Until the 17th and 18th centuries, two institutions ruled without opposition: the kings and the church. The kings ruled with absolute power and no one questioned their authority. The church held the key to religious truth and no one was audacious enough to question its authority. In the 17th and 18th centuries, however, there arose a new ideology in matters of society and religion: the Enlightenment.

The central theme of the Enlightenment was rationalism, the rule of reason. It held that religion and society should be measured by reason alone. Society should be built on the basis of reason, and religion should conform to reason. Political rule should be conducted with reason, and the lives of individuals should be governed by reason.

The distinguished thinkers of the Enlightenment included John Locke (1674–1704), best known for his "Essay Concerning Human Understanding," and Thomas Hobbes (1588–1679), author of *Leviathan,* a work of political philosophy. Also among them was the famous Sir Isaac Newton (1642–1727), who formulated the law of gravitation, the binomial theorem, and the elements of differential calculus.

French Enlightenment thinkers, too, were rationalists. They were greatly influenced as well by the deism of British thinkers. Deism, the belief in God the Creator whose existence is known exclusively through reason, regarded clericalism and elaborate rituals as extraneous elements. Voltaire (1694–1778) is the best-known Enlightenment thinker, one whose anti-Semitic views were given expression in his *Philosophical Dictionary.* Diderot (1713–1784), editor of the French *Encyclopedia,* embraced the rationalism of the Enlightenment, although religious tolerance did not

accompany it, since he described Jews as a nation of bigoted obscurantists. Another important figure was Baron de Montesquieu (1689–1755), whose *The Spirit of the Laws* would have a profound impact on the structure of American government.

What was most significant from the standpoint of Jews was that some thinkers began to speak about religious tolerance. John Locke, for example, was troubled by religious intolerance because he thought it undermined the possibilities of living in a truly peaceful society. In one of his "Letters on Toleration," he wrote:

> . . . neither pagan nor Mahometan [*sic*], nor Jew, ought to be excluded from the civil rights of the commonwealth because of his religion.

ENLIGHTENMENT AND THE JEWS: WESTERN EUROPE

Without question the most important figure in the Jewish Enlightenment, or Haskalah, was Moses Mendelssohn (1729–1786). Mendelssohn was born in Dessau. His father was at first a *schulklapfer,* one who called Jews to gather for the morning prayers; later he became a teacher and a scribe. The younger Mendelssohn studied Talmud. At an early age it became evident that he was an extremely gifted student. He also studied the Bible, the *Tanach,* and fell in love with it early. Even biblical grammar did not escape his attention. He studied it and made efforts to compose prose and poetry in Biblical Hebrew. Mendelssohn probably began then to acquaint himself with Maimonides' philosophical writings.

In 1743 Mendelssohn moved to Berlin, following his Talmud teacher, Rabbi David Hirschel Frankel, who had been called there to serve as chief rabbi. There he continued to study Talmud and its commentaries. He also found opportunity to study Jewish philosophy as

Title page of Book of Psalms, translated into German by Moses Mendelssohn.

well as general philosophy. In his spare time he mastered Latin, French, English, and German. Mendelssohn made such great progress in his philosophical studies that an essay written by him, but submitted anonymously, won a prize offered by the Berlin Academy. His only competition came from the prominent and renowned philosopher Immanuel Kant!

Mendelssohn is remembered best for two of his literary contributions, the *Bi'ur* and *Jerusalem: On Religious Power in Judaism*. The *Bi'ur* is a translation of the Bible into German, begun in 1774 and completed after Mendelssohn's death. It was written in Hebrew characters for Yiddish-speaking Jews to learn proper German.

Mendelssohn translated the five books of the Torah, Ecclesiastes, Psalms, and the Song of Songs. The balance of the *Tanach* was completed by colleagues after Mendelssohn's death, especially Solomon Dubno, who was a fine Talmud scholar, an expert in Bible, and a skilled grammarian. The translation was accompanied by a commentary, written in Hebrew, which was totally traditional in content.

The intention of the *Bi'ur,* Mendelssohn tells us in his introduction, was to give the youth of Germany access to the meaning and message of the Bible in its fullest sense, and an appreciation of its beauty. He felt that a lack of knowledge of Biblical Hebrew was standing in the way. He felt, in addition, that the study of Bible had been shortchanged in Jewish education at the expense of Talmud study.

Reaction to the *Bi'ur* was favorable for the most part. There was, however, some opposition from a number of prominent rabbis in Germany and Poland. Foremost among the opponents was the chief rabbi of Prague, Rabbi Ezekiel Landau, author of a classic work in halakhah, the *Noda b'Yehudah*. The fear was that people would cease studying the Bible in its original language. Some, it was thought, would use the Bible merely as a tool for learning the German language. Were the *Bi'ur* to be introduced in schools, children would have to devote additional time to studying German language and literature just to master the German of the *Bi'ur*; this would take away time from study of Bible and Talmud. Finally, older students would begin to take time away from Torah study and devote it to general studies, since they now would have the key, a thorough knowledge of German.

These were real concerns. Many young people did utilize the *Bi'ur* to acquire knowledge of German; this was the key to general culture, a mode of access to literature, science, and philosophy. Many who until then had been immersed in Talmud study alone began to become masters of languages, sciences, and German literature. On the other hand, the *Bi'ur* provided a major impetus to Bible study, and the commentaries provided a new understanding of the text, its structure, its content, and its ideas.

Mendelssohn's second major literary contribution was *Jerusalem*. In his introduction to this work, Mendelssohn wrote that his goal was to promote the cause of civil emancipation of the Jews by showing how the Jewish religion was compatible with Enlightenment ideas. The book had two parts. Part One dealt with Religion and State, while Part Two dealt with Judaism, attempting to reconcile Jewish tradition with philosophical rationalism.

In Part One, Mendelssohn wrote of the need in society for freedom of conscience and religious tolerance. The purpose of the state is the welfare of its citizens. Sometimes attaining this will require placing limits on its citizens for the sake of the general good; the individual cannot have complete freedom.

There is, however, no justification for the state's imposing limits on beliefs and opinions.

Part Two is subdivided into the realm of beliefs and opinions, on the one hand, and the realm of the ritual and ceremonial, on the other. In beliefs and opinions, said Mendelssohn, Judaism is no more and no less than the ideal religion of the Enlightenment, religion based on universal human reason. Judaism believes in the existence of God, in Divine Providence and immortality of the soul; each of these fundamental teachings is demonstrable by reason and thus part of natural religion. Hence there is nothing unique to Judaism in its beliefs and opinions.

Mendelssohn then turned to the realm of the ritual and ceremonial. It is here that Judaism added to the Enlightenment's natural religion. Judaism should not be seen, however, as revealed religion; rather it should be seen as revealed law. Mendelssohn reflected here the view of the Enlightenment, which rejected revealed religion; a true, valid religion must be based solely on reason.

The notion that Judaism is revealed law is problematic. The Bible and the Talmud, the classical sources of Judaism, do not lend it support, for revelation at Mount Sinai is a central principle of Jewish belief. It may be argued as well that if reason can lead to true beliefs, why can it not lead to mitzvot. What need is there for revelation at Sinai? Finally, fundamental doctrines such as the existence of God, the nature of the world, the responsibilities of man, and the purpose of life underlie the mitzvot. The sources do not separate doctrines from mitzvot.

In any case, *Jerusalem* had a significant impact on non-Jews, because the first part, dealing with Religion and State, advocated freedom of conscience and freedom of belief. For Jews, by contrast, it had lesser impact. Jews were simply not convinced that Judaism could be found to be in accord with Enlightenment teachings.

Among the disciples of Mendelssohn was Naphtali Herz Wessely (1725–1805). Wessely was a poet, a linguist, a Bible commentator, a leader in the effort to revive Biblical Hebrew, and an advocate of the Enlightenment among Jews. In his noted work *Divrei Shalom v'Emet* ("Words of Peace and Truth"), he called for two types of study: *Torat ha-Adam* (human knowledge) and *Torat ha-Shem* (God's laws and teachings). Human knowledge involved etiquette, the ways of morality and good character, civility, and clear, graceful expression; it also included history, geography, astronomy, and the natural sciences. Human knowledge is indispensable if one is to be of benefit to the community, to society as a whole, and to humanity. It also lays the foundations for true *Torat ha-Shem*.

Haskalah was not without its opponents. Rabbi David ben Nathan (d. 1792) of Lissa, Poland, was incensed by Wessely's work. In a sermon attacking Wessely, he said:

> Who of the pious students of God's laws, assuming that he is an intelligent, honest, and understanding student of the Torah, is not a tribute to humanity, even if he has not learned etiquette and languages. Can such a man be lacking in "human knowledge"?

Similar sentiments were expressed by Rabbi Ezekiel Landau, chief rabbi of Prague.

ENLIGHTENMENT AND THE JEWS: EASTERN EUROPE

Haskalah, the Jewish Enlightenment, came to Eastern Europe as well, although not until the 19th century. Russian Jews were provincial, largely because of their being banned from many cities in the Pale of Settlement, and very restricted in their intellectual and cultural interests. They were pious and observant of Jewish law, and most were engaged in farming, small business, or crafts, although barely managing to eke out a living. They had little contact with France and Germany, centers of the Enlightenment and of the Haskalah.

The 19th century, though, brought a dramatic change, as trade with European countries grew enormously and therefore contact with Europe expanded. The Jewish communities were affected particularly in Galicia, because of the reform policies of the Holy Roman Emperor, Joseph II, and in Odessa, a Russian seaport on the Black Sea. These communities became the conduits for trade but also for European ideas. They turned into advocates and disseminators of Haskalah in Russia.

The Haskalah supported and encouraged secular Jewish education. Its thinking was that the bigger businessmen of Russia—and there were some—would be well served with an opportunity to master German or Russian and to study literature, geography, and other secular subjects; such businessmen had frequent business contacts with residents of Berlin and Vienna. It was felt that Jews should also be encouraged to enter more useful, more dignified professions. The *maskilim,* the humanists, believed, in addition, that secular education would improve the image of Jews in the eyes of non-Jews.

The language of the Haskalah in Russia was Hebrew. This was a conscious choice, for it meant dissociation from German Jews. Hebrew is the language of the Bible and of Jewish history. The *maskilim* wanted to remain part of the long history of the Jews, unlike German Jews, who chose instead to use German. One important result of this decision was the creation of a productive, vibrant Hebrew literature in Russia.

There were many prominent figures in the Russian Haskalah. Solomon Rapoport (1790–1867), born in Lemberg, Galicia, received a traditional Jewish education and quickly became recognized for his brilliance as a talmudist. Ordained as a rabbi, he served as rabbi in Lwow and Tarnopol. In 1840 he was selected chief rabbi of Prague.

Influenced by his friendship with Nachman Krochmal, who will be discussed below, Rapoport was attracted to the Haskalah and to secular learning. He studied classical, Semitic, and modern languages, as well as science. He became determined to apply his training in secular studies to the history of the

Abraham Mapu

Jewish people. His first work was a biography of Rashi, and this was followed by five other historical pieces. The quality of Rapoport's work was so notable that scholars throughout Europe began to seek his advice on issues of Jewish history.

Nachman Krochmal (1785–1840) was born in Brody, Galicia, and, like Rapoport, was the son of a well-to-do merchant. Enamored by the Haskalah in Germany, his father had provided him with an excellent education, both secular and Jewish. Krochmal became determined to apply himself to the "scientific" study of Jewish history and Jewish philosophy.

Abraham Mapu (1808–1867) was the creator of the modern Hebrew novel. He is best known for his first novel, Ahavat Zion *("The Love of Zion"), published in Vilna in 1853. Mapu was one of the leaders of the Haskalah, Jewish Enlightenment, in Eastern Europe.*

Born in Slobodka, a poor community near Kovno, Lithuania, he was such an excellent Talmud student that he was deemed fit for independent study at age 12. Married for the first time at 17, he continued his studies at the home of his wealthy father-in-law. He taught himself Latin and acquired proficiency in French, German, and Russian. His interest in the Bible, Hebrew grammar, and modern literature prepared him well for later accomplishments.

Mapu's wife died in 1846 and he moved to Kovno, having been appointed to teach in a gov- *ernment school. There he met his second wife in 1851 and enjoyed ten years of happiness at home, along with better financial circumstances. In Kovno he experienced his most productive literary period.*

Ahavat Zion is a melodrama dealing with the wars and loves of King Ahab of ancient Israel. Its characters are one-dimensional and its plot is hardly believable, yet its impact on the young Jews living in the Pale of Settlement was enormous. It opened to thousands of readers the world of action, love, romance, and even violence. Ahavat Zion remains so popular that it has been published 16 times and translated into many languages, including English, French, German, Russian, Arabic, Judeo-Arabic, Judeo-Persian, Ladino, and Yiddish.

His brilliance in conversation and in teaching led him to be referred to as the "Mendelssohn of Galicia." In truth, his writings were deeper and more original in thought than Mendelssohn's.

Krochmal's most noted work is the *Guide for the Perplexed of Our Time*. The task that Krochmal set for himself was to identify the "spirit" of Judaism and the characteristics that constitute this spirit. His conclusion was to subsume the Jewish religion under the wider concept of Jewish nation. The spirit of Judaism, then, was not Hasidism nor was it Talmudism. Instead it was national in character. The relationship of this idea to early Zionist thinking is readily apparent.

Another figure of distinction among the *maskilim* was Isaac Baer Levinsohn (1788–1860). A native of the northern part of the Pale, Volhynia, and member of a wealthy mercantile family, Levinsohn benefited from a thorough secular education. Unlike most Jews, however, he received instruction in the Russian language. As he grew into young adulthood, Levinsohn spent some time in Brody. There he made the acquaintance of the leading scholars of Galicia and soon became a colleague of theirs. While in Brody, Levinsohn wrote a grammar of the Hebrew language in Russian.

In 1820 Levinsohn returned to Volhynia. There he wrote his most important work, *Te'udah b'Yisrael* ("A Testimony in Israel"), published in 1828. The purpose of this work was to convince Jews that Haskalah was in no way in conflict with Jewish teaching. Haskalah thinking supported the study of Hebrew grammar and Hebrew language and encouraged young Jews to study the sciences, pursue handicrafts, and engage in agriculture. Passages in the Talmud and medieval rabbinic authorities prove this notion to be fully in accord with Jewish historical traditions.

Levinsohn published a second work in 1839, called *Beit Yehudah* ("The House of Judah"). In it he outlined his five-point program for reforming Russian Jewry. This program, which became the official program of the Russian Haskalah, made the following recommendations:

- Modern schools be established for children of both sexes and modern theological seminaries be set up in Warsaw, Vilna, Odessa, and Berditchev. In addition to Jewish studies, students should receive instruction in secular subjects.
- A chief rabbi and council be appointed to have charge of the spiritual life of Russian Jewry.
- Competent preachers be obtained to instruct the people.
- At least a third of the people be encouraged to engage in agriculture.
- Jews be discouraged from luxurious living.

Levinsohn was so committed to modernizing the Jews of Russia that Czar Nicholas I awarded him 1,000 rubles in recognition of his attempts to end Jewish "fanaticism"!

Vilna was the birthplace of another outstanding spokesman for Jewish Enlightenment, Judah Leib Gordon (1831–1892). His father selected as his son's teacher Rabbi Lipa, who used the teaching method of the Vilna Gaon, in which the study of Bible and Hebrew grammar preceded Talmud study. By age 14, Gordon was advanced enough to study without a teacher and still become thoroughly familiar with Rabbinic literature. At 17 he began studying European culture and languages—Russian, German, Polish, French, and English. Graduating from the government teachers' seminary in Vilna at 22, he began teaching in various Jewish government schools in Lithuania. Somewhat later, he served as secretary of the Society for the Promotion of Culture among the Jews of Russia, the Mefizei Haskalah.

Gordon's writings focused on the shortcomings of Jewish life in Russia. In one of his works, one of the characters says:

Isaac Ber Levinsohn

The stranger no longer oppresses us, our despots are the progeny of our own bodies. Our hands are no longer manacled, but our souls are in chains.

What is the solution to this problem? Gordon's answer: Be modern. Dress and talk like Russians; read Russian literature; take an interest in Russian life. Should one forsake his Jewish loyalties? Certainly not—but "be a Jew at home and a man in the street"!

Yiddish Literature

The 19th century brought the rise of Yiddish literature to the Pale of Settlement. Yiddish was the vernacular of Jews in the Pale, a language that Jews had adopted in the Middle Ages when they lived in the German-speaking world. It had come, over time, to include a sprinkling of Hebrew and Slavic words. Until the 19th century, however, Yiddish writing included just romances, folk songs, and religious fables. Only in the 19th century did it become an avenue of literary expression.

The first major figure in Yiddish literature—some would label him the "grandfather" of Yiddish literature—was Sholom Abramovich (1835–1917), known best today by his pen name, Mendele Mokher Seforim ("Mendele the bookseller"). Mendele came from Kapuli in Belorussia, but lived at various times in Berdichev and Zhitomir, and had to support himself as the director of an elementary school, a Talmud Torah, in Odessa.

In his early writings, Mendele criticized the filth, ignorance, and vulgarity of life in the Pale. In one work, a novel called *Benyemin Hasheleshi* ("Benjamin the Third"), he wrote about a Jew wandering through the Pale, encountering everywhere superstition, uncleanliness, and backwardness.

As Mendele matured, his writing matured as well. He polished and repolished, even rewriting stories from his earlier works. His style and his use of Yiddish idiom improved significantly, as did his precision in the use of language. While he continued to satirize Jewish life in the Pale, he now tempered that satire with pathos and emotionalism. He tried to bring that life alive in his writings, to make it truly real.

A second major figure in Yiddish literature was Sholom Rabinovitz (1859–1916), known by his more famous pen name, Sholem Aleichem. Sholem

Mendele Mokher Seforim

Aleichem would become the culture hero of the Pale of Settlement. Born in Pereslav in Ukraine, he was educated in the early years in the traditional *heder*. At age 14 he entered the Russian gymnasium there and graduated in 1876.

Because he was fortunate enough to marry the daughter of a wealthy landowner, he was able to travel and write extensively. He lived in Switzerland for a time and accepted invitations to lecture in Europe and the United States. When World War I started, he relocated to Denmark and from there to the United States, where he settled in 1914. When Sholem Aleichem died in 1916, hundreds of thousands attended his funeral and then accompanied him to his grave.

Sholem Aleichem was an extraordinarily productive writer. From his first Yiddish story in 1883 until the autobiography on which he was working at the time of his death, he produced 40 volumes of stories, novels, and plays. In addition, he founded the distinguished Yiddish literary journal, *Die Yiddishe Bibliothek*.

Sholem Aleichem chose the short story as his medium, and the ordinary people of the typical community in the Pale as his subject matter. Characters in his stories included Tevye the dairyman, a poor man but a Jewish "philosopher," Menahem Mendel, an optimist but a fool, and Hopke, a pockmarked maid. Then there were Rabtchik, the Jewish dog, Methuselah, the Jewish horse, and countless Jewish goats, cats, and chickens. Aleichem's characters suf-

Sholem Aleichem and family.

fered from every well-known affliction of the Pale: scurvy, cataracts, tuberculosis, and asthma.

His writings showed sympathy and humor. He tried to be authentic, to reflect the realities of life in the Pale. He wanted Jews to be able to laugh at themselves and at their suffering.

A third significant figure in Yiddish literature was Isaac Leib Peretz (1852–1915). Born in Zamosc, Poland, Peretz came from a respected traditional family. Tutored privately in Hebrew grammar, German, and Russian, his mother's extreme religious outlook prevented him from receiving a systematic secular education. Still he had access to a large library of Polish and German books, which he read insatiably.

Peretz's parents forced him to marry at 18, a marriage that lasted only three years. A second marriage was significantly happier. He trained as a lawyer and was very successful in this profession, until a false accusation of being involved in a revolutionary movement led to his being disbarred. He was ultimately forced to support his family as the bookkeeper of the Warsaw Jewish Community House. In 1899, his sup-

port of socialism led to being arrested and imprisoned for attending an illegal meeting. Peretz would turn out to be a leading figure in the Jewish socialist movement.

Peretz was a gifted poet and author. He wrote in Hebrew, Polish, and Russian, but not Yiddish. Only after he turned 40 did he begin to write in Yiddish. He was convinced that Yiddish was just a temporary means of educating the Jewish masses until they learned the language of their native country. After the 1881 pogroms, however, which constituted a violent response to the assassination of Czar Alexander II for which Jews were blamed, his attitude toward Yiddish became more positive.

As he looked at the Pale of Settlement, Peretz, a supporter of Jewish Enlightenment, disapproved of the religious fanaticism that he saw, as well as the dirt and needless squalor. At the same time, he retained his unshakable loyalty to his people. A profoundly religious person, he was interested in exploring the private faith of the Jews, their folklore, and their wondrous and supernatural tales. In *Bontsche Shweig,* for example, he writes of a poor, helpless, uncomplaining man, who even in the Kingdom of Heaven asks for only the most modest reward, while in *Even Higher,* a kindly Hasidic rebbe proves his worth even to the most uncompromising opponents of Hasidism.

Peretz's love and respect for the piety of simple people led him to reflect on and consider Hasidim and its values. His tale *Zwischen Zwei Berg* ("Between Two Mountains") affirmed the value of faith in a materialistic world.

Other gifted writers lived and flourished after these three. Sholem Asch and I. J. Singer, for example, wrote novels dealing with Jewish life in Eastern Europe. After the Russian Revolution in 1917, though, it was the state-serving vehicle of sovietization, while in the United States, it was simply a medium for Americanization. Poland remained, however, until the Nazi Holocaust, the main center of Yiddish creative writing.

The Musar Movement

The 1850s brought the creation of the Musar movement. This movement, founded by Rabbi Yisrael Salanter (1810–1873), sought to place stress on

Jewish morality and ethics, thereby improving the quality of religious observance and Torah study. Rabbi Yisrael's own father, Rabbi Zev Wolf Lipkin, was his teacher, and Rabbi Yisrael's ability in talmudic study soon became evident. He was a brilliant young man with a remarkable memory and rapidly became well known for his talmudic scholarship.

Rabbi Yisrael was, however, attracted to the method of study known as *pilpul*. With *pilpul*, seemingly unconnected subjects could be linked to lead to certain halakhic conclusions; sometimes these were legitimate conclusions, but sometimes they were not reached with complete intellectual honesty; thus the system was being abused. Rabbi Lipkin decided to send his son to Salant, where he would encounter a more analytic system of study. Rabbi Yisrael went to Salant and stayed there for more than fifteen years. He married there and gained greater fame for his knowledge and for his genius.

It was in Salant that Rabbi Yisrael met his role model, Rabbi Joseph Zundel (1786–1866). Rabbi Zundel was a pious man of great scholarship. He

A street in Lublin, a major economic center for the Jews of Poland from the 16th century Lublin also became a center for the study of Torah, and was nicknamed Jerusalem of Poland.

taught Rabbi Yisrael that the way to personal greatness and service of God was through musar (Jewish ethical teachings). The text through which an understanding of Jewish ethics could be gained was Rabbi Hayyim Luzzatto's *Mesilat Yesharim.*

In 1840 Rabbi Yisrael moved to Vilna. There he headed a yeshiva and taught Talmud in synagogues and study halls outside his own yeshiva. It became more and more evident that he was one of the leading talmudic scholars of his time. His reputation in Vilna and the respect in which he was held in Vilna allowed him to turn to his life's task, the Musar movement.

In 1845 Rabbi Yisrael set forth his program for the ethical rejuvenation of traditional Jewry, as he sought to elevate Jewish religious life by restoring ethical principles to the center of a religious Jew's focus. In this way, the religious observance and Torah study of the Jew would be enhanced. In his view, all dimensions of Jewish life—education, commerce, and family—were to be held to the standards of musar, traditional Jewish ethics.

How was this to be accomplished? Rabbi Yisrael had a four-part plan:

- the printing and dissemination of musar books
- lectures and speeches on musar topics to be delivered regularly in synagogues and houses of study
- the establishment of special "musar houses" in all communities and neighborhoods, where musar would be taught and studied
- the development of a special cadre of disciples who would commit themselves to spread and strengthen the Musar movement

Rabbi Yisrael's program began in Vilna and his ideas took root there, among both the scholars and the masses.

Vilna was, however, a major center of Haskalah. Rabbi Yisrael was a dynamic, charismatic personality, and his ideas were achieving popularity throughout Vilna. Leaders of the Haskalah mistakenly perceived him as a potential ally. Therefore in 1848, when the Russians established two new official rabbinic seminaries to produce "modern" rabbis, they asked Rabbi Yisrael to teach Talmud in one. Rabbi Yisrael refused and was forced to leave Vilna for Kovno.

In Kovno, Rabbi Yisrael led a yeshiva, to which came many students and disciples. Among them were Rabbi Yitzchak Blaser, Rabbi Naftali Amsterdam, Rabbi Simcha Zisel Ziev, Rabbi Eliezer Gordon, and Rabbi Jacob Joseph. Hundreds of others came to study with Rabbi Yisrael.

The success of the Musar movement can be measured best by its impact in the great yeshivot of Lithuania. The yeshivot of Telshe, Slobodka, Radin, Mir, Kelm, Novardok, Kletzk, and Slutzk were all products of the Musar movement. In addition, the Musar movement brought about major reform in the inner lives of Jews.

Talmud Study and the Yeshivot

All of Talmud study in the 18th century pales before the contributions of Rabbi Eliyahu, the Gaon of Vilna (1720–1797), son of Shlomo Zalman. He was born in Selets in Grodno province, into a well-known rabbinical and scholarly family. Recognized very early as a prodigy, he delivered a learned discourse in a Vilna synagogue at age 6. As he proceeded through his years of study, Rabbi Eliyahu became the scholar par excellence. He combined Talmud scholarship with historical insight and with a vast reserve of knowledge of the sciences, mathematics, philosophy, and music.

The Gaon never served as the rabbi of a community nor did he become the head of a yeshiva. He, like other scholars in the family, was supported by funds left him by his father-in-law, Moses Rivkes. In addition, out of their respect for him, the Vilna community set aside funds and provided him with a rented apartment.

In the wake of the 1648 massacre in Poland and after the failure of the Shabbetai Zevi messianic movement, the Gaon restored talmudic scholarship to its place of respectability in Jewish life. Perhaps his greatest contribution was his editing and standardizing the test of the Mishnah and the Talmud. This was a prodigious task, requiring immense knowledge and enormous skill. His textual emendations yielded both the answers to many questions and the reconciliation of many scholarly controversies.

There were, of course, many other outstanding Talmudists in the 18th century. One example was Rabbi Ezekiel Landau (1713–1793) of Prague, mentioned above. Rabbi Landau authored the talmudic commentary *Tzelach,* which was, and is, very popular. He also wrote the *Noda b'Yehudah,* a classic of rabbinic literature. In addition, there was also Rabbi Yaakov Emden (1697–1776) of Altona, Germany, who was an authority in halakhah and a kabbalist; he was regarded as one of the outstanding scholars of his generation. His contemporary was Rabbi Yehonasan Eybeschuetz (1695–1764). Rabbi Eybeschuetz, who was himself both a talmudist and a kabbalist, served as the rabbi of the "Three Communities," Altona, Hamburg, and Wandsbeck. Another distinguished scholar was Rabbi Pinchas Horowitz (1730–1805), author of two major Talmud commentaries, *Hafla'ah* and *HaMakneh,* both still studied today.

In 1788 Rabbi Aryeh Leib HaCohen Heller (1754–1813) of Stryj, in Galician Poland, wrote *Ketzot haChoshen,* a commentary on that part of the *Shulhan Arukh* dealing with monetary and legal matters. It became a classic text for study of the *Shulhan Arukh.* Rabbi Yaakov Lorbeerbaum (1760–1838) of Lissa produced a companion volume to the *Ketzot,* which he named *Netivot haMishpat;* the two are presently included in standard volumes of the *Shulhan Arukh.*

In the 1760s, another commentary to the *Shulhan Arukh* was published. Authored by Rabbi Yosef Teomim (1712–1792) and entitled *Pri Megadim,* it was intended to explain the comments of Rabbi

The Vilna Gaon

David HaLevi (known as *Taz*), Rabbi Shabsai Cohen (known as *Shach*), and Rabbi Avraham Abale Gombiner (known as *Magen Avraham*). The *Pri Megadim* is also included in standard editions of the *Shulhan Arukh*.

Another outstanding talmudist of the 18th century was Rabbi Akiva Eiger (1761–1837), who served as the rabbi of Posen, Prussia. His remarkable responsa and his insights into Talmud texts have made his work indispensable to today's advanced Talmud student.

The communities of Sephardim produced distinguished talmudists of their own. Rabbi Yehudah Rosanes (1657–1727) of Constantinople wrote a commentary on Rambam's *Mishneh Torah,* called *Mishneh l'Melech.* Rabbi Yom Tov Algazi (1727–1802) of Turkey and Israel wrote responsa called *Rit Algazi.*

The 19th century marks a major turning point, for it was then that the great yeshivot of Lithuania came into being. At the same time, yeshivot were being founded in the Austro-Hungarian Empire.

In Lithuania the first of the yeshivot was Volozhin, which opened its doors in 1803; its founder was Rabbi Chaim Volozhiner (1749–1821), a student of the Gaon of Vilna. In a letter that he sent to all the Jewish communities of Lithuania, he explained what he saw as the necessity to open a central, national house of learning, one that would attract students to talmudic study and provide a proper physical and spiritual environment of support for a high level of intensive study. Rabbi Chaim based his own educational philosophy on four central principles: the necessity for personal influence and interaction between teacher and student; communal study rather than private, isolated study and research; the building of students' self-confidence and personal self-worth as well as psychological and spiritual elevation; and the infusion of the feeling of joy and accomplishment in talmudic studies.

Volozhin quickly became a leading yeshiva. When Rabbi Chaim died in 1821, he was succeeded by his son, Rabbi Yitzchak, known as Rabbi Itzele, a worthy successor to his father as head of the yeshiva. Rabbi Itzele was also very supportive of secular learning and was fluent in German, Russian, and Polish. He died in 1849.

Among the successors of Rabbi Chaim in leading the yeshiva was Rabbi Naftali Tzvi Yehuda Berlin (1817–1893), the *Netziv,* author of the renowned commentary on the Torah called *Ha'amek Davar.* In 1880 Rabbi Chaim Soloveitchik, who had come to Volozhin in 1873, was appointed associate head of the yeshiva. Rabbi Chaim revolutionized Torah study with a method that demanded intensive analysis, clarity of thought, a new terminology for legal concepts, and rigorous intellectual honesty.

In 1815 in the small village of Mir, Lithuania, a second yeshiva opened. The Mirrer yeshiva was founded by Shmuel Tikitinsky, a leading scholar of the community, although he was not a rabbi. Leadership of the yeshiva presented some difficulty, until Rabbi Eliyahu Boruch Kamai took charge. He led the yeshiva in Talmud study that was analytic and loyal to the Talmud text, while at the same time communicating the sense that he cared deeply about each one of his students. When Rabbi Kamai died in 1917, he was succeeded by his son-in-law, Rabbi Eliezer Yehuda Finkel. Rabbi Finkel joined with Rabbi Avraham Tzvi Kamai to administer the yeshiva; Rabbi Yerucham Levovitz, a noted teacher of Musar, became the spiritual guide, the *mashgiach,* of the yeshiva. These three great personalities attracted legions of students to the Mir yeshiva over the eighteen years before World War II.

Several other yeshivot were established during the 19th century. The Yeshiva Knesses Israel was founded in Slobodka, a suburb of Kovno, in 1863. In 1877 its leadership was placed in the capable hands of Rabbi Nosson Tzvi Finkel, who was later joined by Rabbi Yitzchak Yaakov Rabinowitz, a scholar whose genius was sometimes compared to that of Rabbi Chaim Soloveitchik.

A second yeshiva was established in Slobodka in 1897 and named Knesses Beis Yitzchak in memory of the late Rav of Kovno, Rabbi Yitzchak Elhanan Spektor. In 1904 Rabbi Baruch Ber Leibowitz, one of the prime disciples of Rabbi Chaim Soloveitchik and one of the leading talmudic scholars of his time, became its head.

Other great yeshivot of this century include the yeshiva of Radin, founded by Rabbi Yisrael Meir HaCohen Kagan, the Chofetz Chaim, in 1869; the yeshiva of Telshe, founded by Rabbi Eliezer Gordon in 1875; and the yeshiva of Slutzk, founded by Rabbi Yaakov David Willowski in the 1890s. Each of these yeshivot continues to exist today, either in Israel or in the United States.

In the Austro-Hungarian Empire, the largest yeshiva was located in Pressburg (now known as Bratislava, Slovakia). It was founded in 1803 by Rabbi Moses Sofer (1763–1839), the Chasam Sofer. Rabbi Sofer's goals were to raise the stature of Talmud study in the eyes of the community, to combat the threat posed by Reform Judaism, and to make the Pressburg yeshiva into the major institution of Jewish life in the Austro-Hungarian Empire. Within a few years it became evident that these goals were being achieved, as some 250 students were in the yeshiva; it was creating Jews of great piety and deep faith, with loyalty to Torah and mitzvot being central in the students' lives.

Rabbi Sofer died in 1840 and was succeeded as head of the yeshiva by his son, Rabbi Avraham Shmuel Sofer. Like his father, Rabbi Avraham was a man of great talmudic knowledge and of great character. Even the emperor was impressed enough by him that the yeshiva was recognized as an official theological college. This special status exempted students from military service. Rabbi Avraham also worked toward the construction of new buildings for the yeshiva. He was succeeded by his son, Rabbi Simcha Bunim, and the latter was succeeded by Rabbi Akiva Sofer. The yeshiva remained active in Pressburg until World War II, when it relocated to Jerusalem, where it continues to flourish.

In Germany, meanwhile, 1873 brought the establishment of a rabbinical seminary in Berlin that would later become a major institution in Western Europe for the training of Orthodox rabbis, that is, rabbis who believe that all of Jewish religion, as recorded in both the Written Law and the Oral Law, is divinely inspired. This institution was founded and headed by Rabbi Azriel Hildesheimer (1820–1899), who was a rabbi, a scholar, and an educator. He studied Talmud in his youth with Rabbi Jacob Ettlinger (1798–1871) and Rabbi Isaac Bernays (1792–1849), two outstanding talmudists. Later he studied Semitics, philosophy, history, and science and received his doctorate at the University of Halle.

The Berlin Rabbinical Seminary expected that any candidate for admission would bring with him a high level of secular education. Students were to continue their education at the university level while at the seminary. In addition to Hildesheimer, the faculty included David Tzvi Hoffmann (1843–1921), Germany's leading halakhic authority in the early 20th century, a master of modern biblical study and a challenger to biblical criticism; Jacob Barth (1851–1914), one of the world's leading semiticists but also an instructor in biblical exegesis and Jewish philosophy; Alexander Altmann (1906–1987), who taught Jewish philosophy; Jehiel Weinberg (1884–1966), who taught Talmud and codes; and Jacob Freimann (1866–1937), who lectured in rabbinics and Jewish history. The graduates included Alexander Altmann, who served as rabbi in Berlin and then in Manchester, England, before becoming an instructor at Brandeis University in his later years; and Eliezer Berkovits (1908–1992), who served as rabbi in Berlin, in Leeds, England, in Sydney, Australia, and in Boston, before becoming chairman of

Ha-Melitz: The first Hebrew newspaper in Russia.

the department of Jewish philosophy at the Hebrew Theological College in Chicago.

The 19th century also brought the establishment of yeshivot attuned to the ideals of Hasidism; a later chapter will discuss these in greater detail. Thus there were a group of yeshivot aligned with the Hasidim of Lubavitch and several yeshivot associated with the Satmar Hasidim. The Hasidim of Vizhnitz and Gur had their yeshivot as well.

Jewish Philosophy

Rabbi Samson Raphael Hirsch (1808–1888) stands out among the rabbinic figures of 19th-century Germany. His contributions to the German-Jewish world were many, but his writings in Jewish philosophy were particularly significant. In the 1830s Hirsch published two works: *The Nineteen Letters* and *Horeb*.

Nineteen Letters was modeled on the 12th-century *Kuzari* of Judah Halevi. It is an imaginary dialogue, an exchange of letters, between a young university student and a rabbi. In the student's first letter, he observes that the goal of every religion must be to bring happiness and perfection but that Judaism has brought only misery and slavery to its adherents. Moreover, he continues, it is the Torah's laws that are the problem, enforcing Jewish isolation and arousing suspicion and hostility on the part of others. Judaism has made life nothing but prayers and ceremonies! It is entirely impossible, he says, to observe the Torah's laws. They were made for an entirely different time!

The rabbi's responses are contained in the other eighteen letters. Some of the subjects are God and the World, Man, Education, Emancipation, Reform, and Classification of the Commandments. It was Hirsch's intention to formulate the views of Judaism on these issues in a way that would be meaningful to the Jewish youth of the time. Particular challenges were being presented by Jewish emancipation, which came to all of Germany in 1871, and the emerging Reform Movement, which will be discussed in a later chapter.

A companion to the *Nineteen Letters* was *Horeb: A Philosophy of Jewish Laws and Observances,* published in 1838. Hirsch divided this work into six sections: *Toroth*—fundamental principles relating to mental and spiritual preparation for life; *Edoth*—symbolic observances representing truths which form the basis of Israel's life; *Mishpatim*—declarations of justice toward human beings; *Chukim*—laws of righteousness toward those beings that are subordinate to man: toward earth, plants, animals, toward one's own body, mind, spirit, and word; *Mitzvoth*—commandments of love; and *Avodah*—divine Service. He attempted to present the details of the Torah laws in each case and to buttress them with philosophical understanding.

Biblical Exegesis

Mendelssohn's *Bi'ur* has been discussed above. There were other contributions made to biblical study during this period. Hirsch, for example, translated the Torah into German and accompanied his translation with a commentary. This commentary, written between 1867 and 1878, was perhaps the crowning achievement of Hirsch's years in Frankfurt.

David Tzvi Hoffmann wrote commentaries to Genesis, Leviticus, and Deuteronomy, which demonstrate a clear mastery of modern biblical study. Hoffmann emphasized the importance of using rabbinic homiletical and exegetical interpretations in attempting to understand these books. He was also determined to refute the views of the well-known proponent of biblical criticism Julius Wellhausen. It was for this purpose that he wrote a separate book called *Definitive Proofs against Wellhausen,* published in 1916.

Samuel David Luzzatto (frequently referred to as Shadal; 1800–1865) was another distinguished exegete, who lived in Italy. Shadal spent most of his life teaching at the rabbinical college of Padua, where he taught Bible, philology, philosophy, and Jewish history. His commentary is traditional in its orientation. He had the highest regard for the commentary of Rashi, preferring Rashi's comments to those of Ibn Ezra, whose comments were "insincere" in Shadal's opinion. Although he wrote a traditional commentary, he was not at all reluctant to use the modern commentaries of Christian scholars. In addition, his mastery of Hebrew philology, combined with his ability to interpret the poetry and imagery of the biblical text skillfully, made his commentary a unique one.

Rabbi Samson Raphael Hirsch (1808–1888) believed that Judaism should be modernized and the best of world culture adopted, but he rejected the approach of the maskilim in his Nineteen Letters on Judaism.

Samson Raphael Hirsch engaged in biblical exegesis as well. During his time as rabbi in Frankfurt, he spent twelve years translating the Bible into German and writing a commentary on it. In addition, he translated and commented on the Book of Psalms. Hirsch's translation is a literal one. He rejected the aesthetic approach endorsed by his teacher, Isaac Bernays, because he thought that the Bible addresses the heart and intellect rather than the imagination.

A fourth major exegete of the 19th century was *Malbim* (1809–1879); *Malbim* is an acronym for Meir Loeb ben Jehiel Michael. Although born in Volhynia and educated there, he served as rabbi in Prussia and in Romania, thus encountering the Reform Movement. *Malbim* felt that the Reformers would destroy traditional Judaism at its very foundations. His commentary sought to bolster Jews' religious faith through biblical commentary, through improving their familiarity with the Hebrew language, and through interpreting the Bible according to its plain meaning, thereby weakening the influence of the Reformers. In addition, he wanted to demonstrate that the Oral Law was divine in origin and that all its words were necessary and implicit in the biblical text—in short, that the Bible and the Talmud were two complementary parts of one tradition. *Malbim*'s first commentary, on the

book of Esther, was published in 1849. Subsequent parts came out on various occasions, with the commentary reaching completion in 1876.

Kabbalah and Jewish Ethics

Another member of the Luzzatto family, Rabbi Moshe Hayyim (1707–1746), was an outstanding figure in the 18th century. Born in Padua, Italy, he was regarded from childhood as a genius. He had a thorough knowledge of Bible, Talmud, midrash, halakhic literature, and classical languages and literature; he was especially familiar with contemporary Italian culture. He was instructed in poetry, the sciences, and Kabbalah by Isaac Cantarini and Isaiah Bassan.

Rabbi Moshe is best known as the author of a classic work in Jewish ethics, *Mesilat Yesharim.* In this book, which is studied to this day, he provides guidance and direction to those who aspire to ethical and religious perfection. The reader is taken by the hand and led step-by-step to the final goal.

Rabbi Moshe wrote other works in Jewish ethics that are still read today. In his *Derech ha-Shem* and his *Da'at Tevunot* he explores the aim of creation, original sin, divine justice, and related topics while at the same time looking at the everyday problems of ethical and religious life—prayer, the commandments, the *yetzer ha-ra* (evil inclination), and others.

Another major area of interest to Luzzatto was Kabbalah. He wrote a number of works in this area. In some of these—his *Kelah Pithei Hokhmah,* for example—he attempted to formulate the major themes of Lurianic Kabbalah. In others, such as his *Zohar Tinyana,* he dealt with a fundamental theme in Kabbalah, the theme of redemption; the *Zohar Tinyana* was written in Aramaic, the language of the *Zohar,* the classic text of the Kabbalah (see sidebar).

SUMMARY

Jews encountered the Enlightenment, whose central theme was rationalism, in Western Europe and in Eastern Europe. Religion and society should be ruled by reason, said Enlightenment thinkers. Jewish Enlightenment, Haskalah, was the application to Judaism of Enlightenment ideas and themes. In Germany the major figure was Moses Mendelssohn, while in Russia there were Solomon Rapoport, Nachman Krochmal, Isaac Baer Levinsohn, and Judah Leib Gordon.

During the 19th century Yiddish began to be a literary language, not just a spoken language. Mendele Mokher Seforim, Sholom Aleichem, and Isaac Leib Peretz are notable figures in this significant transformation. We have also looked at the Musar movement, led by Rabbi Yisrael Salanter, and considered the emergence of great yeshivot in Poland, Lithuania, and Germany. The Gaon of Vilna was unquestionably the outstanding talmudist of the 18th century. Developments in Jewish philosophy, biblical study, and Jewish ethics have also been considered.

Documents

MOSES MENDELSSOHN VISITS THE SEER OF KOENIGSBERG (1777)

This document presents a student's account of a first visit by Mendelssohn to the renowned philosopher Immanuel Kant. The two quickly developed a warm relationship.

Without paying particular attention to those present, but nonetheless with anxious, quiet steps, a small, physically deformed Jew with a goatee entered the lecture hall and stood standing not far from the entrance. As was to be expected, there began sneering and jeering that eventually turned into clicking, whistling and stamping, but to the general astonishment of everyone the stranger stood with an ice-like silence as if tied to his place. For the sake of showing clearly his interest in waiting for the professor [Immanuel Kant] he took an empty chair and sat. Someone approached him and inquired [why he was there], and he replied succinctly but courteously that he wanted to stay in order to make the acquaintance of Kant. Only Kant's appearance could finally quiet the uproar. His lecture drew the attention of everyone to other matters, and one became so enraptured, so immersed in a sea of new ideas, that one long forgot about the presence of the Jew.

At the conclusion of the lecture, the Jew pushed himself forward with an intensity, which starkly contrasted with his previous composure, through the crowd in order to reach the professor. The students hardly noticed him, when suddenly there again resounded a scornful laughter, which immediately gave way to wonder as Kant, after briefly looking at the

Rabbi Moshe Hayyim Luzzatto was a member of one of the most important, oldest, and most respected families in Italian Jewry. Members of the family were poets, authors, historians, philosophers, and Bible commentators, including Samuel David Luzzatto, also discussed in this chapter.

Rabbi Luzzatto's most significant contribution was his work in Jewish ethics, Mesilat Yesharim. Luzzatto was also a gifted poet. His poems were frequently written in honor or in memory of friends or for weddings. His use of the Hebrew language was masterful and his use of imagery excellent.

More important were his plays in verse. The first of these, Leshon Limmudim, was a treatise on rhetoric. The second, Migdal Oz, was composed in the form of Italian pastoral drama, and the third, La-Yesharim Tehillah, was written as an allegory. These plays were admired by Hebrew writers and intellectuals in Italy and Western Europe. Luzzatto was a kabbalist, but despite their opposition to Kabbalah, the maskilim, proponents of the Haskalah, adopted him as if he were one of their own.

The most important event in Luzzatto's life took place in 1727. Absorbed in the study of Kabbalah, as was his habit, he heard a voice, which he believed to be the voice of a maggid, a divine power inclined to reveal heavenly secrets to human beings. From that time, the maggid spoke to him frequently and Luzzatto made use of these teachings, as he met with the group that came to study with him regularly.

A member of the group, Jekutiel Gordon, wrote letters about the group's activities, and these came to the attention of Rabbi Moses Hagiz, who came to believe that this was a group of followers of Shabbetai Zevi. Shabbetai Zevi was the false Messiah of the previous century, who had raised the hopes of Jews living everywhere for the promised messianic redemption, only to disappoint them by converting to Islam. Hagiz demanded that Luzzatto be stopped, and he persuaded the rabbis of Padua to compel Luzzatto to surrender his writings and to refrain from teaching Kabbalah.

Luzzatto continued to study Kabbalah, however, and in 1734 his books were banned in Italy. Luzzatto left Italy for Germany, but there too, in Frankfurt am Main, he was compelled to take an oath that he would end his study of Kabbalah. Finally he moved to Amsterdam, where he was left alone. In 1743 he moved to Erez Yisrael, settling in Tiberias and dying there in 1746, the victim of a plague.

stranger pensively and exchanging with him a few words, heartily shook his hand and then embraced him. Like a brushfire there went through the crowd, "Moses Mendelssohn. It is the Jewish philosopher from Berlin." Deferentially the students made way as the two sages left the lecture hall hand in hand.

IMMANUEL KANT: LETTER TO MARKUS HERZ (1777)

Kant recounts to Herz his first meeting with Mendelssohn. He apologizes for the inferior quality of his lecture on that occasion.

. . . Dearest Friend,

Today Herr Mendelssohn, your and my honorable friend—as I take pride in calling him—departed from here. Having a man of such gentle disposition, and good spirits and intelligence for a constant and intimate companion in Koenigsberg would be the kind of spiritual nourishment which is completely lacking here, and which, as I grow older, I increasingly miss. I did not (I must admit) know how to enjoy the company of such a rare person, or how to avail myself sufficiently of [his presence in Koenigsberg] in part because I was afraid to interfere with the business that had brought him here. The day before yesterday, he honored me by attending two of my lectures—*à la fortune du pot,* as one might say, since the table was not prepared for such a distinguished guest. The lecture, this time, must have seemed rather tumultuous to him; vacations had interrupted the previous one and most of the time, therefore, was spent on summarizing its content. The summary, naturally, lacked all the clarity and order of the lecture itself. I beg you to help me retain the friendship of this venerable man. . . .

MOSES MENDELSSOHN: JUDAISM AS REVEALED LEGISLATION (1783)

This is a selection from Mendelssohn's *Jerusalem.* He felt that one could be at the same time an observant Jew and an adherent of Enlightenment ideas.

I must, however, also do justice to his [Herr Moerschel's] searching eye. What he saw was, in part, not wrong. It is true that I recognize no eternal truths other than those that are not merely comprehensible to human reason but can also be demonstrated and verified by human powers. Yet Mr. Moerschel is misled by an incorrect conception of Judaism when he supposes that I cannot maintain this without departing from the religion of my fathers. On the contrary, I consider this an essential point of the Jewish religion and believe that this doctrine constitutes a characteristic difference between it and the Christian one. To say it briefly: I believe that Judaism knows of no revealed religion in the sense in which Christians understand this term. The Israelites possess a divine legislation—laws, commandments, ordinances, rules of life, instruction in the will of God as to how they should conduct themselves in order to attain temporal and eternal felicity. Propositions and prescriptions of this kind were revealed to them by Moses in a miraculous and supernatural manner, but no doctrinal opinions, no saving truths, no universal propositions of reason. These the Eternal reveals to us and to all other men, at all times, through nature and thing, but never through word and script. . . .

Now I can summarize briefly my conceptions of the Judaism of former times and bring them into a single focus. Judaism consisted, or, according to the intention of the founder, was to consist of:

Religious doctrines and propositions or *eternal truths* about God and His government and providence, without which man cannot be enlightened and happy. These are not forced upon the faith of the nation under the threat of eternal or temporal punishments, but, in accordance with the nature and evidence of eternal truths, recommended to rational acknowledgement. They did not have to be given by direct revelation, or made known through word and script, which are intelligible only *here* and *now.* The Supreme Being has revealed them to all rational creatures through *things* and *concepts* and inscribed them in the soul with a script that is legible and comprehensible at all times and in all places. For this reason our much-quoted poet sings:

1.

The heavens declare the majesty of God,
And the firmament announceth the work of His hands,
From one day this doctrine floweth into another;
And night giveth instruction to night.
No teaching, no words,
Without their voice being heard.
Their choral resoundeth over all the earth,
Their message goeth forth to the ends of the world,
To the place where He hath set a tent for the sun, etc.

Their effect is as universal as the beneficent influence of the sun, which, as it hurries through its orbit, sheds light and warmth over the whole globe. As the same poet explains still more clearly in another place:

From sunrise to sundown
The name of the Lord is praised.

Or, as the prophet says in the name of the Lord: *From the rising of the sun to its setting, My name is great among the heathens, and in every place frankincense is presented unto My name, even pure oblations, for My name is great among the heathens.*

2. Historical truths, or records of the vicissitudes of former ages, especially of the circumstances in the lives of the nation's forefathers; of their having come to know the true God, of their way of life before God; even of their transgressions and the paternal chastisement that followed them; of the covenant which God concluded with them; and of the promise, which He so often repeated to them, to make of their descendants, in the days to come, a nation consecrated to Him. These historical records contained the foundation for the national cohesion; and as historical truths they can, according to their nature, not be accepted in any other manner than on faith. Authority alone gives them the required evidence; these records were also confirmed to the nation by miracles and supported by an authority which was sufficient to place the faith beyond all doubt and hesitance.

3. Laws, precepts, commandments and rules of life, which were to be peculiar to this nation and through the observance of which it should arrive at national felicity, as well as personal felicity for each of its individual members. The lawgiver was God, that is to say, God not in His relation as Creator and Preserver of the universe, but God as Patron and Friend by covenant of their ancestors, as Liberator, Founder and Leader, as King and Head of this people; and He gave his laws the most solemn sanction, publicly and in a never heard-of, miraculous manner, by which they were imposed upon the nation and all their descendants as an unalterable duty and obligation.

These laws were revealed, that is, they were made known by God, through words and script. Yet only the most essential part of them was entrusted to letters; and without the unwritten explanations, delimitations, and more precise determinations, transmitted orally and propagated through oral, living instruction, even these written laws are mostly incomprehensible, or inevitably became so in the course of time. For no words or written signs preserve their meaning unchanged throughout a generation.

The written as well as the unwritten laws have directly, as *prescriptions for action* and rules of life, public and private felicity as their ultimate aim. But they are also, in large part, to be regarded as a kind of script, and they have significance and meaning as ceremonial laws. They guide the inquiring intelligence to divine truths, partly to eternal and partly to historical truths upon which the religion of this people was founded. The ceremonial law was the bond which was to connect action with contemplation, life with theory. The ceremonial law was to induce personal converse and social contact between school and teacher, inquirer and instructor, and to stimulate and encourage

rivalry and emulation; and it actually fulfilled this mission in the early period, before the constitution degenerated and human folly again interfaced to change, through misunderstanding and misdirection, the good into evil and the useful into the harmful. . . .

NAFTALI HERZ WESSELY: WORDS OF PEACE AND TRUTH (1782)

This selection comes from Wessely's Words of *Peace and Truth.* This was a controversial work that aroused the ire of leading rabbinic figures in Germany and Poland who opposed the Jewish Enlightenment.

Now, in order to educate the youths of Israel in the proper manner, two types of studies should be established. The first type is the study of "human knowledge" [*Torat haadam*], that is, those matters which earn for their possessors the title "man" [*Adam*], since he who lacks this knowledge hardly deserves this title, as shall be explained. The second type is the study of the Torah of God, that is, God's laws and teachings, matters that are above human reason and that were made known to Moses through prophetic revelation. Had the Torah not come to us in this divine fashion, it would have remained hidden from even the most sagacious of men, for its contents cannot be deduced from the fixed laws of nature. Moreover, only the seed of Israel is obligated by the laws of the Torah. . . .

In general, "human knowledge" is comprised of etiquette, the ways of morality and good character, civility and clear, graceful expression; these matters and their like are implanted in man's reason. He who possesses "human knowledge" will gain much from the poetic expression of the divine Torah and from the ways of God that are written therein. . . . Similarly, history, geography, astronomy, and the like—which are inscribed in the mind of man as innate "primary ideas" whose foundation is reason—produce truths in every matter of wisdom. Included in this category of knowledge are the natural sciences, which provide genuine knowledge about all things: animals, plants, minerals, the elements, meteorology (clouds and their effects), botany, anatomy, medicine, chemistry, etc. It is in man's power to study all of these phenomena by means of his senses and reason; he does not need anything divine to comprehend them. . . .

Now, "human knowledge" is anterior to the exalted divine laws. Hence it is proper that in his youth man should crown himself with the fear of God, with the rules of etiquette and with knowledge to which the appellation "human" is appropriate. With this knowledge he will prepare his heart to learn the laws and teachings of God. . . . Therefore he who is ignorant of the laws of God but is versed in "human knowledge," even though the sages of Israel will not benefit from his light in the study of Torah, he will benefit the remainder of humanity. But he who is ignorant of "human knowledge," though he knows the laws of God, gladdens neither the wise of his own people nor the remainder of humanity. . . .

There is one people in the world alone who are not sufficiently concerned with "human knowledge" and who have neglected the public instruction of their youth in the laws of etiquette, the sciences and the arts. We, the children of Israel, who are dispersed throughout all of Europe and who live in most of its states, have turned our backs on these studies. Those among us who dwell in Germany and Poland have been especially negligent in this regard. Many among them are men of intelligence and great understanding, and many are also men of faith and piety, but from childhood their exclusive preoccupation has been God's laws and teachings. They have not heard of or studied "human knowledge." They are ignorant even of the grammar of the holy tongue, and they do not discern the beauty of its diction, the rules of its syntax and the purity of it style—which are wells from which spring wisdom and moral instruction. It goes without saying that they lack proper knowledge of the language of the peoples among whom they live. Many of them do not even know how to read or write the native language. Knowledge of the structure of the earth and the events of history are hidden from them, as are matters of civility, the sciences and the arts. They do not know or understand, for from the start nothing of all this was told to them, neither by their fathers nor by their teachers, who themselves were ignorant of these subjects. Even the fundamental principles of their faith were not taught systematically, so that all the youth might become conversant with them in an orderly fashion. Similarly, our youth were not taught ethics and psychology.

Let it be understood, however, that we ourselves are not responsible for this state of affairs. We should not pour out our anger upon ourselves or direct our complaints against ourselves. Rather, it is the nations who have hosted us for more than a thousand years who are to blame for our misfortune, for they have terribly wronged us by the command of their kings and ministers. Inspired by many evil motives they have risen against us to destroy us and to humble us to the dust, for which purpose they subjected us to irrational decrees. They thereby acted contrary to "human knowledge," for they thrust our bodies to the dust and depressed the spirit within us. . . .

And so now, perhaps the time has come to remove hatred from the hearts of men, an unfounded hatred based on a quarrel which is not theirs and whose source lies in differences of faith and worship. O generation! You have seen that God is good. He has raised up a great man, a savior to mankind, the exalted emperor, His Majesty Joseph II [see chapter 2 for discussion of Joseph II, the Habsburg emperor]. Aside from the tidings of his wisdom, his counsel, and his military might, imperial statements that have recently issued from him have brought us tidings of even more heroic deeds. These statements—words of peace and truth to all his subjects—have been tried in the crucible of reason and are founded on the love of mankind. Moreover, in his many good works he has not forgotten a poor people, long abused, the Jews. He gave us many good and consoling commands, as a father does to his son, a teacher to his pupils and a [benign] ruler to his people. He has unshackled the disabling bonds by permitting the Jews to engage in all forms of cultivation of the land, to work in all crafts, and to trade in all merchandise. In his interest he has also observed that few among us speak the German language . . . accurately and as a result cannot read books, neither history books nor books on etiquette, science, and arts. Neither can we speak in a clear fashion with the inhabitants of the land and their ministers. Taking this into consideration he has commanded us upon a righteous path. He has instructed the Jews to establish schools in which to teach their children to read and write the German language. He has also instructed them to write edifying books according to the Torah, to teach the children understanding and the rules of behavior in society. Arithmetic, geometry, astronomy, history and geography, however, are to be studied from the extant books used by the children of the kingdom, for these sciences do not impinge upon faith, and the ideas of all men concerning these subjects are identical. Knowledge of these subjects can only strengthen the House of Israel and mend the breaches made by the preceding rulers. . . . And thus, the children of Israel will also be men who accomplish worthy things, assisting the king's country in their actions, labor, and wisdom.

JUDAH LEIB GORDON: "AWAKE, MY PEOPLE!" (1866)

The poem Hakiza Ami was composed by J. L. Gordon, the leading Russian Hebrew poet of the Haskalah. He called upon Jews to become modern, dress and talk like Russians, and read Russian literature.

Awake, my people! How long will you slumber?
The night has passed, the sun shines bright.
Awake, lift up your eyes, look around you—
Acknowledge, I pray you, your time and your place. . . .

The land in which now we live and are born—
Is it not thought to be part of Europe?
Europe—the smallest of Earth's regions,
Yet the greatest of all in wisdom and reason.

This land of Eden [Russia] now opens its gates to you,
Her sons now call you "brother"!
How long will you dwell among them as a guest,
And why do you now affront them?

Already they have removed the weight of suffering from
    your shoulder,

They have lifted off the yoke from your neck,
They have erased from their hearts gratuitous hatred and
  folly,
They give you their hand, they greet you with peace.

Raise your head high, straighten your back,
And gaze with loving eyes upon them,
Open your heart to wisdom and knowledge,
Become an enlightened people, and speak their language.

Every man of understanding should try to gain knowledge;
Let others learn all manner of arts and crafts;
Those who are brave should serve in the army;
The farmers should buy plows and fields.

To the treasury of the state bring your strength,
Take your share of its possessions, its bounty.
Be a man abroad and a Jew in your tent,
A brother to your countrymen and a servant to your king. . . .

MENDELE MOKHER SEFORIM: MY SOUL DESIRED YIDDISH (1862)

In this selection, Mendele presents his considerations and some of his concerns as he contemplated writing in Yiddish instead of Hebrew. As things turned out, his Yiddish stories laid the foundations for modern Yiddish literature

. . . Here I am, observing the ways of our people and attempting to write for them stories from Jewish Sources in the holy tongue, yet most of them do not even know this tongue. Their language is Yiddish. And what life is there for a writer, what profit in his labor, if he is of no use to his people? The question—"for whom do I toil"—has not ceased to trouble me. . . . The Yiddish language in my day was an empty vessel, containing nothing but slang and trite, meaningless phrases. . . . The women and the poor would read Yiddish without understanding it, while the rest of the people, even if they didn't know how to read in another language, were ashamed to be caught reading Yiddish, lest this private folly of theirs become public knowledge. And if one of them gave in to temptation and read a Yiddish book and, enjoying it, laughed over it, he immediately justified his reaction by dismissing the book as women's literature, capable of provoking laughter but not thought. Those of our writers who know Hebrew, our holy tongue, and continue to write in it, do not care whether or not the people understand it. These writers look down on Yiddish and greatly scorn it. And if one out of many occasionally remembered the cursed jargon and wrote a few lines in it, he kept his works hidden, so as to escape criticism and ridicule. How perplexed I was then,

when I thought of writing in Yiddish, for I feared it would entail the ruin of my reputation—so my friends in the Hebrew literature movement had warned me. But my love for the useful defeated false pride, and I decided to take pity on the much-scorned language and do what I could for my people. One of my friends [Shiye-Mordkhe Lifshits] joined me in persuading the publisher of *Hameliz* to publish a periodical in Yiddish, the language of our people. The publisher agreed and *Kol Mevaser* began to appear with great success. I was soon inspired to write my first story in Yiddish: *"Dos kleine Menshele, oder a lebens beshraybung fun Avrom Yitzhok Takif," gedrukt b'hishtadlus Mendele Moykher Sforim.* . . . And other stories and books followed.

My first story made a big impact on the Jewish masses and was soon published in a third edition . . . and then in a fourth edition . . . That story laid the cornerstone of modern Yiddish literature. Fom then on, my soul desired only Yiddish, and I dedicated myself entirely to it. . . .

HIRSCH LEIB GORDON: THE MUSAR YESHIVA—A MEMOIR (CA. 1910)

One of the great yeshivot affected by the Musar Movement was in Slobodka. This document gives one a sense of life in that place.

A visitor entering the large hall of the Musar yeshiva in Slobodka—and there was only one hall—could see the supervisor [*mashgiah*] moving like a shadow among the diligent students. But everyone knew that he and his authority were not of essence there. The authority of Musar, and the edifier [*mashpia*] who wielded the authority, played the essential role. Rabbi Netta Hirsch Finkel, who at the time of my studies in Slobodka was not yet called "the Grandfather," would go about the yeshiva in seeming humility. But all knew that the power and rule were vested in him. The aristocratic figure of the head of the yeshiva, Rabbi Moshe Mordecai Epstein, would appear occasionally, but it was obvious that he felt a little strange in the spacious hall, where not the Torah held sway but rather "the Method," the special Musar method beside which the Torah was unimportant.

Rabbi Netta Hirsch would look around constantly as if searching for something in the behavior of the students that was not to his liking or taste. Sometimes he would stop beside the desk of a yeshiva youth and examine his comportment—his chanting, his movements, his reactions to what was going on around him. The youth upon whom Rabbi Netta Hirsch fixed his stare would shake with fear before the penetrating gaze, uncertain as to whether he had found favor and approval in the eyes of his examiner. Rabbi Netta Hirsch stood in the center of all that went on in the yeshiva, and yet stood above it all.

The power and authority of Rabbi Netta Hirsch were at their peak on Sabbath night between *minhah* and *maariv*. Then the hall would be enveloped in shadows and the crowd would surround the chair in the center of the hall on which sat the great *mashpia* like a king in his court. No member of the yeshiva would dare be absent from this session. From the day of the great scandal involving the books of the Musar which had been thrown into the public toilet, the relations between the Musar movement and its opponents in Lithuania became increasingly strained; both friend and foe saw in Rabbi Netta Hirsch the chief protagonist in the battle, and my child's heart went out in devotion to this majestic figure.

I began to visit the great yeshiva in the evenings, especially at dusk on the Sabbath, when the Grandfather would speak in a low and pleasant voice that dropped sometimes to a secret whisper. Hundreds of youths swarmed around him like bees. Most seemed moved by the preaching and the somber voice, although here and there I could detect an expression of doubt, or a secret smile. On one occasion the Grandfather happened to look at me, and wondering at my relative youth he asked me:

"Who are you, little man?"

"I am the son of Rabbi Komay, and I am studying in the yeshiva of Rabbi Hirschel."

"And what are you doing here?"

"I come here in the evenings, that I may gain in piety." (I realized that in my eagerness I was exaggerating a bit.)

The Grandfather smiled and stroked my face affectionately. And whenever he exhorted us in the evenings he would embrace me and hold me in his arms.

The Grandfather would speak in broken phrases, in isolated words and fragments of sentences. I can recall one sermon which he gave in the month of Elul:

. . . repentance . . . repentance and good deeds . . . difficult to accomplish them . . . but one must try anyway . . . nothing can stand in the way of true penitents . . . the Mouth of Hell [*Gehenna*]. . . . He that talks inordinately with women shall inherit Gehenna . . . anyone who swears obscenely . . . anyone who gets angry . . . a flatterer . . . vulgarities . . . one who leaves the path of Torah will fall into Gehenna . . . but one who recites the Shema and observes it faithfully, for him Gehenna is cooled . . . as long as a man lives he has hope . . . today there is still time, but who can know about tomorrow . . . anyone who cries in the night, his voice is heard. . . .

At this point the crowd would burst out weeping. And anyone passing in front of the Holy Ark [in which the Torah scrolls are kept] during the evening prayer after the sermon was like a cantor chanting *Kol Nidrei*.

RABBI DAVID MOSES JOSEPH OF KRYNKI: THE VOLOZHIN YESHIVA (1909)

One of the great yeshivot in Lithuania was in Volozhin. This letter was part of a fund-raising campaign, due to the fact that the building had burned down the previous year.

An important announcement concerning the Torah: I have seen with my own eyes that the honor of the holy yeshiva of Volozhin—which was founded by our holy master, Rabbi Haim Volozhin through prayer and entreaty, and even the shedding of tears—has been brought down and made low. There are those who say: What in fact is the importance of the yeshiva, are there not other yeshivot in the world? There are others who say that with respect to curricula, the yeshivot in other cities are superior to the yeshiva of Volozhin. Everyone seems to feel that there have always been yeshivot in the big cities. I know that this is not the case and that the truth is that the yeshiva of Volozhin is the mother and source of all the yeshivot and Talmud Torahs in the world. The latter are as pipes which come from the source and thus in the blessing of the source they too will be blessed. . . .

Therefore I see it as my duty to proclaim the truth to the world, words of truth for him who wants to know, as it is written (Deut. 32:7), "Ask your father and he will tell you, your elders and they will say to you." Today I am, with God's help, seventy-eight years old, and when our holy rabbi founded the yeshiva I was about fifteen or sixteen years old. I was familiar with the ways of the world, and I noted that before our holy rabbi founded the "house of God" the world was empty, literally without form; it was void, for even the term "yeshiva" was unknown, let alone what activities took place in one. The term "public study of Torah" was also unknown to a world void of Torah. Holy books, such as volumes of the Talmud, were rare and to be found only in the homes of exceptional individuals, such as famous patrons. Even in the communal study halls [*bateh midrash*] of large towns, a complete set of the Talmud was not to be found. This was the case because there was no need for these books. When our holy rabbi founded the yeshiva, an appeal was made for volumes of the Talmud, and it was necessary to send to the large towns for books. When the rabbi of Slavuta saw that there was a need for volumes of the Talmud, he printed a few hundred sets, in large and small formats, and as a result of their popularity, they spread all over the world. In the first year of the yeshiva I noted that many merchants made it their business to travel by way of Volozhin in order to see what this thing called a yeshiva was and what was done there. At the sight of dozens of Torah scholars sitting and studying day and night with a wonderful diligence, they were astonished and amazed, for they had never seen or even imagined anything like it. Many merchants remained for days and did not want to leave.

After a number of years, one of the students of our holy rabbi went to Minsk—this was Rabbi Mordechai Minsker. He studied with awesome discipline, and the sons of the great patroness Bluma of that city became attached to him. He inspired them, and together with their mother they founded a small prayer room and study hall [*kloiz*]. She supported all the students of the *kloiz* at her own expense and covered the other expenses of the *kloiz* out of her own pocket as well. This was the very first *kloiz* in the world, for there was no other. A few years later another patron, I think it was Rabbi Haim Michvantzer, founded another, and after him Rabbi Samuel Rofe and others. Meanwhile in Vilna there was still no yeshiva. I once asked our holy rabbi for permission to give a daily lecture [*shiur*] to students, as was done in the yeshiva [of Volozhin]. He replied with these words: "I get more satisfaction and gratification from the yeshivot of Minsk than from my own yeshiva. With regard to the latter I am troubled by all the details necessary for the running of the yeshiva, whereas at the yeshivot of Minsk I have no worries at all and all [the pleasure] is mine!" After a few years Mordechai Minsker settled in Vilna and founded a yeshiva in the old *kloiz*. Then, with the help of Rabbi Judah Kliatsky he set up a yeshiva in the new *kloiz,* and after that yeshivot and Talmud Torahs multiplied in a number of towns. Were it not for the fact that our holy rabbi founded his yeshiva, the Torah would have—God forbid—been forgotten in Israel. This I often say about our teacher and holy rabbi, "How great are the deeds of your life." My eyes saw all that is written here and it is not from hearsay. . . .

RABBI S. R. HIRSCH: THE NINETEEN LETTERS: LETTER 13

One of Hirsch's *Nineteen Letters* deals with defining *Edoth*. Hirsch attempted to explore and define the philosophical basis of halakhah.

Edoth. However, the mere acknowledgment of the essential principles of life does not suffice for the building up of a life of such endeavors in righteousness and love. There is need; in addition thereto, of symbolic words and acts which shall stamp them indelibly upon your soul, and thus preserve them for you and for others. If a truth is to produce results, it must be impressed upon the heart and mind repeatedly and emphatically. This is the essential concept at the basis of the *Edoth*. The symbols are chiefly those of acts, of practices which serve as signs of an idea. Thus the doctrine that God is the creator and possessor of all, that all

is His, that man is the administrator according to God's will and Israel the teacher of the law of mankind's mission, is symbolized in the commandments concerning *bechor*—the sanctity of the first-born, *chalah*—the offering of the prescribed portion of dough, *orlah*—the prohibition of the use of immature fruit, *chadash*—the prohibition of the use of new grain prior to the offering of the prescribed measure of barley, *Shabbath*—the Sabbath. With specific reference to Israel's holy soil, there are the laws of *shemitah* and *yovel*—the Sabbatical and Jubilee years, *terumah*—the heave-offering, and *bikkurim*—the offering of the first ripe fruits.

The doctrine that God is the Redeemer and Savior of Israel is symbolized by Pesach—the Passover festival, *Shevuoth*—the Feast of Weeks, *Succoth*—the Feast of Tabernacles, and *Shemini Atzereth*—the Eighth Day of Solemn Assembly. The fact that God is to us in exile what He was to our ancestors in the Holy Land is symbolized by *Channukah*—the Memorial of the Rededication of the Temple, and by Purim—the Memorial of the Deliverance from Haman. Acknowledgment that the body can have meaning only through the spirit and freedom only through law is symbolized in the Sefirah, the counting of the days between Passover and the Feast of Weeks. Consideration of the causes of our exile and the warning to shun the sins which have led thereto are taught by the *Taanioth*—fast days. To keep even the body and its organs pure and holy, and to shun everything that leads to bestiality is taught by *milah*—circumcision. To dedicate all the powers of our mind, heart, and body to the service of the All-One is the lesson of *Tefillin*—the phylacteries. To be reminders of the presence of the Unseen One and of His revelation in the past, of the limitation of sensuality as a weapon for battle against evil—this constitutes the purpose of the *Tzitzith*—the show-threads. Consecration of the Jewish home as a sanctuary of God and of the Jewish life therein as a perpetual service of God is the aim of the *mezuzah,* the sacred inscription on the doorposts. Recognition of the "Jacob-like" element in Israel's calling, that is, of the lack of external might and independence, as a requirement of a truly spiritual conception of the mission of Israel to teach the revelation of God, is symbolized in the Matzoh—the bread of affliction, and in *gid ha-nasheh*—the prohibition of the sinew of the hip that was lamed.

The *lulav,* the palm branch, and the *succah,* the booth, both symbols of the Succoth festival, are intended to teach us the wise appreciation and use of our property, so that we may neither scorn nor worship what we possess. The same lesson is taught us with respect to the land of Israel by *Maasoroth,* the tithe offering. Finally, Rosh Ha-Shanah and Yom Kippur, the New Year and the Day of Atonement, Shofar and Rosh Chodesh, the stirring blast of the ram's horn and the ritual of the New Moon, are to remind us to test our own lives by the basic axiom that God is the King, Judge, and Father of us all. We are to realize that, by not fulfilling our life's calling in its entirety, we forfeit our claim to life and existence, and that we must endeavor to raise ourselves up once more to a purer, better future. These symbolic acts and seasons all give expression to ideas, without splitting them up into words as speech must. They come to the mind each a unit, like thought itself, even as the resolve which they should serve to generate. They present themselves with the force of a single, undivided and indivisible appeal to the soul. Therefore they are appropriate vehicles to convey the sentiments of one united nation pervaded with one thought, actuated by one resolve, and are intelligible beyond the confines of the Israelite nation. Every single detail of action or omission in the *Edoth* division of the Law is a written note, a word, a sermon addressed to the reverent soul. They are, all of them, reminders, or vivid expressions of sentiment by means of the significant language of action. The greatest and the least among them, even the one that is the target of so much ridicule, the prohibition of the use of an egg laid on a Sabbath or holiday, are all symbols that teach important lessons. The strict attention paid to so-called trifles is no more worthy of ridicule and no less reasonable than the care you exercise to use a clear and intelligible language or a neat and legible handwriting.

Take, for example, the law of the Sabbath, with its prohibition of *M'lachah,* of a specified number of acts classed as "labor." The day upon which the newly created world first lay spread out in its completeness before man that he might possess it and rule over it, this day was to be to him an eternal testimony of the great truth that all things around him were the property of God, the Creator. He was to realize that it was God who had conferred upon him the power and the right to rule the world, in order that he should administer his trust as the property of God and in accordance with His supreme will. In order to keep this idea ever fresh and vivid in his mind, he was to refrain on this day from exercising his human authority over the things on earth. He was not to place his hand upon any object for the purpose of exercising dominion over it; that is, for employing it for any purpose of his own. He must, as it were, return the borrowed world to its Divine Owner in order to realize that it is only lent to him. Therefore the type of labor forbidden on the Sabbath is chiefly *Melecheth Machsheveth,* that is, productive activity, executed consciously, with a purpose and proper means, in order to obtain a certain result. It must be an action, therefore, which is the outcome of human will and conscious force, not *Kilkul*—"an act which produces no desired result," *Mith'asek*—"occupation without purpose," *She-eno Mitchaven*—"unintentional work," *She-eno tz'richa legufah*—"in itself unnecessary," *Ke-le-achar yad*—"indirectly performed," or not in *Sheur*—"in proper measure and proportion."

Do you not see, then, that every moment of the Sabbath that you restrain your hand from labor, you proclaim God as the sole Creator and Master and yourself as His servant? Do you not see, then, that even the slightest, least arduous productive activity on the Sabbath implies the denial of God as Creator and Lord, and the usurpation on your part of the Throne of God? The desecration of the Sabbath is therefore equivalent to the blunt rejection and negation of the mission of Israel. Do you not recognize that the Sabbath is *B'rith,* a "a covenant," and *Zikaron,* a "sacred memorial," and *Oth,* "an instructive sign"? It is *kodesh,* a sacred day, which was not instituted that man may rest after the labors of the week which is past, but that he may consecrate himself to the task of the week which is to come.

And so, in like manner, every ordinance falling into the category of *Edoth* is of equal importance, with the proper distinction drawn between *de-oraitha*—the plain word of the Scripture, and *de-rabbanan*—those ordinances established by rabbinical interpretation.

RABBI MOSES HAYYIM LUZZATTO: MESILAT YESHARIM

This document is part of the first chapter of Mesilat Yesharim, a classic work of Jewish ethics still studied today, 300 years after its writing. Luzzatto tries to guide his reader to ethical and religious perfection.

The foundation of saintliness and the root of perfection in the service of God lies in a man's coming to see clearly and to recognize as a truth the nature of his duty in the world and the end toward which he should direct his vision and his aspiration in all of his labors all the days of his life.

Our sages of blessed memory have taught us that man was created for the sole purpose of rejoicing in God and deriving pleasure from the splendor of His Presence; for this is true joy and the greatest pleasure that can be found. The place where this joy may truly be derived is the world to come, which was expressly created to provide for it; but the path to the object of our desires is this world, as our sages of blessed memory have said (*Avoth* 4:21), "This world is like a corridor to the world to come."

The means which lead a man to this goal are the mitzvoth, in relation to which we were commanded by the Lord, may His Name be blessed. The place of the performance of the mitzvoth is this world alone.

Therefore, a man was placed in this world first—so that by these means, which were provided for him here, he would be able to reach the place which had been prepared for him, the world to come, there to be sated with the goodness which he acquired through them. As our sages of blessed memory have said (*Eruvin* 22a), "Today for their [the mitzvoth's] performance and tomorrow for receiving their reward."

When you look further into the matter, you will see that only union with God constitutes true perfection, as King David said (Psalms 73:28), "But as for me, the nearness of God is my good," and (Psalms 27:4), "I asked one thing from God; that will I seek—to dwell in God's house all the days of my life." For this alone is the true good, and anything besides this which people deem good is nothing but emptiness and deceptive worthlessness. For a man to attain this good, it is certainly fitting that he first labor and persevere in his exertions to acquire it. That is, he should persevere so as to unite himself with the Blessed One by means of actions which result in this end. These actions are the mitzvoth.

The Holy One, blessed be He, has put man in a place where the factors which draw him further from the Blessed One are many. These are the earthy desires which, if he is pulled after them, cause him to be drawn further from and to depart from the true good. It is see, then, that man is veritably placed in the midst of a raging battle. For all the affairs of the world, whether for the good or for the bad, are trials to a man: Poverty, on the one hand, and wealth, on the other, as Solomon said (Proverbs 30:9), "Lest I become satiated and deny, saying, 'Who is God?' or lest I become impoverished and steal." Serenity, on the one hand, and suffering, on the other; so that the battle rages against him to the fore and to the rear. If he is valorous, and victorious on all sides, he will be the "Whole Man," who will succeed in uniting himself with his Creator, and he will leave the corridor to enter into the Palace, to glow in the light of life. To the extent that he has subdued his evil inclination and his desires, and withdrawn from those factors which draw him further from the good, and exerted himself to become united with it, to that extent will he attain it and rejoice in it.

If you look more deeply into the matter, you will see that the world was created for man's use. In truth, man is the center of a great balance. For if he is pulled after the world and is drawn further from his Creator, he is damaged, and he damages the world with him. And if he rules over himself and unites himself with his Creator, and uses the world only to aim him in the service of his Creator, he is uplifted and the world itself is uplifted with him. For all creatures are greatly uplifted when they serve the "Whole Man," who is sanctified with the holiness of the Blessed One. It is as our sages of blessed memory have said in relation to the light that the Holy One, blessed be He, stored away for the righteous (Hagigah 12a): "When the Holy One, blessed be He, saw the light that He had stored away for the righteous, He rejoiced, as it is said (Proverbs 13:9), 'The light of the righteous rejoices.' " And in relation to the "stones of the place" that Jacob took and put around his head they said (Hulin 91b), "R. Yitzchak said, 'This teaches us that they [the stones] gathered themselves into one spot, each one saying, "Let the righteous one lay his head upon me.' " Our sages of blessed memeory drew our attention to this principle in Midrash Koheleth, where they said (Koheleth Rabbah 7:28) " ' See the work of God.' (Ecclesiastes 7:13). When the Holy One, blessed be He, created Adam, He took him and caused

him to pass before all the trees of the Garden of Eden. He said to him, 'See how beautiful and praiseworthy are My works; and all that I have created, I have created for your sake. Take heed that you do not damage and destroy My world.' "

To summarize, a man was created not for his station in this world, but for his station in the world to come. It is only his station in this world is a means toward his station in the world to come, which is the ultimate goal. This accounts for numerous statements of our sages of blessed memory, all in a similar vein, likening this world to the place and time of preparation, and the next world to the place which has been set aside for rest and for the eating of what has already been prepared. This is their intent in saying (Avoth 4:21), "This world is similar to the corridor," as our sages of blessed memory have said (Eruvin 22a), "Today for their performance and tomorrow to receive their reward." "He who exerted himself on Friday will eat on the Sabbath" (Avodah Zarah 3a), "This world is like the shore and the world to come like the sea" (Koheleth Rabbah 1:36), and many other statements along the same lines.

And in truth, no reasoning being can believe that the purpose of man's creation relates to his station in this world. For what is a man's life in this world! Who is truly happy and content in this world? "The days of our life are seventy years, and, if exceedingly vigorous, eighty years, and their persistence is but labor and foolishness" (Psalms 90:10). How many different kinds of suffering, and sicknesses, and pains and burdens! And after all this—death! Not one in a thousand is to be found to whom the world has yielded a superabundance of gratifications and true contentment. And even such a one, though he attain to the age of one hundred years, passes and vanishes from the world.

Furthermore, if man had been created solely for the sake of this world, he would have had no need of being inspired with a soul so precious and exalted as to be greater than the angels themselves; especially so in that it derives no satisfaction whatsoever from all of the pleasures of this world. This is what our sages of blessed memory teach us in the Midrash (Koheleth Rabbah), " 'And also the soul will not be filled' (Eccelesiastes 6:7) What is this analogous to? To the case of a city dweller who married a princess. If he brought her all that the world possesses, it would mean nothing to her, by virtue of her being a king's daughter. So is it with the soul. If it were to be brought all the delights of the world, they would be as nothing to it, in view of its pertaining to the higher elements." And so do our sages of blessed memory say (Avoth 4:29), "Against your will were you created, and against your will were you born." For the soul has no love at all for this world. To the contrary, it despises it. The Creator, blessed be His Name, certainly would never have created something for an end which ran contrary to its nature and which it despised.

Man was created, then, for the sake of his station in the world to come. Therefore, this soul was placed in him. For it befits the soul to serve God; and through it a man may be rewarded in his place and in his time. And rather than the world's being despicable to the soul, it is, to the contrary, to be loved and desired by it. This is self-evident.

After recognizing this we will immediately appreciate the greatness of the obligation that the mitzvoth place upon us and the preciousness of the divine service which lies in our hands. For these are the means which bring us to true perfection, a state which, without them, is unattainable. It is understood, however, that the attainment of a goal results only from a consolidation of all the available means employable toward its attainment, that the nature of a result is determined by the effectiveness and manner of employment of the means utilized toward its achievement, and that the slightest differentiation in the means will very noticeably affect the result to which they give rise upon the fruition of the aforementioned consolidation. This is self-evident.

It is obvious, then, that we must be extremely exacting in relation to the mitzvoth and the service of God, just as the weighers of gold and pearls are exacting because of the preciousness of these commodities. For their fruits result in true perfection and eternal wealth, than which nothing is more precious.

We thus derive that the essence of a man's existence in this world is solely the fulfilling of mitzvoth, the serving of God and the withstanding of trials, and that the world's pleasures should serve only the purpose of aiding and assisting him, by way of providing him with the contentment and peace of mind requisite for the freeing of his heart for the service which devolves upon him. It is indeed fitting that his every inclination be towards the Creator, may His Name be blessed, and that his every action, great or small, be motivated by no purpose other than that of drawing near to the Blessed One and breaking all the barriers (all the earthy elements and their concomitants) that stand between him and his Possessor, until he is pulled toward the Blessed One just like iron to a magnet. Anything that might possibly be a means to acquiring this closeness, he should pursue and clutch, and not let go of; and anything which might be considered a deterrent to it, he should flee as from a fire. As it is stated (Psalms 63:9), "My soul clings to You; Your right hand sustains me." For a man enters the world only for this purpose—to achieve this closeness by rescuing his soul from all the deterrents to it and from all that detracts from it.

After we have recognized the truth of this principle, and it has become clear to us, we must investigate its details according to its stages, from beginning to end, as they were arranged by R. Pinchas ben Yair in the statement which has already been referred to in our introduction. These stages are: Watchfulness, Zeal, Cleanliness, Separation, Purity, Saintliness, Humility, Fear of Sin, and Holiness. And now, with the aid of Heaven, we will explain them one by one.

Reference Works

H. Goldberg, *Israel Salanter: Text, Structure, Idea*

L. Greenberg, *The Jews in Russia*

R. S. Hirsch, *The Nineteen Letters*

M. H. Luzzatto, *Mesilat Yesharim*

P. Mendes-Flohr and J. Reinharz, *The Jew in the Modern World: A Documentary History*

H. M. Sachar, *The Course of Modern Jewish History*

B. Wein, *Triumph of Survival*

Chronology

1740	Moses Hayyim Luzzatto (1707–1746), Italian poet and kabbalist, writes *Mesilat Yesharim* ("The Path of the Upright").
1753	Hayyim Joseph David Azulai (1724–1806) begins his literary diary, *Ma'agal Tov* ("Good Path"), in which he records information on Jewish scholarship, history, and folklore through 1778.
1813	Joseph Perl (1773–1839), leader of Galician Haskalah, establishes first modern Jewish school there. It combines general and Jewish studies.
1818	Leopold Zunz (1794–1886), a founder of Science of Judaism in Germany, publishes his first work, *Studies in Rabbinical Literature*.
	The first Reform temple opens in Hamburg, Germany.
1823	Isaac Baer Levinsohn (1788-1860), founder of Russian Haskalah, publishes *Te'eudah be-Yisrael* ("Testimony in Israel").
1835	Abraham Geiger (1810–1874) begins publishing *The Scientific Journal for Jewish Theology*, the platform of Reform Judaism.
1836	S. R. Hirsch publishes *The Nineteen Letters*. In 1837 he publishes *Horeb: A Philosophy of Jewish Law and Observance*.
1839	Judah Alkalai (1798–1878), Sephardic rabbi in the Balkans and early Zionist thinker, publishes *Darkei Noam* ("Paths of

Pleasantness"), in which he presents a revolutionary concept of redemption.

1842 Reform Jews of Frankfurt found a society to promote a program rejecting talmudic Judaism, traditional observance, and the belief in the Messiah.

R. Israel Salanter, Lithuanian rabbi, founds the first musar society in Vilna. It advocates moral earnestness as a required addition to ritual observance and talmudic learning.

1843 Isaac Leeser, American rabbi, founds the first Jewish periodical in the United States, *The Occident and American Jewish Advocate.*

1844 Leeser publishes English translation of the Pentateuch.

Translation of the entire Bible takes seventeen years to complete.

1851 Zechariah Frankel founds *Monthly for the History and Scientific Study of Judaism.* The *Monatsschrift* will become the world's major Jewish scholarly periodical.

Nachman Krochmal's *Moreh Nevuchei ha-Zman* ("Guide for the Perplexed of the Time") is published eleven years after his death in 1840. This is the first systematic philosophy of Jewish history.

1852 Heinrich Graetz (1817–1891) begins publication of his *History of the Jews.*

1853 Isaac Mayer Wise publishes *Minhag Amerikah* ("The American Rite") in Hebrew and German. He abolishes prayers about sacrifices, for the coming of the Messiah, and for restoration to Palestine.

1868 Seligman Isaac Baer (1825–1897), German liturgical scholar, publishes an edition of the prayer book with commentary. This becomes the standard *siddur* for the Ashkenazic community.

1873 Israel Meir ha-Kohen publishes his first book, *Hafetz Hayyim.* It deals with the laws of slander, gossip, and talebearing. Israel Hildesheimer, who believed that Orthodox teachings are compatible with the scientific study of Jewish sources, founds a rabbinic seminary in Berlin.

1880 Eliezer Ben-Yehuda (1858–1922) writes *A Burning Question,* a series of articles advocating the use of Hebrew as the language of instruction in Palestine's schools.

Yeshiva of Slobodka is established.

1881 Leo Pinsker (1821–1891) writes *Auto-Emancipation,* in which he analyzes the psychological and social roots of anti-Semitism.

1896 Cairo Genizah is discovered.

1907 Israel Meir ha-Kohen, the *Hafez Hayyim,* publishes the *Mishnah Berurah,* a commentary on part of the *Shulhan Arukh.*

1917 The Jewish Publication Society publishes a new translation of the Bible, which becomes the standard version of the Masoretic text.

1934 Mordechai Kaplan publishes *Judaism as a Civilization.*

1938 Ben-Yehuda begins a 17-volume dictionary of the Hebrew language.

1947 The Dead Sea Scrolls are discovered.

1952 Salo Baron (1895–1989) begins publication of a revised version of his *Social and Religious History of the Jews;* by 1985 it will be 18 volumes.

1965 W. Gunther Plaut writes *The Growth of Reform Judaism,* tracing the development of Reform Judaism.

1966 S. D. Goitein publishes *A Mediterranean Society,* a five-volume work based on the Genizah documents.

1971 The *Encyclopaedia Judaica* is published in Israel.

4

RELIGIOUS REFORM

INTRODUCTION

This chapter considers various attempts to "modernize" Judaism. As was seen in the preceding chapters, the central idea of the Enlightenment was rationalism. Religion and society, said its thinkers, should be measured by reason alone. Reason dictated that there be equal rights for all. Reason called for religious tolerance. Quite naturally, Jews began to anticipate an opportunity for emancipation. While for Mendelssohn and his followers this meant the coming of the Haskalah, or Jewish Enlightenment, for others it meant attempts to "modernize" Judaism, to make it more like Christianity. Out of this approach came Reform Judaism, Positive-Historical Judaism, and Neo-Orthodoxy.

REFORM JUDAISM

In its early period, between 1810 and 1830, the reformation of Judaism was led by laymen. The father of Reform Judaism was Israel Jacobson (1768–1828). Jacobson argued that the Jews were not a nation at all; they were a religious group. The Jews of Germany, then, were "Germans of the Mosaic religion," while the Jews of France were "Frenchmen of the Mosaic religion." This conception led to changes in the prayerbook to remove "objectionable passages." Thus the lamentations recited on Tisha b'Av had to be removed, for they spoke of a Jewish nation. Any prayer for the restoration of Jewish kings had to be removed, for the Jews were not a nation. Any prayers for redemption of the Jewish people and the coming of a Messiah were inappropriate, for the Jews were not a nation.

Reform Jews introduced significant changes into Jewish ceremonial as well. They sought to create a more aesthetic and more dignified worship service, in imitation of German Protestantism. Thus men would come bareheaded, men and women would sit together, there would be a mixed choir, the service would be in German not Hebrew (with the exception of the *Shema* and certain other parts), the rabbi's sermon would be in German, and the reading of the Torah would be accompanied by translation into German.

The first Reform temple was in the school chapel of Israel Jacobson in Seesen, from 1810 to 1815. After 1815 it was in Jacobson's Berlin home. The first regular Reform synagogue, not in a private home, was in Hamburg. The Hamburg temple was constructed in 1818.

Reform Jews chose deliberately to call their synagogues "temples," for they did not hope for the building of a third Temple in Jerusalem. Instead they had their own temples in Germany.

In its later period, beginning with the 1840s, rabbis led the movement. The leader was Abraham Geiger (1810–1874); it was he who formulated an ideology for Reform Judaism, following up on the practical changes that had already taken place.

Geiger was among those who participated in *Wissenschaft des Judentums* (Science of Judaism). Leopold Zunz (1794–1886), founder of the *Wissenschaft* in Berlin in 1819, gathered together 50 young scholars.

Heinrich Graetz, professor and leading modern historian.

Abraham Geiger

The program of this group was to employ modern, up-to-date methods in their study of the history and the literature of the Jews. The assumption of Zunz was that once Germans were able to know Judaism and Jews better through such scholarship, the process of Jewish emancipation would advance more quickly. Geiger studied halakhah, sects in Judaism, Jewish poetry in the Middle Ages, and biblical exegesis.

Geiger followed up the practical changes that were made in Jacobson's time with a definition of doctrines. He said, first of all, that Judaism had a mission to carry out among the nations. That mission was to disseminate "ethical monotheism," that is, a belief in One God who demanded of man ethical behavior, as presented and defined in the Torah and in the writings of the prophets. The goal of this mission was to bring justice and peace to the world. This being the case, *galut* (the Diaspora) became a blessing, since it was the means by which the Jewish mission could be carried out; this conception was in clear opposition to any idea of Jewish nationhood.

Geiger also stressed that Judaism was most interested in the internal, inner dimension of religion. It was interested in how man felt about God and how he perceived his relationship with God. It was the duty of Jewish teachings and teachers to point him in the proper direction. The practical observances of Judaism, the ritual and the ceremonial, had far less significance. They were simply the external forms.

Judaism, said Geiger, had progressed beyond particularism, embracing universalism instead. Jews had no special status in God's eyes—there is no room for the idea of a chosen people. God values every man and every religious belief equally. Thus Reform Jews should remove from the prayerbook any reference to this teaching.

Geiger attached great value to Jewish tradition, but he saw Judaism as a constantly evolving organism. Biblical Judaism should not be equated with classical Rabbinic Judaism, nor should classical Rabbinic Judaism be equated with Medieval Judaism. Modern rabbis of his time were perfectly justified in their attempts to continue the evolution of Judaism, but there should be no revolutionary break with the past.

By contrast with Geiger, Samuel Holdheim (1806–1860) saw Reform Judaism as revolutionary.

The Bible, he said, has two components: the eternally valid religious elements, on the one hand, and the temporally bound parts of the constitution of the ancient Hebrew commonwealth, on the other. Once the Temple was destroyed in 70 C.E., only the religious elements, monotheism and morality, remained valid—everything else, that is, ceremonial law, lost all validity. Holdheim advocated moving the Sabbath to Sunday, abandoning *kashrut* (dietary laws), and viewing intermarriage as the ideal marriage. Holdheim, then, was more radical than Geiger. His ideas would have enormous impact outside Germany, in America, as we will see shortly.

Leaders of the movement for reform within Judaism met at conferences on several occasions. They met at Brunswick in 1844, at Frankfurt in 1845, and at Breslau (Wroclaw) in 1846. Issues of theory were avoided, because there was much disagreement on these. Discussion focused instead on matters of practice. Perhaps the sources justify changes in the prayerbook, it was suggested, or accompaniment with an organ. Perhaps there was room to tone down the requirements of Sabbath observance and to modify the requirements of marriage and divorce.

One participant in the conferences was Zechariah Frankel (1801–1875). Born in Prague, Frankel studied Talmud with distinguished scholars and then studied philosophy, natural sciences, and philology at the University of Budapest, receiving a doctorate there in 1831. He served in the rabbinate between 1831 and 1854, when he was appointed director of the newly founded Jewish Theological Seminary in Breslau.

At the Frankfurt conference the subject was the use of Hebrew as the language of prayer. This was a real issue for two reasons. First, many German Jews were not conversant with the Hebrew language. Second, the use of the Hebrew language in prayer emphasized the national dimension of the Jewish people; its use would suggest that Jews were not sufficiently loyal to Germany.

Geiger favored the use of German. Hebrew was a dead language, unfamiliar to most German Jews. In addition, continuing to use the Hebrew language would raise questions about the loyalty of Jews to their German homeland. Although Geiger did not say so in Frankfurt, he did not favor complete elimination of Hebrew but preferred the integration of German into the prayers.

Frankel took a different position on the issue. He felt Hebrew must remain the language of prayer. Religion and emancipation of the Jews must be distinguished from one another; religion should never be sacrificed on the altar of emancipation. The Jews of France were good evidence that use of Hebrew in prayer would not stand in the way of Jewish emancipation.

Frankel argued further that Hebrew in prayer strengthens the bond between God and the Jewish people. Hebrew was the language of Revelation. Its use in prayer is a constant reminder of the covenant between the Jews and God. He argued, finally, that were Jews not to study and master Hebrew, the Bible would become the private property of the rabbis; it would certainly be inadvisable to divide the Jewish people into separate castes. Introducing some German into the prayer service would be fine, but the first language of prayer must remain Hebrew.

Frankel was so troubled by these discussions of change in Judaism that he left the conference before its conclusion. He thought the changes under consideration were too radical, in contravention of Jewish history. Insufficient attention was being paid to the attachment of Jews to traditional practice. Although he had participated, Frankel now separated himself entirely from the reformers.

REFORM JUDAISM IN AMERICA

Moderation won out in Germany, but the story was a different one in America. Moderate reform was advocated by Isaac M. Wise (1819–1900), while radical reform was supported by David Einhorn (1809–1879). Radical reform became dominant, as became evident in 1885 with the Pittsburgh Platform. This document declared acceptance of moral law but rejection of ceremonial law; all laws governing diet, for example, no longer applied. It spoke of Jews being a religious community, not a nation, so there was no need to pray for restoration to a national homeland. It saw the task of Jews as spreading "ethical monotheism" and bringing truth, justice, and peace to all men. The Pittsburgh Platform remained the credo of Reform Judaism for half a century.

Time brought the realization that Reform Judaism had underestimated the role of traditional observance in Jewish survival. It also brought historical change, as the Zionist movement stirred up hopes for a Jewish homeland and a return to the concept of Jewish peoplehood. These developments brought the Columbus Platform in 1935.

The Columbus Platform embraced Zionism. It spoke of the responsibility of all Jews to support fully the efforts of Palestine to become a Jewish state. Palestine, it said, should function not only as a refuge for the oppressed but also as a center of Jewish culture and spiritual life. In addition, said the Columbus Platform, beyond its moral and spiritual demands, Judaism requires observance of the Sabbath and festivals.

As the 20th century progressed, further changes took place. The Reform movement opened its first day schools. Ritual became more prominent in Reform temples. More Hebrew was incorporated into the prayer book. Still there remain issues that separate Reform Judaism from more traditional forms of Judaism.

Among these issues are the officiating of rabbis at mixed marriages, patrilineal descent, and homosexuality. Although the majority of Reform rabbis refuse to perform mixed marriages, a minority do perform such marriages. Presumably the thinking behind the minority position is that rabbinic officiation will encourage the married couple to become part of the

Title page of the first Reform prayerbook to appear in America. Prepared by a commission consisting of Rabbis Isidor Kalisch, Isaac Wise, and Mayer Rothenheim, it was issued in English, German, and Hebrew.

synagogue community. In actuality, participation of a rabbi endorses the practice of intermarriage.

In 1983 the Reform movement accepted patrilineal descent as its definition of who is a Jew. A person who has one Jewish parent of either gender is a Jew, they said, provided both parents have committed themselves to raising their child as a Jew exclusively, educating the child as a Jew, and observing Jewish rites of passage. In defining Jewish lineage thus, Reform Judaism separated itself from Conservative Judaism. Although the expectation was that Conservative Judaism would then follow this position, it never did. It stood firm with the historical definition of Jewish identity through the matrilinear principle. Moreover, this principle separated Reform Judaism from the State of Israel. The Law of Return, which conferred Israeli citizenship automatically on any Jew, required that the individual be a Jew either through conversion or through the matrilinear line. Someone who claimed to be a Jew only through his or her father would not qualify!

Finally, Reform Judaism accepts gay and lesbian synagogues, as well as gay and lesbian rabbis. While it is certainly the case that American Jews support the need to preserve the civil rights of homosexuals, this does not mean they are prepared to accept the practice of homosexuality. To be served by rabbis who are gay and to recognize same-sex marriages as valid would be to do so. Reform Judaism recognizes the difference between preserving civil rights and accepting the practice of homosexuality, but the popular perception remains that it endorses both heterosexual and homosexual behavior.

At its convention in May 1999, the Central Conference of American Rabbis adopted a Statement of Principles for Reform Judaism. This statement affirmed the central tenets of Judaism: God, Torah, and Israel. It declared that the great contribution of Reform Judaism is that it enabled the Jewish people to introduce innovation while preserving tradition, to embrace diversity while asserting commonality, to affirm beliefs without rejecting those who doubt, and to bring faith to sacred texts without sacrificing critical scholarship.

The statement declared that God is one, even though Jews may differ in their understanding of the Divine presence. Every human being is created in the image of God and therefore every human life is sacred. Jews respond to God daily, through public and private prayer, through study and through performance of mitzvot, sacred obligations to God and to other human beings.

Torah, said the statement of principles, is the foundation of Jewish life. It is God's ongoing revelation to the Jewish people and the record of the people's ongoing relationship with Him. Jews must study the Hebrew language, the language of Torah and Jewish liturgy, so that they might have access to the sacred texts. Jews must engage in lifelong study, in the home, in the synagogue, and in every place where Jews gather to learn and to teach. Jews must commit themselves to the fulfillment of mitzvot that address them as individuals and as a community. Some mitzvot demand renewed attention to them, as the result of the unique context of the modern world. Social action and social justice remain a central focus of traditional Reform Jewish belief and practice. Jews are partners with God in *tikkun olam,* repairing the world. They are bidden to work to bring nearer the messianic age.

Israel is a central part of Jewish religious life. Reform Judaism is committed to the State of Israel. The statement speaks of the special quality of life in Israel and encourages those who choose to immigrate to Israel. Israel must strive to promote full civil, human, and religious rights for all its residents, and must strive for a lasting peace with its neighbors. Jews living in the Diaspora should learn Hebrew and make periodic visits there, thereby deepening their relationship to the land and to its people.

From 1973 to 1996 the president of the Union of American Hebrew Congregations, which represents 1.5 million Jews in more than 900 synagogues, was Rabbi Alexander Schindler. He died in November 2000 at age 75.

Schindler thought that intermarried couples should be included in synagogue life. He supported patrilineal descent. He advocated equality for women in Judaism, as well as the acceptance of gay and lesbian Jews.

Although Schindler favored radical changes, he also embraced Jewish tradition. He was an ardent Zionist and a strong advocate of social justice. Even outside the framework of Reform Judaism, he was a key Jewish leader, serving from 1976 to 1978 as chairman of the Conference of Presidents of Major Jewish Organizations.

Schindler's successor as president of the UAHC was Rabbi Eric Yoffie. Yoffie has encouraged the Reform movement to give greater attention to Torah study and adult literacy, with special emphasis on religious education and youth. He has been deeply involved in issues of social justice and community concern. He has worked tirelessly on behalf of the Jewish state and the rights of Reform Jews in Israel.

Rabbi David Ellenson heads the rabbinical seminary of Reform Judaism, Hebrew Union College–Jewish Institute of Religion. This institution has centers in Cincinnati, New York, Los Angeles, and Jerusalem. Each of the centers provides geographic proximity to Reform congregations and institutions in disparate regions, fosters expanded field work and mentorship opportunities throughout North America, and places students in pulpits, religious schools, college Hillels, and Jewish communal agencies.

The Central Conference of American Rabbis was founded in 1889. It members are mainly part of the organized rabbinate of Reform Judaism. Most have been ordained at Hebrew Union College, but some were ordained at the Conservative Jewish Theological Seminary or the Reconstructionist Rabbinical College. Approximately 1,800 rabbis are members currently.

Leaders of the CCAR are its president, Rabbi Janet Marder, executive vice president Rabbi Paul Menitoff, and executive secretary Rabbi Elliot Stevens. At its yearly conventions, the CCAR considers a variety of issues that have come up since the previous convention and sometimes votes on statements of principle. The CCAR also publishes the *CCAR Journal: A Reform Jewish Quarterly.*

Among the prominent rabbis and scholars of Reform Judaism is W. Gunther Plaut. Plaut has served as rabbi in a number of communities. Presently he is the rabbi emeritus of Holy Blossom Temple in Toronto, Canada. He has been active in the community of rabbis in the United States and Canada and has authored a number of books. His *The Torah: A Modern Commentary* has been reprinted nine times by the UAHC Press.

Eugene Borowitz is professor of education and Jewish religious thought at Hebrew Union College. He is a distinguished teacher and Jewish philosopher, but more important than this, he is unquestionably the most influential theologian of Reform Judaism. His 1974 work, *The Masks Jews Wear,* won a National Jewish Book Award in the field of Jewish thought. He was the founding editor of *Shma: A Journal of Jewish Responsibility,* a magazine of social ethics. Moreover, it was Rabbi Borowitz who drafted the statement of principle, "Reform Judaism: A Centenary Perspective," in 1976, as Reform Judaism celebrated 100 years of existence in America.

Michael A. Meyer is a professor of Jewish history at Hebrew Union College. He is a prolific author of a number of books, articles, and reviews. Meyer wrote a masterful history of Reform Judaism in 1988. This book, *Response to Modernity: A History of the Reform Movement in Judaism,* is recognized as the definitive work on the history of the movement.

In the area of halakhah, the late Rabbi Solomon Freehof set the standard. Between 1960 and 1980 he published seven volumes of responsa, dealing with life-cycle issues, holiday celebrations, medical ethics, conversion, suicide, and so on. After Freehof's

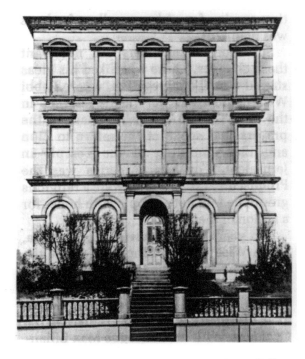

Very early photograph of the Hebrew Union College building in Cincinnati, Ohio.

death, he was succeeded by Rabbi Walter Jacob as chair of the Responsa Committee of the CCAR.

Reform Judaism has established a presence in Israel. In 1963 the Hebrew Union College established a branch in Jerusalem, under the direction of its president, Nelson Glueck, and in the face of intense opposition to Reform Judaism. At the beginning the college was an archaeological center and a place of worship for local Reform adherents, but it has become the phyisical and spiritual focus of Reform Judaism in Israel and throughout the world.

In 1987, under the leadership of its president, Alfred Gottschalk, and its board chairman, Robert Scheuer, the college completed an expansion program. It is now the headquarters of the World Union for Progressive Judaism, conducts an intellectual and cultural program for the people of Jerusalem, and provides facilities for a religious action program. Most significant, it serves as a center for rabbinic training. Candidates for serving as rabbis outside Israel are required to spend the first year of their five-year program in Jerusalem. The college also has a department to prepare Israelis for the Israeli rabbinate.

Reform congregations have been established in various parts of Israel. In the town of Mevasseret Zion, for example, a Reform congregation was founded in 1993. It now has more than 120 member families and is led by Rabbi Maya Leibovic, the first Israeli woman to be ordained in Israel. An older Reform congregation, one of the first in Israel, is Haifa's Or Hadash, founded in 1965. Its spiritual leader is Rabbi Dr. Edgar Nof. At present it has over 250 members and is attracting a growning number of Israeli families. Reform congregations have been established as well in Tel Aviv, Jerusalem, Netanya, and Rishon le-Zion.

As might be expected, the Reform movement has also been active in the field of education. It has conducted Jewish kindergartens in Israel for some 1,500 children and sponsored the writing of curricula and study material on themes relating to the Jewish calendar and life-cycle. It has run in-service training programs for teachers and prepared programs on Jewish values and sources for use in Israeli state schools.

The most important educational institution of Reform Judaism in Israel is the Leo Baeck Education Center in Haifa. Established in 1938 as a small kinder-

garten class for Haifa's German-speaking Jewish imigrants, the Leo Baeck Education Center has grown to become one of Israel's largest institutions of Progressive Judaism. Directed by headmaster Danny Fessler, it includes junior-high and senior-high schools with a total of 1,600 students, an early child care center with 95 pre-schoolers, and a community center offering dozens of social outreach programs.

POSITIVE-HISTORICAL JUDAISM: ZECHARIAH FRANKEL

Zechariah Frankel was one of the scholars who participated in *Wissenschaft des Judentums*. His particular research interest was the history of halakhah, and it was the subject of his book *Darkhei HaMishnah*, which is still regarded highly among scholars.

Beyond his academic research, Frankel contributed a system of ideas that he called Positive-Historical Judaism. "Positive" meant "scientific," while "historical" meant corresponding to the historical experience of the Jews. Jewish tradition and history have established certain beliefs, values, and institutions as fundamental, said Frankel; these are untouchable. How is the identity of these beliefs, values, and institutions to be discovered? Through scientific historical study. Such study will reveal that Judaism has undergone change and will certainly

Zechariah Frankel

The 19th century was a century of noteworthy changes for German Jewry. A profile of 19th-century Berlin, the largest city and the capital of Germany, will be useful in creating the context in which the changes occurred.

An Edict of 1812 gave Prussian citizenship to Berlin Jews. All restrictions on residence and all special taxes were abolished. Formal civic equality would not be attained, however, until July 1860. The Jews of Berlin numbered 3,292 in 1812, 11,840 in 1852, and 108,044 in 1890. The Jews comprised about 2 percent of the total population of Germany in 1840 and 5 percent in 1890. The Jews in Berlin comprised 1.4 percent of German Jewry in 1811–1828 and 7 percent in 1871. Despite a declining birth rate, the Jewish population of Berlin continued to grow through immigration from Eastern Europe, especially from the province of Posen (Poznan).

As Berlin grew in importance as a commercial and industrial center, Jews played an increasingly important role in the city's economic life. Jews were bankers and owners of department stores. They were in the grain and metal trades, in the textile and clothing industries, in building construction, and in the manufacture of railroad engines and cars. Ludwig Loewe headed a large armaments factory in Berlin, while the General Electric Company was founded by the Jewish engineer Emil Rathenau. In 1861 53 percent of Berlin Jews were engaged in commerce, and 17 percent in industry and the manual trades. Some Berlin Jews were prominent in literature, the theater, music, and art.

Berlin was the home of national German-Jewish organizations, such as the Deutsch-Israelitischer Gemeindebund, the Verband der deutschen Juden, the B'nai B'rith, and the Hilfsverein der deutschen Juden. Jewish newspapers and periodicals were published in Berlin, including the communal organ, whose circulation reached 60,000 copies.

The community was administered by a committee of seven members and three alternates and a council of 21 members and 10 alternates. The first elections to the council took place in February 1854, and its first constitution was approved in August 1860.

Education too underwent many changes in 19th century Berlin. New schools were established. A boys' school was founded by the community, headed by Leopold Zunz, as was a school for girls. There were also several Jewish private schools in the city. Teachers' seminaries, one under the direction of Zunz, were opened.

The struggle between Reform Jews and Orthodox Jews had considerable impact in Berlin. Reform Jews pressed for the introduction of an organ and for modification of the liturgy in Berlin's New Synagogue. Abraham Geiger, the formulator of the principal tenets of Reform Judaism, was appointed rabbi in Berlin in 1870. This brought a reaction from the Orthodox, with Azriel Hildesheimer and his followers leaving the main community and establishing the Adass Yisroel congregation.

One condition of Geiger's appointment had been that an Institute for Jewish Research should be established in Berlin, and so in 1872 the Hochschule fuer die Wissenschaft des Judentums opened. One year later, Hildesheimer opened a rabbinical seminary for Orthodox Judaism, Rabbinerseminar fuer das orthodoxe Judentum. The community had 16 synagogues, seven of them Orthodox, the remainder Reform.

continue to change; the validator of any change, past and present, is the Jewish community as a whole.

In conformity with this line of thinking, Frankel introduced changes in his own synagogue, changes which in his eyes been sanctioned by the Jewish community as a whole. Thus he began to deliver his sermons in German and he permitted a boys' choir. In addition, he eliminated *piyyutim*, liturgical poetry, from the prayer service.

As part of his challenge to Reform Judaism, Frankel affirmed that mitzvot were the essence of Judaism. Judaism, he wrote, is not just a collection of religious beliefs; rather, it is mitzvot, which direct the individual to ethical behavior.

Was there Revelation of the Torah at Sinai? Frankel believed, certainly, that the Bible had been revealed. But what about the Talmud? The laws of the Talmud, he said, were not a product of supernatural revelation. Instead they were the product of the living spirit of the Jewish people, of an interaction among the Jewish people, the Bible, and historical circumstances. The substance of Judaism, then, was the forms, institutions, and practices that resulted from this interaction. All of this was in accord with the Divine Will. God gave the Torah to the Jews, and the Jews may be trusted to understand God's Will correctly and preserve the essence of the Torah.

CONSERVATIVE JUDAISM

Conservative Judaism sees its roots in Frankel's "historical Judaism" and its fundamental ideas. There is much to be said for this view, although Conservative Judaism is better seen as an essentially American religious movement. In 1902 Solomon Schechter, a rabbi and scholar living in England at the time, was invited to lead the Jewish Theological Seminary in New York City. He invited distinguished scholars such as Louis Ginzberg, Alexander Marx, and Israel Friedlander to become members of the faculty. Later years would bring Louis Finkelstein, Abraham Joshua Heschel, and Saul Lieberman, each an outstanding scholar in his own field.

It was Schechter's conviction that history and community were critical sources for determining what was legitimate and authoritative in Judaism. On the one hand, Jews should be loyal to their own history, never suggesting changes in halakhah that would violate that history in some way. On the other hand, no change should be introduced unless it was acceptable to the Jewish community at large, to what he called "catholic Israel." For example, the Conservative movement did not remove all references to sacrificial offerings from the prayerbook, as had been done by Reform Judaism. Instead it made them history: we remember the offering of sacrifices but we do not pray for their reinstitution.

Halakhah remained central to Conservative Judaism, but change in Jewish religious life was in-

Solomon Schechter (1847–1915), scholar of Eastern Europe, Germany, and England, called from Cambridge University to head the Jewish Theological Seminary of America in 1902. He gathered the great faculty and library of the Seminary, and gave form to the Conservative movement.

evitable. Change could be made, however, only where biblical and talmudic sources provided precedent. Thus, for example, the Law Committee of Conservative Judaism permitted Jews to drive to and from the synagogue on Shabbat. This permission was granted as a necessary historical accommodation. There remained, though, certain essentials which innovation could not touch: the observance of *kashrut* (dietary laws), the use of Hebrew in the liturgy, and the Sabbath.

Conservative Judaism, like any movement, has confronted challenges. Schechter spoke of "catholic Israel," by which change could occur only if it represented the expressed will of the Jewish community over the ages. Today, though, a majority of Jews are not observant of Jewish law. Has this practice now become the view of "catholic Israel"—the Jews deciding that observance of Jewish law is unnecessary? Conservative leaders have redefined "catholic Israel" to mean the community of Jews committed to halakhah. But the number of Jews committed to Jewish law is so small that they cannot represent "catholic Israel"!

Conservative Jews of today are divided into two camps: traditionalists and liberals. For the traditionalists, Judaism is governed by halakhah. Change has taken place, especially in permitting women full participation in the prayer service, but egalitarianism does not constitute compromising the authority of Jewish law. Patrilineal descent or homosexuals in the rabbinate would constitute violating the halakhah. The principles of the traditionalists are set forth in a 1988 doctrinal statement, *Emet v-Emunah.*

The liberals, by contrast, advocate a "post-halakhic" direction. This view posits that Jews are not bound to accept literally anything found in the Bible or the Talmud; anything found there is subject to review and reevaluation. This is not to say that halakhah has no meaning for the liberals, although there is much more room for innovation. Thus, the liberals would see no difficulty with recognizing gay synagogues and ordaining gay clergy.

Conservative Judaism must deal with another reality. Conservative rabbis spoke of appealing to Jews committed to Jewish law who were open to the critical study of Bible and Talmud and open to modifying the halakhah in light of historical scholarship.

Conservative laity were unprepared to accept the rigors of the halakhah as the Orthodox do, but unwilling to go in the direction of Reform Judaism. They wanted a movement that was Zionistic and that would encourage them to bring up a Jewish family—matters of critical scholarship and halakhah in the light of history mattered to them precious little!

Conservative Judaism faced another challenge, as the Jewish Theological Seminary decided to admit women to its rabbinical school. The class beginning study in the fall of 1984 would include women.

The right wing of the movement responded by forming a new organization, the Union for Traditional Conservative Judaism. This organization would have its own Board of Halakhic Inquiry, challenging the authority of the Conservative movement's Committee on Jewish Law and Standards. In 1990 the organization's name was changed to Union for Traditional Judaism and opened its own rabbinical school, the Metivta, headed by Rabbi David Weiss Halivni as rosh yeshiva.

Rabbi Halivni was ordained by a yeshiva in Sighet, Hungary, and by Mesivta Chaim Berlin in New York. He serves as well as professor of Talmud and Classical Rabbinics at Columbia University. The executive vice-president of the Union for Traditional Judaism and founder of the Metivta is Rabbi Ronald Price. His own ordination was conferred by Rav Halivni in 1992.

The motto of the Metivta is *emunah zerufa v'yosher da'at,* "Genuine Faith and Intellectual Integrity." Its students study Torah in an atmosphere where one can be fully committed to faith and halakhic adherence but comfortable in expressing and researching philosophical and textual questions. Critical methodologies are utilized in the study of the Bible and the Talmud. The Metivta sees such methodologies as a valid approach in the study of sacred texts.

In an attempt to define itself, the Union for Traditional Judaism affirmed its commitment to the primacy of halakhah, in the formulation of all religious policy decisions. Many policy decisions of recent decades, they argued, have shown that the Conservative movement is selectively loyal to halakhah in general and the halakhic process in particular. For example, Conservative Judaism has endorsed prayerbook revision, egalitarianism, the redefinition

of halakhic boundaries of sexual relationships, and the acceptance of conversions that are not halakhic even by Conservative standards. These changes, moreover, often proceeded without prior review by the Conservative movement's own halakhic authorities.

This being said, the fact remains that the Conservative movement has vibrant institutions. Rabbis are members of the Rabbinical Assembly, with decisions in halakhah made by its Law Committee for Conservative Judaism. Laymen and laywomen are members of the United Synagogue of America. Conservative Judaism has an ever-increasing number of Solomon Schechter Hebrew day schools; recent years have seen high schools established as well. The Ramah camps do a wonderful job at informal Jewish education.

Established in 1886, the Jewish Theological Seminary is the spiritual and academic center of Conservative Judaism. It trains the rabbis of the Conservative movement but at the same time is regarded as a first-rate center for academic Judaic studies. Chancellor of the Seminary since 1986 is Dr. Ismar Schorsch.

Dr. Schorsch, a professor of modern Jewish history in addition to being chancellor, has worked throughout

Early photograph of the Jewish Theological Seminary of America in New York City.

his tenure to communicate his vision of Conservative Judaism as the most authentic contemporary expression of rabbinic Judaism. In 1995, he published *Sacred Cluster: The Core Values of Conservative Judaism,* a highly acclaimed monograph outlining the seven fundamental tenets of Conservative Judaism. His most recent book in Jewish history is entitled *From Text to Context: The Turn to History in Modern Judaism.*

Thanks to a generous gift of $18 million from William Davidson of Detroit, Dr. Schorsch's belief that the survival of the Jewish people depends on education resulted in the creation in 1996 of the William Davidson Graduate School of Education. Dr. Schorsch was also the guiding force behind the Solomon Schechter High School of New York, established on the JTS campus in 1992. Having outgrown its space, the school is now located on Central Park West in Manhattan.

The faculty of the Seminary today includes, among others, Dr. Mayer Rabinowitz, professor of Talmud and chair of the Joint Bet Din of the Conservative movement; Dr. Joel Roth, professor of Jewish thought and halakhah and member of the Committee on Jewish Law and Standards; and Dr. Neil Gilman, professor of Jewish philosophy. Many of the faculty members studied with one of the great figures of American Jewry, Rabbi Abraham Joshua Heschel.

Conservative Judaism is also very active in the State of Israel. The official establishment of the Masorti movement occurred in 1979. Before this there had been congregations throughout the country under the auspices of the United Synagogue of Israel and the Rabbinical Assembly of Israel. These two organizations joined to form the Masorti movement.

There were only four congregations in 1972, but since then the movement has grown to include about 50 affiliated Masorti congregations. Most of the original congregations were formed by core groups of immigrants from English-speaking countries familiar with Conservative ideology. Today over half the Masorti movement's members are native-born and veteran Israelis. The rest are immigrants from a variety of countries including Latin America, North America and the former Soviet Union. Masorti's members and affiliates number over 25,000, and over four times that number participate in Masorti's many programs in Israel.

The ideology of the Masorti movement in Israel is based on three primary principles: Torah and Mitzvot, Tolerance and Pluralism, and Zionism. Halakhah expresses the basic principles of Judaism and the Torah in daily living. The study of Jewish tradition and its sources, however, is subject to a critical approach that utilizes the scientific tools of modern research.

All people are created in God's image, entitled to liberty, freedom of thought, and freedom of religious worship. The principles of democracy are central to the view of the Masorti movement.

Finally, the Masorti movement believes in the paramount importance of the State of Israel as the ultimate concretization of Judaism's goals and ideals. The movement sees the building of the land and the nation as a primary mitzvah and believes that Israel must be the center of the Jewish people.

Among the various institutions of the Masorti movement are the Conservative Yeshiva and the Schechter Institute of Jewish Studies. The Conservative Yeshiva was founded in 1995 to meet the need for serious learning in a coeducational and open-minded environment. Since 1995 it has grown from five students to more than fifty. Leading the faculty are Rabbi Joel Roth, *rosh yeshiva,* former dean of the Rabbinical School of the Jewish Theological Seminary, and Rabbi Pesach Schindler, *rosh yeshiva,* assistant professor of Talmud at the Hebrew University.

The Schechter Institute, established in 1984, includes the Rabbinical School of the Masorti movement. Rabbinic training requires undertaking a four-year, full-time program of study. Its students become proficient in all aspects of Jewish studies, including Bible, rabbinics, Jewish thought, and Jewish history. Most students are between the ages of 25–40, are married, and have children. Presently there are 20 students studying toward the rabbinate, eight of whom are women.

Another part of the Schechter Institute is its Graduate School of Advanced Jewish Studies, which offers a master's degree in several areas of Jewish studies. The very distinguished faculty includes among others Rabbi Professor David Golinkin, instructor in Bible, Rabbi Professor Shamma Friedman, instructor in Talmud, and Professor Eliezer Schweid, instructor in Jewish thought.

The Rabbinical Assembly of Israel, numbering about 150 rabbis, is the organization of Masorti rabbis living and working in Israel. It is committed to providing religious services and teaching Torah to its congregations. In matters of Jewish law, the Va'ad Halakhah (Law Committee) makes decisions. This committee is composed of seven rabbis from the Rabbinical Assembly. It is chaired by Rabbi David Golinkin and publishes its responsa each year.

Leaders of the Masorti movement include Dr. Irit Zmora, chairperson of the Masorti movement, and Rabbi Ehud Bandel, president of the Masorti movement. Rabbi Bandel was the first native-born Israeli to be ordained as a Masorti rabbi. As for the Rabbinical Assembly, Rabbi Mauricio Balter is the chairperson, while Rabbi Andrew Sacks is the director.

On several issues the Masorti movement finds itself at odds with the religious establishment in Israel. For example, the position of the Orthodox rabbinate on any issue of religion is the only accepted one. The current monopoly held by the religious establishment prevents Masorti organizations from receiving equal public funds for religious and educational services and denies their rabbis the right to officiate at weddings.

Another issue where there is tension is the status of women in tradition and ritual. The Masorti movement seeks to find ways to assure women's rights and equality. The role traditionally delegated to women was an expression of certain historical and social realities in public and religious life. The Masorti movement wishes to examine, within the framework of halakhah, ways of including women in areas previously closed to them.

Finally, the Jewish Theological Seminary has trained rabbis but is also regarded as a first-rate center for academic Judaic studies.

RECONSTRUCTIONIST JUDAISM

The founder of Reconstructionist Judaism was Rabbi Mordecai Kaplan (1881–1983). Born in Vilna, Lithuania, in 1881, he received a traditional Jewish education there and immigrated along with his family to America in 1889. Remaining traditional in his religious observance, he became increasingly disillusioned by Orthodox theology and was increasingly attracted to non-Orthodox approaches to Judaism. He graduated from City College of New York, was ordained at the Jewish Theological Seminary, and received a master's degree from Columbia University.

As he pondered the nature of Jewish religion, Kaplan began to regard Judaism not as a religion but as a civilization, characterized not only by beliefs and practices but by language, culture, literature, ethics, art, history, social organization, symbols, and customs. In 1935 Kaplan wrote *Judaism as a Civilization,* a book that became the foundation of the new Reconstructionist movement. He argued that we need a reconstruction of the religious foundations of Judaism in light of our understanding that Judaism is a religious civilization.

For Kaplan God was not a supernatural force in the universe, a God active in history, but the power that makes possible personal salvation. God could not abridge the laws of nature, for God was synonymous with natural law. Prayer was necessary because it helped man become conscious of his conscience, because prayer with the community focused attention on the community, and because it offered a release of emotion that could orient man in a positive psychological direction.

Kaplan rejected several traditional Jewish categories. Chosenness, for example, was rejected because too often it was taken as a sign of Jewish superiority, instead of an expression of Jewish obligation to God and humanity. He rejected the idea of a personal messiah. Kaplan wrote his own Sabbath prayerbook in which he removed both concepts from the prayers.

To be sure, Reconstructionists do emphasize the importance of Jewish observance. They observe the halakhah, however, only by personal choice. They do not observe because God commanded observance, but because observance is a valuable cultural remnant.

The number of Jews identifying themselves as Reconstructionists is small when compared to the numbers in Reform or Conservative Judaism. Only 1 percent of the Jews in North America affirm that they are Reconstructionists. Moreover, there are only about 100 Reconstructionist synagogues in the United States and Canada.

Bernhard Felsenthal, U.S. Reform rabbi. Cincinnati, Ohio, American Jewish Archives.

Among the institutions of the Reconstructionists are the Reconstructionist Rabbinical College, the Jewish Reconstructionist Foundation, and the Reconstructionist Rabbinical Association. The Rabbinical College was established in 1968. It is dedicated to studying and teaching Judaism as an evolving religious civilization and to advancing the universal freedom, justice and peace that are Judaism's core values. Its mission is to train rabbis, cantors, and other Jewish leaders. Its first president was Mordechai Kaplan, who was succeeded by his son-in-law, Ira Eisenstein. The current president is Rabbi Dan Ehrenkrantz.

The Jewish Reconstructionist Federation, founded in 1955, is the synagogue arm of the Reconstructionist movement. As mentioned, it serves about 100 congregations. It offers consultation on all key areas of synagogue life, including youth and adult education, leadership development, outreach and community-building initiatives, fundraising, and budgeting.

There is, finally, the Reconstructionist Rabbinical Association, founded in 1974. It is the professional association of Reconstructionist rabbis, with more than 200 members. The association has three primary missions. First, it provides professional and personal support and resources to rabbis. Second, it brings the teachings and traditions of Judaism to bear on contemporary issues and challenges. Third, it represents Reconstructionist rabbis in the larger Jewish and general communities, by participating in programs, commissions, and other activities.

NEO-ORTHODOXY: SAMSON RAPHAEL HIRSCH

Born in Hamburg in 1808, Rabbi Samson Raphael Hirsch (1808–1888) studied in his youth with private tutors. Already at a young age he decided to devote himself to the presentation of Orthodox Judaism in modern, updated form with the greatest effectiveness. The beginnings of Reform Judaism were in Hamburg, where the first Reform temple was built in 1818; these developments were of great concern to Hirsch's family and to other traditional Jews. Moreover, there were no "modernized" Orthodox rabbis ready to do battle with the reformers. Few read German instead of Yiddish, and few wrote or spoke precise German.

Enormous influence on Hirsch came from two remarkable scholars, Hakham Isaac Bernays (1792–1849) and Rabbi Yaakov Ettlinger (1798–1871), both natives of Germany. Bernays, who refused to be called "rabbi" because he thought the Reform Jews had degraded that title, was an outstanding talmudist, a child prodigy. But he was also university educated, with a profound knowledge of philosophy and modern literature. He arrived in Hamburg in 1821, having been appointed chief rabbi of this largest Jewish community in Germany, which numbered 6,000. Bernays had a profound influence on Hirsch.

Ettlinger had an important impact on Hirsch as well. He had studied with Rabbi Asher Wallerstein (d. 1837), son of Rabbi Aryeh Leib ben Asher (d. 1785), author of a classic talmudic work called *Sha'agat Aryeh,* and with Rabbi Abraham Bing; he was ordained by the latter. It is

RELIGIOUS REFORM / 103

One of Rabbi Samson Raphael Hirsch's distinguished teachers was Rabbi Isaac Bernays (1792–1849). Bernays was born in Mainz, Germany, studied at Wuerzburg University and in the yeshiva of Abraham Bing. He was appointed rabbi of Hamburg in 1821.

Bernays delivered his sermons in polished German, spent his life battling the Reform movement, and left German Jews his two great students, Hirsch and R. Azriel Hildesheimer.

At the yeshiva of Wuerzberg, Bernays studied with a younger contemporary, R. Jacob Ettlinger (1798–1871). Bernays helped Ettlinger with Maimonides' philosophical work, Guide to the Perplexed, while Ettlinger helped Bernays study the halakhah of kosher slaughter and of the meat and milk prohibition in the Shulhan Arukh.

Hamburg was the birthplace of the Reform movement, so Bernays' appointment as chief rabbi of Hamburg at age 29 meant that he would have to challenge their views. Bernays was both traditional and modern and could speak to the wider community. He therefore could initiate the Orthodox response to modernity.

Bernays made outward concessions to modernity. Unlike more traditional, less modern rabbis, he donned clerical robes, delivered his sermons every Shabbat in German, and conducted services in an aesthetically pleasing manner. More important, though, he was committed to modern culture and contemporary scholarship. He was a master of German theology and philosophy. Unlike Moses Mendelssohn, however, he was a Talmud scholar of note and was able to integrate his rabbinic learning with modern German thought.

Bernays joined the ban on use of the Reform prayerbook, saying, "This is a prayerbook, but not a Jewish prayerbook." He thought that the Reform movement's rejection of messianic belief undermined the very existence of the Jewish people.

Bernays, who preferred to be called Hakham Bernays rather than Rabbi Bernays, because in his opinion the reformers had demeaned the title "Rabbi," was not a successful leader. He was gifted and brilliant but spoke over the heads of his audience. Still, his contribution to what would be termed Neo-Orthodoxy was immeasurable, for his students, especially Rabbi Samson Raphael Hirsch, succeeded in rebuilding German Orthodoxy.

notable that while a yeshiva student, Ettlinger was pursuing a formal university education. He would become one of the great scholars of his time, writing the 'Arukh la-Ner, a respected commentary on the Talmud, and She'elot u-Teshuvot Binyan Ziyyon, a classic collection of responsa. Clearly it was Ettlinger's view that secular study was critical for any rabbi wishing to function effectively in the modern world.

Ettlinger was chosen to be head of the yeshiva of Mannheim in 1825. Hirsch went there in 1828 to study, receiving rabbinic ordination from Ettlinger. He then went to study at the University of Bonn, where he pursued interests in classical philology, history, philosophy, and experimental physics.

In 1831 Hirsch began his rabbinic career. His first position was in Oldenburg. As he entered the rabbinate, Hirsch found German Orthodox Jewry in crisis as the result of Jewish emancipation. Assimilation and intermarriage were rampant. Attempts were being made to transform Judaism from an all-encompassing way of life into simply a religion. Among the Orthodox, Hirsch saw lifeless, routinized observance.

The rabbis of the "old school," as was noted earlier, were ill equipped to deal with the crisis.

Hirsch came to the conclusion that to prevent the disappearance of Judaism as a way of life and thought,

Isaac Bernays

it was crucial to present the eternal teachings of Judaism in a new form. The fruits of this conviction were his two works, *Nineteen Letters* and *Horeb*, discussed in Chapter 3.

After eleven years in Oldenburg, he spent the next five years in Emden. Then in 1846 he was asked to become chief rabbi of Nikolsburg; during that period he was rabbinic leader of Moravia, which included part of modern Austria and the Czech Republic. He served too as a member of Parliament. It was in large measure through his efforts that Austrian Jewry and Moravian Jewry attained their emancipation.

In 1851 Hirsch was invited to Frankfurt by a small group of Orthodox Jews who wanted to hold on to Orthodoxy in a community where the Reform Jews dominated; the Reform community consisted of some 5,000 Jews. When Hirsch began his work, Frankfurt had no Orthodox community, just a few Orthodox Jews. There was no synagogue and no Jewish school. Hirsch built a large, flourishing Orthodox community of over 400 families. At its core was a major Jewish day school, with 500 students from elementary through high school. The synagogue sat 1,000.

Written on the foundation stone of Hirsch's synagogue was the following wish:

> May we merit to raise up together our sons and daughters to Torah and *derekh eretz*, as we were instructed by the founding fathers of our nation, the true sages.

The credo of Hirsch's school was *yafeh talmud Torah 'im derekh eretz* ("Torah study is good when combined with general culture").

How did Hirsch understand this imperative of the rabbis? Some have argued that his attitude toward general culture cannot be seen as other than an attitude for his time, an attitude taken by one challenged by the Reform movement. Had he not faced this challenge, he would not have advocated openness to general culture. A careful reading of Hirsch's writings belies this understanding.

Hirsch affirms the value of general culture. Knowing full well that his views might be misunderstood—since some might say that Torah and *derekh eretz* have equal value, while others might make Torah subservient to *derekh eretz*—he wrote, in his *Collected Writings* (VI:120–123):

> The more the Jew is a Jew, the more universalist will be his views and aspirations, the less alien will he be to anything that is noble and good, true and upright in the arts and sciences, in civilization and culture. . . . The more the Jew is a Jew, the more gladly will he give himself to all that is true progress in civilization and culture—provided that in this new circumstance he will not only maintain his Judaism but will be able to bring it to ever more glorious fulfillment.

For Hirsch, then, Torah is primary in importance, with *derekh eretz* secondary. The imperative of combining Torah with *derekh eretz* applies to all Jewish communities, in all places, at all times.

How successful was Hirsch in carrying out in practice what he saw as the mandate of the rabbis? First of all, Hirsch preached, taught, and wrote in German. In addition, he was most conversant with general culture; thus he was able to make reference to Greek and Latin literature, to Shakespeare, and to German philosophical literature. In 1859 the hundredth anniversary of the birth of Friedrich von Schiller, the distinguished German dramatist, poet, and historian, was observed in Hirsch's school. When Hirsch addressed the assembly called for this occasion, his address was filled with quotes from Schiller's poetry.

But perhaps it was in the schools founded by Hirsch in Frankfurt that the greatest statement was made; these schools would become models for Orthodox Jewish high schools elsewhere in Germany and Western Europe, and in the United States and Israel later on. It was about these schools that Hirsch wrote, in his *Collected Writings* (VII:413–417):

> Your child would have become a different person if you had taught him to discern the true value of secular wisdom and scholarship by measuring it against the standard of the Divinely given truths of Judaism; if, in making this comparison, you would have noted the fact that is obvious even to the dullest eye, namely, that the knowledge offered by Judaism is the original source of all that is genuinely true, good, and pure in secular wisdom, and that secular learning is merely a preliminary, a road leading to the ultimate, more widespread dissemination of the truths of Judaism. If you had opened your child's eyes to genuine, thorough knowledge in both fields of study, then you would have taught him to love and cherish Judaism and Jewish knowledge all the more.

Hirsch died in 1888. But his neo-Orthodoxy, which argued for Torah observance combined with a positive attitude toward general education and culture, persists as an approach to Judaism. Thus his influence remains in the United States, in Israel, and in parts of Europe.

ORTHODOX JUDAISM IN AMERICA

Orthodox Judaism of today is strong, it is alive and well, although many do not see Orthodox Judaism as Hirsch saw it in the 19th century. Survivors of the Holocaust have invested themselves in preserving Judaism in their new world. The day school movement is a major product of these efforts. Approximately 180,000 students can be found enrolled in day schools. These schools have shown themselves to be the most effective tool for ensuring Jewish survival.

Institutions for higher Jewish education include Yeshiva University in New York City. Over its history this institution has been administered by several distinguished rabbis and scholars, including Dr. Bernard Revel (1885–1940) and Dr. Norman Lamm (b. 1927). In December 2002, Dr Lamm became chancellor and Richard M. Joel (b. 1951) was appointed as the fourth president of the university. Yeshiva University provides its students with both a college education and undergraduate programs in Jewish studies.

Those who graduate and choose to prepare for rabbinic ordination, *semikhah,* must enter the Rabbi Isaac Elhanan Theological Seminary. Rabbi Dr. Joseph Soloveitchik (1903–1993), recognized by all segments in the Orthodox community as a distinguished Talmud scholar, succeeded his father, Rabbi Moses (1876–1941), as *rosh yeshiva* upon the latter's death in 1941. From 1941 until his own death in 1993, Rabbi Soloveitchik ordained more than 1,500 rabbis.

The earliest yeshivot on this continent, established before World War II, were Mesivta Tiferes Yerushalayim, headed by Rabbi Moshe Feinstein (1895–1987) for nearly 50 years until his death in 1987; Yeshivas Ner Israel, headed by Rabbi Yaakov Ruderman (1901–1987), who arrived in America in the

Rabbi Dr. Norman Lamm, 1996

Rabbi Dr. Joseph Soloveitchik (1903–1993)

1930s; Torah Vodaath, headed by Rabbi Yaakov Kamenetzky (1891–1986); and Mesivta Chaim Berlin, headed by Rabbi Yitzchak Hutner (1907–1980), who also came to America in the 1930s. In the early1940s and after World War II, other great East European Talmud scholars, who had escaped Hitler miraculously, came to America. Among them were Rabbis Eliyahu Meir Bloch (1894–1955) head of the Telshe Yeshiva in Cleveland; Rabbi Abraham Kalmanowitz (1891–1964), founder of the Mir Yeshiva in Brooklyn; and Rabbi Yeruchim Gorelik (1922–1984), one of the *roshei yeshiva* at Yeshiva University.

Particularly notable among those who escaped Europe during World War II was Rabbi Aharon Kotler (1892–1964). Rabbi Kotler was an illustrious Talmud scholar and a man of great charisma. Fleeing Poland and admitted under President Roosevelt's special "clergyman" category, he arrived in America in 1940. Shortly after his arrival, he settled in Lakewood, New Jersey, establishing Beth Medrash Govoha. Starting with only ten students, this yeshiva had 250 by the time of Rabbi Aharon's death in 1964. Rabbi Shneur Kotler succeeded his father as *rosh yeshiva*. Today the yeshiva accommodates more than 1,000 students.

Hasidic leaders also established yeshivot. Rabbi Menahem Mendel Schneerson (1902–1994), leader of the Lubavitcher Hasidim, urged his followers to build yeshivot. Other Hasidic leaders did so as well. For example, Rabbi Yoel Teitelbaum (1888–1979), leader of the Satmar Hasidim, the Satmar Rav, built a yeshiva and by the 1980s led a community of tens of thousands in the Williamsburg section of Brooklyn.

Major institutions of the Orthodox community include the Rabbinical Council of America and the Union of Orthodox Jewish Congregations of America. The Rabbinical Council is the largest and most influential Orthodox rabbinical group. Most of its members are pulpit rabbis, but membership is also available to teachers and school administrators. Until his death in 1993, Rabbi Soloveitchik provided spiritual and political leadership to the rabbis, many of whom had been his students at Yeshiva University.

The Union of Orthodox Jewish Congregations is the congregational organization of Orthodox synagogues. Member congregations range from some with mixed seating to others that go beyond the minimal requirements of the halakhah. One significant responsibility assumed by the Orthodox Union is the supervision of *kashrut*, the dietary laws. Food products carrying the union's symbol of approval have been deemed acceptable for eating by rabbinical supervisors, *mashgihim*. Other agencies of kashrut supervision unaffiliated with the Orthodox Union exist as well. They each have their own symbols of approval.

In 1971, Dr. Bernard Lander established Touro College. Since its founding, the college has grown enormously, becoming an international institution and serving nearly 10,000 students. In addition to its undergraduate programs, graduate programs are available in law, health sciences, education and psychology, medicine and business. Moreover, Touro College has branches in New York, California, Moscow, China, and Israel.

The Orthodox community is divided between the modern, or centrist, Orthodox and the right-wing Orthodox. While for either group, Torah study and observance of the mitzvot are central, the modern Orthodox place value on secular education and are supportive of the State of Israel. Secular knowledge is valuable for those whose professions require it: doctors, lawyers, computer professionals, academics, and so on. It is of value too for those whose profession does not require it; it is important to read and study in an effort to confront the challenges of modernity, to accept what can be accepted and reject what cannot. Modern Orthodox Jews support the State of Israel by visiting, contributing, and including *Hallel* in the prayers on Yom ha-Atzma'ut, Israel's Independence Day.

The right-wing Orthodox, by contrast, do not encourage secular education. To them, secular education is helpful, but only as career preparation if seen as necessary, for one's commitment to Torah study is compromised by putting time aside for secular study. Right-wing Orthodox Jews do visit Israel and do contribute, but are unwilling to view the creation of the state as a miracle, which would mandate the recital of *Hallel* on Yom ha-Atzma'ut. In addition, leadership of the right-wing Orthodox comes from the Mo'etzes Gedolei ha-Torah, Council of Torah Sages, distinguished Torah scholars who can provide guidance to the community on whatever issues present themselves.

SUMMARY

In this chapter we have looked at another outcome of the Enlightenment thinking that emerged in the 18th and 19th centuries, attempts to "modernize" Judaism. Reform Judaism began in Germany at this time. Israel Jacobson was its father, redefining Judaism as a religion, not a nation, and introducing some changes in Jewish ceremonial, thus creating a more dignified worship service. Only in later years did Abraham Geiger formulate an ideology for Reform Judaism. Moderate reform prevailed in Germany, but in America radical reform prevailed. We also considered how American Reform Judaism has developed and changed from its beginnings in the 19th century to its present state.

The roots for America's Conservative Judaism are to be found in Zechariah Frankel's Positive-Historical Judaism. Frankel formulated ideas without a movement, but in America a movement was created on the basis of his ideas. We have reviewed his teachings and considered how they have been applied. In recent years Conservative Judaism been divided into two camps, traditionalists and liberals, with commitment to the textual authority of Bible and Talmud being the major separating issue.

The appearance of Reform Judaism presented a special challenge to Orthodox Judaism, a challenge taken on by Rabbi Samson Raphael Hirsch. Hirsch became convinced that, in order to ensure that Judaism would survive, the teachings of Judaism had to be presented in a new form that was meaningful to young German Jews. Hirsch did this in writing and in the community, creating neo-Orthodoxy.

Finally, we looked at how Orthodox Judaism has developed in America: its educational institutions, its organizational structure, and the differences between the modern Orthodox and the right-wing Orthodox.

Documents

THE HAMBURG RABBINICAL COURT: THESE ARE THE WORDS OF THE COVENANT (1819)

This document is a selection from the twenty-two halakhic opinions solicited regarding the acceptability of Reform Judaism. Among the contributors were Rabbi Akiva Eiger of Posen, Prussia (1761–1837), Rabbi Moses Sofer of Pressburg, Hungary (1763–1839), and Rabbi Mordecai Benet, chief rabbi of Moravia (1753–1829).

These are the words of the covenant with Jacob, a law unto Israel, an eternal covenant; the world of God is one forever and ever. [These words are uttered] in accordance with the Torah and by judgment of the court of justice of the holy community of Hamburg—may the Lord bless it well—with the support of the leading men of learning in Germany, Poland, France, Italy, Bohemia, Moravia and Hungary. All of them join together, in an edict decreed by the angels and a judgment proclaimed by the holy ones, to abolish a new law (which was fabricated by several ignorant individuals unversed in the Torah) instituting practices which are not in keeping with the Law of Moses and of Israel. Therefore these pious, learned, holy and distinguished rabbis have risen to render the Law secure [against such infractions].

They have discovered a breach [of the Law] and have sought to contain it with prescriptions forbidding the three cardinal sins [of Reform].

1. It is forbidden to change the worship that is customary in Israel from the Morning Benedictions to "It is our duty to praise [the Lord of all]"; and all the more so [is it prohibited] to make any deletions in the traditional liturgy.
2. It is forbidden to pray in any language other than the Holy Tongue. Every prayerbook that is printed improperly and not in accordance with our [traditional] practice is invalid, and it is forbidden to pray from it.
3. It is prohibited to play a musical instrument in the synagogue on the Sabbath and on the festivals even when it is played by a non-Jew.

Happy is the man who heeds the decree of the sages of the court of justice and the words of the learned, pious and holy. Happy is the man who does not remove himself from the congregation, in order that he may walk in the way of the good. He who desires the integrity of his soul will take utmost care lest he trangress, Heaven forbid, the words of the learned contained in this volume, as the sages of the Talmud, may their memory be blessed, said: "Pay heed to their legacy." Who is the man who fears the Lord and will not fear the words of the forty pious, exalted, and holy men who have affixed their signatures to this book, sparing [thereby] himself and his household.

By Order of the Court of Justice of the Holy Community of Hamburg.

. . . Behold, we had hoped that these men [who introduced Reform] would have attended to our words and listened to the voice of their teachers, who alone are fit to express an opinion on matters concerning what is permitted and what is prohibited. In former times the men of our proud city have listened to the voice of their teachers, who told them the path they were to take. We had thought that our judgment would be honored and that they would not dare to disobey our utterance, for our strength now is as it was formerly.

But we hoped in vain, for these men disobeyed the counsel [of their teachers] and sank into sin. They quickly built for themselves a house of prayer, which they called a temple, and published a prayerbook for Sabbaths and festivals, which has caused great sorrow and brought tears to our eyes over the destruction of our people. For they have added to and deleted from the text of the prayers according to their hearts' desires. They have eliminated the Morning Benedictions and the blessing for the Torah and have discarded Psalm 145, as well as other psalms from the morning prayers. They have set their hands upon the text of the recitation of "Hear, O Israel," and in the wickedness of their hearts have deleted the texts of "To God who rested," "God the Lord," "True and firm," and "There is none to be compared to Thee." Moreover, they have printed most of the prayers in German rather than in Hebrew. Worst of all, they have perpetrated a sore evil by removing all references to the belief in the Ingathering of the Exiles. [Their deletions include] the text "Lead us with an upright bearing to our land" in the benediction "With great love," the text "Who will raise us up in joy to our land?" in the Additional Service [*Musaf*] for the Sabbath and the texts "Bring us in jubilation to Zion your city" and "Gather our scattered ones from among the nations" in the Additional Service for festivals. They have thereby testified concerning themselves that they do not believe at all in the promise of our teacher Moses, may he rest in peace: "If any of thine that are dispersed be in the uttermost parts of the earth, from thence will the Lord thy God gather thee, and from thence will He fetch thee." This belief is one of the major tenets of our holy Torah. All the prophets have been unanimous in affirming that the God of our fathers would gather our scattered ones, and this is our hope throughout our Exile. This belief in no way detracts from the honor of Their Majesties the kings and ministers under whom we find protection, for it is common knowledge that we believe in the coming of the messiah and the ingathering of the exiles. No one has ever dared to object to this belief of ours, because they know that we are obligated to seek the well-being of the peoples who have brought us under their protection. They have bestowed much good and kindness

upon us, may God grant them success in all their actions and works. Our opinion here corresponds to that which the learned men of our time, may their light shine, have elaborated in their letters. He who rejects this belief denies [one of] the fundamental tenets of our religion. Woe to the ears that have heard that men have arisen in Israel to do violence to the foundations of our holy faith.

Yet with all this they are not content, for their hands are still outstretched and they continue to do evil. At the dedication of their house of prayer men and women sang together at the opening of the ark, in contradiction to the law set out in the Talmud and in the Codes: "a woman's voice is indecent." Such [an abomination] is not done in our house of prayer, which has replaced the Temple, throughout the entire Diaspora of the sanctified ones of Israel. Who has heard or seen such a thing? In addition, they play a musical instrument (an organ) on the holy Sabbath and have abolished the silent prayer. They have even abolished the reading of a selection from the Prophets on the Sabbath [after the reading of the weekly portion from the Pentateuch] as well as the reading of the four portions [of the Pentateuch read in addition to the weekly portion on the four Sabbaths preceding Passover]. On Purim the congregation recited the prayer "grant us discernment" instead of the Eighteen Benedictions, and in the evening they read the Book of Esther in German from a printed text [rather than from a handwritten Hebrew scroll]. Lack of space prevents the inclusion of all their pernicious customs and practices by means of which they have chosen to disobey the Holy One of Israel and to defy the holy sages of blessed memory, the court of their city, and the vast majority of our community who are God-fearing and faithful and fulfill the commandments of God.

Thus we have resolved that this is not the time to place our hands over our mouths and to be silent. Were we to remain silent we would be committing a sin, for [the reformers] would say the rabbis are silent and [their] silence [is to be construed] as consent. With honeyed words they would lead astray the God-fearing and the faithful, who in their innocence would follow them. [The reformers] would say to them: "Behold, the path upon which we walk is good. Come, let us join together and be one people." And so the Torah, Heaven forbid, would disappear. Brethren, the children of Israel, it shall not be; Israel has not yet been abandoned. There are still judges in the land who are zealous for God's sake and who will rend the arm, and even crack the skull, of him who pursues the sin [of the reformers]. To these judges we shall hasten for aid. They will rise up and help us abolish the [wicked] counsel [of the reformers] and strengthen our religion. Accordingly, we have girded our loins and written to the famous learned men of the holy communities of Germany, Poland, Bohemia, Moravia, and Italy. We have sent them our legal judgment, which we mentioned above, and we asked them if after close and careful study by means of their clear and pure reason they would confirm all that is in our judgment as being proper. In this way we can make public the abomination that has been committed in Israel. Every pious man who fears the word of God will pay heed to the words of the learned men of our time, may their light shine, and to our words. He shall not follow the counsels of the perverse who walk upon a crooked path.

THE REFORM RABBINICAL CONFERENCE AT FRANKFURT: HEBREW AS THE LANGUAGE OF JEWISH PRAYER (1845)

This document records the proceedings at this 1845 conference, attended by 30 rabbis. Among the notable participants were Zechariah Frankel and Abraham Geiger.

Third Session, morning, July 16, 1845. . . .The President moves that it would seem desirable to discuss the report [of the Commission on Liturgy] immediately.

Question 1: To what degree is the Hebrew language necessary for the public prayer service, and, if not necessary, is its retention advisable for the time being?

Report of the committee: With respect to question one, the Hebrew language is not in every instance *objectively* necessary for the service, nor does the Talmud, with very minor exceptions, prescribe it. But since a large part of the Israelites in contemporary Germany seem to feel a subjective necessity for it, the committee considers the use of the Hebrew language advisable for typical parts of the liturgy: the *barechu,* the *parshat shema,* the three first and three last benedictions of the liturgy and the blessings upon reading of the Torah should be recited in Hebrew; all other parts of the liturgy may be recited in a German adaptation.

The President, in accordance with the proposal of the committee, now poses the question: Is praying in the Hebrew language *objectively, legally necessary?*

Frankel takes the floor. He deems the occasion important enough to begin with a few general observations. This rabbinical conference consists of the guides and teachers of the people. They are familiar with the people's needs and sorrow; it is their duty to satisfy these needs, to alleviate these sorrows, and to prevent any discord [among the people]. It is the duty of the rabbinical conference to show and to attest that it is moved by serious and sacred aspirations. Its spokesmen, therefore, have to begin by stating their principles. It is the pride of Judaism that no person, and no social class, may presume authority, but that every decision must evolve organically from principles and derive its validity therefrom. Points of view may be stated

and put to the vote, but without principles they are merely private opinions. First of all, therefore, the people are entitled to an exposition of our principles. . . . The speaker now explains his principles: He stands for a positive, historical Judaism. [This approach posits that] in order to understand Judaism in the present, one must look back and investigate its past.

The positive forms of Judaism are deeply rooted within its innermost being and must not be discarded coldly and heartlessly. Where would we be if we were to tear apart our inner life and let a new life spring forth from our head as Minerva sprang forth from the head of Jupiter? We cannot return to the *letter of Scripture.* The gap [between it and us] is too wide to be bridged. Even a new exegesis of the Bible is subject to changing phases of scholarship and could not serve as a foundation of a firm edifice. Should we allow any influence of the *Zeitgeist,* of the spirit of the time? But the *Zeitgeist* is as fickle as the times. Besides, it is cold. It may seem reasonable, but it will never satisfy, console, and calm the soul; Judaism, on the other hand, always inspires and fills the soul with bliss.

The reform of Judaism, moreover, is not a reform of faith, but one of religious commandments. These still live within the people and exert their influence. We are not called upon to weaken, but rather to strengthen this influence. We must not consider the individuals who do not abide by them; we are not a party and must therefore take care of the whole. Now it is necessary to conserve the things which are truly sacred to the entire people, to prevent any schism in Israel. Rather than creating new parties, we must make peace between the existing ones. . . .

Fourth Session, afternoon, July 16, 1845. . . . *Geiger* demands a strict adherence to the expression of the problem as consisting of the following two questions:

1. Is the complete exclusion of the Hebrew language from the liturgy in general desirable?
2. Are there momentary considerations in favor of a provisional solution?

Both questions, however, overlap and cannot be strictly separated in the debate. The speaker considers it desirable to pray in the mother tongue, which is the language of the soul. Our deepest emotions and feelings, our most sacred relationships, our most sublime thoughts find their expression in it. He feels compelled to admit that as regards himself—although Hebrew is his first mother tongue which he learned before other languages, and a language he knows thoroughly—a German prayer strikes a deeper chord than a Hebrew prayer.

The Hebrew language, he continues, has ceased to be alive for the people, and the language of [Jewish] prayer is certainly not the language of the Scripture any more. It is obvious, moreover, that even a reading from the Torah tires a large part of the community.

The introduction of the vernacular into the service, it is claimed, effects the disappearance of the Hebrew language and thus undermines the foundations of Judaism. To this objection the speaker replies that anyone who imagines Judaism to be walking on the crutches of a language deeply offends it. By considering Hebrew as being of central importance to Judaism, moreover, one would define it as a national religion, because a separate language is a characteristic element of a separate nation. But no member of this conference, the speaker concluded, would wish to link Judaism to a particular nation. . . .

Fifth Session, morning, July 17, 1845. . . . *Frankel* [takes the floor]. The ongoing debate, far from offering new ideas, has rather confirmed [Frankel's] point of view. Geiger considers a language to be the mark of a separate nationality and claims that the retention of Hebrew would testify to our national aspirations; this point, however, is not essential to the question under consideration. The cause of emancipation has nothing to do with religion, and no religious aspect should be sacrificed for it. Everything pertaining to religion must be retained, and if our nationality were religious, then we should openly confess to it.

In countries [that have granted the Jews full] emancipation, such as Holland and France, he continues, experience has fortunately shown that the Hebrew language does not prevent the Jews from being genuine patriots and from fulfilling all duties towards the state. One has to be very careful with such expressions; our meetings are public, therefore "O Sages, be careful with your words."

If Geiger goes on to claim that a German prayer strikes a deeper chord in him than a Hebrew one, he makes a purely subjective statement. Most speakers of Hebrew will feel differently, because this language is a stronger expression of religious emotions; as witnesses, the speaker calls upon the majority of rabbis assembled here, who are familiar with the Hebrew language.

Hebrew, the speaker argues, is the language of our Scripture, which contains every ingredient of our religion. Religion must provide not only an abstract but also an external bond between us and the deity, this being the reason for precepts such as the *tefilin* and *mezuzah;* in like manner, the use of Hebrew in the prayers serves as an external bond. The language of the Scripture is a constant reminder of our Covenant with God. These various bonds and reminders resemble the sheaf of arrows in the following parable: As long as they remain bound together a sheaf of arrows is unbreakable, but as soon as single arrows are removed from the sheaf it will quickly fall apart. Many characteristic elements of Judaism have been effaced by now, it is time to halt the process.

There is another aspect to be considered as well. The Bible has been given to the Jews as a pledge to be safeguarded; they were called upon to carry it through the world for thousands of years. Mind you, not the priests of Israel alone were called upon to do so, but all of Israel. Samuel already, by establishing schools for prophets, undermined the hierarchy; it is therefore written of him, "Moses and Aaron among His priests, and Samuel among them that call upon His name" [Ps. 99:6; cited in Hebrew], and the Talmud rightly remarks, "Samuel is equivalent to Moses and Aaron." If the original texts of the Scripture were to become the exclusive property of a separate class of rabbis, we should soon have a separation of priests and laymen again. But all of us object to the establishment of a caste of priests and wish to obliterate all memory of it. That is why our youth has to be instructed in the Hebrew language so that it may understand the service and the Scripture.

The speaker adds, however, that it is necessary to conduct part of the service in German; but Hebrew must prevail. The language of revelation, in which God spoke to Moses, must act as an edifying stimulus. Hebrew, in fact, is so essential to our service *that its use should have been secured by* [halakhic] *law;* had anyone ever thought of abandoning the Hebrew language, such a law would certainly have been passed. The sages allowed another language besides Hebrew in the service [i.e., Aramaic] merely out of consideration for the weak who could not find their peace of mind in a Hebrew prayer. They never thought of excluding the Hebrew language from the Temple. . . .

PHILIPPSON: All extremes are to be avoided, and according to the general consensus, neither Hebrew nor German should be excluded from the service. The question, then, is one of proportions. We do not work for the moment and for individual communities; we work for the future and for the whole [of Jewry]. The Hebrew and the German elements must be organically melted into one another.

We shall have to distinguish between *prayer* and public *services.* A prayer is the expression of the particular states and emotions of the soul, of happiness and unhappiness, of joy and of suffering, of sorrow, repentance and penance; here, a full understanding is necessary, and a foreign language utterly useless. The public prayer services, on the other hand, do not refer to the individual [per se]; public prayer is intended to stimulate, to teach, and to express the confession.

The Hebrew language certainly serves as a stimulus. In it, for the first time, the *shema* ["Hear, O Israel," Deut. 6:4], the *unity of God* was expressed; the principle of pure love for mankind, "Thou shalt love thy neighbor as thyself" [Lev. 19:18; cited in Hebrew]; the sentence of the equality of all men before the law, "one law and one ordinance" [Num. 15:16; cited in Hebrew]; Moses spoke to God in Hebrew, "O Lord God, Thou has begun to show Thy servant Thy greatness" [Deut. 3:24]. God had *begun* to reveal Himself to him. By using the original expressions, therefore, the public prayer service acts as a powerful stimulus.

When the Torah is read, the Hebrew language will also act as a teacher. This reading must not be abolished, otherwise the people would lose all contact with the Scripture. . . .

As a *center of the confessions* the Hebrew language is indispensable. The German Jews are Germans, they feel and think in German and wish to live and act as patriots. But Judaism is not German, it is universal. The Diaspora of the Jews is not tantamount to the Diaspora of Judaism; the latter, on the contrary, must keep its unified character. The content of this character is the *confession;* its form is represented in the *Hebrew language.*

As citizens, we all strive towards *unity* with our fellow countrymen; as members of a religion, however, we are allowed, and even obliged, to retain that which distinguishes us. Facing an immense majority, the minority needs some distinguishing features. The Hebrew language fulfills this purpose.

The Hebrew language, moreover, is neither *poor* nor *dead,* as it is claimed. Masterpieces of unperishable value have been written in it, and as a language of religion it has remained fully alive. To repeat, the Hebrew language must be retained, but at the same time it must be organically united with the *German* element.

KAHN: I am only speaking from an objective point of view. I certainly wish to retain the Hebrew language for the time being, but we must gratefully acknowledge that its use for our prayers is nowhere prescribed. Our ideal, therefore, should be the establishment of a purely *German* service, because language by itself does not constitute a religious element.

Our *schools* ought to teach in Hebrew; the service, however, aims at edification, elevation, instruction; it should not be turned into a means for the preservation of the Hebrew language.

It is claimed that the Hebrew expression *Adonai* (i.e., God) sounds more solemn than the German word *Gott.* To this differentiation I must seriously object, because it would cast a heavy doubt on our civil oath. The name *Gott* is as sacred to me as *Adonai,* and I hope that everybody here will agree with me on this. (*General and loud consent.*)

We should not have any religious element wrested from us. Granted. But we must first concur regarding the nature of religious elements. Language is not one of them. The *shema* ["Hear, O Israel"] sounds much more religious to the German when spoken in German, and much more edifying to the Englishman when spoken in English, than when spoken in unintelligible Hebrew. With the elimination of the Hebrew language [from the liturgy], then, nothing would really be lost. . . . I vote for the introduction of a purely German service. . . .

LOEWENGARD: It was said: "We are Germans and want to be Germans!" If this statement has any political implications I should like to remind you that we are not yet emancipated. (Disapproval from all sides. The speaker explains that he merely wants to keep all political aspects out of the debate, because their introduction only causes mis-

understanding.) From the religious point of view, a distinction was made between prayer and service; this was correct. The reading from the Torah, for instance, is meant to demonstrate the unity of Israel established by the Torah, as it is expressed in "And this is the law which Moses set before the children of Israel." Instruction [in the Torah] could be managed without this public reading, because [printed] Bibles are available in sufficient numbers now. As a demonstration [of Jewish unity], however, it should be sufficient to read selections from the Hebrew Pentateuch [at the public service and not also the traditional passages from the prophets].

THE REFORM RABBINICAL CONFERENCE AT FRANKFURT: THE QUESTION OF MESSIANISM (1845)

Inclusion of prayers concerning the doctrine of the Messiah was unacceptable to Reform Judaism. Discussion of this issue took up another session of the Frankfurt Conference.

Eighth Session, July 20, 1845. Agenda: Discussion of questions pertaining to cult. Question 2: To what degree must the dogma of the Messiah, and anything pertaining to it, be taken into consideration in the liturgy?

Before opening the debate, the President considers it necessary to remark that we are not concerned with the establishment of a certain doctrine of the Messiah, and that such doctrines will not be put to the vote; we are only concerned with how the existing liturgy should be evaluated in this respect, or perhaps conveniently changed. Points of view may differ subjectively but it is hoped that a version acceptable to all will emerge. The numerous speakers, especially those who are ardent believers in traditional messianism, should beware of creating any doubt concerning their allegiance to the state. Such contrasts and seeming contradictions are easily resolved within the mind of the believer. Here we are only concerned with the demands of truthfulness, lest we pray for something that does not coincide with our convictions.

The committee report reads as follows: The concept of the Messiah must continue to occupy a prominent place in the liturgy, but all political and national implications should be avoided.

EINHORN: The concept of the Messiah is closely linked to the entire ceremonial law. The believer in the Talmud finds his salvation only in the reconstruction of the state, the return of the people, the resumption of sacrifices, etc. Here lies the cause for all our lamentations over the destruction of the Temple, and our yearnings for the ruins of the altar. Ardent belief and unshakable courage were expressed in these hopes, uttered forth from the dark caves of our miserable streets.

But now our concepts have changed. There is no need any more for an extended ceremonial law. The earlier approach restricted divine guidance to the land [of Israel] and the people; the deity, it was believed, enjoyed bloody sacrifices, and priests were needed for penance. With increasing zeal, the prophets spoke up against this restricted view. Everybody knows the passage: "It hath been told thee, O man, what is good, and what the Lord doth require of thee; only to do justly, and to love mercy, and to walk humbly with thy God" (Mic. 6:8, cited in Hebrew). The decline of Israel's political independence was at one time deplored, but in reality it was not a misfortune, but a mark of progress; not a degradation, but an elevation of our religion, through which Israel has come closer to fulfilling its vocation. The place of the sacrifices has been taken by sacred devotion. From Israel, the word of God had to be carried to the four corners of the earth, and new religions have helped in carrying out the task. Only the Talmud moves in circles; we, however, favor progress.

At one time I took the concept of the Messiah to be a substitute for the idea of immortality, but now I no longer think so. I rather consider it as a hope of both worldly and heavenly salvation. Neither this idea nor the concept of the Chosen People contains anything reprehensible. The concept of the Chosen People, in fact, offers the undeniable advantage, for it creates a beneficial self-consciousness in the face of the ruling church.

HESS: In discussing the concept of the Messiah we run the greatest risk of losing ourselves in diffuse theories. The question is simply whether one wishes to interpret the Scripture in spirit, or literally; whether one conceives of messianism as an ideal, or as the idea of our religious independence, unattainable without the full political equality of the Israelites; whether, moreover, one sees it as a bond with our brethren living under oppressive rulers. Let us therefore hold on to the fact that the concept of a personal and political Messiah is dead for German Jewry, and that we must not petition God for that which we no longer believe. . . .

HOLDHEIM: Two points of misunderstanding must be clarified:

1. The hope for a national restoration contradicts our feeling for the fatherland; some speakers have claimed, on the other hand, that the two may coexist.
2. We are warned not to emphasize the national element, lest there be misinterpretations; but it was rightly remarked, on the other hand, that we should not pay attention to misinterpretations.

The main point, however, is this: We merely represent the religious, not the political interest of the community. The latter is sufficiently represented by other spokesmen. Our nationality is now only expressed in religious concepts and institutions. It is said: Our original nationality has developed towards religion. But this is erroneous; such a de-

velopment is unnatural. One must not mistake a national for a religious phenomenon, otherwise many abuses could be justified.

The wish to return to Palestine in order to create there a political empire for those who are still oppressed because of their religion is superfluous. The wish should rather be for a termination of the oppression, which would improve their lot as it has improved ours. The wish, moreover, is inadmissible. It turns the messianic hope from a religious into a secular one, which is gladly given up as soon as the political situation changes for the better. But the messianic hope, truly understood, is religious. It expresses either a hope for redemption and liberation from spiritual deprivation and the realization of a Kingdom of God on earth, or for a political restoration of the Mosaic theocracy where Jews could live according to the Law of Moses. This latter religious hope can be renounced only by those who have a more sublime conception of Judaism and who believe that the fulfillment of Judaism's mission is not dependent on the establishment of a Jewish state, but rather on a merging of Jewry into the political constellations of the fatherland. Only an enlightened conception of religion can displace a dulled one. Those, however, who believe that religion demands a political restoration must not renounce this belief even under the best of circumstances [in the Diaspora], because religion will content itself with nothing less than the complete satisfaction of its demands. This is the difference between strict Orthodoxy and Reform: Both approach Judaism from a religious standpoint; but while the former aims at a restoration of the old political order [in the interest of religion], the latter aims at the closest possible union with the political and national constellations of their times [as the demand of religion]. . . .

WECHSLER: As soon as we try to pin down the "how" of our hope, the hope immediately disappears. We ought not to vivisect our messianism, but to shape the existing prayers in accordance with our consciousness. We must not disregard the masses. If we had to compose new prayers, the situation would be different.

Therefore, everything already in existence should be admitted as long as it does not run counter to commonly accepted truth. *Political* and *national* do not seem to be the right expressions, anyway. Is *People of Israel* a national or political term? If it were so, the word *People* should not be used, and all passages in the liturgy containing the word should be deleted.

The question only concerns the prayer for our return to Palestine and all its consequences.

In all contemporary additions to the prayerbook our modern conception of the Messiah may clearly be stated, including the confession that our newly gained status as citizens constitutes a partial fulfillment of our messianic hopes. . . .

Resolution adopted by the majority: The messianic idea should receive prominent mention in the prayers, but all petitions for our return to the land of our fathers and for the restoration of a Jewish state should be eliminated from the liturgy. . . .

THE NEW ISRAELITE TEMPLE ASSOCIATION: CONSTITUTION OF THE HAMBURG TEMPLE (1817)

The first Reform temple was dedicated in Hamburg on October 18, 1818. The New Israelite Temple Association, founded by 66 laymen, put together the first systematic Reform worship services.

. . . Since public worship has for some time been neglected by so many, because of the ever decreasing knowledge of the language in which alone it has until now been conducted, and also because of many other shortcomings which have crept in at the same time—the undersigned, convinced of the necessity to restore public worship to its deserving dignity and importance, have joined together to follow the example of several Israelite congregations, especially the one in Berlin. They plan to arrange in this city also, for themselves as well as others who think as they do, a dignified and well-ordered ritual according to which the worship service shall be conducted on the Sabbath and holy days and on other solemn occasions, and which shall be observed in their own temple, to be erected especially for this purpose. Specifically, there shall be introduced at such services a German sermon, and choral singing to the accompaniment of an organ.

Incidentally, the above-mentioned ritual shall not be confined to services in the temple: rather it shall apply to all those religious customs and acts of daily life which are sanctified by the church or by their own nature. Outstanding amongst these are the entrance of the newly-born into the covenant of the fathers, weddings, and the like. Also, a religious ceremony shall be introduced in which the children of both sexes, after having received adequate schooling in the teachings of the faith, shall be accepted as confirmants of the Mosaic religion.

THE PITTSBURGH PLATFORM (1885)

This document expressed the main principles of American Reform Judaism. It remained authoritative for more than 50 years.

In view of the wide divergence of opinion and of the conflicting ideas prevailing in Judaism today, we, as representatives of Reform Judaism in America, in continuation of the work begun at Philadelphia in 1869, unite upon the following principles:

First—We recognize in every religion an attempt to grasp the Infinite One, and in every mode, source, or book of revelation held sacred in any religious system the consciousness of the indwelling of God in man. We hold that Judaism presents the highest conception of the God-idea as taught in our holy Scriptures and developed and spiritualized by the Jewish teachers in accordance with the moral and philosophical progress of their respective ages. We maintain that Judaism preserved and defended amid continual struggles and trials and under enforced isolation this God-idea as the central religious truth for the human race.

Second—We recognize in the Bible the record of the consecration of the Jewish people to its mission as priest of the One God, and value it as the most potent instrument of religious and moral instruction. We hold that the modern discoveries of scientific researches in the domains of nature and history are not antagonistic to the doctrines of Judaism, the Bible reflecting the primitive ideas of its own age and at times clothing its conception of divine providence and justice dealing with man in miraculous narratives.

Third—We recognize in the Mosaic legislation a system of training the Jewish people for its mission during its national life in Palestine, and today we accept as binding only the moral laws and maintain only such ceremonies as elevate and sanctify our lives, but reject all such as are not adapted to the views and habits of modern civilization.

Fourth—We hold that all such Mosaic and Rabbinical laws as regulate diet, priestly purity and dress originated in ages and under the influence of ideas altogether foreign to our present mental and spiritual state. They fail to impress the modern Jew with a spirit of priestly holiness; their observance in our days is apt rather to obstruct than to further modern spiritual elevation.

Fifth—We recognize in the modern era of universal culture of heart and intellect the approach of the realization of Israel's great Messianic hope for the establishment of the kingdom of truth, justice and peace among all men. We consider ourselves no longer a nation but a religious community, and therefore expect neither a return to Palestine, nor a sacrificial worship under the administration of the sons of Aaron, nor the restoration of any of the laws concerning the Jewish state.

Sixth—We recognize in Judaism a progressive religion, ever striving to be in accord with the postulates of reason. We are convinced of the utmost necessity of preserving the historical identity with our great past. Christianity and Islam being daughter-religions of Judaism, we appreciate their mission to aid in the spreading of monotheistic and moral truth. We acknowledge that the spirit of broad humanity of our age is our ally in the fulfillment of our mission, and therefore we extend the hand of fellowship to all who cooperate with us in the establishment of the reign of truth and righteousness among men.

Seventh—We reassert the doctrine of Judaism, that the soul of men is immortal, grounding this belief on the divine nature of the human spirit, which forever finds bliss in righteousness and misery in wickedness. We reject as ideas not rooted in Judaism the belief both in bodily resurrection and in Gehenna and Eden (hell and paradise) as abodes for everlasting punishment or reward.

Eighth—In full accordance with the spirit of Mosaic legislation which strives to regulate the relation between rich and poor, we deem it our duty to participate in the great task of modern times, to solve on the basis of justice and righteousness the problems presented by the contrasts and evils of the present organization of society.

ZECHARIAH FRANKEL: ON CHANGES IN JUDAISM (1845)

In this selection, Frankel tries to articulate a middle position between Orthodoxy and Reform Judaism. Although he does not name it here, he would later call it "Positive-Historical Judaism."

. . . Maintaining the integrity of Judaism simultaneously with progress, this is the essential problem of the present. Can we deny the difficulty of a satisfactory solution? Where is the point where the two apparent contraries can meet? What ought to be our point of departure in the attempt to reconcile essential Judaism and progress, and what type of opposition may we expect to encounter? How can we assure rest for the soul so that it shall not be torn apart or be numbed by severe doubts while searching for the warm ray of faith, and yet allot to reason its right, and enable it to lend strength and lucidity to the religious feeling which springs from the emotions? The opposing elements which so seldom are in balance must be united, and this is our task. . . .

Judaism is a religion which has a direct influence on life's activity. It is a religion of action, demanding the performance of precepts which either directly aim at ennobling man or, by reminding man of the divine, strengthen his feelings of dependence on God. And because of this trait neither pure abstract contemplation nor dark mysticism could ever strike root in Judaism. This, in turn, guaranteed that the lofty religious ideas were maintained in their purity, with the result that even today the divine light shines in Judaism.

By emphasizing religious activity, Judaism is completely tied to life and becomes the property of every individual Jew. A religion of pure ideas belongs primarily to the theologians; the masses who are not adapted to such conceptions concern themselves little with the particulars

of such religions because they have little relationship to life. On the other hand, a religion of action is always present, demanding practice in activity and an expression of will, and its demands are reflected in the manifold life of the individual, with the result that the faith becomes the common property of every follower.

Thus we have reached the starting point for the consideration of the current parties in Judaism. The viewpoint of the Orthodox party is clear. It has grown up in pious activity; to it the performance of precepts is inseparable from faith, for to it, the two are closely and inwardly connected. Were it to tear itself away from observance and give up the precepts, then it would find itself estranged from its own self and feel as though plunged into an abyss. Given this viewpoint, the direction and emphasis of the Orthodox party is clear. Where else, save in the combination of faith and meticulous observance of the precepts, can it find that complete satisfaction which it has enjoyed in the heritage of the fathers? When it will reject that which it has so long kept holy and inviolable? No—that is unthinkable.

Against this party there has arisen of late another one [Reform] which finds its aim in the opposite direction. This part sees salvation in overcoming the past, in carrying progress to the limit, in rejecting religious forms and returning merely to the simple original idea. In fact, we can hardly call it a party in Judaism, though its adherents still bear the name Jew, and are considered as such in social and political life, and do not belong to another faith. They do not, however, belong wholly to Judaism, for by limiting Judaism to some principles of faith, they place themselves partly outside the limits of Judaism.

We will now turn to a third party which has arisen from the first party, and not only stands within the bound of Judaism, but is also filled with real zeal for its preservation and endeavors to hand it over to the descendants and make it the common good of all times.

This party bases itself upon rational faith and recognizes that the task of Judaism is religious action, but it demands that this action shall not be empty of spirit and that it shall not become merely mechanical, expressing itself mainly in the form. It has also reached the view that religious activity itself must be brought up to a higher level through giving weight to the many meanings with which it should be endowed. Furthermore, it holds that we must omit certain unimportant actions which are not inherently connected either with the high ideas or with the religious forms delineated by the revealed laws. We must, it feels, take into consideration the opposition between faith and conditions of the time. True faith, due to its divine nature, is above time, and just as the nobler part of man is not subjected to time, so does faith rise above all time, and the word which issued from the mouth of God is rooted in eternity. But time has a force and might which must be taken account of. There is then created a dualism in which faith and time face each other, and man chooses either to live beyond time or to be subjected to it. It is in this situation that the Jew finds himself today; he cannot escape the influence of the conditions of the time and yet when the demands of faith bring him to opposition with the spirit of time, it is hoped that he will heed its call—find the power to resist the blandishments of the times. This third party, then, declares that Judaism must be saved for all time. It affirms both the divine value and historical basis of Judaism and, therefore, believes that by introducing some changes it may achieve some agreement with the concepts and conditions of the time.

In order to have a conception of what changes should and can be introduced, we must ask ourselves the question—does Judaism allow any changes in any of its religious forms? Does it consider all of them immutable, or can they be altered? Without entering into the citation of authorities pro and con, we may point out that Judaism does indeed allow changes. The early teachers, by interpretation, changed the literal meaning of the Scriptures; later scholars that of the Mishnah, and the post-talmudic scholars that of the Talmud. All these interpretations were not intended as speculation. They addressed themselves to life precepts. Thanks to such studies, Judaism achieved stabilization and avoided estrangement from the conditions of the time in various periods. . . . [The rabbis] established a rule which was intended as a guardian and protector against undue changes. It reads as follows: That which was adopted by the entire community of Israel and was accepted by the people and became a part of its life, cannot be changed by any authority.

In this fundamental statement there lies a living truth. Through it there speaks a profound view of Judaism which can serve for all times as a formula for needed changes and can be employed both against destructive reform and against stagnation.

This fundamental statement helps to make clear to us what changes in Judaism are justified and how they can be realized. True, Judaism demands religious activity, but the people is not altogether mere clay to be molded by the will of theologians and scholars. In religious activities, as in those of ordinary life, it decides for itself. This right was conceded by Judaism to the people. At such times as an earlier religious ordinance was not accepted by the entire community of Israel, it was given up. Consequently, when a new ordinance was about to be enacted it was necessary to see whether it would find acceptance by the people. When the people allows certain practices to fall into disuse, then the practices cease to exist. There is in such cases no danger for faith. A people used to activity will not hurt itself and will not destroy its practices. Its own sense of religiosity warns against it. Only those practices from which it is entirely estranged and which yield it no satisfaction will be abandoned and will thus die of themselves. On the whole there is always a great fund of faith and religious activity to afford security against negation and destruction.

We have, then, reached a decisive point in regard to moderate changes, namely, that they must come from the people and that the will of the entire community must decide. Still, this rule alone may accomplish little. The whole community is a heavy, unharmonious body, and its will is difficult to recognize. It comes to expression only after many years. We must find a way to carry on such changes in the proper manner, and this can be done by the help of the scholars. Judaism has no priests as representatives of faith, nor does it require special spiritual sanctimoniousness in its spokesmen. The power to represent it is not the share of any one family, nor does it pass from father to son. Knowledge and mastery of the law supply the sanctity, and these can be attained by everybody. In Jewish life, spiritual and intellectual ability ultimately took the place of the former priesthood which, even in early times, was limited in its function primarily to the sacrificial cult. Even in early days, Judaism recognized the will of the people as a great force, and because of this recognition a great religious activity came into being. But this activity, in turn, was translated into a living force by the teachers of the people through the use of original ordinances and through interpretation of the Scriptures. At times these actions of the sages lightened the amount of observance; at times they increased it. That the results of the studies and research of the teachers found acceptance among the people proves, on the one hand, that the teachers knew the character of their time, and, on the other hand, that the people had confidence in them and that they considered them true representatives of their faith.

Should Jewish theologians and scholars of our time succeed in acquiring such a confidence, then they will attain influence with the introduction of whatever changes may be necessary. The will of the community of Israel will then find its representatives, and knowledge will be its proper exercise.

The scholars thus have an important duty in order to make their work effective. It is to guard the sense of piety of the people and to raise their spirit to the height of the great ideas. For this they need the confidence of the people. Opposition to the views of the people, such as some reformers display, is unholy and fruitless. The teacher thereby loses the power to make the essence of faith effective, for in place of that confidence which is the basis of correct relations between teacher and community there comes mistrust and an unwillingness to follow. The truths of faith must be brought nearer to the people so that they may learn to understand the divine content within them and thus come to understand the spiritual nature and inner worth of the forms which embody these truths. Once the people are saturated with an awareness of the essential truths and the forms which embody them, a firm ground will have been established for adhering to Jewish practices. And if the people then cease to practice some unimportant customs and forms of observances it will not be a matter of great concern. And it will not, as recent changes have, lead some Jews into shock and hopelessness. They will no longer see all such changes as leading to the disappearance of our faith and language, as their pusillanimity leads them to believe, the end of the existence of Judaism.

JEWISH WOMEN CALL FOR A CHANGE (MARCH 1972)

This document presents some of the changes in Conservative Jewish practice sought by a group of women who called themselves Ezrat Nashim.

The Jewish tradition regarding women, once far ahead of other cultures, has now fallen disgracefully behind in failing to come to terms with developments of the past century.

Accepting the age-old concept of role differentiation on the basis of sex, Judaism saw woman's role as that of wife, mother, and home-maker. Her ritual obligations were domestic and familial: *nerot, challah,* and *taharat ha-mish-pachah.* Although the woman was extolled for her domestic achievements, and respected as the foundation of the Jewish family, she was never permitted an active role in the synagogue, court, or house of study. These limitations on the life-patterns open to women, appropriate or even progressive for the rabbinic and medieval periods, are entirely unacceptable to us today.

The social position and self-image of women have changed radically in recent years. It is now universally accepted that women are equal to men in intellectual capacity, leadership ability and spiritual depth. The Conservative movement has tacitly acknowledged this fact by demanding that their female children be educated alongside the males—up to the level of rabbinical school. To educate women and deny them the opportunity to act from this knowledge is an affront to their intelligence, talents and integrity.

As products of Conservative congregations, religious schools, the Ramah Camps, LTF, USY, and the Seminary, we feel this tension acutely. We are deeply committed to Judaism, but cannot find adequate expression for our total needs and concerns in existing women's social and charitable organizations, such as Sisterhood, Hadassah, etc. Furthermore, the single woman—a new reality in Jewish life—is almost totally excluded from the organized Jewish community, which views women solely as daughters, wives, and mothers. The educational institutions of the Conservative movement have helped women recognize

their intellectual, social and spiritual potential. If the movement then denies women opportunities to demonstrate these capacities as adults, it will force them to turn from the synagogue, and to find fulfillment elsewhere.

It is not enough to say that Judaism views women as separate but equal, not enough to point to Judaism's past superiority over other cultures in its treatment of women. We've had enough of apologetics: enough of Bruria, Dvorah, and Esther; enough of *eshet hayil.*

It is time that:

women be granted membership in synagogues

women be counted in the minyan

women be allowed full participation in religious observances—*aliyot, baalot keriah, shelihot zibbur*

women be recognized as witnesses before Jewish law

women be allowed to initiate divorce

women be permitted and encouraged to attend Rabbinical and Cantorial schools, and to perform Rabbinical and Cantorial functions in synagogues

women be encouraged to join decision-making bodies, and to assume professional leadership roles, in synagogues and in the general Jewish community

women be considered as bound to fulfill all *mitzvoth* equally with men.

For three thousand years, one-half the Jewish people have been excluded from full participation in Jewish communal life. We call for an end to the second-class status of women in Jewish life.

EMET V' EMUNAH (1988): THE IDEAL CONSERVATIVE JEW

This document is a doctrinal statement of Conservative Judaism.

Throughout most of its history, Jewish life was an organic unity of home and community, synagogue and law. Since the Emancipation, however, Judaism has been marked by increasing fragmentation. Not only do we find Jewish groups pitted against one another, but the ways in which we apprehend Judaism itself have become separate and distinct. That unified platform upon which a holistic Jewish life was lived has been shattered. Participating in a majority culture whose patterns and rhythms often undermine our own, we are forced to live in two worlds, replacing whole and organic Judaism with fragments: ritual observance or Zionism, philanthropy or group defense; each necessary, none sufficient in itself.

Facing this reality, Conservative Judaism came into being to create a new synthesis in Jewish life. Rather than advocate assimilation, or yearn for the isolation of a new ghetto, Conservative Judaism is a creative force through which modernity and tradition inform and reshape each other.

During the last century and a half, we have built a host of institutions to formulate and express and embody our quest. As important as these are, they in themselves cannot create the new Jewish wholeness that we seek. In spite of the conditions of modern life, we must labor zealously to cultivate wholeness in Jewish personalities.

Three characteristics mark the ideal Conservative Jew. First, he or she is a *willing* Jew, whose life echoes the dictum, "Nothing human or Jewish is alien to me." This willingness involves not only a commitment to observe the mitzvot and to advance Jewish concerns, but to refract all aspects of life through the prism of one's own Jewishness. That person's life pulsates with the rhythms of daily worship and Shabbat and Yom Tov. The moral imperatives of our tradition impel that individual to universal concern and deeds of social justice. The content of that person's professional dealings and communal involvements is shaped by the values of our faith and conditioned by the observance of *kashrut,* of Shabbat and the holidays. That person's home is filled with Jewish books, art, music, and ritual objects. Particularly in view of the increasing instability of the modern family, the Jewish home must be sustained and guided by the ethical insights of our heritage.

The second mark of the ideal Conservative Jew is that he or she is a *learning* Jew. One who cannot read Hebrew is denied the full exaltation of our Jewish worship and literary heritage. One who is ignorant of our classics cannot be affected by their message. One who is not acquainted with contemporary Jewish thought and events will be blind to the challenges and opportunities which lie before us. Jewish learning is a lifelong quest through which we integrate Jewish and general knowledge for the sake of personal enrichment, group creativity and world transformation.

Finally, the ideal Conservative Jew is a *striving* Jew. No matter the level at which one starts, no matter the heights of piety and knowledge one attains, no one can perform all 613 mitzvot or acquire all Jewish knowledge. What is needed is an openness to those observances one has yet to perform and the desire to grapple with those issues and texts one has yet to confront. Complacency is the mother of stagnation and the antithesis of Conservative Judaism.

Given our changing world, finality and certainty are illusory at best, destructive at worst. Rather than claiming to have found a goal at the end of the road, the ideal Conservative Jew is a traveler walking purposefully towards "God's holy mountain."

RABBI S. R. HIRSCH: THE NINETEEN LETTERS: LETTER 18

In this eighteenth letter, Hirsch advises the perplexed university student regarding the proper path to take to discover religious truth.

And what is our present state? Today, two opposing parties confront each other. The one party has inherited uncomprehended Judaism as a mechanical habit, *mitzvoth anashim melumodoh* without its spirit. They bear it in their hands as a sacred relic, as a revered mummy, and fear to awaken its spirit. Some of the others are indeed filled with noble enthusiasm for the welfare of the Jews, but they look upon Judaism as a lifeless framework, as something which should be interred in the grave of a past long since dead and buried. They seek its spirit and find it not, and are in danger, with all their efforts to help the Jew, of severing the last life-nerve of Judaism out of sheer ignorance. And today, when, despite a thousand shades and variations of difference, these two opposing elements are alike in the one great respect, that they are both in the wrong—what shall be done? What is the way to salvation? Does it suffice for the salvation of Judaism to establish our schools upon such a two-fold basis, and to reform our mode of worship? This spirit, the inner harmonious principle of life, is lacking, and that you cannot supply by polishing the outer frame.

There is one way to salvation—atonement must begin where the sin was committed. That one way is to forget the inherited views and prejudices concerning Judaism; to go back to the true sources of Judaism, to the Bible, Talmud and Midrash; to read, study and comprehend them in order to live by them; to draw from them the teachings of Judaism concerning God, the world, mankind and Israel, according to history and precept; to know Judaism out of itself; to learn from its own utterances its wisdom of life. The beginning should be made with the Bible. Its language should first be understood, and then, out of the spirit of the language, the spirit of the speakers therein should be inferred. The Bible should not be studied as an interesting object of philosophical or antiquarian research, or as a basis for theories of taste, or for amusement. It should be studied as the foundation of a new science. Nature should be contemplated with the spirit of David; history should be perceived with the ear of an Isaiah, and then, with the eye thus aroused, with the ear thus opened, the doctrine of God, world, man, Israel and Torah should be drawn from the Bible and should become an idea, or system of ideas, fully comprehended. It is in this spirit that the Talmud should be studied. We should search in the Halachah only for further elucidation and amplification of those ideas we already know from the Bible, and in the Aggadah only for the figuratively disguised manifestation of the same spirit.

This is the path you should pursue, unconcerned as to the opinion which others may hold in reference to your methods of study. You are studying in order to know the light, the truth, the warmth and the sublimity of life, and when you have attained this end you will understand Israel's history and Israel's Law, and that life, in its true sense, is the reflection of that Law, permeated with that spirit. One spirit lives in all, from the construction of the Holy Tongue to the construction of the universe and the plan of life; one spirit, the spirit of the All-One!

Ah, what a task for the disciples of science! But the results of such study must be carried over into life, transplanted by the schools. Schools for Jews! The young saplings of your people should be reared as Jews, trained to become sons and daughters of Judaism, as you have recognized and understood and learned to respect and love it as the law of your life. They should be as familiar with the language of the Bible as they are with the language of the country in which they live. They should be taught to think in both. Their hearts should be taught to feel, their minds to think. The Scriptures should be their book of law for life, and they should be able to understand life through the word of that Law.

Their eye should be open to recognize the world around them as God's world and themselves in God's world as His servants. Their ear should be open to perceive in history the narrative of the education of all men for this service. The wise precepts of the Torah and Talmud should be made clear to them as designed to spiritualize their lives for such sublime service to God. They should be taught to understand, to respect and to love them, in order that they may rejoice in the name of "Jew" despite all which that name implies of scorn and hardship. Together with this type of instruction they should be trained for breadwinning, but they should be taught that breadwinning is only a means for living, but not the purpose of life, and that the value of life is not to be judged according to rank, wealth, or brilliance, but solely in terms of the amount of good and of service to God with which that life is filled. They should be taught not to subordinate the demands of their spiritual mission to those of physical pleasure and comfort, but the reverse. While this training goes on, and until such time as Israel's house will be built up of such sons and daughters, the parents should be implored and entreated not to interfere with the work of the school, not to crush tender shoots of Jewish sentiment in the breasts of their children with a cold unsympathetic attitude. The school should also endeavor to awaken within the hearts of the parents the nobler impulses latent there. If this should prove impossible, at least they should be brought to respect the sentiments which they cannot themselves understand. If an earnest effort were made to attain these ends, things would be different in Israel.

RABBI S. R. HIRSCH: JUDAISM ETERNAL

In this selection, Hirsch offers his opinion regarding the value of studying world history.

It shows us all this in order that, in the midst of a world seeking its salvation in the pursuit of self-interest and power, one people might be introduced which, as the direct creation of a Divine revelation, should adopt an outlook contrary to that of all the other peoples; which without land or material power, should find its existence in God and its strength only in the fulfillment of His Law; which should be a constant reminder of God and of the mission of mankind, and consequently an instrument for the eventual assembling of the peoples in the service of God and the Law of God for the performance of man's function. It goes on to tell us how to this people was to be entrusted the legacy of God to humanity; how it was to be allowed to perish as a state in the conflicts with the Assyrian-Babylonian, Persian-Median, Macedonian-Syrian and Roman monarchies, and with its Divine legacy to humanity to be scattered among the nations as the "Divine seed" in order that its redemption might prefigure the redemption of the whole of humanity. To guide it in its course through the centuries and among the nations it was to be provided with men with the "open eye" who should foretell to it the fate of these great powers in their rise and fall and its own course over their graves, and who should arm it with the Divine promises in order that in its periods of deepest darkness it might march on full of confidence to meet its own dawn and that of the whole of humanity.

The Jewish people is a product of the progressive development of humanity. It has been sent into the midst of the nations to further that development, and for this end the whole course of history has been mapped out before it. Should not then an acquaintance with world history be for its children not only not superfluous but actually indispensable? Can they even dimly comprehend the old prophetic saying about the three different missions of the peoples without some knowledge of the Japhetic-Hellenistic influence on the development of culture up to this day? They will no doubt hear a story about the "sending of Moses," which tries to make of this "Moses" a disciple of Egyptian priests and of the Mosaic legislation a product of Egyptian wisdom. If they are to dismiss this story as the pitiable invention which it is, must they not first see clearly the boundless contrast between the Egyptian wisdom which founded its caste system on the annihilation of the freedom of the individual and the Sinaitic legislation which founded its state on Justice? Will they not find fresh evidence for the Divine origin of the Law given to them by Moses in studying the life and politics of the time in which this Law was given to their ancestors, when through this study they realize how, in contrast to Egyptian tyranny and Syrian depravity, they were given a Law which in its insistence on justice, humanity and morality far surpassed not only all the systems then existing on the earth but all which have since appeared, and which still represents for humanity the ultimate goal of moral progress? Will they not properly understand the prophecies of Isaiah, Jeremiah, Ezekiel, Hosea, Nahum, Obadiah and Habakkuk about Tyre and Babylon, Egypt and Nineveh, etc., and the "Mene Tekel" warning of Jewish men of God to kings feasting on their plunder, only when they have learnt about the history of these peoples, their culture, their battles and wars, etc., from the chronicles of the times? Will they understand the past of their people, its tasks in the present and its hopes, along with those of all mankind, for the future, without some instruction in world history?

In teaching them the languages of the civilized nations and introducing them to their literature we give them the key with which, when they are grown up, they can gain entrance to the intellectual creations of the peoples and feed and enrich their minds with all that is good and noble and true in the contributions of the noblest spirits to the realm of knowledge. In doing this we do not at the same time prepare them for realizing how, since the time when seeds of light from the divine flame on Sinai were sown in the bosom of the peoples, the old night has faded more and more from the earth, how the living thought of God, the conception of the world and of man as sprung from God, the idea of the unity of God and of the human race, of man's task in life to cultivate truth and goodness, justice and morality, of the Divine and eternal significance of every fleeting moment on earth spent in the fulfillment of duty, of the establishment of a kingdom of God on earth to which all men must give their noblest labours—how these seeds of light from the Divine fire on Sinai have won for themselves an ever larger place in the minds of men, and are continuing to work for the improvement and happiness of mankind? Do we not with all this at the same time help them to understand that their fathers did not strive and hope in vain, that their prophets communicated to them no dreams and fairy tales, that the intellectual and moral dawn of which they were the heralds at midnight is already announcing its approach, and that the vision placed thousands of years ago by the Divine spirit in the mouths of Jewish prophets has already been realized by numbers of gifted youths who—consciously and unconsciously—are working for its fulfillment, namely, the redemption of humanity through the obedience of all to the Divine moral law? And is this knowledge of no benefit for giving our youth a Jewish outlook on life?

Reference Works

S. Bayme, *Understanding Jewish History*

J. L. Blau, *Modern Varieties of Judaism*

S. R. Hirsch, *Judaism Eternal*

S. R. Hirsch, *The Nineteen Letters*

J. R. Marcus, *The American Jewish Woman: A Documentary History*

R. Mendes-Flohr and J. Reinharz, *The Jew in the Modern World: A Documentary History*

M. A. Meyer, *Response to Modernity: A History of the Reform Movement in Judaism*

N. Rosenbloom, *Tradition in an Age of Reform*

H. M. Sachar, *The Course of Modern Jewish History*

M. Sklare, *Conservative Judaism*

Chronology

1818	The first Reform Temple is constructed in Hamburg, Germany.
1819	*Wissenschaft des Judentums* (Science of Judaism) is founded in Berlin by Leopold Zunz.
1840	Abraham Geiger formulates the ideology of Reform Judaism.
1851	Rabbi Samson Raphael Hirsch is invited to serve as rabbi in Frankfurt.
1854	Zechariah Frankel, author of *Darkhei HaMishnah*, is appointed the director of the Jewish Theological Seminary in Breslau.
1902	Solomon Schechter is invited to lead the Jewish Theological Seminary in New York City.
1912	Young Israel, a modern Orthodox movement, is founded on the Lower East Side of New York City.
1934	*Judaism as a Civilization*, authored by Rabbi Mordechai Kaplan, is published. This book becomes the foundation for Reconstructionist Judaism.
1964	R. Aharon Kotler, founder of the Beth Medrash Govoha in Lakewood, New Jersey, dies.

1971	Touro College is founded by Dr. Bernard Lander.
1976	Dr. Norman Lamm inaugurated as 3rd President of Yeshiva University
1979	The Conservative Masorti Movement is founded in Israel.
1986	Dr. Ismar Schorsch, professor of modern Jewish history, is appointed to head the Jewish Theological Seminary.

1986	100th Anniversary of Yeshiva University
1987	Rabbi Moshe Feinstein, rosh yeshiva of Mesivta Tiferet Yerushalayim in New York, dies.
1999	Central Conference of Reform Rabbis adopts Statement of Principles for Reform Judaism.
2003	Richard Joel inaugurated as 4th President of Yeshiva University

5

HASIDISM

INTRODUCTION

During the first half of the 17th century, Polish Jewry reached its peak. Approximately 500,000 Jews lived in Poland, enjoying enormous economic success, as they filled an important need for a middle class. Jews found themselves in an excellent political situation, due in great measure to their economic prominence.

Jews also had almost complete political autonomy: they were governed by the Council of the Four Lands, Great Poland, Little Poland, Volhynia, and Lithuania, each of which sent representatives to the Council. Although the Polish government saw the Council as responsible only for the collection of taxes, its range of activities was actually wider. It censored publications, negotiated with the Sejm, the Polish parliament, governed the economic practices of communities, and adjudicated disputes between local communities.

The Jews of Poland reached the highest levels of Torah study as well. Great Talmud scholars who lived there included R. Shalom Schachna (d. 1558), R. Solomon Luria (1510–1574; known as Maharshal), and R. Moshe Isserles (1530–1572). R. Isserles authored the normative code of halakhah for Ashkenazic Jews which he called the *Mappah* ("Tablecloth"). The Jewish world turned to Poland whenever it sought rabbis and spiritual leadership.

TURNING POINT IN POLAND

Everything changed, however, in 1648. The Cossacks, bands of Greek Orthodox fighting men living in a part of Poland called Ukraine, revolted against the Polish nobility. The revolt was led by Bogdan Chmielnicki. Strong support for the Cossacks came from the peasantry of Ukraine. Jews became involved because many were employed as *arendars,* overseers, by absentee Polish landlords. Because they were seen as sharing guilt with Polish nobles, they were made the focus of the peasants' resentment at being squeezed.

Between 1648 and 1658 at least 100,000 Jews were killed in Poland and 700 communities were destroyed. The status of Polish Jewry declined. The nobles became stronger than the kings, who were the protectors of the Jews. There was much anti-Jewish activism among the clergy, which generated an overall rise in anti-Semitism. Economic difficulties led to poverty among Jews. Taxes demanded by the government were high, and bribes had to be offered to nobles and clergymen; Jews, for example, had to pay for the right to appoint their own rabbis.

The internal life of Polish Jews suffered as well. The failure of the false messiah Shabbetai Zevi led to enormous decline in the morale of the Jews. In 1764 the government declared an end to the Council of the Four Lands, thereby taking away a primary source of the strength and unity of the Polish-Jewish community. The level of Torah study went into decline. Mitzvot were observed, but without passion and commitment, without life.

The Ba'al Shem Tov

It is against this background that there appears the founder of Hasidism, Rabbi Yisrael ben Eliezer (1700–1760), known as the Ba'al Shem Tov, or Besht. Born in Podolia, which was then part of Poland, Rabbi Yisrael spent seven years in solitude and meditation in the Carpathian Mountains, a major mountain range which runs through southwestern Russia, the Czech Republic, and Romania. There he became a *ba'al shem,* one who heals through the power of faith, and there he laid the foundations of Hasidism.

The Ba'al Shem Tov spoke of a new form of religious leadership, based on personality and charisma rather than scholarship. This was the doctrine of the zaddik. He taught that there was divinity everywhere and that it was the task of the Hasidim, under the guidance of the zaddik, to release the "divine sparks" hidden within the material world.

God was to be worshipped through joyful prayer, taught the Besht, rather than through study; he emphasized the value of the prayer of the poor and of those who could neither read nor write. All of life should be the service of God with joy. There was no place for sorrow and sadness or for asceticism in religious life.

On Rosh HaShanah in 1747 the Ba'al Shem Tov had a major mystical vision in which he saw his soul ascending heavenward and receiving a Divine message. The message was that once the doctrines of Hasidism became widespread in the Jewish world, the Messiah would arrive. This vision led the Besht to decide to devote his life to achieving this lofty goal.

Students of the Ba'al Shem Tov

The Besht had two distinguished students: R. Dov Baer of Mezhirech (d. 1772) and R. Yaakov Yosef of Polnoye (d. 1782). R. Dov Baer, better known as the Maggid (Preacher), was a great talmudist and a great kabbalist. His most significant achievement was the transformation of Hasidism from a system of ideas and customs into a movement. He began by transferring the center of Hasidism from Podolia to Volhynia, which was closer to central Poland. In so doing, he made Hasidism available to all parts of Poland. In addition, he took his finest students and began preparing them to spread the teachings of Hasidism. These students were then sent as emissaries to all corners of Eastern Europe, including Poland, Lithuania, and Ukraine. Their task was to spread the teachings of Hasidism.

The efforts of the Maggid met with much success. Because of his reputation as an outstanding Talmud scholar, people listened to him. Beyond this, his charismatic personality drew them to his words. The Maggid was the unchallenged leader of Hasidism, the zaddik without any competition.

Another major contribution of the Maggid, although an ironic one, was the decentralization of Hasidic leadership. He established several communities of Hasidim and placed one of his greatest students at the head of each; each of his students would then designate his own greatest student as successor. Among the outstanding

The Baal Shem Tov, the Master of the Holy Name.

students of the Maggid were R. Levi Yitzhak of Berditchev, R. Yehiel Michel of Zlochov, R. Elimelech of Lizensk, and R. Aharon of Karlin.

The second great student of the Besht was R. Yaakov Yosef of Polnoye, who was the rabbinic leader of the city of Sharogrod. He stood in complete opposition to the views of the Besht at first. He felt that Torah study was the central form of serving God and saw value in some degree of asceticism. The Besht, however, saw great potential in R. Yaakov Yosef. He sat and talked and argued with him, and they met for such discussions on several occasions until the Besht finally prevailed. The residents of Sharograd were very displeased with R. Yaakov's "conversion" to Hasidism, however, and dismissed him from his rabbinic position.

R. Yaakov wanted to lead the Hasidim after the Besht, but for various reasons, the Maggid was selected instead. R. Yaakov took a different route, becoming the architect of Hasidic teachings. His book *Toledot Yaakov Yosef,* which appeared in 1780, is the first published work presenting the ideology of Hasidism.

The Zaddik

Eighteenth-century Polish Jewry was experiencing spiritual decline. R. Yaakov blamed its leadership, the rabbis, the scholars, and the teachers. There was now

The town of Berditchev, in Ukraine, was an important center of Hasidism in the last quarter of the 18th century. Let us take a closer look at this community.

No Jewish community existed in Berditchev before 1721. Jews settled there when Berditchev began to develop as a fair town in 1765. According to a census in that year, the Jewish population was 1,220 (out of a total population of 1,541). By 1789 they numbered 1,951 (out of 2,460).

In 1797, Prince Radziwill, the owner of the town, granted seven Jewish cloth merchants a monopoly of the cloth trade, and in the first half of the 19th century, the town's commerce was concentrated in Jewish hands. Jews founded trading companies and banking establishments. Jews also served as agents on the neighboring estates of the nobility.

From 1785 until his death in 1810, R. Levi Yitzhak served as Hasidic zaddik and rabbi in Berditchev. He was one of the students of R. Dov Baer of Mezhirech, became one of his closest disciples, and eventually grew to be one of the most famous personalities of early Hasidism. R. Levi Yitzhak stressed the element of joy in the worship of God and emphasized the principle of devekut ("adhesion, cleaving") to God. His book of sermons, Kedushat Levi, was published during his lifetime.

R. Levi Yitzhak did not found a Hasidic dynasty, but had many pupils and left an indelible mark on Hasidism. He also became a popular hero in Jewish poetry and fiction both in Hebrew and in Yiddish.

a need for a new type of religious-spiritual leader, he said, one who would lead through personality and character and way of life, not through Talmud scholarship. The Besht had spoken of such leaders, calling them zaddikim, but R. Yaakov now committed the idea to writing.

The zaddik had a dual role. On the one hand, he was a source of religious authority and knowledge of God's will; it was he who would bring the Divine earthward. On the other hand, the zaddik would lift the Jews to a higher spiritual level, drawing them closer to God. The Jewish people had to be led in a way that would make them able to release the "divine sparks" hidden in the material world; to do this they needed the leadership of the zaddik. The zaddik was to live a life of paradox: he was to be alone with God, but at the same time he was to guide the wider Jewish community.

Devekut

A second fundamental teaching of Hasidism is *devekut* (cleaving, adhering to God). This concept is a key to understanding what is special in Hasidism. *Devekut*, for the Hasidim, is the purpose of all mitzvot and of all spiritual life. All areas of life present opportunities for *devekut*. *Devekut* is possible for every Jew.

Hasidism says that there are two paths to *devekut*. The first path has man draw closer to God through his own efforts. He fulfills mitzvot, he studies Torah, he engages in prayer, all with intention to achieve *devekut*. The second path has man achieve *devekut* with help from the zaddik. The two paths must be used together, for no matter how much the Jew invests in achieving *devekut*, he needs the zaddik to help him. Moreover, there are Jews who have no opportunity to study and do mitzvot, for they must struggle to earn a living; others have opportunity but cannot achieve a constant state of *devekut*. It is here that the zaddik must become involved.

Opposition to Hasidism

Opposition to Hasidism centered in Vilna, home of the Gaon of Vilna, R. Eliyahu. In 1772 an edict of excommunication was pronounced against the Hasidim living there. Leaders of the Hasidim were banished from Vilna.

The community of Vilna called upon other communities to take similar action. Wherever Hasidism was strong, such calls were ignored. Thus in southern Poland, in Volhynia, in Podolia, and in Ukraine, no action was taken. In Lithuania and White Russia, however, a number of communities followed the lead of Vilna, issuing edicts of excommunication against the Hasidim.

These edicts forbade speaking or associating with Hasidim. They banned any renting of living quarters to them. They obligated Hasidim to leave the community that had declared the edict. They forbade the reading of Hasidic texts.

The synagogue of the Baal Shem Tov.

What was on the minds of the opponents of Hasidism, the Misnagdim? First, they saw the Hasidim as distancing themselves from the wider Jewish community, creating a split community. In addition, Hasidim were neglecting the fixed times of prayer as mandated by the halakhah. Beyond this, they had introduced a new prayer format, called the *Nusach ha-Ari*. They were advocating the study of Kabbalah, Jewish mysticism, and of ethical works in place of Torah study. Finally, the halakhah requires that slaughter knives be both sharp and smooth. Although the halakhah did not insist on this, Hasidim were using knives honed to a razor-sharp edge, refusing to eat meat slaughtered without meeting this special requirement.

The year 1781 brought a second edict in Vilna, in response to the publication of *Toledot Yaakov Yosef.* This time the Gaon of Vilna signed the edict and all the communities of Lithuania endorsed it.

What concerned the Gaon about Hasidism? How could one serve God even with the *yetzer ha-ra,* the evil inclination? This notion was likely to blur the boundary, said the Gaon, between the sacred and the profane, the permitted and the forbidden. He was troubled by their emphasis on the internal dimension of religion, feeling that this was likely to lead to violation of one's practical obligations, to violation of the halakhah.

The Hasidim also opposed the study of Torah with some external motivation— honor, respect from scholars, wealth, and so on; the Gaon felt that such an approach would lead Jews to complete avoidance of Torah study. He was bothered as well by the pantheism in the *Tanya,* authored by R. Shneur Zalman of Lyady (1745–1813); the idea that the "sparks of holiness" can be found anywhere in the material world was objectionable. Finally, the Gaon rejected the doctrine of the zaddik. This was too close to idolatry. Moreover, many of the zaddikim were ignorant Jews, not scholars.

The hostility that characterized relations between Hasidim and Misnagdim was intense. The Vilna Gaon said that Hasidim were not just violaters of the law, they were heretics! This being so, it became permissible to slander them and turn them over to the non-Jewish authorities.

This was in fact done to R. Shneur Zalman. The rulers of Russia were informed that the Hasidim were disloyal to Russia, hated non-Jews and were smuggling money to Turkey to be used to support the Jews of Palestine. R. Shneur Zalman was arrested and brought to St. Petersburg for questioning about these accusations but later released by the authorities.

To be sure, Hasidim and Misnagdim were in conflict, but although the battle of the Gaon of Vilna against Hasidism failed, the positive impact of Hasidism on Lithuanian Jewry, the fortress of the Misnagdim, cannot be understated. Lithuanian Jewry was strengthened and unified by the struggle. The great yeshivot of Lithuania were established at that time, for it was necessary for the Misnagdim, to solidify their own faith, to become more familiar with Jewish traditional belief, before going to battle with the Hasidim.

In addition, the appearance of Hasidism had enormous impact on Jews throughout Eastern Europe, beyond Poland and Lithuania. The Hasidic communities and the Lithuanian yeshivot were united in opposition to Haskalah and to Reform Judaism. Moreover, despite their struggle against one another, Hasidim and Misnagdim shared a commitment to Jewish tradition, the only question being which form of faith and which form of tradition.

Hasidism in the 19th and 20th Centuries

Despite certain basic unities of ideology among the zaddikim at the beginning, the 19th century saw the emergence of differences in approach and emphasis among them and hence among their followers. For example, Rabbi Simcha Bunim (d. 1829) advocated inwardness and was opposed to the external forms of Hasidic practice. He dressed in European clothes and studied European languages. His approach was individualism; he wanted to be alone and not be bothered by his Hasidim, rejecting the zaddik's responsibility to lead. He placed rational, disciplined Talmud study and study of the writings of R. Judah Loeb ben Bezalel (1525–1609), the famous Maharal of Prague, above ecstasy and feeling. Because he felt that no one in his generation could understand the Kabbalah properly, he discouraged its study.

One who developed the approach of R. Simcha Bunim to the fullest was his student R. Menachem Mendel (1787–1859) of Kotzk. The Kotzker Rebbe favored the study of the Bible—Torah, Prophets, Hagiographa—and urged his followers to study Talmud with commentaries. He emphasized intentionality and thought, telling his Hasidim that they must not act without prior thought. He encouraged his followers to distance themselves from others, to set up a separate society for themselves.

One of the great students of both R. Simcha Bunim and R. Menachem Mendel was R. Isaac Meir Alter (1789–1866), who would become the first Gerer Rebbe; the Gerer Hasidim remain a vibrant, active group today in Israel. Like his teachers, R. Alter placed Torah study at the center of Jewish spiritual life. For him, too, Maharal's writings remained central. He instructed his followers to seek religious truth but never to be satisfied with superficial explanation in place of profound interpretation and explanation. They were to strive continuously after self-perfection.

R. Alter rejected, however, the idea of the zaddik's distancing himself from others. He interested himself in the day-to-day problems of his Hasidim and made himself available to all. Jews did not have a pleasant life in Poland and R. Alter was well acquainted with the problems of their lives. He battled to preserve the traditional Jewish way of life, including resistance to the changes in dress mandated by the Polish government. Even when imprisoned by the government, he refused to make concessions.

R. Isaac Meir was also a distinguished talmudist. His work, entitled *Hiddushei ha-Rim,* contained insightful comments on Talmud and the *Shulhan Arukh.* It rapidly became a basic text for yeshiva students.

Another figure who took a different approach to Hasidism, emphasizing different themes, was R. Shneur Zalman of Lyady, mentioned previously. His thinking is given expression in his book *Likkutei Amarim* ("Collected Sayings"), known better as the *Tanya;* this book has become a classic Hasidic work. For R. Shneur Zalman, the Hasid had to engage in regular Torah study and pursue regular spiritual exercise to achieve lasting results. In addition, he had to be exacting in his performance of the mitzvot and he had to work toward worshipping God with joyousness, not melancholy. From this philosophy there emerged the new ethical concept of the *beinoni,* "the average man"; this will be elaborated upon below.

Although R. Simcha Bunim opposed the study of Kabbalah, R. Shneur Zalman favored its study. He believed it was a way to strengthen one's faith in God and to arouse the heart to God's service. In fact R. Shneur Zalman constructed a psychological system based on the principles of the Kabbalah, a system in which he attempted to penetrate the depths of the human soul.

The zaddik, too, played a different role for R. Shneur Zalman. He was seen as a spiritual leader and guide for his Hasidim, but the Hasidim were to find their own path to God. Each individual Hasid was expected to find his way independently. The Hasidic community was not needed to assist him, nor was the zaddik. The zaddik was an exceptional type, whose characteristics were inborn and who directed all spiritual efforts to God, but such individuals are rare. The ideal Jew was the *beinoni.*

The *beinoni* is one who is unable to achieve complete spiritual identity with God, yet in his everyday life, as in his emotions and intellect, he strives toward perfection. Every Jew should attempt to be a *beinoni*—this is an attainable goal. The *beinoni* must resist evil in his life by means of subjecting it to good; doing this requires spiritual powers, but it can be achieved. As he struggles against the *yetzer ha-ra,* the evil impulse, writes R. Shneur Zalman, the recognition that "the brain rules the heart from birth" and persevering in meditation will give strength. Meditation on God's greatness and on love and reverence for Him will elevate man's most primitive feelings to a higher degree of "love and rational reverence." Attention to the requirements of accepted Jewish ethical behavior will give additional support to the aspiring *beinoni.*

The movement of Gerer Hasidim remained vital after the death of R. Isaac Meir in 1866. Succeeding R. Isaac was his grandson, R. Judah Aryeh Leib Alter (1847–1905), who had been orphaned while a child and educated by his grandfather. R. Judah Leib involved himself in public life, dealing with the everyday problems of Polish Jews. He worked very hard to promote Torah study, and many young Jews heard his message in this area.

R. Judah Leib was a distinguished Torah scholar, although humble and modest. His commentary on the Torah, called *Sefat Emet,* is studied today by many Jews. His comments are profound, presented clearly and influenced greatly by the writings of the Maharal of Prague. He also contributed commentaries on sections of the Talmud.

Successor to R. Judah Leib was his son, R. Abraham Mordechai Alter (1866–1948). He brought Gerer Hasidism to its greatest level of influence. He was the most prominent figure in European Orthodox Jewry before the Holocaust and was one of the founders of Agudas Yisrael, an organization that attempted to unite Torah-observant Jews in the pursuit of common goals. R. Abraham Mordechai was especially devoted to young people and their needs, investing much time in establishing schools and youth organizations. During the Holocaust years and after, he was active in rescue work and in the spiritual and material rehabilitation of refugees.

R. Israel Alter (1892–1977) succeeded his father. R. Israel had impact on the Jewish world far beyond his immediate followers. The reputation of Gerer

Lubavich representative use a variety of vehicles to service outlying Jewish communities. The representatives from Minneapolis use a chartered plane for a trip to LaCrosse, Wisconsin.

hasidut and its influence grew under his leadership. Thousands of visitors went to Jerusalem yearly to see him and to receive his blessing.

R. Israel died in 1977 and was succeeded by his brother, R. Simcha Bunim (1898–1992), who would himself be succeeded by his nephew, the current leader of the Gerer Hasidim, R. Pinchas Menachem (b. 1926).

R. Shneur Zalman was succeeded by his son, Dov Baer (1773–1827). He settled in the town of Lubavich, which became the center of Habad *hasidut.* It was R. Dov Baer who gave direction to Habad, defining its principles. He gave particular stress to meditation, *hitbonnenut,* urging his Hasidim to engage in meditation on the greatness of God and on love and reverence for God. This activity, he taught, would elevate the primitive feelings in the sacred soul to higher levels. He also strengthened the intellectual aspect of Habad by presenting the study of Hasidism as not just the means to an end but an end in itself.

R. Dov Baer was succeeded by his son-in-law, Menahem Mendel (1789–1866), who was also a grandson of R. Shneur Zalman. R. Menahem Mendel was a prolific scholar and was acknowledged as one of the greatest Torah scholars of his generation. His collection of responsa, *Zemach Zedek,* is still a highly esteemed halakhic work. The Russian government recognized his leadership of Russian Jewry by conferring upon him the hereditary title of "honored citizen."

A later successor to R. Shneur Zalman was R. Shalom Dov Baer (1866–1920). He, like his predeces-

Rabbi Shneur Zalman of Lyady

sors, was a scholar, but it was his charismatic personality that attracted many to him. His greatest achievement, however, was the founding of the first yeshiva of Habad in 1897. It was called Tomchei Temimim and it paved the way to the development of organized, effective religious education within the Habad movement.

R. Shalom Baer's son, R. Joseph Isaac (1880–1950), succeeded him, assuming leadership after the Revolution of 1917, which brought Communism to Russia, followed quickly by civil war. R. Joseph Isaac sought to rebuild Jewish religious life under the Communist regime, soon becoming the leader of Russian Jewry. Within just a few years, Habad became the center of a strong Jewish spiritual revival. The Communists were not going to tolerate this situation forever, though, and R. Joseph Isaac was forced to leave Russia for Riga (Latvia), where he organized new Habad centers and from where he founded Habad centers worldwide. Later he moved to Poland, organizing a network of Habad yeshivot. When World War II came, he was forced to leave Poland for Brooklyn. There he began again, founding modern Habad organizations, a network of schools and yeshivot, a flourishing publishing house, and numerous welfare organizations.

Rabbi Menachem Mendel Schneerson, 1902—1994

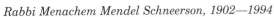

R. Menahem Mendel Schneerson (1902–1994), son-in-law of R. Joseph Isaac, succeeded him; he died in 1994, and there is currently no successor to him. R. Menachem Mendel was a dynamic Hasidic leader. He expanded the institutions of Habad and increased the number of adherents to more than 25,000. He sent his Hasidim to all corners of the world, striving to bring Jews back to Orthodox belief and traditions. He tried to spread the influence of Hasidism beyond the

Rabbi Menahem Mendel (1730–1788) of Vitebsk was a Hasidic leader active in Belarus, Lithuania, and Eretz Yisrael. He was a student of R. Dov Baer, the Maggid of Mezhirech, and was the teacher of R. Shneur Zalman of Lyady, the founder of Habad Hasidism.

Opposition to Hasidism was strong, especially in Vilna. R. Menahem Mendel visited there twice, once accompanied by R. Shneur Zalman, attempting to meet with the leader of the Misnagdim, the Vilna Gaon. The intention was to explain to the Gaon the merits of Hasidism. The Gaon, however, refused to meet with his two distinguished guests.

R. Menahem Mendel headed a synagogue in Minsk, but the opposition of the Misnagdim led him to leave Minsk and to settle in Gorodok. From there he spread the teachings of Hasidism in the provinces of Vitebsk and Mogilev.

In 1777 R. Menahem Mendel moved to Eretz Yisrael, accompanied by a group of 300, not all of whom were Hasidim. As a result of encountering hostility from Misnagdim, he decided to move to Tiberias, in the north of Eretz Yisrael. There he built a Hasidic synagogue. While serving as leader of Hasidim in Eretz Yisrael, he remained the spiritual leader of the Hasidim in Belarus, who corresponded with him; he guided them in their conduct and instructed them in the principles of Hasidism.

A fundamental teaching of Hasidism is devekut (cleaving, adhering to God). R. Menahem Mendel's comments on devekut are interesting.

Devekut requires the individual to concentrate fully, to remove all distractions. The ability to enjoy the pleasures of this world is an indication of the degree of one's capacity to achieve spiritual devekut. Spiritual devekut survives the body and is the means of immortality and eternal pleasure in God.

R. Menahem Mendel's comments on religious faith are notable as well. God has blessed all men with the gift of faith. Some use this gift well, some do not. Does this mean that those who do not have fallen short? No, this is not the case. Comparing individuals in regard to their moral and spiritual standing is wrong. Only God can make a valid judgment of one's religious faith.

Hasidic community, attempting to touch the mainstream of Jewish life.

SUMMARY

The Ba'al Shem Tov reshaped and reinterpreted Jewish tradition as he introduced Hasidism in the 18th century. His students, the Maggid and R. Yaakov Yosef, as well as their students, took the responsibility of disseminating the new teachings, chiefly the leadership of the zaddik and *devekut* as the purpose of all spiritual life, transforming Hasidism into a vibrant movement throughout Poland and Lithuania. Despite tensions with the Misnagdim and opposition to their teachings, Hasidism held firm even during the period of the Holocaust, and it remains alive in America, Israel, and elsewhere in the 21st century.

DOCUMENTS

R. ZEVI ELIMELECH OF DINOV: BNEI YISASCHAR, ADAR 3, DERUSH 2

This is a selection from a classic Hasidic work, the *Bnei Yisaschar,* authored by R. Zevi Elimelech (1783–1841).

The Jew is not permitted to reason on matters of faith. True service of God is to have faith because of tradition. Our Creator said of Abraham: "For I have known him to the end that he may command his children. . . that they may keep the way of God" (Gen. 18:19). I have known him means that I have given him knowledge [of God] from which faith will proceed naturally to his descendants. Similarly, David said to his son Solomon: "Know the God of your father" (1 Chron. 28:9). This alludes to faith based on ancestral tradition. David did not say: "[Know] God through your own personal process of reasoning."

Faith based on ratiocination is called sight, for intellectual conceptions are akin to physical perceptions. Our sages said, "I see the words of Admon." Thus there is faith through sight, so to speak. But faith based on tradition is likened to the sense of hearing with the ears.

R. Yosef Ya'avetz wrote that those who reasoned about matters of faith during the decrees in Spain [i.e., the Expulsion] changed their religion [lit. their honor] on the day of wrath. The women and the "intellectual lightweights" whose faith was based on tradition, however, hallowed the glorious and awesome Name [of God], thereby passing the test of purification. We have explained a reason for this. Those who enter into the divine mysteries know that the Breaking [of the Vessels] is related to the category of eyes. The category of ears, however, is related to the mystery of the perfect restoration. Therefore, faith related to sight can be destroyed and nullified. But faith related to hearing cannot be destroyed or nullified. This is what is meant by "Hear, and your soul shall live" (Isa. 55:3). Understand it.

Furthermore, faith by tradition is an inheritance from Abraham, of whom God said, "For I have known him."

God granted Abraham the power of knowledge. Since faith of this kind derives from the Ein-Sof [kabbalist name for God], it is endless. But faith attained through human reasoning comes from a finite being and therefore can, heaven forbid, be terminated. . . .

Even if you are inclined to think about faith by rationally contemplating good and evil, i.e., [even if] you seek to achieve faith on the basis of evidence obtained but an intellective process and are not content with faith based upon tradition, this too is forbidden. For Abraham's descendants, faith comes as an inheritance from Abraham. . . .

Remember that you must believe absolutely, without doubts and without hidden complaints. Philosophical speculation is a disgrace for the Jew because faith comes naturally to the descendants of Abraham. If you are not content with faith based on tradition and want to engage in philosophical speculation, it is as if you were confessing, heaven forbid, that you are not a link in the genealogical chain of Abraham's descendants.

R. MENACHEM MENDEL OF VITEBSK: PERI HA-ARETZ TO KI TISSA

R. Menechem Mendel (1730–1788), the oldest disciple of R. Dov Baer, the Maggid of Mezhirech, was active in Belarus, Lithuania, and later in Eretz Yisrael. This is a selection from his biblical commentary

Devekut requires that there be no impediment between man and God; only then is *devekut* possible. As in the parable of the Besht, it is impossible to join silver coins together with glue unless some of the coin is scraped away where the attaching takes pace. Only then will they hold well and become as one. If, however, there is rust or some other intervening substance, the pieces cannot be joined together. This indicated the meaning of "If thou seek her as silver, then shalt thou understand the fear of the Lord and find the knowledge of God" (Prov. 2:4). Such must be the *devekut* to God. You must scrape away part of yourself to make sure that there is no rust or other substance capable of creating an obstructive partition. Only then can *devekut* take effect. However, there is no connection when you hold on to something other than the divine. As is known, attachment to the corporeal causes pleasure so strong that the mind is unable to think about anything else; one's thoughts are focused only upon that one thing. This holds true for every form of pleasure, such as the love of money, which takes up all man's thoughts.

The general rule is that [studying] Torah and [performing] mitzvot will all be useless, heaven forbid, if they are done without *devekut*, as mentioned. Man's potential degree of *devekut* may be surmised from his capacity for *devekut* in corporeal matters. People differ from each other in this respect. All depends upon what the individual experiences in this particular *devekut*, i.e., physical pleasure: to that degree is he obligated in the service of Lord and in *devekut* with Him. For all there is to man is intellect, [appropriate] attributes, and *devekut*. All of man's above-mentioned perceptions must therefore be directed toward the Eternal Creator, in order to ensure the immortality [of his soul] after he dies and it separates from the body. If man succeeds in using all these perceptions in *devekut*, God will give him much pleasure. However, if he does not so train his perceptions and pleasures while he is still alive, but allows them to dwell upon ephemeral and transient physical things, when he sheds his material self, and his body perishes and is lost, what blessing will he leave after him? How will he begin the life of delight, using his personal capacities [for spiritual *devekut* and pleasure] if he does not learn the way of the living and eternal God while he is still alive?

R. ELIMELECH OF LIZHENSK: NOAM ELIMELECH, VA-ETCHANAN

This selection is from another popular Hasidic work, the *Noam Elimelech*. R. Elimelech (1717–1787) was another disciple of the Maggid.

We read in the Talmud, "The Holy One decrees, and the zaddik annuls," as it is written, "Thou shalt also decree a thing and it shall be established unto thee" (Job 22:28). Now, how does this verse prove that the zaddik can annul judgments, i.e., harsh decrees which the Holy One ordains? The obvious meaning of the verse is that when the zaddik ordains, the Holy One fulfills the decree. However, we may understand this passage according to what has been said earlier. When the zaddik ordains here below, there is no *din* ("judgment") up above, and thus the decrees vanish themselves.

However, we must endeavor to understand: From where does the zaddik derive the ability to heal the sick through his prayers and to sustain him in the continued life? After all, even the zaddik does not live forever; his life is only contingent. How can a contingent being give life to a per-

son? The blessed Lord, who exists and lives forever and whose life is absolute, can bestow life upon a man who is merely a contingent being. But this cannot be done by man whose own life is contingent.

The answer is that the zaddik attaches (*medabbek*, from *devekut*) himself to God, and his life is thus connected to the eternal and absolute life of God. The life of the zaddik, too, thus becomes absolute and eternal because of this intimate attachment, like organs of the same body.

In this manner does the zaddik have the power to bring life to the sick.

However, one might ask: If so, should not the zaddik live forever? That is impossibile, because the zaddik is not always in *devekut*. Sometimes he is interrupted from his *devekut*, because that is the nature of the world; complete *devekut* can be approached but not fully maintained (lit. "reached and not reached"). The zaddik must always move up from level to level, and in his desire to rise to the very highest level he must sometimes regress and descend to a somewhat lower level, and then rise to the highest one. When the time comes for the zaddik to go the way of all the earth, to the "world of truth," and he is interrupted in his *devekut*, he then passes away and is gathered unto his people.

Indeed, this is the will and desire of God, that all of us be in *devekut* with Him. That is what the commandments "I am the Lord thy God" and "There shall be no other gods" are all about. "I am" is the positive precept, and "There shall not be the negative percept," concerning Godliness, and both are matters of *devekut*. Thus God Himself spoke to us, saying that we shall be in *devekut* with Him, with eternal life.

R. YAAKOV YOSEF OF POLNOYE: TOLEDOT YAAKOV YOSEF TO VA-YISHLACH

This section comes from the first Hasidic book published, a classic and fully reliable source for the teachings of the Ba'al Shem Tov. R. Yaakov Yosef (d. ca. 1782) was himself a disciple of the Besht.

There are two methods in the great principle of serving the Lord. One is to cleanse your thoughts first and then perform the mitzvah, whether of deeds or words, so that it will be pure and lucid, without any ulterior motive.

That is the mystery of [the verse] "And Isaac went out to meditate in the field at the eventide" (Gen. 24:63). Eventide refers to alien and evil thoughts, of which Isaac would carefully rid himself before he began to pray. By so doing he made sure that his prayer would be as clear as the very heavens, as bright as day.

But there is another way, deeper than the first. . . . I heard from my master [the Besht] that we should begin studying Torah, praying, or performing a mitzvah in association with the evil urge, and not for their own sake. In this way, we prevent the *yetzer ha-ra* from attacking us, so that we will be able to complete [our session of studying Torah, praying, or doing mitzvot] for its own sake.

The conclusion is to first try to deceive the evil urge by cooperating with it, and then, showing ourselves to be mighty as lions, to perform the Lord's service for its own sake.

Admittedly there is danger involved [in this approach]. You may be captivated by the *yetzer ha-ra* while associated with it, and then there is no telling who will emerge victorious. Perhaps you will no longer be able to separate from it afterwards.

Nevertheless, remember that if you are careful you may succeed, and pray to God to help you in the struggle against the evil urge. This way may well turn out to be better than the first one mentioned above.

HASID OF INWARDNESS: R. SIMCHA BUNIM

R. Simcha Bunim (1762–1827) was a student of R. Yaakov Yitzchak, the Seer of Lublin. Reluctant to become a Hasidic rebbe, he was convinced by his students to do so. These are some tales about him told by his students.

How to Serve God: Four Tales

Repetition

Rabbi Bunem once said to Rabbi Mendel, his disciple: "What do I need so many Hasidim like these for? A few who really are Hasidim would be enough for me."

"Why did the former zaddikim not do the same?" answered Rabbi Mendel. Long afterward, when his master had been dead for many years and he himself was the rebbe of Kotsk [Kock], Rabbi Mendel once said to his disciple, Rabbi Hirsh of Tomaszow: "What do I need so many Hasidim like these for? A few who are really Hasidim would be enough for me."

"Why did the former zaddikim not do the same?" answered Rabbi Hirsh.

By Night

Two hours every night, as he lay in bed, Rabbi Bunem would listen to this disciple Mendel, later the rabbi of Kotsk, while he read to him out of the *Book of Splendor* [Zohar]. Sometimes, Rabbi Bunem fell asleep for a little while, and the reading was interrupted. When he awoke, he himself resumed it.

But once when he woke, he said to his disciple: "Mendel, I have been thinking it over: Why should I go on living as I do? People keep coming to me and prevent me from serving God. I want to give up my service as a rabbi; I want to devote myself to the service of God." He

repeated this again and again. His disciple listened and said nothing.

Finally, Rabbi Bunem dozed again. After a few breaths, he sat up and said: "Mendel, no rabbi has been permitted to do so, I am not permitted to do it either."

The Order That Was Rescinded

The Russian government gave orders that the Hasidim were no longer to be allowed to visit the zaddikim. Temerl, a noble lady who had provided for Rabbi Bunem in his youth and in whose service he used to sail down the Vistula to take lumber to Danzig [Gdansk], spoke to the governor of Warsaw and succeeded in having the order rescinded.

When Rabbi Bunem was told about it, he said: "Her intentions were good. But it would have been better had she induced the government to build a wall about every zaddik's house, and surround it with Cossacks to allow no one to enter. Then they would let us live on bread and water and do our job."

In a Brothel

A lumber merchant once asked Rabbi Bunem to take his son, who was to attend to some business for him, to Danzig, and begged him to keep an eye on the youth.

One evening, Rabbit Bunem could not find him at the inn. He left immediately and walked along the street until he came to a house where he heard someone playing the piano and singing. He went in. When he entered, the song had just come to an end, and he saw the lumber merchant's son leave the room. "Sing your best selection," he said to the girl who had been singing, and gave her a gulden. She sang, the door to the room opened, and the youth returned.

Rabbi Bunem went up to him and said in a casual tone, "Oh, so there you are. They have been asking for you. How about coming right back with me?" When they reached the inn, Rabbi Bunem played cards with the youth for a while and then they went to bed. The next evening, he went to the theater with him. But when they returned, Rabbi Bunem began to recite psalms and spoke with great force until he had extricated the youth completely from the power of materiality, and brought him to the point of perfect turning.

Years later, the zaddik once told his friends: "That time in the brothel, I learned that the Divine Presence can descend anywhere and if, in a certain place, there is only a single being who receives it, that being receives all of its blessings."

THE BRODY HEREM, (1772)

Objections of the Misnagdim, opponents of Hasidism, are recorded in this document. They claim that the Hasidim seek to separate themselves from the community, create new laws, and throw off the yoke of the Torah.

a. Listen, O Holy Congregation...

Whereas it is proclaimed throughout the camp of the Hebrews that because of our sins there have arisen in our midst new groups and sects who separate themselves from the community, make new customs, institute new evil laws, throw off the yoke of Torah and prefer a dissolute life. . . .

These people. . . . build altars for themselves so that they may be set apart from the Holy Congregation. They maintain separate quorums [minyans] for prayer and do not pray. . . . in the regularly appointed synagogues or houses of study. They have changed the order of prayer. . . . and do not recite the *Sh'ma* or the *Amidah* at the prescribed time. They recite a version of the prayers which is different from that established. . . . in these parts by our ancient Gaonim. . . . They have cast off the heavenly yoke and have taken leave of Eternal Life; they spend their days in singing. . . . They scorn the Oral Law and study only the Kabbalah. . . . They use the Siddur of the Ari, that holy man of God, which they no doubt corrupt! Add to this that they use knives for slaughtering which have been sharpened by firing, a practice for which there is no support in all the Talmud or in any of the interpretations of the Law. . . .

When in the past there appeared such evil-doers in our midst, the wise men of the time and the Parnassim and the leaders of the Four Lands pursued them and made public their shame until we were rid of them. But in our time that is no longer possible and there is no one to stand up against evil-doers. . . . How long will they remain a stumbling block for the House of Israel? . . . How long can we tolerate this wicked group which conjures up . . . new customs? . . .

Therefore do we declare the great and awful ban . . . with all the curses and maledictions of the Torah . . . the excommunication of Joshua ben Nun. . . . From this day on all the synagogues and Minyanim in our communities. . . . are forbidden to introduce any change in the order of the prayers; likewise are they prohibited from using the prayerbook of the Ari or of any other kabbalist. . . . We also do decree that on pain of excommunication no one may wear white clothes on the Sabbath and holidays, with the exception of those few men who are known to us as learned and steeped in the Talmud and the legal literature, men who fear God and who are occupied with Torah and mitzvot. . . . Whosoever shall go about in white clothes. . . . shall be made to stand in the middle of the street and he will be held up in mockery and ridicule as an example to others. . . . And as for slaughtering knives which are sharpened by firing and not by hand . . . we warn you that you are forbidden to eat meat slaughtered by these knives . . . for such slaughtering borders on heresy and it is not kosher. . . .

Should a visitor come to our city and refuse to eat meat slaughtered by the shohetim of this community, or if he should practice a new custom to pray from the Siddur of the Ari, his host must inform the parnas to drive that man out of the city. . . .

We do this for the glory of the Blessed God and His Holy Torah so that neither He not His Torah are desecrated.

R. SHNEUR ZALMAN OF LYADY: TANYA, CHAPTER 3

R. Shneur Zalman (1745–1813) was a disciple of the Maggid and the founder of Habad Hasidism. This selection is from his *Tanya*, as is the next selection.

The intellect, which is [located] in the intellectual soul and which comprehends everything, is called "Wisdom" (Hokhmah), "the power of everything." "Understanding" (Binah) is the actualizing of this potential through intellectual reflection upon a certain concept in order to understand it thoroughly and in depth. These two [Wisdom and Understanding] are the "father" and "mother" from which love and fear of God are born. Fear of God is born of the intellect's deep reflection upon God's greatness: how He fills all worlds and encompasses all worlds and the fact that everything is as naught before Him. Through this "exhalted fear" (yirat ha-romemut) fear is awakened in man's mind and thought. Man fears and is humbled by God's infinite greatness.

This fear will in turn inflame man's heart with "strong love," as with flashes of fire, passionately, yearningly, and longing for the greatness of the blessed Ein-Sof. This is the "yearning of the soul," as it is written: "My soul yearneth yea, even pineth, for the courts of the Lord" (Ps. 84:3); "My soul thirsteth for God" (ibid. 63:2). This "thirst" derives from the element of fire which is in the divine soul, as the natural philosophers have stated. It is similarly stated in *Etz Hayyim* [by R. Hayyim Vital] that the element of fire is in the heart, and the source of water and moisture is the mind; so is it stated in *Etz Hayyim*, gate 50, that [water] is associated with Wisdom (Hokhmah), which is therefore called "the water of the divine soul." The rest of the attributes (middot) are all derived from the love and fear and their derivations. . . .

Da'at (knowledge) [the third sefirah] is derived from "And Adam knew" (yada) Eve (Gen. 4:1) and implies attachment and union. One binds his intellect, through very strong and mighty bonds, with the greatness of the Ein-Sof. Otherwise, not true fear and love result, but rather false imaginations. Hence, knowledge is the [source of] the existence and sustenance of the moral attributes and [the sefirah of Tiferet] includes Hesed [the sefirah of Love] and Gevurah, which is to say love and its derivatives, and fear and its derivatives.

Therefore, even the most worthless and the transgressors of Israel, in the majority of cases, sacrifice their lives for the sanctity of God's unity, even if they are boors and ignoramuses and do not know God's greatness. For whatever little knowledge they do possess, they do not reflect upon it at all, and so they sacrifice their lives not because of knowledge or contemplation. It is [to them] as if it were simply impossible to deny God's unity under any circumstance. This is because the one God illuminates and animates the entire soul, through being clothed under the aspect of Wisdom (*hokhmah*), which is beyond any graspable knowledge or intelligence.

Reference Works

L. Dawidowicz, *The Golden Tradition*

N. Lamm, *The Religious Thought of Hasidism*

A. Nadler, *The Faith of the Mitnagdim*

E. J. Shochet, *The Hasidic Movement and the Gaon of Vilna*

Chronology

1736	Israel ben Eliezer (1700–1760), later known as the Ba'al Shem Tov, begins the founding of Hasidism.
1740	The Ba'al Shem Tov establishes himself in Medzhibezh, Podolia, and he will remain there until his death.
1760	R. Dov Baer (1710–1772) of Mezhirech succeeds the Besht. He is called the Maggid (Preacher) of Mezhirech.
1772	The Vilna Gaon issues a ban on Hasidism; the ban is repeated in 1781.
1780	Rabbi Yaakov Yoseph of Polnoye (d. 1782) publishes the first Hasidic work, *Toledot Yaakov Yoseph* ("History of Jacob Joseph").
1796	R. Shneur Zalman of Lyady (1745–1813), founder of Habad Hasidism, publishes *Tanya*, a systematic presentation of Habad Hasidism.
1815	R. Shalom Rokeach (1779–1855), rabbi in Belz, is recognized as a zaddik; he has thousands of followers, and Belz becomes a center of Hasidism in Galicia.
1927	R. Joseph Isaac Shneersonn (1880–1950), the Lubavitch Rebbe, obtains permission to leave the Soviet Union.
1940	R. Abraham Isaac Alter (1866–1948), the Gerer Rebbe, goes to Palestine.
1950	R. Menachem Mendel Schneerson (1902–1994) becomes head of Habad movement in United States.
1957	The Belzer Rebbe, R. Aaron, dies. Succeeded by a nephew, R. Issachar Dov (1948–). R. Issachar Dov establishes a Hasidic center in Jerusalem.
1972	The Talner Rebbe, R. Meshulam Zusya Twersky, a descendant of R. Menachem Nachum of Chernobyl (1730–1787), dies in Boston. He is succeeded by his son, R. Yitzchak Twersky (1930–1997), who served at the same time as Professor of Near Eastern Languages and Literatures at Harvard University.
1977	The Gerer Rebbe, R. Isarel Alter, dies. Succeeded by R. Bunim, who dies in 1992. Current Rebbe is R. Pinchas Menachem.
1979	Satmar Rebbe, R. Yoel Teitelbaum (1887–1979), dies. Succeeded by son, R. Moses. Approximately 50,000 Satmar Hasidim live in Brooklyn's Williamburg neighborhood.
1994	R. Menachem Mendel Schneersohn, the Lubavitcher Rebbe, dies. As of 2004, no successor has been named.
2000	R. Schlomo Halberstam (1907–2000), the Bobover Rebbe, dies. Succeeded by son, R. Naftali, as Rebbe.

6

HOLOCAUST

THE WEIMAR REPUBLIC

Germany was defeated in World War I. German Emperor Wilhelm II fled to Holland, leaving Germany to rebuild. The decision was made to declare a republic at Weimar, and the proclamation was made on November 9, 1918. German leaders thought that the Allies would be more receptive to a republic and would offer better terms to a government more like their own. Friedrich Ebert and Philipp Scheidemann, socialists, were designated to run the new Weimar Republic.

The new government was not entirely new, though. It introduced no new reforms to Germany, whether in politics, in society, or in economics. Moreover, important positions in the judiciary, the military, and the financial community continued to be held by the same people. Aristocrats, who supported the army, lost no privileges.

The new Weimar Republic was plagued with violence. Many former army officers, aristocrats from the upper class, remained unsympathetic to the principles of democratic government. They chose to join armed groups, the *Freikorps* (free corps), that roamed through Germany, murdering, looting, seeking out enemies, those they saw as responsible for taking away their privileged lives.

The reparations requirements imposed on Germany were outrageous. The Allies were demanding $33 billion. Walther Rathenau, the foreign minister, a wealthy Jew who had been successful in organizing the supply of scarce war materials during the war, hoped they would reduce this demand when they realized such a sum could not be paid. Rathenau was murdered, however, on June 24, 1922, before this issue was resolved. He was faulted by the right-wing extremists for signing a treaty with the Communists, the Soviets.

Massive inflation came to Germany in 1923. In January 1923 the dollar was worth 1,200 German marks, but later in the same year it was worth 4.2 billion marks. Inflation was brought under control, how-ever, by a moderate Center-Right coalition led by Gustav Stresemann, so that between 1924 and 1929, the economy was righted.

Defeat in war, violence, unemployment, reparations demands, and inflation all set the stage for a new politics, for the Nazi Party. Germans desperately wanted strong leadership to help them bring an end to the crisis.

HITLER'S RISE TO POWER

The German Workers' Party was founded in January 1919, after the war. It was anti-Christian, racist, and violently anti-Semitic. Its chosen symbol was the swastika. The party called Jews the "mortal foe of the German people."

Adolf Hitler, as a young man, was greatly influenced by the German nationalist and racist thinking in Austria and Germany of the early 20th century. At the same time he was opposed to any arguments for democracy and for equality suggested by the Social Democrats. In 1919 he joined the German Workers' Party, which soon changed its name to National Socialist German Workers' Party, or Nazi Party.

In early 1920 he and Anton Drexler, founder of the party, wrote a 25-point party program. This program demanded the abrogation of the Versailles Treaty and the restoration of the German colonies. The state should stand supreme, it said, and individuals should subject their own needs to the common good. Working-class Marxist movements were opposed, as well as large retail stores. Foreigners and foreign influences—that is, the Jews—were the major source of Germany's problems.

Between 1920 and 1923 the Nazi Party grew and its ideology developed further; during these years it was confined to Bavaria. Hitler became the leader, although his leadership was challenged by some. Among those who joined were Major Ernst Rohm, who became the leader of the brown-clad Storm Troops, the SA; Hermann Goering, an intellectual and a fighter pilot, who could not make his peace with the defeat of the Germans in World War I; Dr. Josef Goebbels, a journalist, who felt the world did not appreciate his talents; and Heinrich Himmler, a farmer who rebelled against his strict middle-class Catholic upbringing.

As the Nazi Party grew, claiming a membership of 4,500 and growing support among the extreme right-wing circles of Bavaria, Hitler decided to imitate Mussolini's successful efforts to take power in Italy. The local government in Munich was to be removed from power and then the Nazis would march to Berlin.

The seizure of power, "scheduled" for November 8, 1923, came to be known later as the "Beer Hall Putsch." Hitler, Goering, and some 60 SA men appeared in a large beer hall in Munich and threatened the 3,000 present there. They arrested Otto von Lossow, the commander of the local garrison. Those present were "persuaded" to sign a document handing over power to Hitler. Next morning, however, Lossow repudiated his signature, and his troops fired upon the Nazis, who had marched through Munich to take over the government buildings. Eighteen Nazis were killed, although Hitler managed to escape.

Shortly afterward, however, Hitler was arrested and brought to trial. He was sentenced to five years in prison but was released by Christmas 1924. While in prison, he wrote the manifesto of the Nazi Party, *Mein Kampf* ("My Struggle").

The "star" of *Mein Kampf* is certainly the Jew. The Jew is the incarnation of evil, the Satan of the 20th century, wrote Hitler. The Jew is responsible for Bolshevism; Jews are anti-democracy. The Jews are responsible for the defeat of Germany in World War I and for the deaths of 30 million in the Bolshevik Revolution.

The Jews are determined to destroy the Aryan race, he continued, by destroying its racial foundation, by defiling Aryan blood; thus they seek to seduce Aryan virgins to achieve this purpose. The Jew is a parasite with no roots in Aryan soil, a foreigner in Germany. Although the most difficult struggle against the Jew is in Germany, he is involved in an international conspiracy to seize world power—Zionism.

The Jews rule the press and the economic life of Europe. The Jew is the enemy of all that is good: he undermines the political foundations of states, he defiles their culture, and he mocks all religion and morality. Hitler saw himself as the redeemer, and the battle against the Jews as his "holy war."

The Jew, then, was central in Nazi thinking. He was in no way ancillary. Still, there was a long way to go from the ideas of *Mein Kampf* to mass murder.

The years that followed the publication of *Mein Kampf* were disappointing ones for the Nazis. Germany was recovering from World War I. Its economy was being rebuilt and Germany was enjoying prosperity again. The 1928 election brought the Nazis just 12 of 489 seats in Germany's Reichstag.

In 1929, however, the New York Stock Exchange collapsed, provoking a worldwide economic crisis. Millions were suddenly unemployed everywhere. Germans wanted strong leadership to help them bring an end to the crisis.

The years from 1929 to 1933 brought political crisis after political crisis. The Germans were deeply divided over the question of maintaining the republic or ending it. The Social Democrats and Catholic Centrists favored the republic but could not attain a parliamentary majority; the Nazis, the Communists, and the Nationalists opposed a republic, but they too could not secure a majority. Repeated elections were held, with no progress, although in 1930 the Nazis won 107 seats and in 1932 they won 196. The Nazis were drawing on the discontent of the middle and lower-middle classes. There were 7 million unemployed in Germany. Nazi vote totals were very similar to unemployment figures, both peaking in 1932 at over 6 million.

German President Paul von Hindenburg, 85 years old, deaf, partly blind, and senile, sought a government that he could control. Article 48 of the Weimar Constitution permitted him to appoint a chancellor

Members of the German general staff and Adolf Hitler.

who would rule by decrees issued in his name. This being so, he decided to appoint a government including three Nazis: Wilhelm Frick, Hermann Goering, and Adolf Hitler. Hitler, Hindenburg's advisers said, could be controlled in such a government, for he would have to yield to the conservative majority. Hitler became Chancellor in January 1933.

To be sure, Hitler was now Chancellor of Germany but he wanted a majority of seats in the Reichstag. He convinced Hindenburg to dissolve the parliament, the Reichstag, and new elections were called for March 5, 1933. Hitler then went to work on his opposition, the Socialists and the Communists.

On February 27, 1933, the Reichstag burned down. The Nazis accused a Dutch anarchist, Marinus van der Lubbe, of heading a Communist plot to set the fire. They used the fire as an excuse for arresting Communist leaders and Reichstag members.

The day after the Reichstag fire, February 28, a number of emergency decrees were announced, for the purpose of preventing "Communist acts of violence which are endangering the State." The decrees eliminated fundamental freedoms—freedom of speech, freedom of the press, freedom of assembly, and freedom from search without a warrant. They also declared that there would be severe punishment for treason, for arson, and for railroad sabotage. These decrees were accompanied by a propaganda storm about an imminent Communist revolution.

The proportion of seats held by the Nazis increased in the March election, but only to 44 percent. The Nazis were compelled to form a coalition with the Deutschnationale Volkspartei, or Nationalists.

The Nazis now turned to terror in an attempt to pass an Enabling Act. Under its provisions, the government would have the power to enact any law during a four-year period, even a law that did not conform to the German constitution, without consulting the Reichstag. On March 26, 1933, such a law was passed, providing Hitler with legal authority for dictatorship.

BOYCOTT

The first step taken against the Jews was the boycott of April 1, 1933. But before we examine this action, a few words of introduction are necessary. The enthusiasm of the ordinary Germans for anti-Jewish

activity was not great. Hitler had promised the electorate of Germany three things: first, he would bring an end to the economic and political problems that Germany was experiencing; second, Germany would enjoy national rejuvenation; and third, a solution would be offered for the problem of the Jews. The German people voted for Hitler because they saw the need for new approaches to economic and political problems and for the national rejuvenation that would result from these. The views of the Nazis on the Jewish problem were not of primary concern to them.

The anti-Jewish activity of the Nazis was fueled by their mythology about Jews. The Jews were dirty and were Bolsheviks, were easily identified, and were participants in an international Jewish conspiracy. The reality was entirely different, however, for the German Jew was assimilated and difficult to identify, with no involvement whatsoever in an international Jewish conspiracy. He saw himself as a German first and foremost. This conflict between the Jew of Nazi propaganda and the Jew of experience stood in the way of the Nazis' implementing any anti-Jewish actions.

This being said, let us consider the boycott, which was the first official anti-Jewish act carried out after the Nazis took power. The Nazis had not planned a large-scale anti-Jewish program to be carried out as

Anti-Jewish poster issued by the Minister of Propaganda, Berlin, in 1940, with the slogan "Behind the enemy, the Jew" and in French from 1942, with the slogan "And behind the Jew."

soon as they were in control. On the contrary, a 1932 Nazi Party document stated:

> Should the NSDAP [the Nazi Party] receive an absolute majority, Jews will be deprived of their rights by legal process. If, however, the NSDAP receives power only through a coalition, the rights of German Jews will be undermined through administrative means.

Hitler desired to act "legally" and systematically. He was concerned that only two of his ministers, Frick and Goering, were Nazis. In addition, he feared the reaction of the world, fearing that any "illegal" actions might end up weakening the German economy.

The Storm Troopers, or SA, the party militia of the Nazis, wanted to take more extreme action and actually began to do so without Hitler's approval. The boycott would serve, then, to channel the drive of the SA into more acceptable, less destructive forms.

At the end of March 1933 Hitler decided to impose an economic boycott on all Jews. A committee of 14 members was constituted, chaired by Julius Streicher, editor of the rabidly anti-Jewish daily *Der Sturmer,* and perhaps the most extreme anti-Semite in the Nazi Party. The committee set the boycott for April 1, 1933. It would continue until the Jews were removed from the German economy. The world outside was to be told that the boycott was to exert pressure on German Jews and on the foreign press to cease their attacks on the Nazi government.

The boycott was to include artisans and craftsmen; theaters and actors; movie houses and producers of films; doctors, lawyers, and judges; and newspaper sellers. It would not include, however, any Jews from outside Germany living in Germany. The Nazis feared that boycotting this group would provide ammunition for "foreign propagandists." Supervisors of the boycott would be the SA, the private army of the Nazi Party, and the SS (Defense Corps), whose task it was to protect the party leaders.

On March 28 the German public was made aware of the boycott. There was immediate response in the Berlin stock market, as prices fell dramatically. There was also opposition from Hindenburg and others. A rally on March 27 in New York's Madison Square Garden had raised concern among other government leaders about Germany's economy. They were worried about possible actions that might be taken by "international Jewry."

But Hitler could not call off plans for the boycott. There was pressure coming from the SA and the Nazi Party. The whole purpose of the boycott, moreover, was to give the SA a way to express its extremism in a more acceptable fashion. In addition, to cancel the boycott would be to step back from a basic ideological position: anti-Semitism and anti-capitalism.

Despite the hesitations, it was announced just twenty-four hours before the boycott that it would last for only one day. If, however, the Jews of the world did not halt their anti-German activity, the boycott would begin again on Wednesday, April 5.

The boycott began on Saturday, April 1, but in the middle of the afternoon Julius Streicher announced that it would not be renewed on April 5. The boycott failed because it had no public support, and also because the Nazis had not prepared themselves. They did not understand the complexity of Jewish economic involvement in Germany, nor did they understand well how economic acts against the Jews would affect a German economy weakened by the 1929 crash of the stock market.

ANTI-JEWISH LEGISLATION

April 1933 brought another form of anti-Jewish actions: legislation that drew a distinction between Jews and Aryans, those of German or kindred blood. Hitler was convinced absolutely that a solution had to found for the Jewish problem, but the first of the laws were a response to pressure that came, on the one hand, from outside the Nazi Party and, on the other hand, from inside the party. From other countries came insistence that the Nazis act legally and systematically; this insistence on order and system was echoed by Hindenburg. From inside the Nazi Party, the SA, came pressure to act quickly against the Jews; the SA in fact acted before any legislation had been passed.

Four laws were passed in April 1933. The first two, enacted on April 7, came in response to pressure from the SA. One was called Restoration of the Professional Civil Service. It disqualified three groups from civil service: political opponents, those without proper training for civil service, and non-Aryans. The second law was called Regarding Admission to the Bar; non-Aryans were disqualified from service as lawyers and were rejected as applicants for the bar.

Hindenburg insisted on the inclusion of the Hindenburg clause, which exempted anyone who had served in the German army in World War I, or whose father had served. The impact of these laws was tempered somewhat by the inclusion of this clause. In any case, there were few Jews in the upper levels of the civil service affected by the first law; of the 3,000 Jewish lawyers in Germany, many fell under the Hindenburg clause.

On April 22 a law excluded non-Aryan doctors from the national health insurance system. This was a terrible blow to Jewish doctors.

April 25 brought a law regarding overcrowding in German schools. World War I and the economic crisis had prevented the building of schools. This law solved the problem by restricting enrollment, especially the enrollment of Jews. Quotas were set. Wherever the Jewish population was under 5 percent, the quota was 1.5 percent; wherever it exceeded 5 percent, the quota was 5 percent. Here, too, the impact was reduced somewhat by those included in the Hindenburg clause.

Other laws were passed later in 1933. In July a law was passed permitting the cancellation of Reich citizenship of those who had settled in Germany after November 9, 1918. In July a clarification was offered: this law was to be applied first to the 150,000 *Ostjuden* (Jewish immigrants, mostly from Poland) living in Germany. The problem was that only some of the *Ostjuden* had become citizens—even the Nazis could not remove citizenship from one who was not a citizen! In addition, where would the *Ostjuden* go? Poland was unwilling to take them back. This law was useless.

Three more laws were passed in 1933. The first was the Hereditary Farm Law, which forbade a Jew to own land or to be a farmer, so as not to contaminate Aryan soil. The problem was that there were almost no Jewish farmers.

The other two laws were very effective, however, because they placed Jewish cultural life and the newspaper profession under the supervision of Goebbels's propaganda office. The first law required anyone active in films, theater, music, art, or literature to be licensed by Goebbels's propaganda office. The second

required the same for the newspaper profession. These laws put thousands of Jews out of work in their chosen professions.

The extremists and the SA, however, were not satisfied. To be sure, there was immediate removal of Jews from the professions and severe limitations had been placed on the opportunities for Jews to enter the professions, but no action had been taken on what was the central question in their eyes: the racial-biological issue.

More important, the less extreme elements were not satisfied. The major problem was the Hindenburg clause. Less than 50 percent of the Jewish judges were affected by the law on the bar, and only 30 percent of the Jewish lawyers and no more than one quarter of Jewish doctors were affected.

Once again the Nazis were insufficiently prepared.

THE NUREMBERG LAWS

Nineteen thirty-four was a quiet year. The Nazis had apparently decided to allow the Jews an economic base for continued existence. The Aryan clause was declared invalid in the area of business. June 1934 brought the "Night of the Long Knives," a purge of the extreme elements, particularly the SA; even the leader of the SA, Ernst Rohm, was killed.

The Jews read the signs—and drew the wrong conclusions. Whereas approximately 37,000 Jews left Germany in 1933, only 27,000 left in 1934. In the first months of 1935, 10,000 Jews came back to Germany, hoping that the situation of Jews there would improve. Unfortunately they were only dreaming.

In September 1935 the annual convention of the Nazi Party was held in the city of Nuremberg. It was supposed to conclude on Sunday, November 15, with a special ceremonial meeting of the German parliament, the Reichstag. Two days before that meeting, Hitler, much impressed by the enthusiastic crowds who had gathered, ordered Frick, minister of the interior, to prepare a law dealing with Aryan–Jewish relations; this law would be passed on Sunday, November 15.

Hitler wanted marriage between Aryans and Jews to be forbidden. He wanted sexual relations between Aryans and Jews outside of marriage to be forbidden. He also wanted Jews to be forbidden to employ Aryan housekeepers. The law would be called Law

*Racist attitides in Germany developed from the idea
that the Aryan-Nordic race was superior to all other
races. To the Nazis, the Teuton stood for goodness, and
strength. The Aryan myth existed prior to the Nazis,
they turned it into a reality which was readily applied
to society.*

for the Protection of German Blood and German
Honor. Within two days, then, a law addressing the
heart of the Jewish problem was to be prepared.

Late on Saturday night Hitler added another request. A Law of Citizenship in the Reich should be
prepared. His requests were fulfilled and Sunday
brought the announcement of the Nuremberg Laws.

Jews, like Aryans, had the status of citizens of the
state, thus obligating the Reich to protect them. The
new status given the Aryans by the Nuremberg Laws
was citizens of the Reich, which allowed them to
vote, a privilege which Jews did not have. By this
time, however, there was only one party for which
they could vote, the Nazi Party.

As for the Law for the Protection of German Blood
and German Honor, the original law failed to determine who was regarded as a Jew under this new law.
It took another two months to decide who qualified as
a Jew. The one responsible for the formulation of the
Nuremberg Laws, moreover, was Dr. Bernhard
Losener. He was an anti-Nazi and worked to the utmost to reduce the negative impact on Jews.

In sum, then, the Nuremberg Laws affected the
Jews very little. There was no real practical impact on
the Jews of Germany. Again the Nazis had failed to
prepare themselves sufficiently.

EMIGRATION

The various parts of the Nazi bureaucracy were working on different approaches to the solution of the
Jewish problem. Thus, as early as 1934 the leadership
of the SS (Defense Corps) was considering emigration of Jews as a real option. A report prepared in
June 1934 regarding emigration as a policy showed
that the SS had a better grasp of reality. They understood the problems of mass emigration. Palestine was
improbable and impractical. The doors of neighboring countries would not remain open forever. The SS
was prepared to accept the limited existence of a
Jewish community in Germany.

Between 1935 and September 1, 1939, the beginning of World War II, the prime focus of SS policy on
the Jews was emigration. Hitler wanted order, but
immigration was a slow process, with many requirements regarding documentation. Was the potential
immigrant in good health? What was his economic
situation? What was his psychological state?

Other factors entered into the issue of mass emigration as well. The world was in economic crisis.
Countries suffering from high unemployment were unlikely to take in a large number of immigrants. In addition, the Jews of Germany were middle-class
professionals, not the more desirable farmers, artisans,
and factory workers. Moreover, 35 percent of the Jews
of Germany were age 50 and above; this fact made immigration more difficult psychologically and reduced
the chances of successful absorption in a new country.
Perhaps the greatest obstacle was the attachment of
German Jews to Germany. German culture, German
literature, German rabbinic tradition were all part of
more than a thousand years of Jewish life in Germany.

Several thousand Jews benefited, however, from
the Transfer Agreement (*Ha'avarah*) signed in 1933
by the Nazi Ministry of Economic Affairs and representatives of the Jewish Agency. The agreement obligated potential emigrants from Germany to buy
machinery or other finished products in Germany

with German marks and have these items shipped to Palestine, where they would be sold to local builders or industrialists. Upon the immigrants' arrival in Palestine, they would be compensated in the currency of Palestine. Thus Germany benefited by the sale of exports, while Palestine benefited by Jews' being permitted to leave Germany freely and settle in Palestine. Approximately $36 million changed hands, allowing the absorption of many thousands of Jews between 1933 and 1939.

Despite the good fortune of these Jews, the causes noted above led only 21,000 Jews to leave Germany in 1935, 25,000 in 1936, 23,000 in 1937, and 20,000 in 1938. There was a steady decline in emigration, and by 1938 only 25 percent of the 650,000 German Jews had left Germany.

The failure of emigration led Adolf Eichmann, head of the Central Office for Jewish Emigration, to take responsibility for drawing up a more comprehensive plan. This happened in 1937, though, when the nations of the world were closing their doors to immigrants. Palestine was a possibility, but the Nazis decided in the end that they would not contribute to the birth of an independent Jewish state.

SS Colonel Adolf Otto Eichmann was chief of operations in the scheme to exterminate all of European Jewry. At the end of the war, he escaped to Argentina, but in 1960 was captured by Israeli agents. Eichmann was tried before the Jerusalem District Court and was sentenced to death by hanging. Eichmann was the only criminal ever put to death in Israel. His body was cremated and his ashes were scattered over the Mediterranean.

Thus the boycott failed. Anti-Jewish legislation failed, largely because of the Hindenburg clause. Emigration failed because of the factors mentioned above. The Nazis lacked an organized program until 1938.

MORE ANTI-JEWISH ACTIVITY

How did the Jews in Germany respond to what was happening to them between 1933 and 1938? The documents available to us reveal three things about the Jews' response. They saw their major task as helping those affected by anti-Jewish legislation to find work. The Jews—even the Orthodox—saw themselves as rooted in German soil; thus it became desirable to find ways of ensuring an economic basis for their lives in Germany. There was, nevertheless, a readiness to aid those desiring to leave Germany and settle in Palestine. Still, there was no sense of impending tragedy.

The great turning point in the Third Reich came in 1938. By the end of that year, an organized, centrally directed anti-Jewish policy emerged. The main personalities were Goering, Heydrich, and Eichmann. They were realists, who had the full support of Hitler. No one was paying any more attention to the extremists.

During 1938 the legislative attack was renewed. In March the Jewish communities were told they could no longer demand compulsory contributions from members. This meant that the Nazis were not thinking any more about permitting the ongoing existence of Jewish communities in Germany.

Many Jews were arrested. In May 1938 all Jews from the Soviet Union were arrested, as were all the "anti-social elements" and all the "criminals" among the Jews of Germany. These people were sent to concentration camps, although those who were prepared to emigrate would be released.

Progress was made in Aryanization, which meant the transfer of Jewish businesses into the hands of Aryans. There had been some progress in "voluntary" Aryanization, but now preparations were being made for mandatory Aryanization. This required identifying and labeling Jewish businesses as well as defining what was meant by "Jewish business."

The decrees of April 1938 included a requirement that by June 30 every Jew provide an estimate of his

After World War II, Adolf Otto Eichmann (1906–1992) was called "the great transport officer of death." He was born in Solingen, Germany, and when he was eight years old, his family moved to Linz, Austria. Eichmann attended elementary school and high school and later technical school, but he was not much of a student. From 1928 to 1933 he worked as a traveling salesman for the Socony Vacuum Company.

In 1932 Eichmann joined the Nazi Party. He became a member of the SS in 1933 and was sent to one of the German SS camps for military training. He then served as SS corporal in the concentration camp at Dachau, his first encounter with systematic terror and violence. At the end of 1934 he volunteered for the SD, the Nazi Secret Service, and began to work in its Jewish section.

Specializing in the area of intelligence, Eichmann traveled to the Near East, including Palestine. Making himself more and more familiar with Judaism and with Jewish organizations, he also attempted to learn some Yiddish and some Hebrew. His expeditions and his studies combined to make him an expert authority on Zionist organizations and Jewish emigration.

Germany conquered Austria in March 1938 and Eichmann was sent there to work on Jewish emigration. He was determined to force Jews to emigrate and organized their expulsion so well that the procedures of his Center for Jewish Emigration in Vienna were replicated in Prague in 1939. In 1939 Eichmann returned to Berlin as director of the Reich Center for Jewish Emigration.

In 1941 Eichmann became head of the Gestapo's section IVB4, which dealt with Jewish affairs and the expulsion of populations. When the Nazis had decided on the complete physical extermination of the Jewish people as their "final solution," Himmler and Heydrich put Eichmann in charge of every aspect of this process. Until the collapse of the Third Reich, Eichmann remained head of the Department of Jewish Affairs, and he was fervently devoted to carrying out his responsibilities.

After the Wannsee Conference, which he prepared and organized, Eichmann directed the deportations of Central European Jews to the death camps. He made decisions about the pace and timing of deportations and he handled requests for the exemptions of Jews, deciding to grant them or—more commonly—to reject them. He was responsible as well for planning the sterilization of people who were only partly Jews and for deceiving the outside world, hiding the facts about the mass murder of Jews.

After the war Eichmann was taken prisoner, his true identity having been concealed in the postwar confusion, but he managed to escape and settle in Argentina in 1950. Only in May 1960 was he discovered by Israeli agents and flown to Israel to stand trial there.

The trial of Eichmann before the Jerusalem District Court lasted from April to December 1961. Israeli Supreme Court Justice Moshe Landau presided, Israel's attorney general, Gideon Hausner, led the prosecution team, and Robert Servatius, a German lawyer, defended Eichmann. Eichmann was found guilty on all charges. His appeal to the president of Israel was rejected. He was hanged at the Ramleh prison, his body was cremated, and the ashes were scattered over the Mediterranean Sea.

holdings and present a report on property owned. Any German who concealed a Jewish business was threatened with fines and imprisonment. A Jewish business for the Nazis was one that belonged to a non-Aryan as defined by the Law of Citizenship in the Reich.

Additional decrees called for the closing of all Jewish doctors' offices and law offices that had previously been excluded by the Hindenberg clause. Similarly, all Jewish stores and real estate concerns had to be closed or sold by a certain date.

In 1938 Jews were brought under total control of the SS. The first part of this process was to simplify identification of Jews by forbidding them to have Aryan names and requiring them to add "Israel" or "Sarah" where they did not have an acceptable name. In addition, Jews were required to submit their passports to the Nazis. These would be returned with a large letter "J" stamped on them, as suggested by Swiss officials.

The decrees enacted after the Reichstag fire in February 1933 were designed to prevent "Communist acts of violence which are endangering the state." Those suspected of engaging in arson or treason were to be taken into "protective custody." The definition of "protective custody" was now broadened to include "people whose conduct endangered the existence and the security of the *Volk* [native Germans] and the state"—in other words, the Jews.

KRISTALLNACHT ("NIGHT OF BROKEN GLASS")

Jews remember November 9, 1938, as *Kristallnacht* ("Night of Broken Glass"). This was a pogrom

This beautiful Berlin synagogue was completely destroyed during Kristallnacht.

The Nazi death camp of Auschwitz. Thousands of Jews were gassed, shot, and burned to death there.

planned and organized by Goebbels and implemented by the SA; the SS opposed such actions, preferring instead the cold terror of a police state. This action was a last, desperate attempt of the SA extremists to take control of the Reich.

The pretext was the assassination in Paris of a German diplomat, Ernst vom Rath, who was not even a Nazi. He was shot on November 7 by a 17-year-old Polish Jew named Herschel Grynszpan. Grynszpan's parents were Polish Jews in Germany who had never obtained German citizenship and were about to be deprived of their Polish passports by an act of Poland. Germany feared being stuck with thousands of stateless foreign Jews. Therefore the Gestapo (Secret State Police) had taken 50,000 Polish Jews and relocated them close to the Polish border, forcing them to live under the worst conditions. Grynszpan was lodging his own kind of protest.

The pogrom resulted in the burning of nearly every synagogue and many other Jewish institutions. More than 7,000 Jewish businesses were destroyed. Almost 100 Jews were killed and thousands were injured. Thirty thousand were put in concentration camps at Sachenhausen, Buchenwald, and Dachau, but most were freed when emigration could be arranged.

Kristallnacht, however, had discredited the radicals. As a result, Goering was now made responsible for the Jews. On January 24, 1938, he ordered Heydrich to organize the emigration of Jews from Germany in accord with the experience of Eichmann in Austria. Within six months, though, it became clear that emigration would not work either. Some other solution was needed for the "Jewish problem."

INVASION OF POLAND

On September 1, 1939, Germany invaded Poland. Shortly thereafter Russia invaded Poland from the east. The two great powers divided Poland.

The invasion of Poland provided Hitler with an opportunity to carry out his intentions regarding the Jews. The part of Poland now held by Germany was itself divided in two. One part, the *Wartheland,* became part of the Reich, while the second part, the General Government, was to be under German administration. Anyone who was not a pure Aryan was to be evicted from the *Wartheland.* At the same time, close to one-half million Aryans were to be brought from Nazi Germany to establish settlements in what used to be Poland.

Hans Frank headed the German civil administration of the General Government, although at times he found himself in conflict with the SS. To this area were to be brought those Poles and Jews who had been evicted from the *Wartheland.* Educated Poles, priests, and other potential leaders of opposition and resistance were to be killed immediately, while the working class were to engage in hard labor. The Jews were to be concentrated in major centers but separated from the non-Jews.

On September 21, 1939, Heydrich and the heads of the *Einsatzgruppen* ("special-duty groups") met in Berlin. Heydrich introduced the racist policies that he intended to put in place in Poland and then detailed the role to be played by the *Einsatzgruppen* in effecting these policies. An important document, known as a *Schnellbrief* (Telex, similar to a fax), was sent to the heads of the *Einsatzgruppen* and served as a written record of the Berlin meeting.

The *Schnellbrief* spoke of the establishment of ghettos and of the role to be played by the Jewish Councils, the *Judenrats*. Let us consider each of these separately.

GHETTOS

The Nazis began to work with the idea of having ghettos in 1939, as evidenced by the *Schnellbrief*. The first major ghetto was in Lodz, Poland. The plans were approved in February 1940 and the ghetto was sealed on May 1, 1940, with 160,000 Jews inside. The second major ghetto was in Warsaw. By November 1940 almost half a million Jews were locked inside 100 square blocks; that is, 33 percent of Warsaw's population was in 2.5 percent of the city's area. In the cities and towns of Poland and Lithuania, there were many other smaller ghettos.

What was life like for the Jews compelled to live in the ghettos? In general terms, there was terrible overcrowding and lack of proper sanitary facilities. The central problems, however, were starvation and disease.

The policy of the Nazis was to starve the Jews. They supplied less than the amount of food necessary for physical sustenance, and even this was frequently rotten. The Jews became obsessed with hunger, and this affected their spirits and behavior. Jewish organizations outside Poland simply could not raise enough funds to make a dent. One report of the Joint Distribution Committee said that it would take $100,000 per month just to provide one meal per day to those in need in one ghetto. The JDC's entire annual budget in 1939 was about $1.2 million for all operations worldwide.

Connected with starvation was disease. The most widespread disease was typhus. It is estimated that there were between 100,000 and 150,000 cases of typhus in the Warsaw ghetto during the years of the war. In general, hunger lasting months and years fatally weakened masses of Jews. Approximately 600,000 Jews died of "natural" causes in the ghettos.

Another practice that made life in the ghettos extremely difficult was forced labor. At first Jews would be grabbed off the streets to perform tasks demanded by day-to-day life—street cleaning or snow removal, for example. Later the enormous potential of Jews as a work force was drawn upon in a more organized fashion. Fixed tasks were assigned, whether factory work or more difficult, demanding outdoor work like woodcutting in the forest or ditch-digging. Work would be done from dawn to sunset, every day, with no payment. In some places all males ages 14 to 60 had to work; in others, the local Jewish Council would set up a rotation.

How could life be made more bearable, with conditions of disease, hunger, overcrowding, terrible sanitation, forced labor, and possible deportation? One way was to smuggle food into the ghettos, thereby preventing death by starvation of most of the ghetto Jews. Young children played an important role here, for small children were hard to catch. Even when they were caught, the mercies of the Jewish ghetto police or of the Nazis could be drawn upon. Some have argued that food smuggling was a form of unarmed resistance. The goal of the Nazis was to starve the Jews, but the Jews discovered a way to frustrate them in achieving this goal.

The Nazis also attempted to dehumanize the Jews. The Jews responded by cultivating education and culture in the ghettos. The General Government as of September 1941 permitted Jews to run elementary school classes but forbade post-elementary education. Typical of totalitarian societies, the Nazis regarded education and knowledge as subversive.

The Jews defied this policy. Even before the permission given in September 1941, there were numerous elementary schools for the study of Bible and Talmud. There were also elementary-level schools, called *com-*

Jewish partisan group, operating in and near Vilna. Abba Kovner (center), the poet, was an active member of the group.

Abba Kovner (1918–1987), born in Sevastopol, Russia, was a longtime member of the Ha-Shomer Ha-Tsa'ir (Progressive Zionist) youth movement when the war broke out. From 1940 to 1941, he was one of the movement's underground leaders in Vilna, Lithuania. When the Nazis took Vilna in June 1941, he found temporary shelter in a Dominican convent. Upon returning to the newly established Vilna Ghetto, Kovner heard about the massacres of Jews, concluding that the only adequate response was armed resistance. From this point on, he devoted himself to the creation of a Jewish fighting force.

In December 1941, Kovner drafted a manifesto to be distributed to the ghetto population. The manifesto said:

Hitler plans to kill all the Jews of Europe. Lithuanian Jews are the first in line. Let us not go like sheep to the slaughter!

This was the first time that a public document described the situation as part of a Nazi overall plan to exterminate the Jews. One month later, the F.P.O. (United Partisans Organization) was created, with Kovner as one of its leaders. In July 1943, he took command of the organization.

When the Germans began the final liquidation of the Vilna Ghetto in September 1943, Kovner led the resistance and managed to escape with his men into the forests. He fought with the partisans until the end of the war.

After the war, he was one of the architects of the Bericha movement, which tried to get war survivors into British-controlled Palestine. He was also the driving spirit behind the East European Jewish Survivors Associations.

In 1945, Kovner went to Palestine on a mission to request support for the creation of special units, which would carry out revenge in postwar Europe. On his way back to Europe, he was arrested by the British, returned to Palestine, and imprisoned. When released in 1946, he joined Kibbutz Ein Hachoresh and achieved national fame as a poet. He was the founder of the Moreshet ("Heritage") Institute of Holocaust Research in Givat Haviva. He was also the spiritual father of Beit Hatefutsot, the Diaspora Museum in Tel Aviv.

Abba Kovner died on his kibbutz in 1987.

---

plets, for general studies. Complets usually had classes of four to eight students, who met in secret with their teachers. After the permission was granted for elementary schools, clandestine high schools functioned. In addition, professional courses were offered, in pharmacology, technical drawing, and nursing. High-level courses were offered in education and chemistry. In the Warsaw ghetto one could even study medicine.

The Jews turned to music and to the theater as well. There were orchestras in Warsaw, Lodz, Vilna, and Kovno. There were also theaters in Warsaw, Lodz, and Vilna. The Jews saw comedy, revues, and serious drama. There were lending libraries. Warsaw had scores of underground Jewish newspapers in Polish, Yiddish, and Hebrew.

Culture was an enormous booster of morale. It was a declaration of one's humanity. It was a refusal to allow the human spirit to be crushed. It too was a form of resistance.

For children, education meant shelter, physical warmth, sanitary medical attention, food, and emotional support; the atmosphere was a counter to the bleakness of the outside world. It meant as well a strengthening of Jewish unity.

For adults, their children's education was an expression of hope for the defeat of the Nazis, a hope that there would be a future. It was a declaration of humanity and a strengthening of Jewish unity and of Jewish identity. It was, then, a form of resistance.

JUDENRAT

An order from Hans Frank on November 28, 1941, directed every Jewish community in the General Government to establish a Jewish Council, a Judenrat. A community with fewer than 10,000 citizens would be served by a Judenrat of 12, while a community with more than 10,000 would be served by a Judenrat of 24.

At first the Judenrat served merely as an administrative body for the Jewish community, but it slowly became the instrument for the implementation of Nazi policy. It would publish regulations, be held responsible for the fulfillment of Nazi demands, and prepare the lists necessary for forced labor and "resettlement."

Adam Czerniakow, a 62-year-old member of the prewar Jewish community council in Warsaw, was told by the Nazis that he would head the Warsaw Judenrat and he was instructed to set it up. An engineer by profession, he had been an instructor in vocational schools before the war.

Czerniakow met with fellow members of the Jewish citizens' committee and together they began the task of selecting the *Judenrat*. It was agreed that one-third of the *Judenrat* would be members of the prewar community council. The others would be people who had been leaders in the Jewish community. Thus a judge on a commercial court was selected, as were two attorneys. One of the members came from the trade unions, while another was prominent in the Jewish Socialist Party. One was a rabbi and another a physician. Two bankers were selected, as was a leading merchant.

On October 13, 1939, Chaim Mordechai Rumkowski, age 70, a member of the community board before the war, was designated by the Nazis to head the Lodz *Judenrat*. The Nazis instructed him to him to choose a consultative committee, and so he sent letters to 31 well-known members informing them that they had been selected and that they could not refuse to serve.

On November 7 all members were told to appear at the Gestapo offices. There, all but Rumkowski and two others were arrested and sent to a camp near Lodz, where most of them died. On February 5, 1940, Rumkowski announced the formation of a new *Judenrat* of 21 members. Rumkowski's strategy was obedience to the Germans and making the ghetto indispensable to the Nazi war machine. This strategy worked well for a while, as the ghetto was producing clothes and other items needed by the German economy. In 1944, however, the Nazis sent Rumkowski and most of the other ghetto inhabitants to the gas chambers.

Judenrat members confronted major moral dilemmas, some more difficult to resolve than others. The first of these was whether to join. To accept would be to collaborate; to refuse would be to abandon one's own people. Assuming one accepted, should one agree to take a census—it was difficult to ascertain its purpose; perhaps it was to distribute food, but perhaps it was draw up lists for forced labor.

Should one volunteer to organize forced labor? The tasks varied in level of difficulty. Some would certainly die when carrying out a difficult task. In addition, not everyone worked. The wealthy could buy their way out by bribing the Nazis.

Some dilemmas were more clearly life-and-death issues. In a case where the amount of medication is limited, to whom should it be given? To the young? To the wealthy? To everyone? On March 5, 1942, the Nazis banned all Jewish births, the last permitted date being August 15, 1942. How should births be prevented? Should mothers be told to abort and forced to do so if they refuse? At which stage of pregnancy—

Chaim Mordechai Rumkowski, portrayed as head Jewish official in the Lodz ghetto, by H. Szylis, 1940. Jerusalem, Yad Vashem Archives.

Raoul Wallenberg

Some righteous gentiles were involved in rescue efforts during the Holocaust, risking their lives and sometimes giving their lives in the process. Perhaps the best-known of them was Raoul Wallenberg (1912–1947?). Wallenberg was a Swedish diplomat who became a legend through his work to save Hungarian Jewry at the end of World War II.

In July 1944, the Swedish Foreign Ministry, at the request of Jewish organizations, sent him on a rescue mission to Budapest, as an attaché to the Swedish embassy. By then 467,000 Hungarian Jews had already been deported to the death camps. Wallenberg's main responsibility was to distribute Swedish certificates of protection, granted at first to Jews who had some connection with Sweden. He exerted some pressure on the Hungarian government to allow Jews to work with him, so that his department, "Section 3—for Humanitarian Aims," eventually employed 300 Jews.

When the Arrow Cross, the most extreme of the Hungarian Fascist movements, seized power in October 1944, Wallenberg established the "international ghetto." This allowed about 33,000 Jews, 7,000 of whom had Swedish protection, to find refuge in houses displaying the flags of neutral countries.

In November 1944, thousands of Budapest Jews, including women and children, were forced on a "death march" to the Austrian border. Wallenberg and Per Anger, the embassy's secretary, followed after the Jews with a convoy of trucks carrying food and clothing. Wallenberg himself distributed medication to the dying, and food and clothing to the marchers. Somehow he managed to free about 500 and bring them back to Budapest.

In Budapest, Wallenberg organized "International Labor Detachments," and even a "Jewish Guard," consisting of Aryan-looking Jews dressed in S.S. and Arrow Cross uniforms. He established two hospitals and soup kitchens. Adolf Eichmann threatened to kill him, referring to him as Judenhund Wallenberg ("Jewdog Wallenberg").

During the liberation of Hungary, Wallenberg presented himself to Soviet army guards, who were searching the streets of Budapest. He was last seen on January 17, 1945, traveling with a Russian driver to Soviet army headquarters. In 1951–52, it was discovered that Wallenberg was in a forced labor camp. The response of the Soviet Union to inquiries from the Swedish Foreign Ministry was that Wallenberg had died in his cell on July 17, 1947, of a sudden heart attack. The actual circumstances of his final disappearance remain a mystery.

even in the eighth month? If a birth does take place, should the child be killed?

The Nazis gave "life cards" to the *Judenrat* members. Anyone holding one of the cards would be permitted to remain in the ghetto. The others would be "resettled." To whom should the cards be given?

The last dilemma was the most difficult one—to provide a quota of Jews to be sent to the death camps. On July 20, 1942, Adam Czerniakow, head of the Warsaw *Judenrat*, received such an order. It was his responsibility to provide 6,000 Jews per day to be "resettled."

DEATH CAMPS

The first part of the "final solution" to the Jewish problem was the mass murder of the Jews of the East, the Soviet Union, by the *Einsatzgruppen*. The decision to proceed with the mass murder of Jews most likely came in mid-March 1941. By that time it had become clear that the idea of a Jewish reservation in Madagascar, a French colony off the east coast of Africa, was no longer feasible, since a successful campaign against Russia would bring another 5 million Jews into the picture. Moreover, the only neutral power in the West, the United

Jews executed in Lodz, Poland. Courtesy Yad Vashem Archives, Jerusalem.

would bring another 5 million Jews into the picture. Moreover, the only neutral power in the West, the United States, had not protested the Nazi treatment of Jews, nor had the Vatican; no international objection had been made to the intensification of Nazi brutality to Jews. In addition, the invasion of Russia would provide the necessary cover for the mass murder of civilians—eliminating Jews would become a "military necessity."

The *Einsatzgruppen,* numbering 3,000 men, were assigned different areas. By the end of 1942, 1.4 million Jews had been killed. When the "work" was completed in late 1943, 2.4 million Jews had been lost at the hands of the *Einsatzgruppen,* assisted by local henchmen or Ukrainian and Latvian volunteers.

Why could not Western and Central European Jewry be dealt with in similar fashion? It was concluded that mass murder within the sight of local populations might provoke opposition. Moreover, it would be difficult to present mass murder as a "military necessity" in Western and Central Europe. It was decided, then, to set up an apparatus of mass murder in the East, where secrecy could be maintained more easily.

In January 1942, a conference was called by Heydrich, head of the Main Security Office, to comply with Goering's order. This conference was held in Wannsee, a suburb of Berlin. The participants were mid-level officials representing every major division of the German government.

The conference began with a survey of the current status of European Jewry. Its population was estimated at 11 million, including those in neutral and Allied countries such as Great Britain, Sweden, and Switzerland. Emigration of Jews was discounted, for this would be difficult to implement in wartime. It was affirmed, however, that the evacuation of Jews to the East had emerged as "a further solution possibility."

The real importance of Wannsee, though, was that the entire German bureaucracy had become involved in the conscious mass murder of Jews.

By 1939, concentration camps were in existence at Dachau, Sachsenhausen, Esterwegen, Buchenwald, Mauthausen, and Ravensbruck. These were originally just overflow prisons, holding only a few thousand prisoners in 1939. Eventually, though, they were expanded into a vast empire of thousands of camps exploited for slave labor.

Three types of camps existed: transit camps, labor camps, and concentration camps. Once the decision was made regarding the "final solution," death camps were set up, either as separate institutions or as divisions of concentration camps.

The first death camp was established at Chelmno on December 8, 1941, in the western Polish territory annexed by Nazi Germany, not far from the city of Lodz. Tens of thousands were killed there. Trucks were converted into hermetically sealed vans and their exhaust pipes were bent and inserted into the passenger area of the vehicle. As the vehicle moved along, the hundred or so Jews inside were choked to death by carbon monoxide from the exhaust. When the vans arrived at Chelmno, the corpses were unloaded into pits and covered with a layer of earth.

Three more death camps were established in 1942. Belzec, in eastern Poland, opened in March; it was intended to kill the Jews of Lwow and Lublin. Sobibor, located near Lublin, opened in May; Jews from Poland, Holland, and France were sent there. Treblinka, about 50 miles from Warsaw, was set up to kill Jews from Warsaw and other areas of Poland and Eastern Europe. The estimated numbers of Jews killed in these camps: Belzec, 600,000; Sobibor, 250,000; and Treblinka, 840,000.

Other camps served different needs. Majdanek, for example, was set up to use Jewish skilled labor to produce arms and ammunition. At the same time, it served as a center for mass murder. It housed about 50,000 inmates at any one time, and by the end of the war 200,000 had been killed there.

Of all the death camps, the most famous—or infamous—is Auschwitz. Auschwitz started as a concentration camp for Poles and then Soviet prisoners of war. By 1941, however, it became a death camp for Jews. It was divided into three areas: Auschwitz One—the main camp, where apart from prisoners, the camp commander's headquarters, the administration, and the Gestapo offices were located; Auschwitz Two—Birkenau a huge area that held over 100,000 slave laborers, as well as four combination gas chamber–crematorium buildings capable of killing over 8,000 Jews daily; and Auschwitz Three—Monowitz, a slave labor camp, where the factories of I. G. Farben, producing synthetic rubber, were located.

From May 1940 to the end of 1943 the commander of Auschwitz was Rudolf S. Hoess. Hoess was tried in Poland after the war and hanged at Auschwitz in April 1947. He testified that Himmler had told him in the summer of 1941 to turn Auschwitz into an extermination center for Jews. From April 1942 to November 1944 the lives of perhaps 1.5 million Jews were taken there, along with over 100,000 non-Jews, who were abused, tortured, shot, and hanged, but generally not gassed.

Some Jews were selected to comprise the *Sonderkommando* units. These had the responsibility of herding the victims into the gas chambers and helping them undress. Later they extracted gold teeth from the bodies and removed rings from them. They also sorted the possessions of the dead for reuse.

Eventually the *Sonderkommando* members would be killed themselves, so that no eyewitnesses to the Nazi deeds would remain alive.

Thousands of individuals became dazed and apathetic through starvation, thirst, and sheer exhaustion. They were automatons and had lost all will to live. They were nicknamed *Musulmanner* ("Muslims").

The camp system was designed to strip its inmates of all humanity. Thus inmates wore uniforms and experienced extreme deprivation. At Auschwitz, numbers were tattooed on inmates' arms; other prisoners there wore number badges and were referred to only as numbers, not by their names. As a result, to maintain any sense of humanity and human behavior was a great victory, and significant numbers did so.

Sonderkommandos at an extermination camp rushing to perform their duties. They too ended up in gas chambers and in mass graves

A session of the International Military Tribunal, Nuremberg, 1945–1946. In the dock are (1) Hermann Goering, (2) Rudolf Hess, (3) Joachim von Ribbentrop, (4) Wilhelm Keitel, (5) Ernst Kaltenbrunner, (6) Alfred Rosenberg, (7) Hans Frank (8), Wilhelm Frick, (9) Julius Streicher, (10) Walther Funk, (11) Hjalmar Schacht, (12) Karl Doenitz, (13) Erich Raeder, (14) Baldur von Schirach, (15) Fritz Sauckel, (16) Alfred Jodl (17), Franz von Papen, (18) Artur Seyss-Inquart, (19) Albert Speer, (20) Konstantine von Neurath, (21) Hans Fritzsche.

SUMMARY

After its defeat in World War I, Germany was in disarray. Emperor Wilhelm II fled Germany and a republic was declared on November 9, 1918, with the hope that a government of this Western type might lead the Allies to demand less in a peace treaty. The republic was named the Weimar Republic after the city of Weimar, in which it was declared.

Germany faced many challenges after the war, including unemployment, reparation payments demanded by the Allies, inflation, murders and looting by armed groups, the *Freikorps*. The crash of the New York Stock Exchange, and the resulting worldwide economic crisis, was perhaps the greatest challenge of all.

Germany looked for strong leadership to help it overcome the crises. This situation allowed for the emergence of the Nazi Party. The party was established in 1919, but only in 1933 did it take control of Germany, under the leadership of Adolf Hitler. Hitler's regime restored order to Germany, but it also brought anti-Semitism. A boycott of Jews' businesses, anti-Jewish legislation, the Nuremberg Laws, Aryanization, and attempts to have Jews emigrate followed.

On September 1, 1939, World War II began. For Jews this would mean the establishment of ghettos in Poland, administered by the *Judenrat,* the murder of 2.4 million Jews in Russia by the *Einsatzgruppen,* and the construction of death camps, created for the annihilation of Jews.

Documents

ADOLF HITLER: MEIN KAMPF

This document is an excerpt from Hitler's famous work *Mein Kampf* ("My Struggle"). Imprisoned after the failed "Beer Hall Putsch" (November 8, 1923), Hitler dictated this manifesto of the Nazi Party to his cellmate Rudolf Hess.

. . . The Jewish doctrine of Marxism rejects the aristocratic principle of Nature and replaces the eternal privilege of power and strength by the mass of numbers and their dead weight. Thus it denies the value of personality in man, contests the significance of nationality and race, and thereby withdraws from humanity the premise of its existence and its culture. As a foundation of the universe, this doctrine would bring about the end of any order intellectually conceivable to man. And as, in this greatest of all recognizable organisms, the result of an application of such a law could only be chaos, on earth it could only be destruction of the inhabitants of this planet.

If, with the help of his Marxist creed, the Jew is victorious over the other peoples of the world, his crown will be the funeral wreath of humanity and this planet will, as it did thousands of years ago, move through the ether devoid of men.

Eternal Nature inexorably avenges the infringement of her commands.

Hence today I believe that I am acting in accordance with the will of the Almighty Creator: *by defending myself against the Jew, I am fighting for the work of the Lord.*

. . . To what an extent the whole existence of this people is based on a continuous lie is shown incomparably by the *Protocols of the Elders of Zion,* so infinitely hated by the Jews. They are based on a forgery, the *Frankfurter Zeitung* moans and screams once every week: the best proof that they are authentic. . . . For once this book has become the common property of a people, the Jewish menace may be considered as broken.

. . . His unfailing instinct in such things scents the original soul in everyone, and his hostility is assured to anyone who is not spirit of this spirit. Since the Jew is not the attacked but the attacker, not only anyone who attacks passes as his enemy, but also anyone who resists him. But the means with which he seeks to break such reckless but upright souls is not honest warfare, but lies and slander.

Here he stops at nothing, and in his vileness he has become so gigantic that no one need be surprised if among our people the personification of the devil as the symbol of all evil assumes the living shape of the Jew.

The ignorance of the broad masses about the inner nature of the Jew, the lack of instinct and narrow-mindedness of our upper classes, make the people an easy victim for this Jewish campaign of lies.

While from innate cowardice the upper classes turn away from a man whom the Jew attacks with lies and slander, the broad masses from stupidity or simplicity believe everything. The state authorities either cloak themselves in silence or, what usually happens, in order to put an end to the Jewish press campaign, they persecute the unjustly attacked, which, in the eyes of such an official ass, passes as the preservation of state authority and the safeguarding of law and order.

Slowly fear and the Marxist weapon of Jewry descend like a nightmare on the mind and soul of decent people.

They begin to tremble before the terrible enemy and thus have become his final victim.

The Jew's domination in the state seems so assured that now not only can he call himself a Jew again, but he ruthlessly admits his ultimate national and political designs. A section of his race openly owns itself to be a foreign people, yet even here they lie. For while the Zionists try to make the rest of the world believe that the national consciousness of the Jew finds its satisfaction in the creation of a Palestinian state, the Jews again slyly dupe the dumb *Goyim*. It doesn't even enter their heads to build up a Jewish state in Palestine for the purpose of living there; all they want is a central organization for their international world swindle, endowed with its own sovereign rights and removed from the intervention of other states: a haven for convicted scoundrels and a university for budding crooks.

It is a sign of their rising confidence and sense of security that at a time when one section is still playing the German, Frenchman, or Englishman, the other with open effrontery comes out as the Jewish race.

How close they see approaching victory can be seen by the hideous aspect which their relations with the members of other peoples takes on.

With satanic joy in his face, the black-haired Jewish youth lurks in wait for the unsuspecting girl whom he defiles with his blood, thus stealing her from her people. With every means he tries to destroy the racial foundations of the people he has set out to subjugate. Just as he himself systematically ruins women and girls, he does not shrink back from pulling down the blood barriers for others, even on a large scale. It was and it is Jews who bring the Negroes into the Rhineland, always with the same secret thought and clear aim of ruining the hated white race by the necessarily resulting bastardization, throwing it down from its cultural and political height, and himself rising to be its master.

For a racially pure people which is conscious of its blood can never be enslaved by the Jew. In this world he will forever be master over bastards and bastards alone.

And so he tries systematically to lower the racial level by a continuous poisoning of individuals.

And in politics he begins to replace the idea of democracy by the dictatorship of the proletariat.

In the organized mass of Marxism he has found the weapon which lets him dispense with democracy and in its stead allows himself to subjugate and govern the peoples with a dictatorial and brutal fist.

He works systematically for revolutionization in a twofold sense: economic and political.

Around peoples who offer too violent a resistance to attack from within he weaves a net of enemies, thanks to his international influence, incites them to war, and finally, if necessary, plants a flag of revolution on the very battlefields.

In economics he undermines the states until the social enterprises which have become unprofitable are taken from the state and subjected to his financial control.

In the political field he refuses the state the means for its self-preservation, destroys the foundations of all national self-maintenance and defense, destroys faith in the leadership, scoffs at its history and past, and drags everything that is truly great into the gutter.

Culturally, he contaminates art, literature, the theater, makes a mockery of natural feeling, overthrows all concepts of beauty and sublimity, of the noble and the good, and instead drags men down into the sphere of his own base nature.

Religion is ridiculed, ethics and morality represented as outmoded, until the last props of a nation in its struggle for existence in this world have fallen.

Now begins the great last revolution. In gaining political power the Jew casts off the few cloaks that he still wears. The democratic people's Jew becomes the blood-Jew and tyrant over peoples. In a few years he tries to exterminate the national intelligentsia and by robbing the peoples of their natural intellectual leadership makes them ripe for the slave's lot of permanent subjugation.

The most frightful example of this kind is offered by Russia, where he killed or starved about thirty million people with positively fanatical savagery, in part amid inhuman tortures, in order to give a gang of Jewish journalists and stock exchange bandits domination over a great people.

The end is not only the end of the freedom of the peoples oppressed by the Jew, but also the end of this parasite upon the nations. After the death of his victim, the vampire sooner or later dies too.

NUREMBERG LAWS (1935)

The annual convention of the Nazi Party took place in Nuremberg, and concluded with a ceremonial meeting of the Reichstag. On this occasion the Nuremberg Laws were enacted.

Reich Citizenship Law, September 15, 1935

The Reichstag has unanimously enacted the following law, which is promulgated herewith:

§1 (1) A subject is anyone who enjoys the protection of the German Reich and for this reason is specifically obligated to it.

(2) Nationality is acquired according to the provisions of the Reich and state nationality law.

§2 (1) A Reich citizen is only that subject of German or kindred blood who proves by his conduct that he is willing and suited loyally to serve the German people and the Reich.

(2) Reich citizenship is acquired through the conferment of a certificate of Reich citizenship.

(3) The Reich citizen is the sole bearer of full political rights as provided by the laws.

§3 The Reich Minister of the Interior, in agreement with the Deputy of the Führer, will issue the legal and administrative orders required to implement and supplement this law.

Nuremberg: September 15, 1935
at the Reich Party Congress of Freedom

The Führer and Reich Chancellor
The Reich Minister of the Interior

First Decree to the Reich Citizenship Law, November 14, 1935

Pursuant to § 3 of the Reich Citizenship Law of September 15, 1935 (Reichsgesetzblatt I, p. 1146), the following is decreed:

§1 (1) Until further regulations concerning the certificate of Reich citizenship are issued, subjects of German or kindred blood who on the effective date of the Reich Citizenship Law possessed the right to vote in Reichstag elections, or to whom the Reich Minister of the Interior, in agreement with the Deputy of the Führer, granted provisional Reich citizenship, will be provisionally deemed Reich citizens.

(2) The Reich Minister of the Interior, in agreement with the Deputy of the Führer, may revoke provisional Reich citizenship.

§2 (1) The provisions of § 1 also apply to subjects who are Jewish *Mischlinge*.

(2) A Jewish *Mischling* is anyone who is descended from one or two grandparents who are fully Jewish as regards race, unless he is deemed a Jew under § 5, Paragraph 2. A grandparent is deemed fully Jewish without further ado, if he has belonged to the Jewish religious community.

§3 Only a Reich citizen, as bearer of full political rights, can exercise the right to vote on political matters, or hold public office. The Reich Minister of the Interior or an agency designated by him may, in the transition period, permit exceptions with regard to admission to public office. The affairs of religious associations are not affected.

§4 (1) A Jew cannot be a Reich citizen. He is not entitled to the right to vote on political matters; he cannot hold public office.

(2) Jewish civil servants will retire by December 31, 1935. If these civil servants fought at the front during the

World War for the German Reich or its allies, they will receive the full pension according to the salary scale for the last position held, until they reach retirement age; they will not, however, be promoted according to seniority. After they reach retirement age, their pension will be newly calculated according to the prevailing salary scales.

(3) The affairs of religious associations are not affected.

(4) The conditions of service of teachers in Jewish public schools remain unchanged until the issuance of new regulations of the Jewish school system.

§5 (1) A Jew is anyone descended from at least three grandparents who are fully Jewish as regards race. §2, Paragraph 2, Sentence 2 applies.

(2) Also deemed a Jew is a Jewish *Mischling* subject who is descended from two fully Jewish grandparents and

a. who belonged to the Jewish religious community when the law was issued or has subsequently been admitted to it;

b. who was married to a Jew when the law was issued or has subsequently married one;

c. who is the offspring of a marriage concluded by a Jew, within the meaning of Paragraph 1, after the Law for the Protection of German Blood and German Honor of September 15, 1935 (RGBl. I, p. 1146) took effect;

d. who is the offspring of extramarital intercourse with a Jew, within the meaning of Paragraph 1, and will have been born out of wedlock after July 31, 1936.

§6 (1) Requirements regarding purity of blood exceeding those in § 5 that are set in Reich laws or in directives of the National Socialist German Workers Party and its units remain unaffected.

(2) Other requirements regarding purity of blood that exceed those in § 5 may be set only with the consent of the Reich Minister of the Interior and the Deputy of the Führer. Insofar as requirements of this kind already exist, they will become void as of January 1, 1936, unless approved by the Reich Minister of the Interior in agreement with the Deputy of the Führer. Application for approval is to be made to the Reich Minister of the Interior.

§7 The Führer and Reich Chancellor may grant exemptions from provisions of the implementation decree.

The Führer and Reich Chancellor
The Reich Minister of the Interior
The Deputy of the Führer

Law for the Protection of German Blood and German Honor, September 15, 1935

Imbued with the insight that the purity of German blood is prerequisite for the continued existence of the German people and inspired by the inflexible will to ensure the existence of the German nation for all times, the Reichstag has unanimously adopted the following law, which is hereby promulgated:

§1 (1) Marriages between Jews and subjects of German or kindred blood are forbidden. Marriages nevertheless concluded are invalid, even if concluded abroad to circumvent this law.

(2) Only the State Attorney may initiate the annulment suit.

§2 (1) Extramarital intercourse between Jews and subjects of German or kindred blood is forbidden.

§3 Jews must not employ in their households female subjects of German or kindred blood who are under 45 years old.

§4 (1) Jews are forbidden to fly the Reich and national flag and to display the Reich colors.

(2) They are, on the other hand, allowed to display the Jewish colors. The exercise of this right enjoys the protection of the state.

§5 (1) Whoever violates the prohibition in § 1 will be punished by penal servitude.

(2) A male who violates the prohibition in § 2 will be punished either by imprisonment or penal servitude.

(3) Whoever violates the provisions of §§ 3 or 4 will be punished by imprisonment up to one year and by a fine, or by either of these penalties.

§6 The Reich Minister of the Interior, in agreement with the Deputy of the Führer and the Reich Minister of Justice, will issue the legal and administrative orders required to implement and supplement this law.

§7 The law takes effect on the day following promulgation, except for § 3, which goes into force January 1, 1936.

Nuremberg, September 15, 1935
at the Reich Party Congress of Freedom

The Führer and Reich Chancellor
The Reich Minister of the Interior

The Reich Minister of Justice
The Deputy of the Führer

First Decree for Implementation, November 14, 1935

§3 (1) Subjects who are Jewish *Mischlinge* with two fully Jewish grandparents may conclude marriages with subjects of German or kindred blood, or with subjects who are Jewish *Mischlinge* having only one fully Jewish grandparent, only by permission of the Reich Minister of the Interior and the Deputy of the Führer, or of an agency designated by them.

(2) In making the decision, special attention is to be paid to the physical, psychological, and character attributes of the applicant, the duration of his family's residence in Germany, his own or his father's service in the World War, and other aspects of his family history. . . .

§4 No marriage is to be concluded between subjects who are Jewish *Mischlinge* having only one fully Jewish grandparent. . . .

RESPONSE OF THE REICHSVERTRETUNG (NATIONAL REPRESENTATION OF THE JEWS IN GERMANY) TO THE NUREMBERG LAWS

This document presents the German Jews' view of their priorities in response to the Nuremberg Laws.

The Reichsvertretung der Juden in Deutschland announces the following:

I

The Laws decided upon by the Reichstag in Nuremberg have come as the heaviest of blows for the Jews in Germany. But they must create a basis on which a tolerable relationship becomes possible between the German and the Jewish people. The *Reichsvertretung der Juden in Deutschland* is willing to contribute to this end with all its powers. A precondition for such a tolerable relationship is the hope that the Jews and Jewish communities of Germany will be enabled to keep a moral and economic means of existence by the halting of defamation and boycott.

The organization of the life of the Jews in Germany requires governmental recognition of an autonomous Jewish leadership. The *Reichsvertretung der Juden in Deutschland* is the agency competent to undertake this. It has the support, with few exceptions, of the totality of the Jews and Jewish Communities, particularly the State Association of Jewish Communities (*Landesverbände*) and all the City Communities, as well as the independent Jewish organizations: Zionist Federation of Germany (*Zionistische Vereinigung für Deutschland*), Central Organization of Jews in Germany (*Zentralverein der Juden in Deutschland*), Union of Jewish Veterans (*Reichsbund jüdischer Frontsoldaten*), Association for Liberal Judaism (*Vereinigung für das religiös-liberale Judentum*), the Organized Orthodox Community (*die organisierte Gemeinde-Orthodoxie*), Union of Jewish Women (*Jüdischer Frauenbund*), Reich Committee for Jewish Youth Organizations (*Reichsausschuss der jüdischen Jugendverbände*).

The most urgent tasks for the *Reichsvertretung*, which it will press energetically and with full commitment, following the avenues it has previously taken, are:

1. Our own Jewish educational system must serve to prepare the youth to become upright Jews, secure in their faith, who will draw the strength to face the onerous demands which life will make on them from conscious

solidarity with the Jewish community, from work for the Jewish present and faith in the Jewish future. In addition to transmitting knowledge, the Jewish schools must also serve in the systematic preparation for future occupations. With regard to preparation for emigration, particularly to Palestine, emphasis will be placed on guidance toward manual work and the study of the Hebrew language. The education and vocational training of girls must be directed to preparing them to carry out their responsibilities as upholders of the family and mothers of the next generation.

An independent cultural structure must offer possibilities of employment to Jews who are artistically and culturally creative, and serve the separate cultural life of the Jews in Germany.

2. The *increased need* for emigration will be served by large-scale planning, firstly with respect to *Palestine*, but also to all other available countries, with particular attention to young people. This includes study of additional possibilities for emigration, training in professions suited for emigrants, particularly agriculture and technical skills; the creation of ways and means to mobilize and liquidate the property of persons who are economically independent, the broadening of existing means of transferring property, and the creation of additional such means.

3. Support and care of the needy, sick, or aged must be assured through further systematic expansion of the Jewish *welfare services* provided by the communities to supplement government social services.

4. An impoverished community cannot carry out these varied and difficult tasks. The *Reichsvertretung* will try by every means to safeguard the economic position of the Jews by seeking to *protect the existing means of livelihood*. Those who are economically weak will be assisted by the further development of such economic aids as employment bureaus, *economic advice,* and personal or mortgage loans.

5. *We are given strength in the present and hope for the future by the vitality of the progress in the construction of a Jewish Palestine.* In order to draw the Jews of Germany even more closely into this development, the *Reichsvertretung* itself has joined the *Palestine Foundation Fund* (Keren Hayesod) and appeals warmly to Jewish communities and organizations to follow its example. The *Reichsvertretung* offers its services to establish organizational links between the institutions of the Jews in Germany and the work of reconstruction in Palestine.

*

In full awareness of the magnitude of the responsibilities involved and the difficulties of the task, the *Reichsvertretung* calls on the Jewish men and women, and on all Jewish youth, to join together in unity, to maintain high Jewish morale, to practice strictest self-discipline, and show a maximum willingness to make sacrifices.

II

In accordance with a proposal made in the presidium of the *Reichsvertretung,* the *Reichsvertretung,* the state Federations, and the communities are requested to cooperate closely in taking such organizational and personnel measures as are required in the Jewish bodies in order to ensure the vigorous and systematic carrying out of the new working program by all Jewish official bodies.

SCHNELLBRIEF (TELEX) (SEPTEMBER 21, 1939)

This communication to the heads of the *Einsatzgruppen,* the "special-duty groups," detailed their responsibilities in Nazi-occupied Poland.

Heydrich's Instructions to Chiefs of *Einsatzgruppen,* September 21, 1939

The Chief of the Security Police
SECRET   Berlin: September 21, 1939
To: Chiefs of all *Einsatzgruppen* of the Security Police
Subject: Jewish Question in the occupied territory

I refer to the conference held in Berlin today and once more point out that the planned overall measures (i.e., the final aim) are to be kept strictly secret.

Distinction must be made between:

(1) The final aim (which will require extended periods of time), and

(2) The stages leading to the fulfillment of this final aim (which will be carried out in short terms).

The planned measures demand the most thorough preparation in their technical as well as economic aspects.

It is obvious that the tasks that lie ahead cannot be laid down in full detail from here. The instructions and guidelines below will at the same time serve the purpose of urging the chiefs of the *Einsatzgruppen* to give the matter their practical thought.

I

For the time being, the first prerequisite for the final aim is the concentration of the Jews from the countryside into the larger cities.

This is to be carried out with all speed.

In doing so, distinction must be made:

(1) between the areas of Danzig and West Prussia, Posen, Eastern Upper Silesia, and

(2) the rest of the occupied territories.

As far as possible, the area mentioned (in *item 1*) is to be cleared of Jews; at least the aim should be to establish only a few cities of concentration.

In the areas mentioned in *item 2,* as few concentration points as possible are to be set up, so as to facilitate subsequent measures.

In this connection, it is to be borne in mind that only cities which are rail junctions, or at least are located along railroad lines, are to be designated as concentration points.

On principle, Jewish communities of fewer than 500 persons are to be dissolved and to be transferred to the nearest city of concentration.

This decree does not apply to the area of *Einsatzgruppe 1,* which is situated east of Cracow and is bounded roughly by *Polanico, Jaroslaw,* the new line of demarcation, and the former Slovak-Polish border. Within this area, only an improvised census of Jews is to be carried out. Furthermore, Councils of Jewish Elders, as discussed below, are to be set up.

II

Councils of Jewish Elders [Jüdische Ältestenräte]

(1) In each Jewish community, a Council of Jewish Elders is to be set up, to be composed, as far as possible, of the remaining influential personalities and rabbis. The council is to comprise up to 24 male Jews (depending on the size of the Jewish community).

The council is to be made *fully responsible,* in the literal sense of the word, for the exact and punctual execution of all directives issued or yet to be issued.

(2) In case of sabotage of such instructions, the councils are to be warned of the severest measures.

(3) The Jewish councils are to take an improvised census of the Jews in their local areas—broken down if possible by sex (age groups): (a) up to 16 years of age, (b) from 16 to 20 years of age, and (c) over, as well as by principal occupational groups—and are to report the results in the shortest possible time.

(4) The Councils of Elders are to be informed of the dates and deadlines for departure, departure facilities, and finally departure routes. They are then to be made personally responsible for the departure of the Jews from the countryside.

The reason to be given for the concentration of the Jews into the cities is that Jews have most influentially participated in guerrilla attacks and plundering actions.

(5) The Councils of Elders in the cities of concentration are to be made responsible for appropriately housing Jews moving in from the countryside.

For general reasons of security, the concentration of Jews in the cities will probably necessitate orders altogether barring Jews from certain sections of cities, or, for example, forbidding them to leave the ghetto or go out after a designated evening hour, etc. However, economic necessities are always to be considered in this connection.

(6) The Councils of Elders are also to be made responsible for appropriate provisioning of the Jews during the transport to the cities.

No objections are to be voiced in the event that migrating Jews take their movable possessions with them, to the extent that this is technically possible.

(7) Jews who do not comply with the order to move into the cities are to be allowed a short additional period of grace where circumstances warrant. They are to be warned of strictest punishment if they should fail to comply with this latter deadline.

III

On principle, all necessary measures are always to be taken in closest accord and cooperation with the German civil administration agencies and locally competent military authorities.

In carrying them out, care must be taken that the economic security of the occupied territories not be impaired.

(1) Above all, the needs of the army must be considered. For example, for the time being it will hardly be possible to avoid leaving behind some Jew traders here and there, who in the absence of other possibilities simply must stay for the sake of supplying the troops. In such cases, however, prompt Aryanization of these enterprises is to be sought and the emigration of the Jews is to be completed later, in accord with the locally competent German administrative authorities.

(2) For the preservation of German economic interests in the occupied territories, it is obvious that Jewish-owned essential or war industries and enterprises, as well as those important for the Four Year Plan, must be kept up for the time being.

In these cases also, prompt Aryanization is to be sought, and the emigration of the Jews is to be completed later.

(3) Finally, the food situation in the occupied territories must be taken into consideration. For instance, as far as possible, real estate owned by Jewish settlers is to be provisionally entrusted to the care of neighboring German or even Polish farmers, to be worked by them together with their own, so as to assure harvesting of the crops still in the fields or renewed cultivation.

With regard to this important question, contact is to be made with the agricultural expert of the Chief of the Civil Administration.

(4) In all cases in which the interests of the Security Police on one hand and those of the German Civil Administration on the other cannot be reconciled, I am to be informed in the fastest way before the particular measures in question are carried out, and my decision is to be awaited.

IV

The chiefs of the *Einsatzgruppen* will report to me continuously on the following matters:

(1) Numerical survey of the Jews present in their territories (broken down as indicated above, if possible). The numbers of Jews who are being evacuated from the countryside and of those who are already in the cities are to be reported separately.

(2) Names of cities which have been designated as concentration points.

(3) Deadlines set for the Jews to migrate to the cities.

(4) Survey of all Jewish-owned essential or war industries and enterprises, as well as those important for the Four Year Plan, within their areas.

If possible, the following should be specified:

a. Kind of enterprise (also statement on possible conversion into enterprises that are truly essential or war-related, or important for the Four Year Plan);

b. Which of these enterprises need to be Aryanized most promptly (in order to forestall any kind of loss)? What kind of Aryanization is suggested? Germans or Poles? (This decision depends on the importance of the enterprise.)

c. How large is the number of Jews working in these enterprises (including leading positions)?

Can the enterprise simply be kept up after the removal of the Jews, or will such continued operation require assignment of German or Polish workers? On what scale?

Insofar as Polish workers have to be introduced, care should be taken that they are mainly brought in from the former German provinces, so as to begin the weeding out of the Polish element there. These questions can be carried out only through involvement and participation of the German labor offices which have been set up.

V

For the attainment of the goals set, I expect total deployment of all forces of the Security Police and the Security Service.

The chiefs of neighboring *Einsatzgruppen* are to establish contact with each other immediately so that the territories concerned will be covered completely.

VI

The High Command of the Army, the Plenipotentiary for the Four Year Plan (Attention: Secretary of State *Neumann*), the Reich Ministries of the Interior (Attention: Secretary of State *Stuckart*), for Food and for Economy (Attention: Secretary of State *Landfried*), as well as the Chiefs of Civil Administration of the Occupied Territory have received copies of this decree.

ELECTION OF ELKES AS HEAD OF THE JUDENRAT IN KOVNO

This document describes the selection of a reluctant Dr. Elkes to head the *Judenrat* of Kovno, Lithuania.

. . . In the first days of August, Kaminsky informed the Jewish Committee that the ghetto in Slobodka would be headed by an *Ältestenrat* (Council of Elders) which would be elected by the Jews themselves. But first of all they would have to elect a "Head of the Jews"—that was the demand of *Hauptsturmführer* Jordan, who was responsible for Jewish affairs in Kovno. This created a very grave problem for the Kovno Jews: whom to elect to this position of exceptionally great responsibility, which was at the same time difficult and dangerous. For this purpose the Council called an enlarged meeting of all those who had been active in public affairs of any kind and had remained in the city. The meeting was held on August 5 in the offices of the Council on Daukshos Street, and about 30 persons attended.

This Jewish meeting, the last in the city of Kovno itself before it was left by its Jewish residents, was unusually dramatic. Everybody was deeply aware that a solution must be found for a problem which literally involved their lives. It was not easy to find a suitable candidate for this unusual position. The candidate would have to know how to find a common language with the Germans, and know also how to appear before them as the representative of the ghetto. Even if it was understood from the outset that the man elected would be only "Head of the Jews," that is, the lowly representative of the "accursed Jews"—in the defiled vocabulary of the Germans—nevertheless it was also understood that everything possible must be done that the man elected would, despite everything, have a certain authority in the eyes of the Germans and that they would take into consideration what he said. Everybody understood that the man elected must have qualities that enabled him to influence the Germans to a certain degree. It was also necessary that the man who would stand at the head of the ghetto must have a clean public record, be a good Jew and a good man, discerning and clever, courageous and of strong character, so that he would not be easily discouraged and would not bend his knees when he had to stand before the Germans as the tragic messenger of an unhappy Jewish community, without salvation and surrounded by ravening beasts.

Several candidates were proposed at the meeting. However, none of them could unite those taking part in the meeting around himself. In addition, the candidates proposed all refused to accept this task. A great feeling of depression spread through the meeting. After lengthy discussions Dr. Z. Wolf, the chairman of the meeting, proposed the candidacy of Dr. E. Elkes, a loyal and Zionist Jew, and a famous doctor in the city of Kovno. The proposal was accepted immediately by the whole assembly, and with great enthusiasm. But Dr. Ekes refused to accept this appointment. Again there was great confusion of spirit. Rabbi Schmukler then rose from his place and made a speech that was moving and full of pain, and shook everyone deeply. "How terrible is our position"— he said in a trembling voice—"that we are not offering the revered Dr. Elkes the respected position of head of the Jewish Community of Kovno, but the shameful and humiliating one of 'Head of the Jews,' who is to represent us before the Germans. But please understand, dear and beloved Dr. Elkes, that only to the Nazi murderers will you be 'Head of the Jews,' in our eyes you will be the head of our Community, elected in our most tragic hour, when blood runs from all of us and the murderer's sword is suspended over our heads. It has fallen to your part to accept duties of unequalled difficulty, but at the same time it is also a great privilege and a deed of charity, and you do not have the right to escape from it; stand at our head, defend us, you shall be with us and we will all be with you, until we arrive at the great day of salvation!" When Rabbi Schmukler had finished speaking he wept, and all the assembly wept bitter tears with him. Dr. Elkes stood pale and silent. All could see what was happening in the depth of his soul, and all felt that in these tragic moments Dr. Elkes understood that it was his duty to make this great sacrifice that a cruel fate had imposed upon him. A feeling of relief descended on all, and a ray of secret hope shone into the broken hearts of all those present.

THE BAN ON BIRTHS IN SHAVLI (1942)

On March 5, 1942, the Nazis banned births, with the latest permitted date being August 5, 1942. This presented the *Judenrat* with the need to formulate a plan of action in response to this ban.

July 4, 1942

. . . Dr. Charny drew the attention of the Jewish delegation to the Order concerning births. The Order was first issued on March 5, 1942. The latest date for authorized births was August 5, 1942. He would extend the date to August 15, 1942. In the event of a birth taking place in a Jewish family after this date the whole Jewish family would be "removed" [i.e., killed] and the responsibility would rest with the Jewish delegates.

July 13, 1942

Re: Security Police Order

In accordance with the Order of the Security Police, births are permitted in the ghetto only up to August 15, 1942. After this date it is forbidden to give birth to Jewish children either in the hospitals or in the homes of the pregnant women. It is pointed out, at the same time, that it is permitted to interrupt pregnancies by means of abortions. A great responsibility rests on the pregnant women. If they do not comply with this order, there is a danger that they will be executed, together with their families. The delegates [i.e., the *Judenrat*] are making this matter widely known. In warning the women of the possible consequences, they believe that the women concerned will remember it well . . . and will take the necessary measures during the registration of pregnant women which will take place during the next few days, and subsequently.

The Delegation

Protocol of the meeting of the Shavli *Judenrat* on March 24, 1943

Those present: M. Lejbowicz, B. Karton, A. Heller, and A. Katz of the Delegation; the doctors: Burstein, Blecher, Goldberg, Dyrektorowicz, L. Pesachowicz, and others. The Agenda: *How should births be prevented in the ghetto?* M. Lejbowicz: We will go back to the question of the births. The ban on giving birth to children which has been imposed on the Jews applies with the utmost severity to all the ghettos. There was a birth recently in Kovno and all members of the family were shot and killed. But no attention is being paid to this and people are behaving most irresponsibly here. There are already several cases of pregnancy and no measures have been taken against them. Dr. Blecher asks: Can the pregnant women be forced to have abortions performed? Are there statistics on the women who are pregnant? Dr. L reports: We have had three births since August 15 of last year; he did not know how they took place because he did not treat the cases. At the present time there are about 20 pregnant women in the ghetto, most of them in the first few months, but some who are already in the fourth or fifth month and one even in the eighth month. Only two of the pregnant women refuse to have an abortion; for one of them this would be a third abortion and she is threatened by the danger of subsequent childlessness, and the other is the one who has reached the eighth month. Dr. P.: They must be persuaded to agree to have an abortion. They must be told what happened in Kovno and Riga. If necessary one must make use of a white lie in this emergency and tell them that the Security Police is already looking for these cases. Dr. Burstein proposes that the whole medical team, including the midwives, should be forbidden to attend to births. Dr. Bl. proposes that all cases of pregnancy should be registered and the pregnant women persuaded to have abortions. M.L.: We must not make propaganda against births in public! The matter could reach ears that should not hear it. We must discuss the matter only with those concerned. He proposes that the pregnant women be summoned to the clinic, that they be warned in the presence of the doctor and a representative of the Delegation, and the full danger that awaits them be explained. Dr. L.: How can one perform an abortion on a woman who has already reached the eighth month of her pregnancy? Surely we must understand the feelings of the mother. It will surely be impossible to convince her. And what will happen to the infant if we cause a premature birth? We cannot carry out an operation like that in a private home, and it is forbidden to leave the child at the hospital. And what will happen if despite everything the child is born alive? Shall we kill it? I cannot accept such a responsibility on my conscience. Dr. Bl. adds that the position is really very difficult in a case like this, for no doctor will take upon himself the responsibility of killing a live child, for that would be murder. Dr. P asks: Perhaps we should let the child be born and give it to a Christian? M.L.: We cannot allow the child to be born because we are required to report every case of a birth. We have been asked three times whether there were any births and each time we answered in the negative. B.K.: What can we do when the ghetto is in such danger? If the danger were only to the family of the infant we could leave the matter to the responsibility of the person concerned, but it endangers the whole ghetto. The consequences are liable to be most terrible.

FACING FACTS: THE BLOODY NIGHT—APRIL 17, 1942

This document presents accounts of the arrests and the killings carried out by the Gestapo in the ghettos of Occupied Poland in March and April of 1942.

The Fascist beast bared its teeth and let loose. On Friday night into Saturday (April 17th into 18th), arrests according to lists were carried out in the Warsaw ghetto by Gestapo officers. Forty-eight of the arrested were shot right away in the yards or side streets by other Gestapo men who were waiting for the victims.

On Saturday, after Friday's bloody night, the ghetto was silent. Shrouded in deep sorrow, heads bowed before the dead bodies of the bestially murdered martyrs, the Jewish population of Warsaw asked what the next night would bring. What is being prepared, what is the bloody executioner devising for us?

On Sunday strange rumors began to spread through the ghetto. The Germans had indeed murdered Jews, but not just so, without cause. They shot Jews who "were engaged in matters that were not their business." The Jews they shot had busied themselves with *"politics,"* had published *illegal* newspapers. It was *Socialists* who were shot. They are the ones who bring misfortune to the ghetto.

This filthy, disgusting stream of reports began to flood the ghetto. All those who live high and mighty under the bloody rule of Hitler's regime, all those fine Jews who rejoice in the "autonomy" bestowed upon us in the form of this cursed ghetto, they all began whispering and murmur-ing, dropping names, judging and condemning. They, the filthy scum of our time, have become the judges and the dunners for the "injury" which the "politics," the "Socialists" brought on the Warsaw ghetto!

But was that the cause of the bloody night? Let the facts speak.

Beginning in mid-February until the end of March, the following events took place in *Tarnów.* Every day Gestapo and SS men entered the Jewish residential quarter, killing innocent Jews whom they encountered by chance on the streets, in the yards, and in their homes. In *Radom,* in March, in one night 70 Jews of various strata of the population were arrested. That same night 24 of the arrested were murdered right away and the rest were sent off to Oświęcim (Auschwitz). In *Cracow* at the beginning of April, over 50 Jews were arrested from lists and were murdered in the same bestial way as in Warsaw.

And what about *Lublin,* where from March 15 until April 10, 25,000 Jews were sent out in sealed trains in an "unknown direction"? During this action all the children of the Jewish orphanage, all the old people in the old-age home, and all the sick in both Jewish hospitals were murderously, outrageously shot. Besides that, *over 2,000 Jews were shot* in the streets and in their homes. That happened—we emphasize this—at the end of March, the beginning of April 1942.

Need we mention the terrible poison-gassing in Chelmno, where 5,000 Jews from the Kolo district and 35,000 Jews from the Lodz ghetto were put to death?

These are all facts of the last 3–4 months. But we must not forget what happened in the fall of 1941 in *Vilna,* where 50,000 Jews were murdered, and in the entire Vilna district and in the Kovno area of Lithuania, where altogether 300,000 Jews were slaughtered. And what about *Slonim* with 9,000 murdered Jews; what about *Równe* with 17,000 Jews shot? What of the whole of Eastern Galicia where there is not a single townlet of which at least half of its Jewish population has not been murdered?

Then let the dogs be silent who dare to bark on the graves of those who fell during the bloody Friday night in Warsaw. Let them not dishonor the peace of the martyrs. Let them not try to argue that it was Socialists who brought on the misfortune. That Friday night in the Warsaw ghetto was only one *small* link in the *great* chain of the bestial murders of the Jews by Hitler.

Yes, we know well enough that the Jewish leeches, the vampires who, under the protection of Hitler's wings, suck out the last bit of strength of the Jewish populace, really want the ghetto to appear as one cemetery, that deathly stillness should reign here, which will not disturb them while they do the work of jackals and hyenas.

EVIDENCE OF R. HOESS, COMMANDER OF AUSCHWITZ

This document is an excerpt from R. Hoess, *Commandant of Auschwitz: The Autobiography of Rudolf Hoess.*

In the summer of 1941, I cannot remember the exact date, I was suddenly summoned to the *Reichsführer* SS, directly by his adjutant's office. Contrary to his usual custom, Himmler received me without his adjutant being present and said in effect:

"The Führer has ordered that the Jewish question be solved once and for all and that we, the SS, are to implement that order.

"The existing termination centers in the East are not in a position to carry out the large *Aktionen* which are anticipated. I have therefore earmarked Auschwitz for this purpose, both because of its good position as regards communications and because the areas can easily be isolated and camouflaged. At first I thought of calling in a senior SS officer for this job, but I changed my mind in order to avoid difficulties concerning the terms of reference. I have now decided to entrust this task to you. It is difficult and onerous and calls for complete devotion notwithstanding the difficulties that may arise. You will learn further details from *Sturmbannführer* Eichmann of the Reich Security Main Office who will call on you in the immediate future.

"The departments concerned will be notified by me in due course. You will treat this order as absolutely secret, even from your superiors. After your talk with Eichmann you will immediately forward to me the plans for the projected installations.

"The Jews are the sworn enemies of the German people and must be eradicated. Every Jew that we can lay our hands on is to be destroyed now during the war, without exception. If we cannot now obliterate the biological basis of Jewry, the Jews will one day destroy the German people."

On receiving these grave instructions, I returned forthwith to Auschwitz, without reporting to my superior at Oranienburg.

Shortly afterward Eichmann came to Auschwitz and disclosed to me the plans for the operations as they affected the various countries concerned. I cannot remember the exact order in which they were to take place. First was to come the eastern part of Upper Silesia and the neighboring parts of Polish territory under German rule, then, depending on the situation, simultaneously Jews from Germany and Czechoslovakia, and finally the Jews from the West: France, Belgium, and Holland. He also told me the approximate number of transports that might be expected, but I can no longer remember these.

We discussed the ways and means of effecting the extermination. This could only be done by gassing, since it would have been absolutely impossible to dispose by shooting of the large numbers of people that were expected, and it would have placed too heavy a burden on the SS men who had to carry it out, especially because of the women and children among the victims.

Eichmann told me about the method of killing people with exhaust gases in lorries, which had previously been used in the East. But there was no question of being able to use this for these mass transports that were due to arrive in Auschwitz. Killing with showers of carbon monoxide while bathing, as was done with mental patients in some places in the Reich, would necessitate too many buildings, and it was also very doubtful whether the supply of gas for such a vast number of people would be available. We left the matter unresolved. Eichmann decided to try and find a gas which was in ready supply and which would not entail special installations for its use, and to inform me when he had done so. We inspected the area in order to choose a likely spot. We decided that a peasant farmstead situated in the north-west corner of what later became the third building sector at Birkenau would be the most suitable. It was isolated and screened by woods and hedges, and it was also not far from the railway. The bodies could be placed in long, deep pits dug in the nearby meadows. We had not at that time thought of burning the corpses. We calculated that after gas-proofing the premises then available, it would be possible to kill about 800 people simultaneously with a suitable gas. These figures were borne out later in practice.

Eichmann could not then give me the starting date for the operation because everything was still in the preliminary stages and the *Reichsführer* SS had not yet issued the necessary orders.

Eichmann returned to Berlin to report our conversation to the *Reichsführer* SS.

A few days later I sent to the *Reichsführer* SS by courier a detailed location plan and description of the installation. I never received an acknowledgement or a decision on my report. Eichmann told me later that the *Reichsführer* SS was in agreement with my proposals.

EVIDENCE FROM J. WIERNIK ON TREBLINKA

This document is an excerpt from J. Wiernik's *A Year in Treblinka by an Eye Witness.*

. . . I stood in the line opposite my house in Wolynska Street, and from there we were taken to Zamenhof Street. The Ukrainians divided up the loot amongst themselves before our eyes. They fought amongst themselves, valued and sorted everything. Despite the great number of people, there was silence in the street. A silent and cruel despair fell upon all. Oh what despair it was! They photographed us as though we were animals from before the Flood. There were also some who remained calm. I myself hoped that we would go home again. I thought they would check our documents. An order was given, and we moved off from our places. Woe to us! The naked truth was revealed before our eyes. Railway cars. Cars that were empty. That day was a fine, hot summer's day. It seemed as though the sun was protesting against the injustice. What was the guilt of our wives, our children, our mothers? What was it? The sun disappeared behind thick clouds. It is beautiful, warms and shines and does not wish to witness our suffering and humiliation.

An order is given to get into the cars. Eighty are pushed into each car. The way back is sealed off. I had on my body only trousers, a shirt, and shoes. A back-pack with other things and high boots had stayed at home. I had prepared it because there were rumors that we would be sent to the Ukraine for work. The train was shunted from one siding to another. I knew this rail junction well and realized that we were staying in the same place. Meanwhile we could hear the Ukrainians amusing themselves, the sound of their shouting and cheerful laughter reaching us. It was becoming increasingly suffocating inside the car, and from minute to minute there was less air to breathe; it was all despair, blackness, and horror. . . . With indescribable suffering we finally arrived at Malkinia. We stopped there all night. Ukrainians came into the car and demanded valuables. Everybody gave them up in order to preserve their lives a little while longer.

. . . In the morning the train moved and we reached Treblinka station. I saw a train that passed us and in it people who were hungry, ragged, and half naked. They said something to us but we did not understand them. The day was burning hot. They lack of air was terrible. As a result we were very thirsty. I looked out of the window. The peasants brought water and charged 100 zloty for each bottle. I had no money, apart from 10 gold coins. Also a 2, a 5, and a 10 in silver, with a portrait of the Marshal, that I had kept as a memento. So I was forced to do without water. Others bought it. They paid 500 zloty for a kilogram of black bread. I was tortured by thirst until mid-day. Then the future *Hauptsturmführer* came in and picked 10 men who brought us water. I assuaged my thirst a little. An order was given to take out the dead, but there were none. At four in the afternoon the train moved off. We arrived at Treblinka in a few minutes. It was only there that the blinkers dropped from our eyes. Ukrainians with rifles and machine-guns stood on the roofs of the huts. The whole area was strewn with bodies, some dressed and some naked. Their faces were distorted with fear and horror. They were black and

swollen. Their eyes were frozen wide open. Their tongues hung out, brains were spattered around and the bodies twisted. There was blood everywhere. Our innocent blood. The blood of our children, our brothers and sisters. The blood of our fathers and mothers. And we are without hope, we realize that we will not escape our fate. . . .

There is an order to get out of the cars. Belongings are to be left behind. We are taken to the yard. There were huts on either side. There were two large notice boards with orders to hand over gold, silver, precious stones, and all valuables. Failure to do so would bring the death penalty. On the roofs of the huts were Ukrainians with machine-guns. The women and children were ordered off to the left and the men told to sit down in the yard, on the right. Some distance away from us people were working: they were sorting the belongings taken from the train. I managed to steal over among the workers, and began to work; I suffered the first lash from the whip of a German whom we called Frankenstein. The women and children were told to take off their clothes.

. . . When we carried, or more correctly, dragged, the bodies away we were made to run, and were beaten for the least delay. The dead had been lying there for a long time. They had already begun to decompose. There was a stench of death and decomposition in the air. Worms crawled on the wretched bodies. When we tied on the belts, an arm or a leg would frequently drop off. We also labored on graves for ourselves until dusk, without food or drink. The day was hot, and thirst plagued us greatly. When we reached the huts in the evening each one of us began to search for the people he had known the day before—in vain—they were not to be found, they were no longer among the living. . . .

EVIDENCE AT NUREMBERG ON AUSCHWITZ

This document comes from the Trial of Major War Criminals conducted at Nuremberg, Germany, from November 1945 to October 1946.

M. Dubost: What do you know about the Jewish transport that arrived from Romainville about the same time as you?

Vaillant-Couturier: When we left Romainville the Jewish women who were together with us remained behind. They were sent to Drancy and finally arrived in Auschwitz, where we saw them again three weeks later. Of 1,200 who left, only 125 arrived in the camp. The rest were taken to the gas chambers immediately, and of the 125 not a single one was left by the end of the month.

The transports were carried out as follows: at the beginning, when we arrived, when a Jewish transport came there was a "selection." First the old women, the mothers and the children. They were told to get on trucks, together with the sick and people who looked weak. They kept only young girls, young women and young men; the latter were sent to the men's camp.

In general, it was rare for more than 250 out of a transport of 1,000 to 1,500 to reach the camp, and that was the maximum; the others were sent to the gas chambers straight away.

At this "selection" healthy women between 20 and 30 years old were also chosen, and sent to the Experimental Block. Girls and women, who were a little older or not chosen for this purpose, were sent to the camp and, like us, had their heads shaved and they were tattooed.

In the spring of 1944 there was also a block for twins. That was at the time of the immense transport of Hungarian Jews, about 700,000 persons [actually, 430,000]. Dr. Mengele, who was carrying out the experiments, kept back the twin children from all transports, as well as twins of any age, so long as both twins were there. Both children and adults slept on the floor in this block. I don't know what experiments were made apart from blood tests and measurements.

M. Dubost: Did you actually see the "selection" when transports arrived?

Vaillant-Couturier: Yes, because when we were working in the Sewing Block in 1944, the block in which we lived was situated just opposite the place where the trains arrived. The whole process had been improved: Instead of carrying out the "selection" where the trains arrived, a siding took the carriages practically to the gas chamber, and the train stopped about 100 meters from the gas chamber. That was right in front of our block, but of course there were two rows of barbed wire between. Then we saw how the seals were taken off the trucks and how women, men, and children were pulled out of the trucks by soldiers. We were present at the most terrible scenes when old couples were separated. Mothers had to leave their daughters, because they were taken to the camp, while the mothers and children went to the gas chambers. All these people knew nothing of the fate that awaited them. They were only confused because they were being separated from each other, but they did not know that they were going to their death.

To make the reception pleasanter there was then—in June and July 1944, that is—an orchestra made up of prisoners, girls in white blouses and dark blue skirts, all of them pretty and young, who played gay tunes when the trains arrived, the "Merry Widow," the Barcarolle from the "Tales of Hoffman," etc. They were told it was a labor camp, and as they never entered the camp they saw nothing but the small platform decorated with greenery, where the orchestra played. They could not know what awaited them.

Those who were taken to the gas chambers—that is, the old people, children, and others—were taken to a red brick building.

M. Dubost: Then they were not registered?

Vaillant-Couturier: No.

Dubost: They were not tattooed?

Vaillant-Couturier: No, they were not even counted.

Dubost: Were you yourself tattooed?

Vaillant-Couturier: Yes.

(The witness shows her arm)

They were taken to a red brick building with a sign that said Baths. There they were told to get undressed and given a towel before they were taken to the so-called shower room. Later, at the time of the large transports from Hungary, there was no time left for any degree of concealment. They were undressed brutally. I know of these particulars because I was acquainted with a little Jewess from France, who had lived on the Place de la Republique. . . .

Dubost: In Paris?

Vaillant-Couturier: In Paris; she was known as "little Marie" and was the only survivor of a family of nine. Her mother and her seven sisters and brothers had been taken to the gas chambers as soon as they arrived. When I got to know her she worked on undressing the small children before they were taken to the gas chamber.

After the people were undressed they were taken into a room that looked like a shower room, and the capsules were thrown down into the room through a hole in the ceiling. An SS man observed the effect through a spy-hole. After about 5 to 7 minutes, when the gas had done its job, he gave a signal for the opening of the doors. Men with gas-masks, these were prisoners too, came in and took the bodies out. They told us that the prisoners must have suffered before they died, because they clung together in bunches like grapes so that it was difficult to separate them.

Reference Works

Y. Arad (ed.), *Documents on the Holocaust* (*Yad Vashem*)

Y. Bauer, *A History of the Holocaust*

L. Dawidowicz (ed.), *A Holocaust Reader*

———, *The War Against the Jews*

R. Hilberg, *The Destruction of the European Jews*

Chronology

1920	Nazi Party publishes a 25-point program. The main thrust is nationalist, the creation of a "Greater Germany." The party has 60 members.
1923	The Beer Hall Putsch—Adolf Hitler is jailed until 1924. Nazi Party is banned. The party has 60,000 members in Bavaria.
1925	Hitler's *Mein Kampf* is published.
1933	Hitler comes to power in Germany. Reichstag fire—February 27, 1933. Dachau, near Munich, is opened as the first Nazi concentration camp.
1935	Nuremberg Laws are enacted.
1936	Gestapo is established. Himmler is made chief of SS and Gestapo.
1937	Buchenwald is opened.
1938	Anschluss—the Nazis invade Austria in March.
1938	H. Grynszpan assassinates a German diplomat in Paris, providing a pretext for *Kristallnacht.* Jews must add "Israel" or "Sarah" to their Aryan first names. Eichmann is placed in charge of Center for Jewish Emigration in Vienna.
1939	Heydrich holds conference of *Einsatzgruppen* chiefs.

1940	Auschwitz is established. Lodz ghetto—encloses 164,000 Jews. Warsaw Ghetto—encloses 400,000 Jews.
1941	First Death Camp—Chelmno. 2,000 Jews are killed at Bialystok in June. 48,000 Jews will be killed by end of 1941 at Ponary, outside Vilna.
1941	10,600 Jews from Riga ghetto are executed in November. 25,000 more are executed in December. 1.1 million Jews are murdered in 1941.
1942	Wannsee Conference is called to plan implementation of the "Final Solution." 250,000 Jews are killed in 18 months at Sobibor, beginning in May. 250,000 Jews are killed at Treblinka in two months, July and August. 400,000 Jews are killed in Occupied Europe in August. In 1942, 2.7 million Jews murdered.
1943	By end of April, 600,000 Jews are murdered at Belzec.
1944	By June 17, 1944, 340,000 Hungarian Jews are sent to Auschwitz. By end of 1944, 600,000 Jews have been murdered.
1945	Nuremberg Trials begin.
1946	Verdicts are rendered in October 1946.

7

ZIONISM

The area known as Palestine, the region that today includes the Land of Israel west of the Jordan River and the kingdom of Jordan to the east, was a real backwater of the Ottoman Empire. There was almost no direct governance by the Sultan of Turkey. Although populated by about 400,000 in 1840, Palestine was a place of enormous poverty, disease, and illiteracy. It had few roads, no seaport, and no railroad until 1892. Most who lived there were farmers who raised a few sheep and goats, although they were hindered frequently by drought and locusts.

There were internal tensions among the Arabs. The urban Arabs were separated from the rural, who were themselves separated from the nomads. There was a large gap between the urban gentry and the rural peasantry. In addition, rivalries between and among the villages and the nomads caused additional tensions.

Religious divisions and tensions also characterized Palestine. There were constant rivalries between and among the Sunni Muslims, the Shi'ite Muslims, the Druze, the various groups of Christians, and the Jews.

Palestine was populated at the beginning of the 19th century by approximately 6,000 Jews. By 1856 there were more than 17,000. Roughly half of these lived in Jerusalem, and the balance were divided among Tiberias, Safed, and Hebron.

Living conditions in Jerusalem were difficult. There was rampant disease, resulting largely from terrible hygiene. Neighborhoods were congested within the walls of the Old City. The Jews of Jerusalem had no means of support apart from donations from the communities of the Diaspora. The Muslim community of Jerusalem persecuted its Jews. Few could anticipate the growth of a Zionist movement at the end of the 19th century.

FORERUNNERS OF ZIONISM

Zionism is the Jewish nationalist movement that espouses the return of the Jewish people to their historic homeland, the Land of Israel, and the renewal of their collective spiritual, political, and economic life there in the framework of an independent Jewish state. The first person to use the word "Zionism" was Dr. Nathan Birnbaum. In 1893 he wrote of Zionism in his nationalist-Zionist newspaper, whose language was German.

The Zionist ideal of a Jewish homeland in Palestine could not be realized before people began to publish books and essays and circulate ideas favoring the concept. The first of these was R. Zvi Hirsch Kalischer (1795–1874), who authored a book called *Drishat Zion* ("Seeking Zion") in 1862. He wrote of "natural redemption," advocating the settlement of Jews in Palestine. Jews laboring on the land would lessen the

Zvi Hirsch Kalischer

161

need to import food from outside Palestine. They would be able to fulfill the commandments of tithing, of leaving some of their crops for the poor, of the Sabbatical year, and of the Jubilee year.

A second book prefiguring Zionism was *Rome and Jerusalem,* written by Moses Hess (1812–1875) and published in 1862. Hess was a close friend of Karl Marx and was a leading figure in German socialism. At first estranged from Judaism, Hess returned to it largely because of the Damascus Affair in 1840, in which Jews were accused of abducting and killing a Catholic monk. Although the Jews were clearly innocent, they underwent torture and two Jews were killed in the process. For Hess, this event was clear evidence that anti-Semitism would never disappear.

Emancipation was never going to be a solution to the Jewish problem, wrote Hess; it was destined to fail. The only real solution would be establishing Jewish settlements in Palestine, with the eventual goal of establishing a Jewish state. To be sure, the Jewish state would not attract all Jews to it, but it would serve as their spiritual center in any case.

A third precursor to Zionism was Dr. Leo Pinsker (1821–1891) of Odessa. The year 1881 was a major turning point in Pinsker's life. Before then, he had been active in an organization that encouraged Jews to acquaint themselves with the Russian language and culture. In 1881 Czar Alexander II was assassinated. Jews were thought to have carried out this assassination and a wave of pogroms resulted. As was noted in chapter 1, Czar Alexander III enacted the May Laws in 1882. Pinsker came to the conclusion that there was no possibility of overcoming the hatred of Jews. The cause of Russian anti-Semitism was the view that Jews were foreigners in Russia. The only solution was the establishment of a Jewish national center.

Pinsker's book, *Auto-Emancipation,* examined the social and psychological roots of anti-Semitism. It advocated the establishment of a national Jewish home. This book was very influential and came to be highly admired.

By the late 1870s there were Zionist circles and clubs in hundreds of towns in the Pale of Settlement. Meetings of the Lovers of Zion (Hovevei Zion) were illegal and secret. The members shared the view that there was a need to establish a Jewish nation in Palestine. These clubs, however, were not yet a movement, with central direction. It was here that Pinsker took the initiative.

In 1884 Pinsker called a national conference of Hovevei Zion, to be held in the German city of Kattowitz (now Katowice, Poland) in order to avoid the Russian authorities. The 34 delegates to this conference came to a consensus that their first priority should be "practical Zionism," the financing of Jewish settlement in Palestine. They established a central office in Odessa and elected Pinsker president. His assigned task was to encourage and support Jewish colonization in Palestine.

Pinsker died in 1891, but the 1890s saw rapid growth of Hibbat Zion in many parts of Europe. Although many of the Jews involved were not observant, distinguished rabbis urged their followers to participate nevertheless. R. Naftali Zvi Berlin (1817–1893), the head of the Volozhin yeshiva for 40 years, joined Hibbat Zion at its very beginning and was a member of its executive board. R. Isaac Elhanan Spektor (1817–1896) of Kovno supported Hibbat Zion, hosting the preparatory meetings for the Kattowitz conference in his own home. Hibbat Zion formed by far the strongest base for Theodor Herzl's Zionist movement.

The First Aliyah ("Immigration") came in the 1880s, beginning in 1882 and ending in 1903. The assassination of Czar Alexander II, for which some blamed the Jews, was a major contributing element. Approximately 25,000 immigrated to Palestine from Russia and Romania and established agricultural colonies. The immigrants lacked funding and agricultural knowledge. Baron Edmond de Rothschild came to their aid, however, providing financial support and sending personnel to train them in agriculture, especially grape-growing and wine production.

THEODOR HERZL

The Zionist movement needed leadership, though, and this came from Theodor Herzl. Herzl (1860–1904) was born in Budapest. He received an excellent secular education but a limited Jewish education. He came from a typical enlightened German-Jewish family, more German than Jewish.

Theodor Herzl

Herzl studied law in Vienna but chose to become a journalist. From October 1891 until July 1895 he was the Paris correspondent of the leading Vienna newspaper, the *Neue Freie Presse.*

In Paris Herzl became interested for the first time in the problem of anti-Semitism. Despite their having been emancipated 100 years before, the Jews of France were still encountering prejudice. Herzl proposed first the organized conversion of Jews to Christianity, followed by their becoming socialists. Then he offered a second solution: public discussion of the issue. For this purpose he wrote a play, *Das Ghetto,* which he thought would promote a relationship based on mutual respect and tolerance. Herzl's final views, however, were determined by the Dreyfus Trial.

Captain Alfred Dreyfus, the first Jew to serve on the General Staff of the French army, was accused of spying for France's enemy, Germany. The accusation was based on fabricated evidence, but Dreyfus was sentenced in 1895 to life imprisonment on Devil's Island. In 1896 the real spy was discovered, but his guilt was concealed, on the grounds that the French army would be dishonored as it prepared for war with Germany. Only in 1906 was Dreyfus legally rehabilitated, promoted to major, and decorated with the Legion of Honor.

The Dreyfus Trial convinced Herzl that anti-Semitism was an incurable Gentile "disease." It was present even in those countries that had emancipated their Jews. The only real solution was for the Jews to leave Europe and settle in an area that would be their own.

Having concluded that this and only this was a solution to the problem of anti-Semitism, Herzl published a pamphlet called *Der Judenstaat* ("The Jewish State"). In this work, he argued that anti-Semitism was not merely a social issue, whereby it was asserted that Jews were rich and exploiting the non-Jews. Nor was it simply a religious question whereby the Jews were accused of killing Jesus. It was, instead, a national question. The Jews had no place even in civilized Western Europe.

Herzl proposed the establishment of a Jewish national homeland. This would come about through a combination of political efforts to gain the approval of governments and practical colonization, which would, by necessity, follow the political successes.

Two agencies should be set up: the Society of Jews and the Jewish Company. The Society of Jews, a legal body constituting the representatives of the Jewish nation, would determine policy. The Jewish Company was to be an executive body assigned to carry out the policy. It would do the practical work, raising funds, organizing trade, supervising construction, and so on.

The Jewish State was well received in Eastern Europe. Copies were smuggled into the Pale of Settlement in order to circumvent Russian censorship. There was enormous excitement, but not because Herzl had put forth new ideas. The Jews sensed that a leader of the Zionist movement had now appeared.

In line with his political Zionism, Herzl used his contacts to secure interviews with political leaders.

The degradation of Captain Dreyfus

He met with the Kaiser of Germany and with the foreign minister of the Turkish Sultan. He met as well with Baron Edmond de Rothschild. Despite the foreign minister's passing on Herzl's appeal, the Sultan refused to consider issuing a charter for Jewish settlement in Palestine. Rothschild, meanwhile, angrily rejected the whole idea of Jewish statehood.

FIRST ZIONIST CONGRESS

Clearly unsettled by these meetings, Herzl decided to stir up the Jewish masses. He became determined to build support among them and to put the Jewish Question on the agenda for public discussion. The result was the decision to hold the First Zionist Congress, an international representative gathering of Jews supportive of the Zionist cause, in Basel, Switzerland, from August 29 to August 31, 1897.

When the Congress convened, 204 representatives came from 15 countries. Most came from Russia, Germany, and the Austro-Hungarian Empire, but some came from England, France, the United States, and Palestine.

Herzl set two goals for this First Congress. The first goal was to unite all Zionist groups in terms of purposes and actions, to establish a Zionist movement. The second goal was to reopen public discussion of the Jewish Question.

In his opening speech, Herzl expressed these themes and elaborated on them. Zionism must aim at reviving national feelings among Jews and improving their material situation. To achieve the goals of Zionism would require a strong organization. The establishment of a Jewish national home must be done legally, with the recognition of nations; there must be a commitment to political Zionism.

There was a formulation and adoption of the Basel Program. This program declared the aim of Zionism to be a publicly recognized, legally secured home in Palestine for the Jewish people. It endorsed political Zionism. It expressed its support for planned, programmatic settlement, beginning with agricultural workers, laborers, and tradesmen.

A Zionist Organization was formed which would operate between the annual congresses. The format of future congresses would include a discussion of the Jewish situation in the world, lectures on Palestine and settlement of Jews there, and debates on cultural issues. An executive committee of 23 would work between congresses. Anyone 18 or older who contributed one shekel (25 cents or one shilling in 1897) and accepted the Basel Program would have the right to vote for delegates.

Herzl advocated political Zionism in place of the practical Zionism of Hibbat Zion. Asher Zvi Ginsberg (1856–1927), who took the pen name of Ahad Ha-Am ("One of the People"), thought that Zionism should be more than a political movement. Zionism should seek to establish a Jewish homeland that would be a spiritual center for world Jewry, wherever they might live. A homeland for the Jews could be only in its historical home, the Land of Israel. There a rich national culture could be developed, one that would nourish Jewishness and Jewish identity everywhere in the Diaspora.

Herzl's position was that if Zionism was to be more than a political movement, it would stir up the old battles over the role of religion and Jewish law in Jewish life. Ahad Ha-Am's response was that without the setting up of a spiritual center in Palestine, the issue of Jewish survival would not be addressed. Political Zionism would not guarantee the survival of Jews. Jews would continue the process of assimilation and loss of Jewish identity. Herzl eventually triumphed over the challenge offered by Ahad Ha-Am, but it posed a threat, for a time, to political Zionism.

Ahad Ha-Am

One of the most fascinating figures in the history of Zionism was Asher Hirsch Ginsberg (1856–1927), known better by his pen name, Ahad Ha'am. A Hebrew essayist and thinker, he was also one of the leaders of the Hibbat Zion movement.

Born near Kiev in Russia, he received a traditional Jewish education in the home of his father, a Hasid who was a wealthy village merchant. He studied Talmud and medieval Jewish philosophy with a private teacher. He read the literature of the Haskalah and studied Russian, German, French, English, and Latin without any teacher. After marrying in 1867, he continued to study philosophy and science at home. He never entered a university, remaining self-taught. His own rationalism led him first to abandon Hasidism and then all religious faith.

In 1884 Ahad Ha'am settled in Odessa, an important center of Hebrew literature and Hibbat Zion. He stayed there until 1907, becoming active in Hibbat Zion. Visiting Eretz Yisrael in 1891, he published on his return a strongly critical survey of the economic, social, and spiritual aspects of the Jewish settlements. He also became manager of the Ahi'asaf publishing house and editor of the monthly Ha-Shilo'ah *in 1896.* Ha-Shilo'ah, *the most important organ of Zionism and Hebrew literature in Eastern Europe, served a large readership and contributed to the development of modern Hebrew literature. More important, it provided Ahad Ha'am a means to make his own views known.*

Involved as he was in Hibbat Zion, Ahad Ha'am had serious concerns about practical Zionism. Zionism was a great and noble cause but a cause that should not be advanced precipitately. He was not convinced that the Zionist program was the solution to the Jewish problem. His own preference was to solve the Jewish problem by revitalizing Jewish spiritual creativity and by strengthening Jews' identification with their heritage and history.

Ahad Ha'am did not see the ingathering of the exiles in Eretz Yisrael as the ultimate long-term goal. Most Jews would continue to live in exile, working with the assumption that their social and economic situation would ultimately improve and they would achieve equality of rights. Only some Jews would settle in Eretz Yisrael. There they would maintain a Jewish state that would serve as a "spiritual center" for the Diaspora. Jewish society there would constitute a focus of emotional identification with Judaism and the spiritual values created there would nourish all parts of the Jewish people and ensure its continued existence and unity.

Ahad Ha'am died in 1927 but every type of Zionism has been challenged by his writings and his thinking. Even after the establishment of the State of Israel, his writings are still studied and are an influential factor in Jewish thought in the Diaspora and in Israel. In a word, Ahad Ha'am was one of the most significant authors and thinkers of his generation.

LABOR ZIONISM

The Second Aliyah ("Immigration"), which occurred between 1905 and 1914, brought about 30,000 Jews to Palestine. Most who came were Russian Jews who had experienced a series of bloody pogroms in response to the failed Russian Revolution of 1905.

Many Russian Jews had been attracted by the increasingly popular ideology of socialism. Socialism viewed capitalist society as one in which rich capitalists exploited workers, using the hard work of the working class to become wealthy. Socialism called for the reform of society to be brought about by class struggle. The resulting society would be a just one, in which economic, social, and political power was shared.

This was an attractive ideology, but Russian Jews concluded eventually that it was impossible for Jews to benefit from socialist reforms, because of anti-Semitism. They began to preach a fusion of socialism with Zionism, advocating a Jewish society in Palestine constructed along socialist lines.

The major spokesman for Socialist or Labor Zionism was Nachman Syrkin, but the one who wrote about the centrality of labor and the worker was A. D. Gordon (1856–1922). Jews in the Diaspora, wrote Gordon, have been "abnormal," depending on the manual labor of others. Labor binds a people to the soil and establishes their possession of the soil. A living, vital culture is built upon labor, since only a healthy national life produces a vital culture, and a healthy national life depends on labor.

Among those included in the Second Aliyah was David Ben-Gurion, who would become the first Prime Minister of Israel. In addition, Labor Zionism, the chosen ideology of these immigrants, would become the official ideology of today's Ma'arach (Labor Alignment).

RELIGIOUS ZIONISM

Religious Zionism presented a different kind of challenge. Observant Jews participated in the Zionist movement, seeing Zionism as a political movement that had little to say about one's religious observance. One's relationship to tradition was entirely personal and individual. At the 1901 Zionist Congress, however, a resolution passed making educational work compulsory for Zionists. Since most early Zionists were not observant Jews, this meant education with a secular, nationalist orientation.

Observant Jews were very concerned by this resolution. It seemed to them that secularism was taking over the Zionist movement. This course was likely to alienate traditional Jews and drive them away. In 1902 the decision was made to found a new party, called Mizrachi, an abbreviation for *mercaz ruchani* ("spiritual center"). The founder of this new party was Rabbi Isaac Jacob Reines (1839–1915).

Mizrachi set its own religious-educational agenda, which it planned to foster both in and outside Palestine. It wanted to build and strengthen commitment to religious Zionism. Its audience was traditional, Orthodox circles in Europe; it hoped to attract such Jews with the vision of a revitalized Jewish religious life in Palestine.

Mizrachi held the conviction that Jewish survival as a nation depended on return to Palestine. It believed that full actualization of Torah obligations was possible only in Palestine; its slogan was "The land of Israel for the people of Israel according to the Torah of Israel." Mizrachi was determined to work within the Zionist organization for its broader political goal, a Jewish homeland, while using its own organization to promote its religious and educational aims.

The Third Aliyah, which followed World War I and the Russian Revolution, brought many young, observant workers from Poland and Lithuania. These immigrants formed their own organization with the stated ideology of *Torah v'Avoda* ("Torah and Labor"). Ultimately this became the dominant religious Zionist party, absorbing Mizrachi to form today's Mafdal (National Religious Party).

BALFOUR DECLARATION

On November 2, 1917, the British government issued the Balfour Declaration, in the form of a letter from Lord Balfour to Edmond de Rothschild, who represented the Jews of the world. This declaration professed the support of Great Britain for establishing a national home for the Jewish people in Palestine.

A number of motives lay behind this declaration. Lord Balfour and Prime Minister Lloyd George were pious Christians who took the Bible very seriously. They understood the extent of its contribution to Christianity and to the British national character, and so they valued an opportunity to help those who had given the world the Bible.

There were political considerations as well. The British wanted to sway public opinion in the United States and in Russia so that these nations would stand behind them in World War I. The idea was that if American and Russian Jews were on the British side, general public opinion in these countries would follow.

There were, finally, strategic considerations. Control of Palestine meant control of an important strategic area. Palestine was close to the Suez Canal and to the land and water routes to India. Britain was also interested in preventing France from taking the Suez Canal. By creating a buffer between Syria and Egypt, this move could be prevented.

In April 1920 the San Remo Peace Conference, which followed World War I, assigned a Mandate over Palestine to Great Britain, and in March 1921 Great Britain subdivided the Mandate, creating Transjordan (called Jordan today). On July 1, 1922, the Churchill White Paper provided official "clarification" of how Great Britain viewed its Mandate over Palestine, and on July 24, 1922, the official text for the Mandate was approved by the League of Nations. By 1922, the number of Jews living in Palestine had risen to 120,000.

Under the terms of the Mandate, Britain obligated itself to put the Balfour Declaration into effect, to establish a Jewish national home. This obligation stemmed from the moral claim of the Jews to have a national home in Palestine, which itself emanated from the Jews' historical connection to Palestine.

Britain, as the holder of the Mandate, was to have full powers of legislation and administration. It had no obligation to move quickly toward establishing autonomous rule for the residents of Palestine, as did France, which held a Mandate over Syria and Lebanon. Nevertheless, Britain was obligated to allow the creation of a "Jewish Agency," which would work with them in matters of social and economic organization and structure and in the development of Palestine. This agency would involve itself, then, in the development of natural resources, the building of roads, the setting up of public utilities, and the like.

Hebrew was to be an official language of the Mandate, appearing on all currency and on all legal documents. Immigration and settlement of Jews in Palestine were to be permitted, even facilitated and encouraged by the British. Immigration would be limited, however, to the "economic and absorptive capacity" of Palestine.

ARAB NATIONALISM

The greatest threat to the establishment of a Jewish homeland was the emergence of Arab nationalism. The Arabs feared massive immigration of Jews into Palestine. The Jews would take all of Palestine, they thought, evicting all Arabs from it.

The central figure in Arab nationalism was Haj Muhammad Amin al-Husseini, appointed the Mufti of Jerusalem in 1922. The Mufti held the highest religious position in Palestine but at the same time headed the Muslim Supreme Council. Thus he joined enormous religious influence with enormous political power. This combination allowed him to spread Arab nationalism and opposition to the British Mandate.

Despite the Mufti's efforts, things remained relatively calm in Palestine. There did occur outbreaks of violence in May 1921. Riots, burnings, and killings began in Tel Aviv but spread to the villages of Petach Tikva, Kfar Saba, Hadera, and Rehovot. Casualties were minimal, however, fewer than a hundred on each side.

Other than this, the 1920s brought no major incidents. The year 1929, though, changed everything. On August 23, 1929, the Mufti called upon the Muslim masses to "defend" the al-Aqsa mosque, located on the Temple Mount in Jerusalem, to rise up against the Orthodox Jews of Jerusalem. The violence spread beyond Jerusalem to Tel Aviv, Haifa, and Jaffa. There were attacks on agricultural villages. The Jewish settlement in Hebron was devastated by the attacks, as 60 Jews perished and 50 were wounded. Order was restored in Palestine on August 28, but 135 Jews had died, and 400 were wounded; 90 Arabs had died, with 90 wounded.

As the clouds gathered over Europe's Jews, immigration to Palestine increased. By 1936 there were 400,000 Jews living in Palestine. The Arabs of Palestine, of whom there were 960,000, began to argue that the responsibilities of the British had now been completed. A Jewish homeland existed. The time had now come to end the Mandate and give Palestine its independence. This meant, naturally, a Palestine that would be ruled by its majority, the Arabs.

The concern about increased immigration combined with the Mufti's anti-Jewish feelings. In May 1936 he announced a strike of all Arab workers, protesting the British immigration policy. It was to last seven months. In the middle of the summer, an armed revolt began. Jewish farms were attacked, cattle and produce were destroyed, and Jewish civilians were killed. By October, 200 Arabs were killed, as were 80 Jews and 28 British.

The British promised a Royal Commission of Inquiry before which the Arabs could present their complaints. The Arabs agreed to stop the rebellion and to suspend their strike.

On November 11, 1936, the British established the Peel Commission. It had three tasks: to examine the causes of the violence, consider the complaints of both sides, and make recommendations for the future. The central conclusion of the commission's report was that any compromise was impossible. The recommendation was partition. Palestine would be divided into three parts: a Jewish state, an Arab state, and an area that would remain in British hands.

The idea of partition was acceptable to the British. The Arabs, however, were divided in opinion. Some, like King Abdullah of Transjordan, were inclined to accept. The Mufti and his followers, however, rejected the idea outright. The Jews were inclined to

Vladimir (Zev) Jabotinsky (1880–1940) was a Zionist activist, soldier, orator, writer, poet, and founder of the Jewish Legion during World War I. Fluent in Russian, Hebrew, Yiddish, English, French, and German, he drew large audiences everywhere he spoke and was often the highlight of Zionist Congresses.

As head of the Betar movement, an activist Zionist youth movement founded in Riga, Latvia, in 1923, he inspired thousands of young Jews, especially in Eastern Europe. In 1925 he left the Zionist movement and established the Revisionist Party, which advocated the restoration of the Jewish Legion to protect against Arab hostility. It also called for a political offensive aimed at changing British policy, so that, through mass immigration, a Jewish majority would be in Palestine, including Transjordan, that part of Palestine declared by the British off limits to Jews.

Jabotinsky supported "illegal" immigration of Jews to Palestine and was intent on interfering with British regulations on immigration. Between 1936 and 1940 this activity was the major focus of the Revisionists. Relations between Arabs and Jews in Palestine were deteriorating during the 1930s, and the 1936 Arab riots led Jabotinsky to think that they should be countered with violent retaliation. This was certainly already the view of the Irgun Zvai Leummi, founded by Revisionists and members of Betar in 1937 and receiving orders from Jabotinsky.

Jabotinsky died in 1940. Among his followers of were Menachem Begin (1913–1992), commander of the Irgun from 1944 to 1948 and Israel's sixth Prime Minister, and Binyamin Netanyahu, its tenth Prime Minister.

---

accept partition, with the exception of Vladimir Jabotinsky and the Revisionists, who rejected this option without hesitation.

The next three years brought a renewal of the Arab Revolt. Over the course of three years, 2,400 Jews

Vladimir Jabotinsky (1880–1940) in the uniform of the Jewish Legion, which he founded in World War I. Jabotinsky was imprisoned by the British for organizing the Haganah. Later, he founded the Zionist Revisionist movement and the Irgun Zvai Leumi.

were killed, as were 3,800 Arabs and 600 Britons. By early 1939 the British had abandoned the idea of partition entirely. The Arab ferment contributed to this decision, as did the concern that the Arabs might join the Axis powers.

Together with abandonment of the partition idea came the announcement of a conference to be held in London in February 1939. Among the invited were the Zionists and the Arabs of Palestine, but representatives of Arab states bordering Palestine were also invited to participate.

The conference ended on March 17, 1939, but its conclusions were not published until a White Paper came out in May 1939. It was here that Britain made known its intentions for the future of Palestine. Britain envisioned the emergence of an independent state of Palestine within a period of ten years. Those living in Palestine would play a growing role in its government. The settlements of Jews and of Arabs and the holy places would be protected, as would British strategic interests.

Of far greater significance, however, were the statements about Jewish immigration to Palestine. There would be a special one-time act of compassion allowing 25,000 Jews to enter. After this, only 10,000 Jews would be admitted each year. After 1944 no Jews would enter without Arab approval.

The Zionists agreed to oppose this British policy. The Arabs were satisfied, although many would have liked even fewer Jews to be admitted. In Britain there was powerful opposition from the press and from important politicians, especially Churchill. Nevertheless, the White Paper was approved by a slim majority in the British Parliament.

WORLD WAR II

World War II began on September 1, 1939. Three major developments affected the Zionist movement during the war. First, Churchill found himself at odds with the British Foreign Office and the mandatory authorities. Churchill gave enormous support to the Zionist movement, promising Dr. Chaim Weizmann an acceptable solution to the problem of Palestine after the war. This would include partition and the immigration of 1.5 million refugees into Palestine over a period of ten years; there would be immediate immigration of 150,000 orphans. He could not, however, overcome the opposition of the Foreign Office and the mandatory authorities.

In addition, the Zionist Congress of May 1942, held in New York City at the Biltmore Hotel because of the war, produced the Biltmore Program. This program stated that there would be no solution to the problem of Palestine that did not include a Jewish state, with complete Jewish sovereignty. This was the first time the Zionist movement insisted on a Jewish state.

The war period also brought increased anti-British violence on the part of Lechi (Lochamei Herut Yisrael), known as the Stern Gang. This group had separated itself from the Irgun (Irgun Zvai Leummi, National Military Organization), preferring to force the British out of Palestine through violence. On November 6, 1944, Lord Moyne, the representative of Britain in Egypt, was assassinated by Lechi. The Zionist leadership condemned this action, but it was certainly a sign that patience with the British had come to an end and there would no longer be British-Zionist cooperation.

In July 1945 Churchill was defeated. The Labour Party came to power, under the leadership of Clement Attlee, although the most influential figure in Attlee's government was the foreign minister, Ernest Bevin. During the years of the war, the Labour Party was most supportive of the Zionists. When it took over, Zionist leaders were convinced

that the road to Jewish statehood was now open. They were mistaken.

British policy after the war concerned itself with two things. First, England was experiencing serious economic crisis. It was necessary to protect access to the oil lines in Iraq, Qatar, and Kuwait. These oil lines, however, passed through other Arab countries. It became critical, then, to maintain friendly relations with all Arab countries.

Second, the Soviets aspired to take over the Arab countries bordering the Persian Gulf. Friendly relations with these Arab countries would help overcome this threat.

The British concluded that they needed to proceed more slowly on Palestine. Bevin's view was that the loyalty of the Arabs ought to be "cultivated." He suggested that America be enlisted in the effort to find another place of shelter for the Jews.

President Truman, however, responded with a letter to Attlee, urging that 100,000 Jews be admitted to Palestine immediately. Troubled by the situation of the 250,000 displaced persons, survivors of the Holocaust with no homes and no choice but to remain in camps in Germany, he saw Palestine as a solution. The British, however, refused to admit 100,000. As a result, the Haganah (Army of Defense), the Irgun, and Lechi agreed to work together. From November 1945 to May 1946, there were systematic attacks on British installations.

Menachem Begin headed the Betar movement before he was 20 years old. Because of his Zionist activities, the Russians sentenced him to a Siberian labor camp. In 1942 he immigrated to Palestine, where he organized the armed Jewish underground struggle against the British. He evaded police by disguising himself as a bearded rabbi. Begin founded the Herut (Freedom) Party and in 1977 became Prime Minister.

In November 1945, Attlee proposed the establishment of an Anglo-American Committee of Inquiry, whose task would be to examine the problem posed by Jewish displaced persons and to recommend a solution. Truman agreed, on the one condition that the focus be on Palestine as a solution.

The proposed committee was formed. Its 25 members visited the United States, England, Palestine, Egypt, and the displaced persons camps in Germany, in an effort to hear from all sides. The demands of the Arabs were extreme. They said that immigration of Jews should be halted, the Mandate should conclude, and the Balfour Declaration should be repudiated. Palestine should become an independent Arab state.

The Jews saw Palestine as the only solution to the problem presented by the 250,000 displaced persons in postwar Europe. Palestine, they said, could certainly absorb a million and a quarter immigrants over a ten-year period.

In its report, the committee recommended immediate admission of 100,000 Jews. It recommended as well that Palestine be a bi-national state.

Truman accepted the recommendations. Britain rejected them. Ben-Gurion rejected them as well. His feeling was that only an independent Jewish state could ensure that Jewish immigration would never cease.

It was now that all Jewish forces adopted the approach of Lechi, permitting even the killing of British soldiers. On June 17, 1946, all bridges connecting Palestine to its neighbors were bombed—this episode was called the Night of the Bridges. On July 22, 1946, there was an explosion in the British headquarters at the King David Hotel, killing 91 people.

During the same years, the Jewish Agency renewed its support of illegal immigration of Jews into Palestine. By the fall of 1946 more than 1,000 were leaving the displaced persons camps every month, making their way to Palestine. The British did have some success in stopping ships and preventing their passengers from entering Palestine. Approximately 50,000 were forced to go to Cyprus, where they remained in camps.

END OF BRITISH MANDATE

In February 1947, the British decided to end their Mandate over Palestine. They placed the problem of Palestine in the hands of the United Nations. On May 31, 1947, the United Nations formed its first committee, which it named United Nations Special Committee on Palestine. Eleven countries participated and presented their report on August 31, 1947.

On most questions there was agreement. The Mandate had to end and Palestine had to be independent. The new state (or states) had to be a democracy. The economic unity of Palestine had to be preserved. The holy places of all three religions had to be protected and accessible to all. The General Assembly had to solve the problem of the 250,000 displaced persons immediately.

On two issues there was disagreement among the members. First, should there be one state or two? The minority favored one state, with Jerusalem as the capital. The state would be a federation of cantons, some populated by Jews, some by Arabs. Internal affairs would be handled by each canton. Immigration, foreign policy, and security would be the responsibility of the central government. The majority favored two states.

A second area of disagreement was Jewish immigration. The minority thought that immigrants should be permitted to enter Palestine for just three

Rabbi Meir Berlin (left), American president of the Mizrachi World Organization, talking with Jewish Agency leader David Ben-Gurion.

years and only in accordance with its ability to absorb them. The majority favored the immigration of 150,000, 6,250 per month, during an interim period of two years. After this interim period, 60,000 would be admitted per year.

The Zionists accepted the recommendation of the majority, although the limits established were not to their liking. The most critical elements were there, nevertheless: there would be sovereignty and unlimited immigration, at least in the immediate future. The Arabs rejected the majority recommendation outright, threatening to go to war.

The matter was put to a vote in the United Nations on November 29, 1947. The majority recommendation was accepted by a 33–13 vote. The key players were the United States and Russia. On one side, Truman wanted to come to the aid of those who had suffered under the Nazis, and on the other, Russia wanted to establish a presence in the Middle East.

SUMMARY

We have reviewed the early history of Zionism, beginning with its precursors, R. Zvi Hirsch Kalischer, Moses Hess, and Leo Pinsker. We looked then at Theodor Herzl, his book *The Jewish State* and the reception it was given, and the first international gathering of Zionists, the First Zionist Congress.

Labor Zionism, a combination of socialism with Zionism, was attractive to many Zionists. Others, observant Jews, preferred religious Zionism. On

A banner headline announces the birth of the new state. Although the State of Israel was proclaimed on Friday afternoon, May 14, 1948, the paper is dated Sunday, May 16, because no papers in Israel are printed on the Jewish Sabbath

November 2, 1917, the British issued the Balfour Declaration, declaring their support for a national home for the Jews in Palestine and, at the post–World War I peace conference, were given a Mandate over Palestine. The Mandate lasted for 30 years, but the British eventually despaired of resolving the conflict between Jews and Arabs, placing Palestine in the lap of the United Nations. The United Nations Special Committee on Palestine recommended partition of Palestine. In November 1947 this recommendation was approved by a vote in the United Nations.

Documents

Z. H. KALISCHER: DERISHAT ZION
(1862)

In this selection, one of the precursors to the Zionist movement, Rabbi Z. H. Kalischer, urges Jews to go and settle in Palestine, thus beginning their promised redemption.

The redemption of Israel, for which we long, is not to be imagined as a sudden miracle. The Almighty, blessed be His Name, will not suddenly descend from on high and command His people to go forth. He will not send the Messiah from heaven in a twinkling of an eye, to sound the great trumpet for the scattered of Israel and gather them into Jerusalem. He will not surround the Holy City with a wall of fire or cause the Holy Temple to descend from the heavens. The bliss and the miracles that were promised by His servants, the prophets, will certainly come to pass—everything will be fulfilled—but we will not run in terror and flight, for the Redemption of Israel will come by slow degrees and the ray of deliverance will shine forth gradually.

My dear reader! Cast aside the conventional view that the Messiah will suddenly sound a blast on the great trumpet and cause all the inhabitants of the earth to tremble. On the contrary, the Redemption will begin by awakening support among the philanthropists and by gaining the consent of the nations to the gathering of some of the scattered of Israel into the Holy Land.

The prophet Isaiah (27:6 and 12–13) expressed this thought as follows: "In the days to come shall Jacob take root, Israel shall blossom and bud; and the face of the world shall be filled with fruitage. And it shall come to pass in that day, that the Lord will beat off his fruit from the flood of the River unto the Brook of Egypt, and ye shall be gathered one by one, O ye children of Israel. And it shall come to pass in that day, that a great horn shall be blown; and they shall come that were lost in the land of Assyria, and they that were dispersed in the land of Egypt; and they shall worship the Lord in the holy mountain at Jerusalem." He thus revealed that all of Israel would not return from exile at one time, but would be gathered by degrees, as the grain is slowly gathered from the beaten corn. The meaning of "In the days to come Jacob shall take root" in the first verse above, is that the Almighty would make those who came first—at the beginning of the Redemption—the root planted in the earth to produce many sprigs. Afterward Israel will blossom forth in the Holy Land, for the root will yield buds which will increase and multiply until they cover the face of the earth with fruit. This conception of the Redemption is also implied in the statement (Isaiah 11:11): "And it shall come to pass in that day, that the Lord will set His hand again the second time to recover the remnant of His people, that shall remain from Assyria and from Egypt." It is evident that both a first and a second ingathering are intended: the function of the first will be to pioneer the land, after which Israel will blossom forth to a most exalted degree.

Can we logically explain why the Redemption will begin in a natural manner and why the Lord, in His Love for His people, will not immediately send the Messiah in an obvious miracle? Yes, we can. We know that all our worship of God is in the form of trials which He tests us. When God created man and placed him in the Garden of Eden, He also planted the Tree of Knowledge and then commanded man not to eat of it. Why did he put the Tree in the Garden, if not as a trial? Why did He allow the Snake to enter the Garden and tempt man, if not to test whether man would observe God's command? When Israel went forth from Egypt, God again tested man's faith with hunger and thirst along the way. The laws given us in the Torah about unclean animals which are forbidden us as food are also a continuous trial—else why did the Almighty make them so tempting and succulent? Throughout the days of our dispersion we have suffered martyrdom for the sanctity of God's Name; we have been dragged from land to land and have borne the yoke of exile through the ages, all for the sake of His holy Torah and as a further stage of the testing of our faith.

If the Almighty were suddenly to appear, one day in the future, through undeniable miracles, this would be no trial. What straining of our faith would there be in the face of the miracles and wonders attending a clear heavenly command to go up and inherit the land and enjoy its good fruit? Under such circumstances what fool would not go there, not because of his love of God, but for his own selfish sake? Only a natural beginning of the Redemption is a true test of those who initiate it. To concentrate all one's energy on this holy work and to renounce home and fortune for the sake of living in Zion before "the voice of gladness" and the "voice of joy" are heard—there is no greater merit or trial than this.

I have found support for this view in *The Paths of Faith:* "When many Jews, pious and learned in the Torah, volunteer to go to the Land of Israel and settle in Jerusalem, motivated by a desire to serve, by purity of spirit, and by love of holiness; when they come, by ones and twos, from all four corners of the world; and when many settle there and their prayers increase at the holy mountain in Jerusalem— the Creator will then heed them and hasten the Day of Redemption." For all this to come about there must first be Jewish settlement in the Land; without such settlement, how can the ingathering begin?

There are many who will refuse to support the poor of the Holy Land by saying: "Why should we support people who choose idleness, who are lazy and not interested in working, and who prefer to depend upon the Jews of the Diaspora to support them?" To be sure, this is an argument put forth by Satan, for the people of Palestine are students of the Torah, unaccustomed from the time of their youth to physical labor. Most of them came from distant shores, risking their very lives for the privilege of living in the Holy Land. In this country, which is strange to them, how could they go about finding a business or an occupation, when they had never in their lives done anything of this kind? Their eyes can only turn to their philanthropic brethren, of whom they ask only enough to keep body and soul together, so that they can dwell in that Land which is God's portion on earth.

Yet, in order to silence this argument once and for all, I would suggest that an organization be established to encourage settlement in the Holy Land, fro the purpose of purchasing and cultivating farms and vineyards. Such a program would appear as a ray of deliverance to those now living in the Land in poverty and famine The pittance that is gathered from the entire Jewish world for their support is not enough to satisfy their hunger; indeed, in Jerusalem, the city which should be a source of blessing and well-being, many pious and saintly people are fainting of hunger in the streets.

The situation would be different if we were inspired by the fervor of working the land with our own hands. Surely, God would bless our labor and there would be no need to import grain from Egypt and other neighboring countries, for our harvest would prosper greatly. Once the Jews in the Holy Land began to eat of their own produce the financial aid of the Diaspora would suffice.

Another great advantage of agricultural settlement is that we would have the privilege of observing the religious commandments that attach to working the soil of the Holy Land. The Jews who supervised the actual laborers would be aiding in the working of the land and would therefore have the same status as if they had personally fulfilled these commandments.

But, beyond all this, Jewish farming would be a spur to the ultimate Messianic Redemption. As we bring redemption to the land in a "this-worldly" way, the rays of heavenly deliverance will gradually appear.

Let no stubborn opponent of these thoughts maintain that those who labor day and night will be taken away from the study of the Torah and from spiritual to secular concerns. This counterargument is shortsighted. On the contrary, the policy we propose will add dignity to the Torah. "If there is no bread, there can be no study"; if there is bread in the land, people will then be able to study with peace of mind. In addition, we are sure that there are many in the Holy Land who are not students of the Torah and who long to work the land. These will support the physically infirm scholars to whom no man would dare say: Work the land! But to whom all would say that they should devote themselves entirely to serving the Lord.

Such a policy would also raise our dignity among the nations, for they would say that the children of Israel, too, have the will to redeem the land of their ancestors, which is now so barren and forsaken.

Why do the people of Italy and of other countries sacrifice their lives for the land of their fathers, while we, like men bereft of strength and courage, do nothing? Are we inferior to all other peoples, who have no regard for life and fortune as compared with love of their land and nation? Let us take to heart the examples of the Italians, Poles, and Hungarians, who lay down their lives and possessions in the struggle for national independence, while we, the children of Israel, who have the most glorious and holiest of lands as our inheritance, are spiritless and silent. We should be ashamed of ourselves! All the other peoples have striven only for the sake of their own national honor; how much more should we exert ourselves, for our duty is to labor not only for the glory of our ancestors but for the glory of God who chose Zion!

THEODOR HERZL: THE JEWISH STATE *(1896)*

This is an excerpt from Herzl's famous book *The Jewish State,* published in 1896.

The Jewish question still exists. It would be foolish to deny it. It is a remnant of the Middle Ages, which civilized nations do not even yet seem able to shake off, try as they will. They certainly showed a generous desire to do so when they emancipated us. The Jewish question exists wherever Jews live in perceptible numbers. Where it does not exist, it is carried by Jews in the course of their migrations. We naturally move to those places where we are not persecuted, and there our presence produces persecution. This is the case in every country, and will remain so, even in those highly civilized—for instance, France—until the Jewish question finds a solution on a political basis. The unfortunate Jews are now carrying the seeds of anti-Semitism into England; they have already introduced it into America.

I believe that I understand anti-Semitism, which is really a highly complex movement. I consider it from a Jewish standpoint, yet without fear or hatred. I believe that I can see what elements there are in it of vulgar sport, of common trade jealousy, of inherited prejudice, of religious intolerance, and also of pretended self-defense. I think the Jewish question is no more a social than a religious one, notwithstanding that it sometimes takes these and other forms. It is a national question, which can only be solved by making it a political world-question to be discussed and settled by the civilized nations of the world in council.

We are a people—one people.

No one can deny the gravity of the situation of the Jews. Wherever they live in perceptible numbers, they are more or less persecuted. Their equality before the law, granted by statute, has become practically a dead letter. They are debarred from filling even moderately high positions, either in the army or in any public or private capacity. And attempts are made to thrust them out of business also: "Don't buy from Jews!"

Attacks in Parliaments, in assemblies, in the press, in the pulpit, in the street, on journeys—for example, their exclusion from certain hotels—even in places of recreation, become daily more numerous. The forms of persecution varying according to the countries and social circles in which they occur. In Russia, imposts are levied on Jewish villages; in Romania, a few people are put to death; in Germany, they get a good beating occasionally; in Austria, anti-Semites exercise terrorism over all public life; in Algeria, there are traveling agitators; in Paris, the Jews are shut out of the so-called best social circles and excluded from clubs. Shades of anti-Jewish feeling are innumerable. But this is not to be an attempt to make out a doleful category of Jewish hardships.

I do not intend to arouse sympathetic emotions on our behalf. That would be a foolish, futile, and undignified proceeding. I shall content myself with putting the following questions to the Jews: Is it not true that, in countries where we live in perceptible numbers, the position of Jewish lawyers, doctors, technicians, teachers, and employees of all descriptions becomes daily more intolerable? Is it not true that the Jewish middle classes are seriously threatened? Is it not true that the passions of the mob are incited against our wealthy people? Is it not true that our poor endure greater sufferings than any other proletariat? I think that this external pressure makes itself felt everywhere. In our economically upper classes it causes discomfort, in our middle classes continual and grave anxieties, in our lower classes absolute despair.

Everything tends, in fact, to one and the same conclusion, which is clearly enunciated in that classic Berlin phrase: *Juden Raus!* ("Out with the Jews!")

I shall now put the question in the briefest possible form: Are we to "get out" now, and where to?

Or, may we yet remain? And, how long?

Let us first settle the point of staying where we are. Can we hope for better days, can we possess our souls in patience, can we wait in pious resignation till the princes and peoples of this earth are more mercifully disposed toward us? I say that we cannot hope for a change in the current of feeling. And why not? Even if we were as near to the hearts of princes as are their other subjects, they could not protect us. They would only feel popular hatred by showing us too much favor. By "too much," I really mean less than is claimed as a right by every ordinary citizen, or by every race. The nations in whose midst Jews live are all either covertly or openly anti-Semitic.

The common people have not, and indeed cannot have, any historical comprehension. They do not know that the sins of the Middle Ages are now being visited on the nations of Europe. We are what the ghetto made us. We have attained pre-eminence in finance because medieval conditions drove us to it. The same process is now being repeated. We are again being forced into finance, now it is the stock exchange, by being kept out of other branches of economic activity. Being on the stock exchange, we are consequently exposed afresh to contempt. At the same time, we continue to produce an abundance of mediocre intellects who find no outlet, and this endangers our social position as much as does our increasing wealth. Educated Jews without means are now rapidly becoming socialists. Hence we are certain to suffer very severely in the struggle between classes, because we stand in the most exposed position in the camps of both socialists and capitalists. . . .

The Plan

The whole plan is in its essence perfectly simple, as it must necessarily be if it is to come within the comprehension of all.

Let the sovereignty be granted us over a portion of the globe large enough to satisfy the rightful requirements of a nation; the rest we shall manage for ourselves.

The creation of a new state is neither ridiculous nor impossible. We have in our day witnessed the process in connection with nations which were not largely members of the middle class, but poorer, less educated, and consequently weaker than ourselves. The governments of all countries scourged by anti-Semitism will be keenly interested in assisting us to obtain the sovereignty we want.

The plan, simple in design, but complicated in execution, will be carried out by two agencies: The Society of Jews and the Jewish Company.

The Society of Jews will do the preparatory work in the domains of science and politics, which the Jewish Company will afterward apply practically.

The Jewish Company will be liquidating agent of the business interests of departing Jews, and will organize commerce and trade in the new country.

We must not imagine the departure of the Jews to be a sudden one. It will be gradual, continuous, and will cover many decades. The poorest will go first to cultivate the soil. In accordance with a preconceived plan, they will construct roads, bridges, railways and telegraph installations; regulate rivers; and build their own dwellings; their labor will create trade, trade will create markets and markets will attract new settlers, for every man will go voluntarily, at his own expense and his own risk. The labor expended on the land will enhance its value, and the Jews will soon perceive that a new and permanent sphere of operation is opening here for that spirit of enterprise which as heretofore met only with hatred and obloquy.

If we wish to found a state today, we shall not do it in the way which would have been the only possible one a thousand years ago. It is foolish to revert to old stages of civilization, as many Zionists would like to do. Supposing, for example, we were obliged to clear a country of wild beasts, we should not set about the task in the fashion of Europeans of the fifth century. We should not take spear and lance and go out singly in pursuit of bears; we would organize a large and active hunting party, drive the animals together, and throw a melinite bomb into their midst.

A. D. GORDON: "PEOPLE AND LABOR" (1911)

A. D. Gordon was the Zionist movement's secular mystic and saint. Until age 47 he lived in Russia, supporting himself by managing a firm. When the lease ran out on this firm, though, he needed to consider his options. He chose to settle in Palestine. In his writings, Gordon emphasizes the centrality of labor.

The Jewish people has been completely cut off from nature and imprisoned within city walls these 2,000 years.

We have become accustomed to every form of life, except to a life of labor—of labor done at our own behest and for its own sake. It will require the greatest effort of will for such a people to become normal again. We lack the principal ingredient for national life. We lack the habit of labor—not labor performed out of external compulsion, but labor to which one is attached in a natural and organic way. This kind of labor binds a people to its soil and to its national culture, which in turn is an outgrowth of the people's soil and the people's labor.

Now it is true that every people has many individuals who shun physical labor and try to live off the work of others. But a normal people is like a living organism which performs its various functions naturally, and labor is one of its basic and organic functions. A normal people invariably contains a large majority of individuals for whom labor is second nature. But we Jews are different. We have developed an attitude of looking down on manual labor, so that even those who are engaged in it work out of mere compulsion and always with the hope of eventually escaping to "a better life." We must not deceive ourselves in this regard, nor shut our eyes to our grave deficiencies, not merely as individuals but as a people. The well-known talmudic saying, that when the Jews do God's will their labor is done for them by others, is characteristic of our attitude. This saying is significant. It demonstrates how far this attitude has become an instinctive feeling within us, a second nature.

Who among us thinks about this problem? Who is sensitive to it? We have no labor—and yet we are not aware that anything is missing. We take no notice of it even when we talk of our national rebirth. Labor is not only the force which binds man to the soil and by which possession of the soil is acquired; it is also the basic energy for the creation of a national culture. This is what we do not have—but we are not aware of missing it. We are a people without a country, without a living national language, without a living culture—but that, at least, we know and it pains us, even if only vaguely, and we seek ways and means of doing what needs must be done. But we seem to think that if we have no labor it does not matter—let Ivan, or John, or Mustapha do the work, while we busy ourselves with producing a culture, with creating national values, and with enthroning absolute justice in the world.

After very prolonged and very stubborn battles, the ideal of culture has finally won a place in our national (Zionist) movement. But what kind of culture is it?

By culture we usually mean what is called in Zionist circles "the rebirth of the spirit," or a "a spiritual renaissance." But the spirit which we are trying to revive is not the breath of real life which permeates the whole living organism and draws life from it, but some shadowy and abstract spirit, which can express itself only within the recesses of heart and mind. Judging by the deliberations at the Zionist Congress, culture is entirely a matter of ideas or ideology. Such being the case, culture may mean to some of us the ideology of Hermann Struck and Rabbi Reines, i.e., the religious orthodoxy of Mizrachi, while to others it may signify the outlook of the school of Marx and Engels.

A vital culture, far from being detached from life, embraces it in all its aspects. Culture is whatever life creates for living purposes. Farming, building, and road-making—any work, any craft, any productive activity—is part of culture and is indeed the foundation and the stuff of culture. The procedure, the pattern, the shape, the manner in which things are done—these represent the forms of culture. Whatever people feel and think both at work and at leisure, and the relations arising from these situations, combined with the natural surroundings—all that constitutes the spirit of a people's culture. It sustains the higher expressions of culture in science and art, creeds and ideologies. The things we call culture in the most restricted sense, the higher expressions of culture (which is what is usually meant when culture is discussed in our circles)—this is the butter churned out of culture in general, in its broadest sense. But can butter be produced without milk? Or can a man make butter by using his neighbor's milk and still call the butter all his own?

What are we seeking in Palestine? Is it not that which we can never find elsewhere—the fresh milk of a healthy people's culture? What we are come to create at present is not the culture of the academy, before we have anything else, but a culture of life, of which the culture of the academy is only one element. We seek to create a vital culture out of which the cream of a higher culture can easily be evolved. We intend to create creeds and ideologies, art and poetry, and ethics and religion, all growing out of a healthy life and intimately related to it; we shall therefore have created healthy human relationships and living links that bind the present to the past. What we seek to create here is life—our own life—in our own spirit and in our own way. Let me put it more bluntly: In Palestine we must do with our own hands all the things that make up the sum total of life. We must ourselves do all the work, from the least strenuous, cleanest, and most sophisticated, to the dirtiest and most difficult. In our own way, we must feel what a worker feels and think what a worker thinks—then, and only then, shall we have a culture of our own, for then we shall have a life of our own.

It all seems very clear: From now on our principal ideal must be Labor. Through no fault of our own we have been deprived of this element and we must seek a remedy. Labor is our cure. The ideal of Labor must become the pivot of all our aspirations. It is the foundation upon which our national structure is to be erected. Only by making Labor, for its own sake, our national ideal shall we be able to cure ourselves of the plague that has affected us for many generations and mend the rent between ourselves and Nature.

Labor is a great human ideal. It is the ideal of the future, and a great ideal can be a healing sum. Though the purpose of history is not, to be sure, to act the teacher, still the wise can and must learn from it. We can learn from our condition in the past and in the present, for we must now set the example for the future. We must all work with our hands.

We need a new spirit for our national renaissance. That new spirit must be created here in Palestine and must be nourished by our life in Palestine. It must be vital in all its aspects, and it must be all our own.

What we need is zealots of Labor—zealots in the finest sense of the word.

Any man who devotes his life to this ideal will not need to be told how difficult it is, but he will also know that it is of immense importance.

MIZRACHI MANIFESTO (1902)

This document presents the main principles of the Mizrachi party.

In the lands of the Diaspora the soul of our people—our Holy Torah—can no longer be preserved in its full strength, nor can the commandments, which comprise the entire spiritual life of the people, be kept in their original purity, because the times are besieging us with difficult demands. It is impossible for us to respond to those demands without ignoring the holy treasure entrusted to us at Sinai, without God forbid, turning it into a thing of little value in our eyes, as each of us strays further and further away from the other. Against his will each loses his Jewish self in the [non-Jewish] majority, for only in their midst can he fulfill all those secular requirements which the times demand of him. The people has found one remedy for this affliction—to direct their hearts to that one place which has always been the focus of our prayers, that place wherein the oppressed of our people will find their longed-for respite: Zion and Jerusalem. We have always been united by that ancient hope, by the promise which lies at the very roots of our religion, namely, that only out of Zion will the Lord bring redemption to the people of Israel. The emancipation which our German brethren so desired did much to divide us and keep us scattered in the countries of our dispersion. When the limbs are dispersed, the body disintegrates, and when there is no body, the spirit has no place to dwell in this world.

It has therefore been agreed by all those who love the spirit of their people and are faithful to their God's Torah, that the reawakening of the hope of the return to Zion will provide a solid foundation as well as lend a special quality to our people. It will serve as a focus for the ingathering of our spiritual forces and as a secure fortress for our Torah and its sanctity.

RAV A. Y. KOOK: "THE LAND OF ISRAEL" (1910–1930)

Rav A. Y. Kook (1865–1935) was the first chief rabbi of Palestine. He was respected by all, both observant and secular Jews. In this selection he expresses some thoughts about the holiness of Eretz Yisrael.

Eretz Israel is not something apart from the soul of the Jewish people; it is no mere national possession, serving as a means of unifying our people and buttressing its material, or even its spiritual, survival. Eretz Israel is part of the very essence of our nationhood; it is bound organically to its very life and inner being. Human reason, even at its most sublime, cannot begin to understand the unique holiness of Eretz Israel; it cannot stir the depths of love for the land that are dormant within our people, cannot begin to understand the unique holiness of Eretz Israel; it cannot stir the depths of love for the land that are dormant within our people. What Eretz Israel means to the Jew can be felt only through the Spirit of the Lord which is in our people as a whole, through the spiritual cast of the Jewish soul, which radiates its characteristic influence to every healthy emotion. This higher light shines forth to the degree that the spirit of divine holiness fills the hearts of the saints and scholars of Israel with heavenly life and bliss.

To regard Eretz Israel as merely a tool for establishing our national unity—or even for sustaining our religion in the Diaspora by preserving its proper character and its faith, piety, and observances—is a sterile notion; it is unworthy of the holiness of Eretz Israel. A valid strengthening of Judaism in the Diaspora can come only from a deepened attachment to Eretz Israel. The hope for the return to the Holy Land is the continuing source of the distinctive nature of Judaism. The hope for the Redemption is the force that sustains Judaism in the Diaspora; the Judaism of Eretz Israel is the very Redemption.

Jewish original creativity, whether in the realm of ideas or in the arena of daily life and action, is impossible except in Eretz Israel. On the other hand, whatever the Jewish people creates in Eretz Israel assimilates the universal into characteristic and unique Jewish form, to the great benefit of the Jewish people and of the world. The very sins which are the cause of our exile also pollute the pristine wellspring of our being, so that the water is impure at the source. Once the unique wellspring of Israel's individuality has become corrupt, its primal originality can express itself only in that area of loftiest universal creativity which belongs to the Jew—and only in the Diaspora, while the homeland itself grows waste and desolate, atoning for its degradation by its ruin. While the life and thought of Israel are finding universal outlets and are being scattered abroad in all the world, the pristine well of the Jewish spirit stops

running, the polluted streams emanating from the source are drying up, and the well is cleansing itself, until its original purity returns. When that process is completed, the exile will become a disgust to us and will be discarded. Universal Light, in all its power, will again radiate from the unique source of our being; the splendor of the Messiah who is to gather in the exiles will begin to be manifest; and the bitter lament of Rachel weeping for her children will find sweet and glorious consolation. The creativity of the Jew, in all its glory and uniqueness, will reassert itself, suffused with the all-encompassing riches of the spirit of the greatest giant of humankind, Abraham, whom the Almighty called to be a blessing to man.

A Jew cannot be as devoted and true to his own ideas, sentiments, and imagination in the Diaspora as he can in Eretz Israel. Revelations of the holy, of whatever degree, are relatively pure in Eretz Israel; outside it, they are mixed with dross and much impurity. However, the greater is one's yearning for and attachment to Eretz Israel, the purer his thoughts become, for they then live in the air of Eretz Israel, which sustains everyone who longs to behold the Land. In the Holy Land man's imagination is lucid and clear, clean and pure, capable of receiving the revelation of Divine Truth and of expressing in life the sublime meaning of the ideal of the sovereignty of holiness; there the mind is prepared to understand the light of prophecy and to be illumined by the radiance of the Holy Spirit. In gentile lands the imagination is dim, clouded with darkness and shadowed with unholiness, and it cannot serve as the vessel for the outpouring of the Divine Light, as it raises itself beyond the lowness and narrowness of the universe. Because reason and imagination are interwoven and interact with each other, even reason cannot shine in its truest glory outside the Holy Land.

Deep in the heart of every Jew, in its purest and holiest recesses, there blazes the fire of Israel. There can be no mistaking its demands for an organic and indivisible bond between life and all of God's commandments; for the pouring of the spirit of the Lord, the spirit of Israel which completely permeates the soul of the Jew, into all the vessels which were created for this particular purpose; and for expressing the word of Israel fully and precisely in the realms of action and idea.

In the hearts of our saints, this fire is constantly blazing up with tongues of holy flame. Like the fire on the altar of the Temple, it is burning unceasingly, with a steady flame, in the collective heart of our people. Hidden away in the deepest recesses of their souls, it exists even among the backsliders and sinners of Israel. Within the Jewish people as a whole, this is the living source of its desire for freedom, of its longing for a life worthy of the name for man and community, of its hope for redemption—of the striving toward a full, uncontradictory, and unbounded Jewish life.

This is the meaning of the Jew's undying love for Eretz Israel—the Land of Holiness, the Land of God—in which all of the divine commandments are realized in their perfect form. This urge to unfold to the world the nature of God, to raise one; heard in His Name in order to proclaim His greatness in its real dimension, affects all souls, for all desire to become as one with Him and to partake of the bliss of His life. This yearning for a true life, for one that is fashioned by all the commandments of the Torah and illumined by all its uplifting splendor, is the source of the courage which moves the Jew to affirm, before all the world, his loyalty to the heritage of his people, to the preservation of its identity and values, and to the upholding of its faith and vision. An outsider may wonder: How can seeming unbelievers be moved by this life force, not merely to nearness to the universal God but even toward authentic Jewish life—to expressing the divine commandments concretely in image and idea, in song and deed? But this is no mystery to anyone whose heart is deeply at one with the soul of the Jewish people and who knows its marvelous nature. The source of this Power is in the Power of God, in the everlasting glory of life.

BALFOUR DECLARATION (NOVEMBER 2, 1917)

The Balfour Declaration was an extremely important document in the history of Zionism.

Foreign Office
November 2nd, 1917

Dear Lord Rothschild,

I have much pleasure in conveying to you, on behalf of His Majesty's Government, the following declaration of sympathy with Jewish Zionist aspirations which has been submitted to, and approved by, the Cabinet.

His Majesty's Government view with favour the establishment in Palestine of a national home for the Jewish people, and will use their best endeavours to facilitate the achievement of this object, it being clearly understood that nothing shall be done which may prejudice the civil and religious rights of existing non-Jewish communities in Palestine, or the rights and political status enjoyed by Jews in any other country.

I should be grateful if you would bring this declaration to the knowledge of the Zionist Federation.

Yours,

James Balfour

BRITISH MANDATE (JULY 24, 1922)

In this document, the British present their understanding of the commitments made in the Balfour Declaration.

Whereas the Principal Allied Powers have agreed, for the purpose of giving effect to the provisions of Article 22 of the Covenant of the League of Nations, to entrust to a Mandatory selected by the said Powers the administration of the territory of Palestine, which formerly belonged to the Turkish Empire, within such boundaries as may be fixed by them; and

Whereas the Principal Allied Powers have also agreed that the Mandatory should be responsible for putting into effect the declaration originally made on November 2, 1917, by the Government of His Britannic Majesty, and adopted by the said Powers, in favor of the establishment in Palestine of a national home for the Jewish people, it being clearly understood that nothing should be done which might prejudice the civil and religious rights of existing non-Jewish communities in Palestine, or the rights and political status enjoyed by Jews in any other country; and

Whereas recognition has thereby been given to the historical connection of the Jewish people with Palestine and to the grounds for reconstituting their national home in that country; and

Whereas the Principal Allied Powers have selected His Britannic Majesty as the Mandatory for Palestine; and

Whereas the mandate in respect of Palestine has been formulated in the following terms and submitted to the Council of the League for approval; and

Whereas by the afore-mentioned Article 22 (paragraph 8) it is provided that the degree of authority, control or administration to be exercised by the Mandatory, not having been previously agreed upon by the Members of the League, shall be explicitly defined by the Council of the League of Nations;

Confirming the said mandate, defines its terms as follows:

Article 1: The Mandatory shall have full powers of legislation and of administration, save as they may be limited by the terms of this mandate.

Article 2: The Mandatory shall be responsible for placing the country under such political, administrative and economic conditions as will secure the establishment of the Jewish national home, as laid down in the preamble, and the development of self-governing institutions, and also for safeguarding the civil and religious rights of all the inhabitants of Palestine, irrespective of race and religion.

Article 3: The Mandatory shall, so far as circumstances permit, encourage local autonomy.

An appropriate Jewish agency shall be recognized as a public body for the purpose of advising and co-operating with the Administration of Palestine in such economic, social and other matters as may affect the establishment of the Jewish national home and the interests of the Jewish population in Palestine, and, subject always to the control of the Administration, to assist and take part in the development of the country.

The Zionist organization, so long as its organization and constitution are in the opinion of the Mandatory appropriate, shall be recognized as such agency. It shall take steps in consultation with His Britannic Majesty's Government to secure the co-operation of all Jews who are willing to assist in the establishment of the Jewish national home.

BILTMORE PROGRAM (MAY 1942)

This document represents the first time the Zionist movement declared its intention to establish a sovereign, independent Jewish state.

1. American Zionists assembled in this Extraordinary Conference reaffirm their unequivocal devotion to the cause of democratic freedom and international justice to which the people of the United States, allied with the other United Nations, have dedicated themselves, and give expression to their faith in the ultimate victory of humanity and justice over lawlessness and brute force.

2. This Conference offers a message of hope and encouragement to their fellow Jews in the Ghettos and concentration camps of Hitler-dominated Europe and prays that their hour of liberation may not be far distant.

3. The Conference sends its warmest greeting to the Jewish Agency Executive in Jerusalem, to the *Vaad Leumi,* and to the whole *yishuv* in Palestine, and expresses its profound admiration for their steadfastness and achievements in the face of peril and great difficulties. The Jewish men and women in field and factory, and the thousands of Jewish soldiers of Palestine in the Near East who have acquitted themselves with honor and distinction in Greece, Ethiopia, Syria, Libya and on other battlefields, have shown themselves worthy of their people and ready to assume the rights and responsibilities of nationhood.

4. In our generation, and in particular in the course of the past twenty years, the Jewish people have awakened and transformed their ancient homeland; from 50,000 at the end of the last war, their numbers have increased to more than 500,000. They have made the waste places to bear fruit and the desert to blossom. Their pioneering achievements in agriculture and in industry, embodying new patterns of cooperative endeavor, have written a notable page in the history of civilization.

5. In the new values thus created, their neighbors in Palestine have shared. The Jewish people in its own work of national redemption welcomes the economic, agricultural and national development of the Arab peoples and states. The Conference reaffirms the stand previously adopted at the Congress of the World Zionist Organization, expressing the readiness and the desire of the Jewish people for full cooperation with their Arab neighbors.

6. The Conference calls for the fulfillment of the original purposes of the Balfour Declaration and the Mandate which recognizing *"the historical connection of the Jewish people with Palestine"* was to afford them the opportunity, as stated by President Wilson, to found there a Jewish Commonwealth. The conference affirms its unalterable rejection of the White Paper of May 1939 and denies its moral or legal validity. The White Paper seeks to limit, and in fact to nullify, Jewish rights to immigration and settlement in Palestine, and, as stated by Mr. Winston Churchill in the House of Commons in May 1939, constitutes "a breach and repudiation of the Balfour Declaration." The policy of the While Paper is cruel and indefensible in its denial of sanctuary to Jews fleeing from Nazi persecution; and at a time when Palestine has become a focal point in the war front of the United Nations, and Palestine Jewry must provide all available manpower for farm and factory and camp, it is in direct conflict with the interests of the Allied war effort.

7. In the struggle against the forces of aggression and tyranny, of which Jews were the earliest victims, and which now menace the Jewish National Home, recognition must be given to the right of the Jews of Palestine to play their full part in the war effort and in the defense of their country, through a Jewish military force fighting under its own flag and under the high command of the United Nations.

8. The Conference declares that the new world order that will follow victory cannot be established on foundations of peace, justice and equality, unless the problem of Jewish homelessness is finally solved.

The Conference urges that the gates of Palestine be opened; that the Jewish Agency be vested with control of immigration into Palestine and with the necessary authority for upbuilding the country, including the development of its unoccupied and uncultivated lands; and that Palestine be established as a Jewish Commonwealth integrated in the structure of the new democratic world.

Then and only then will the age-old wrong to the Jewish people be righted.

MOSHE SHERTOK: "BI-NATIONALISM IS UNWORKABLE" (JULY 17, 1947)

Some argued in favor of a bi-national Jewish-Arab state. In this document, Shertok presents his opposition to this idea. Shertok, who Hebraized his name to Sharett, became Israel's second Prime Minister.

The [Arab–Jewish conflict in Palestine] can certainly not be met by the adoption of a bi-national solution based on parity. Such a solution, to be operative, presupposes two collective wills acting, by and large, in unison.

It is not a question of individuals combining on some minor matters. Individuals may combine across the barriers of race or community or religion, but on major matters, what one would have to face for a considerable time—heaven knows for how long—would be two national entities, each with a collective will of its own. And to imagine that such a state would be something workable is to presuppose a willingness to walk together on the part of those two national entities.

These prerequisites do not exist, and therefore the issue, I am afraid, is a purely academic one. If, for the sake of argument, I am to assume that it may be practical politics—which I do not—then I would have to say that it would either lead to a state of permanent deadlock on major matters, or that it would lead to the virtual abolition of independence. For in this case again, in order to save the situation from a state of perpetual deadlock, a third party would have to be introduced either as a result of foresight or as a result of an *espirit d'escalier.*

I do not think I am fully competent to judge the subject from the point of view of comparative constitutional law, but I am not aware of any precedent for such an arrangement. There are bi-national and multi-national states in the world, and in all of them, I believe, sovereignty in the ultimate resort is vested in the majority of the population or the majority of some elected assembly. In the last resort the majority prevails, and nowhere do you find two equally balanced communities set against each other. It would have been more logical to expect such an arrangement in those countries than in a country like Palestine, because in those countries there are no such fundamental cleavages and no such diametrical divergencies as we have to face in Palestine. It is not a workable solution.

I must stress again and again that the question is not whether Jews and Arabs can live together within the framework of one state. They can. They do. They will. The question is whether they can operate a state machinery by pulling an equal weight in its councils. They will pull apart. The problem in this country is not how to compose the differences between two static sections of the country's population. If that were the case, it would not be so difficult. The problem is how to reconcile independence with the dynamic development of the Jewish section and of the country as a whole. Perhaps I could formulate it a little differently, and that perhaps would be more correct. The problem is how to make of independence an instrument of development and not a stranglehold on development. But if you assign equality to both statics and dynamics, then the statics will have the advantage. Equality of veto will mean Jewish defeat. What can a Jewish veto do to the Arabs, vitally, crucially? The Arabs are here. Nobody in his senses would try to eradicate them; anyhow you won't do it by a veto. What positive act can doom the hopes of the Arabs to live here, to enjoy prosperity? But an Arab veto could and would prevent Jewish immigration, and that is the most fundamental issue for the Jews.

You do not solve the problem by taking immigration out of the context and entrusting it to some ad hoc authority. It cannot be taken out of context. The problem of immigration is bound up with the whole machinery of government, with economic policy, with fiscal policy. It is not merely a question of issuing visas and letting people in. It means absorbing those people, providing for them, so shaping the country's economic policy as to enable us to absorb immigrants. If there is harmony between the ad hoc immigration authority and the state machinery, then it is all right. But if there is complete discord, the possibility of it, the certainty of it, then it will not work, and the immigration powers which you might grant to the ad hoc authority would prove a delusion. . . . Again, in a bi-national state . . .we shall be irresistibly driven to the installation of a third party wielding real power with all the negative results—primarily, no independence.

UNITED NATIONS GENERAL ASSEMBLY: RESOLUTION ON PALESTINE (NOVEMBER 29, 1947)

This is the United Nations Resolution on Palestine. Thirty-three nations voted in favor of establishing an independent, sovereign Jewish state.

The General Assembly . . . Considers that the present situation in Palestine is one which is likely to impair the general welfare and friendly relations among nations;

Takes note of the declaration by the mandatory power that it plans to complete its evacuation of Palestine by August 1, 1948;

Recommends to the United Kingdom, as the mandatory power for Palestine, and to all other Members of the United Nations the adoption and implementation, with regard to the future government of Palestine, of the Plan of Partition with Economic Union set out below;

Requests that (a) the Security Council take the necessary measures as provided for in the plan for its implementation; . . .

Part I

A. *Termination of Mandate, Partition and Independence.*

1. The Mandate for Palestine shall terminate as soon as possible but in any case not later than August 1, 1948.
2. The armed forces of the mandatory power shall be progressively withdrawn from Palestine, the withdrawal to be completed as soon as possible but in any case not later than August 1, 1948.

   The mandatory power shall advise the Commission, as far in advance as possible, of its intention to terminate the Mandate and to evacuate each area.

   The mandatory power shall use its best endeavors to ensure that an area situated in the territory of the Jewish State, including a seaport and hinterland adequate to provide facilities for a substantial immigration, shall be evacuated at the earliest possible date and in any event not later than February 1, 1948.
3. Independent Arab and Jewish States and the Special International Regime for the City of Jerusalem, set forth in part III of this plan, shall come into existence in Palestine two months after the evacuation of the armed forces of the mandatory power has been completed but in any case not later than October 1, 1948. . . .

D. *Economic Union and Transit*

1. The Provisional Council of Government of each State shall enter into an undertaking with respect to Economic Union and Transit. . . .

Part III—City of Jerusalem

A. *Special Regime*

The City of Jerusalem shall be established as a *corpus separatum* under a special international regime and shall be designated to discharge the responsibilities of the Administering Authority on behalf of the United Nations.

Reference Works

S. Avineri, *The Making of Modern Zionism*

I. Bickerton and M. N. Pearson, *The Arab–Israeli Conflict: A History*

A. Hertzberg (ed.), *The Zionist Idea*

W. Laqueur, *A History of Zionism*

W. Laqueur and B. Rubin (eds.), *The Israel–Arab Reader*

P. Mendes-Flohr and J. Reinharz (eds.), *The Jew in the Modern World: A Documentary History*

H. M. Sachar, *A History of Israel*

Chronology

1862	Moses Hess (1812–1875), distinguished German Socialist, publishes *Rome and Jerusalem,* in which he argues for the establishment of a Jewish state in Palestine.
	R. Zvi Hirsch Kalischer (1795–1874), Orthodox rabbi and early Zionist thinker, writes *Derishat Zion.* The redemption of the Jews, he says, will come through their return to Palestine.
1884	First Conference of Hibbat Zion takes place in Kattowitz, Germany, led by Leo Pinsker.
1890	Odessa, Russia, becomes head office of Hibbat Zion, with permission of the Russians. Hibbat Zion will exist until 1919.
1894–1895	The Dreyfus Affair.
1896	Herzl publishes *The Jewish State.*
1897	First Zionist Congress meets in Basel, Switzerland
1898	Second Zionist Congress meets. Herzl meets with Kaiser Wilhelm II but fails to win him over.
1899	Third Zionist Congress meets.
1902	Mizrachi movement is founded.
1903	The British suggest Uganda as Jewish homeland. Herzl brings this idea before the Sixth Zionist Congress—it is rejected.
1906	David Ben-Gurion (1886–1973) leaves Russia for Palestine.
1907	Yitzchak Ben-Zvi (1884–1963) leaves Russia for Palestine.

	Eighth Zionist Congress meets. Weizmann speaks of merging practical Zionism and political Zionism, creating "synthetic Zionism."
1909	City of Tel Aviv is founded. Kibbutz Degania is founded.
1917	Balfour Declaration
1920	Histadrut (General Federation of Jewish Labor) is founded.
	Haganah (Army of Defense) is established. Two chief rabbis are selected: Rabbi Abraham Isaac Kook (1865–1935) for the Ashkenazim and Rabbi Jacob Meir (1856–1939) for the Sepharadim.
1921	Sir Herbert Samuel, British High Commissioner in Palestine, appoints Haj Amin al-Husseini Grand Mufti (expounder of Muslim law) of Jerusalem.
1929	Widespread Arab riots. Hebron massacre.
1936	Arab Revolt. Peel Commission proposes partition.
1939	British White Paper published. World War II begins.
1942	Biltmore Conference.
1945	Assassination of Lord Moyne. Attlee elected Prime Minister of Britain. Anglo-American Committee of Inquiry.
1946	Night of the Bridges.
1947	UN votes to end Mandate.

8

THE STATE OF ISRAEL

ESTABLISHMENT OF THE STATE

The State of Israel came into being on May 14, 1948. Between November 29, 1947 and May 14, 1948, British policy had been total non-cooperation in implementing the United Nations recommendation to split into two states, an Arab state and a Jewish state. The soon-to-be Jewish state could not purchase arms, ruled the British, although at the very same time they were selling arms to Iraq and Transjordan. Jews were still prohibited entry into Palestine. Police fortresses were transferred to the Arabs, but Jews were forbidden to organize a militia.

The British were responding, on the one hand, to their own need for Arab oil and, on the other, to their bitterness about Jewish terrorism and illegal immigration. They were also assuming Arab victory over the Jews in any war that might come.

Between November 1947 and May 1948 the Arabs responded to the partition resolution with attacks on Jews within and outside of Palestine. Supporters of the UN resolution began to have doubts about partition, especially the United States, for their concern was that Israel could not defend itself against Arab attacks. The American government advised postponing the declaration of a state until order could be restored. The Jewish leadership, led by Ben-Gurion, decided to declare a state, and the United States granted recognition within two hours.

DECLARATION OF INDEPENDENCE

The proclamation of the State of Israel affirmed that the Land of Israel was the birthplace of the Jewish people. The spiritual, religious, and national identity of the Jews had been created there. Eretz Yisrael had remained central in the prayers of the Jews and in their history, as they looked forward to national restoration.

The proclamation reviewed the history of the Zionist movement, recalling the First Zionist Congress, the Balfour Declaration, the tragedy of the Holocaust, and the United Nations vote for partition. No Jew would ever again be homeless, it declared, as the gates of the State of Israel would be open to all.

The new state would adhere to the principles of liberty, justice, and peace as articulated in the biblical prophets. The sanctity of the holy places of all religions would be upheld; full freedom of conscience, worship, education, and culture would be guaranteed. The state would ensure full social and political equality to all, no matter what race, creed, or sex.

WAR OF INDEPENDENCE

Israel's War of Independence immediately followed the declaration of the state. The armies of six Arab nations invaded the new State of Israel: Lebanon, Syria, Transjordan, Egypt, Iraq, and Saudi Arabia. Only Israel's tiny population of 600,000 stood in the way of these military forces.

The war lasted from May 14, 1948, until January 8, 1949. By the time it ended, it had taken 6,000 lives and 30,000 had been wounded. Arab casualties exceeded this amount, but the Arabs never announced the numbers to the world. For a nation of only 600,000, then, 1 percent of its residents had given their lives. In addition, the price of war was high. The estimated cost was close to $500 million. In the course of the war, moreover, many of Israel's fields and many of its citrus groves were destroyed.

There were truces agreed upon at various stages; an armistice agreement was signed by Israel and Egypt on February 24, 1949. Shortly thereafter, agreements were signed with Lebanon, Jordan, and Syria. Only Iraq remained steadfast in its refusal to sign. The hope of all parties was that a permanent peace treaty would follow the armistice agreements, but this did not happen.

The victory of Israel in its war against the Arab armies was remarkable. It was, however, a mixed blessing. The United Nations resolution called for two states, but the new state of Palestine never came into existence. Instead the West Bank, the area west of the Jordan River, was annexed by Jordan, and the Gaza Strip, a small section of land bordering Egypt, became part of Egypt. Jerusalem was divided between Israel and Jordan, and Jews were not permitted to pray at its holy places, although the armistice agreement had guaranteed them access. In addition, the Jordanian occupation of the Old City resulted in the desecration of its Jewish holy places.

The war had created a State of Israel larger than what the UN resolution had intended, however. Israel now extended southward all the way from the border with Lebanon to Eilat, which was located on the Red Sea.

Arabs who had fled Palestine during or after the war were another issue. More than 700,000 Arabs had left Palestine. Should they be repatriated? Should a peace treaty precede any repatriation? Should the Arab countries absorb them?

The issue was complicated by the question of why these Arabs had left. The Arabs claimed that the Israelis had incited them to leave their homes. They made reference to the incident at the village of Deir Yassin, when the Irgun had massacred Arab civilians. Incidents like this led Arabs to conclude that they would be better off outside Israel. The Israelis countered by arguing that Arab governments had encouraged Israel's Arabs to leave, promising an early return once the war was over. This issue remains on the table whenever the Israelis and the Arabs engage in any negotiation, as Arabs seek to return to their prewar homes.

A final consequence, perhaps the most important of all, was the failure of Arab governments to recognize the reality of there being a State of Israel. Arabs remained convinced that they could eliminate it. So long as this was the case, the Arab-Israeli conflict could never be resolved.

FORMATION OF GOVERNMENT

From the declaration of the state until March 10, 1949, Israel was governed by a Provisional Council of State.

Thirty-seven individuals comprised this council, 13 of them serving as its executive. Those who participated had been members of either the Va'ad Leumi (National Council of Palestinian Jewry) or the Jewish Agency Executive prior to the creation of the state.

Many of the government ministries were simply a continuation of the departments and bureaus that had existed during the Mandate. The departments of health, religious affairs, and social welfare, for example, became ministries of health, religious affairs, and social welfare in the state. In similar fashion, the financial, immigration, and foreign affairs departments became the ministries of finance, immigration, and foreign affairs.

Before the establishment of the state, David Ben-Gurion was elected chairman of a Provisional Zionist Council of State. He could not become Prime Minister until there was a State of Israel. On May 16, 1948 Chaim Weizmann was elected president of the Provisional Council, but he similarly could not be the President of the State of Israel until the first election in January of 1949.

The Israeli parliament, the Knesset (Assembly), has 120 members, chosen in general, national, secret, equal, direct, and proportional elections. All laws passed in the Knesset apply to everyone, no matter what race, creed,

Beneath the portrait of Theodor Herzl, David Ben-Gurion, Prime Minister of Israel, reads the Declaration of Independence.

or sex. The Knesset oversees the functions of government, defines the structure of government, and determines the distribution of power among the various authorities. It is the legislative branch of Israel.

The executive branch of the State of Israel is the government. The government remains in power so long as it has the confidence of a majority of the Knesset. It must apply the laws passed there and carry out the policies approved there. Elections are held every four years, although a no-confidence vote in the Knesset might lead to the fall of the government and a call for new elections before the four years are over. Each citizen votes twice—once for Prime Minister, once for a political party list.

The first Prime Minister of the State of Israel was David Ben-Gurion. His contributions to the Zionist movement and to the government of Israel were immense. Some others who served as Prime Minister were Moshe Sharett, Levi Eshkol, Golda Meir, Yitzchak Rabin, Menachem Begin, Yitzchak Shamir, Shimon Peres, Binyamin Netanyahu, Ehud Barak, and Ariel Sharon.

The first President of the state was Chaim Weizmann. The Knesset chooses the President, who serves for five years. He signs every law passed by the Knesset, opens the first session of a new Knesset, receives reports as to government decisions and activities, receives the credentials of foreign diplomats, and appoints the state comptroller and the governor of the Bank of Israel. The President asks the victor in the election for Prime Minister to form a government. Among the presidents who have served are Yitzchak Ben-Zvi, Zalman Shazar, Ephraim Katzir, Yitzchak Navon, Chaim Herzog, Ezer Weizmann, and Moshe Katzav.

In the first Knesset election, 21 parties offered candidates. Among these were left-wing parties like Mapai (Israel Workers' Party) and Mapam (United Workers' Party); center-right-wing parties like Herut (Freedom) and the General Zionists; and religious parties, like Mizrachi (National Religious Party) and Agudat Yisrael (Union of Israel).

Mapai was the party of Ben-Gurion. It had built the Histadrut (Labor Federation) and nurtured its growth. It had established the Haganah, which would later become the Israel Defense Forces and be responsible for Israel's victory in its War of Independence. Labor Zionism was its credo, but the party was more pragmatic than dogmatic. It promoted its views in the largest federation of kibbutzim. A well-organized party with united, integrated leadership, it succeeded in maintaining control over economic and human resources entering the country.

Mapam advocated agricultural socialism, that is, collectivism. It wanted a classless society with leadership coming from the kibbutzim and worth attached to manual labor on farms and in factories. It believed Arabs should enjoy equality before the law and their villages should not be ruled by the military. In foreign policy, Israel should be "neutral," which meant oriented toward the Soviet Union.

Herut (Freedom) party members were the ideological heirs of Jabotinsky. The name of the party affirmed that if the goals of Zionism were to be achieved, they needed to be redefined. Herut supported militancy and wanted no compromise; all of Palestine that was included in the British Mandate, not just that part west of the Jordan River. In foreign policy, Israel should look to the countries of the West, and the economy of Israel should embrace capitalism. Mass immigration should be encouraged.

The General Zionists were interested more in the overall goals of Zionism than in any specific policies. They did, however, support free enterprise and a limited role for government.

The Mizrachi party took as its slogan: "The land of Israel for the people of Israel according to the Torah of Israel." Its leaders felt there could be no compromise in spiritual matters. It established schools committed to the ideals of the Torah and the Jewish people. It expected that its young men would serve in the Israeli Army.

The Agudat Yisrael party involved itself in building yeshivot and fostering Orthodox education. It chose to play a limited political role. Students in its yeshivot were exempt from army service, as ongoing study of Torah was their contribution to the spiritual well-being of the Jewish people.

In the first election to the Knesset, Mapai captured 46 seats, while the other Labor Zionist party, Mapam, got only 19. Herut and the General Zionists (later to be called Liberals) took 21, while the religious parties took 16. Some smaller parties captured between 2 and 7 seats.

Once the War of Independence was over, the new state had to confront other difficulties. The greatest of these was the mass immigration of Jews to Israel. Prior to the creation of the state, many Jews had lived in various Arab countries. For example, there were 260,000 Jews living in Morocco and 130,000 Jews in Iraq. Within the first three years of the State of Israel, however, its population doubled as 600,000 Jews came and settled.

Immigration on such a large scale presented enormous economic difficulties. Israel sought assistance from Jewish communities around the world, and the assistance came. Still, there was need to house the new immigrants and to provide health care for them. This was costly. Thus Israel was forced to impose high taxes, as well as to ration food.

One way to carry the cost was to accept war reparations from Germany. Needless to say, this was a very emotional issue, since many of Israel's residents had been touched by the Holocaust in some way. Ben-Gurion favored accepting reparations, but many

were unalterably opposed, including Menachem Begin. No "blood money" should be taken from Germany, he said. No "compensation" could be offered for the liquidation of Jews. Ben-Gurion won out, but Begin saw this decision as "the ultimate abomination, the like of which we have not known since we became a nation."

THE ARAB-ISRAELI CONFLICT

The new Jewish state experienced many wars, as the Arabs made several attempts to destroy it. The first war was the Sinai Campaign. In 1954 Gamal Abd al-Nasser became President of Egypt. In his view Israel was holding Arab territory that should be liberated. In addition, he believed the British should be removed from the Suez Canal. The Egyptian armed forces should be built up so that they could challenge Israel. Finally, the natural resources of Egypt should be enhanced. This meant the construction of a huge dam at Aswan, across the Nile River; Egypt could then control the Nile, using its waters for irrigation and hydroelectric power.

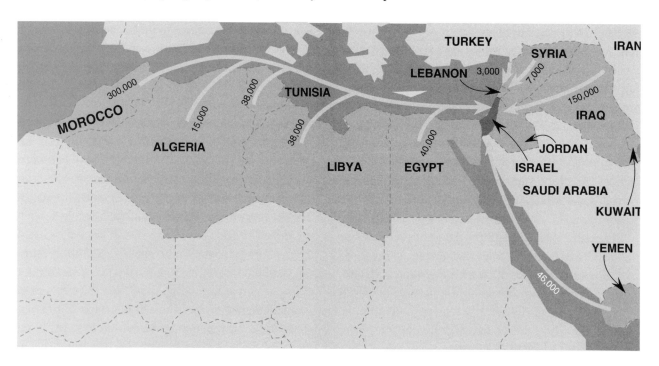

Israeli independence had a tremendous effect on Jewish communitie in Arab lands. Most of the Arab countries instituted severe restrictions on their Jewish citizens. The hostile governments deprived them of their properties, their home, and their businesses. These repressive measures initiated a huge exodus of Jews. Most of them arrived penniless, with only the clothes on their backs. In 1949, Operation Magic Carpet evacuated 50,000 Jews from Yemen.

Nasser's intentions to destroy Israel were never concealed. Between May and July 1954, Israel issued nearly 400 complaints to the Israel-Egypt Mixed Armistice Commission of intensified assaults from Gaza. By October 1954, fedayun (terrorist) squads, trained and equipped by Egyptian army units, were penetrating deep into Israel. Roads, bridges, and water pipes were mined, large quantities of equipment and livestock stolen. In February 1955 alone, 45 incidents occurred. The attacks resumed, after a brief pause, extending to the outskirts of Tel-Aviv and inflicting dozens of civilian causalties each month.

The attacks of the fedayun abated for a while, but in March 1956, they began again. On March 22, eleven Israeli settlers were wounded near the Gaza Strip. On April 4, three Israeli soldiers were killed. A few days later, a new series of raids took place, and by April 11, nearly a dozen Israeli civilians had been killed. The Egyptian press aclaimed the fedayun as "heroes back from the battlefield."

Nasser was still intent on the complete destruction of Israel. Between July 29 and September 25, fedayun assaulted Israel from bases in Gaza, Jordan, and Syria, killing another 19 Israelis and wounding 28. Rightly concerned with Nasser's long-range intentions, Israel attacked Egypt in October 1956.

Britain and France supported Israel. Britain's Prime Minister, Anthony Eden, felt that dictators like Nasser needed to be confronted and was angry at Nasser's rejection of the Baghdad Pact, an agreement of mutual cooperation whose intention was to block Soviet influence in the Middle East. France was concerned with Nasser's support for Algerian rebels and wanted to humiliate him, thus undermining his support.

Britain and France planned an attack on Egypt together with Israel. Israel advanced quickly through the Sinai Peninsula to the Suez Canal. The United States exerted pressure in the UN, however, and Britain and France gave in. By March 1957 all Israeli troops were withdrawn.

A number of factors contributed to the likelihood of another Arab-Israeli war in the 1960s. First, despite many similarities, the Arab nations of Egypt, Syria, and Jordan were very different from one another; the only source of unity was the identity of the enemy, the State of Israel. Second, Syria was bombarding Jewish settlements from the Golan Heights, and Israel was retaliating; Jordan and Israel were in dispute over water rights, the shared use of the Jordan River. Third, the Palestinians had awakened, becoming an effective military force. Fourth, the Ba'ath, an extremist party, had seized power in Syria, which led to clashes in the demilitarized zone. Finally, Syria and Egypt signed a defense agreement, creating the United Arab Republic.

In 1967 Nasser was subjected to increasing criticism. The UN forces stationed in Egypt were there to protect Egypt from Israeli attack, but Nasser had been allowing Israel to import arms through the Gulf of Aqaba to Eilat. Nasser's response was to ask the UN Secretary-General to withdraw troops and close the Gulf of Aqaba to Israeli ships bringing arms to Eilat.

Nasser's actions were acts of war in the eyes of international law. His actions led to the Six-Day War, which began on June 5 and concluded on June 10, 1967. Israel looked for assistance in forcing Nasser to reopen the Straits of Tiran but found no international support. Perceiving itself as facing destruction at the hands of the Arabs, Israel decided to strike first.

Attacks from the air disabled the air forces of Egypt and Syria completely. In the course of this short war, Israel's army won control of the Sinai Peninsula, the West Bank, including East Jerusalem, and the Golan Heights. The Arabs suffered a major defeat and a massive loss of territory.

Israel found itself in a position of strength, able to sit comfortably with new borders. Of particular importance was the conquest of the Jewish quarter of Jerusalem, which included the Western Wall. This wall had surrounded the Second Temple, which the Romans destroyed in 70 C.E.

The response of the Arabs to their great defeat was a simple one: defiance. There was no desire to seek diplomatic solutions. In August 1967, the foreign ministers of 13 Arab states met at Khartoum, Sudan, and emerged with three "no's": no peace with Israel, no negotiation with Israel, no recognition of Israel. They also vowed to support the "maintenance of the rights of the Palestinian people in their nation."

This attitude typified the Arab stance after the 1967 war. Between March 1969 and July 1970, Nasser engaged in the War of Attrition. This was an attempt to destroy the line of fortifications set up by the Israelis along the Suez Canal. By July 1969 Israeli casualties had reached 70 a month. The Israelis decided to bombard Egyptian positions from the air, an act that reduced their losses considerably.

Nasser died in September 1970 and was succeeded by Anwar al-Sadat. Sadat was Nasser's Vice-President, but he had shared no power and had minimal influence. Once he became Egypt's President, however, Sadat moved away from Nasser's inclination toward socialism by announcing a ten-year development plan designed to encourage European and American investment. He lifted restrictions on imports and permitted an influx of consumer goods. He displayed no interest, moreover, in Pan-Arabism, showing more interest in his domestic agenda.

In truth, though, Sadat was preparing for war with Israel. In 1967 Leonid Brezhnev, President of the Soviet Union, had released many Jews from Russia to further the goal of achieving détente with the United States. Sadat saw this move as support for Israel, however, so in March 1972, he "released" 15,000 Soviet advisers and experts.

This action led Israel to believe that the chances of war were negligible. Moshe Dayan, who was Israel's Defense Minister, and Prime Minister Golda Meir were confident that there would be no war. The leaders of Western Europe and the United States agreed. How could the Egyptians use Soviet weapons without Soviet assistance?

Sadat, however, saw the need to disrupt the prevailing situation through war. The Israelis were not interested in negotiation. The Americans were taken up with the Vietnam War and the Watergate scandal. War would capture everyone's attention.

There were economic benefits to war as well. It was costly to maintain armed forces. While the army stood ready, moreover, the economy stagnated. Sadat hoped that, at the very least, a partial victory might enable him to reopen the Suez Canal, providing much-needed revenue to Egypt.

The war began on October 6, 1973; it was Yom Kippur, the holiest day on the Jewish calendar. The Egyptians experienced early success, as they advanced into the Sinai. By October 15, though, the Israelis began to counterattack. By October 24, when a cease-fire went into effect, Israeli tanks had crossed the Suez Canal and were in Egypt, close to Cairo. On the northern front, Damascus was within range. About 11,000 Egyptians and Syrians died in this war, while only 2,500 Israelis lost their lives.

In 1982 a war broke out between Israel and PLO forces stationed in Lebanon. This conflict was named Operation Peace for the Galilee. Its goal was to protect the towns of the Galilee from PLO shelling across the Lebanese border. In the view of the Minister of Defense, Ariel Sharon, the larger goal was to destroy the PLO's military dominance of Lebanon and install a new Lebanese government prepared to sign a peace treaty with Israel.

Israel has almost 30 political parties, 13 of which held seats in the Knesset after the January 2003 election. One of the parties, Shas (Shomrei Torah Sephardim—Sephardi Torah Guardians), began as a local municipal list in 1984. It developed quickly into a full-fledged national political party.

The Agudat Israel ("Israelite Union") party sees itself as representing the interests of Ashkenazic Jews. Its constituency is Jews whose family origins are in Eastern Europe. Shas represents an alternative to the Agudat Israel for Sephardic Jews, Jews of North African and Middle Eastern descent. Like Agudat Israel, which is guided by a Council of Torah Sages, Shas has its own Council of Torah Sages. Its true spiritual leader, however, is the former Sephardic Chief Rabbi (Rishon Letzion), Rabbi Ovadiah Yosef.

The party chairman of Shas is Eli Yishai. In the area of foreign policy, this party believes that no credible peace partner exists and favors strengthening the settlements in the West Bank. It is not, however, opposed to negotiations with the Palestinians. In terms of its domestic policy, Shas supports the expansion of religious legislation, supports tax and economic initiatives to benefit the poor and middle classes, and operates many community social welfare projects.

Unlike Agudat Israel, Shas sees no contradiction between its religious beliefs and Zionism. In addition, it seeks representation for its adherents in all government bodies, Zionist institutions, and the Jewish Agency.

Prior to the 1999 election, it was anticipated that Shas would end up holding fewer than the 12 Knesset seats it held, but instead it increased its seats to 17. In the 2003 election, by contrast, its seats fell to just 11.

The larger goal involved Israel in a siege of Beirut, brought widespread international condemnation—including from the United States—and led to antiwar protests within Israel itself. This conflict did succeed in expelling the PLO from Beirut, but Israel placed too much trust in the Gemayel family as partners of Israel. Bashir Gemayel, a Maronite Christian and the elected President of Lebanon, was assassinated. Maronite Christians massacred Palestinians in the camps of Sabra and Shatila, an event for which the Israeli government was held indirectly accountable.

The PLO certainly had been forced to leave Lebanon, but the cost was too high. It is estimated that the Israeli invasion of Lebanon cost over 20,000 lives, most of them Lebanese and Palestinian civilians. The war ended with the withdrawal of Israeli troops in June 1985, although the Israelis continued to control a "security zone" in southern Lebanon until 2000.

By the mid-1980s there was much frustration among the Palestinians living under Israeli occupation. Lacking civil rights and having their economic status dependent on Israel's economy, they found themselves with an unclear, unresolved political status. They had little faith in Arabs living outside Palestine and little faith in the efforts of the PLO to secure Palestinian self-determination. Israeli settlements beyond the Green Line, that is, in the territory conquered from Jordan in the 1967 war, have contributed to the Arabs' uncertain political status.

Eventually the frustration showed itself in the Intifada ("uprising," "shaking off"), which began in December 1987 and continued for six years, into the 1990s. Over 700 Palestinians and 40 Israelis were killed. Arab leaders were deported; universities, colleges, and schools were closed; houses were demolished; and curfews were applied. Israel was unable, however, to stop the rock throwing, fire bombs, burning tires on the roads, and massive demonstrations that characterized the Intifada.

The peace process continued during Intifada I but stalled in the summer of 2000, so Intifada II began in the fall of 2000. Rock throwing, fire bombs, the burning of tires, and massive demonstrations continued to be the pattern. A new strategy of rebellion was developed, however, as Arabs were encouraged

The Hebrew word for Intifada is "hitan'arut." The photo appeared in a special issue of the Hebrew paper Ha'aretz devoted to the Palestinian uprising.

to become suicide bombers, and thus martyrs to the cause.

Although Israel prevented many suicide bombings, a number were successful. Frequently buses, bus stops, and bus stations were the targets. In December 2001 a suicide bomber blew up a bus in Haifa, killing 15 and injuring 40. In June 2002 a car bomb exploded next to a bus in Megiddo, causing the bus to burst into flames, killing 14 and injuring more than 20.

Suicide bombings had other targets. A particularly horrible incident took place on the first night of Passover in 2002 in Netanya, as a suicide bomber entered the Park Hotel during the Passover seder and placed a bomb there, killing 29 people and injuring many others. Several bombings occurred in Jerusalem, at a coffee house, in a marketplace, and in an ultra-Orthodox neighborhood, all resulting in casualties. In December 2001, suicide bombers killed 11 and injured 188 on Ben Yehuda Street, a pedestrian mall at the center of Jerusalem.

Israeli Prime Minister Sharon remained insistent that no negotiations would take place until Yasser

Arafat condemned the actions of the suicide bombers and put an end to other terrorist activities. Arafat refused to do this, despite ongoing pressure from the United States. His reliability and trustworthiness were compromised further when Israel captured the *Karine A,* a ship carrying advanced heavy weaponry from Iran to the Palestinian Authority.

Largely in response to the suicide bombings, the Israel Defense Forces called up reservists and moved them into Palestinian towns. Some moved into Bethlehem, and armed Palestinian terrorists responded by entering the Church of the Nativity and remaining there until some agreement was reached with the Israelis. Others moved into Jenin and its refugee camps, from which Israeli intelligence believed many of the suicide bombers had come.

In March 2002 the Israeli army occupied Ramallah, site of Arafat's headquarters, and told Arafat that he would not be permitted to leave until he allowed Israel to take some of the terrorists hiding in his office. This did not happen until early May 2002, when Arafat agreed to have some terrorists exiled and others sent to Gaza.

The United States became involved in the Middle East as well. Secretary of State Colin Powell attempted to get peace talks going between Israel and the Palestinians, but with little success. Saudi Arabia surprised everyone, however, with a peace proposal by which all Arab countries would recognize Israel, Israel would return to its pre-1967 borders, and the Arab insistence on the refugees' right to return to their homes in Israel before 1948 would be waived.

Much has changed since then. More suicide bombings have occurred. A second Gulf War took place, aimed at overthrowing Iraq's leader, Saddam Hussein, suspected of possessing weapons of mass destruction. The Palestinians selected a Prime Minister Mahmoud Abbas, also known as Abu Mazen. Finally, a proposed "road map" for peace was presented to Israel and to the Palestinians.

By May 2003 Intifada II had been going on for 31 months and had claimed the lives of at least 2,000 Palestinians and 750 Israelis. Suicide bombings continued. On May 18, a commuter bus entering

Jerusalem was bombed, killing at least seven people and wounding 19 others. On the same day, a suicide bomber killed an Israeli couple in Hebron. The couple had been on their way to the Tomb of the Patriarchs, a holy site for both Jews and Muslims. Hamas took credit for these bombings.

On May 19, a suicide bomber entered a mall in the northern city of Afula and detonated a bomb that killed three people and wounded dozens more. For this bombing the Al Aqsa Martyrs' Brigade and Islamic Jihad took joint credit. This was the mode chosen by the Palestinians to protest the impending meeting between Prime Minister Sharon and the new Palestinian Prime Minister Mahmoud Abbas.

The first Gulf War began on January 19, 1991. In August 1990, Iraq had invaded and occupied the small Arab state of Kuwait with the order to invade coming from Iraqi dictator Saddam Hussein. The entire world was surprised by this invasion. President George H.W. Bush had little difficulty winning the support of the country for potential war against Iraq.

The war against Iraq, called Operation Desert Shield and led by General Norman Schwarzkopf, resulted from this invasion. The United States established a broad-based international coalition to confront Iraq. Among the many countries that joined the coalition were France, Germany, Italy, Saudi Arabia, Syria, and Kuwait. Saudi Arabia and Kuwait were the main financial supporters of the war.

Terrorist attacks against Israel include the bombing of passenger buses.

Israel was close enough to Iraq to be on alert for attack and Israel was in fact attacked from the air by Scud missiles. Significant damage resulted in some cases. Israel had been requested by the United States to stay out of the war, lest the Arab countries leave the coalition by virtue of Israel's involvement.

The war concluded on February 28, 1991. Under the terms of the cease-fire, Iraq agreed to pay reparations to Kuwait, reveal the location and extent of its stockpiles of chemical and biological weapons, and eliminate its weapons of mass destruction. United Nations inspectors complained later, however, that the Iraqi government was frustrating their attempts to monitor Iraqi compliance with the terms.

The year 2003 brought another war with Iraq. Iraq was still under the leadership of dictator Saddam Hussein. In his annual State of the Union address, President George W. Bush, son of former President George H.W. Bush, condemned Iraq for showing "utter contempt" for United Nations weapons inspectors, for not accounting for thousands of chemical and biological arms and missiles.

Bush called on the United Nations Security Council to meet to hear Secretary of State Colin Powell present intelligence on Iraq's activities. He said that the U.S. had intelligence that Iraq was hiding arms from inspectors and that Iraqi military officers were posing as scientists for interviews with inspectors

Unlike his father, who had international support for the war against Iraq, Bush ran into difficulties getting support. France and Germany refused support, indicating they would vote against any Security Council resolution supporting the war. Russia, another permanent Security Council member, indicated that they too would vote against such a resolution. Only the United Kingdom expressed support for a resolution supporting the war.

The United States set March 17 as a deadline for Iraqi disarmament. The deadline was allowed to pass and the war began on March 20. Called Operation Iraqi Freedom, the war effort was led by General Tommy Franks. American and British forces invaded Iraq and the war continued for approximately five weeks. The Iraqi government of Saddam Hussein fell quickly and many Iraqis on the United States list of most-wanted were either captured or turned themselves in. The fate of Saddam Hussein remained unclear. for a while, but in any case, his government had fallen. He was finally captured in November. The task that now lay before the United States and Great Britain was to rebuild the government of a Saddam-less Iraq.

For Israel the fall of Saddam brought several benefits, including the elimination of an enemy; the security of being the only state in the region with nuclear weapons; a political shift in the regional balance toward more moderate Arab states; new U.S. pressure on Syria not to hide members of the old Iraqi regime; and the expected congressional approval of $1 billion in military aid and $9 billion in loan guarantees.

Another significant development was the selection by the Palestinian Authority of Mahmoud Abbas as Prime Minister of Palestine. Abbas served in the position for only for only six months, however, and was succeeded by Ahmed Qurei. Yasser Arafat, the President of Palestine, had always resisted any reduction of his authority, but the United States insisted that it would never engage in peace discussions with him.

Despite his brief term of service, the appointment of Abbas provided the Quartet of Middle East mediators, the United States, the European Union, the United Nations, and Russia, with a special opportunity to advance the cause of their U.S.-backed "road map" to Palestinian statehood. In addition, the defeat

Mahmoud Abbas (Abu Mazen) and Yasir Arafat

of Saddam Hussein may have opened the door to new opportunities for negotiations.

What is the "road map"? Its ultimate goal is a final and comprehensive settlement of the conflict by 2005. The settlement will include an independent, democratic, and viable Palestinian state living side-by-side in peace and security with Israel. The plan seeks to end the occupation that began in 1967, when Israel captured the West Bank, Gaza, and East Jerusalem. To reach a solution, however, the Palestinians need leadership acting decisively against terror. The Quartet will meet regularly at senior levels to evaluate the parties' performance.

In Phase I, the Palestinian Authority must issue an unequivocal statement reiterating Israel's right to exist in peace and security and calling for an immediate and unconditional cease-fire, undertake efforts to arrest, disrupt and restrain individuals and groups conducting violence on Israelis, dismantle terrorist capabilities and infrastructure, bring all security under the control of the Interior Minister, and hold free, open, and fair elections.

Israel must issue an unequivocal statement affirming its commitment to the two-state vision of an independent, viable, sovereign Palestinian state and calling for an immediate end to violence against Palestinians, freeze all construction in Jewish settlements and dismantle illegal settlement outposts built since March 2001, end demolitions of the homes of Palestinian militants, and withdraw progressively from the Palestinian autonomous zones that it has recoccupied during the conflict.

In Phase II (as early as the end of 2003), Israel moves to enhance maximum territorial contiguity for the Palestinians, a Palestinian constitution is ratified, and an international conference launches the process leading to the establishment of a Palestinian State with provisional borders.

In Phase III (2004–2005), a second international conference will finalize the permanent-status solution for a Palestinian state in 2005, including borders, Jerusalem, refugees, settlements, and peace between Israel and other Arab states.

Certain issues will doubtless remain subject to disagreement. For example, the Palestinians will demand that Arab refugees be permitted to return to their former homes in Israel. Prime Minister Sharon has stated that some Jewish settlements will be traded for peace, but will he even consider this demand for return? Who will determine which settlements might be returned? What is meant by control of terrorism? Who will determine that terrorism is under control? How will the final borders be determined? How can agreement be reached about control of Jerusalem? Each of these questions will have to be resolved if there is to be a "final and comprehensive settlement."

Has Phase I of the "road map" to Palestinian statehood been realized? Not yet. The Palestinians have declared no cease-fire and terrorism continues. Israel has not ceased construction in Jewish settlements and has not withdrawn progressively from Palestinian autonomous zones occupied during the conflict.

Further complicating the "road map" question, Mahmoud Abbas resigned his post as Prime Minister, convinced that he could never operate freely and independently. Yasser Arafat would always stand in the way of Palestinian statehood. Ahmed Qurei, another close associate of Arafat, took Abaas's place as Prime Minister.

Israel has decided, in addition, to construct a 25-foot-tall barrier, a line of walls, trenches, fences, and razor wire that would frustrate terrorist attempts to enter Israel. This remains a controversial measure even within Israel, but has been effective in achieving its goal. More problematic, however, is the perception of Palestinians that this barrier will represent a unilateral determination by Israel of the final borders separating the two states.

PEACE TREATIES

Israel and Egypt

Although Sadat was defeated in the 1973 war, he was seen as a hero. He had stood up to Israel and not been humiliated. Sadat wanted to regain Egyptian rule over the Sinai, though. He announced that he was willing to come to Jerusalem and address the Knesset. Sadat's visit to Jerusalem, the first visit by an Arab head of state to Israel, did much to break down the psychological barriers separating the two countries, barriers which stood in the way of peace.

On March 6, 1979, the first peace treaty between Israel and an Arab country was signed, in Washington, D.C. Although there was desire for peace on both sides, discussions ran up against some brick walls. President Jimmy Carter became involved. He invited Prime Minister Begin (see sidebar) and President Sadat to spend some time with him at a presidential retreat, Camp David. Out of Camp David came two documents: (1) the draft of an Israel-Egypt peace treaty to be signed within three months and (2) an agreement to conduct negotiations between Jordan, Israel, and "representatives of the Palestinian people" relating to the West Bank and Gaza.

Israel and the PLO—the Oslo Accords

Peace negotiations between Israel and the Palestinians are based in the Oslo accords. These accords, called the "Declaration of Principles," were negotiated secretly by Israeli and Palestinian delega-

tions in 1993 in Oslo, Norway, under the supervision and guidance of the Norwegian Foreign Minister, Johan Jorgen Holst. They were signed in a historic Washington ceremony hosted by President Bill Clinton on September 13, 1993, during which PLO Chairman Arafat and Israeli Prime Minister Yitzhak Rabin grasped hands in an uneasy, yet unforgettable handshake.

The goals to be achieved in the peace process, as defined at Oslo I, are the complete withdrawal of Israeli troops from the Gaza Strip and the West Bank, and the Palestinians' right to self-rule in those territories. By October 1996, Israeli troops had withdrawn from much of the West Bank.

"Letters of Mutual Recognition" accompanied the "Declaration of Principles." Israel, for the first time, officially recognized the PLO as the legitimate representative of the Palestinians. The PLO recognized Israel's right to exist, renounced terrorism, rescinded its call for Israel's destruction, and accepted the principle of land for peace.

Oslo II, known as the Taba agreement, laid down the timetable and conditions under which the majority of Palestinians would gain autonomy. It called for the election of the Palestinian Council and a President and divided the West Bank into three areas; voting took place on January 20, 1996.

Prime Minister Menachem Begin welcomes President Anwar Sadat of Egypt at Ben-Gurion Airport, November 21, 1977.

In addition, the PLO committed itself to rescind the articles of the Palestinian National Charter that refer to the destruction of Israel. This commitment was met in April 1996.

Despite the Oslo accords, the Israel-Palestinian conflict continued. In October 1998, a summit conference, hosted by President Clinton, was convened at Wye River, Maryland. The Israeli delegation included Prime Minister Benjamin Netanyahu and, among others, Foreign Minister Ariel Sharon, currently Israel's Prime Minister. The Palestinian delegation was just Yasser Arafat. On October 23, 1998, an agreement was signed. The issues covered in this agreement were security and terrorism, the controversial articles of the PLO Charter, and the redeployment of Israeli military forces.

Intifada I and II continued during all negotiations. Ongoing and escalating terrorism, moreover, continued to interfere with the peace process. On April 30, 2003, as discussed above, President George W. Bush presented his "road map" for a solution to the Israel-Palestinian conflict. The government of Israel approved it on May 25, 2003.

Israel and Jordan

King Hussein met frequently with Israeli leaders, but always in secret. This situation changed in mid-1994, when Hussein met them openly. Negotiations began during the summer months, and most of the issues of dispute were resolved quickly. The ceremony of signing the peace treaty was held on October 26, 1994, at a new border crossing area north of Eilat. The guest of honor for the occasion was President Bill Clinton. The agreement was signed by Yitzhak Rabin and Abed el-Majali, the Prime Minister of Jordan.

Among the matters dealt with in the agreement were the allocation of water, cooperation in the development of energy, the problem of refugees, the proper treatment of the holy places of each religion, the boundaries of the two states, economic relations between the two states, and the exchange of ambassadors within one month of the treaty's approval. In the eyes of Israel, the allocation of water was of great importance, since its water sources are limited.

King Hussein died in 1999 and was succeeded by his son, Abdullah.

Menachem Begin (1913–1992) was the sixth Prime Minister of Israel, leading the state from 1977 to 1983. Born and educated in Brest-Litovsk (Brisk), Poland, he later received a law degree from Warsaw University.

In 1929 Begin joined Betar, an activist Zionist movement; he became a member of its leadership in Poland in 1931 and head of the movement in 1939. During the Palestine riots of 1936–1938 he organized a mass demonstration near the British Embassy in Warsaw and was imprisoned by the Polish police as a result. When the Germans invaded Poland, he escaped to Vilna, where the Soviet authorities caught him and sentenced him in 1940 to eight years of hard labor. He was released, however, at the end of 1941, but only because he was a Polish citizen.

He reached Palestine in 1942, and in 1943 he assumed command of the Irgun, an underground military force. In January 1944 he declared armed warfare against the British, beginning a determined underground struggle for Jewish political independence. The British offered a reward for his apprehension.

In 1948 Begin was elected to the first Knesset and served there until he retired as Prime Minister. In 1952 he led the fight against accepting reparations payments from West Germany. In 1967 he was named minister without portfolio in the Government of National Unity, formed just before the Six-Day War.

After having served in the Knesset since 1948, Begin, leader of the Likud (Union) Party, was elected Prime Minister in 1977. The Labor Party had led Israel for thirty years, but now Begin was to lead the country.

Perhaps the most remarkable product of the Begin administration was the Egypt-Israel peace treaty. President Sadat shocked the world by announcing in November 1977 his intention to visit Israel and speak in the Knesset. In 1979 a peace treaty was signed. Begin, Sadat, and American President Jimmy Carter were awarded the Nobel Peace Prize in recognition of this achievement.

Begin retired as Prime Minister in 1983, without providing an explanation. Some have speculated that he was saddened by the many casualties in the 1982 war in Lebanon, a war that did not achieve the government's desired end. Begin died in 1992.

SUMMARY

The State of Israel was founded on May 14, 1948. Unfortunately its history has been one of wars in 1948, 1956, 1973, and 1982. We have discussed the formation of government and the structure of government, as well as the major political parties and holders of political office. The chapter concludes with an examination of the treaties signed by Israel with Egypt, Jordan, and the PLO.

Documents

ISRAEL'S DECLARATION OF INDEPENDENCE (MAY 14, 1948)

This document is Israel's Declaration of Independence. It affirms that the spiritual, religious, and national identity of the Jews was created in the Land of Israel.

The Land of Israel was the birthplace of the Jewish people. Here their spiritual, religious and national identity was formed. Here they achieved independence and created a culture of national and universal significance. Here they wrote and gave the Bible to the world.

Exiled from Palestine, the Jewish people remained faithful to it in all the countries of their dispersion, never ceasing to pray and hope for their return and the restoration of their national freedom.

Impelled by this historic association, Jews strove throughout the centuries to go back to the land of their fathers and regain their statehood. In recent decades they returned in their masses. They reclaimed the wilderness, revived their language, built cities and villages and established a vigorous and ever-growing community, with its own economic and cultural life. They sought peace yet were prepared to defend themselves. They brought the blessings of progress to all inhabitants of the country.

In the year 1897 the First Zionist Congress, inspired by Theodor Herzl's vision of the Jewish State, proclaimed the right of the Jewish people to national revival in their own country.

This right was acknowledged by the Balfour Declaration of November 2, 1917, and reaffirmed by the Mandate of the League of Nations, which gave explicit international recognition to the historic connection of the Jewish people with Palestine and their right to reconstitute their national home.

The Nazi Holocaust, which engulfed millions of Jews in Europe, proved anew the urgency of the reestablishment of the Jewish State, which would solve the problem of Jewish homelessness by opening the gates to all Jews and lifting the Jewish people to equality in the family of nations.

The survivors of the European catastrophe, as well as Jews from other lands, proclaiming their right to a life of dignity, freedom and labor, and undeterred by hazards, hardships and obstacles, have tried unceasingly to enter Palestine.

In the Second World War the Jewish people in Palestine made a full contribution in the struggle of the freedom-loving nations against the Nazi evil. The sacrifices of their soldiers and the efforts of their workers gained them title to rank with the peoples who founded the United Nations.

On November 29, 1947, the General Assembly of the United Nations adopted a Resolution for the establishment of an independent Jewish State in Palestine, and called upon inhabitants of the country to take such steps as may be necessary on their part to put the plan into effect.

This recognition by the United Nations of the right of the Jewish people to establish their independent state may not be revoked. It is, moreover, the self-evident right of the Jewish people to be a nation, like all other nations, in its own sovereign state.

Accordingly, we, the members of the National Council, representing the Jewish people in Palestine and the Zionist movement of the world, met together in solemn assembly today, the day of the termination of the British Mandate for Palestine, and by virtue of the natural and historic right of the Jewish people and of the resolution of the General Assembly of the United Nations, hereby proclaim the establishment of the Jewish State in Palestine, to be called Israel.

We hereby declare that as from the termination of the Mandate at midnight, this night of the fourteenth to the fifteenth of May, 1948, and until the setting up of the duly elected bodies of the State in accordance with a Constitution, to be drawn up by a Constituent Assembly not later than the first day of October 1948, the present National Council shall act as the Provisional State Council, and its executive organ, the National Administration, shall constitute the Provisional Government of the State of Israel.

The State of Israel will be open to the immigration of Jews from all countries of their dispersion; will promote the development of the country for the benefit of all its inhabitants;

will be based on the precepts of liberty, justice and peace taught by the Hebrew Prophets; will uphold the full social and political equality of all its citizens, without distinction of race, creed or sex; will guarantee full freedom of conscience, worship, education and culture; will safeguard the sanctity and inviolability of the shrines and Holy Places of all religions; and will dedicate itself to the principles of the Charter of the United Nations.

The State of Israel will be ready to cooperate with the organs and representatives of the United Nations in the implementation of the Resolution of the Assembly of November 29, 1947, and will take steps to bring about the Economic Union over the whole of Palestine.

We appeal to the United Nations to assist the Jewish people in the building of its State and to admit Israel into the family of nations.

In the midst of wanton aggression, we call upon the Arab inhabitants of the State of Israel to return to the ways of peace and plan their part in the development of the State with full and equal citizenship and representation in all its bodies and institutions, provisional or permanent.

We offer peace and amity to all the neighboring states and their peoples, and invite them to cooperate with the independent Jewish nation for the common good of all. The State of Israel is ready to contribute its full share to the peaceful progress and development of the Middle East.

Our call goes out to the Jewish people all over the world to rally to our side in the task of immigration and development and to stand by us in the great struggle for the fulfillment of the dream of generations—the redemption of Israel.

With trust in the Rock of Israel, we set our hand to this Declaration, at this session of the Provisional State Council, in the city of Tel Aviv, on this Sabbath eve, the fifth of Iyar, 5708, the fourteenth day of May, 1948.

THE LAW OF RETURN (JULY 5, 1950)

The Law of Return established who would qualify to be a citizen of the new State of Israel.

---

1. Every Jew has the right to immigrate to the country.
2. (a) Immigration shall be on the basis of an immigrant's visa. (b) An immigrant's visa shall be granted to every Jew who has expressed his desire to settle in Israel, unless the minister of immigration is convinced that the applicant (1) is acting against the Jewish people, (2) is likely to endanger public health or the security of the state.
3. (a) A Jew who comes to Israel and after his arrival expresses his desire to settle there, is entitled, while he is still in Israel, to obtain an immigrant certificate. (b) The reservations detailed in section 2(b) will also be in force regarding the granting of an immigrant certificate, but a

person will not be considered as endangering the public health as a result of an illness he contracted after his arrival in Israel.
4. Every Jew who immigrated to Israel before this law entered into effect, and every Jew born in the country, whether before or after this law entered into effect, shall be considered as having immigrated according to this law.
5. The minister of immigration is responsible for the enforcement of this law, and he is empowered to enact regulations in all matters concerning its implementation as well as the granting of immigrant visas and immigrant papers to minors under the age of eighteen.

DAVID BEN-GURION. ADDRESS TO THE KNESSET ON THE LAW OF RETURN (JULY 3, 1950)

In this address to the Knesset, Israel's parliament, Ben-Gurion attempts to present some background to the Law of Return.

. . . The Law of Return and the Law of Citizenship that you have in front of you are connected by a mutual bond and share a common conceptual origin, deriving from the historical uniqueness of the State of Israel, a uniqueness vis-à-vis the past and the future, directed internally and externally. These two laws determine the special character and destiny of the State of Israel as the state bearing the vision of the redemption of Israel.

The State of Israel is a state like all the other states. All the general indications [of statehood] common to the other states are also to be found in the State of Israel. It rests on a specific territory and a population existing within this territory, it possesses sovereignty in internal and external affairs, and its authority does not extend beyond its borders. The State of Israel rules only over its own inhabitants. The Jews in the Diaspora, who are citizens of their countries and who want to remain there, have no legal or civil connection to the State of Israel, and the State of Israel does not represent them from any legal standpoint. Nevertheless, the State of Israel differs from the other states both with regard to the factors involved in its establishment and to the aims of its existence. It was established merely two years ago, but its roots are grounded in the far past and it is nourished by ancient springs. Its authority is limited to the area in which its residents dwell, but its gates are open to every Jew wherever he may be. The State of Israel is not a Jewish state merely because the majority of its inhabitants are Jews. It is a state for all the Jews wherever they may be and for every Jew who so desires.

On the fourteenth of May, 1948 a new state was not founded *ex nihilo*. Rather, the crown was restored to its pristine splendor 1,813 years after the independence of Israel was destroyed, during the days of Bar Kokhba and Rabbi Akiba. . . .

The establishment of the Jewish state was not an event limited to the place and time of its emergence. Rather, it is a world event, in the sense of time as well as place, an event summarizing a prolonged historical development. This event has introduced radical reforms and itself serves as a source for alterations and changes exceeding its temporal and spatial framework.

It is not accidental that the Proclamation of Independence began with cogent and succinct passages concerning the perpetual link between the Jewish people and its ancient homeland. Neither is it accidental that as a primary and essential principle governing the direction of the state it was declared before anything else that "the state of Israel shall be open to Jewish immigration and the ingathering of exiles." . . . Just as it was clear that the renewal of the State of Israel is not a beginning, but a continuation from days of yore, so, too was it understood that this renewal is not an end and conclusion but another stage in the long path leading to the full redemption of Israel.

The Diaspora has not ceased with the foundation of the state. In fact, this Diaspora is not a recent phenomenon, having preceded by a long period of time the destruction of our independence. Already in the seventh century B.C.E., simultaneous to the destruction of the First Commonwealth, we find Jews in foreign lands. . . .

In the last meeting of the Zionist Executive in Jerusalem a debate arose concerning the question: ingathering of exiles or ingathering of all the exiles? This debate will not be decided by ideology or by political resolutions; only Jewish history can offer a solution. Nevertheless, it is a fact worth noting that foreign volunteers from fifty-five various countries representing all five continents of the world served in the Israel Defense Force [during the war of Independence]. Further, with respect to its scope, dimensions, pace and diversity, the return of the exiles taking place in our days has no precedent, even in the annals of the Jewish nation. This is the great, decisive event of our generation that will determine the fate of the State of Israel and fashion the image of the Hebrew nation for many generations; no event in our life from our emergence as a people until the present has been so decisive.

The motives at work in the Jewish immigration [to the land of Israel] in all the generations, including our own, have been many and varied. Longings for redemption, ancient memories, religious feeling, love of homeland and above all, distress—With the foundation of the state a new factor has been added whose strength will continually increase: the power of appeal and attraction [embedded] in the State of Israel. The pace and scope of the exiles will in no small part be dependent upon our capacity to augment this appeal and

to turn the State of Israel into the center for the realization of the longings of the nation and for the satisfaction of its material and spiritual needs. In addition, this capacity may very well be the primary factor in attracting immigration from the countries of the New World.

The Law of Return is one of the Basic Laws of the State of Israel. It comprises the central mission of our state, namely, ingathering of exiles. This law determines that it is not the state that grants the Jew from abroad the right to settle in the state. Rather, this right is inherent in him by the very fact that he is a Jew, if only he desires to join in the settlement of the land. In the State of Israel the Jews have no right of prority over the non-Jewish citizens. The State of Israel is grounded on the full equality of rights and obligations for all its citizens. This principle was also laid down in the Proclamation of Independence. . . . The right to return preceded the State of Israel and it is this right that built the state. This right originates in the unbroken historical connection between the people and the homeland, a connection which has also been acknowledged in actual practice by the tribunal of the peoples.

UNITED NATIONS RESOLUTION 242 (NOVEMBER 22, 1967)

Five months after the Six-Day War, the United Nations Security Council passed this resolution. The obligations of Israel, as well as the obligations of the Arab states, are spelled out.

The Security Council,

Expressing its continued concern with the grave situation in the Middle East,

Emphasizing the inadmissibility of the acquisition of territory by war and the need to work for a just and lasting peace in which every state in the area can live in security,

Emphasizing further that all Member States in their acceptance of the Charter of the United Nations have undertaken a commitment to act in accordance with Article 2 of the Charter.

1. *Affirms* that the fulfillment of Charter principles requires the establishment of a just and lasting peace in the Middle East which should include the application of both the following principles.

    1. Withdrawal of Israel armed forces from territories occupied in recent conflict.

    2. Termination of all claims or states of belligerency and respect for and acknowledgement of the sovereignty, territorial integrity and political independence of every State in the area and their right to live in peace within secure and recognized boundaries free from threats or acts of force.

2. *Affirms further* the necessity

a. For guaranteeing freedom of navigation through international waterways in the area;

b. For achieving a just settlement of the refugee problem;

c. For guaranteeing the territorial inviolability and political independence of every State in the area, through measures including the establishment of demilitarized zones;

3. *Requests* the Secretary-General to designate a Special Representative to proceed to the Middle East to establish and maintain contacts with the States concerned in order to promote agreement and assist efforts to achieve a peaceful and accepted settlement in accordance with the provisions and principles in this resolution;

4. *Requests* the Secretary-General to report to the Security Council on the progress of the efforts of the Special Representative as soon as possible.

THE PALESTINIAN NATIONAL CHARTER (JULY 1968)

In addition to launching the War of Attrition, the Arab states put their collective weight behind the Palestine Liberation Organization in order to break the deadlock in Arab–Israel relations. Frequently these states sought to further their own competing policies and approaches by manipulating factions of the PLO—or even by organizing new factions.

After drafting the original Palestinian National Charter in 1964, the PLO underwent several important changes. Ahmad Shuqeiri, the first chairman, was replaced in 1967 by Yahya Hamuden, who was in turn replaced in 1969 by Yasser Arafat, head of al-Fatah. During the transitional period that followed the June 1967 war, the PLO became increasingly independent of the Arab states and served as an umbrella organization of semiautonomous Palestinian groups. Fatah, the largest of these, has continued to dominate it. Following the May 1983 Lebanese–Israel agreement, Arafat's leadership of Fatah was seriously challenged for the first time.

The Popular Front for the Liberation of Palestine (PFLP), headed by George Habash, was organized in December 1967. In 1968 Nayef Hawatmeh and his followers seceded from the PFLP to form the Popular Democratic Front for the Liberation of Palestine. The Palestine Liberation front was reorganized by Ahmad Jibril into the Palestine Front for the Liberation of Palestine—General Command. In 1968 the Syrian Ba'ath party established Al-Saiwa—Vanguard of the People's War of Liberation the Arab Liberation Front, which later also gained the support of Libya.

The first charter of the Palestine Liberation Organization was drafted in 1964. Many changes in leadership and structure took place after this date. For this reason, a new charter was formulated and adopted in July 1968. This document presents the aims and goals of the PLO.

On April 24, 1996, the Palestinian National Council, convening in Gaza, voted 504 to 54, with 14 abstentions, as follows:

- The Palestinian National Charter is hereby amended by canceling the articles that are contrary to the letters exchanged between the P.L.O. and the Government of Israel 9–10 September 1993.

- Assigns its legal committee with the task of redrafting the Palestinian National Charter in order to present it to the first session of the Palestinian central council.

In December 1998, the Palestinian National Council convened in Gaza, in the presence of U.S. President Clinton, to reaffirm this decision.

This Charter shall be known as "the Palestine National Charter."

Articles of the Charter:

1. Palestine, the homeland of the Palestinian Arab people, is an inseparable part of the greater Arab homeland, and the Palestinian people are a part of the Arab nation.

2. Palestine, within the frontiers that existed under the British Mandate, is an indivisible territorial unit.

3. The Palestinian Arab people alone have the legitimate rights to their homeland and shall exercise the right of self-determination after the liberation of their homeland, in keeping with their wishes and entirely of their own accord.

4. The Palestinian identity is an authentic, intrinsic and indissoluble quality that is transmitted from father to son. Neither the Zionist occupation nor the dispersal of the Palestinian Arab people as a result of the afflictions they have suffered can efface this Palestinian identity.

5. Palestinians are Arab citizens who were normally resident in Palestine until 1947. This includes both those who were forced to leave or who stayed in Palestine. Anyone born to a Palestinian father after that date, whether inside or outside Palestine, is a Palestinian.

6. Jews who were normally resident in Palestine up to the beginning of the Zionist invasion are Palestinians.

7. Palestinian identity, and material, spiritual and historical links with Palestine are immutable realities It is a national obligation to provide every Palestinian with a revolutionary Arab upbringing, and to instill in him a profound spiritual and material familiarity with his homeland and a readiness for armed struggle and for the sacrifice of his material possessions and his life, for the recovery of his homeland. All available educational means and means of guidance must be enlisted to that end, until liberation is achieved.

8. The Palestinian people is at the stage of national struggle for the liberation of its homeland. For that reason, differences between Palestinian national forces must give way to the fundamental difference that exists between Zionism and imperialism on the one hand and the Palestinian Arab people on the other. On that basis, the Palestinian masses, both as organizations and as individuals, whether in the homeland or in such places as they now live as refugees, constitute a single national front working for the recovery and liberation of Palestine through armed struggle.

9. Armed struggle is the only way of liberating Palestine, and is thus strategic, not tactical The Palestinian Arab people hereby affirm their unwavering determination to carry on the armed struggle and to press on towards popular revolution for the liberation of and return to their homeland They also affirm their right to a normal life in their homeland, to the exercise of their right of self-determination therein and to sovereignty over it.

10. Commando action constitutes the nucleus of the Palestinian popular war of liberation. This requires that commando action should be escalated, expanded and protected, and that all the resources of the Palestinian masses and all scientific potentials available to them should be mobilized and organized to play their part in the armed Palestinian revolution. It also requires solidarity in national struggle among the different groups within the Palestinian people and between that people and the Arab masses, to ensure the continuity of the escalation and victory of the revolution.

11. Palestinians shall have three slogans: national unity, national mobilization, and liberation.

12. The Palestinian Arab people believe in Arab unity. To fulfill their role in the achievement of that objective, they must, at the present stage in their national struggle, retain their Palestinian identity and all that it involves, work for increased awareness of it, and oppose all measures liable to weaken or dissolve it.

13. Arab unity and the liberation of Palestine are complementary objectives; each leads to the achievement of the other. Arab unity will lead to the liberation of Palestine, and the liberation of Palestine will lead to Arab unity. To work for one is to work for both.

14. The destiny of the Arab nation, indeed the continued existence of the Arabs, depends on the fate of the Palestinian cause. This interrelationship is the point of departure of the Arab endeavor to liberate Palestine. The Palestinian people are the vanguard of the movement to achieve this sacred national objective.

15. The liberation of Palestine is a national obligation for the Arabs. It is their duty to repel the Zionist and imperialist invasion of the greater Arab homeland and to liquidate the Zionist presence in Palestine. The full

responsibility for this belongs to the peoples and governments of the Arab nation, and to the Palestinian people first and foremost. For this reason, the task of the Arab nation is to enlist all the military, human, moral, and material resources at its command to play an effective part, along with the Palestinian people, in the liberation of Palestine. Moreover, it is the task of the Arab nation, particularly at the present stage of the Palestinian armed revolution, to offer the Palestinian people all possible aid, material, and manpower support and to place at their disposal all the means and opportunities that will enable them to continue to perform their role as the vanguard of their armed revolution until the liberation of their homeland is achieved.

16. On the spiritual plane, the liberation of Palestine will establish in the Holy Land an atmosphere of peace and tranquility in which all religious institutions will be safeguarded and freedom of worship and the right of visit guaranteed to all without discrimination or distinction of race, color, language, or creed. For this reason the people of Palestine look to all spiritual forces in the world for support.

17. On the human plane, the liberation of Palestine will restore to the Palestinians their dignity, integrity and freedom. For this reason, the Palestinian Arab people look to all those who believe in the dignity and freedom of man for support.

18. On the international plane, the liberation of Palestine is a defensive measure dictated by the requirements of self-defense. This is why the Palestinian people, who seek to win the friendship of all peoples, look for the support of all freedom-, justice-, and peace-loving countries in restoring the legitimate state of affairs in Palestine, establishing security and peace in it and enabling its people to exercise national sovereignty and freedom.

19. The partition of Palestine, which took place in 1947, and the establishment of Israel, are fundamentally invalid, however long they last, for they contravene the will of the people of Palestine and their natural right to their homeland and contradict the principles of the United Nations Charter, foremost among which is the right of self-determination.

20. The Balfour Declaration, the Mandate Instrument, and all their consequences, are hereby declared null and void. The claim of historical or spiritual links between the Jews and Palestine is neither in conformity with historical fact nor does it satisfy the requirements for statehood. Judaism is a revealed religion; it is not a separate nationality, nor are the Jews a single people with a separate identity; they are citizens of their respective countries.

21. The Palestinian Arab people, expressing themselves through the Palestinian armed revolution, reject all

alternatives to the total liberation of Palestine. They also reject all proposals for the liquidation or internationalization of the Palestine problem.

22. Zionism is a political movement that is organically linked with world imperialism and is opposed to all liberation movements or movements for progress in the world. The Zionist movement is essentially fanatical and racialist; its objectives involve aggression, expansion and the establishment of colonial settlements, and its methods are those of the Fascists and the Nazis. Israel acts as cat's paw for the Zionist movement, a geographic and manpower base for world imperialism and a springboard for its thrust into the Arab homeland to frustrate the aspirations of the Arab nation to liberation, unity 'and progress. Israel is a constant threat to peace in the Middle East and the whole world. Inasmuch as the liberation of Palestine will eliminate the Zionist and imperialist presence in that country and bring peace to the Middle East, the Palestinian people look for support to all liberals and to all forces of good, peace and progress in the world, and call on them, whatever their political convictions, for all possible aid and support in their just and legitimate struggle to liberate their homeland.

23. The demands of peace and security and the exigencies of right and justice require that all nations should regard Zionism as an illegal movement and outlaw it and its activities, out of consideration for the ties of friendship between peoples and for the loyalty of citizens of their homelands.

24. The Palestinian Arab people believe in justice, freedom, sovereignty, self-determination, human dignity and the right of peoples to enjoy them.

25. In pursuance of the objectives set out in this charter, the Palestine Liberation Organization shall perform its proper role in the liberation of Palestine to the full.

26. The Palestine Liberation Organization, as the representative of the forces of the Palestinian revolution, is responsible for the struggle of the Palestinian Arab people to regain, liberate and return to their homeland and to exercise the right of self-determination in that homeland, in the military, political and financial fields, and for all else that the Palestinian cause may demand, both at Arab and international levels.

27. The Palestine Liberation Organization shall cooperate with all Arab countries, each according to its means, maintaining a neutral attitude vis-à-vis these countries in accordance with the requirements of the battle of liberation, and on the basis of that factor. The Organization shall not interfere in the internal affairs of any Arab country.

28. The Palestinian Arab people hereby affirm the authenticity and independence of their national revolution and reject all forms of interference, tutelage or dependency.

29. The Palestinian Arab people have the legitimate and prior right to liberate and recover their homeland, and shall define their attitude to all countries and forces in accordance with the attitude adopted by such countries and forces to the cause of the Palestinian people and with the extent of their support for that people in their revolution to achieve their objectives.

30. Those who fight or bear arms in the battle of liberation form the nucleus of the popular army which will shield the achieved merits of the Palestinian Arab people.

31. The Organization shall have a flag, an oath of allegiance and an anthem, to be decided in accordance with appropriate regulations.

32. Regulations, to be known as Basic Regulations for the Palestine Liberation Organization, shall be appended to this Charter. These regulations shall define the structure of the Organization, its bodies and institutions, and the powers, duties and obligations of each of them, in accordance with this Charter.

33. This Charter may only be amended with a majority of two thirds of the total number of members of the National Council of the Palestine Liberation Organization at a special meeting called for that purpose.

ISRAEL-EGYPT PEACE TREATY (MARCH 26, 1979)

This document is the Israel–Egypt Peace Treaty. Although there were hopes for a "normal relationship" between the two countries, this has yet to materialize. There have been no wars between the two countries, however, since the signing of the treaty.

The Government of the Arab Republic of Egypt and the Government of the State of Israel;

Preamble

Convinced of the urgent necessity of the establishment of a just, comprehensive and lasting peace in the Middle East in accordance with Security Council Resolutions 242 and 338;

Reaffirming their adherence to the "Framework for Peace in the Middle East Agreed at Camp David," dated 17 September 1978;

Noting that the aforementioned Framework as appropriate is intended to constitute a basis for peace not only between Egypt and Israel but also between Israel and each of its other Arab neighbors which is prepared to negotiate peace with it on this basis;

Desiring to bring to an end the state of war between them, and to establish a peace in which every state in the area can live in security;

Convinced that the conclusion of a Treaty of Peace between Egypt and Israel is an important step in the search for comprehensive peace in the area and for the attainment of the settlement of the Arab–Israel conflict in all its aspects;

Inviting the other Arab parties to this dispute to join the peace process with Israel guided by and based on the principles of the aforementioned Framework;

Desiring as well to develop friendly relations and co-operation between themselves in accordance with the United Nations Charter and the principles of international law governing international relations in times of peace;

Agree to the following provisions in the free exercise of their sovereignty, in order to implement the Framework for the Conclusion of a Peace Treaty Between Egypt and Israel:

Article I

1. The state of war between the Parties will be terminated and peace will be established between them upon the exchange of instruments of ratification of this Treaty.
2. Israel will withdraw all its armed forces and civilians from the Sinai behind the international boundary between Egypt and mandated Palestine, as provided for in the annexed protocol (Annex I), and Egypt will resume the exercise of its full sovereignty over the Sinai.
3. Upon completion of the interim withdrawal provided for in Annex I, the Parties will establish normal and friendly relations, in accordance with Article III(3).

Article II

The permanent boundary between Egypt and Israel is the recognized international boundary between Egypt and the former mandated territory of Palestine, as shown on the map at Annex II, without prejudice to the issue of the status of the Gaza Strip. The parties recognize this boundary as inviolable. Each will respect the territorial integrity of the other, including their territorial waters and airspace.

Article III

1. The Parties will apply between them the provisions of the Charter of the United Nations and the principles of international law governing relations among states in times of peace. In particular:
   a. they recognize and will respect each other's sovereignty, territorial integrity and political independence;
   b. They recognize and will respect each other's right to live in peace within their secure and recognized boundaries;
   c. They will refrain from the threat or use of force, directly or indirectly, against each other and will settle all disputes between them by peaceful means.
2. Each Party undertakes to ensure that acts or threats of belligerency, hostility, or violence do not originate from and are not committed from within its territory, or by any forces subject to its control or by any other forces stationed on its territory, against the population, citizens or property of the other Party. Each Party also under-

takes to refrain from organizing, instigating inciting, assisting or participating in acts or threats of belligerency, hostility, subversion and violence against the other Party, anywhere, and undertakes to ensure that perpetrators of such acts are brought to justice.
3. The Parties agree that the normal relationship established between them will include full recognition, diplomatic, economic and cultural relations, termination of economic boycotts and discriminatory barriers to the free movement of people and goods, and will guarantee the mutual enjoyment of citizens of the due process of law. The process by which they undertake to achieve such a relationship parallel to the implementation of other provisions of this treaty is set out in the annexed protocol (Annex III).

Article IV

1. In order to provide maximum security for both Parties on the basis of reciprocity, agreed security arrangements will be established including limited force zones in Egyptian and Israeli territory, and United Nations forces and observers described in detail as to nature and training in Annex I, and any security arrangements the Parties may agree upon.
2. The Parties agree to the stationing of United Nations personnel in areas described in Annex I:
   The Parties agree not to request withdrawal of the United Nations personnel and that these personnel will not be removed unless such removal is approved by the Security Council of the United Nations, with the affirmative vote of the five Permanent Members, unless the Parties otherwise agree.
3. A Joint Commission will be established to facilitate the implementation of the Treaty, as provided for in Annex I.
4. The security arrangements provided for in paragraphs 1 and 2 of this Article may at the request of either party be reviewed and amended by mutual agreement of the Parties.

Article V

1. Ships of Israel, and cargoes destined for or coming from Israel, shall enjoy the right of free passage through the Suez Canal and its approaches through the Gulf of Suez and the Mediterranean Sea on the basis of the Constantinople Convention of 1888, applying to all nations. Israeli nationals, vessels and cargoes destined for or coming from Israel, shall be accorded non-discriminatory treatment in all matters connected with usage of the canal.
2. The Parties consider the Strait of Tiran and the Gulf of Aqaba to be international waterways open to all nations for unimpeded and non-suspendable freedom of navigation and overflight. The Parties will respect each other's right to navigation and overflight for access to either country through the Strait of Tiran and the Gulf of Aqaba.

Article VI

1. This Treaty does not affect and shall not be interpreted as affecting in any way the rights and obligations of the Parties under the Charter of the United Nations.
2. The Parties undertake to fulfill in good faith their obligations under this Treaty, without regard to action or inaction of any other party and independently of any instrument external to this Treaty.
3. They further undertake to take all the necessary measures for the application in their relations of the provisions of the multilateral conventions to which they are parties, including the submission of appropriate notification to the Secretary General of the United Nations and other depositories of such conventions.
4. The Parties undertake not to enter into any obligation in conflict with this Treaty.
5. Subject to Article 103 of the United Nations Charter, in the event of a conflict between the obligations of the Parties under the present Treaty and any of their other obligations, the obligations under this Treaty will be binding and implemented.

Article VII

1. Disputes arising out of the application or interpretation of this Treaty shall be resolved by negotiations.

2 Any such disputes which cannot be settled by negotiations shall be resolved by conciliation or submitted to arbitration.

Article VIII

The Parties agree to establish a claims commission for the mutual settlement of all financial claims.

Article IX

1. This Treaty shall enter into force upon exchange of instruments of ratification.
2. This Treaty supersedes the Agreement between Egypt and Israel of September, 1975. All protocols, annexes, and maps attached to this Treaty shall be regarded as an integral part hereof.
3. The Parties undertake not to enter into any obligation in conflict with this Treaty.
4. The Treaty shall be communicated to the Secretary General of the United Nations for registration in accordance with the provisions of Article 102 of the Charter of the United Nations.

Done at Washington DC, this 26th day of March, 1979, in triplicate in—the English, Arabic, and Hebrew languages, each text being equally authentic. In case of any divergence of interpretation, the English text shall prevail.

Reference Works

I. J. Bickerton and M. N. Pearson, *The Arab-Israeli Conflict: A History*

P. Mendes-Flohr and J. Reinharz, *The Jew in the Modern World*

I. Rabinovich and J. Reinharz, *Israel in the Middle East*

H. M. Sachar, *A History of Israel*, 2 vols.

Chronology

1947	UN General Assembly adopts the Palestine partition plan by a two-thirds majority.
1948	Massacre by Irgun troops takes place in the Palestinian village of Deir Yassin.
	The State of Israel is proclaimed on May 14. The Arab states reject the partition plan and their armies enter Palestine on May 15.
1948–1949	War in Palestine ends in Israeli victory. Armistice agreements are signed between Israel and the neighboring Arab states. Israel becomes a member of the UN.
1949	UN Resolution 1194 is adopted, proclaiming the right of Palestinian refugees to return to their homes.
1950	The West Bank is annexed by Transjordan. Egypt establishes its control of Gaza.
1951	Israel rejects UN peace plan which is accepted by Egypt, Syria, Lebanon, and Jordan.
1956	Israel, France, and Britain attack Egypt, in response to Nasser's nationalization of the Suez Canal on July 26.
1958	Egypt and Syria form the United Arab Republic (UAR)
1959	Congress of Fatah is founded in Kuwait.
1964	The Palestine Liberation Organization (PLO) is created.
1967	Israel attacks Egypt, Syria, and Jordan. Following a six-day lightning war, Israel occupies Sinai, the Golan, the West Bank,

Gaza, and East Jerusalem. Settlement begins in the summer.

The UN Security Council adopts Resolution 242.

Fifth session of the Palestine National Council. Yasser Arafat becomes chairman of the PLO's executive committee.

1970   Serious clashes occur between the PLO and the Jordanian government. The PLO is expelled from Jordan, and the leadership of the Palestinian resistance moves to Lebanon.

1972   A group belonging to the Palestinian "Black September" organization attacks at the Munich Olympic Games. Eleven Israeli athletes and coaches are killed.

Arafat addresses the UN General Assembly. The UN recognizes the right of the Palestinians to independence and self-determination. The PLO obtains observer status.

1973   Israeli operation in Beirut takes place in April. Three PLO leaders are killed. There are mass demonstrations of solidarity with the Palestinian resistance in Lebanon.

Palestinian National Front is formed in the occupied territories.

Egyptian and Syrian armies launch attack to recover the territories occupied by Israel. The Yom Kippur War begins.

Security Council Resolution 338 is adopted. Fighting stops a few days later.

Arab League summit takes place in Algiers. A resolution is passes recognizing the PLO as the "sole legitimate representative of the Palestinian people." Jordan abstains.

1977   Thirteenth session of the Palestine National Council meets in Cairo. It accepts the idea of an independent Palestinian state in part of Palestine.

The right wins the Israeli elections for the first time. Its leader, Menachem Begin, becomes Prime Minister.

U.S.-Soviet declaration on peace in the Middle East, supported by the PLO. President Anwar Sadat of Egypt goes to Jerusalem.

1981   Israeli-Palestinian war breaks out on the Lebanese border in July. Israelis bomb Beirut.

President Sadat is assassinated in October. The day after martial law is declared in Poland, Israel annexes the Golan.

1982   Israel completes its withdrawal from Sinai in April.

Israeli invasion of Lebanon starts, followed by siege of Beirut. The PLO begins to withdraw from Beirut in September, under the protection of the Multinational Force.

The final resolution of the Arab League summit in Fez is adopted in September, calling for the creation of an independent Palestinian state, recognizing the PLO as the sole legitimate representative of the Palestinian people and the right of "all the states of the region" to live in peace.

New Lebanese president Beshir Gemayel is assassinated. Israelis enter West Beirut. Massacre in the Sabra and Shatilah Palestinian camps.

1984   Elections take place in Israel. National Unity Government is formed.

1985   Israel completes withdrawal from Lebanon, except for a strip along the southern border controlled by the South Lebanon Army.

1987   The Palestinian uprising in the occupied territories known as the Intifada begins in Gaza and then in the West Bank.

1988   King Hussein of Jordan announces on television the severance of his country's "legal and administrative ties" with the West Bank, annexed by his grandfather Abdullah in 1950 and occupied by Israel since 1967.

1989   Arafat declares the Palestinian National Charter "null and void."

1990   The emigration of Soviet Jews to Israel is accelerated suddenly. The monthly number of arrivals continues to rise right through to December (34,000), making a total of almost 200,000 for the year.

Iraqi forces cross the border into Kuwait. Security Council Resolution 660 demands "that Iraq withdraw immediately and unconditionally all its forces." Unlike the majority of Arab countries, the PLO supports Saddam Hussein.

1991   Following the agreement of the Palestine National Council and a final round of consultations, U.S. Secretary of State James Baker, accompanied by his Soviet counterpart, announces in Jerusalem the convening of a peace conference in Madrid on October 30. Diplomatic relations between the Soviet Union and Israel, broken off in 1967, are reestablished.

The Madrid Conference is opened by U.S. and Soviet Presidents Bush and Gorbachev, followed by the first bilateral negotiations between Israel and its Arab neighbors, with the Palestinians included as part of a joint Jordanian-Palestinian delegation. The negotiations continue, not without difficulty, in December and February, and the multilateral negotiations begin in Moscow on January 28, 1992.

1992   Yitzhak Rabin wins the Israeli election. Rabin envisages a "limited withdrawal" from the Golan in exchange for "total peace with Syria."

1993   Mutual recognition by Israel and the PLO. The PLO and the government of Israel, in the presence of Yitzhak Rabin and Yasser Arafat, sign the Declaration of Principles on Interim Self-Government at the White House.

1994   Arafat returns to Gaza. Arafat, Rabin, and Peres are co-recipients of the Nobel Peace Prize. Peace treaty is signed between Israel and Jordan.

1995   Despite a further attack in Jerusalem in August, Arafat and Rabin sign in Washington, in the presence of President Clinton, President Mubarak, and King Hussein, the Oslo II agreement in September, providing for the extension of autonomy to the West Bank In November, Yitzhak Rabin is assassinated by right-wing extremist student Yigal Amir. He is succeeded by Shimon Peres Israel completes its withdrawal from the Palestinian towns, except Hebron.

1996   Yasser Arafat is elected president of the Palestine Authority and his supporters win two-thirds of the 80 seats in the Legislative Council. In reprisal for the murder of its master bombmaker, Yehia Ayache, by the Israeli secret services, Hamas carries out a series of bloody terrorist attacks in Jerusalem, Tel Aviv, and Ashkelon At its first session to be held in Palestine, the Palestine National Council meets in Gaza and removes from its Charter all the articles incompatible with Israel's right to exist. The Israeli elections are won by a coalition of right-wing, far-right, and religious parties led by Binyamin Netanyahu, who becomes Prime Minister.

1999   The Jewish municipality of Jerusalem opens a tunnel under the Mosque Esplanade, provoking an outburst of violence, the most serious since the Intifada, that spreads to all the occupied territories (76 deaths). Yasser Arafat makes his first official visit to Israel, in response to an invitation to Caesarea from the head of state, Ezer Weizman. In Israeli elections for Prime Minister and the 120 members of the Knesset, the Labor candidate, Ehud Barak, degeats Likud leader Binyamin Netanyahu by the large margin of 56 percent to 44 percent. A September 4 Memorandum signed by Yasser Arafat and Ehud Barak at Sharm el-Sheikh redefines the timeline for application of the Wye River Memorandum on further redeployment of the Israeli army. It provides for the opening of two safe passages between the Gaza Strip and the West Bank, further release of prisoners, and the conclusion of a comprehensive agreement on all permanent status issues by September 13, 2000, at the latest. King Hussein of Jordan dies. He is succeeded by his son, King Abdullah II.

2000   The Israeli army hastily withdraws from South Lebanon, originally planned for July 7 following the Hezbollah offensive and the collapse of the South Lebanon Army (SLA). Syrian President Hafez al-Assad dies. His son, Bashir, prepares to assume power. Intifada II begins. Violence begins as rock throwing but moves quickly to machine gun and mortar fire, suicide bombings, and lethal road ambushes.

2001   Israel captures boatload of illegal arms intended for the Palestine Authority. In the election for Prime Minister, Ariel Sharon defeats Ehud Barak in a landslide. Labor Party agrees to join a coalition with Likud. In March Prince Abdullah of Saudi Arabia proposes a peace plan. Israel will withdraw from the occupied territories and the Arabs will recognize Israel. Suicide bombing in June in a crowded discotheque in Tel Aviv kills at least 17. More than 70 are injured. In August, 15 are killed at a Jerusalem pizzeria. Jerusalem Brigade, a wing of Islamic Jihad, claims responsibility

2002   Suicide blast on the first day of Passover kills 19 at Park Hotel in Netanya: 100 people injured.

Israel begins Operation Defensive Shield in March. Palestinian leaders are arrested. Arafat is imprisoned in Ramallah, and Palestinian militants shelter themselves in Bethlehem's Church of Nativity.

Sieges are ended in Ramallah and the Church of Nativity in May. Militants in the Church of the Nativity are exiled, while militants in Ramallah are imprisoned in Jericho.

President Bush calls upon Palestinian people to replace Arafat, electing a leader "not compromised by terror."

2003   Palestinian Authority selects Mahmoud Abbas as Prime Minister of Palestine.

U.S.-British Coalition invades Iraq and defeats the armies of Saddam Hussein, creating new realities in the Middle East. Suicide bombings continue. In a May 18 bombing in Jerusalem, seven are killed and 19 wounded. On May 19, a suicide bomber enters a mall in Afula, a town in northern Israel, and detonates a bomb that takes the lives of three and wounds dozens.

A "road map" to peace, formulated by the United States, the European Union, Russia, and the United Nations, is presented to the Israelis and the Palestinians. The Israeli cabinet endorses this peace plan on May 25. Only 12 members voted in favor, however, with seven opposed and four abstaining.

Abbas resigns as Palestine's Prime Minister. Ahmed Qurei takes his place.

9

THE JEWS IN AMERICA

EARLY SETTLEMENT

The earliest settlement of Jews in North America took place in 1654. Jews fleeing religious oppression in Europe had gone to South America, as far away as possible from the threat of the Inquisition. Some had found refuge in Brazil, especially in the city of Recife, which was the world's largest source of refined sugar. Jews achieved great financial success in Recife and similar communities. Many of them became the owners and operators of Brazil's sugar refineries.

These Jews were *conversos* (New Christians) who had escaped the Inquisition through conversion. In Brazil as well they found themselves under constant watch, in case they returned to being Jews. Change came in 1620, when the Dutch took control of Recife and granted civil equality to all its residents, including its Jews. The promise of Dutch rule led many of the New Christians to declare themselves as Jews. It also attracted Jews from Amsterdam, England, the Balkans, and Central and Eastern Europe.

A flourishing Jewish community was established in Recife, including the first Jewish congregation in the New World. A rabbi was brought from Amsterdam, Hebrew schools were created, and a kosher slaughterhouse began to function. By the middle of the 17th century, the Jews of Recife numbered 1,500, a third of Recife's white residents. In Dutch Brazil they enjoyed fuller rights than did the Jews living in Holland itself.

This idyllic life was not to last, though. The Portuguese recaptured Recife in 1654. The conquering general, an enlightened man, promised the Jews a full pardon for their participation on the Dutch side and assured them of religious tolerance. He was ultimately obligated, however, to bring the Inquisition to Brazil. This led the Jews to depart in early 1654.

Jews sought to settle in various places in the Western Hemisphere. Some settled in Aruba or

Isaac Aboab, the first rabbi in the Western Hemisphere. In 1642 he was called to the Dutch Jewish community of Recife, but he returned to Amsterdam when the Portuguese conquered the colony and brought in the Inquisition.

Curaçao. Others sought to find their place in the capital of New Netherlands, New Amsterdam, known today as New York City. Twenty-three professing Jews—four men, six women, and thirteen children—made this city their choice. The governor of New Amsterdam, Peter Stuyvesant, opposed their entry, but he was overruled by the Dutch West India Company, which desired to increase the number of taxpayers in New Netherlands and responded to pressure by Jewish shareholders in the company.

Although Stuyvesant was compelled to admit the Jews, this directive did not prevent his harassing them. Despite orders from the Dutch West India Company, he forbade Jews to trade with Indians, buy homes or business premises, open shops for retail trade, vote, hold office, or serve in the militia. The Jews found ways to support themselves, though. They worked as butchers, metalworkers, importers, and peddlers. They rented housing, purchased their own burial ground, and even found ways to care for the orphaned and the poor.

In March 1655 another group of Jews arrived in New Amsterdam. Five families and three unmarried men came directly from Holland. These Jews were not poor at all. Moreover, they made it clear from the outset that they intended to organize a congregation and conduct their own religious services. Stuyvesant protested, but, inasmuch as there were prominent Jewish stockholders in the Dutch West India Company, his protests fell on deaf ears. He was told that Jews should be permitted to settle, worship, and trade in New Netherlands.

Only ten years later, however, in 1665, the British conquered the Dutch colony. Life under the British was significantly different for Jews. Whereas in Europe the Jews awaited emancipation, this was not the case in America. Emancipation was granted in almost all British colonies, in recognition that the Jews were human beings and deserved full and equal rights. Although some restrictions remained in certain of the colonies, they were usually simply ignored.

Did this mean that the Jews were citizens? It did not. The British, however, had guaranteed to all inhabitants of the former New Netherlands—including Jews—full rights of worship, trade, individual property, and inheritance. Jews were forbidden to build a synagogue and had to pay taxes to the Anglican Church, but these restrictions were ignored within a few decades. By the beginning of the 18th century the Jews living in New York were voting in elections and serving on juries. By the middle of the century they were enjoying most of the political rights of the Protestant majority, many more rights than were enjoyed by Catholics!

As stated, Jews were forbidden to build a synagogue, but this restriction did not prevent them from worshipping openly. In 1730 they finally were permitted to build their first synagogue, Shearith Israel.

The degree of religious freedom extended to Jews varied from colony to colony. In New England, for example, Jews, because they denied the divinity of Jesus Christ, were forbidden to live in Massachusetts, Connecticut, and New Hampshire. Rhode Island, by contrast, welcomed them. Similarly, they were permitted to reside in Quaker Pennsylvania and Anglican New Jersey. South Carolina's constitution, authored by English philosopher John Locke, guaranteed the right of residence to "Jews, heathens and dissenters."

JEWS AND THE AMERICAN REVOLUTION

By 1776 there were 2,000 Jews living in colonial America. Most of them supported the colonies during the Revolution. They were attracted by the possibility of building a new nation in which Jews would be equals. The various colonial bills of rights supported the concept of Jewish equality.

Among those who participated in the Revolution were Mordechai Sheftal of Savannah, the deputy commissary general for Georgia, and Colonel Solomon Bush, the adjutant general of the Pennsylvania militia. In addition, Lieutenant Colonel David Franks served as adjutant to General Benedict Arnold, and Dr. Philip Moses Russell served as George Washington's surgeon.

Other Jews contributed as blockade runners, civilian contractors, and financiers. Civilian contractors were of great importance in the Revolution. They provided the army with uniforms, gunpowder, lead, and other needed equipment.

The most famous Jewish financier of the Revolution was Haym Salomon, who immigrated to New York in 1772. One of his great services was providing interest-free loans to government officials. Among the beneficiaries were James Madison, Thomas Jefferson, and several generals of the Continental Army.

GERMAN JEWRY IN AMERICA

The Congress of Vienna, conducted in 1815, redesigned Europe after the defeat of Napoleon. A new German Confederation, in which Austria took the leading place, linked the 38 separate German states.

Chicago's memorial to Haym Salomon, seen standing to the right of George Washington while Robert Morris stands on his left, both supporting him in his fight for freedom.

Holland was strengthened by the incorporation of Belgium. Prussia was given extensive territories in the Rhineland. Sardinia was enlarged by the addition of Genoa. The other Italian states, except the Papal States, were put under the rule of the Habsburg family. Most of Poland was awarded to Russia, compensating Prussia with most of Saxony and Austria with Italian lands.

This period is known as the "German Period" in American Jewish history, despite the fact that Jews from German-speaking lands formed only a fraction of the Jewish immigrants. Jews came from Poland, from elsewhere in Europe, and from outside Europe. It was, however, largely German Jews writing in the German language who gave this period its distinctive character.

Jews came to America on the whole for the same reasons: economic distress, outrageous persecutions, restrictive laws, and the failure of movements aimed at revolution and reform. The early stages of the Industrial Revolution compounded the economic changes in Europe. Jews were confronted as well with anti-Jewish legislation. In 1820, 3,500 Jews lived in America, by 1840 there were 15,000, and by 1847 there were 50,000.

The immigrants were largely poor and undereducated. They came from small towns and most were single men. Many had no alternative but to engage in country peddling. Success in peddling eventually led them into retailing and wholesale businesses. This success led to a better economic situation, but also to decreased religious observance. More time away from home meant less time devoted to religious observance.

Complicating the situation even more was a lack of spiritual leadership in the new immigrant communities. For ordained rabbis trained in Europe in authentic rabbinic learning, America was a cultural wasteland. There were no seminaries and no rabbinic scholarship. Leadership was provided, then, by those who could serve as cantor, reader, preacher, educator, *mohel* (performer of circumcisions), and kosher slaughterer to untutored local congregations.

In the absence of spiritual leadership, the children and grandchildren of immigrants tended to set aside what they viewed as outdated religious practice. They began to pray in English, to hear sermons in English, and to allow men and women to sit together at prayer. These small changes paved the way for the development of Reform Judaism in America.

The moving force in the emergence of Reform Judaism was Isaac Mayer Wise (1819–1900). A native of Bohemia, he studied in a series of yeshivot and then attended the University of Vienna. He came to the United States in 1846 with his wife and child.

At first he was a roving preacher, invited to speak in New Haven, Syracuse, and Albany. His enormous intellect and oratorical skills, however, brought him the offer of a pulpit in Albany, which he accepted. His success there allowed him to introduce innovations in

Rabbi Isaac Mayer Wise

the synagogue. He permitted an organ and a choir for Sabbath services, allowed men and women to sit together, and eliminated anachronistic prayers for the restoration of "David's throne" and the renewal of sacrifices in Jerusalem.

Wise's reputation as a patriot, modernist, and charismatic pastor led him to be offered a position in Cincinnati, where he spent the rest of his life. There he published a popular English-language newspaper, the *Israelite,* and was present at the dedication of almost every new Reform congregation in the Midwest and the South.

Most important of his contributions were the establishment of the Union of American Hebrew Congregations in 1873 and the founding of Hebrew Union College in 1875. Thirty-four Reform temples in the Midwest were invited to send representatives to a founding conference. They accepted the invitation and joined to found the organization. Within three years, major Reform congregations of the Eastern states joined. By 1878, 100 congregations had become members.

Hebrew Union College opened in 1875. The faculty included Wise, as unpaid president, two local rabbis, and one paid layman. Since the plan was to begin with a preparatory program for teenagers, the first students were 14 teenagers.

Four years later the college department began. Wise was able to attract quality academics to serve on his faculty. Appointed to the faculty were the rabbinical scholar Moses Mielziner, the historian Gotthard Deutsch, the Hebraist Max Margolis, and the Bible scholar Moses Buttenwieser. Courses offered included Bible, Talmud, the history of Judaism, Hebrew, Syriac, and Arabic. In July 1883 the first four rabbis were ordained at Hebrew Union College.

Two years later, in 1885, the core principles of American Reform Judaism were formulated at a conference convened in Pittsburgh. The Bible was to be understood as reflecting "the primitive ideas of its own age." Only the moral injunctions and ceremonials that "elevate and sanctify our lives" were binding. Talmudic rules on *kashrut* (dietary laws), dress, the second-day observance of festivals, and the separation of sexes were subject to review. The traditional prayerbook's allusions to messianism and Zion were

considered outdated. "We consider ourselves no longer a nation, but a religious community," said the assembled rabbis.

One of the major issues in 19th-century America was slavery. Four million black slaves lived in the states of the South. Of the 15,000 to 20,000 Jews in the South, one quarter were slave-owners. Some Jews were professional slave dealers.

Little, if any, opposition to slavery was voiced. Solomon Cohen, a merchant in Savannah, wrote: "I believe that the institution of slavery was refining and civilizing to the whites . . . and at the same time the only human institution that could elevate the Negro from barbarism and develop the small amount of intellect with which he is endowed."

Nor did the rabbis of the South object to slavery. Some of them were slave-owners themselves.

In the states of the North, opinions varied. Some, like Isidor Bush of St. Louis, a member of the Missouri legislature, were abolitionists. August Bondi participated with the famous abolitionist John Brown in the battles of Black Jack and Osawatomie.

Some rabbinic leaders, such as Rabbis Gustav Gottheil (1827–1903) in New York and David Einhorn (1809–1879) in Baltimore, were abolitionists, but others were anti-abolitionists. Rabbi Morris Raphall (1789–1868) of New York, for example, delivered and published a sermon rationalizing slavery as biblically sanctioned. Rabbis Raphall and Einhorn debated the issue of slavery in a public forum.

When the Civil War began, the overriding issue became that of loyalty to the Union or to the Confederacy. Perhaps 9,000 Jews served in the respective armed forces, roughly 6,000 on the Union side and 2,000 to 3,000 in the Confederate forces. Some Jews held high positions in the armies. Major General Frederick Knefler, for example, rode with General Sherman through Georgia.

EAST EUROPEAN IMMIGRATION

America experienced massive immigration from Eastern Europe between 1880 and 1915. The life of Jews in Russia in the Pale of Settlement was less than pleasant. They lived in poverty and were often plagued by pogroms. Czar Alexander II was assassinated in

1881 and Jews were accused of carrying out the assassination. This accusation led to pogroms in the Pale.

Economic factors played a far greater role, however. Competition from America led to the drying up of markets in Europe for grain and meat. In addition, the Industrial Revolution was in its earliest stages. The availability of alternative forms of employment such as factory work was limited. The promise of a better life for one's family in America was another consideration.

Jews concluded that immigration to the New World was the path to take. Not just Jews immigrated, though. By 1907, 338,000 Poles, Slovaks, Croats, and Serbs had left their homelands. By 1910, 200,000 southern Italians had left Italy.

From the Russian Empire, however, 3 million had left, two-thirds of them Jews. Whereas there had been 250,000 Jews in America in 1880, there were 3 million in America in 1914! The enormous growth of the American Jewish community in just 35 years is remarkable.

Some attempts were made to settle immigrant Jews outside major metropolitan areas. For example, Jewish leaders proposed the Galveston Project, which planned to take immigrants to Texas and then distribute them throughout the Mississippi Valley. Jews were more attracted to America's large cities, however.

As early as 1890, the Jewish population of New York City reached 200,000, while in Philadelphia there were 26,000. Boston, Baltimore, Cleveland, and Chicago each had 20,000 Jewish residents. Only 30 years later, the Jewish population in each city had quadrupled or quintupled.

In each of these cities a Jewish neighborhood grew up. In Chicago, for example, approximately 50,000 Jews settled on the West Side, a commercial district adjacent to the railroad stations. Maxwell Street, the main street of the neighborhood, was full of pushcarts and market stalls. Jews lived in three- and four-story double-decker apartment buildings, in an area that was only 2 miles wide and 3 miles long. Similar communi-

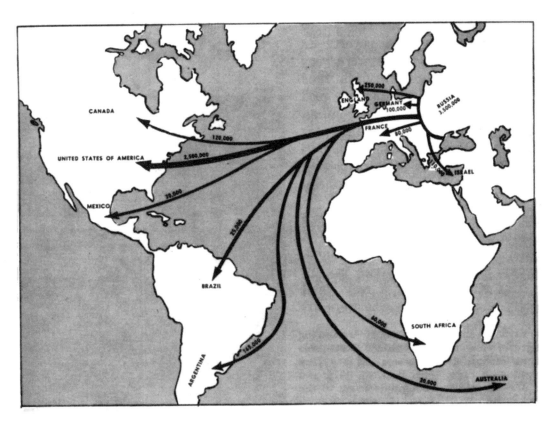

This map shows where Jews went from Eastern Europe between the years 1880 and 1934. The vast majority came to the United States.

ties were established on Philadelphia's South Side, Boston's North End, and in East Baltimore.

The heart and center of Jewish immigrant settlement, however, was New York. The Lower East Side was the ghetto neighborhood of New York. There, just a short walk from where they had disembarked from ships, lived 330,000 Jews at the beginning of the 20th century. They made up by far the overwhelming ethnic majority of the district—all of them living within a 40-block area.

Most of them were crammed into tenements, which had no more than four toilets per building and one faucet per apartment. Residents of tenements ordinarily slept three or four to a room. Despite the trying conditions, no less than 70 percent of the new immigrants to the New World chose to remain in New York City.

How did the immigrant Jews support themselves? Some became the owners of tiny retail stores—cigar shops, delicatessens, seltzer-and-newspaper kiosks, fruit stands. Others were peddlers and sidewalk tradesmen, and some were junkmen—buyers of old clothes, old rags, old bits of metal for resale or recycling. Some made use of their Old World skills, working as bakers, carpenters, plasterers, bookbinders, jewelers, and similar trades.

Most important among the occupational pursuits of immigrant Jews, however, was their involvement in the garment industry. Many Jews living in Russia's Pale of Settlement had survived there as tailors and milliners. These skills were certainly transferable. It was, of course, helpful that the vast majority of those who owned the garment shops or managed them were Jews.

Jewish immigrants worked in conditions that were far from ideal. To be sure the garment industry was known as the Jewish industry, but the Jews working in that industry did so in sweatshops. These were tiny, dirty, unventilated, and often located in the employer's dwelling. Employees worked 65 hours a week. During the busy season, they had to work 75 hours. They had to provide their own needles, thread, irons, and occasionally their own sewing machines.

The trade-union movement began among Jews in the 1880s, but made little progress before 1900. After 1900, larger clothing factories became more common. The period of successful organization is from 1909 to 1916, coinciding with the beginning of trade unionism in the United States.

It was women who were the leaders of the garment industry's "Great Revolt." Rose Schneiderman, for example, was active in the International Ladies' Garment Workers Union and worked tirelessly for worker's and women's rights. Fannie Cohn was the ILGWU's only woman vice-president. Bessie Abramowitz helped organize the Chicago strike of 33,000 men's-clothing workers at age 20! Pauline Newman was the first women's organizer of the historic shirtwaist industry strike.

The "Great Revolt" occurred between 1909 and 1914. The largest of the shirtwaist factories belonged to the Triangle and Leiserson companies. They employed nearly a thousand workers, 70 percent of whom were women. In September 1909, workers voted to join the United Hebrew Trades, the consciousness-raising organizers of Jewish-staffed industry. Triangle's management fired the "troublemakers" and advertised for replacements. In response, Local 25 of the ILGWU called for a strike.

The strike took place, but as the young women walked the picket lines, they were taunted, threatened, jostled by the company thugs. Some were arrested for vagrancy and incitement. Five weeks of this pressure, of hunger, and physical weakness, took their toll.

In November, the leadership of the ILGWU convened an emergency meeting. Three thousand women attended and were addressed by the Lower East Side's working-class heroes, Meyer London, Morris Hillquit, Joseph Barondess, and Samuel Gompers. Each appealed for labor unity, for financial and "moral" support.

When a 19-year-old worker named Clara Lemlich rose to speak, the atmosphere changed dramatically. She described the pain and humiliation of factory labor. She called for united action against not only the Triangle Company but against all shirtwaist manufacturers. Her impassioned speech captured the attention of the crowd. In response to her appeal for support, over 20,000 shirtwaist workers, all of them women, joined the Triangle workers in a city-wide walkout.

Management soon realized that despite all efforts to the contrary, public opinion was on the workers' side. They felt they had to negotiate. After two weeks of discussion, an agreement was reached. The manu-

The Jewish Daily Forward (Yiddish: Forverts) is a legendary name in American journalism and a revered name in American Jewish life. The Forward, a Yiddish-language daily newspaper, began publication on April 22, 1897. It served the immigrant population of New York City as a defender of trade unionism and a voice for moderate, democratic socialism.

The founding editor of the Forward was Abraham Cahan, who remained its editor for a full half-century until his death in 1950. Under Cahan's leadership, the Forward came to be known as the voice of the Jewish immigrant and the conscience of the ghetto. It fought for social justice, helped generations of immigrants enter American life, and was among the nation's most eloquent defenders of democracy and Jewish rights.

The readership of the Forward grew steadily, and by the 1930s its circulation topped 275,000. Its editorial staff included nearly every major luminary in the then-thriving world of Yiddish literature, from the beloved "poet of the sweatshops," Morris Rosenfeld, to the future Nobel laureate Isaac Bashevis Singer. Cahan, both as editor and writer, including especially his timeless advice column, the Bintel Brief, set the populist, down-to-earth tone that was characteristic of the Forward.

With the end of World War II, the Forward entered a period of decline. The vast Yiddish-speaking world of East European Jewry was no more. Thus in 1983 the paper cut back to a weekly publishing schedule and launched an English-language supplement. In 1990 the Forward Association, the newspaper's non-profit holding company, decided to remake the English-language Forward as an independent, high-profile weekly newspaper committed to covering the Jewish world with the same crusading journalistic spirit as Cahan's Jewish Daily Forward.

The Forward's current editor, the veteran journalist and author J. J. Goldberg, who took over in July 2000, has continued and expanded the paper's commitment to prestigious, hard-hitting reportage, while at the same time returning to the populist, progressive spirit that was the hallmark of the Forward in its early years. Under his leadership the paper has reached its largest-ever English-language circulation, while firmly cementing its reputation as American Jewry's essential newspaper of record.

facturers agreed to reduce the work-week to 52 hours and to provide four legal holidays with pay. Employees were no longer expected to provide their own tools. A joint grievance committee would negotiate issues as they arose.

While women were the majority of workers in the shirtwaist industry, men were more numerous in the cloak and suit industry. Working conditions were the usual ones in the women's garment trades, which meant 12- and 14-hour days, fees for tools, and fines for damage. The time had come for the men to emulate the women.

A major figure in the general effort to create trade unions in the United States, not just among the Jews, was Samuel Gompers. Gompers, himself an immigrant, settled with his family on the Lower East Side of New York City in 1863. He joined a local of the Cigar Makers' National Union and quickly rose to its leadership. In 1886 he helped establish the American Federation of Labor, becoming its president and major spokesman. Gompers was a major influence on the American labor movement.

In an effort to aid in preparation for the strike, Gompers raised funds from other AFL unions. The strike was called for July 1910, with 65,000 cloak makers walking off the job.

This time, however, the well of public sympathy had dried up. The summer wore on, but the manufacturers

Samuel Gompers (1850–1924), a British-born Jew who started as a cigar-maker in New York and became founder and president for 38 years of the American Federation of Labor.

held firm. The economic effects of the strike were felt throughout the Lower East Side.

Late in the summer of 1910, influential Jews outside the garment industry became involved. Jacob Schiff and other stalwarts of the German-Jewish establishment urged management and workers to take advantage of the skills of Louis D. Brandeis, a renowned Boston lawyer with much experience in handling industrial-relations cases. In September, an agreement was reached.

The employers accepted the principle of a 50-hour work-week, ten paid legal holidays, payment of time and a half for overtime, and a joint committee to monitor physical conditions in the factory. They even accepted the union shop, where preference would be given to union over non-union members.

One more event made Jewish workers an organized presence on the industrial scene. On Saturday afternoon, March 25, 1911, some 800 young women and several dozen young men were at work on the top three floors of the ten-story Triangle Shirtwaist Company building. Someone working on the eighth floor carelessly tossed a cigarette into piles of oil-soaked straps lying under the sewing machines. Flames leaped immediately through the workroom, from machine to machine, then from floor to floor, turning the factory into an inferno. The owners fled the building in panic without unlocking its door.

By the time the fire was brought under control, 147 women and 21 men had died. Many others had critical burns and broken limbs. The Shirtwaist Makers Union arranged for a mass funeral. Over 100,000 workers marched in a silent cortege though the streets and the victims were buried in a common grave. From this point on, it became clear to everyone that the trade-union movement was irreversible.

Not all immigrant Jews worked in the garment industry or supported themselves through petty trades. Some, like Abraham Cahan (1860–1951), engaged in literary work. Born in a town near Vilna, Lithuania, Cahan was educated at the government Teachers' Seminary there. He arrived in America in 1882, having spent 18 months trying to elude the Russian police due to his socialist views. In 1897 he helped found the great Yiddish newspaper, the *Jewish Daily Forward*, and headed its staff for almost half a century.

Cahan was an editor, author, and socialist leader, but he was also a fine author. His books *Yekl, a Tale of the New York Ghetto* (1896), *Imported Bridegroom* (1898), and *The White Terror and the Red* (1905) were well received. *The Rise of David Levinsky* (1905), however, became the classic novel of the urban immigrant experience.

Another distinguished immigrant writer was Mary Antin. Born in Poland and the daughter of immigrant parents, she came to America as a youngster. She lived in a Boston Jewish ghetto, attending public school there. After graduating high school, she studied at Wellesley College.

Antin's book, *The Promised Land* (1912), achieved extraordinary success. It was the first book by an American Jew to become a bestseller, going through 34 printings and selling 85,000 copies. The book focused on the poverty that the immigrant Jews experienced in their new home in America.

Like Antin, Anzia Yezierska dealt with the immigrant's struggle for financial security. Born in poverty in a Polish village, she came to America at the turn of the century. She lived the familiar immigrant's life of sweatshop labor, night school English, and ghetto claustrophobia. Three years after arriving in America, though, she was awarded a scholarship to Columbia.

In 1915, her first short story of immigrant life, "Free Vacation Stories," was published. Other stories followed and were published in 1920 as a collection, *Hungry Hearts*. The stories were clearly autobiographical, dealing with all the nuances of immigrant Jewish life.

The immigrant Jews, like Jews native to America, encountered instances of anti-Semitism. Consider the case of Leo Frank in 1913, which resulted in a lynching. Frank, a native of Brooklyn living in Atlanta, Georgia, was accused of raping and murdering a 13-year-old, Mary Phagan. The evidence brought in support of the charge was less than convincing. Witnesses confirmed Frank's claim that he was at home at the time of the murder. In addition, on the day of the conviction, a handyman confessed to the crime. Thus the governor of Georgia commuted the sentence of the court.

Anti-Semitism certainly contributed to the conviction of Frank. Jews were seen as foreigners in the

South. The governor's action so enraged the citizens of Georgia that a violent mob responded by lynching Frank.

Anti-Semitism also interfered with Jews' making their way up the economic ladder. Even a distinguished intellectual like Henry Adams thought the Jews were corrupting America, undermining its ethos and spirit, for the Jews could never join the WASP elite.

Universities were, of course, the training ground for the future leaders of America. Advocates of restrictionism said that the participation of Jews in higher education should be limited. Columbia University responded by lowering its enrollment limit of Jews from 40 percent to 20 percent. Other Ivy League schools introduced similar quotas on Jewish enrollment.

The vehicles of American Jewish minority politics in the 20th century were public education, political lobbying, diplomatic representation, and even mass demonstrations. The American Jewish Committee was formed in 1906 as a means to speak to the American government on behalf of Russian Jewry after the Kishinev pogrom. The Anti-Defamation League was founded in 1913 as part of a public relations effort to free Leo Frank. These first efforts created what would become a pattern for American Jews speaking on behalf of Jewish interests.

WORLD WAR I AND THE RUSSIAN REVOLUTION

America was a latecomer to involvement in World War I. Jews had their own viewpoint on this issue. Jews who had come from Germany had never lost their links with Germany. German language and German culture remained alive in homes and synagogues. In addition, like East European Jews, they wanted to see the czars overthrown.

Jews advocated pacifism. The United Hebrew Trades of New York urged President Wilson to keep America out of a war being conducted "on the bodies of the working people of Europe." Other prominent Jews, such as Henry Morgenthau and Felix Frankfurter, urged America to stay out of the war.

Rabbis Felix Adler, Emil Hirsch, Judah Magnes, and Stephen Wise also condemned the war.

Everything changed, however, with the Russian Revolution of March 1917 and the resulting political emancipation of Russian Jews. In a sermon in which he welcomed this development, Stephen Wise said: "What we have so often reiterated has become true— the Jewish question has been solved in Russia. . . . I consider [the Russian Revolution] to be the most important historic event since the French Revolution." In a rally organized by the Bund (Jewish Socialists), the Socialist Party, the Russian Social Democrats, the United Hebrew Trades, and the Workmen's Circle, 15,000 East Side Jews gathered in Madison Square Garden to celebrate the Revolution.

On April 6, 1917, the United States entered the war. The International Ladies' Garment Workers Union purchased $100,000 in Liberty Bonds. The Amalgamated and the Workmen's Circle passed resolutions supporting the war. The United Hebrew Trades and the Furriers Union raised $12 million on the Lower East Side in their bond drives.

In 1918, Jews constituted 3.3 percent of the American population; 5.7 percent of the U.S. armed forces were Jews. Of 250,000 Jewish soldiers and sailors, 51,000 were enlistees. Some 3,400 were killed in action, 14,000 were wounded, and 1,130 were awarded decorations (four of these the Medal of Honor).

By 1925 the Jewish population of the United States reached 4.24 million. They were engaged in a variety of economic pursuits. Jews were prominent in the garment industry, so that by 1940 the needle trades employed 700,000 men and women nationwide. Jews founded and developed the three largest scrap metal companies: Luria Brothers of Philadelphia, Hyman Michaels of Chicago, and Luntz Iron and Steel of Canton, Ohio. Jews also manufactured cigars and cigarettes; the P. Lorillard tobacco company was founded by Jews.

Jews engaged in real estate as well. Some saved enough for a down payment on a building on the Lower East Side of New York City. Others had enough money to build medium-priced apartment buildings; in the 1920s, Jews put up 157,000 apartments in

Brooklyn and the Bronx. Still others had grander visions. Louis Horowitz, who arrived from Russia at age 13, built $600 million worth of skyscrapers in Manhattan, including the Woolworth Building, the Chrysler Building, and the Waldorf-Astoria Hotel.

Some found their fortunes in cosmetics. Three of the nation's largest beauty firms—Revlon, Max Factor, and Helena Rubinstein—were founded by first-generation East European Jews. Others went into motion pictures, including Samuel Goldwyn and Louis Mayer, founders of MGM.

Others made their mark in musical theater. Irving Berlin, for example, arrived from Russia in 1893 at age five. Living a typical impoverished boyhood on the Lower East Side, he worked as a singing waiter, as a saloon composer, and later as a staff lyricist for a music publisher. Berlin had no formal music education but an excellent ear for melody. Only in the first decade of the 20th century, however, during the ragtime era, did he become famous and wealthy, with his "Alexander's Ragtime Band." This tune sold a million copies of sheet music within three months of its publication.

In the 1930s, he turned out musical hits and wrote the music for a series of Hollywood musicals. Ironically, it was Irving Berlin, an immigrant Jew, who wrote the nation's most popular songs about Christmas and Easter, "White Christmas" and "Easter Parade." Moreover, it was he who composed America's most widely sung patriotic song, "God Bless America."

George Gershwin was not himself an immigrant, but he was the son of Russian-Jewish immigrants. His father, Morris Gershowitz, worked as a foreman in a Lower East Side shoe factory. It is Gershwin who represents, by consensus, the highest level of American musical genius.

Gershwin was assisted in part by his brother Ira, who provided lyrics. In 1924, at the request of orchestra leader Paul Whiteman, he composed a modern jazz concerto, *Rhapsody in Blue.* In 1928, he composed the equally famous and popular *An American in Paris.* In 1935, the Gershwin brothers decided to write a folk opera called *Porgy and Bess.* This work came to be regarded as America's greatest

musical drama. Unfortunately, George Gershwin died in 1937 of a brain tumor at age 38.

While some saw Irving Berlin as the "father" of the modern American musical theater, others saw Jerome Kern as a more outstanding figure. Kern was born in New York City in 1885, the son of a comfortable German-Jewish family. He worked for a time in London, but returned to the United States in 1914. *The Girl from Utah* was the first Broadway musical to feature his songs.

Kern was untiring in his work. In some seasons he had as many as six Broadway productions to his credit. He is most famous for his adaptation of the Edna Ferber novel *Show Boat,* with book and lyrics by Oscar Hammerstein II. The production opened on Broadway in 1927. It was a great success and is probably the most influential American musical ever produced.

Kern's work influenced another postwar composer whose background was similar to his. Like Kern, Richard Rodgers was born in 1902 to the comfort of an Upper West Side New York home. His mother's family was German-Jewish, while his father, of Russian-Jewish ancestry, was American-born and a physician. He and a classmate, Lorenz Hart, also a son of German Jews, collaborated at Columbia on several campus musical comedies.

Rodgers and Hart, the former a gifted composer and the latter a gifted lyricist, broke into Broadway while still very young. During the 1930s they produced an interrupted string of hits, from *On Your Toes* to *Pal Joey.* In 1938 they appeared on the cover of *Time* magazine as "the American Gilbert and Sullivan."

In the post–World War I years, in addition, Jews began to dominate the American concert stage. The pianists Artur Schnabel, Rudolf Serkin, Vladimir Horowitz, and Artur Rubinstein attained international musical reputations. Violinists like Josef Szigeti, Mischa Elman, Jascha Heifetz, Nathan Milstein, Isaac Stern, and Yehudi Menuhin achieved great prominence among the performers of classical music.

Jews of both Central and East European background also conducted the nation's principal symphony orchestras. Thus Serge Koussevitzky became conductor of the Boston Symphony Orchestra in 1924 and transformed it into one of the premier concert ensembles in the United States. The Hungarian-born Eugene Ormandy conducted the Minneapolis Symphony Orchestra in the early 1930s, then took over as music director of the Philadelphia Orchestra in 1938, holding that position for an unprecedented 42 years.

The second generation of American Jewish writers were not immigrants but American born. This generation included Ludwig Lewisohn, a fascinating figure. Lewisohn was born in Germany into an assimilated and fervently patriotic family. They left Berlin due only to business failures, immigrating to America in 1890. Lewisohn's father was bankrupt, so when a brother-in-law promised employment, he took his wife and son, age seven, to St. Matthew, South Carolina.

Lewisohn's family encouraged him to attend Methodist Sunday school, where he was encouraged to "accept the Gospel story and the obvious implications for Pauline Christianity without question." Two years later, the family settled in Charleston, still avoiding any association with Jews. Lewisohn saw himself as "an American, a Southerner, and a Christian." He did not realize that others might not see him that way.

Lewisohn attended the College of Charleston, but no fraternity would accept him. He excelled in his study of English literature and was a published author of literary criticism even before graduation from college. He anticipated being selected to teach at the local Episcopal academy, but was told that the board found his name and face "characteristically Jewish" and they turned down his application.

Ludwig Lewisohn, U.S. writer. Courtesy S. Liptzin, Jerusalem.

At age 20, Lewisohn left to pursue a master's degree in English literature at Columbia University in New York City. He earned his degree with highest honors, but no scholarship followed for continued graduate study. His department chairman informed him that opportunities were closed for Jews in fields "unique to Anglo-Saxon ways of thinking."

Lewisohn left Columbia and began to publish, producing a novel, a dramatic poem, several articles, and stories. In 1910, he finally secured an academic appointment to teach German literature at Ohio State University. In the next seven years, Lewisohn edited and translated the dramas of Gerhart Hauptmann, published a classic interpretive study of modern German literature, and produced articles and smaller volumes on other German authors.

With the arrival of World War I, however, Germany was the enemy and anything German, including its culture, was unpopular. In 1919, Lewisohn was dropped from the faculty. Fortunately, he was asked to serve as associate drama and fiction editor for the *Nation*. His stream of books and articles on French and German literature, together with his novels and short stories, kept his name well-known in the literary world.

The 1920s and the early 1930s brought Lewisohn to Paris. There he published two masterly works on American thought and literature, *Expression in America* (1932) and *Creative America* (1933). He also published a novel, *The Case of Mr. Crump* (1926).

It was in Paris that Lewisohn began to give increasing attention to his Jewish heritage. In 1922, he published *Up Stream*. This work was autobiographical. He wrote of his family's life in Germany, the early years in America, his father's assimilationism, his own determined acculturation, and the shock experienced when his career opportunities were destroyed by anti-Semitism.

Continuing to study Jewish history and culture, he wrote books and articles, fiction and non-fiction, asserting the need for Jewish self-assertion. In 1928, he published a novel, *The Island Within*. This work became his most popular "Jewish" book. It won unqualified critical acclaim. A critic writing for the *Nation* called it "the most nearly perfect thesis novel of our generation."

Lewisohn's work was a turning point in a transitional postwar era. It made the case for acceptance of the Jewish past as a moral imperative for the intellectual Jewish conscience. The pressures of a majority culture led many to acculturation. Lewisohn argued that this was a truly misguided choice.

THE GREAT DEPRESSION

The year 1929 brought with it the crash of the stock market—the Great Depression. For those immigrants who labored in the garment industry, everything collapsed. Progress had been achieved through the process of collective bargaining, but these gains were now reversed. Wages were reduced and the workweek was increased to 55 and sometimes 60 hours. Entire families had to work just to survive, just as in the old sweatshop days.

White-collar workers suffered as well. Most were in small commercial or handicrafts operations. The economic collapse was catastrophic for them too. Many small businesses were unable to survive.

A 1931 nationwide review of 30 Jewish welfare agencies showed a 42 percent increase in relief recipients. Furthermore, many Jews were embarrassed at having to apply for charity and so did not apply. Community institutions suffered as well. Synagogue construction had to be stopped before completion. Orphanages, old-age homes, and health clinics could not be supported by the East European community.

PRESIDENT ROOSEVELT AND THE NEW DEAL

Franklin Roosevelt was elected President in 1932. Prior to this he served as governor of the state of New York from 1928 to 1932. His lieutenant governor was a Jew, Herbert Lehman. Lehman was an able politician and administrator, and, when Roosevelt was elected President, Lehman ran as a candidate for governor. He was elected by a plurality of close to a million votes. He was reelected subsequently for four more terms in 1934, 1936, 1938, and 1940.

Roosevelt felt it necessary to put things back in order in America. He promised America the New Deal program, which called for federal support of the economy and social programs. Roosevelt felt that no man of talent should be overlooked, even if he was a Jew.

Among those to whom Roosevelt turned was Bernard Baruch. During World War I Baruch had supervised industrial mobilization, and in later years he had provided financial assistance to Democratic Senate candidates in areas of the country seen by the leadership of the Democrats as critical. Roosevelt's predecessor, Herbert Hoover, called Baruch the most powerful Democrat in the capital.

Baruch recommended that Roosevelt appoint General Hugh Johnson, one of his assistants during World War I, to head the National Recovery Administration. Roosevelt agreed. What this appointment meant was that Baruch would be keeping a close eye on the activities and policies of the NRA.

Another major contributor to the Roosevelt administration was Louis Brandeis, who had been a Justice of the Supreme Court since 1916. Although three successive Republican administrations had ignored him, Roosevelt did not. Brandeis understood fully, as did no one else in his time, the nation's economic system. He understood, as well, the relationship of legal judgments to economic facts and the danger of allowing large corporations to govern the economy.

Roosevelt held Brandeis in the highest regard. The two consulted from time to time on key legislation, including the National Labor Relations Act, the Securities Exchange Act, and the Social Security Act. Each of these would become an essential part of the New Deal.

A third major figure in the Roosevelt years was Felix Frankfurter. Frankfurter attended City College and then Harvard Law School. He was an outstanding student, who received glowing recommendations upon graduation. Moving back to New York, he served as assistant United States attorney for New York under Henry Stimson. When Stimson was appointed Secretary of War by President Taft, he invited Frankfurter to come to Washington as his assistant.

In 1914 Frankfurter was invited to join the faculty of Harvard Law School. Brandeis kept his permanent home in Boston, and for the next 23 years he and Frankfurter were able to meet there and confer at length. Frankfurter would also send his best students to serve as clerks for Brandeis.

Louis Dembitz Brandeis (1856–1941), Justice of the Supreme Court and Zionist leader. A champion of liberal causes, he became interested in Judaism and Zionism when he met Jewish garment workers during settlement of a strike in 1910. He said that following Jewish ideals made one a better American.

Frankfurter knew Roosevelt well, both of them having served in the Wilson administration. When Roosevelt was elected, Frankfurter became Brandeis's principal emissary. In addition, their friendship allowed Frankfurter to advise on key New Deal legislation. His students, now in Washington, would consult with him frequently by letter and by telephone as they drafted legislation.

Other Jews were prominent in the Roosevelt administration. Henry Morgenthau, Jr., for example, served as Secretary of Treasury. Benjamin V. Cohen was the general counsel of the Treasury Department. David Lilienthal was the first chairman of the Tennessee Valley Authority.

ANTI-SEMITISM IN THE ROOSEVELT YEARS

Did Jews face anti-Semitism in the Roosevelt years? Did the prominence of Jews in the New Deal lead to their being blamed for it? The answer to both questions is yes.

Father Charles Coughlin, a Canadian-born Catholic priest, was the major anti-Semitic figure in the 1920s and 1930s. In 1926 he bought radio time to air his "Golden Hour from the Shrine of the Little Flower," a program in which he spoke of the importance of brotherly love. With the arrival of the Great Depression, though, he saw an opportunity to express his political views. He spoke of a Communist conspiracy within the United States, a conspiracy that he linked to the social evils of divorce, birth control, and free love.

But who was at fault? It was big business, especially the "international bankers," who were starving honest workers. It was the "Shylocks" in London and on Wall Street, who were concerned only with returns on their investments. It was the President and his "New Deal intellectual" advisers, who were preparing America for the "Kuhn-Loebs, the Rothschilds . . . the scribes and Pharisees, the Baruchs." In short, it was the Jews.

How influential was Coughlin? By early 1939 his periodical *Social Justice* was read by 200,000 people. In the same year, 50 to 75 rallies were taking place in New York each week, encouraging people to physical violence against Jews.

There was also the more "respectable" anti-Semitism of the corporate economy, where Jews were kept out of every level of employment, from management to salesmen and secretaries. Newspapers showed anti-Semitism. The *New York Daily News,* for example, gave much space to the speeches of Coughlin. The *Los Angeles Times* presented Jews as ranking second only to Italians as the nation's least-trusted ethnic group. Anti-Semitism even had its spokesmen in Congress. Senator Robert Reynolds, Democrat of North Carolina, published a weekly newsletter that borrowed much from Coughlin's *Social Justice.*

AMERICA AND THE HOLOCAUST

An earlier chapter has dealt with the Holocaust, but something must be said about America and the Holocaust years. In 1938 Hitler invaded Austria (the *Anschluss*), making it part of the Third Reich. The Nazis subjected 200,000 Jews to expropriation of property and physical persecution. This situation led Roosevelt and the State Department to reconsider immigration policies. The decision was to combine the quotas for Germany and Austria and raise them to 26,000. The quota system had to remain in place, though, without modification, so that the fragile Democratic coalition of Northern urban liberals and Southern restrictionists would not be endangered.

Roosevelt concluded that a new approach was needed. Under Secretary of State Sumner Welles suggested that the representatives of 50 governments be invited to an international conference on refugees. Roosevelt accepted the suggestion. Of the 50 governments to which invitations were sent, only 32 countries agreed to participate. The conference was scheduled for early July 1938 in Evian-les-Bains, France.

Representing the United States at Evian was Myron C. Taylor, former chairman of United States Steel. He was accompanied by two State Department "technical advisers," whose function was to ensure that the United States immigration policy remained in place. Taylor declared that the policy of immigration quotas would remain and that some permanent solution for the Jewish refugees would have to be sought elsewhere.

This did not happen. Consider the words of the Australian delegate, who said, "As we have no real racial problem, we are not desirous of importing one," or of the Canadian delegate, who repeated the observation of Frederick Blair, commissioner of immigration, that the Jews themselves were responsible for their own suffering. In short, the Evian Conference was an abject failure.

No other attempts to deal with the problem took place until the establishment of the War Refugee Board in January 1944. A report prepared by younger (non-Jewish) members of the Treasury Department had revealed that the State Department had been engaged in "procrastination and willful failure to act . . . even of willful attempts to prevent action from being taken to rescue Jews from Hitler." Morgenthau brought this report to Roosevelt, who immediately removed immigration policy from the State Department and assigned it to the newly created War Refugee Board. This board would consist of representatives of the Treasury, War, and State Departments, the latter department's participation being only nominal.

John Pehle, an up-and-comer in the Treasury Department, served as the board's director. Staff members were assigned to Switzerland, Turkey, Sweden, North Africa, and Portugal. The Axis powers were clearly losing the war, so the governments of Hungary, Bulgaria, and Romania seemed to be interested in using the hundreds of thousands of Jews still in their control for bargaining purposes.

In the course of its work, the board rescued approximately 200,000 Jews, with some 15,000 evacuated physically from Axis territory. The German SS, however, sent 474,000 Hungarian Jews to Auschwitz in the spring and summer of 1944. Involved in the board's efforts at rescue were the famous Raoul Wallenberg of Sweden, active in Hungary, and Cardinal Angelo Roncalli, later Pope John XXIII, who provided baptismal certificates to the papal representative in Hungary. One only wonders how many Jews might have been saved had the War Refugee Board been established earlier than 1944.

With the conclusion of World War II, the United States began a period of recovery. This involved paying tribute to those who had given their lives in the war, reintegrating war veterans into American society through the G.I. Bill, and bringing Nazis to trial at Nuremberg. It also involved paying attention to the 250,000 displaced Jews who had no homes to which they could return after the Holocaust.

President Truman, who succeeded Franklin Roosevelt after the latter's death, was very much preoccupied with the situation of the displaced persons. As was discussed in Chapters 7 and 8, he viewed Palestine as a real option for them, but the British resisted, unwilling to arouse concern among the Arabs. Only after the British returned their Mandate over Palestine to the United Nations was there a change, ultimately leading to the establishment of a Jewish state.

JEWS IN AMERICA IN THE 1950s

Approximately 5 million Jews lived in the United States in 1950, continuing to pursue a wide variety of economic opportunities. The garment trades, like the liquor industry, entertainment, and mass merchandising, remained with the Jews. Some, like the Lazarus family of Columbus, Ohio, took the family clothing business and expanded it through Ohio, eventually associating themselves with Filene's of Boston and with the Bloomingdale stores. The new company was called Federated Department Stores.

Jews became prominent in investment banking. Among the best-known firms were Lehman Brothers and Lazard Freres. Lehman Brothers helped finance department stores, Hollywood film studios, and liquor, airline, and communications studios.

In journalism, too, Jews stood out. Adolph Ochs purchased the *New York Times* in 1896, raising its circulation in two years from 9,000 to 25,000 and in 40 years to 500,000. Ochs would be succeeded by his son-in-law, Arthur Hays Sulzberger and, later, Sulzberger's son, Arthur Ochs Sulzberger. The *Washington Post* was purchased after World War I by Eugene Meyer. He and his daughter, Katherine Graham, made the paper second in influence only to the *New York Times*.

In real estate, one Jew, William Levitt, had extraordinary impact. The housing shortage that affected America after World War II led Levitt to borrow funds to buy 400,000 acres of land near Hempstead on Long Island, outside of New York City. There, using cut-rate, mass production techniques, he built 17,000 single-family homes. These were available, to veterans only, at a price that young families could afford. "Levittown" became a clean and pleasant community of 82,000 people. This town became a model for producing affordable housing to middle-income Americans.

Adolph Ochs (1858–1935) developed the New York Times into one of the world's most influential newspapers.

ANTI-SEMITISM IN THE 1950s

Was anti-Semitism now just a memory? By no means. As the House reconvened in January 1945, Congressman John Rankin of Mississippi proposed the revival of the House Special Committee on Un-American Activities. Rankin declared that this proposal was being offered at the suggestion of the American Legion. The House gave reluctant approval to reviving the committee.

Rankin was troubled by the enormous power held by Frankfurter, Morgenthau, and other Jews. He announced on one occasion that Communism was an instrument devised by world Jewry to extirpate Christianity. On another occasion he told his colleagues that the murder of 30 million Russian Christians during World War II had been perpetrated by "the same gang that composed the Fifth Column of the Crucifixion. They hounded the Savior during the days of his ministry, persecuted him to his ignominious death. . . . For nearly two millennia they have overrun and virtually destroyed Europe. Now they are trying to undermine and destroy America."

The committee turned its attention to Hollywood as it began an investigation of the film industry. This investigation reached its peak when it moved to Washington in October 1947. The charge of Communist influence on film could not be substantiated, but ten witnesses refused to answer questions posed to them. As a result, the "Hollywood Ten" were indicted, convicted, and given one-year sentences. The Motion Picture Association of America, most of whose members were Jews, was sent into panic by those who had refused to answer questions. These leaders of the film industry created a blacklist, expelling the Hollywood Ten until such time as they declared under oath that they were not Communists. The blacklist would continue to affect the film industry for almost a decade.

Even more unsettling was the Rosenberg Affair. In 1949 the American public was stunned to learn that the Soviet Union, the Communist enemy, had detonated its own atomic bomb. In the same year the FBI, which had been working on the case, discovered that the party at fault was Klaus Fuchs, a German-born British atomic scientist. Fuchs confessed that in 1944 and 1945 he had turned over information to the Russians. Eventually a number of others were discovered to have been involved and were indicted. These included Julius and Ethel Rosenberg, David Greenglass and Morton Sobell, and Anatoly Yakovlev, the Soviet vice-consul in New York. Each defendant was charged with conspiracy to commit espionage in violation of the Espionage Act of 1917.

The trial began in March 1951 in the District Court for the Southern District of New York in Manhattan. The prosecutor was Irving Saypol, who had been very successful in recent trials of Communists. He wanted the death sentence for the Rosenbergs and stiff prison sentences for the others. The Rosenbergs protested their innocence, but the jury did not believe them. In April 1951 all the accused were found guilty on all counts of conspiracy to commit sabotage. On April 5 the sentences were pronounced. Greenglass was sentenced to serve 15 years in prison, while Sobell received 30 years without parole. Judge Irving Kaufman sentenced the Rosenbergs to die during the week of May 21, 1951. They were executed on Friday, June 18.

The Rosenberg Affair, although Jews were involved, was not about anti-Semitism. It related to concern about Communism. Still, the impact of this event on American Jews should not be dismissed. Anna M. Rosenberg (not related to the accused spies), for example, was a candidate for appointment as Assistant Secretary of Defense. A number of hate groups joined to block this candidacy, although the American Jewish Committee and the Anti-Defamation League saved it by providing data to the Senate Armed Services Committee exposing the anti-Semitic background of the accusers.

Jews were certainly the focus of the House Un-American Activities Committee. The prominence of Jews in the film industry, coupled with the anti-Semitism of Rankin and others, made them a target. This was combined with the anti-Communism of the time, as Rankin made abundantly clear.

JEWS IN AMERICA IN THE 1960s

In the 1960s Jews continued their involvement in department stores, the tobacco and liquor industries,

and wholesale food. Some were especially successful. Armand Hammer, for example, son of a Russian immigrant physician who was a charter member of the Communist-leaning American Labor Party, turned the Occidental Petroleum Company into a $20 billion food, chemical, and energy giant.

Jews also continued to involve themselves in real estate. For example, Harris Uris and his son Harold became major players in commercial construction in New York City. Between 1945 and 1971 the Uris Corporation put up 13 percent of all office buildings in Manhattan since the end of World War II. The Tishman Corporation, led by Lawrence and Preston Tisch, developed a vast conglomerate of hotels and office buildings, turning their business into a post–World War II empire.

Jews turned as well to radio and television. William Paley became the president of the Columbia Broadcasting System at age 27. At first it was just radio, but it quickly moved into television. Leonard Goldenson, similarly, developed the American Broadcasting System into a great media empire.

The great star in this area, however, was David Sarnoff. He had dropped out of school before reaching the ninth grade. At age 15, Sarnoff began to work as a junior operator for the American branch of the Marconi Wireless Company. In his spare time he im-

David Sarnoff (1891–1971) began as a messenger boy and wireless operator. He rose to become head of the Radio Corporation of America. He was active on behalf of Jewish causes.

mersed himself in manuals on mathematics, science, and telecommunications. At 18 he was appointed chief wireless operator for Marconi.

Sarnoff saw the potential for developing radio as a mass medium. He saw as well the potential revenue to be earned from advertising and from sales of what Sarnoff called the "radio music box." The company liked his vision, and so in 1919 American Marconi and General Electric joined to establish an independent American company, the Radio Corporation of America. Sarnoff was appointed commercial manager and de facto chairman. In 1926 RCA created its own radio network, the National Broadcasting Company. After World War II Sarnoff turned all his attention to television, and RCA eventually produced a patented color-television tube. As the leader of RCA, Sarnoff became one of America's wealthiest men.

Jews realized early that they ought to vote for Democrats. They saw that their security depended on a healthy economy and strong judicial barriers between church and state. Jews also understood the importance of social-welfare issues and their impact on minorities.

Jews provided 74 percent of the vote for Adlai Stevenson in 1952 and 1956. In 1960, Jews gave Kennedy 81 percent of their votes, and in 1964, 89 percent of the Jewish vote went to Lyndon Johnson. In 1968, 89 percent went to Hubert Humphrey.

Jews also contributed funds to political candidates, directing their money toward their ideological convictions. Thus Dewey Stone, Philip Klutznick, and Arthur Krim were major contributors to the campaigns of Kennedy and Johnson. Of the 21 people who lent $100,000 or more to Hubert Humphrey's 1968 campaign, 15 were Jews.

JEWS AND THE CIVIL RIGHTS MOVEMENT

In 1954 the United States Supreme Court presented its judgment in *Brown vs. Board of Education,* striking down racial segregation in the public schools. This decision was followed within the next dozen years by a series of federal laws and court orders setting aside any legal support for racial segregation.

The Jews of the South, who made up barely 1 percent of the area's population, agonized over how to conduct themselves. Those who lived outside large, modern cities like New Orleans and Atlanta chose to adopt a low profile on the issue. A majority of the rabbis in the South agreed to remain inactive in the civil rights movement, at their congregants' request. No more than six or seven in the entire South worked openly for civil rights.

The choice to adopt a low profile did not ensure that the Jews of the South would continue to live peacefully with their segregationist neighbors. On the contrary, in one year, from November 1957 through October 1958, synagogues and other Jewish community centers were bombed in Atlanta, Nashville, Jacksonville, and Miami. In addition, some rabbis received telephone death threats.

It was the active participation of Jews from the North in the civil rights movement of the 1950s and 1960s that thwarted the desire of Southern Jews to be quietly supportive. The Supreme Court accepted the conclusion of sociologist Kenneth Clark that segregation led black children to receive an inferior education. Clark's study had been commissioned by the American Jewish Committee, which submitted it to the Court. The Anti-Defamation League and the American Jewish Congress supported the cause as well. Once the Court ruled, these organizations began to file legal briefs in civil rights cases dealing with housing, employment, education, and public accommodations.

Jewish involvement went beyond institutional affiliation, however. In the 1960s, when the focus was on the registration of black voters, up to 90 percent of the civil rights lawyers present were Jews, according to the estimates of one black leader in Mississippi. These lawyers examined welfare standards, the bail system, arrest procedures, justice-of-the-peace rulings, and the like. Moreover, Jews were at least 30 percent of the white volunteers who rode freedom buses to the South, registered blacks to vote, and picketed segregated establishments.

An unfortunate incident connected to the civil rights movement took place in 1964. Two young New Yorkers, Michael Schwerner and Andrew Goodman, joined with a black Mississippian, James Cheney, as volunteers in a voter-registration drive. They were attacked and killed by members of the Ku Klux Klan, and their bodies were dumped in a secret grave. The tragic discovery of their corpses contributed, in large measure, to the swift passage of the Voting Rights Act of 1965.

Chapter 8 discussed the Israeli–Arab Six-Day War of June 1967. How did President Johnson relate to this conflict? Was he supportive of Israel, or did he prefer to take a neutral position, as President Eisenhower did during the Sinai Campaign in 1956?

President Johnson and the United States were pre-occupied with the Vietnam War, so little military help could be offered. Nevertheless, Johnson worked through the United Nations and with allies to try to break the Egyptian stranglehold over Israel. This effort was unsuccessful, but Israel was granted full access to American military equipment. In addition, the Sixth Fleet was positioned in the eastern Mediterranean to prevent the Soviets from intervening on behalf of the Arabs. After the war, in the United Nations Security Council debate, the United States supported Israel's refusal to return territory without Arab acceptance of Israel's independence and security.

JEWS IN AMERICA IN THE 1970s AND 1980s

In the 1970s and 1980s Jews continued to be involved in radio and television. Similarly, they continued to expand their real estate holdings. The Crown family of Chicago, for example, acquired railroads, Great Lakes ore vessels, airplane factories, hotels, banks, agribusinesses, and more real estate. Tobacco and liquor remained Jewish businesses for the most part.

The American economy began to favor science and technology in these years, as the government funded large contracts for research and development, allowing the Xerox Corporation and the Polaroid Corporation to develop new ideas and bring them to production.

Jews found that now they could gain access to architecture and engineering schools, as the quotas for acceptance were finally dropped. Quotas for acceptance to law schools were dropped as well, so that by the late 1960s it became a rarity to find a big city law firm without at least one Jewish senior partner. Medical

schools, too, eliminated quotas. By 1986, 39 percent of medical students in the leading medical schools were Jews, and by 1989, of 50 American Nobel laureates in the medical sciences, including biochemistry, physiology, and genetics, 17 were Jews.

As in the time of Roosevelt's New Deal, Jews were involved in government. In the 1970s and 1980s, however, they did not just make political contributions, as they had in the 1960s, they became candidates. Abraham Beame became the first Jewish mayor of New York City; Edward Koch, who succeeded Beame, became the first mayor to serve three consecutive terms. Abraham Ribicoff, a Democrat, was elected governor of Connecticut. He was asked by Kennedy to serve as Secretary of Health, Education and Welfare and was later elected twice as United States senator. Jews were also elected governors of Pennsylvania, Maryland, Oregon, Vermont, and Rhode Island.

Another distinguished senator was Jacob Javits from New York. He was a powerful supporter of the Civil Rights Act and strong enough in his convictions to refuse to support Barry Goldwater, the 1964 Republican candidate for the presidency. Jewish senators represented, at various times, Connecticut, Florida, Nebraska, Oregon, Michigan, Minnesota, Ohio, Pennsylvania, Wisconsin, Maine, New Jersey, New York, and Alaska. Jews also began to win seats in the U.S. Congress, representing districts in nearly half the states.

Probably the most famous Jew to serve in government was Henry Kissinger. He was "discovered" by Richard Nixon, perhaps the most unlikely President to appoint a Jewish refugee from Germany to a position of influence in his administration. When Nixon assumed the presidency in 1969, Kissinger was brought to Washington to serve as national security adviser. By 1973 Nixon decided to appoint Kissinger as his Secretary of State.

Although Kissinger wanted to avoid any involvement in the Arab–Israeli conflict, the October 1973 Israel–Egypt war forced him to be involved. As it turned out, Kissinger's skills in negotiating an end to the conflict and working out disengagement agreements between the parties paved the way for what would be negotiated at Camp David and signed at the peace treaty accords in 1978–1979.

JEWS IN AMERICA FROM 1990 TO 2003

The year 1992 brought the election of a Democrat from Arkansas, Bill Clinton. Israel continued to be a central issue for Jews. Much progress was made in this area, as has been discussed in Chapter 8. Unfortunately the years 2000–2003 featured Intifada ("uprising") II. Several hundred Palestinians and more than 100 Israelis were killed in these violent clashes. Israeli Prime Minister Barak offered major concessions to the Palestinians, but they were rejected. Clinton involved himself actively in efforts to reach a resolution, but these efforts failed. The Bush administration, which came into office in 2000, lent its support to the "road map" for peace, developed together with the United Nations, the European Union, and the Russians. This peace proposal is outlined and discussed in Chapter 8.

Jews continue to serve as mayors, governors, representatives, and senators. Michael Bloomberg was elected mayor of New York City in 2001. The states of Hawaii and Pennsylvania elected Jews as their governors in 2002, Linda Lingle in Hawaii and Ed Rendell in Pennsylvania.

The number of U.S. representatives remained at 26 after the 2002 election. Included among the Jewish members are Tom Lantos of California, Barney Frank of Massachusetts, and Jerrold Nadler of New York. The number of Jews in the Senate rose from 10 to 11. Prominent among the senators are Dianne Feinstein of California, Joseph Lieberman of Connecticut, Arlen Specter of Pennsylvania, and Charles Schumer of New York.

A remarkable step forward for Jews was the selection by the Democratic presidential candidate, Albert Gore, of an Orthodox Jew, Joseph Lieberman, as candidate for Vice President. No Jew had ever been selected as candidate for Vice President, let alone a practicing Orthodox Jew. Gore was defeated by George W. Bush in the 2000 election, though, so Lieberman never got to sit as Vice President. In 2002 Lieberman declared himself a candidate for the 2004 Democratic Party presidential nomination.

Anti-Semitic incidents continued to take place during this time period. The Anti-Defamation League, which audits anti-Semitic incidents annually, reported that there were more than 1,500 across the

Joseph Lieberman

United States in 2002, a slight increase over approximately 1,400 in 2001. Anti-Semitic incidents involve physical and verbal assaults, harassment, property defacement and vandalism, hateful e-mail messages, and other expressions of anti-Jewish sentiment. The most serious reported episodes in 2002 were three arsons, three attempted arsons, one attempted bombing, six bomb threats, and seven cemetery desecrations.

Perhaps most disturbing is the increase in anti-Semitic incidents on college campuses. Only 85 acts were reported in 2001, but 106 in 2002, an increase of 24 percent. Many of the 2002 incidents grew out of anti-Israel or "anti-Zionist" demonstrations, or other actions in which some participants engaged in overt expression of anti-Jewish sentiments, including name-calling directed at Jewish students, placards comparing the Star of David to the swastika, or vandalism of Jewish property, such as Hillel buildings.

One of the most disturbing occurrences took place at the University of Colorado. Jewish students were confronted by an angry, threatening crowd yelling "Nazis!" and other epithets as they held a peace vigil in September 2002. In later weeks, "Jews rot in Hell" was spray-painted on a Jewish fraternity house and a sukkah was defaced with a swastika.

The Internet plays an important role in the spread of anti-Semitism. Hate literature is transmitted through hundreds of sites on the Web and through bulletin boards, chat rooms and e-mail messages. Web sites operated by anti-Semites are found easily on the Internet and provide haters with the ability to reach a potential audience of millions with literature and recruitment materials.

Intermarriage is a major threat to Jewish continuity and to the related loss of Jewish identity. As the end of the 20th century approached, this continued to be a concern. A national Jewish population study in 1990 showed that some 33 percent to 50 percent of American Jews were intermarrying. Research carried out in 1998 showed a 60 percent rate of intermarriage among Reform Jews. It also showed that 52 percent of Jews married after 1985 married non-Jews.

The Leadership Council of Conservative Judaism issued a Statement on Intermarriage in March 1995. This statement indicated commitment to a three-tiered approach to intermarriage. The first step was to try to prevent intermarriage; the second, to promote conversion of the non-Jewish spouse; and the third, and final step, to attempt to bring the intermarried couple closer to the Jewish community, to integrate them into the Jewish community.

On September 11, 2001 terrorists hijacked four commercial airliners. They succeeded in flying three of the aircraft into the twin towers of New York City's World Trade Center and the Pentagon. Thousands were killed in these attacks and American Jews joined all other Americans in shock, especially in view of these attacks having occurred on home soil.

For some days it was unclear who was responsible for the attacks, but by the end of the week the administration reached the conclusion that the Saudi billionaire Osama bin Laden was the chief suspect. President Bush announced that the United States was prepared to put together a broad-based coalition that would support a war against terrorism. The war against terror would begin with the Al Qaeda terrorist network that bin Laden directed from Taliban-controlled Afghanistan.

American Jewish leaders now faced a new set of concerns. The Bush administration appealed to countries that supported terrorism themselves to join the battle against terror. Moreover, it refused to treat Yasser Arafat and the terrorist groups operating out of Palestine as equivalent to the Taliban and bin Laden. In addition, it would not include Hamas and Hezbollah among the suspected terrorist groups whose assets would be frozen.

On October 7, the United States began its strikes against Afghanistan. Jewish leaders were encouraged by an apparent reconciliation between Bush and Prime Minister Sharon on the issue of American pressure on Israel, as well as promises that Hamas, Hezbollah, and other anti-Israel terrorist groups would soon make the list of targeted terrorist organizations. They decided to state clearly their strong support for the war against terrorism.

In November, assurances that the battle against terrorism would not disregard the terrorist attacks against Israel bore fruit. The Justice Department included a terrorist organization associated with Hezbollah and the Martyrs of Al-Aqsa Brigades among the 46 groups named as "terrorist organizations" whose members would be precluded from entering the United States and whose funds would be frozen.

In December, the administration signaled that the war on terrorism would target groups carrying out attacks against Israel. Following attacks for which Hamas took credit, the Treasury Department an-

The Twin Towers of the World Trade Center.

nounced that the assets of three charitable organizations with links to Hamas, including the Texas-based Holy Land Foundation for Relief and Development, would be frozen. The Holy Land Foundation was accused of directly transferring its funds to offices of charity groups in Palestinian-controlled areas that had links to, or were controlled by, Hamas.

SUMMARY

In this chapter we looked at the history of Jews in America. Beginning with the earliest settlement of Jews who were seeking to flee religious oppression in Western Europe, we then considered the participation of Jews in the American Revolution. American Reform Judaism emerged in the middle of the 19th century. Jews took different positions on slavery, the great issue of the time, and joined the armies of both sides in the Civil War. The end of the 19th century brought massive immigration from Eastern Europe, so that by 1914 there were 3 million Jews living in America.

Like everyone else, Jews experienced the Great Depression of the 1930s; Roosevelt's New Deal policies were eventually successful in getting the American economy turned around. We looked at America and the Holocaust, when too little was done too late. The economic and political activities of Jews in the 1950s and 1960s and the Jews' involvement in the civil rights movement of the 1960s were considered as well.

As we looked at the Jews in the 1970s, the 1980s, 1990s, and the first years of the 21st century, special attention was given to greater Jewish involvement in political life. Jews were also prominent in law, medicine, science, and technology. Moreover, they contributed their skills and various talents to the world of business.

Anti-Semitic incidents continued to occur during the latter half of the 20th century, as indicted by the annual audit of the Anti-Defamation League. Jewish leaders remained very concerned as well about the possibility of Jews losing their identity as Jews through intermarriage.

The September 11, 2001 terrorist attack on the World Trade Center and the Pentagon shocked all Americans. The Bush administration declared war on terror and assembled a broad-based coalition committed to support all U.S. efforts to defeat terrorists. Osama bin Laden, who lived in Afghanistan, was identified as the chief suspect in the World Trade Center attacks and so the war against terror began with an attack on Taliban-controlled Afghanistan. The United States committed itself as well to close down and freeze the assets of all organizations providing financial support to terrorist groups attacking Israel.

Henrietta Szold (1860–1945) was born in Baltimore, Maryland, shortly after her parents arrived in the United States from their native Hungary. In 1859 her father, Rabbi Benjamin Szold, accepted a rabbinic position at Congregation Ohab Shalom

In the private school located in the basement of the synagogue, Henrietta's father taught her English, secular studies, and Jewish tradition. In addition to German, the family's household language, he taught her French and Hebrew. After completing high school at the Western Female High School, she taught French, German, botany, and mathematics for 15 years at the Misses Adams' School while also teaching in the Ohab Shalom school and giving Bible and history classes for adults.

Like other American communities, Baltimore was affected by the immigration of Russian Jews beginning in 1881. As of 1890, there were 20,000 Jews living in Baltimore, but 30 years later the number approached 80,000. As was the case in New York and

Chicago, a ghetto of Russian Jews was created in Baltimore. Many of the immigrants, especially the Jewish intellectuals, were attracted to the Szolds.

Henrietta Szold suggested that a night school be established for immigrants. Her suggestion was accepted and she was asked to teach in this program and supervise it, which she did. When the program was taken over by the city in 1898, it had instructed more than 5,000 students, Jews and Christians, and had become the model for what would become the predominant pattern of Americanization of immigrants.

During this period, Henrietta Szold began to work for the Jewish Publication Society, working as its secretary but also doing translation work. She was involved as well in the compilation of the Jewish Encyclopedia. *In 1902 Rabbi Szold died and Henrietta and her mother decided to move to New York. There she continued her work for the Jewish Publication Society.*

Henrietta Szold (1860–1945), scholar, humanitarian, and Zionist leader. After a distinguished career as educator and editor, she founded Hadassah, and settled in Jerusalem, where she supervised Hadassah's medical and social services, and headed Youth Aliyah.

While working among the Russian immigrants in Baltimore, Szold had become a Zionist. She felt that Zionism provided some compensation for the wounds inflicted by history on the Jewish people. On a visit to Palestine in 1909, she was impressed with the beauty of Palestine but also troubled by the misery and disease among the people. As a result, in 1914 she joined 38 women in founding Hadassah Women. She was elected the first president of Hadassah.

By 1916 Hadassah had 4,000 members. In that year, Henrietta Szold was asked to assume responsibility for organizing the American Zionist Medical Unit, involving doctors, nurses, administrators, vehicles, and drugs. She accepted. In the same year, American Zionists united in the Zionist Organization of America and placed her in charge of Zionist educational and public relations work.

Her final 25 years were spent in Palestine, supervising the medical unit there. The unit was enlarged in 1922 and was now called Hadassah Medical Organization. In 1930 Szold was asked by the Va'ad Leummi, the National Council of Jews in Palestine, to govern social welfare in Palestine. This job involved, among other things, rehabilitation of juvenile delinquents and the establishment of vocational schools.

In 1933, as the rise of the Nazi Party induced some young Jews to leave Germany, Szold was placed in charge of Youth Aliyah, an organization created to prepare young people in Germany to settle in Palestine. By 1948, 30,000 young people had taken advantage of Youth Aliyah.

Henrietta Szold died in 1945. Her contributions to the Jewish people on several different fronts were truly remarkable.

Documents

THE VIRGINIA ACT OF 1785

This document commits to the freedom of religion in Virginia. This same commitment would be made later in the U.S. Bill of Rights.

The General Assembly, on the sixteenth day of December, seventeen hundred and eighty-five, passed an act in the words following, to wit:

Whereas, Almighty God has created the mind free; that all attempts to influence it by temporal punishment, or burthens, or by civil incapacitations, tend only to beget habits of hypocrisy and meanness, and are a departure from the plan of the Holy Author of our religion, who, being Lord both of body and mind, yet chose not to propagate it by coercions on either, as was in his Almighty power to do; that the impious presumption of legislators and rulers, civil as well as ecclesiastical, who being themselves but fallible and uninspired men, have assumed dominion over the faith of others, setting up their own opinions and modes of thinking as the only true and infallible, and as such endeavoring to impose them on others, have established and maintained false religions over the greatest part of the world, and through all time, that to compel a man to furnish contributions of money for the propagation of opinions which he disbelieves, is sinful and tyrannical, and even the forcing him to support this or that teacher of his own religious persuasion, is depriving him of the comfortable liberty of giving his contributions to the particular pastor whose morals he would make his pattern, and whose powers he feels most persuasive to righteousness, and is withdrawing from the ministry those temporary rewards which, proceeding from an approbation of their personal conduct, are an additional incitement to earnest and unremitting labors, for the instruction of mankind; that our civil rights have no dependence on our religious opinions any more than our opinions in physics or geometry; that therefore the proscribing any citizen as unworthy the public confidence by laying upon him an incapacity of being called to offices of trust and emolument, unless he profess or renounce this or that religious opinion, is depriving him injuriously of those privileges and advantages to which, in common with his fellow-citizens, he has a natural right; that it tends only to corrupt the principles of that religion it is meant to encourage, by bribing, with a monopoly of worldly honors and emoluments, those who will externally profess and conform to it; that though, indeed, those are criminal who do not withstand such temptation, yet neither are those innocent who lay the bait in their way; that to suffer the civil magistrate to intrude his powers into the field of opinion, and to restrain the profession or propagation of principles on supposition of their ill tendency, is a dangerous fallacy, which at once destroys all religious liberty, because he, being of course judge of that tendency, will make his opinions the rule of judgment, and approve or condemn the sentiments of others only as they shall square with or differ from his own; that it is time enough for the rightful purposes of civil government, for its officers to interfere, when principles break out into overt acts against peace and good order; and finally, that truth is great and will prevail, if left to herself; that she is the proper and sufficient antagonist to error, and has nothing to fear from the conflict, unless by human interposition disarmed of her natural weapons, free argument and debate; errors ceasing to be dangerous when it is permitted freely to contradict them:

Be it enacted by the General Assembly, That no man shall be compelled to frequent or support any religious worship, place or ministry whatsoever, nor shall be enforced, restrained, molested or burthened, in his body or goods, nor shall otherwise suffer on account of his religious opinions or belief; but that all men shall be free to profess, and by argument to maintain, their opinions in matters of religion, and that the same shall in no wise diminish, enlarge or affect their civil capacities.

And though we well know that this Assembly elected by the people for the ordinary purposes of legislation only, have no power to restrain the acts of succeeding assemblies constituted with powers equal to our own, and that, therefore, to declare this act to be irrevocable would be of no effect in law; yet we are free to declare, and do declare, that the rights hereby asserted are of the natural rights of mankind; and that if any act shall be hereafter passed to repeal the present, or to narrow its operation, such act will be an infringement of natural right.

THE MANHATTAN BEACH AFFAIR
(1879)

Social anti-Semitism affected Jews in the late 19th century. This document illustrates ways in which this was expressed.

The war against the Jews, which was carried on at Saratoga two years ago, is apparently to be revived at Coney Island. This time it is in a quarter where the Jewish residents of New York City are particularly aimed at. Several days ago a rumor was circulated to the effect that Austin Corbin, the President of the Manhattan Beach Company, had taken an open stand against admitting Jews to the beach or hotel. This report was on Sunday strengthened by a statement from Mr. P.S. Gilmore, the leader of the Manhattan Beach band, who said that Mr. Corbin told him he was going to oppose the Jews, and that he would rather "sink" the two millions invested in the railway and hotel than have a single Israelite take advantage of its attractions. A representative of the *Herald* called upon Mr. Corbin at his banking establishment in the new Trinity building, No. 115 Broadway, yesterday, to ascertain what foundation there was for these most extraordinary rumors. Mr. Corbin at first exhibited some timidity about talking on the subject, but finally invited the reporter into his private office, where he was joined by his brother and partner, Daniel C. Corbin.

"You see," he began, "I don't want to speak too strongly, as it might be mistaken for something entirely different from its intended sense. Personally I am opposed to Jews. They are a pretentious class, who expect three times as much for their money as other people. They give us more trouble on our road and in our hotel than we can stand. Another thing is, that they are driving away the class of people who are beginning to make Coney Island the most fashionable and magnificent watering place in the world."

"Of course, this must affect business?"

"Why, they are hurting us in every way, and we do not want them. We cannot bring the highest social element to Manhattan Beach if the Jews persist in coming. They won't associate with Jews, and that's all there is to it."

"Do you intend to make an open stand against them?"

"Yes, I do. They are contemptible as a class, and I never knew but one 'white' Jew in my life. The rest I found were not safe people to deal with in business. Now, I feel pretty warm over this matter, and I will write a statement which you can publish."

Mr. Corbin sat down at his desk and wrote a few sentences on a slip of paper, as follows:

"We do not like the Jews as a class. There are some well behaved people among them, but as a rule they make themselves offensive to the kind of people who principally patronize our road and hotel, and I am satisfied we should be better off without than with their custom."

"There," said he, handing the statement to the reporter, "that is my opinion, and I am prepared to follow up the matter. It is a question that has to be handled without gloves. It stands this way: We must have a good place for society to patronize. I say that we cannot do so and have Jews. They are a detestable and vulgar people. What do you say, eh, Dan?"

This last sentence was addressed to his brother, Mr. Daniel Corbin, who had taken an active part in the conversation. Dan said, with great emphasis, "Vulgar? I can only find one term for them, and that is nasty. It describes the Jews perfectly."

Mr. Austin Corbin then spoke warmly of the loss sustained by the Manhattan Beach Company in consequence of Israelitish patronage.

"Do you mean, Mr. Corbin, that the presence of Jews attracts the element of ruffianism?" asked the reporter.

"Not always. But the thing is this. The Jews drive off the people whose places are filled by a less particular class. The latter are not rich enough to have any preference in the matter. Even they, in my opinion, bear with them only because they can't help it. It is not the Jews' religion I object to; it is the offensiveness which they possess as a sect or nationality. I would not oppose any man because of his creed."

"Will the other members of the Manhattan Beach Company support you in your position?"

"I expect them to. They know just as much about it as I do, and no reasonable man can deny that the Jews will creep in a place just as it is about to become a grand success and spoil everything. They are not wanted at the Beach, and that settles it."

"Have you spoken to any other members about it?"

"No; but I guess they know my opinions."

Mr. Corbin rose from the chair he had been sitting in and paced the floor. "I'll tell you," said he, running his fingers through his hair, "if I had had my way and there was no one to consult in the matter but myself, I would have stopped the Jews from coming long ago. You just publish my statement. It covers the whole ground, and I mean every word of it."

Mr. Corbin concluded the conversation by telling the reporter to be sure and not give the impression that he was warning against the Jewish religion, but he stigmatized the Jews as having no place in first-class society.

A. CAHAN, "THE RUSSIAN JEW IN AMERICA"

In this selection, Abraham Cahan (1860–1953), a prominent figure in Yiddish-language publishing, describes Jewish life on the Lower East Side of New York.

. . . The Jewish population in the United States has grown from a quarter of a million to about one million. Scarcely a large American town but has some Russo-Jewish names in its directory, with an educated Russian-speaking minority forming a colony within a Yiddish-speaking colony, while cities like New York, Chicago, Philadelphia, and Boston each have a Ghetto rivaling in extent of population the largest Jewish cities in Russia, Austria, and Rumania. The number of Jewish residents in Manhattan Borough is estimated at two hundred and fifty thousand, making it the largest center of Hebrew population in the world. The Russian tongue, which twenty years ago was as little used in this country as Persian, has been added to the list of languages spoken by an appreciable portion of the polyglot immigrant population.

Have the newcomers justified the welcome extended to them from Chickering Hall? Have they proved a desirable accession to the American nation?

"Let another man praise thee, and not thine own mouth; a stranger, and not thine own lips," is a proverb current among the people who form the subject of this paper; and being one of them, I feel that it would be better, before citing figures and facts, to let Gentile Americans who have made a study of the New York Ghetto answer the question. Here is what Mr. Jacob A. Riis, an accepted authority on "how the other half lives," has to say of Jewish immigrants:

They (the Jews) do not rot in their slum, but, rising, pull it up after them. . . . As to their poverty, they brought temperate habits and redeeming love of home. Their strange customs proved the strongest ally of the Gentile health officer in his warfare upon the slum. The death-rate of poverty-stricken Jewtown, despite its crowding, is lower always than that of the homes of the rich. . . . I am a Christian, and hold that in his belief the Jew is sadly in error. So that he may respect mine I insist on fair play for him all around. I am sure that our city has to-day no better and no more loyal citizen than the Jew, be he poor or rich, and none she has less to be ashamed of. . . .

The question of limiting immigration engages the attention of Congress at frequent intervals, and bills aiming at reform in this direction are brought before the Senate and the House. In its bearings upon the Russian, Austrian or Rumanian Jew, the case is summed up by the opinions cited. Now let us hear the testimony of facts on the subject. The invasion of foreign illiteracy is one of the principal dangers which laws restricting immigration are meant to allay, and it is with the illiteracy of the New York Ghetto that we shall concern ourselves first.

The last report of the commissioner-general of immigration gives twenty-eight per cent as the proportion of illiterates among the immigrants who came during the past year from Russia. The figure would be much lower should the computation be confined to immigrants of the Mosaic faith instead of including the mass of Polish and Lithuanian peasants, of whose number only a very small part can read and write. It may not be generally known that every Russian and Polish Jew, without exception, can read the Hebrew bible as well as a Yiddish newspaper, and that many of the Jewish arrivals at the barge office are versed in rabbinical literature, not to speak of the large number of those who can read and write Russian. When attention is directed to the Russian Jew in America, a state of affairs is found which still further removes him from the illiterate class, and gives him a place among the most ambitious and the quickest to learn both the written and the spoken language of the adopted country, and among the easiest to be assimilated with the population.

The cry raised by the Russian antisemites against the backwardness of the Jew in adopting the tongue and the manners of his birthplace, in the same breath in which they urge the government to close the doors of its schools to subjects of the Hebrew faith, reminds one of the hypocritical miser who kept his gate guarded by ferocious dogs, and then reproached his destitute neighbor with holding himself aloof. This country, where the schools and colleges do not discriminate between Jew and Gentile, has quite another tale to tell. The several public evening schools of the New York Ghetto, the evening school supported from the Baron de Hirsch fund, and the two or three private establishments of a similar character are attended by thousands of Jewish immigrants, the great majority of whom come here absolutely ignorant of the language of their native country. Surely nothing can be more inspiring to the public-spirited citizen, nothing worthier of the interest of the student immigration, than the sight of a gray-haired tailor, a patriarch in appearance, coming, after a hard day's work at a sweat-shop, to spell "cat, mat, rat," and to grapple with the difficulties of "th" and "w." Such a spectacle may be seen in scores of the class-rooms in the schools referred to. Hundred of educated young Hebrews earn their living, and often pay their way through college, by giving private lessons in English in the tenement houses of the district—a type of young men and women peculiar to the Ghetto. The pupils of these private tutors are the same poor overworked sweat-shop "hands" of whom the public hears so much and knows so little. A tenement house kitchen turned, after a scanty supper, into a class-room, with the head of the family and his boarder bent over an English school reader, may perhaps claim attention as one of the curiosities of life in a great city; in the Jewish quarter, however, it is a common spectacle.

Nor does the tailor or peddler who hires these tutors, as a rule, content himself with an elementary knowledge of the language of his new home. I know many Jewish workmen who before they came here knew not a word of Russian, and were ignorant of any book except the Scriptures, or perhaps the Talmud, but whose range of English reading places them on a level with the average college-bred American.

The grammar schools of the Jewish quarter are overcrowded with children of immigrants, who, for progress and deportment, are rated with the very best in the city. At least 500 of 1677 students at the New York City College, where tuition and books are free, are Jewish boys from the East Side. The poor laborer who will pinch himself to keep his child at college, rather than send him to a factory that he may contribute to the family's income, is another type peculiar to the Ghetto.

The innumerable Yiddish publications with which the quarter is flooded are also a potent civilizing and Americanizing agency. The Russian Jews of New York, Philadelphia and Chicago have within the last fifteen years created a vast periodical literature which furnishes intellectual food not only to themselves, but also to their brethren in Europe. A feverish literary activity unknown among the Jews in Russia, Rumania and Austria, but which has arisen here among the immigrants from those countries, educates thousands of ignorant tailors and peddlers, lifts their intelligence, facilitates their study of English, and opens to them the doors of the English library. The five million Jews living under the tsar had not a single Yiddish daily paper even when the government allowed such publications, while their fellow countrymen and co-religionists who have taken up their abode in America publish six dailies (five in New York and one in Chicago), not to mention the countless Yiddish weeklies and monthlies, and the pamphlets and books which to-day make New York the largest Yiddish book market in the world. If much that is contained in these publications is rather crude, they are in this respect as good—or as bad—as a certain class of English novels and periodicals from which they partly derive their inspiration. On the other hand, their readers are sure to find in them a good deal of what would be worthy of a more cultivated language. They have among their contributors some of the best Yiddish writers in the world, men of undeniable talent, and these supply the Jewish slums with popular articles on science, on the history of institutions of the adopted country, translations from the best literatures of Europe and America, as well as original sketches, stories, and poems of decided merit. It is sometimes said (usually by those who know the Ghetto at second hand) that this unnatural development of Yiddish journalism threatens to keep the immigrants from an acquaintance with English. Nothing could be further from the truth. The Yiddish periodicals are so many preparatory schools from which the reader is sooner or later promoted to the English newspaper, just as the several Jewish theatres prepare his way to the Broadway playhouse, or as the Yiddish lecture serves him as a stepping-stone to that English-speaking, self-educational society, composed of working-men who have lived a few years in the country, which is another characteristic feature of life in the Ghetto. Truly, the Jews "do not rot in their slum, but, rising, pull it up after them."

CHARLES BERNHEIMER: "SWEATSHOPS IN PHILADELPHIA" (1905)

Bernheimer (1868–1960), a social worker active in Jewish affairs, describes the sweatshops of early 20th-century Philadelphia in this selection.

We enter a sweatshop in Lombard, Bainbridge, Monroe or South Fourth Street. It may be on one of the several floors in which similar work is going on. The shop is that of the so-called contractor—one who contracts with the manufacturer to put his garments together after they have been cut by the cutter. The pieces are taken in bundles from the manufacturer's to the contractor's. Each contractor usually undertakes the completion of one sort—pants, coats, vests, knee pants or children's jackets. There is probably one whole floor devoted to the making of this one kind of garment. It may be that two contractors divide the space of a floor, the one, perhaps, being a pants contractor, and the other a vest contractor, with an entirely distinct set of employees. To his employees the contractor is the "boss," as you find out when you inquire at the shop. Before you have reached the shop, you have probably climbed one, two or three flights of stairs, littered with debris. You readily recognize the entrance to one of these shops once inside the building. The room is likely to be ill-smelling and badly ventilated: the workers are afraid of draughts. Consequently, an abnormally bad air is breathed which it is difficult for the ordinary person to stand long. Thus result the tubercular and other diseases which the immigrant acquires in his endeavor to work out his economic existence.

There are the operator at the machine, the presser at the ironing table, the baster and the finisher with their needles—the latter young women—all bending their backs and straining their eyes over the garments the people wear, many working long hours in [the] busy season for a compensation that hardly enables them to live, and in [the] dull season, not knowing how they will get along at all.

If we apply our ordinary standards of sanitation to these shops they certainly come below such standards. By frequent visits we may grow accustomed to the sights and smells, and perhaps unconsciously assume that such shops

must in the nature of things be in bad condition. But a little reflection will readily show the error of such an assumption.

It is all the more harrowing that the workers have a tenacity of life due to a rich inheritance of vitality, and that through sickness and disease, through squalor and filth, they proceed onward, often managing to pull themselves out of the economic slough, though retaining, perhaps, the defects of bad physical development and surroundings. . . .

The shops are chiefly conducted by the contractors, entirely independent of the manufacturers and the various manufacturers for whom they work assume no liability with reference to them or their employees. They merely agree to pay so much per piece of the garments they give out, and expect the garments to be returned to their establishments as agreed upon by the contractors. Few in this city have "inside" shops, that is, shops in which the entire garment is completed inside the establishment, or in a separate building, under their own supervision. Wherever these inside shops have been established the conditions are very much better; the shop is much cleaner, the light good, the air bearable and the compensation usually more steady.

The last statement requires elucidation. In one clothing manufacturing establishment, there is in the rear a so-called inside shop with a regular contractor in charge. The firm furnishes its first work to this contractor and thus enables him to give, in turn, steady employment, but claims it could not extend such a shop without adding considerably to the expense, as the rental and the assurance of regularity involve a larger outlay than arranging with contractors who compete on the basis of low rentals and the smallest possible expense.

The contractor is usually an operator or other worker who becomes imbued with the desire to set up for himself. Excessive competition among the small contractors has contributed to the bad economic state of affairs in the garment trades. The contractor is between the upper millstone of the manufacturer and the nether mill-stone of the workman, forced to take the prices of the one and trying to make the utmost possible out of the other. Some few have saved enough to become manufacturers themselves. Some of the old established manufacturing firms have retired from business as the result of the competition of this new element.

In actual money gains, the contractors whose earnings have been estimated are not better off than their workmen. Many said that if they could get their little capital back they would probably return to their former occupation—at least for a time, for the desire to be a "boss" is strong and would doubtless lead to other attempts. . . .

In [the] busy season the employees are required to work long hours, sometimes as high as fifteen, perhaps, eighteen, a day. In [the] slack season they must wait for the work that is doled out to them. Where time enters at all into the measurement of the pay, the employers endeavor to stretch it without giving corresponding pay. There seem to be numerous devices by which the workers can be taken advantage of. The character of the work varies so much in any one trade that it seems difficult to regulate the prices unless by the most iron-clad arrangement, backed by the force of strong organization. But the weakness of the organizations has been apparent in the past. Sometimes they have been affiliated with one general labor organization, sometimes with another. They are now welded together under the United Garment Workers of America, into which they have gone during the past few years. With the exception of the Cutters' Union the membership of these organizations is almost entirely composed of Russian Jews.

JACOB H. SCHIFF: "THE GALVESTON PROJECT" (OCTOBER 25, 1907)

Jacob H. Schiff (1847–1920) was regarded for many years as the head of American Jewry. He proposed and financed the Galveston Project, described in this selection.

I had a conference yesterday with Messrs. Cyrus Sulzberger, Oscar Straus, and Professor Loeb upon the project about which we have been recently corresponding, and we have reached the conclusion that the Removal Office at New York, with the experience and connections it has already secured, would be well in position to undertake the carrying out of my project, as far as the labor on this side is concerned.

With this in view, it is proposed that the Removal Office create an organization at New Orleans or Galveston, or both, to receive arriving immigrants and at once forward them to their destination, which latter is to be previously arranged for through the New York organization of the Removal Office. To accomplish this properly, it is thought that the Removal Office should have sixty days' previous notice of the initial embarkation of emigrants for New Orleans or Galveston, and that the first shipment should not exceed 500 persons.

It would be left to the ITO [Jewish Territorial Organization], allied in this, as I hope, with Dr. Paul Nathan's Hilfsverein, to father the movement in Russia, to gather the proposed emigrants, to arrange steamship routes, etc., and for any expense attached to this the funds would have to be found in Europe. On the other hand, I shall undertake to place at the disposal of the Removal Office the $500,000 which it is my intention to devote to the initiation of the project. Based upon the cost per head of carrying on the present removal work, which is steadily going forward, half a million dollars should suffice to

place from 20,000 to 25,000 people in the American "Hinterland," and I believe, with the successful settlement of such a number, others would readily follow of their own accord, and that then a steady stream of immigration will flow through New Orleans and Galveston into the territory between the Mississippi River on the east, the Pacific Ocean on the west, the Gulf on the south and the Canadian Dominion on the north.

This project is now to a great extent in your own and your friends' hands, and I shall look forward with deep interest to see what can be done with it. . . .

THE ANTI-DEFAMATION LEAGUE: A STATEMENT OF POLICY (MAY 1915)

This document presents the policies of the Anti-Defamation League in 1915. The ADL was to concern itself with education about Judaism through books and lectures. It was also to be vigilant about any plays and motion pictures dealing with Jews, making sure that no objectionable portraits of Jews were presented.

The Anti-Defamation League of America, founded under the auspices of the Independent Order of B'nai B'rith, is the result of a demand by the Jewish people for concerted action against the constant and ever increasing efforts to traduce the good name of the Jew. . . . For the present the League contemplates the following activities:

Educational:
1. Public and university libraries will be furnished with lists of books on Jewish subjects, which, in the opinion of the League tend to show the facts regarding Jewish ethics, customs, history, religion and philosophy.

   Where it is found that the endowment of institutions, either private or public, does not permit the procurement of a fairly comprehensive number of books on these subjects, it will be the aim of the League to supply them. Investigations show that a majority of the public libraries of the country do not even possess a Jewish history written by a Jewish historian.

   Investigations will be made of the bibliography on Jewish subjects in libraries. Wherever it is found that books which maliciously and scurrilously traduce the character of the Jew are kept for general circulation— especially in public stackrooms—the proper authorities will be urged to withdraw such books from general circulation, or, at least, to place a restriction on their use.
2. The services of prominent lecturers and publicists, regardless of religious affiliation, will be enlisted for the purpose of delivering lectures on Jewish subjects at universities, public schools and at appropriate gatherings.

The League will provide also for the dissemination of literature designed to give the public a true understanding of the Jew and Judaism.

3. The League recognizes the fact that the mind of the growing child must be safeguarded against even a suggestion of prejudice; therefore, where in our educational system, either public or private, text books are used which tend to pervert the mind of the child and create prejudice, a determined campaign will be waged to eliminate all such books from the curriculum.

Vigilance Work:

1. The services of clipping bureaus have been secured to keep the League advised as to matters of interest affecting the Jewish people. Information regarding defamation and discrimination should be promptly sent to the Executive Committee of the League.

2. The League will secure corresponding representatives of every State, who will submit to the central office in Chicago all matters pertaining to these subjects which come within the scope of the League.

3. We should find our strongest allies in newspapers, periodicals and magazines, the great mediums for expression and exchange of thought. We therefore heartily endorse and commend the action of certain newspapers in adopting the policy of eliminating mention of the religious denomination of malefactors. We shall bend every energy toward making this policy universal.

4. Where articles appear which present the Jew in a false and unworthy light, we shall endeavor to secure correction either by retraction, or by an answer in the next or early issue of the same publication, thereby reaching the same reading public.

5. The League will attempt to secure the co-operation of the Press in eliminating from foreign and domestic news items, all matters which give an untrue impression of the Jew.

Theaters and Moving Pictures: Investigation will be made of all plays which deal with the Jew. If, after careful study, it is apparent that a play gives an untrue or unfair portrayal of the Jew, the League will endeavor to prevent its production in its offensive form, or if already staged, to secure the elimination of the objectionable matter. Similar measures will be taken in connection with moving picture films.

Legislation:

1. With a view of preventing the presentation, in moving picture theaters, of films which are malicious and scurrilous caricatures, or are objectionable in other respects, the League will endeavor to secure, in the various states of the Union, the enactment of statutes similar to the one recently passed in the State of Ohio, providing for the appointment of a Board of State Censors. Where the passage of such a statute cannot be attained, similar relief will be sought from the various municipalities by securing the enactment of appropriate ordinances.

2. The League will endeavor to secure the passage of laws, where the same is practicable, making it unlawful for any hostelry, directly or indirectly, to publish, circulate, issue, display, post or mail any written or printed communication, notice or advertisement, to the effect that any of the accommodations of such places shall be refused, withheld, or denied to any person on account of his creed. . . .

Situation in 1913: When the League was organized in the fall of 1913, an extraordinary situation confronted it. It seemed that whenever film manufacturers desired to depict a hardhearted money-lender, a blackmailer, a fire-bug, a depraved gambler, a swindler, a grafter or a white-slaver, they determined upon a Jewish name for the person in question, and directed the actor to simulate what is popularly regarded as a "Jewish type." There was nothing so unusual in this, as the tendency has been evident since the time of [Christopher] Marlowe's "Barabas" [in *The Jew of Malta,* 1588]. The extraordinary element, however, was that what previously reached the attention of an infinitesimal fraction of the populace, and that fraction a matured and cultured part, was most vividly presented before the eyes of millions of the unmatured, ignorant or the uncultured. A careful survey of the existing situation showed that there were scores of films on the market which were extremely prejudicial to the welfare and happiness of our people. In addition to the criminal characterization, the Jew was often shown in caricature, in a manner similar to that employed on the burlesque and vaudeville stages. These caricaturizations were supposed to be funny, but in many instances the laughter which they stimulated was that which arises from the malicious discomfiture of another. Under the guise of fun, the most sordid, vulgar and unclean characteristics were frequently attributed to Jews in general.

"A BINTEL BRIEF"

This is a short selection from the advice column of the *Jewish Daily Forward* in early 20th-century America.

Dear Editor,

I come from Europe, where I was brought up by a father who was a Talmud scholar and a cantor. I took after my father both in learning and voice, and when I became a Bar Mitzvah, my leading the congregation in prayer impressed everyone. My name became known in many cities and people came to hear me conduct the services.

When I turned eighteen a respected man from a town near Kovne took me as a son-in-law, gave me four hundred rubles and five years of room and board. I married his pretty sixteen-year-old daughter, moved into my father-in-law's house, ate, drank and devoted myself to the study of Torah. Once in a while, on a special Sabbath or a holiday, I led the prayers in shul, but I took no money for that.

After the five years I was left with a pretty young wife, two children, and my dowry money. My father-in-law then established for me, or I should say for my wife, a small grocery and told me, "You will continue to study Torah and your wife will make a living for you." But my wife wasn't very good at business and the money went fast. Meanwhile, my father-in-law died, my mother-in-law went to her son in Kovne, and we were left alone.

I began to talk to my wife about going to America, and after long deliberation we left home. When we came to this country, our *landsleit* helped us a little to get settled, and when the High Holy Days came, I earned a hundred and eighty dollars as a cantor leading the Musaph prayers. I began to make a living as a cantor, and people hired me for weddings, funerals, and other affairs.

As time went on my horizons broadened. I read all kinds of books, I accumulated worldly knowledge and I began to look at life quite differently.

In short, I can't reconcile myself to continue making a living as a cantor, because I am no longer religious. I can't act against my conscience, and the right thing to do is to give up my present livelihood. I want to learn a trade now, perhaps become a peddler or find another means of earning a living that has nothing to do with religion.

My wife, who held onto her own beliefs and is still fanatical, doesn't even want to hear of my plans. She argues that serving as a cantor is honorable. It is also questionable whether I can earn enough to support a family from working in a shop or peddling.

Now there are arguments about this between me, my wife, and our close friends, and we all decided to place the question in your hands. I want to hear what you have to say about it.

Your reader,
The Progressive Cantor

Answer

Freethinkers as well as religious people will answer this question in the same way. Even the rabbi will say that, according to Jewish law, only a pious Jew may be a cantor. His wife and his religious friends who are trying to convince him to remain a cantor are really committing the worst sin according to their beliefs.

For a non-believer to be a cantor for an Orthodox congregation is without a doubt a shameful hypocrisy.

A JEWISH FAMILY AND THE DEPRESSION (1936)

This selection relates to the ways in which Jewish families dealt with the special challenges of the Great Depression.

Berger Family

Status   WPA   Home Relief Supplementation
Religion Jewish
Man: born 1893 Poland   to U.S.A. 1913
Citizen 1934
Wife: born 1895 Poland   to U.S.A. 1920
Citizen 1939

Education
Man: Very little formal education. Attended Hebrew school Poland.
Wife: No formal education.

Medical Status
Man: Healthy.
Wife: Healthy.

Woman's Work History   Never worked outside of home.
Married   1912, Poland.
Number of Children in the Home   Two   Ages—14 and 17 years.
Basic Occupation Before Relief   Grocery clerk. Previously small businessman.
Average Income Before Relief $20 to $30 weekly.
Private Employment Terminated   October, 1936.
First Accepted for Relief   November, 1936.

Summary

Home Relief   From November 2, 1936, to November 23, 1936. Closed to WPA.
WPA   November, 1936, to date with the exception of: Home Relief for two weeks in August, 1939, following WPA layoff because of 18-month ruling. Reinstated on WPA September, 1939.
Applied for and received Home Relief Supplementation of WPA wages, March 1940, to date. Earlier applications rejected.
Few reclassifications or shifts while on WPA— was a laborer; at present—watchman, $52.80 a month.

Abstract of Home Relief Record

Oct., 1936   *First Application:* (Social Service Exchange—no record.) Family is living in four rooms at a rental of $28 and has lived here since 1934. Their rent is paid to October 31st. The man was a grocery clerk from 1929 to October, 1936, when he was laid off because the owner's brother-in-law was in need of a job. Mr. Berger earned $20 a week and on this the family managed fairly well. Their rent had been $25 a month until last year, when it was raised to $28. Mr. and Mrs. Berger are said to have been panic-stricken at the thought of public assistance. They are especially concerned about their rent, which they have always paid in advance. The man stated that they had always managed adequately, but had not been able to save any money because of their low income. Therefore, they had no resources and it was necessary for them to come to Home Relief only two weeks after Mr. Berger lost his job. The man said that he is "too proud to stay on Home Relief long."

NOV. 2, 1936   Investigator visited Mr. Berger's former employer, the grocer, who said that Mr. Berger is a "most honest, diligent, conscientious worker" and that he was sorry to let him go. He said that his wife's brother was unemployed and that she had prevailed upon him to give this brother the job.

NOV. 2, 1936   *Case Accepted.*

NOV. 17, 1936   *Man assigned to WPA* as a laborer at $60.50 monthly.

NOV. 23, 1936   *Case Closed to WPA.*

NOV. 9, 1937   *Applied for Home Relief supplementation.* There is an estimated budget deficit of $4.05 semimonthly. Family is still living in the same apartment; their rental is now $31. It was raised recently and it is for this reason that Mr. Berger is asking for help. He says that he applied for supplementary assistance at Borough Hall, when first assigned to WPA, and was told that a family with only two children was not eligible for supplementation. The investigator questioned the family's management to date. Both Mr. and Mrs. Berger said that they managed somehow by doing without meat, fruit, etc., by purchasing no new clothing, and by saving in every possible way. Mrs. Berger cried as she talked about their difficulties. She explained that she watches every penny; that her

husband takes his lunch with him and that her boy walks to school because they do not have the carfare to give him.

NOV. 16, 1937   Investigator visited the grocer to whom the Bergers owe a debt of $25. The grocer said that he extended credit to them because they are the type of family who try their best. He knows that they would not apply for assistance unless their need was great.

DEC., 1937   *Case Rejected* "because it does not seem possible for this family to have managed without some other kind of assistance."

JAN. 4, 1938   *Reapplied for Supplementation:* Mr. Berger says that the last time he applied for supplementation he was ashamed to say that he had borrowed money in order to manage. He says that he borrowed from a friend, $10 or $15 at a time as he needed it for rent, and then paid it back when he got his check. He now owes two friends $15 each. He pays a little on these debts and then borrows again when the need for rent or utility bills becomes acute. Mrs. Berger showed investigator the contents of the kitchen cupboard. There seemed to be little more than potatoes. Mr. Berger showed investigator his old, torn coat. Investigator reports that "during the interview, Mr. and Mrs. Berger were not resentful at any time. Mr. Berger was resigned to the interview and slightly disgusted." He did not see the reason for such an intensive investigation. "Investigator still not able to understand the family's ability to manage on about $5 a week for food." The woman was told to keep a daily record of food expenses for the next few days. Man says that he has talked with other men on the job who have families the size of his. They are two or three months in arrears with their rent. He says that he could not stand this; that he has to feel that his rent is paid no matter what else happens.

JAN. 25, 1938   Mr. Berger presented a diet list kept by his wife. The family seems to have been living on a diet which excludes milk, meat, or fish. They use potatoes, evaporated milk, canned fish, etc., as indicated by the list for a week.

FEB. 8, 1938   Man at the District Office. Still no decision by Home Relief. According to investigator, "visitor stated that the list of foods composed by his wife seemed to create some doubt in our minds of the ability of the family to manage over a period of a year on such a diet without there being some apparent decline in health." The decision on the case is left up to the nutritionist. Man states that the family's need is great; that otherwise he would not have applied. He says that the $3 increase in rent brought about the present emergency. He says that they also hope to be able to get some clothing if they are accepted for supplementation.

FEB. 15, 1938   The nutritionist stated that in her opinion "the family could not have lived on this budget for any length of time without seriously impairing their health."

FEB. 15, 1938   *Case Rejected.* "It seems apparent that the family has not explained management freely."

AUG. 16, 1939   *Reapplied for Full Home Relief.* Man was dismissed from WPA, August 10, 1939, because of the 18-month ruling. Questioned again about how the family has been able to manage, they replied they have managed somehow so far. Their rent was increased to $33. They have a roomer who pays $10 a month and Isaac, who was graduated from high school this June, received $3.80 a month from NYA [National Youth Administration] while at school. Mrs. Berger is unable to say how much she needs for living expenses, repeating what she has frequently said in the past, that she managed with what she had on hand. The home is described as crowded, with a boy and girl sleeping in the living room so that the roomer may have a room of his own. Man is anxious for work. He says that he wants to return to WPA rather than stay on Home Relief.

AUG. 31, 1939   *Case Accepted.*

SEPT. 12, 1939   *Reassigned to WPA* as a laborer at $52.80.

SEPT. 14, 1939   *Case Closed to WPA.*

FEB., 1940   *Reapplied for Home Relief Supplementation.* When asked why they had not applied sooner they said Isaac had received $15 a month from NYA while at City College, which he entered last fall, and that he had given it all to his mother to use for the household expenses. She gave him carfare and he took his

lunches from home so that he used little of the $15 himself. He was dropped from the NYA rolls this semester because his average fell below C.

The rent was raised two months ago and is now $34. They were able to make ends meet until this month with the help of the $10 from the roomer and Isaac's $15 income. Their rent is paid to date but they still owe $15 to the grocer. He has been lenient because they pay something regularly, but recently they have failed to keep the bill down and were told that the grocer must have something on account before extending further credit.

MAR., 1940   *Case Accepted for Home Relief supplementation.*

MAY, 1940   *Last Entry*—clothing check for $5 granted.

TEENAGERS' TESTAMENTS (1958)

At the conclusion of the academic year, Rabbi Dr. Victor Reichert of Cincinnati asked members of his confirmation class to write "ethical wills" in which they communicated the values they would pass on to their children. The following two testaments were written by girls in their mid-teens.

A

I wear lipstick, heels, and chemise dresses, but I am still a child. I go to formals, read historical novels and current affairs, but the thought of snow and water pistols still produces a happy, impish feeling. I know that my heart is divided into many rooms; the first contains goodness; the second, selfishness, thoughtlessness; the third, sadness. And as the delicate lilac absorbs from its growing place the tiny drops of dew and gives forth fragrance, so does my heart admit and release those qualities of goodness, thoughtlessness and sadness. This has been my year of learning. Through happy and disappointing experiences I think that I have become a little more tolerant and understanding of people. I mention these facts about myself because I wonder if I am mature enough to make an ethical will.

The dictionary defines ethical as "relating to moral action, motive or character." I bequeath the qualities of character or motive which I think help produce moral action. The first is sympathy and understanding for the feelings of others. Although parents seem to perceive their child's dreams and emotions, they say to a friend, "How lucky she is, not having anything to worry about. Little does my child know of the harsh world." How little do the parents remember the agitation and uncertainty of childhood, unless they can relive their own, the little things . . . the broken doll, the yearning for a sled, the feeling of a left out child.

To all young people I bequeath a sense of justice. To see another viewpoint than your own is the hardest work in the world. To be fair in your dealings with others, you must be honest with yourself. When I argue with my best friend, I try to remember that she thinks she is right, too. This is very difficult. Not so hard is seeing injustice when it doesn't concern you. When I see a little child overpowered by a bigger one, I grow angry. When I see someone persecuted who cannot help himself, I do not like it. I try to help. Trying to make fair the unjust is one quality I believe makes a better person.

To all young people I bequeath tolerance. If a child goes to a foreign school and dresses oddly and speaks with an accent, I think she should not be laughed at. Even if a child is American but behaves differently from his schoolmates, I don't think he should be ridiculed. A little kindness will help the one who receives and the one who gives.

To all young people, I bequeath a love of learning. Learn, always learn, for learning is life. Learning blooms at sunrise and fades away at dusk. Learning is like sewing. One takes one stitch, then another. It is not always easy. Sometimes the light grows dim, but the finished dress makes the struggle worthwhile.

To all young people, I bequeath high standards, the strength to do what is right, because it is right.

To all young people, I bequeath courage. Courage is one of the hardest qualities to develop. President [Franklin D.] Roosevelt who conquered polio, said during a time of great fear, "the only thing to fear is fear itself." Fear paralyzes; courage makes one able to do the things that are necessary in moments of unhappiness and crisis.

To all young people, I bequeath gallantry so that they can meet disappointment with good grace. Gallantry which flourished in the Middle Ages is little valued in the rocket age, but the sportsmanship and consideration it represents can make a person more valuable.

One of the greatest qualities I bequeath is love, of people, animals, nature. The gift of love returns a hundred times to the giver.

Last of all, to all young people, I bequeath faith, faith in God, their fellowmen, and faith in themselves, to learn "To do justice, to love mercy, to walk humbly with thy God."

B

To my children:

To you, my children, I would like to pass on some of my thoughts and beliefs which I have gained through experiences both happy and sorrowful.

I hope that through my efforts and those of your father, that you have come to love and revere the Lord and have found a place in your heart for Judaism. Your father and I have tried to give you a home that made you feel that it and its inhabitants belonged to the Jewish faith. I hope that you have truly felt that attachment for your religion that I have felt.

Though at the time you may have felt greatly taxed at being forced to go to Sunday School, I do hope that you will send your children. I also hope that you yourselves will take an interest in the Sunday School while your children are attending there. From experience, I know that there is possibly the feeling that you would not want to "force" your children to go, because of your distaste of it (if you hold such a distaste). But I would like to recall to you that I felt that I lacked a sufficient knowledge of Judaism because I did not attend Sunday School regularly until eighth grade.

The most important phase of religion is living it. You must not let your religion become mechanical, but make it a part of your daily life and give it its true merit. Attend services as much as possible and set an example for your children. Do not go if you do not feel the urge within you. Do not go just to be "one of the crowd" or just out of habit.

Do not think that once you are confirmed that you know all that there is to know. Continue to study as much as possible even when you are adults. I have often heard and have noticed how uninformed some Jews are concerning their religion. Be sure to learn all you can about it. But on the other hand, do not become bigoted; become well-rounded and as proficient as possible in all fields.

If you ever feel that things are dark for you, there is one sure way to help yourselves. Do not feel sorry for yourself and be a burden to others. Do the exact opposite. Get out and do something to help others. By getting out to help these people, and out from below your own difficulties, you will realize there are many people in much worse conditions than you are. By helping others you will also be helping yourself. Never succumb to letting your difficulties mushroom out of proportion, for you will not only be doing yourself an injustice but you may get to the point where you can not see over the top.

I realize some of the requests I have asked will be hard to uphold, but I hope your lives can be as profitable and as happy as possible. These are the things which I have experienced throughout my life, and I hope you can learn something from them. I believe one important thing to always remember is to keep your opinion of yourself on par with your actual person.

RIOTING IN PHILADELPHIA (AUGUST 1965)

In August 1965, riots took place in Philadelphia. This document attempts to understand and explain these outbreaks.

The major victims of the August riots were the small businessmen of North Central Philadelphia. In all, 726 stores and offices were damaged—523 within the official riot zone, 203 in adjoining neighborhoods and a few several miles removed.

Judging by the number of stores ransacked, the prime targets appeared to be food stores (69), bars and other liquor outlets (67), clothing stores (67), and furniture and appliance stores (44). At the suggestion of the Jewish Community Relations Council of Greater Philadelphia, Mayor Tate quickly appointed a special committee to work on restitution claims. Damage claims upon the city ranged from $500 to $25,000; reimbursements from $65 to $2,000. The destruction was heaviest along Columbia and Ridge Avenues, the two major arteries of the district.

Some civil-rights workers and Negro civic leaders have theorized that most of the stores that were hit had earned the enmity of the area's residents, while merchants with good neighborhood relations were passed over. Actually, this theory has little basis in fact. An analysis of the riot pattern shows that in the two areas of greatest damage, west of Broad Street, the violence was wholesale, the stores clearly identified as Negro-owned being virtually the only exceptions. In a third, minor storm center east of Broad, and other areas that were less thoroughly devastated, indications are that the rioters were motivated more by the desire for loot than for revenge.

A food store belonging to the most chronic scofflaw in the annals of the Health Department was not molested, while retailers known to have good neighborhood relations suffered severe losses. In fact, David Kronick, assistant director of the Milk and Food Section of the Environmental Health Division of the Department of Health, reported later that in none of the riot areas did the department "find any correlation between the number of violations incurred by a store and the treatment it received during the riots."

The first outbreak, on Friday night, was more destructive than any that followed. Within a five-block radius of "riot ground zero," where the Bradford incident took place, only 54 properties out of 170 escaped damage. All but two were easily identified as Negro-owned or -operated; most had window signs to that effect. Of the two properties that came through unscathed, one was a Chinese restaurant which bore a sign reading, "We are colored too"; the other belonged to an osteopath who was indicted as an abortionist a year later.

Negro proprietors who lived some distance from their establishments and were unable to get to their stores in time to put identifying signs in their windows did not fare as well as their resident neighbors; the few Negro stores that were ransacked had no identifying insignia. Clearly the enemy was not all merchants, or even all bad merchants, but the white merchants; not all owners of property, but the *white* establishment, most visible, best symbolized and most vulnerable behind the plate glass windows in the black ghetto.

The second hardest hit section was Strawberry Mansion in the northwest corner of the riot area—the last of the North Central Philadelphia Jewish neighborhoods to turn Negro and still a district with a higher percentage of homeowners, a higher annual income and a higher level of education than other sections of the riot zone.

Two of North Philadelphia's three newspapers are based in Strawberry Mansion. One is a conventional neighborhood weekly; the other, *Nite Life,* is a booster of blackness which many white businessmen look upon as a "hate sheet." It devotes the third page in each of its weekly issues to attacks against unidentified "dishonest merchants," and to ads for neighborhood stores, most of which are unmistakably identified by pictures of the Negro proprietors. A streamer above these ads reads: "These Merchants are Part of You and Your Community. Spend Your Dollar with Them, Because They Respect You and Your Dollar. These Merchants are for Advancement of Our Community." Some of the white merchants are convinced that such "buy-black" appeals helped fan the riot flames.

Although looting accompanied most of the attacks on stores and property, few would argue that this was the sole motivation for the onslaughts. When the fury of the riots had subsided, some civilian leaders suggested that resentment against the practices of some merchants and other economic pressures on the poor had contributed to the holocaust.

Cash and Credit

Negroes, like everybody else, tend to shop in their own neighborhood because it is at hand and because they feel more comfortable there. This tendency is reinforced by the clothing store's "lay-away" plans and the furniture appliance dealer's "easy-credit" offers.

Even when they buy for cash, poor Negroes are ready prey for sharp practice. Often illiterate and largely ignorant of their lawful rights, they are tempting subjects for overcharging, shortchanging and misrepresentation. And the further away Negro consumers move from cash transactions, the more opportunities they open for their own financial defeat.

Lay-away plans invite buyers to reserve an item for which they have insufficient ready cash by making a small deposit and a promise of payments that will eventually make the merchandise theirs. If the merchandise is clearly price-tagged and the lay-away purchase properly receipted—and if the customer keeps a careful record of all his payments—his only penalty may be the higher price often charged for merchandise in the area. If the purchase is not properly receipted, or the customer keeps no record, and the proprietor is unscrupulous, the transaction can become very expensive indeed.

But even more costly to the Negro consumer is the practice of buying goods on credit, a method of financing employed by some clothing stores and most furniture and appliance dealers in North Philadelphia as in other poor neighborhoods, Negro and white, in all parts of the country.

The "easy-credit" system need not involve higher than lawful interest rates in order to spell trouble for poor buyers. Bait advertising lures customers into the stores and high-pressure salesmen push untagged merchandise at whatever price the traffic will bear, with the tempting notion of paying a little bit down and enjoying the use of the merchandise while the balance is paid off, a little each week. People who start out with the intention of paying cash for a moderately priced item often find themselves buying much more luxurious—or simply much higher priced—merchandise than they had originally intended.

"Bait advertising and high-pressure techniques are used on everybody," explains the Reverend William Gray, "but Negroes are more likely to succumb. People tell me—I don't know how many times I've heard it—that they see a TV advertised on sale for $120 and that they end up buying a color set for $700."

The result is that many families in North Philadelphia are saddled with heavy credit obligations which reach crisis proportions when income is suddenly reduced by illness or unemployment. . . . When the financially disabled buyer is unable to meet the regular payments to which he has committed himself—or the added burdens of late penalties and constable court fees—his purchase is "repossessed" by the merchant or the loan company to whom the latter has discounted the credit contract. All that has already been paid—often as much as 50 or 60 per cent of the total cost—is lost. It's all quite legal, of course, but it makes the man who has lost both his money and his television set sullen and angry. And if, as sometimes happens, he later sees, or thinks he sees, the same television set or window fan or kitchen range in the home of his sister or his cousin or his aunt, who has started payments anew, repossession looks suspiciously like confiscation and sullen anger turns to seething range.

Even buyers with the ability to pay frequently find themselves with merely the fiction of possession because the products they have purchased break down before the payments are completed. Lacking any information about legal recourse available to them, some buyers resignedly continue payment on the faulty merchandise; others simply stop payments only to discover that in these circumstances they, and not the merchant who cheated them, are on the wrong side of the law.

Food

Food stores, with few exceptions, sell for cash; hence, there are no credit entanglements behind the North Philadelphians' resentment of the food merchants. Nor does the resentment stem primarily from price policies, although a random check of standard food items in a Columbia Avenue supermarket and one in center city indicated that North Central Philadelphia food prices were about 5 per cent higher than downtown. (Independent grocery stores are more expensive in both areas but comparable to each other.) Nevertheless, the rioters reserved some of their wildest ravages for the 69 food stores they invaded.

Some observers believe that the food stores attracted many rioters simply because their goods are portable and of universal value. Others, however, are convinced that the rioters were reacting to the food merchants' reputation for underweighing, shortchanging and selling stale or rotten food.

According to City Commissioner Maurice Osser, the food merchants are guilty of proportionately more offenses with respect to underweighing and shortchanging than other proprietors in the area. The charge that food merchants sell rotten food is for the most part not true, but there has been evidence of the practice in the past.

"Up until six or seven years ago," Health Department official David Kronick acknowledged, a "fast trade in salvaged food" brought tons of burnt-out and train-wrecked stock to the shelves of North Philadelphia stores. But in recent years, he declared, "Columbia Avenue has been average in regard to the number of violations."

Perhaps the most important fact about consumer relations in North Philadelphia is that most people are either unaware that there are agencies to help them or have no faith in their desire to do so. They rarely call upon the services of private and quasi-public organizations like the Better Business Bureau and the Legal Aid Society. And, not unlike the vast majority of consumers, they have virtually no contact with the Bureau of Weights and Measures, whose job it is to enforce state and Federal standardization laws, insure the use of accurate measuring devices and uncover unfair merchandising practices.

It can be questioned whether the Bureau of Weights and Measures in Philadelphia displays the maximum concern for its most abused wards. "Let them holler," declared one high official to a researcher. "Who listens?"

"The Columbia Avenue shopping area," acknowledged City Commissioner Osser, is one of the worst in the city for violations like shortweighing and overpricing. "But," he added, "we make more routine visits there. More charges are made there than in any other area of the city."

Deputy Commissioner Anthony Sadowski, in charge of the Bureau, confirmed the commissioner's appraisal. "Certainly, Columbia Avenue is a problem area," he admitted. "But every merchant who is cited is brought before a magistrate." However, the Bureau has consistently refused to open its records of complaints and convictions to the public.

Despite charges of sharp practice, the merchants of the Columbia Avenue area are not making inordinate profits. Columbia Avenue is not the place to get rich quick. (A high rate of credit default and an excessive amount of stealing are the merchants' most frequent complaints.)

Almost all of the members of the Columbia Avenue Businessmen's Association have been on the street between 20 and 30 years. Few new businesses have been added in the past five years. The bankruptcy rate is 50 per cent during the first year; 50 per cent of the remaining businesses go under by the fifth year. "Nowadays," commented longtime resident and civic leader, Robert Alexander, Negro manager of Milady's Shoe Store, "when a business closes up, the place stays empty. It is very hard to get new business here. And every time a store goes, some jobs go for the people who live here. We need these jobs."

Negroes and Jews

Since the overwhelming majority of the white businessmen in the riot zone are Jewish, the question has been raised whether the merchants were attacked because they were white or because they were Jewish. The residents of the area are very much aware of the ethnic and religious differences, and there is, in fact, some anti-Jewish sentiment, which grows, in part, out of the economic facts of life. But not one eyewitness to the riot recalls the mobs shouting anti-Semitic slogans, although anti-white epithets abounded. Nor is there anything to suggest that the results would have been appreciably different had the majority of the white merchants been of Italian, Swedish or German background.

The history of the Jews and of North Philadelphia combined to make the Jewish merchants the major representatives of the white establishment in the area. But it was as whites and as merchants and realtors rather than as Jews *per se* that they bore the brunt of the Negroes' attack. Anti-Semitism was not a primary factor in the rioting.

Nevertheless, the Jews do have a special and ambiguous position in the Negro ghetto. In every large city, Jewish organizations and individuals have long been in the forefront of the civil-rights campaign. In Philadelphia, two white board members of the NAACP are Jews, as is the only white elected official from North Central Philadelphia, State Senator Charles Weiner. The two Negro-oriented radio stations in the city are owned by Jews. It is likely that many, if not most, of North Philadelphia's residents are treated by Jewish doctors, advised by Jewish lawyers and served by Jewish community agencies.

But the landlord, too, is likely to be Jewish, as is the grocer and the man who owns the appliance store on the corner. All too often the Negro sees himself as a victim of their exploitation, and the contrast between himself and the more affluent businessmen of the community generates bitterness and resentment.

And finally, there is a widespread feeling among Negroes that Jews, as members of a group so often victimized by prejudice, owe a special solidarity to the Negro people. The demand, conscious or unconscious, is that Jews behave better than other whites in their dealings with Negroes. Whenever this expectation fails to materialize, there is an added feeling of disappointment and betrayal. The result is often a particularly irrational Negro anti-Semitism, which responsible elements in the community, both Negro and white, work hard to combat.

"HEY, JEW BOY" (1968)

This is a poem composed by a black New York City teenager about relations between black and Jews.

Hey, Jew boy, with that yarmulka on your head
You pale-faced Jew boy—I wish you were dead;
I can see you Jew boy—no you can't hide,
I got a scoop on you—yeh—you gonna die.

When the U.N. made Israel a free independent state
Little four- and five-year-old boys threw hand grenades
They hated the black Arabs with all their might
And you, Jew boy, said it was all right.

Then you came to America, land of the free,
And took over the school system to perpetuate white
    supremacy;
Guess you know, Jew boy, there's only one reason you
    made it—
You had a clean white face, colorless and faded.
I hated you Jew boy, because your hang-up was the Torah,
And my only hang-up was my color.

TABLES: 1. ATTITUDES TOWARD JEWS—NEW YORK CITY, 1969 2. ATTITUDES TOWARD JEWS—UNITED STATES, 1978

These tables are instructive regarding attitudes toward Jews among New York City blacks in 1969 and among black residents of the United States in 1978.

ATTITUDES TOWARD JEWS: NEW YORK CITY, 1969

	Total Non-Jewish Whites	Blacks
NEGATIVE:		
Most slum lords are Jewish		
Agree	34%	73%
Disagree	21	8
Not sure	45	19
Jews are richer than other people		
Agree	36	69
Disagree	44	16
Not sure	20	15
Jews more a race than a religion		
Agree	32	57
Disagree	53	26
Not sure	15	17
Jews are irritating because too aggressive		
Agree	21	49
Disagree	59	28
Not sure	20	23
Between money and people, Jews will choose money		
Agree	23	71
Disagree	51	11
Not sure	26	18
Jewish businessmen will try to put over a shady deal on you		
Agree	17	62
Disagree	66	17
Not sure	17	21
Too ambitious for their own good		
Agree	11	39
Disagree	72	37
Not sure	17	24
Feel superior to other groups		
Agree	27	53
Disagree	50	22
Not sure	23	25
Stick to their own and never give outsider a break		
Agree	20	49
Disagree	67	31
Not sure	13	20

More loyal to Israel than to America		
Agree	18	52
Disagree	57	21
Not sure	25	27

Note: The total sample of blacks was 1,041.

ATTITUDES TOWARD JEWS: UNITED STATES, 1978

	Total Public	Total Blacks	Total Whites
Jews have suffered from persecution through the centuries			
Agree	75%	61%	76%
Disagree	15	17	15
Not sure	10	22	9
The same people who would like to keep the Jews down would also like to keep other minorities down			
Agree	62	67	62
Disagree	19	10	20
Not sure	19	23	18
When it comes to choosing between people and money, Jews will choose money			
Agree	34	56	32
Disagree	42	14	45
Not sure	24	30	23
Jews have supported rights for minority groups more than other white people			
Agree	29	38	28
Disagree	36	25	37
Not sure	35	37	35
Jews are more loyal to Israel than to America			
Agree	29	37	28
Disagree	42	14	45
Not sure	29	49	27
Jews are irritating because they are too aggressive			
Agree	27	29	27
Disagree	55	37	57
Not sure	18	34	16

Jews have to work harder because they're discriminated against in so many places			
Agree	27	37	25
Disagree	55	37	57
Not sure	18	26	18
Most of the slumlords are Jewish			
Agree	20	41	17
Disagree	36	19	38
Not sure	44	40	45

JEWISH WOMEN'S GROUPS: SEPARATE—BUT UNEQUAL? (1970)

This selection, written by Doris Gold, deals with the apparently "second-class" status of women in Jewish organizational life. The power and influence were invariably held by men.

A public bus on New York City's Fifth Avenue moves by, bearing a brightly lit blue and white arrow advertising HADASSAH. We think about being a Jewish woman on our way to a women's organization event at midday. While there is a burst of pride in our visibility, we wonder whether the phenomenon of almost a million women members in 18 to 25 separate Jewish women's groups is appropriate at a time when there is again a female emancipatory trend in the land.

It was in this mood that we talked and corresponded with several national Jewish women's organization leaders, a woman editor of a Jewish publication, some Jewish women "actives," and queried a rabbi and some Jewish male professionals for balance. We asked all of them for an opinion on a key question: whether the existence of Jewish women's organizations, both independent and "divisions" of male-dominated organizations, indicated that women lacked equal status in Jewish community life? Other questions dealt with the possible barriers experienced by women in working together with men in the Jewish Establishment; the preference of Jewish women for voluntary rather than paid professional jobs in the Jewish community; the "feminizing" of synagogue life, and last, what seemed to be the future trend of Jewish women's organizations.

Most of the women's leaders were emphatic in their contention that their separation in no way indicated that they were second-class citizens of the Jewish community. . . .

Even if one does accept the view that Jewish woman's organizational separatism may be a stage in the transitional process of her greater emancipation in Jewish life, it is this writer's observation after many years in and out of the Jewish Establishment, that it is more possible to buck the resistance to her intellectual acceptance, her personal worth, in fact, through having, as Virginia Woolf put it, "a room of one's own." It seems to us that the force of male authority and patriarchy is still very strong in the institutional life of the Jewish community, and one which has originally assigned certain tasks to Jewish women to do its "housekeeping."

We believe there are other reasons to be found for the proliferating separatism of the women and the concomitant increased duplication and fragmentation of Jewish community life. It seems to us that somewhere along the way in their American advance, Jewish women took a more comfortable detour (as did non-Jewish women, cited by Dr. Jessie Bernard, a sociologist) from self-awareness or serious vocational preparation. They opted for the role of "organization woman" who could attain status and yichus [importance] in the eyes of the men, even incidentally "beating them at their own game" in being as good or better money-raisers and becoming their own "power elite," albeit as "sorority sisters." It is evident that even those many women who are Jewishly educated and highly competent do not seriously vie for a place in the Jewish community, with the exception of some in Zionist circles and among Yiddishists.

All this does not imply that the many outstanding leaders of national Jewish women's organizations who labor mightily in their vineyards, exhibiting sophisticated Jewish identity and humanistic scope, are not "achievers." But their very stance of modesty, reticence and moral concern may be too much of a good thing for their own self-development and for greater maturity in male–female relationships in the American Jewish community.

The most striking example of the reticence of Jewish women to take up cudgels in their own behalf is the fact that only two independent women's groups are represented in the Conference of Presidents of Major Jewish Organizations. The others are represented via their male parent sponsors, or not at all. Mrs. Virginia Snitow, American Jewish Congress' Women's Division President, told us of movements afoot to consolidate Jewish women leaders at least into a consultative group, and remarked that ". . . the whole idea of standing up to be counted," of "feminism as the women see it, makes them timid of expressing themselves. They seem to feel that when they have an idea or want to raise an issue they must look for a man to 'represent' them, to give it 'legitimacy.' " . . .

It is clear that Jewish women's groups have already created a mass Jewish women's culture and style. In meeting the warm, gracious and often compelling personalities of the women leaders, one sees the blending of the "suburban ideal" and Jewish morality in word and deed. It is probable that the women's divisions or auxiliaries will become more like the large independent women's groups, with their already enlarged smorgasbord of activities to please every woman's palate (and also to retain the new younger members).

While there is no doubt of the good works that will be achieved for Jewry through giant efforts such as these, there persists the feeling that what the Jewish woman may also need is greater self-esteem and individuation. Will organized Jewish women turn to themselves for self-discovery, for doubting their best-of-all-possible-worlds stance? Will the Jewish "organization woman" provide a wider choice to the Jewish women of the "emerging seventies" beyond fund-raising or community service? Will she become a truly equal partner in American Jewish community life?

BELLA ABZUG: NEW YORK CITY CONGRESSWOMAN (1971–1975)

Bella Abzug was the second Jewish woman to serve in the United States Congress. Prior to this, she had been the president of her class at Hunter College and an editor of the *Columbia Law Review*. In this autobiographical fragment, she reflects on the major issues of her time. This selection also sheds much light on her relationship to Jews and Judaism.

Bella on Bella

When I was elected to the House in 1970, I was only the second Jewish woman in the history of our nation to serve in Congress. [The first was Florence Kahn, a Republican from California, who filled her husband's Congressional term after he died in 1925 (1924), then was reelected in her own right.] I was lonely at first, an oddity—a woman, a Jew, a New Yorker, a feminist, a Nixon opponent from way back, a peace activist who passionately opposed American involvement in Indochina and just as strongly favored aid to democratic Israel. And I was past 50.

In my third term, I no longer feel lonely. The Congress is changing. It is younger, livelier, more independent. There are more women, more Jews, more minorities.

A theory has developed that while women were deliberately excluded from the political process, particularly elective office, Jews excluded *themselves,* preferring the anonymity of behind-the-scenes power to the public vulnerability of office-holding. It isn't true. We now have 21 Jews in the House, compared with 12 last year; three of us are women. But while the number of Jews has almost doubled and now reflects our percentage of the population, women remain scandalously underrepresented—only 19 out of 435 members of the House, none out of 100 in the Senate. [1976]

Sometimes I'm asked when I became a feminist, and I usually answer, "The day I was born." If I was born a rebel, I attribute it to my family heritage. My father, Emanuel

Savitzky, fled to the United States from Czarist Russia when the Russo-Japanese War of 1905 broke out [1904–1905]. He hated war. Once he told me how depressed he felt when America entered World War I. While President Wilson was proclaiming his 14-point peace settlement, my father painted his own one-point peace plank outside his butcher shop on Ninth Avenue in Manhattan. He renamed it "The Live and Let Live Meat Market."

My father did not do very well in business: "Live and Let Live" is not exactly a formula for commercial success. An extraordinarily sweet-tempered man, his real love was music. On Friday nights, after the big traditional Sabbath meal, he would sing Yiddish and Russian folk songs for us in his fine tenor. My sister, Helene, would play the piano. I scraped bravely away at the violin. (An interviewer once asked my mother what she thought of my political career. "Oh, I knew Bella would be a success," she said, "because she always did her homework and practiced her violin.")

When my father wasn't singing, his favorite Caruso records were on the victrola. Our seven-room railroad flat would be filled with the plaintive melody of the "Pearl Fisher's Lament." We weren't rich; but we never lacked for anything essential.

My father and mother, who remembered the East European ghettos, considered themselves incredibly lucky to be living in the South Bronx, now one of the worst urban disaster areas in the country, but then a pleasant, almost rural neighborhood, paradise compared to the unspeakable (then and now) immigrant slums of the Lower East Side.

In my childhood fantasies, God and my grandfather were indistinguishable. Wolf Tanklefsky was my mother's father; three times a day, he went to shul, and, when I wasn't in school, he would take me along. I learned the prayers by heart, and my grandfather delighted in standing me on a table and having me demonstrate to his cronies my precocity in Hebrew. Then I would be sent to sit in the balcony with the women. When I asked why, I was told: "That's the way it is." I couldn't accept that.

We were living in the Kingsbridge section of The Bronx when my father's weak heart gave out, and he was dead at 52. I was almost 13, and every morning before school for the following year, I went to our synagogue to say *Kaddish* for him. In retrospect, I could describe that as one of the early blows for the liberation of Jewish women. But in fact, no one could have stopped me from performing the duty traditionally reserved for a son, from honoring the man who had taught me to love peace, who had educated me in Jewish values.

So it was lucky that no one ever tried.

When I was 12, I joined Hashomer Hatzair [The Young Guard], a Zionist youth organization. From then on, I was an enthusiastic Zionist who dreamed of working in a kibbutz, helping to build a Jewish national home in what was then called Palestine. Dressed in brown uniforms and ties, my friends and I rode the subways and stood in the cold on street corners, collecting pennies for our cause. It was my first venture into political campaigning, and also my first experience as a leader.

I'm not sure whether my leadership was based on ability, or on my friends' awe at what they regarded as my superior economic status. My family was lower middle class. The others in Hashomer were *really* poor. When they talked about migrating to Israel, they envisioned a land where they would be better off economically. My approach was more romantic. I had never missed a meal or worked really hard; for me, going to [a] kibbutz would be roughing it. I felt drawn to Hashomer Hatzair because of its moral fervor, social idealism and pioneering militancy. Years later, when I read that the Warsaw Ghetto uprising was commanded by a young Hashomer Hatzair leader, I was not surprised. I would not have expected anything else.

Franklin Delano Roosevelt and his New Deal were already shaping my social consciousness when I entered Walton High, an all-girls school rated among the best academic public schools in the city. My mother, always a good manager, supported us by working as a cashier or saleswoman in department stores to augment the insurance my father had left. Helene became a piano teacher; I did *not* become a violin teacher. I worked summers as a sports counselor in camps, and on weekends as a Hebrew teacher at the Kingsbridge Heights Jewish Center. I became friends with our new young rabbi, Israel Miller, who is now Chairman of the Conference of Presidents of Major Jewish Organizations, and still a friend.

When I got to Hunter College, the tuition-free, all-women's division of the City University, the Hitler regime and persecution of the Jews were on the rise. I was also taking courses at the Jewish Theological Seminary. For the students of my generation, the war in Spain, the need for collective action to oppose the threat of Nazism and the persecution of the Jews, were the searing issues of the day. We had demonstrations, marches, campus strikes; we swapped our silk stockings for lisle in protest against the sale of the Sixth Avenue El as scrap iron for Japan. I transferred much of the intensity I had learned in Hashomer Hatzair to the political campaign to save democratic Spain from the Fascists, who were being openly supported by Hitler and Mussolini while our government and the rest of the western democracies remained neutral. I still remember the gloom, the foreboding we felt in 1939 when the Spanish Republican Army finally collapsed and World War II followed within months. I remember our outrage when, the morning after the Japanese bombed Pearl Harbor, we went to school to find our professors calmly discussing the English Romantic poets while President Roosevelt was coming before Congress to get a declaration of war.

My class graduated into an America at war, and for the next few years, all our thoughts and activities were bound up in the helping to win that struggle. I worked for a defense contractor for a while, and then enrolled at Columbia Law School. By the time the war ended, I had met and married Martin Abzug, a young businessman who sat up nights working on his novels. Soon we were raising a family and at the same time I was trying to make my way in the legal profession.

Many of my Columbia classmates went into Wall Street firms or government. I specialized in labor law and later opened my own office, handling mostly tenants' rights and civil liberties cases. In the years that followed, I became active in Reform Democratic politics and in the women's movement to halt nuclear testing and the proliferation of nuclear weapons. Finally, I was elected to Congress.

I have moved from Orthodoxy to a Conservative synagogue affiliation; I no longer eat only kosher food; usually I'm in shul only on holidays—and for speaking engagements, which I can never resist because my grandfather would be so proud to see me in a pulpit. I've visited Israel several times, but I'm not going to settle there on [a] kibbutz [collective settlement]. Yet it was a dream worth every minute of the dreaming, because it made me a Zionist, it made me a political activist, it kept me a rebel.

Sometimes, in Congress, I get pressure from Jewish constituents who take a narrow view of American foreign policy.

A few people asked me to modify my stand against the Vietnam War, to go along with State Department policy in Southeast Asia so as not to jeopardize American support for Israel. Secretary Kissinger tried to play on these fears when, in the final days of the conflict, he raised the same argument in a hopeless attempt to gather support for military aid to the crumbling regime of President Thieu. I always thought it was insulting to link Israel, a unified and courageous democracy, to a corrupt dictatorial regime like Thieu's, and I never accepted this view, nor did most supporters of Israel.

Similarly, during the height of the impeachment crisis, I received some telegrams from Jewish constituents, sternly advising me not to dare say a word against President Nixon for fear it might hurt the U.S. relationship with Israel. Again, I could not accept that. And I was glad to see that the vast majority of America's Jews never allowed their fears for Israel to overwhelm their sense of what was the right behavior for our country on other issues. (I've always wondered how Rabbi Korff felt when he read Nixon's anti-Semitic remarks in the tape transcripts.) [Rabbi Baruch Korff was a devoted friend of Nixon.] How could it possibly help Israel to tie our relationship with her to the fate of a discredited President or to the continuation of a discredited war?

We have to fight for what we believe in, no matter what the pressure against us. As Congressional adviser to our delegation at the International Women's Year Conference in Mexico City last June [1975], I urged our delegates to reject the totally unacceptable statement that Zionism must be eliminated along with colonialism and apartheid. The attack on Israel was not what we women came to Mexico for. We should have been contributing to a global dialogue on the subject of peace; instead, the anti-Israel bloc manipulated the women, utilizing the women's conference for political purposes, and we got the Declaration of Mexico, tainted with the UN anti-Zionist rhetoric that set the stage later for adoption of the outrageous General Assembly resolution. [November 10, 1975, the United Nations General Assembly adopted an Arab-backed resolution that Zionism was "a form of racism and racial discrimination."]

I am proud that the United States delegations voted against both statements. As a member of Congress, I was even prouder when both the House and the Senate, in an action of solidarity with Israel and the Jewish people, unanimously voted to condemn the Assembly action and when women members of Congress joined me in an appeal to the Assembly not to approve the Declaration of Mexico.

I have never enjoyed a speaking engagement so much as my appearance before the First National Conference on the Role of Women in Jewish Life, in New York, February, 1973. The organizers felt the time had come to examine Jewish law and custom through the sensitized eyes of feminist consciousness, to adapt Jewish traditions to a contemporary society in which women sought equality with men in all aspects of their lives.

It was all very new at the time—but in the ensuing years, there has been a significant shifting of attitudes, a shake-up in the traditional feminine roles in the Jewish community. "That's the way it is" no longer is an adequate answer.

For me, the new consciousness in the Jewish community and throughout the country was perfectly expressed the day I arranged for Rabbi Sally Priesand to deliver the opening prayer at the House of Representatives.

She was the first Jewish woman to do so.

She was the first *woman* to do so.

At that moment, I felt that two movements for social progress had merged and come of age. And I really felt at home in Washington.

JEWISH RENEWAL AT HOME (1979)

This selection comes from the campaign literature of the United Jewish Appeal, an umbrella organization for local Jewish federations all over the country. It presents the agenda and concerns of the American Jewish community. Israel's Jewish Agency is a major beneficiary of funds raised in America to support its programs in social services, education, absorption of immigrants, and so on.

Jewish Renewal at Home: The Role of the American Jewish Community

A Definition

Achieving much but falling short . . . difficulties in expanding or even maintaining programs in the face of persistent inflation . . . curtailed and postponed services . . . unmet needs . . .

The words describing what our regular campaigns have done—and failed to do—in support of human needs in Israel can be applied as well to our local services and programs.

As the new era of Jewish Renewal begins, what must also be applied in our communities is the same zeal the people of Israel have shown in:

identifying unmet needs;

determining where and how serious shortcomings in current services are denying needed aid and comfort; and

formulating realizable goals and achievable programs.

The immediate effect will be to move our campaigns off the dead center of plateau giving to new peaks.

The long-range effect will be to move our communities substantially ahead in our life-renewing work at home.

Interdependence of Jewish Renewal

In naming their vast program of social rehabilitation for 45,000 immigrant families "Project Renewal," the people of Israel have sounded the keynote of our 1979 campaign.

All contributors will have the privilege of participating in that project through capital fund opportunities and special fund giving—the form to be determined by each community. *The privilege will be available only on the basis of an increased pledge to the regular campaign.*

In structuring the 1979 campaign in this way, we acknowledge the interdependence of Jewish life the world over. We recognize that we can only give strength and a heightened quality of life to our fellow Jews overseas on the basis of the strength and quality of life we achieve at home.

In organizing and planning our Jewish Renewal programs, we must also recognize that the structure of our life here is undergoing change, creating new realities, particularly affecting:

Jewish *family life;*

Our treatment of our *aging;*

The *education,* values and opportunities we give our youth;

The way we arrange the *resettlement* of the newcomers among us.

The Family

Many contemporary pressures are leading to upheaval and attrition in American Jewish family life.

Fifteen percent of households involving parents in the 20–29 year range are now headed by one parent . . .

More than half of the heads of Jewish households have no synagogue affiliation . . .

Inter-city movement of Jewish families is mounting . . .

Mid-career joblessness is affecting many American Jewish providers.

Jewish Renewal at Home means increased regular campaign funding and improved services to stabilize and strengthen Jewish family life:

Family Life Education programs;

Family-based experiences in community centers;

Expanded programs meeting the special needs of single parents;

Special group experiences for the adolescent children of divorced parents;

Big-brother and big-sister programs for children of one-parent families;

Pre-school and day care services in aid of working single parents;

Vocational services geared to families hit by mid-career joblessness;

A full range of personal and family counseling.

The Aging

The Jewish elderly, 65 years of age and over, now comprise almost 13 percent of the national Jewish population. Projections say this proportion will reach 15 percent by 1990.

One out of every five Jewish households is headed by a person of 65 or more . . . the incomes of most do not exceed $6,000 per year . . . one in every four has some degree of physical or emotional disability requiring supportive services.

Jewish Renewal at Home means increased regular campaign funding and improved services to provide the Jewish elderly with the total at-home institutional supports they need . . . for the active, productive, self-dependent lives they want to lead:

Expanded therapy services;

Vocational retraining;

Aids to neighborhood stabilization;

New apartments and residential opportunities;

Strengthened "at-home" services: transportation, housekeeping, visiting, counseling, meals-on-wheels;

Augmented recreational, cultural and educational programming;

Modernized institutional care and expanded facilities where needed;

Improved nutritional programs;

Opportunities for volunteer service.

Jewish Education, Youth Programs

Enrollment in Jewish schools at all levels has declined from 600,000 in 1961 to about 400,000 currently.

The search for values by Jewish teenagers and college students outside the Jewish heritage continues unabated. Too many of our youngsters remain unaware of the treasures of Judaism.

Community services for Jewish youths in high schools and on college campuses have been largely minimal.

For many young Jews, Israel is another "foreign country," its role in Jewish destiny unknown or misjudged.

Jewish Renewal at Home means increased regular campaign funding and improved services to make Jewish education a vital force in our communities, Judaism an enduring fountainhead of values and Jewish identity a matter of affirmation:

Increased subsidies and active recruitment programs for greater enrolment in Jewish day schools;

Intensification of the Jewish content of community camp programs;

Enriched Jewish programming in community centers;

Recruitment and training of high-quality teachers for Jewish schools;

Active participation in expanded programs of Jewish studies at universities;

Strengthened college campus programs in Jewish responsibilities for both faculty and students;

Increased community support of youth trips to Israel.

Resettlement of New Immigrants

American Jewish communities have been experiencing—and actively participating in—the first substantial new wave of immigration of Jews to the United States in many decades, largely from the Soviet Union.

Soviet Jewish immigration to North America in the first half of 1978 all but equaled the total of the entire year of 1977. This human flow will increase in 1979.

Jewish Renewal at Home means increased regular campaign funding and improved services to help the Jews of this modern exodus adjust to their new freedom and experience with democracy through expanded programs of:

Social, psychological and practical counseling and orientation;

English language training;

Retraining and employment aid toward swift self-support;

Housing and relocation;

Jewish and general education.

Jewish Renewal in Israel: The Role of the Jewish Agency

Action

The people of Israel have acted decisively in issuing in the era of Renewal.

They have committed themselves to the rejuvenation of 300,000 people—200,000 of them children—living in conditions of physical and social distress in 160 neighborhoods.

They have extended free education through high school for every child in the land.

Risking immediately increased hardship and austerity, they have opened up their economy by sharply devaluing the pound, removing or reducing subsidies on most staples, lifting monetary restrictions and curtailing government spending.

Vision

The hoped-for long-range results?

A society based on social justice and equality of opportunity, with every man, woman and child contributing to the fullest.

An end to the social gap between favored and deprived elements of the population.

More foreign investment, revitalized exports, a reduction in the unfavorable balance of trade.

Slowdown in the inflation rate, economic self-sufficiency, fiscal solvency.

Reality

The gap between vision and reality, however, remains large and troubling. On the horizon—a free, healthy, growing society and economy. Right now—continuing denial and hardship, most heavily affecting tens of thousands of Israel's marginal immigrant families:

Limited funds for social services in distressed neighborhoods, because of curtailed government budgets.

The threat of continuing school dropouts despite free tuition because economy measures have cut funds for books and supplies, hot lunch programs and special tutoring.

An inflation rate that will far exceed the hoped-for 30 per cent . . . imported goods up a minimum of 25 per cent . . . a balance of trade deficit still hovering around $3 billion. . . . a rise of up to 40 per cent in the price of basic commodities.

THE JEWISH AGENCY BUDGET FOR THE YEAR 1978/79 AND REDUCTIONS FROM 1977/78

Function	Budget 77/78	Budget 78/79	Reductions
Immigration & Absorption	$ 77.8 million	$ 66.5 million	–$11.3
Social Welfare Service	51.6 million	31.6 million	–20.0
Health Services	8.7 million	1.7 million	–7.0
Education	50.0 million	36.3 million	–13.7
Institutions of Higher Learning	52.4 million	47.4 million	–5.0
Youth Care & Training	48.8 million	37.9 million	–10.9
Absorption into Agricultural Settlements	55.6 million	30.0 million	–25.6
Immigrant Housing	37.0 million	25.6 million	–11.4
Debt Service	64.0 million	50.0 million	
Other	25.8 million	23.0 million	
Total	$471.7 million	$350.0 million	

Vision

Bridging the gap has always been the responsibility of world Jewry, through the programs of the Jewish Agency.

For 30 years, our lifeline partnership with Israel's people has been based on our commitment to assume our full share of the cost of transporting, resettling and absorbing all incoming immigrants.

The achievement has been substantial. We have helped bring more than 1.6 million immigrants to Israel, contributed to the establishment of 540 agricultural settlements and 29 development towns, and provided funds for housing, employment and a wide range of Jewish Agency health, education and welfare services to newcomers.

But we have never truly, totally carried out our partnership responsibility.

Reality

For we have never given enough. Year after year, except in response to war, we have fallen short of providing our expected share of the Jewish Agency budget. This has led to:

Budgets of austerity and desperation. For three successive years, almost every major Jewish Agency budget line—each one a thread of human hope—has had to be cut.

Deficit financing. The money we have not provided has had to be borrowed. More than 14 percent of the current budget is lost to debt repayment.

Curtailed services. Shortage of funds has stretched every Agency program to the thinnest edge—in a year when new immigration is expected to rise by 3,600.

Renewed life postponed. Tens of thousands of immigrant families we helped bring to Israel still live in substandard conditions, unabsorbed

Action

In 1979, it is up to us to reverse that process, through our campaign for Jewish Renewal.

We must meet our full share of the cost of the Agency's ongoing, life-renewing services—and of our vital community services—through a *substantially increased regular campaign.*

17. JEWISH IMMIGRATION INTO THE UNITED STATES: 1881*–1948

This table presents available figures on Jewish immigration between 1881 and 1948.

1881	8,193[†]	1899	37,415[‡]	1916	15,108	1933	2,372
1882	31,807	1900	60,764	1917	17,342	1934	4,134
1883	6,907	1901	58,098	1918	3,672	1935	6,252
1884	15,122	1902	57,688	1919	3,055	1936	6,252
1885	36,214	1903	76,203	1920	14,292	1937	11,352
1886	49,967	1904	106,236	1921	119,036	1938	19,736
1887	56,412	1905	129,910	1922	53,524	1939	43,450
1888	62,619	1906	153,748	1923	49,989	1940	36,945
1889	55,851	1907	149,182	1924	10,292	1941	23,737
1890	67,450	1908	103,387[§]	1925	10,267	1942	10,608
1891	111,284	1909	57,551	1926	11,483	1943	4,705[ǀ]
1892	136,742	1910	84,260	1927	11,639	July 1943 to	
1893	68,569	1911	91,223	1928	11,639	Dec, 1945	18,000[#]
1894	58,833	1912	80,595	1929	12,479	1946	15,535
1895	65,309	1913	101,330	1930	11,526	1947	25,885
1896	73,255	1914	138,051	1931	5,692	1948 (Jan,	
1897	43,434	1915	26,497	1932	2,755	to Oct,)	12,300
1898	54,630						

* We have no exact figures for Jewish immigration prior to 1881. Some 50,000 German Jews arrived up to 1848. No statistics are available about arrivals from Central Europe after 1848. From 1869, when greater numbers of Jewish immigrants began to arrive from Russia, through 1880, an estimated total of 30,000 landed in the United States. Of smaller contingents of Jews from Austro-Hungary and Romania who immigrated up to 1880 we have likewise no statistics.

[†] For 1881 to 1898 statistics are available only for the number of Jews admitted at the ports of New York, Philadelphia and Baltimore.

[‡] For 1899 to 1907 figures are available for Jewish immigrants at all ports of the United States.

[§] Since 1908, statistics of departure as well as of arrivals have been kept on record. For slightly different figures see Simon Kuznets, "Immigration of Russian Jews to the United States: Background and Structure," *Perspectives in American History* 9 (1975), pp. 35–124.

[ǀ] That is, the fiscal year July 1942 to June 30, 1943.

[#] The figure for July 1943 to December 1945 is an estimate.

SECRETARY OF STATE COLIN L. POWELL, REMARKS AT THE 24TH ANNUAL NATIONAL LEADERSHIP CONFERENCE OF THE ANTI-DEFAMATION LEAGUE

Colin L. Powell, former head of the Joint Chiefs of Staff and the first black to serve as Secretary of State, was a graduate of City College in New York. He has been deeply involved in efforts to bring peace to the Middle East.

Thank you very much, ladies and gentlemen for that warm welcome. . . .

The Anti-Defamation League and its work is desperately needed in a 21st-century world that is still torn by centuries-old conflicts, a world where all too often differences of color, culture and creed are treated as threats rather than as assets. The attacks of September 11th were a chilling demonstration of the extremes to which hatred can take human beings. People of every conceivable belief and background were killed, some 3,000 souls from 80 different countries.

We also saw how people of every conceivable belief and background reached out to one another, went to one another's rescue, prayed together, grieved together, went through this terrible experience together. And we saw how people of every belief and background answered President Bush's call for a global coalition against terrorism.

As a nation, we can be proud that in the darkest hours of our rage, in the darkest hours of our grief, President Bush and the American people chose the path of responsible action. We did not lash out indiscriminately. President Bush stood up before America and all the world and he made it clear that the perpetrators and abettors of the attacks were our enemies, not people of any particular faith or ethnicity.

The President made it clear that worldwide terrorism is our adversary, not Islam. And to your everlasting credit, the Anti-Defamation League and other opinion leaders all across America did exactly the same thing. And when isolated acts of hatred did occur against members of our Muslim community, our Muslim brothers and sisters, we swiftly and strongly condemned them. Our law enforcement went after those who committed those ugly crimes. And our communities rallied to the protection of their Muslim members.

America's principled response to September 11th speaks powerfully to the fundamental decency of the American people. It testifies to the human civic values that all of us share as Americans. It's part of our legacy, it's part of our strength, it's part of what makes us so admired in the world. And it tells me that the ADL's decades of educating the public about tolerance has had a real impact on the way

people think and on the way people behave in our country. It tells me that ADL's inspiring work for nearly a century has helped our society develop habits of tolerance that overwhelmingly held up, even in the most traumatic of national circumstances. . . .

Last week I met with United Nations Secretary General Kofi Annan, Foreign Prime Pique of Spain and High Representative Solana of the European Union and Russian Foreign Minister Igor Ivanov. Our "Quartet," as we call ourselves, this organization of four, committed itself to working for the realization of the vision of the Middle East, the vision of the Middle East offered by President Bush on April 4th, a Middle East where two states, Israel and Palestine, live side by side in peace and security with an internationally recognized border.

We, the Quartet, have pledged to work with the parties, with Arab governments and within the international community, to restore the hope of all the people in the region for a peaceful, secure and prosperous future. And Saudi Crown Prince Abdullah's initiative, recently endorsed by the Arab League, will also play an important role alongside President Bush's vision and the other ideas that are coming forward from a variety of quarters as we move forward.

Our strategy will consist of three elements. First, a restoration of security from terror and violence for Israelis; and for Palestinians as well, an end to the violence that is destroying their own dream. There can be no way forward unless the terror and the violence end once and for all.

Second, we must address urgent humanitarian needs and we must help build strong, accountable, democratic, market-oriented institutions for Palestinians as the basis for a vibrant state.

Third, the promotion of serious and accelerated negotiations, and to that end we are working on a meeting to be held later in the summer where we can begin to bring together the different ideas, the different visions that exist with respect to security, with respect to economic development, and with respect to a political way forward.

All three elements need to be integrated: security, a political way forward, and humanitarian and economic activity. It is crucial that the parties in the region end the violence; it is also crucial that they each have hope, both economic hope and political hope. . . .

Ladies and gentlemen, as Secretary of State, I must look at the world with clear eyes. I must listen to all points of view. I must have an open mind to all ideas. Much of what I see is troubling, from rising tensions in volatile regions, to the spread of weapons of mass destruction, and the tide of hate propaganda on the Internet. . . .

[But] despite all of the problems that I have to deal with every day, when I go home at night I reflect on a world that is still, thankfully, full of hope, full of promise. That isn't surprising for me because I look at the world through the eyes not of a Secretary of State, but through the eyes of the son of hard-working Jamaican immigrants, people who came to this country 70 years ago looking for a better life, looking for an opportunity, looking for a place to raise a family.

I see it through the eyes of the son of those hard-working Jamaican immigrants who was given the opportunity to rise and to serve his country in a number of capacities. I see the world through the eyes of a black kid from Kelly Street in the Bronx whose boyhood pals came from every ethnic background imaginable, except white Anglo-Saxon Protestant in those days. . . .

It was a time when intolerance in my own country said that I was never going to get very far in life because of the color of my skin or my background. I see all that changed. Those enemies are gone. Our nation has changed because there are people such as you, there are people all over this country, and increasingly people all over the world, who recognize that intolerance must be destroyed, that everybody must be given the right to pursue their destiny as God has given them the vision to pursue that destiny. . . .

It is that same tolerant, embracing, hopeful spirit that animates the wonderful work of the ADL and which our world needs now more than ever. By promoting tolerance, the Anti-Defamation League does invaluable service to the American people and to all mankind. For what they say about the Torah is also true about tolerance; its ways are ways of pleasantness, and all its paths are peace

---

THE RABBINICAL ASSEMBLY: STATEMENT ON INTERMARRIAGE (1972)

The Rabbinical Assembly is the organization of Conservative rabbis. It issued this statement in response to the rising rate of intermarriage and the decision of Reform Judaism to accept patrilineal descent in determining Jewishness.

Therefore, we reaffirm the following standards as set forth by the Committee on Jewish Law and Standards of The Rabbinical Assembly:

1. Matrilineal descent.
2. Rabbis and cantors affiliated with the Conservative Movement may not officiate at the marriage of a Jew to a non-Jew, may not coofficiate with any other clergy, and may not officiate or be present at a purely civil ceremony.
3. Only Jews may be members of Conservative congregations and affiliated organizations. However, non-Jewish partners are welcome to attend services and to participate in educational and social programs.
4. Ritual honors, such as *aliyot* to the Torah, are granted only to Jews. Some congregations offer non-ritual roles in life cycle events to non-Jewish family members.
5. Intermarriages should not be publicly acknowledged in any official synagogue forum. Congratulations may be extended to the parents or the grandparents of a child born to an intermarried couple provided that the child is Jewish (born of a Jewish mother, or, in the case of a non-Jewish child, if both parents have committed themselves to converting the child).
6. Sincere Jews by choice are to be warmly welcomed by our community.
7. Sensitiviy should be shown to Jews who have intermarried and their families. We should offer them opportuinities for Jewish growth and enrichment.

In the midst of our confusion and pain we should not ask of Judaism to adopt strategies which do violence to its integrity.

While the Conservative Movement acknowledges the individual and social circumstances that have given rise to an increased rate of intermarraige, it is committed to the ideological imperatives of encouraging endogamous marriages and conversions. As always, at the very heart of this movement stands our belief that we must find the proper application of traditional Jewish norms and values to the modern context.

Reference Works

S. Bayme, *Understanding Jewish History*

A. Hertzberg, *The Jews in America: Four Centuries of an Uneasy Encounter*

I. Howe, *World of Our Fathers*

J. R. Marcus, *The American Jewish Woman: A Documentary History*

P. Mendes-Flohr and J. Reinharz, *The Jew in the Modern World: A Documentary History*

M. L. Raphael, *Jews and Judaism in the United States: A Documentary History*

S. Rezneck, *Unrecognized Patriots: the Jews in the American Revolution*

H. M. Sachar, *A History of the Jews in America*

Chronology

1654	Peter Stuyvesant greets Jews.
1655	Stuyvesant is ordered by Dutch West India Company to allow Jews of New Amsterdam to engage in trade and own real estate.
1665	Jews in New York are granted freedom of worship by English governor
1730	She'arith Israel opens Mill Street Synagogue, first synagogue in North America.
1749	Jews in Charleston, S.C., found Kahal Kadosh Beth Elohim.
1755	She'arith Israel opens synagogue and community all-day school.
1763	Jews of Newport, R.I., open their synagogue, Touro Synagogue.
1781	Haym Salomon raises funds to finance the Revolutionary War.
1791	George Washington replies to letters sent to him by Jewish congregations.
1794	Charleston, S.C., dedicates first synagogue building, Congregation Beth Elohim.
1826	Congregation Bnai Jeshurun is founded in New York by German Jews.
1831	Isaac Leeser (1806–1868) of Congregation Mikveh Israel of Philadelphia is the first Jewish minister to preach in English.
1840	Jews—of whom there are 15,000—assemble in a number of cities to protest Damascus Blood Libel.
1846	First congregation in Chicago is founded—Kehillath Anshe Ma'arav—with 15 Jews. First Ashkenazic synagogue (of English, German, Polish Jews) is established in Montreal, Canada—later to be known as Sha'ar ha-Shamayim.
1848	A failed revolution in Germany spurs emigration to America
1852	Judah P. Benjamin (1811–1884) is elected to U.S. Senate; he is offered a seat on the Supreme Court by President Millard Fillmore but declines the offer.
1853	Oheb Shalom is established in Baltimore, the first Positive-Historical congregation; it is headed by Benjamin Szold (1829–1902).
1854	Congress enacts the Kansas-Nebraska Act, establishing the territories of Kansas and Nebraska and allowing them to decide whether to permit or abolish slavery.

1855	Castle Garden, located at the tip of Manhattan Island, becomes the nation's first formal immigrant receiving station.
1860	Abraham Lincoln elected President.
1861	Civil War begins.
1865	Civil War ends with the surrender of the Confederate armies. President Lincoln is assassinated. The 13th Amendment, prohibiting slavery, is ratified.
1868	Reform Temple Emanu-El, is opened in New York City.
1869	Susan B. Anthony and others found the Women's Suffrage Society.
1873	Union of American Hebrew Congregations is founded.
1874	Hebrew Union College is founded.
1879	Thomas A. Edison invents the first practical electric incandescent lamp.
1855	Nineteen rabbis of the Union of American Hebrew Congregations in Pittsburgh produce a radical statement of the principles of Judaism called the Pittsburgh Platform.
1882	The first federal immigration law is enacted.
1886	Jewish Theological Seminary is founded. Eitz Chaim yeshiva is founded. First synagogue for East European Jews opens. The American Federation of Labor is organized by Samuel Gompers.
1888	Rabbi Jacob Joseph is invited to become New York's chief rabbi.
1897	Rabbi Isaac Elhanan Theological Seminary (RIETS) is founded.
1898	East European immigrants found the Union of Jewish Congregations of America.
1899	The International Ladies' Garment Workers' Union (ILGWU) is founded.
1911	A fire kills 147 women and 21 men at the Triangle Shirtwaist Company in New York City
1913	Solomon Schechter founds United Synagogue of America, lay organization of the Conservative movement.
1914	Bernard Revel reorganizes RIETS and merges it with Eitz Chaim yeshiva. World War I begins. President Wilson declares American neutrality.
1917	United States declares war on the Central Powers. Bolshevik Revolution occurs in Russia.

1919	Rabbinical Assembly of America is established, the central rabbinical organization of the Conservative Movement.		Atomic bombs dropped on Hiroshima and Nagasaki. Japan surrenders. United Nations is founded.
1920	The 19th Amendment grants suffrage to women.	1949	NATO is established.
		1950	Korean War begins.
1922	Mordecai Kaplan founds Society for the Advancement of Judaism.	1954	*Brown vs. Board of Education of Topeka.* The Supreme Court rules against the doctrine of "separate but equal" in public education.
1928	Yeshiva College opens, the first liberal arts college under Jewish auspices combining traditional religious education with general studies at the college level.	1955	The Rabbinical Assembly rules that women may be called to the Torah.
		1960	John F. Kennedy elected President.
1929	The stock market crashes, signaling onset of the Great Depression.	1962	President Kennedy appoints Arthur Goldberg to replace Felix Frankfurter, who has resigned from Supreme Court because of poor health.
1932	Benjamin Nathan Cardozo is appointed associate justice of the Supreme Court.	1963	Kennedy assassinated. Lyndon Johnson succeeds him.
1933	First New Deal legislation enacted.	1964	Congress passes Civil Rights Act.
1935	Rabbinical Council of America is organized.	1965	Race riots take place in Los Angeles. American troops sent to Vietnam.
1936	Rabbi Moshe Feinstein (1895–1986) emigrates to the United States from Russia. Central Conference of American Rabbis supersedes Pittsburgh Platform with Columbus Platform, which is more traditional and favors Zionism.	1973	The Rabbinical Assembly rules that women may be part of a prayer quorum (minyan).
		1974	President Nixon impeached and later resigns.
		1977	Rabbi Norman Lamm succeeds Rabbi Belkin as head of Yeshiva University.
1939	Agudas Yisrael of America is founded. Felix Frankfurter is appointed to the Supreme Court, replacing deceased Benjamin Cardozo. World War II begins.	1982	Severe recession begins. Marines killed in terrorist attack in Beirut.
		1983	The Central Conference of American Rabbis votes to recognize as Jews persons with one Jewish parent, even if it is the father; Conservative Judaism rejects this position. The Jewish Theological Seminary votes to admit women to its rabbinical course of study.
1940	Rabbi Menachem Mendel Schneersohn, the Lubavitcher Rebbe, flees Nazism, settling in the Crown Heights section of Brooklyn. Saul Lieberman (1898–1983), an outstanding scholar of Talmud, joins the faculty of the Jewish Theological Seminary.	1986	Democrats regain control of Senate.
		1988	The Rabbinical Assembly issues *Emet VeEmunah*, the first official statement of the principles of Conservative Judaism.
1941	Rabbi Aaron Kotler arrives in the United States from Japan. He settles in Lakewood, N.J., and establishes the Beth Medrash Govoha. Japan attacks Pearl Harbor. United States declares war on Japan, soon after declares war on Germany.	1991	Soviet Union dissolves after failed coup attempt.
		1992	Bill Clinton elected President.
		1996	Congress passes and Clinton signs major welfare reform bill, minimum wage increase, and health-insurance reform.
1943	Rabbi Samuel Belkin (1911–1976) becomes president of Yeshiva College.	1999	Clinton impeached and acquitted.
1944	Allies invades Normandy. Roosevelt reelected for a fourth term as President.	2000	George W. Bush elected President.
		2001	Terrorists destroy New York's World Trade Center and damage Pentagon. Military action against Afghanistan.
1945	Germany surrenders.	2003	War against Iraq.

10

THE JEWS IN CANADA

EARLY SETTLEMENT

Until the British conquered New France in 1759, there was no Jewish community in Canada. Jews, like Protestants, were forbidden by the French to settle in Canada. The charter of the Company of New France, granted in 1627, stipulated that the colony was to be populated by Catholics of French stock. The British conquest changed things, however, and Jews were now permitted to live in Canada.

The first Jews in Canada were soldiers in the army of Major-General Lord Jeffrey Amherst. These military men were soon joined by other Jews from Britain and from the Thirteen Colonies. The Jewish community, however, remained small. The first official census, taken in 1831, showed 107 Jews, while the census of 1841 showed only 154.

For the most part, Jews lived in Montreal. They were a small group, usually well-to-do and brought up in the prevailing language and culture. Jews were regularly invited to the governor's parties. They participated in gatherings of such groups as the Saint George's Society, the Saint Andrew's Society, and the Saint Patrick's Society. Young Jewish men were fre-

Aaron Hart

quently invited to join His Majesty's militia, and many accepted this offer.

Among the first Jews in Canada was Aaron Hart. Born in England in 1724, he came to Canada as commissary officer to Amherst's troops. He remained in Canada, becoming prominent in the fur trade and in other ventures. It has been suggested that he, more than any other individual, was responsible for the development of the town of Trois Riviéres into a vital trading center. When he died in 1800, British newspapers described him as one of the wealthiest British subjects living outside the British Isles.

Another prominent Jew was Henry Joseph. Born in England in 1775, he came to Canada at the close of the 18th century. Together with his brother-in-law, Jacob Franks, and his father-in-law, Levy Solomons, he established one of the largest chains of trading posts in Canada through the then wild and thinly populated Northwest. He also owned and chartered so many ocean-going ships for freight traffic between England and Canada that some feel he virtually founded the Canadian merchant marine.

The second half of the 19th century brought a significant increase in Jewish immigration to the Americas. Europe was torn by war, revolution, and prejudice, while the New World was underpopulated and wanted immigrants to come. An immigrant population would also provide a badly needed labor force.

The first to move to the Americas were thousands of German Jews, as discussed in Chapter 9. Few of these Jews came to Canada, settling in the United States instead. Later in this period, however, a virtual tidal wave of Jews came to North America from Russia, Poland, Latvia, Lithuania, Romania, and parts of Austria and Hungary. This migration had considerably greater impact in Canada.

The period between 1871 and 1901 was one of rapid development in Canada, as its population rose

The section of Canada's Bill of Rights granting equal rights to Jews.

from 3.7 million to 5.4 million. Immigration accounts in large measure for the growth, as the government saw it as a way to fill the country, especially western Canada. It is estimated that roughly 15,000 of the immigrants were Jews.

The real flood of immigration from Eastern Europe began in 1900. From 1900 to 1925, the population of Canada grew from 5.4 million to 8.8 million. In the same period, however, its Jewish population went from under 17,000 to roughly 125,000.

The number of Jews had grown exponentially. Most Jews continued to live in major urban centers like Montreal and Toronto, each having 15,000 or more Jews in their population. The census indicated that the provinces with the largest Jewish populations in 1921 were Quebec (47,977) and Ontario (47,798). Some Jews, though, elected to live in smaller towns, with fewer than 100 Jewish residents.

The Great Depression of the 1930s brought a tightening of restrictions and very small immigration. The government's insistence that farmers were the only desirable immigrant and anti-immigration (as well as anti-Jewish) sentiment combined to keep the Jewish immigration figure low. Between 1930 and 1940, just 11,005 Jewish immigrants entered Canada. Two hundred families (about 900 persons), most of them refugees, were settled on farms throughout the country.

Approximately 40,000 Jews immigrated to Canada between 1945 and 1960. The Canadian Jewish Congress, founded in 1919 to assist East European

Jewry, worked hard to recruit and bring Jews from the displaced persons camps, survivors of the Holocaust, to Canada to work in the clothing, millinery, and fur trades. It succeeded in bringing 2,500 persons. Of these, 60 percent were Jews. Other immigrants included 4,500 Hungarian Jews fleeing Hungary after the 1956 uprising, as well as immigrants from Morocco, other North African countries, and some Middle Eastern countries, who came in the late 1950s.

During the 1960s and the 1970s, trends in Jewish immigration to Canada usually followed the general pattern of the country's admission policy. The general pattern has based admission to Canada on several factors: population growth, needs of the labor market, reunion of relatives, and humanitarianism. The weight given to each factor varied with the contingencies of the time.

Based on the above considerations, Jewish immigrants came to Canada between 1960 and 1980 from some 20 countries. Immigration from Morocco continued in these years, as did immigration from Romania, Czechoslovakia, and Poland. Jews came from Israel and Iraq, and Jews arrived from the Soviet Union. The largest groups came from Morocco, Israel, and the Soviet Union.

The year 1990 was a time of change in the Soviet Union. The economic situation worsened, while there was political disintegration and ethnic discord. Moreover, there was an easing of political controls in general and of emigration requirements in particular as part of Gorbachev's policies of *perestroika* (restructuring), *glasnost* (cultural freedom), and democratization. Jews found themselves especially concerned with the economic crisis, the political turmoil, and the ethnic unrest.

In 1989 about 72,500 Jews left the Soviet Union, while, in dramatic contrast, about 200,000 left the Soviet Union in 1990. Some settled in the United States, some in Israel, some in Germany or other countries. By 1996, about 10,000 Jews had come to settle in Canada. More than 60 percent resided in Toronto, while about 15 percent lived in Montreal.

In July 1999 the total population of Canada was 30.5 million, with 77 percent living in urban areas. The Jewish population was 356,000. Canada's largest

Jewish communities were Toronto (175,000) and Montreal (100,000), followed by Vancouver (30,000), Winnipeg (15,000), Ottawa (12,000), Calgary (7,500) Hamilton (5,000) and Edmonton (5,000). Between 1990 and 2000, largely due to immigration, Canadian Jewry grew by 14 percent, making it one of the fastest-growing communities in the Diaspora. A quarter of the Jews who immigrated to Canada during this period were born in the Soviet Union or its successor states, while 20 percent were born in Israel.

Anti-Semitism before World War II

Organized anti-Semitism did not appear in Canada until the 1930s under the impact of international Nazism. Adrien Arcand founded a fascist movement in the province of Quebec. The movement had a clearly anti-Semitic direction and sought to exploit French Canadian nationalist sentiments. Nationalism was encouraged by the Roman Catholic Church and was intensified by economic decline, making the Jew a convenient scapegoat.

Arcand published three weekly newspapers, filled with anti-Semitism and playing upon religious and nationalistic sentiments in Quebec. He even republished the infamous *Protocols of the Elders of Zion,* which alleged that there was an international Jewish conspiracy to rule the world.

Leaders of the Canadian Jewish Congress at the groundbreaking ceremony for the Samuel Bronfman House, national CJC headquarters in Montreal. Samuel Bronfman, honorary president, is flanked by Monroe Abbey, Q.C., president (left) and Saul Hayes, Q.C. executive vice-president. Photo Canadian Jewish Congress, Montreal.

In English Canada too there were Nazi-minded groups, but none had the impact of Arcand's movement. Arcand's movement faded, however, when he and others were interned during World War II by the Canadian government.

Canada and the Holocaust

Canada's record during the years of the Nazi Holocaust is a shameful one. During the 1930s and the 1940s Canada could find no room for the Jews. The United States accepted more than 200,000 refugees; Palestine, 125,000; embattled Britain, 70,000; Argentina, 50,000; penurious Brazil, 27,000; distant China, 25,000; and tiny Bolivia and Chile, 14,000 each. Canada, however, found room for fewer than 5,000! To every plea for permission to immigrate to Canada, the response was the same: "Unfortunately, though we greatly sympathize with your circumstance, at present Canada is not admitting Jews. Please try some other country." Usually there was no other country.

Prime Minister Mackenzie King seemed to want to placate the anti-Semitic politicians of Quebec, although he hid these concerns behind a desire for national unity. Almost every French-language newspaper had warned the government against admitting any Jews. Beyond this, the Minister of Immigration, Frederick Charles Blair, was an anti-Semite and a narrow-minded bureaucrat. He expressed concern that Canada might be "flooded with Jewish people." Moreover, Vincent Massey, Canada's High Commissioner in London, was no supporter of Jewish immigration. All of these factors contributed to preventing the immigration of more than 5,000 Jews to Canada during the Second World War.

Anti-Semitism after World War II

Until the 1960s anti-Semitism characterized only fringe groups, those on the margins of society. In the 1960s, however, a neo-Nazi movement appeared in Ontario. Led by two youthful propagandists, David Stanley and John Beattie, the group shocked the people of Toronto by holding open-air meetings in a park in the center of the city. Their Nazi regalia and inflammatory speeches were provocative in the extreme. The group attracted a great deal of attention, and its meetings were punctuated by scuffles and occasional fist fights. Jewish organizations found themselves hampered by statutes guaranteeing free speech. A coalition of Holocaust survivors finally decided to carry out an organized campaign of harassment and physical confrontation during the neo-Nazi meetings. The willingness of this group to engage speakers in combat finally led the Toronto police department to ban the meetings of the neo-Nazis. The group disbanded shortly thereafter.

In the 1980s, anti-Semitism took on a new form, as it now became paired with denial of the Holocaust. James Keegstra, a high school social studies teacher and mayor of a small town in Alberta, was charged under the anti-hate law because he had been teaching anti-Semitic ideas for years. Among his teachings were denial of the Holocaust and international conspiracy theories regarding Jews.

Another case was that of Ernst Zundel, a German immigrant in the printing business in Toronto. Zundel was accused of distributing anti-Semitic hate literature in Canada and abroad, especially material denying the historical authenticity of the Holocaust. He was convicted in 1985 and sentenced to 15 months in prison.

In each of these cases, Jewish community organizations, especially the Canadian Jewish Congress, discussed below, and B'nai B'rith, exerted steady pressure on government to act. This reflected a consensus in the Jewish community that public displays of anti-Semitism had to be dealt with severely, using the power of the law when available.

In 2000 the violence between Israel and the Palestinians led to an upsurge in anti-Semitic incidents in various parts of Canada.

Synagogues

Synagogues are a vital institution in the Jewish community, and Canada has every type of synagogue. Some are Orthodox, some are Conservative, and some are Reform. Some congregations define themselves as Reconstructionist, Traditional, or Humanistic.

Consider, for example, the two largest communities of Jews in Canada, Montreal and Toronto. Montreal has more than 40 Orthodox synagogues, five Conservative congregations, one Reform temple,

The Holy Blossom Temple in Toronto (*below*) has its origins in the small-scale immigration of the 1840s. Then there were only a handful of Jews in Toronto: now it is a thriving community of over 100 000, with some 40 synagogues and ten Jewish schools, including the Associated Hebrew Schools where this Hanukkah ceremony is being held (*left*).

Holy Blossom Temple, Toronto.

and one Reconstructionist congregation. Toronto too has more than 40 Orthodox synagogues, eight Conservative congregations, two Traditional congregations, four Reform temples, one Reconstructionist congregation, and one Humanistic congregation.

Although community sizes are smaller in the other provinces, the distribution is similar. Thus in Winnipeg, Manitoba, there are seven Orthodox synagogues, two Conservative synagogues, and only one Reform temple. In Vancouver, British Columbia, there are four Orthodox congregations, two Conservative congregations, one Traditional congregation, two Reform temples, and one Reconstructionist congregation.

JEWISH EDUCATION

Jewish continuity depends in large measure on investing the resources of the community in Jewish education. The Toronto Jewish community has 30 elementary day schools and 14 high schools that serve more than 9,000 students. Supplementary schools are available to those families that choose to send their children to the public schools.

Among the various high schools is the Community Hebrew Academy of Toronto, a community high school with two branches and about 1,400 students. The modern Orthodox community is served by two schools, the Or Chaim Yeshiva for boys and the Ulpanat Orot for girls, while the more right-wing Orthodox are served by other high schools and yeshivot, like the Ner Yisrael yeshiva. Some 40 percent of Jewish children in Toronto attend Jewish primary schools, while 12 percent attend Jewish high schools.

The community of Montreal also has Jewish primary schools and Jewish high schools. Recently the United Talmud Torahs of Montreal celebrated its one-hundredth anniversary. At present the school occupies two campuses, each of which comprises an

Samuel Bronfman, Canadian industrialist.

elementary school and a high school. It is unaffiliated with any movement or synagogue, although its seeks to ground students in traditional Judaism. Its current enrollment is 1,020 students.

Another high school in Montreal is the Bialik High School, which is the high school of the Jewish People's Schools and Peretz Schools system. Bialik is a Jewish coed school with an enrollment of over 560 and a staff of 60. For those committed to the ideology of Conservative Judaism, an alternative choice is the Solomon Schechter High School.

The first synagogue in Canada was established in the city of Montreal.

The Shearith Israel Synagogue, known today as the Spanish-Portuguese Synagogue, was founded in 1768.

The Spanish-Portuguese Synagogue is the oldest Jewish institution in Montreal, in Quebec, and in Canada. The first Jewish settlers began to arrive in 1760, meeting for prayer in private homes until the synagogue was formally established in 1768. In 1993 there was an ongoing series of celebrations marking the synagogue's 225th anniversary.

The synagogue is a sister congregation to other Spanish-Portuguese congregations in the New World, such as in Curaçao, New York, Philadelphia, and Newport, Rhode Island. Each of these congregations was established by traders coming from the more established communities of Amsterdam and London.

The Spanish-Portuguese tradition follows the rites and customs of the Jews expelled from Spain and Portugal beginning in 1492 who sought refuge in European lands. Other Sephardi, i.e., Spanish or

Iberian, Jews left for Mediterranean, mostly Muslim, lands. They became known as the Sephardi Oriental Jews. During the past half-century many hundreds of families from these communities have come to Montreal and have joined the synagogue, reconnecting with kin from whom their ancestors were separated 500 years ago.

The historical significance of the Spanish-Portuguese Synagogue was recognized by the government of Canada when in the 1970s the National Archives of Canada requested all its early documents and minute books. The synagogue presented its first Torah scroll to the Archives as well. It was the first scroll in Canada and is on display at the National Archives in Ottawa.

The synagogue today serves over 700 families who come from almost every country in the world in which Jews have ever lived. It is a multicultural community, reflecting Montreal life and Canadian pluralism. Although established mainly by English-speaking Jews, it has now become a bilingual community due to the arrival of numerous French-speaking families from North Africa and the Middle East.

Building of the Asociated Hebrew Schools of Toronto.

A fourth high school is the Hebrew Academy of Montreal, an Orthodox Jewish school founded in 1967. It seeks to provide an intensive program of Jewish studies integrated with a strong program of secular studies. Its curriculum stresses the religious significance of the land of Israel and the State of Israel. Another option is the Yeshiva Gedolah of Montreal, an Orthodox institution established in 1965. Its current enrollment is about 400 students.

In Montreal some 60 percent of Jewish children attend Jewish primary schools, while 30 percent attend Jewish high schools.

Montreal confronted an exceptional challenge in the late 1950s and the 1960s. Approximately 10,000 Jews came from French-speaking Morocco in the years between 1958 and 1980. The shortage of Jewish French-language services and institutions created difficulties for the Montreal Jewish community. There were no schools, synagogues, social service organizations, immigration services, or housing agencies to address the needs of the new immigrants to Canada.

Despite the enormous challenges now faced by the community, at least the needs of the immigrants for Jewish educational institutions were addressed quickly. A special Sephardic day school was opened in 1968, with significant financial assistance provided by the Ashkenazic Jewish community in Montreal. The language of instruction in this school, however, remained English.

In 1969, though, two Jewish day schools in which the language of instruction would be French were opened,

Ecole Maimonide and Ecole Sepharade. Moreover, French-language classes in the other Montreal Jewish day schools were expanded, with strong financial incentives from the Quebec government.

Although Toronto and Montreal are the largest Jewish communities in Canada, some of the smaller communities have day schools as well. There are Jewish schools, for example, in Calgary, Vancouver, Winnipeg, and Ottawa. Winnipeg and Vancouver also have high schools.

MAJOR JEWISH ORGANIZATIONS

The Canadian Jewish Congress was founded in 1919, its primary task to assist East European Jewry. The CJC represented all sectors of the Jewish community, although Reform Jews only joined in 1933. The upheaval of World War I, the desperate situation of Jews in Eastern Europe after the war, and the rise in Jewish nationalism and Zionism in many countries led Jews to campaign for a body that would represent the entire community and would speak for all Canadian Jews.

From the mid-1920s until 1934, the Congress did not function, until it was reorganized to deal with rising anti-Semitism in Canada. During the Second World War, the CJC engaged in combating Nazism, raising funds for the American Jewish Joint Distribution Committee, and settling refugees in Canada through its Refugee Committee. These efforts made the Congress the accepted representative organ of Canadian Jews and its acknowledged official voice.

Today the Congress is a representative body in which all Canadian organizations participate. It deals with matters affecting the status, rights, and welfare of Canadian Jewry, investigating and combating any anti-Semitism. It assists in efforts to improve the social, economic, and cultural conditions of Jewry, and to mitigate their sufferings throughout the world.

Delegates are appointed or elected from hundreds of organizations throughout the country, educational institutions, social and national organizations, philanthropic, labor, Zionist, and synagogue institutions. The officers and national council of the Congress are elected at a national assembly every three years. An executive committee of about 75 members is chosen by the officers and national council.

Canada also has numerous Zionist organizations. For example, Na'amat Canada, a Labor Zionist group, works to support a broad spectrum of social, educational and advocacy services operated by Na'amat Israel. Mizrachi Canada, a group of Religious Zionists, supports Torah institutions in Israel. One Zionist group, Hadassah-WIZO of Canada, an organization dedicated to the support of health, social welfare, and educational programs in Israel, has at present over 15,000 members in 247 local chapters across Canada. Although each group has its own agenda, these organizations have generally cooperated on matters of Zionist public relations and other matters of common concern.

The official representative of the organized Canadian Jewish community on matters pertaining to Canada-Israel relations is the Canada-Israel Committee. This committee communicates regularly with members of Parliament, senators, federal civil servants, provincial and municipal governments, journalists, academics, and others who have an impact on public opinion in Canada. The CIC maintains offices in Ottawa, Montreal, and Toronto.

Jews in Canadian Politics

Canada is governed currently by Paul Martin, head of the Liberal Party. The main opposition parties are the new Canadian Alliance (a reshaped Reform Party), the separatist Bloc Québecois, the New Democratic Party, and the Progressive Conservative Party. All ten provinces are led by the Progressive Conservative Party (six provinces), the Liberal Party (two provinces), or the New Democratic Party (two provinces).

Until the April 2003 election, the predominantly French-speaking Quebec was governed by the Parti Québecois, led by Premier Bernard Landry. Landry predicted during his campaign that within 1,000 days Quebec would become a sovereign state, although he failed to explain how Quebec would leave Canada and become independent. Landy and the Parti Québecois were buried in a landslide by Jean Charest and the Liberal Party. The Liberals won 46 percent of the vote,

while the Parti Québecois got only 33 percent and the Action Democratique 18 percent. More important, the Liberals gained control of the Quebec National Assembly, which selects the provincial government.

Jews have participated actively in Canadian political life, especially in Quebec and Ontario. Starting around the time of World War I, there was always a Jewish member in the Quebec Assembly, regularly elected from the Montreal riding of St. Louis and always a member of the Liberal Party. Peter Bercovitch held this seat, succeeded by Louis Fitch, who, in turn was succeeded by Maurice Hartt. In 1960, at long last, a Jew, Harry Blank, was elected to the Quebec Legislature; he was re-elected in 1962 and 1966.

In 1966, Victor Charles Goldbloom, a Liberal from the Montreal riding of D'Arcy-McGee, was elected by the largest majority of any other member in that provincial election, over 23,000 votes. Goldbloom was active in the Jewish community of Montreal and vitally concerned with any legislation affecting social reform and human welfare. In 1970, following the Liberal victory in Quebec, Premier Robert Bourassa named him to his cabinet, appointing him Associate Minister of Education. Thus Goldbloom became the first Jew in the history of Quebec to serve in the provincial cabinet. In the 1980s he served as National Commissioner of Official Languages.

Jews have been prominent in Ontario politics as well. In 1934 David Croll became the first Jewish provincial cabinet member in Canada's history. He served first as mayor of Windsor and was then elected in 1934 to the Ontario Parliament. Shortly thereafter, he was appointed Minister of Labour, Public Welfare, and Municipal Affairs. The first Jew to serve as a member of the federal cabinet was Herbert Gray, appointed in 1969 by Prime Minister Pierre Trudeau to be Minister-without-Portfolio.

Allan Grossman served in the Conservative cabinets of Premiers Leslie Frost and John Robarts, first as Minister-without-Portfolio and later as Minister of Correctional Institutions. Dr. Morton Shulman, a physician, represented the largely Christian riding of High Park as a member of the NDP. Elected to the Ontario Parliament in 1967, he fought for reforms in mental hospitals, in the treatment of prisoners, and in the regulatory procedures of financial and commercial institutions. Stephen Lewis, son of David Lewis, a leader of the NDP, was an active member of the Ontario House.

In the 1980s a number of Jews played prominent roles in public life. Robert Kaplan, Herbert Gray, Senator Jack Austin, and Gerald Weiner served in the federal cabinet. Norman Spector worked as chief of staff to Prime Minister Brian Mulroney and later as ambassador to Israel. Stanley Hartt and Hugh Segal also served as chiefs of staff. Allan Gottlieb represented Canada as ambassador to the United States, while Stephen Lewis served as ambassador to the United Nations.

Canada has had many Jewish political leaders, among them Herbert Gray, David Croll, current British Columbia Premier David Barrett, and David and Stephen Lewis. The New Democrats have exceptional Jewish leaders like the Lewises and Barrett, but federally the NDP is just a tiny party. The Liberals have never had a Jewish candidate for party leadership. Hugh Segal has contended, although unsuccessfully, for leadership of one of the two oldest parties, the Progressive Conservative Party. The prospects of a Jew being a serious candidate for Prime Minister seem remote at this point in time.

In the 2000 election, Prime Minister Chrétien was reelected. His Liberal Party increased its seats in the House of Commons by 11, winning 172 of the 301 seats. The new Canadian Alliance Party won 66 seats, while the Bloc Québecois, the Progressive Conservatives, and the New Democrats trailed far behind.

Six Jews were elected, all as Liberals: Anita Neville, a new member from Manitoba, and incumbents Herbert Grey and Elinor Caplan from Ontario and Irwin Cotler, Raymond Falco, and Jacques Saada from Quebec. Grey and Caplan retained their cabinet posts.

In 2003 Paul Martin was elected leader of the Liberal Party and replaced Chrétien as Prime Minister. He appointed Irwin Cotler as Justice Minister and Attorney General. Two other Jews, Jack Austin and Jacques Saada, were appointed government leaders, respectively, in the upper and lower houses of Parliament.

Jews in the Judiciary

Jews have served in the Canadian judiciary system since 1873, when Moses Judah Hays and Benjamin Hart were named magistrates. Only in 1950, however, was a Jew named to the high court, as Harry Batshaw of Montreal was appointed to the Quebec Superior Court. Judge Batshaw was a fine lawyer and a distinguished Jewish leader in Montreal.

Since his appointment there have been Jewish judges in most provinces. In the 1980s, Charles Dubin became chief justice of Ontario, while Rosalie Abella and Morris Fish were appointed to the Ontario and Quebec Courts of Appeal. Alan Gold served for several years as chief justice of the Quebec Superior Court.

The first Jew to be named to the Supreme Court of Canada was Bora Laskin, appointed in 1970. Laskin was a leading professor of law, who had joined the Ontario Court of Appeal in 1965. He was only 57 at the time of his appointment, but had authored important legal books and was regarded as "an architect of legal thought." One of the nine justices sitting on today's Supreme Court is another distinguished Jewish justice, Madam Justice Louise Arbour.

SUMMARY

This final chapter examined the history of Jews in Canada. The first Jews in Canada settled there after the British conquest of 1759. Only in the second half of the 19th century, however, did the Jewish population reach about 15,000, as many of those leaving Europe due to war, revolution, and prejudice, immigrated to Canada. From 1900 to 1925, though, came massive immigration, so that by 1925, the Jewish population grew to about 125,000. By the end of the 20th century, the Jewish population of Canada was 356,000.

This chapter also took a brief look at anti-Semitism in Canada. There was little anti-Semitism before the Second World War but much more during the war years. While the United States found room for 200,000 Jews, Canada found room for fewer than 5,000. Anti-Semitism after World War II took on different forms, as it became paired with denial of the Holocaust.

The Canadian Jewish community has committed itself to Jewish education, whether day schools and high schools, or supplementary schools. The communities of Montreal and Toronto are especially notable in this regard.

This chapter also examined major Jewish organizations. The Canadian Jewish Congress, for example, serves as the democratically elected, national organizational voice of the Canadian Jewish community. Especially influential in the area of Canada-Israel relations is the Canada-Israel Committee.

Finally, the roles played by Jews in Canadian politics and in the legal profession were considered. Jews have become more prominent in politics in recent decades, holding a wide variety of positions. Jews have also been judges. Judge Bora Laskin, for example, was the first Jew ever to serve in the Supreme Court of Canada.

Beyond question, the best-known Canadian Jewish writer is Mordecai Richler (1931–2001). Born in Montreal, Quebec, on January 27, 1931, he grew up in a working- class area near St. Urbain Street. His grandfather, a rabbinical scholar, had settled there after arriving in Canada in 1904, fleeing the pogroms of Eastern Europe. Richler's father, Moses Isaac, worked as a scrapyard dealer.

Richler majored in English at Sir George William University in Montreal, but left for Europe without completing a degree. He went first to Paris, then to London, where he lived from 1959 to 1972. In 1972 he returned to Canada, splitting his time between London and the eastern townships of Quebec. Richler died of cancer at age 70 in 2001, survived by his wife, Florence, and their children Daniel, Noah, Emma, Martha, and Jacob.

Richler authored several novels, among them The Acrobats, Son of a Smaller Hero, A Choice of Enemies, Cocksure, The Incomparable Atuk, Joshua Then and Now, *and* Barney's Version. *In addition, he wrote the popular children's books* Jacob Two-Two Meets the Hooded Fang *and* Jacob Two-Two and the Dinosaur.

Richler is best known for his award-winning novel, The Apprenticeship of Duddy Kravitz. *In this work he vividly portrays Jewish immigrant life in Montreal. His description of Jewish life, however, was very unsympathetic and drew much criticism from the Jewish community.*

Richler was born into a religiously observant family with a rich immigrant tradition. As a boy growing up in Montreal, he studied Talmud, leading his parents to think he might become a rabbi. He left this setting, however, at 19 to live in Europe for 20 years, in which time he produced five novels.

At some point in his life, moreover, Richler left religious tradition. Some features of Jewish tradition apparently troubled him too much. His works touch frequently on themes relating to Richler's exploration of his own Jewish identity.

The Apprenticeship of Duddy Kravitz *was published in 1959, but sold only 1,000 copies in Canada. After the release of the film version in 1974, however, sales of the book took off in Canada and around the world. Richler soon had enough income to assure him the time he needed to devote himself entirely to writing.*

Documents

HENRI BOURASSA'S CORRESPONDENCE

Henri Bourassa (1868–1952) was the father of French-Canadian nationalism. He led open opposition to Canada's participation in the Boer War in South Africa in 1899, resigning his seat in the Canadian House of Commons in protest. In his search to preserve Canadian autonomy, he founded the influential French-language newspaper Le Devoir, thinking this would be an instrument for expressing his views on the issue. His relationship with the Jews of Quebec was a complicated one, as his letters demonstrate.

1. Part of a letter to a French-Canadian Constituent (1915)

Perhaps I am mistaken, but the tendency of certain Catholics to explain everything as the action of Freemasonry and International Jewry has always seemed false to me. I am not contesting the considerable influence of Freemasonry in certain countries, nor the fact, which is very natural, indeed, that many Jews are very closely connected with the international movement. But neither of these—Freemasons and international Jews or anarchists—have acquired such influence with the widespread participation of nationals in the countries where they operate. In many cases, the enemies of the Church and the Fatherland have done without Jews and Freemasons nicely in achieving their work of destruction. These people are, in my eyes, infinitely more blameworthy than Jews and Freemasons. Besides, attributing so much effective power to Freemasonry enlarges its influence to no purpose.

I hope you will not be scandalized if I tell you that repeated reading of the works of Drumont has cured me of anti-Semitism. By dint of studying the social ills which he exposed—with some exaggeration, nonetheless—I especially retained the impression from it of the bourgeois contempt for the masses, and the scorn of certain Catholic conservatives who do not know how to, or do not want to, perform their social role. These are the two elements which are primarily responsible for social and religious decadence in all countries.

5. Part of a Letter to M. S. Bessler (1934)

Since you understand French, allow me to reply in that language to your letter of February 5th, for which I thank you cordially. I deplore as you do the stupid and coarse attacks against the Jews, without distinction between respectable and non-respectable Jews, a distinction found among all peoples and all countries at all times in history. But I have no authority to repress these attacks. All I can do—and I have done so at times, as you do well to point out—is to express my disapproval.

Besides, it seems to me that your compatriots are taking these attacks too seriously. They especially do not distinguish sufficiently between their declared enemies and certain well-intentioned although possibly ill-informed men who are suspicious of a certain number of Jews whose spirit of monopoly is becoming manifest in public or private enterprises. Instead of confusing them under the same name of anti-Semite, you should rather distinguish them clearly, despise the former and convince the latter that they are wrong. You should also urge some discretion and moderation upon certain of your defenders. Thank you for your letter.

W. L. MACKENZIE KING ON THE JEWS

William Lyon Mackenzie King (1874–1950) was a member of the Liberal Party and its leader from 1919 to 1948. He was the longest-serving Prime Minister of Canada, governing from 1926 to 1930 and then from 1935 to 1948. Mackenzie King guided Canada through World War II and introduced social programs such as unemployment insurance and family allowances. This selection was written shortly after his graduation from the University of Toronto in 1897.

The Jewish Population

Next to the Germans the Jews constitute the largest foreign population in Toronto. As is generally known, the Jews of this generation come from almost every quarter of the earth save Jerusalem, and there are accordingly Jews of many nationalities represented in Toronto. Of these, the Russian and Polish Jews are the most numerous; then there are many from Galicia, a number of German Jews, and a small minority of English. The total Jewish population is in the neighbourhood of 2,500, of which the Polish and Russian Jews constitute about three-fifths. There are from four to five hundred German Jews and from two to three hundred English. Forty years ago there was in Toronto a mere handful all told. Recent accessions have come mainly from Russia, Poland, and Galicia, in consequence of the persecutions to which the Jews were subjected in those countries. In many cases they were denied the right to possess property, the right of education, and even of residence itself outside of restricted areas. Whilst many have come direct from the continent of Europe, others have come here from the United States. The English Jews are the oldest residents, and, together with the German Jews, have been the most intelligent and prosperous of their race. It was chiefly the desire for commercial advancement that led to their coming here. Of the English and German Jews it may be said that at least 25 or 30 have gained more than ordinary prominence in commercial life and some of the best business concerns have been managed by them for a good time past. The great majority, however, whilst they are engaged in mercantile pursuits, have not attained as yet positions of much importance. A large number are occupied in the clothing trade, the manufacture and sale of jewellery and watches, diamond-cutting, the hardware business, and the manufacture and sale of boots and shoes. Almost all the second-hand clothing stores and junk shops in Toronto are owned by Jews, but the total number of these does not exceed fifty-eight. Owing, however, to a peculiarity in the city by-law which requires all such establishments to be licensed, the words "goods, wares, and merchandise," as applied to second-hand stores, do not include goods purchased at public auctions, bones, bottles, waste paper, pianos, sewing machines, or rags, and these articles, with the possible exception of pianos and sewing machines, and the addition of old iron, are precisely those which a large number of Polish and Russian Jews are busied in collecting and selling from one year's end to the other. The number of Jewish peddlers who go about the city and out among the farmers in the country is fairly large, and the quantities of old rubbish they collect and utilize is something amazing. Almost the entire rag and scrap iron trade is carried on by Jews, and of the eight pawn shops in Toronto they are the owners of four. Very few are engaged in the manufacturing industries, but a good many are contractors for the manufacture of ready-made clothing, and some have tailoring establishments of their own.

Relative Positions

The greatest disadvantage to the Russian or Polish Jews is their almost entire unfamiliarity with the English tongue, and the great difficulty they find in gaining any mastery of it. In the days of their persecutions amongst other sufferings many of them were deprived of the right of obtaining an education, and the result is that even their own language is to them of little service save as a medium of immediate conversation. Education is such a novelty to the Russian and Polish Jews that they are anxious for their children to gain the advantages of education. Accordingly, the latter are sent regularly to the Public Schools, and are kept at their books often at a considerable sacrifice to their parents. On the other hand, the language of their fathers is little used among them and promises soon to be forgotten. It is surely not an unfair inference to draw that, taking advantage as they are of the schools of this city, the younger generation of Jews will prove to be better than their fathers before them.

Their Religious Zeal

What has been accomplished in the case of their religion is already too well known to need comment here. The new synagogue on Bond Street so impressively dedicated a short time ago is an edifice which testifies more forcibly than words to the religious zeal of the Jewish people and to the place which they hold in the community today. While it is unquestionably one of the finest structures in Toronto, it is also one of the very few of the many churches in the city which are without a cent of debt. Services are held there during the morning and afternoon of every day in the week, in addition to the regular services on Saturday. A feature of importance to be noted is that the services are conducted in English. Instruction is given in Hebrew and Jewish History to the children on Saturday and Sunday.

Social Characteristics

Their families are usually large, and the houses of the poor are invariably small, but it is seldom, if ever, that two families are found living in the same house, or that sickness prevails to any extent among them. Here, again, religion has operated to affect their material condition. The "unclean thing" is rejected by the Jew; and even to the poorest among them the custom of keeping separate sets of dishes in the "milky" cupboard and the "fleshy" cupboard, is rigorously maintained. Moreover, the Jews are a very abstemious people. It is a great rarity to see a Jew the worse of liquor. They do not frequent the saloons, but when they drink have the beer brought to their houses, where it is shared by men, women and children alike. There are practically no criminals among them, and it is only when they quarrel among themselves that they give any trouble to the police. Very few of them are in a destitute condition, and it is seldom that they apply for relief outside their own members. They have in Toronto two benevolent societies, the one the Toronto Hebrew Benevolent Society, which received an annual grant of $150 from the city; and the Montefiore Ladies' Hebrew Benevolent Society. These two societies do practically all the relief work among the Jews, and their efforts are called for mostly in the case of new families who have been in the city but a short time. Many Jews are members of the local benevolent societies, the Masons, Oddfellows, Foresters, Knights of Pythias, and the Maccabees.

Most of the older Jewish residents have become naturalized, but it cannot be said that they take a very active interest in politics, although they avail themselves of the franchise. Hardly any Jews are in the employ of the city; there is, however, one of their number a letter carrier in the Post Office Department. Very few of the men are members of trade unions, chiefly because there are few unions in the trades which they follow. On the other hand, some of the most zealous advocates of unionism are Jews. and in the garment trades one of their number in particular has been unceasing in his efforts to benefit the conditions of his fellow-workers.

F. C. BLAIR ON THE JEWS

F. C. Blair, as Canada's director of immigration, attended the 1938 Evian Conference. His concerns about the immigration of Jews to Canada are expressed in the following selection.

If the nations now asked to cooperate to save the Jews of Germany and Austria, manage by sacrifice to accomplish this purpose it will please the Germans who want to get rid of this group . . . and it will encourage other nations to do likewise and this is probably the greatest danger. Can immigration countries afford to encourage such an eventuality? It is akin in a sense to the paying of ransom to Chinese bandits.

LETTER OF A. A. HEAPS TO MACKENZIE KING

A. A. Heaps of Winnipeg was a Jewish member of Parliament during the years of the Holocaust. In this letter to his friend Mackenzie King, written after the 1938 Evian Conference, he argued passionately that Canada ought to admit Jews as immigrants.

The existing regulations are probably the most stringent to be found anywhere in the whole world. If refugees have no money they are barred because they are poor, if they have fairly substantial sums, they are often refused admittance on the most flimsy pretext. All I say of existing regulations is that they are inhuman and anti-Christian. . . . Practically every nation in the world is allowing a limited number to enter their countries. . . . The lack of action by the Canadian government is leaving an unfortunate impression. . . . I regret to state that the sentiment is gaining ground that anti-Semitic influences are responsible for the government's refusal to allow refugees to come to Canada.

Percent of total

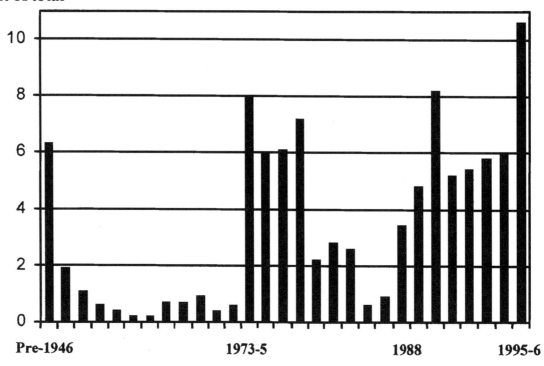

Emigration from the Former Soviet Union
*Most of those who came to Canada from the former Soviet Union arrived in two post–Second World War waves, one
between 1973 and 1980, the second between 1988 and 1996. This table presents some data on these waves of immigration.*

DR. BERNARD SHAPIRO, PRESIDENT OF MCGILL UNIVERSITY

Dr. Bernard Shapiro served as president of McGill University in Montreal from July 1994 until January 2003, when he became president emeritus. He began his academic career at Boston University, later moving to the University of Western Ontario. Before taking the position at McGill, he served in the cabinet of the province of Ontario as Deputy Minister of Education. In this selection, he reflects on Jewish day school education and on his own observance of Jewish tradition.

Government service is something I've begun as a third career. I've had an academic career, which was my second, and my first was, of course, business When I graduated from McGill (my brother and I are identical twins so we did this together) my father was in the restaurant business, but he died immediately after. And so, for about eight years we ran a restaurant business—Ruby Foo's. We sold it because we wanted to leave Montreal to pursue our academic life. He's now an academic also but not in Canada. He's the President of the University of Michigan in Ann Arbor.

I want for my own children and for many Jewish children things that are mutually exclusive in many contexts.

That is, I want them both to have a substantial Jewish education, and to be a substantial part of the wider society in which they live. And those are contradictions in terms because the only access we have to substantial Jewish education is the day school, which automatically removes you from the society in which you live. I think for parents who send their children to day school, they have a particularly strong obligation to try and balance that experience with other kinds of experiences so that it gives you some sense of the wider world. For example, if you are going to day school, I would encourage children to have a summer that wasn't so oriented simply to other Jewish experiences; it should be oriented to other kinds of experiences, if at all possible. Obviously you can't send a child to a camp where he can't eat the food, if you're that observant.

Both of my children went to elementary school in Jewish day schools but not after that. Most Jewish day schools do not take up seriously their obligation to be open to all Jewish children. They are open to all who are willing to cope with the standards of their curriculum. I regard that as unfortunate but, nevertheless, it's true for most—certainly not true of all—but it's certainly true of most. The curriculum of day schools is complex and difficult and most day schools have not responded adequately to the challenge of what to do with children who want this

EDUCATIONAL ATTAINMENT OF REFUGEES IN CANADA FROM MAJOR REFUGEE-PRODUCING COUNTRIES IN CANADA, 1978-87 (IN PERCENT)

| Country | Highest Level of Educational Attainment | | | |
	Less than Secondary	Secondary	University Graduate	Total
USSR	46.8	31.8	21.4	100.0
Romania	33.3	46.5	20.2	100.0
Poland	41.3	38.8	19.9	100.0
Iran	56.7	26.3	17.0	100.0
Afghanistan	67.5	18.1	14.4	100.0
Czechoslovakia	47.7	40.2	12.1	100.0
Nicaragua	76.3	15.0	8.7	100.0
Hungary	41.6	50.5	7.9	100.0
Ethiopia	69.2	23.6	7.2	100.0
Sri Lanka	59.4	34.3	6.3	100.0
Guatemala	80.1	16.3	3.6	100.0
Chile	76.6	20.9	2.5	100.0
El Salvador	81.7	16.0	2.3	100.0
Vietnam	90.0	8.1	1.9	100.0
Laos	93.3	5.9	0.8	100.0
Kampuchea	94.9	4.5	0.6	100.0

Educational Attainment of Refugees in Canada from Major Refugee-Producing Countries in Canada
This table presents data regarding the educational attainment of refugees coming to Canada between 1978 and 1987. It is notable that immigrants from the former Soviet Union had the highest level of educational attainment.

kind of education, whose parents want it for them but who aren't as good or as efficient learners—who aren't as linguistically-oriented as I was. And I regard that as a failing of their religious responsibilities, but that's a whole other hobby horse.

In terms of affiliation, I have always, and still do, belong to a Conservative Synagogue. So in Montreal it was the Shaar Hashomayim, and in Toronto it's the Beth Sed. In terms of practice, which I guess is the more relevant issue, I guess I express my Judaism in a couple of ways. I'm certainly not very observant. I don't find synagogue services at all reinforcing. I just don't find them meaningful. I attend them on a sort of semi-regular basis. I go on all the Holy Days and I go from time to time in between, because it's part of what I understand as being affiliated with the Jewish community. It's part of my definition of what it means to be 'Jewish'. I do not eat non-Kosher food, either at home or out. I like to celebrate the Holidays. I just get a lot of pleasure from it whether it's the High Holidays or Hanukkah or any of the Holidays. I think I consider them all equal. These are occasions for reminding myself, and expressing, what it is that I regard myself as a member of.

HONORABLE CONSTANCE GLUBE, CHIEF JUSTICE OF THE SUPREME COURT OF NOVA SCOTIA

Constance Glube has served in her career as city manager, lawyer, and judge. Since September 1977, she has been on the Supreme Court of Nova Scotia, and in November 1982, she was appointed Chief Justice of the Supreme Court of Nova Scotia, the first woman Chief Justice in Canada. She still holds the position of Chief Justilce. In this selection, she reflects on her own experiences with anti-Semitism.

I think I had more trouble doing law because I was a woman than because I was a Jew. I went to law school at Dalhousie, and I got an articleship through friends of my husband's family. That's two articles over the nine months at that time that we had to article. After I was admitted to the bar, I did stay home for about four, five years with the children. When I went back to work it was really quite difficult. I went to a few places, and most of the places were not particularly interested in me. I don't think it was anything other than the fact that I was a woman, and they couldn't really see how I was going to be practising law for any reasonable length of time, especially with children—we had three children by then. So I went back to work with the same firm where I had articled. I started on a part-time basis; and I think that I was more or less of a back-room lawyer; I went to the Registry of Deeds and searched titles.

I grew up in Ottawa during the War, so of course, there was a lot of anti-Semitism at that time. We lived on a one-block-long street and I used to play with a little girl all the time; and then during the War, all of a sudden when I was old enough to remember, I remember one day someone saying, 'Oh, well, you can't go to her house anymore.' And that was because we were Jewish. Those things would happen at times, but that was in the early forties, so whether or not it's anti-Semitism. Well, there's always people that have problems with somebody who's Jewish. I remember someone I met who was working for the city in Ottawa. He said that he was part Jewish. One day I was getting on the elevator and I said something about a Jewish High Holiday to him—and there were a number of people on the elevator. Afterwards he came up and he said to me, 'Gee, you really shouldn't have said anything about the fact that I was Jewish because I have been sort of observing some of these people; they haven't known me, and you wouldn't believe the amount of anti-Jewish feeling that's around this place.' By that time I think I was City Manager. I perhaps wasn't as aware of it as I might have been. But I don't look for it and, actually, I let people know what I am and, therefore, if they object to it or if they have got problems with it, then I don't need to associate with them.

When we went off to McGill, we lived in residence; and whether we were right or wrong, we felt that there was a quota on Jewish girls permitted into the residence. We could be very wrong, but we always felt that way, 'cause there were very, very few who lived in residences. Jewish people in Montreal, for example, tend to ghettoize themselves; and that bothered me particularly because I'd not grown up in that environment. I remember one girl saying to my sister and myself—we both went to university at the same time—saying she didn't quite understand how we could live with the people we were living with, and how we could associate with the people we were living with. We said, 'Why?' 'Well, because they're not Jewish.' And I said, 'Well, most of the people I've grown up with are not Jewish, so I really don't understand that.' 'Well,' she said, 'I just feel uncomfortable.' Now this was coming from a Jewish girl, a college student.

When I first moved to Halifax in 1952 when I was married, we could not belong to any of the yacht clubs locally. We did belong to one eventually, and we do belong to another one now; but we couldn't initially. The golf club was a closed golf club, and so there was a new one started as a result.

I remember once my husband wanted to go and play bridge with somebody and who was not a member, being

taken by a member of this particular club; and when the member found out who was going to be the partner of this other non-member, they said, 'We're sorry. You can't go.' That's still in the fifties.

CANADIAN JEWISH CONGRESS MISSION STATEMENT

The programs and the priorities of the Canadian Jewish Congress have varied through its long history. This mission statement presents its main concerns at the beginning of the 21st century.

Mission Statement

Canadian Jewish Congress is the democratically elected, national organizational voice of the Jewish community of Canada. It serves as the community's vehicle for defence and representation. Committed to preserving and strengthening Jewish life, CJC acts on matters affecting the status, rights and welfare of the Canadian Jewish community, other Diaspora communities and the Jewish people in Israel.

CJC combats antisemitism and racism, promotes human rights, fosters inter-faith, cross-cultural relations and strives for tolerance, understanding and goodwill among all segments of society in a multicultural Canada.

CJC speaks on a broad range of public policy, humanitarian and social-justice issues on the national agenda that affect the Jewish community and Canadian society at large.

Through its charitable operations, **CJC** provides domestic and international relief aid on a non-sectarian basis, following natural disasters and to isolated Jewish communities in need.

The **CJC** national office is located in Ottawa and works closely with CJC regions and affiliated offices across the country.

CANADA-ISRAEL COMMITTEE MISSION STATEMENT

The task of the Canada-Israel Committee is to work in Canada on behalf of the State of Israel. Its major sponsors are B'nai B'rith Canada, Canadian Jewish Congress, UIA Federations Canada and the Jewish communities of Canada. Each of these groups is represented on the Board of Directors, CIC's policy-making body.

Mission Statement

As mandated by the organized Jewish community in Canada, our objectives are:

- To advance a strong and dynamic relationship between the peoples of Canada and Israel
- To make the Canadian public sensitive to Israel's perspective on Arab-Israel relations

- To help facilitate increased collaboration between Canada and Israel in the pursuit of a just and lasting peace in the Middle East
- To articulate to the Canadian government and the media our concern regarding unfair treatment of Israel in all fora and to communicate the Jewish community's perspective on developments affecting Israel
- To work in concert with all fair-minded and tolerant individuals and groups in Canada and abroad to counter the myths, inaccuracies and oversimplifications concerning Israel and the Arab-Israeli conflict
- To support all efforts within the Jewish community to celebrate Israel, the Jewish people and the realization of their timeless aspirations of Zionism: the return of the Jewish people to their aboriginal homeland as a free and democratic nation

LEAGUE OF HUMAN RIGHTS

One division of B'nai B'rith Canada is the League of Human Rights. The table shown below is the League's audit of anti-Semitic incidents for 1995.

Year	Vandalism	Harassment	Total
1982	19	44	63
1983	25	23	48
1984	60	66	126
1985	52	43	95
1986	23	32	55
1987	18	37	55
1988	52	60	112
1989	63	113	176
1990	60	150	210
1991	50	201	251
1992	46	150	196
1993	105	151	256
1994	92	198	290
1995	80	251	331

Chronology

1759	City of Quebec capitulates to the British military forces.
1760	Aaron Hart becomes the first Jew to settle permanently in Canada. He settled in Three Rivers.
1763	Treaty of Paris is signed. French government ceases to exist in North America.
1768	Shearith Israel Congregation, fourth-oldest congregation on the North American continent, is founded in temporary premises on St. James St. in Montreal.
1791	British divide the "old province of Quebec" into two separate provinces: Upper Canada and Lower Canada.
1807	Ezekiel Hart, son of Aaron Hart, is elected member for Three Rivers to the Legislative Assembly for Lower Canada. He is refused, however, the right "to sit or vote in the Legislative Assembly" because he professes the Jewish religion.
1812	United States attacks Canada, but British and Canadian troops fight back. The War of 1812 decides much of Canada's borders of today.
1828	Jewish residents of Montreal petition the Legislature of Lower Canada for the incorporation of a Jewish religious corporation. The rabbi would have power to celebrate marriages and keep registers of births, marriages, and deaths. The petition's request was granted and became law in January 1831.
1830	A bill is passed by the Legislature of Lower Canada declaring "that all persons professing the Jewish religion are entitled to the full rights and privileges of other subjects of His Majesty." The Jewish population of Canada: 107.
1835	Frank N. Hart becomes the first Jew to graduate from McGill College with the degree of M.D.
1840	The Act of Union unites Upper and Lower Canada, forming the United Province of Canada.
1846	Congregation of English, German, and Polish Jews, subsequently named the Shaar Hashomayim congregation, is formed in Montreal, the first Ashkenazic congregation in Canada.
1856	The Sons of Israel Congregation, the first synagogue in Toronto, is founded as an Orthodox congregation. In 1869 it becomes

a Reform temple and is renamed the Holy Blossom Congregation.

1857   McGill University confers the honorary degree of LL.D. upon the Rev. Abraham de Sola, rabbi of Shearith Israel Congregation and full professor at McGill. He is the first Jew to receive an honorary degree from a Canadian university.

1867   On July 1, the British North America Act unites New Brunswick, Nova Scotia, and the Province of Canada into the Dominion of Canada. Sir John A. Macdonald is named Canada's first Prime Minister.

1870   Manitoba becomes a province.

1871   British Columbia becomes a province. Henry Nathan is elected by acclamation as first member of the Parliament of Canada from British Columbia. He is reelected in 1872.

1873   Prince Edward Island becomes a province.

1877   Jesse Joseph is appointed a director of the Montreal Street Railway Company and president of the company in 1884.

1882   Several thousand Jewish refugees fleeing from the wave of anti-Jewish pogroms in Russia, arrive in Montreal and Toronto, more than doubling the small Jewish communities in those cities.

1885   Canadian Pacific Railway is completed, uniting Canada from coast to coast.

1886   David Oppenheimer is elected mayor of Vancouver and reelected for successive periods of office until 1891.

1897   *Jewish Times,* a biweekly, the first Anglo-Jewish periodical in Canada, is founded by Lyon Cohen.

1905   Alberta and Saskatchewan become provinces.
First Yiddish public library in Canada is opened in Montreal in a rented room.

1911   Jewish population of Canada: 76,200

1912   Peretz School is founded in Montreal.

1914   *Canadian Jewish Chronicle* commences publication in Montreal.
World War I begins.

1916   Federations of Jewish Philanthropies are incorporated in Montreal and Toronto.

1917   Five Talmud Torahs in Montreal are united under the name of the United Talmud Torahs of Montreal.

1919   First Plenary Session of the Canadian Jewish Congress is held in Montreal, attended by 209 delegates from 48 Jewish communities throughout Canada. Over 2,500 spectators attend as well.

1920   Peretz School in Winnipeg opens first Jewish day school in Canada.

1927   Joseph Cohen is elected member of Quebec Provincial Legislature from Montreal.

1931   Treaty of Westminster legislates full legal power to the Canadian Parliament.

1933   Public protest meetings are held in Montreal, Toronto, and Winnipeg against Nazi persecution of Jews in Germany.

1934   From 1919 to 1934, the Canadian Jewish Congress did not function. The First Plenary Session of the reorganized Canadian Jewish Congress is held in Toronto.

1935   The Supreme Court of Canada is formed.

1939   World War II begins.

1949   Newfoundland becomes a province.

1966   Universal Medicare is legislated.

1968   First Sephardic day school is founded in Montreal.

1969   Ecole Maimonide and Ecole Sepharade, both francophone schools, are created in Montreal.

1982   Constitution Act is enacted by vote of British Parliament. From this point on, only Canada's Parliament is empowered to legislate for Canada.

1985   Ernst Zundel is put on trial for publishing and distributing anti-Semitic and Holocaust-denial literature.

1990   Rabbi W. Gunther Plaut, rabbi emeritus of Holy Blossom Temple in Toronto, publishes *The Torah: A Modern Commentary.* Since publication, this book has been reprinted 12 times.

1992   Rabbi Gedalia Felder, distinguished Toronto rabbi and scholar, dies at age 70.

1995   Referendum in Quebec on sovereignty is defeated by a margin of less than 1 percent.

1998   UIA Federations Canada is established, as the result of a merger between the United Israel Appeal and the Council of Jewish Federations.

1999   Nunavut ("Our Land") officially becomes Canada's third territory. Partitioned from the Northwest Territories, Nunavut has a total land and offshore area of 1.6 million square kilometers. Population of this territory is 80 percent Inuit.

BIBLIOGRAPHY

Adler, C. *Jacob H. Schiff: His Life and His Letters.* Garden City, NY: Doubleday, Doran and Company, 1929.

Altmann, A., *Moses Mendelssohn: A Biographical Study.* Philadelphia: Jewish Publication Society, 1973.

Arad, Y., (ed.). *Documents on the Holocaust (Yad Vashem)* Jerusalem: KTAV Publishing House, 1981.

Arian, A., *Politics in Israel: The Second Generation.* Chatham, NJ: Chatham House Publishers, 1989.

Avineri, S., *The Making of Modern Zionism.* New York: Basic Books, 1981.

Bard, M., *Myths and Facts: A Guide to the Israeli–Arab Conflict.* Chevy Chase, MD: American-Israeli Cooperative Enterprise, 2001.

————. *The Complete Idiot's Guide to Middle East Conflict.* Indianapolis: Alpha Books, 1999.

Barnavi, E., (ed.). *A Historical Atlas of the Jewish People.* New York: Schocken Books, 1992.

Baron, S. W., *The Russian Jew Under Tsars and Soviets.* New York: Macmillan Company, 1964.

Bauer, Y., *A History of the Holocaust.* New York: Franklin Watts, 1982.

Bayme, S., *Understanding Jewish History.* New York: KTAV Publishing House, 1997.

Berkovitz, J., *The Shaping of Jewish Identity in 19th-Century France.* Detroit: Wayne State University Press, 1989.

Bickerton, I. and M. N. Pearson, *The Arab–Israeli Conflict: A History.* Melbourne, Australia: Longman Cheshire, 1993.

Blau, J. L., *Modern Varieties of Judaism.* New York: Columbia University Press, 1964.

Bleich, J., "Between East and West: Modernity and Traditionalism in the Writings of Rabbi Yehi'el Ya'akov Weinberg" in M. J. Sokol (ed.). *Engaging Modernity.* Northvale, NJ: Jason Aronson, 1997.

————. *Jacob Ettlinger,* "His Life and Works: The Emergence of Modern Orthodoxy in Germany." Unpublished doctoral dissertation, New York University, 1974.

Breuer, M., *The "Torah-Im-Derekh-Eretz" of Samson Raphael Hirsch.* New York: Feldheim Publishers, 1970.

Cassirer, E. *The Philosophy of the Enlightenment.* Princeton, NJ: Princeton University Press, 1951.

Chazan, R. and Raphael, M. L. (eds.). *Modern Jewish History: A Source Reader.* New York: Schocken Books, 1974. (See Mendes-Flohr and Reinharz, p. ix for other references.)

Cohen, N. *Jacob H. Schiff: A Study in American Jewish Leadership.* Hanover, NH: University Press of New England, 1999.

Dawidowicz, L. (ed.). *A Holocaust Reader.* New York: Behrman House, 1976.

————. *The Golden Tradition.* New York: Holt, Rinehart and Winston, 1966.

————. *The War Against the Jews.* New York: Bantam Books, 1975.

De Lange, N., *Atlas of the Jewish World.* New York: Facts on File, 1984.

———— (ed.). *The Illustrated History of the Jewish People.* New York: Harcourt Brace and Company, 1997.

Ehrmann, E. L., (ed.). *Readings in Modern Jewish History.* New York: KTAV Publishing House, 1977.

Ellenson, D., Rabbi Asriel Hildesheimer and the Creation of a Modern Jewish Orthodoxy. Tuscaloosa: University of Alabama Press, 1991.

Eliach, Y., *Hasidic Tales of the Holocaust.* New York: Oxford University Press, 1982.

Encyclopedia Judaica, s.v. Frankel, Zechariah; Holdheim, Samuel; Hildesheimer, Esriel; Hoffmann, David Zevi; Jacobson, Israel; Volozhin; Luzzatto, Moses Hayyim; Luzzatto, Samuel David; Hirsch, Samson Raphael; Mendelssohn, Moses; Wissenschaft des Judentums; Salanter, Israel; Gordon, Y. L.; Krochmal, N.; Shneur Zalman of Lyady.

Freedman, R., (ed.). *Soviet Jewry in the 1980s.* Durham and London: Duke University Press, 1989.

Friesel, E., *Atlas of Modern Jewish History.* New York: Oxford University Press, 1990.

Gilbert, M., *The Arab–Israeli Conflict: Its History in Maps.* London: Weidenfeld and Nicolson, 1981.

Gillman, N., *Conservative Judaism.* West Orange, NJ: Behrman House, 1993.

Gitelman, Z., *A Century of Ambivalence: The Jews of Russia and the Soviet Union, 1881 to the Present.* New York: Schocken Books, 1988.

————. *Jewish Nationality and Soviet Politics.* Princeton, NJ: Princeton University Press, 1972.

Goldberg, H., *Israel Salanter: Text, Structure, Idea.* New York: KTAV Publishing House, 1982.

Greenberg, L., *The Jews in Russia.* New York: Schocken Books, 1976.

Gribetz, J., Greenstein, E., and Regina Stein, Regina, *The Timetables of Jewish History.* New York: Simon and Schuster, 1993.

Halpern, B. and Reinharz, J., *Zionism and the Creation of a New Society.* Hanover and London: University Press of New England, 2000.

Hazony, Y., *The Jewish State: The Struggle for Israel's Soul.* New York: Basic Books, 2000.

Hertzberg, A., (ed.). *The Zionist Idea.* New York: Atheneum, 1970.

————. *The French Enlightenment and the Jews.* New York: Columbia University Press, 1968.

————. *The Jews in America: Four Centuries of an Uneasy Encounter.* New York: Simon and Schuster, 1989.

Hilberg, R., *The Destruction of the European Jews.* 3 vols. New York: Holmes and Meyer, 1989.

Hirsch, S. R., *The Nineteen Letters.* New York: Feldheim Publishers, 1969.

————. *Judaism Eternal I.* London: The Soncino Press, 1956.

Hitler, A., *Mein Kampf.* New York: Houghton Mifflin, 1969.

Howe, I., *World of Our Fathers.* New York: Harcourt Brace Jovanovich, 1976.

Idel, M., *Hasidism: Between Ecstasy and Magic.* Albany: State University of New York Press, 1995.

Jerusalem Post. *Anatoly and Avital Shcharansky: The Journey Home.* New York: Harcourt Brace Jovanovich, 1986.

Johnson, P., *A History of the Jews.* New York: Harper and Row Publishers, 1987.

Katz, J., *Out of the Ghetto: The Social Background of Jewish Emancipation, 1770–1870.* Cambridge, MA: Harvard University Press, 1973.

————. *Tradition and Crisis.* New York: Schocken Books, 1993.

Katz, S., *Battleground: Fact and Fantasy in Palestine.* New York: Taylor Productions, 2002.

Lamm, N., *The Religious Thought of Hasidism.* Hoboken, NJ: KTAV Publishing House, 1999.

————. *Torah Umadda.* Northvale, NJ: Jason Aronson, 1990.

Laqueur, W., *A History of Zionism.* New York: Schocken Books, 1976.

Laqueur, W. and Rubin, B., *The Israel–Arab Reader.* New York: Penguin Books, 1984.

Leiman, S., "Rabbinic Openness to General Culture in the Early Modern Period in Western and Central Europe" in J. J. Schacter (ed.). *Judaism's Encounter with Other Cultures.* Northvale, NJ: Jason Aronson, 1997.

Luzzatto, R. M. H., *Mesilat Yesharim.* New York: Feldheim Publishers, 1969.

Mahler, R., *Hasidism and the Jewish Enlightenment.* Philadelphia: Jewish Publication Society, 1985.

Marcus, J. R., *The American Jew, 1585–1990: A History.* Brooklyn, NY: Carlson Publishing, 1995.

————. *The American Jewish Woman: A Documentary History.* New York: KTAV Publishing House, 1981.

————. *The Jew in the American World: A Source Book.* Detroit: Wayne State University Press, 1996.

McNeill, W. H., *History of Western Civilization: A Handbook.* Chicago: University of Chicago Press, 1986.

Mendes-Flohr, P. and Reinharz, J. (eds.), *The Jew in the Modern World: A Documentary History.* New York: Oxford University Press, 1980, 1995.

Meyer, M., *The Origins of the Modern Jew: Jewish Identity and European Culture in Germany, 1749–1824.* Detroit: Wayne State University Press, 1967.

————. *Response to Modernity: A History of the Reform Movement in Judaism.* New York: Oxford University Press, 1988.

Nadler, A., *The Faith of the Mitnagdim.* Baltimore: Johns Hopkins University Press, 1997.

Oren, M., *Six Days of War: June 1967 and the Making of the Modern Middle East.* New York: Oxford University Press, 2002.

Rabinovich, I., and Reinharz, J. (eds.). *Israel in the Middle East.* New York: Oxford University Press, 1984.

Raphael, M. L., (ed.). *Jews and Judaism in the United States: A Documentary History.* New York: Behrman House, 1983.

Rappoport, L., *Stalin's War Against the Jews.* New York: The Free Press, 1990.

Rezneck, S., *Unrecognized Patriots: The Jews in the American Revolution.* Westport, CT: Greenwood Press, 1975.

Rosenbloom, N., *Tradition in an Age of Reform.* Philadelphia: Jewish Publication Society, 1976.

Rubenstein, J., *Soviet Dissidents: Their Struggle for Human Rights.* Boston: Beacon Press, 1985.

Rubenstein, J., and Naumov, V. P. (eds.). *Stalin's Secret Pogrom: The Postwar Inquisition of The Jewish Anti-Fascist Committee*. Trans. L.E. Wolfson. New Haven, CT: Yale University Press, 2001.

Sachar, H. M., *The Course of Modern Jewish History*. New York: Vintage Books, 1990.

————. *A History of Israel*. v. 1: Philadelphia: Jewish Publication Society, 1976; v. 2: New York: Oxford University Press, 1987.

————. *A History of the Jews in America*. New York: Alfred A. Knopf, 1992.

Schochet, E. J., *The Hasidic Movement and the Gaon of Vilna*. Northvale, NJ: Jason Aronson, 1994.

Shapiro, E., *A Time for Healing: American Jewry since World War II*. Baltimore: Johns Hopkins University Press, 1992.

Sklare, M., *American Jews: a Reader*. New York: Behrman House, 1983.

————. *Conservative Judaism*. New York: Schocken Books, 1985.

Thomas, B., *How Israel Was Won*. Lanham, MD: Lexington Books, 1999.

Waxman, M., (ed.). *Tradition and Change: The Development of Conservative Judaism*. New York: Burning Bush Press, 1958.

Wein, B., *Triumph of Survival*. Monsey, NY: Shaar Press, 1990.

Wengeroff, P., *Rememberings: The World of a Russian Jewish Woman in the Nineteenth Century*. Trans. H. Wenkart. Ed. B. Cooperman. College Park: University Press of Maryland, 2000.

Wessely, N. H., *Divrei Shalom v'Emet*. Vienna: Anton Schmid, 1826.

Wiesenthal, S., *The Sunflower*. New York: Schocken Books, 1998.

Wolpin, N., (ed.). *Jewish Luminaries*. Brooklyn, NY: Mesorah Publications, 1994.

INDEX